Archives, Ancestors, Practices

Archives, Ancestors, Practices

Archaeology in the Light of Its History

Edited by
Nathan Schlanger and Jarl Nordbladh

Berghahn Books
New York • Oxford

In memory of
Karl Axel Moberg
Bruce Trigger

Education and Culture

Culture 2000

First published in 2008 by
Berghahn Books
www.berghahnbooks.com

Library of Congress Cataloging-in-Publication Data
A C.I.P. record for this book is available from the Library of Congress

British Library Cataloguing in Publication Data
A catalogue record for this book is available from the British Library

Printed in the United States on acid-free paper

ISBN 978-1-84545-066-3 paperback

Contents

Part III : VISUALISING ARCHAEOLOGY

Part IV : QUESTIONS OF IDENTITY

List of Figures

List of Plates

List of Contributors

Luis Alejandro Auat (Ph.D., 2000, UCSF) teaches Argentine and Latin American Philosophy, Social and Political Philosophy at University of Santiago del Estero, Argentina. His research areas include citizenship and identities, political cultures and democracy. buho@arnet.com.ar

Marcello Barbanera (Ph.D., 1996, La Sapienza) teaches Classical Archaeology at La Sapienza, Rome. His interests include the history of classical archaeology, the reuse of Antiquity, archaeological theory, museography, Greek sculpture and Greek artistic theory. His publications include *L'Archeologia degli Italiani* (1998), *Ranuccio Bianchi Bandinelli. Biografia di un grande archeologo* (2003), *Storie dell'Arte antica* (2004). mbarbanera@hotmail.com

Juan Pedro Bellón Ruiz (BA, 1995, University of Jaén) is a member of the Andalusian Center for Iberian Archaeology and of the AREA project. His interests include the archaeology and the historiography of the Iberians, on which he has published *The History of Iberian Archaeology: one archaeology for two Spains*. He is currently working on his doctoral thesis on the Archive Gómez-Moreno. jbellon@ujaen.es

Emma Bentz is a Ph.D. student at the Department of Archaeology and Ancient history, Lund University, Sweden. Her research interests include, among others, the historiography of archaeology and medieval archaeology, with a special emphasis on the medieval countryside. Emma.Bentz@ark.lu.se

Jan Bergman (M.Sc., 1961, The Royal Institute of Technology, Stockholm) has returned, following his 2001 retirement from a professional career in Forest Industry, to pursue his interests in archaeology and geoscience at Göteborg University. janbergman36@telia.com

Sebastian Brather (Ph.D., 1995, Humboldt University Berlin; habilitation, 2002, Freiburg University) directs the Institute for prehistoric and medieval archaeology at Freiburg University. His interests include archaeology and identity, medieval archaeology, and the history of archaeology. sebastian.brather@ufg.uni-freiburg.de

Giovanna Ceserani (Ph.D., 2000, University of Cambridge) is Assistant Professor of Classics at Stanford University. Her interest is in the classical tradition with an emphasis on the intellectual history of classical scholarship, archaeology and historiography since the 18th century. She is currently writing a book on the modern study of Magna Graecia. ceserani@stanford.edu

Margarita Díaz-Andreu (Ph.D., 1990, Complutense University) is a Senior Lecturer in the Department of Archaeology, Durham University. Her research focuses on the politics of identity in archaeology (nationalism and colonialism, history of archaeology, ethnicity and gender) and the prehistoric archaeology and art of Western Europe. Her publications include *The Archaeology of Identity* (2005), and *A World History of Nineteenth-Century Archaeology: Nationalism, Colonialism and the Past* (2007). m.diaz-andreu@dur.ac.uk

Gisela Eberhardt has recently completed her doctoral thesis on German excavations in the 19th and early 20th century at the Institute of Classical Archaeology of the Humboldt University Berlin. Besides the history of the discipline, her interests various aspects of the Neolithic, as well as scientific journalism. Giselaeberhardt@aol.com

Martijn Eickhoff (Ph.D., 2003, Universiteit van Amsterdam) is a researcher at the Netherlands Institute for War Documentation (NIOD) and teaches Cultural History at the Radboud Universiteit Nijmegen. His main field of interest is the relations between archaeology and national socialism on which he has published in *Archaeological Dialogues*. eickhoff@tiscali.nl

Christopher Evans is the Director of the Cambridge Archaeological Unit of the University of Cambridge. He has directed a range of major fieldwork projects in both Britain and abroad (Nepal, Inner Mongolia and Cape Verde), and has widely published on the history of archaeology and, also, its modes of representation. cje30@cam.ac.uk

José Farrujia de la Rosa (Ph.D., 2003, Universidad de La Laguna, Tenerife). His interests include method, theory and history of archaeology, politics, identity and archaeology, and Canarian and Saharan rock art. He has published *Imperialist archaeology in the Canary Islands. French and German studies on prehistoric colonization at the end of the 19th century* (2005), and *Arqueología y franquismo en Canarias* (2007). afarruji@hotmail.com

Susana González Reyero (Ph.D., 2005, Autonoma University, Madrid) is at the Spanish Council for Scientific Research (CSIC) researching on visual archaeology, the representation of the past and the history of archaeology in Spain. She has published *La fotografía en la arqueología española (1860-1960)* (2006) and *Juan Cabré Aguiló y la construcción de la cultura ibérica en la primera mitad del siglo XX* (forthcoming, 2007). sgreyero@ih.csic.es

Ruurd Halberstma (Ph.D., 1995, University of Leiden) is curator of Greek and Roman Antiquities in the Rijksmuseum van Oudheden (National Museum of Antiquities) in Leiden, the Netherlands. He lectures on museology and the history of archaeology at Leiden University, and researches the history of collections and of museums. r.halbertsma@rmo.nl

Curtis M. Hinsley is Regents' Professor in the Department of Humanities, Arts and Religion at Northern Arizona University. He is author of *The Smithsonian and the American Indian: Making a Moral Anthropology in Victorian America* (1994) and more than fifty other books and articles on the history of American anthropology and archaeology. He lives in Sedona, Arizona, with his wife, historian Victoria L. Enders. Curtis.Hinsley@nau.edu

Visa Immonen (MA, 2001, University of Turku) is a member of the Finnish Graduate School of Archaeology. His interests include historical archaeology, material culture studies, artefacts of precious metals, and feminist archaeology. visa.immonen@utu.fi

Marc-Antoine Kaeser Marc-Antoine Kaeser is director of the Latenium – Archaeology Park and Museum, Neuchâtel and associate professor for prehistory at the University of Neuchâtel (Switzerland). His interests include theory, epistemology, and history of archaeology. Among his publications are *Les Lacustres: Archéologie et mythe national*, and *Un savant séducteur: Louis Agassiz (1807–1873)*.

Ana Teresa Martinez (Ph.D., 2004, University of Buenos Aires) teaches social sciences epistemology and the sociology of culture in several Universities in Northwest Argentina. Her interests include local sociology of culture and the sociology of religion. anateres@yahoo.com.ar

Ana Cristina Martins (Ph.D., 2006, University of Lisbon) belongs to the Centre for Archaeology of the University of Lisbon (UNIARQ). Her research interests include the History of Portuguese Archaeology, on which she has presented and published several papers, in both national and international contexts. ana.c.martins@netcabo.pt

Maria Gabriella Micale in completing her Ph.D. in Oriental Archaeology at the University of La Sapienza, Rome. Her interests include history of Near Eastern archaeology, modern Near Eastern archaeological and cultural politics. Her doctoral research concerns architectural representations on neo-Assyrian bas-reliefs. She is member of the Missione Archeologica Italiana in Syria -Ebla (MAIS) since 2000. mgmlucy@libero.it

Tim Murray is Professor of Archaeology at La Trobe University. His interests include the history and philosophy of archaeology, theoretical archaeology, Australian prehistoric and historical archaeology, and archaeological heritage management. His recent monographs include *Keeping up with the Macnamaras* (2005), on the archaeology of 19th immigration to Australia, and *Milestones in Archaeology* (2007). T.Murray@latrobe.edu.au

Jarl Nordbladh (Ph.D., 1980, Göteborg University) has retired as emeritus from a professorship in archaeology at Göteborg University. His research interests include the history of archaeology, Scandinavian rock art and in scientific illustrations. He has taken part in the EU funded AREA project from its beginnings. J.Nordbladh@archaeology.gu.se

Nadezhda Igorevna Platonova (Ph.D., 1988, USSR Academy of Sciences: Institute of Archaeology, Leningrad Branch) is a Senior researcher at the Institute of the History of Material Culture (Russian Academy of Sciences). Her interests include the history and archaeology of Ancient Rus' and the history of archaeological thought and institutions in 19th century Russia. niplaton@peterlink.ru

Megan Price is a mature student at the University of Oxford. She has just completed her D.Phil. on the intellectual relationships between 'town and gown' in late 19th century Oxford, focusing particularly on the growing interest in British prehistory. She is continuing her research into the growth of British and European prehistory at Oxford. megan.price@wolfson.oxford.ac.uk

Arturo Ruiz Rodríguez is Professor of Prehistory and Iberian Archaeology at the University of Jaén (Spain), and director of the Andalusian Center for Iberian Archaeology. His interests include the archaeology and the historiography of the Iberians, on which he has published *The Archaeology of the Iberians* and the *The History of Iberian Archaeology: one archaeology for two Spains*. He is the principal researcher of the AREA project in Jaén. arruiz@ujaen.es

Alberto Sánchez Vizcaíno (Ph.D., 1997, University of Jaén) is lecturer in Prehistory at the University of Jaén (Spain). He is currently member of the Andalusian Center for Iberian Archaeology and of the AREA project. His interests include the archaeology and the historiography of the Iberians, on which he has published *The History of Iberian Archaeology: one archaeology for two Spains*. vizcaino@ujaen.es

Nathan Schlanger (Ph.D., 1995, University of Cambridge) is the scientific coordinator of the AREA project (2000- 2007). His interests include prehistory, material culture studies, archaeology in France and Africa, and the history and politics of archaeology. He is now promoting international research and development at the *Institut national de recherches archéologiques préventives* in Paris. nathan.schlanger@inrap.fr.

Alain Schnapp is Professor of archaeology at the University of Paris I (Panthéon-Sorbonne). His work is dedicated to Greek iconography and to the origins of antiquarianism and archaeological practices. His book *La conquête du passé* (1993) has been translated in several languages. Presently he is directing the European AREA project. alain.schnapp@inha.fr

Ulrike Sommer (Ph.D., 1999, University of Frankfurt) is a lecturer in European Prehistory at the Institute of Archaeology, University College London. Her interests include archaeological formation processes, the archaeology of ethnicity and the history of archaeological research. u.sommer@ucl.ac.uk

Jussi-Pekka Taavitsainen (Ph.D., 1990, University of Helsinki) is Professor in the Department of Archaeology at the University of Turku. His interests include ancient hillforts, medieval archaeology, archaeology of wilderness areas, and artefact studies. jussi-pekka.taavitsainen@utu.fi

Constanza Taboada (Ph.D., Tucumán University) is a researcher and teacher at the Archaeology Institute and Museum at Tucumán University and at the Argentinean CONICET. Her research interests include architecture and pre-hispanic uses of space, interaction processes in the Argentinean northwest plains and valleys, and the history of local archaeology. constanzataboada@gmail.com

Leo Verhart works as curator of the Dutch Prehistoric Department in the National Museum of Antiquities, Leiden, the Netherlands. His interests include the Mesolithic and Neolithic with special attention to the transition, on which he published his Ph.D. thesis: *Times fades away*. l.verhart@rmo.nl.

Christine Walter (Ph.D., 2001, Ecole du Louvre, Paris) works in the Louvre Museum in Paris. Her interests include the Greek Painting and methods of classification in archaeology and in history of art, on which she has published several contributions. Christine.walter@louvre.fr

David R. Wilcox is Senior Research Anthropologist, and formerly Curator of Anthropology, at the Museum of Northern Arizona in Flagstaff. He has co-authored and co-edited several books, including *Philadelphia and the Development of Americanist Archaeology* (2003), *Zuni Origins: Toward a New Synthesis of Southwestern Archaeology* (2007), and *The Archaeology of Perry Mesa and Its World* (2007). DWilcox@MNA.mus.az.us

Preface and Acknowledgements

Nathan Schlanger and Jarl Nordbladh

The book now in your hands is, unashamedly, a conference volume. It is true that such publications often suffer from poor press in academic circles: editors of multi-authored proceedings tend to downplay this fact, and publishers too are often reticent to deal with them. It is also true that planning a conference and editing a book are quite different matters, and similarly that a brilliant orator may prove a poorly structured author, that twenty minutes will not necessarily make twenty pages, and indeed that these ever so valued requirements of 'coherence' and 'novelty', bolstered by the effervescence of the conference itself, may seem with hindsight and changed media somewhat less compelling. As editors we are not oblivious to such pitfalls, of course, and nor can we pretend to have avoided them all. Nevertheless, we do believe that the origins of this volume in a particular conference deserves to be specifically highlighted – both for the benefit of the present publication, its genuine coherence and novelty, and more generally, if we may be so bold, for the sake of this emerging field of research, the history of archaeology.

The conference in question, titled 'Histories of archaeology. Archives, ancestors, practices', was held at the Department of Archaeology, University of Göteborg, Sweden, on 17–19 June 2004. In both chronological and conceptual terms, this conference represents the culmination of an important phase of activity of the European-wide research network known as AREA – Archives of European Archaeology. The AREA network is probably unique in being specifically dedicated to research and documentation on the history of archaeology, with a strong emphasis on the archives of the discipline. Since its launching in 1998, the AREA network has gone through four funding phases, each including a growing number of partner institutions from across the continent – university departments and institutes, museums, research centres and public bodies – working together within a common European framework.[1] The AREA network, the Göteborg conference and the resulting book are obviously connected. Some conceptual and methodological links will be mentioned in our editorial Introduction (and of course in the chapters themselves), so here we simply point at some specificities of the conference in terms of its structure and its composition.

AREA partners, who had planned together the conference and its themes, were of course present and well represented on the day. It was agreed however that AREA members should not themselves give any papers (but only contribute to the poster session). Besides serving to bypass issues of selection and representation within the network itself, this withdrawal also made room available for welcoming other scholars, other voices, other experiences. Some of these scholars were specifically contacted by the scientific committee – and here is the place to acknowledge the very useful and lively participation of Alice Kehoe, the good wishes sent to us by Bruce Trigger who unfortunately could not attend, and more specifically the contribution of Leo Klejn, who was unable to travel to the meeting, but who provided instead on the basis of the extended abstracts a penetrating commentary which was included in the conference booklet. Most speakers however simply responded to the call for paper, and submitted their proposals along the indicated guidelines. Those selected were then happy to realise that their costs were taken care of by the conference organisers – the AREA network. Altogether, 23 papers were presented at the conference, and the vast majority are published here, reworked and edited as the case might be. Several speakers did not see their papers through to publication (A. Doulgeri-Intzesiloglou, S. Wiell, M. Svedin), and likewise some additional papers were accepted from authors who could not attend (A.T. Martinez et al.), or who had only presented posters (J. Bergman, U. Sommer, M. Diaz-Andreu, J.-P. Bellón et al.). The contributors to this volume range from well-established academics to emerging scholars, some at doctoral or post-doctoral stage, and others relatively new to the field. In line with the intrinsically international character of archaeology itself, and the vocation of the AREA network and its EC funding programme, these contributors came from all over Europe, from St Petersburg to Portugal and the Canaries Islands, and from the Mediterranean through to Scandinavia, and also from North and South America, as well as Australia.

The conference itself was structured into four major themes, namely 'Sources and methods for the history of archaeology', 'Archaeological practice', 'Visualising archaeology' and 'Questions of identity'. Papers were submitted and selected in function of these themes (see further in the editorial Introduction). From the onset, it was decided not to hold separate or parallel sessions, but on the contrary to remain together for the whole duration of the conference. Practical considerations aside – the auditorium at our disposal was of a proper 'human' scale for the c. 100 participants that we were – this decision followed from reasons of principle: on balance, the history of archaeology is really not sufficiently advanced or established to permit itself the luxury (if such it is) of further fragmentation into specialism. Not only did all the participants, audience and speakers alike, wish to attend all the presentations, also the very attribution of some papers to this or that theme proved quite difficult and arbitrary to maintain – so much so that several papers presented under one theme at the conference, ended up better placed under another theme in the publication. Last but not least, bringing all the participants together under one roof certainly encouraged longer and wider ranging discussions (held mostly in English, our chosen 'working' language). Many of these lively exchanges continued throughout the social programme of the conference, including a fabulous evening cruise along the Göteborg archipelago, and of course in the weeks and months following the conference itself, thus confirming one of its tacit objectives: to further broaden the network of contacts, competencies and commitment dedicated to the history of archaeology.

As indicated, the conference at the origin of this volume was not only organised but also funded by the AREA network – and here again we must acknowledge the very generous support of the Culture 2000 programme of the DG Education and Culture of the European commission. The *Institut national d'histoire de l'art* – INHA, then project-leader of the AREA network, provided further assistance in terms of funding, logistics and information technology: special thanks are due to Alain Schnapp, to Dominique Barillé and to Pascal Presle and his team. In Göteborg, financial and logistical support were received from Göteborg University, the Jubilee Foundation and the Department of Archaeology, the Magnus Bregvall Foundation, the Wenner-Gren Foundation, the National Heritage Board, the Royal Academy of Letters, History and Antiquities, the Wilhelm and Martina Lundgren Research Foundation I, and the Göteborg Municipality. The conference itself, and the sortie with the Bohuslän, the last remaining passenger steamer boat on the Swedish West Coast, were smoothly organised by the conference organising firm Inspiro Event with Henrik Svensson. In addition, Jarl Nordbladh thanks the archaeology students Malin Börjes, Mikael Cerbing, Maria Persson and Andreas Skredsvik for their devoted assistance with practical matters during the conference. Lastly, Nathan Schlanger wishes to thank Marion Berghahn and Mark Stanton for their support and much needed patience during the production of this volume, the first in the 'Histories of archaeology' series.

Note

1. Support for the AREA network was generously awarded by the Raphael programme (AREA phase I, 1998–1999), and subsequently by the Culture 2000 programme of the European Commission's Directorate General for Education and Culture (AREA phase II, 1999–2000, an experimental measure, and AREA phase III, 2001–2004, followed by AREA phase IV, 2005–2008, both multiannual cultural collaboration projects). Initiated by Sander van der Leeuw, Giovanni Scichilore and Alain Schnapp, AREA has continued under the leadership of the latter and with the scientific coordination of David van Reybrouck (AREA I, II) and Nathan Schlanger (AREA III, IV). Institutional project leaders were the Maison des sciences de l'homme – MSH (AREA I, II), the Institut national d'histoire de l'art – INHA (AREA III), and the Maison de l'archéologie et de l'ethnologie – CNRS (AREA IV). European consultancy was provided throughout the project by Gian Guiseppe Simeone and Culturelab. The following institutions were and are partners of the AREA network (in parenthesis is indicated the AREA phase in which they participated): National Archive of Monuments, Hellenic Ministry of Culture, Athens, Greece (AREA I, II, III, IV); Centro Andaluz de Arqueologia Ibérica, Jaén, Spain (I, II, III, IV); Department of Archaeology, University of Göteborg, Sweden (I, II, III, IV); Fondation Maison des sciences de l'homme – MSH, Paris, France (I, II); Institut national d'histoire de l'art – INHA, Paris, France (II, III, IV); Maison de l'archéologie et de l'ethnologie – CNRS, Nanterre, France (IV); Deutsches Archäologisches Institut, Berlin, Germany (I, II); McDonald Institute for Archaeological Research, Cambridge, United Kingdom (I, II); Service de Préhistoire, Université de Liège, Belgium (I, II); Archeologisch Diensten Centrum, Bunschoten, Netherlands (II); Università degli Studi di Roma La Sapienza, Rome, Italy (II, IV); Ashmolean Museum, University of Oxford, United Kingdom (III); The Butrint Foundation, London / University of East Anglia, United Kingdom (III); Department of Archaeology, University College Cork, Ireland (III); Patronato de la Alhambra y Generalife, Granada, Spain (III); Department of History, Katholieke Universiteit Leuven, Belgium (III); Institut für Ur- und Frühgeschichte und Archäologie des Mittelalters, Freiburg University, Germany (III, IV); Poznan Archaeological Museum, Poznan, Poland (III, IV); Department of Archaeology, University of Durham, Durham, United Kingdom (IV); Institute of Archaeology of the Academy of Sciences, Prague, Czech Republic (IV); Institutul de Arheologie 'vasile Parvan', Bucharest, Romania (IV); Museu Monográfico de Conimbriga, Coimbra, Portugal (IV); Professur für Ur- und Frühgeschichte der Universität Leipzig, Leipzig, Germany (IV).

General Introduction

Archaeology in the Light of its Histories

Nathan Schlanger and Jarl Nordbladh

The sheer mass of the volume you are now holding, with its twenty six chapters and over three hundred and fifty pages, is indicative, so we believe, of the genuine commitment and seriousness of purpose which characterises current enquiries into the history of archaeology. Or should we not rather say 'histories'? After all, this cautiously used plural is not only to acknowledge the more relevant insights of reflexive relativism, but also – in line with the title given to the series of which this is the first volume published – to endorse a certain variability of perspectives and aims, and indeed to welcome diversity in both subject matters and investigative standpoints. In any case, this acknowledged plurality represents something of a departure from the historiographic habits prevailing twenty or fifteen years ago, when conventional writings on the history of archaeology effectively built upon and bolstered a unifying grand narrative of inexorable progress, across time, towards truth. To be sure, such an orientation does make (some) sense in the framework of 'disciplinary histories', which is what most of these texts effectively are – and which quite a few historical overviews or introductory paragraphs in contemporary publications continue, often unwittingly, to be. Basically, such accounts serve to establish the discipline, identify its knowledge claims and lineages of authority, and then confirm to its members its accredited domains and norms of inquiry. A firmer sense of institutional identity and disciplinary cohesion may certainly result from such edifying histories, but also a tendency to entrench norms and outlooks, and then align the path of progress along a single overarching beacon – the one the discipline currently favours.

Fortunately, there is rather more than that to the history of archaeology – indeed to its histories. This unabashedly presentist and pragmatic approach just outlined differs considerably, in both objectives and methodology, from the more critical and contextual histories we adhere to, encourage and set to exemplify throughout this volume. Such histories, which are not so much for archaeology as about archaeology, imply a healthy dose of reflexivity enriched by contacts with historians and sociologists of science, a willingness to delve into the theoretical and methodological intricacies of the discipline with something like ethnographic zeal, an attitude that is at once highly attentive and immune from veneration, neither overly dazzled nor retrospectively dismissive, and thus well able to keep biography from turning into hagiography or, at the other extreme, into patricide. More generally, such critical and contextual histories come with a commitment to explore archaeology from aside as much as from inside, as a situated scientific, cultural and ideological undertaking, trying to understand what archaeology is, and claims to be (or not to be) about, at different times and places, in different social, economic and political contexts, for different actors, protagonists, audiences and publics. And this 'aboutness' – when the results sought after are not necessarily evaluated in terms of their disciplinary relevance or utility, but rather with regards to the light they shed, the aspects they enable to perceive and to examine, the perspectives they imply or call into question – this 'aboutness' quite evidently thrives on 'histories', in the plural.

Having welcomed this plurality of perspectives and subject matters, it does not follow that the coming chapters are bound to be disjointed, inward looking or idiosyncratic, too disparate to size and present together in some recognisable and consequent manner. Indeed, the twenty five chapters of this volume are grouped in what seems to us a fairly coherent and satisfying arrangement, essentially based on their thematic contents. This overarching structure is actually less trivial than it sounds, as can be gathered by first evoking some other structuring possibilities which were not followed. We may begin here with the default option, which is simply to abide by the alphabetical order of the name of the principal authors. This intrinsically arbitrary sequence would lead us from Barbanera, Bentz and Bergman to Taboada, Verhart and Walter. Another possibility would have been to present the chapters according to the archaeological period or periods under discussions, from Murray on Palaeolithic human antiquity, through Platonova on paleo-ethnology, to Micale on Babylonia, Martins on Iron Age Portugal, Ceserani on Roman Capua, ending with Bentz on Medieval settlements in North-Western Europe.

Considerably more familiar and influential are the following two arrangements that are not adopted here. First, we could have taken as the guiding criteria the notion of academic and linguistic traditions, and associate together papers relating to such research traditions, be they recognised and well documented like the British (Evans, Murray, Price) or the German (Brather, Eberhart, Sommer), or less well known – in English, that is – like the Spanish (Ruiz et al., González Reyero, Díaz-Andreu, Farrujia) or the Dutch (Eickhoff, Halbertsma, Verhart). Second, we could have adhered to the chronology or dating of the events under consideration, and thus begun with discussions of historical deeds or personalities prior to the mid-nineteenth century (in the chapters by Halbertsma, Sommer, Barbanera), moving on to the second half of that century (Kaeser, Hinsley & Wilcox, Ceserani, Martins, Farrujia, etc.), the early days of the twentieth (Platonova, Martinez et al., Immonen & Taavitsainen, etc.), to finally reach the more recent events and protagonists of the Second World War and beyond (Eickhoff, Bentz).

There is no doubting the pertinence of such 'chronological' and 'traditional' arrangements (as we may call them) within the framework of disciplinary history; from our perspective, their conventional nature represents however something of an impediment. When based on given geographical regions or languages of expression, historical accounts tend to be self-contained to the point of insularity, imperceptibly sliding towards self-serving assessments regarding this or that 'national' or regional tradition. Traditions do of course exist, and they are important factors that need to be taken into account, but it is also the case that they are made and unmade, deployed or downplayed following considerations that are often broader than idiom and location alone. Likewise the standard chronological coverage, with its inevitable directionally and its stadial-developmental sequence (involving the likes of 'pre-scientific pioneers', 'formative years', 'first syntheses' etc.), often results in records of unfolding that are rather too satisfying and teleological, with their retrospective realignment of selected milestones, with their casting of the current state of the art (as beheld by their chronicler) as an evident pinnacle, and with their well oriented goals as motivating prospects for the future. The point is obviously not to jettison chronological history or to overlook the dangers of anachronism – it is simply to recognise that the narrative injunction to 'begin at the beginning' may actually be artificial and reductive, and also to recall that in history as in evolution, contrary to common expectations, the mere passage of time still leaves everything yet to explain.

The chapters in this volume follow a certain thematic grouping which, if nothing else, can bring about some unexpected juxtapositions with regards to 'chronology' and 'tradition', casting next to each other or in close succession discussions touching on Classical and on Prehistoric Archaeology, on exhibitions and on photography, on national identity and on National Socialism, on Mediterranean archaeology and on Southwestern archaeology, on French archaeologists in Argentina and on Swedish archaeologists in Central Asia. Far more importantly, the chapters are linked by certain characteristics and dispositions, being for the most part micro-historical studies focusing on specific problem-areas and episodes, for which they provide concentrated and well documented analyses. In doing so, most chapters rely heavily on archival sources for researching and illuminating their subject matter. This stance not only takes them beyond more traditional historiographies often limited to the published literature, but also places them well in line with the overarching objectives of the AREA network, whose core activities (as noted in the Preface) focus precisely on archaeological archives, their valorisation and historical exploitation.

Archival materials such as correspondence, internal reports, notebooks and diaries, manuscript drafts, marginal annotations, diagrams, photographs, papers, scraps and minutiae of various descriptions, accumulated over the past centuries as a matter of scientific duty or administrative routine in dust-gathering repositories, all share the characteristics of not being seen by their authors and beholders as formal or accredited statements intended for public consumption – because these archival materials are considered to be 'mere' or 'raw' data, or trivial, or premature, or obsolete, or again too evident to mention, or not part of Science, or on the contrary far too important and revelatory to be left to unsupervised scrutiny in the academic or public domains. Archives, to be sure, are not some miracle panacea, independent of the perspectives and biases of their producers (and custodians): it would be fallacious to embrace them in the same positivist terms we otherwise critique and withhold from the archaeological evidence itself! Nevertheless, there is something appealingly veridical about archives, when considered as the tangible memory of archaeology: whether they have been systematically or haphazardly accumulated, they are as treasure troves – or indeed trash baskets – whose contents can, with a certain immediacy, disclose machinations or reveal discrepancies and thus nudge the kaleidoscope into unexpected and novel configurations. Together with published sources, but also in comparison with the formal, tradition-bound and (usually) self-controlled genre that are publications, archival materials can help us reach further into the 'substrate' of archaeology – those operational and practical aspects normally taken for granted and left unsaid – into its 'forefront' – that is, the initial expression of ideas and intuitions, first jotted down in correspondences or in the grey literature – and finally into its 'core' – where constraints and motivations of ideological or political order can transpire and be apprehended.

The possible transformations of archival materials into historical sources are a central concern in the first thematic section of this volume, dealing with 'sources and methods for the history of archaeology'. The first two chapters focus on two individuals and, in a sense, on their biography. The nineteenth century Swiss naturalist and archaeologist E. Desor, studied by Marc-Antonie Kaeser, is however less important here for his own doings as for the networks of connections between individuals, nationalities and disciplines which he embodies and brings to light. Likewise the career of the pioneering Dutch archaeologist C.C. Reuvens, several decades earlier, serve Runard Halbertsma to reach a wider perspective on archaeological practice in both the Netherlands and across the shores of the Mediterranean. Needless to say, archaeologists rarely if ever act and secure recognition in isolation, outside of some collective or organisational context. Curtis Hinsley & David Wilcox focus on an archaeological expedition to the American Southwest which they present through its personalities – notably F.H. Cushing – and its newly accessible archival productions. Nadezhda Platonova for her part draws on the activities and archives of the Institute for the History of Material Culture in St. Petersburg to challenge enduring assessments regarding the theoretical and methodological paucity of pre-Soviet archaeology. In Tim Murray's case, the annual meetings, publications and correspondence of the British Association for the Advancement of Science serve to grasp some of the personal and ideological conflicts surrounding the 'science of man' as it emerged in the 1860s and 70s. Thus touching on individuals initiatives as well as institutional structures, these chapters exemplify some methodological orientations for archaeological historiography.

For various reasons, the topic of 'archaeological practice' (dealt with in the next section) often ends up neglected or taken for granted in many disciplinary histories, where conceptual debates and theoretical constructs usually overshadow the stubborn determination and serendipity involved in the production of archaeological knowledge. There is undoubtedly scope for paying much closer attention, notably through archival sources, to these more 'material' aspects of archaeological fact-making – field techniques, excavations and stratigraphy, collections and classifications, reconstructions and analyses – if only to show that they are intertwined with both archaeological interpretations and ideological dispositions. Field practices are considered in this light in Giovanna Eberhardt's discussion of their underlying archaeological principles, and also in Gisela Ceserani's use of a specific episode in the study of site stratigraphy to uncover unexpected connections across the 'great divide' between Classical and Prehistoric archaeology. Connections of a different sort are prised out by Emma Bentz, who tracks in her chapter the emergence of a distinctive area of medieval studies across Britain, Germany and Scandinavia, while Sam Bergman rather follows the archaeological practices of one individual across highly contrasting settings, in Sweden and in China. More localised focus is provided by Megan Price, who follows the career of the 'antiquarian and grocer' H.M.J. Underhill between the amateur and professional worlds of late nineteenth-century Oxford, and also by Margarita Díaz-Andreu, who examines spreading networks of academic power and patronage in early twentieth century Spain. Finally, Christopher Evans looks in his chapter at one of the end results of the process, the model-based display in the nineteenth century, and examines what these contraptions tell us about archaeological performance and representation.

This of course ties in with the next section, dealing with 'visualising archaeology'. Here too one senses at times a partial historiographic occlusion, possibly because these visual elements are by now integral and indeed expected components of archaeological discourse, and therefore seldom scrutinised with the full attention they deserve. Reconstructions of past lifeways and monuments are a visual theme which provides ample opportunity for the rendition of clichés and imaginary aspirations. In her chapter, Maria Gabriella Micale shows how influential have been Andrae and Koldeway's early twentieth century reconstructions of Mesopotamian architecture on their contemporaries and followers. In his chronological tripartite study, Mancello Barbanera highlights the importance of visual displays and installations, and considers archaeological exhibitions of Etruscan and Roman remains in a wider comparative framework. In comparison, technical representations do not aim to enliven or illustrate, but rather to reproduce, schematise or abstract. As Christina Walter shows in her chapter, the drawing of Greek vases was motivated since Furtwängler and Beazley by a quest for styles and artists, but also by ambitions of scientific objectivity and accuracy. These scientific properties are of course widely attributed to the technique of photography which, as Susana González Reyero discusses with regards to Juan Cabré in Spain, has long been used in archaeology to document, represent and at times literally stand for the past. The inescapable situatedness of the photographic view is highlighted by Leo Verhart, who uses photographs from the early days of Dutch archaeology to secure unexpected glimpse at the practices and methods of the times.

Both the practices of archaeology and the pasts that are thereby apprehended, reconstructed and visualised are thoroughly enmeshed in 'questions of identity', to which the last section of this volume is dedicated. It has already been established that archaeological pasts, by virtue of their practical and discursive construction, always leave room for appropriation and instrumentalisation, for their producers and their beholders alike. The possibility of drawing and illustrating long term narratives in which affiliations and resemblances can justify (or impose) common destinies is an obvious asset, and so is the opportunity to engage in some mises en scènes of sites of memories or of material paraphernalia. All this to bolster a sense of political or civic belonging (notably to the nation-state), but also to forge other complementary or parallel identities, including amateur, professional, urban, provincial, regional, metropolitan, colonial, citizen and indigenes. Ulrike Sommer takes us in her chapter to an important moment early in the nineteenth century when archaeology was transformed from localised antiquarian erudition to a scientific discipline, partly on the wake of emerging nationalism. A century later, an almost opposite process is highlighted by Ana Teresa Martínez, Constanza Taboada & Alexander Auat regarding the émigrés Wagner brothers, whose mythical bolstering of a remote Argentinean province comes at the expense of scientific credibility. Farrujia present in their chapter yet another case, when issues of prehistoric and anthropological origins in the Canaries islands are addressed by European powers as well as local actors. Martins for her part focuses on late nineteenth century debates within the Portuguese scientific community, regarding the autochthonous origins or foreign influences on local Iron Age societies. As Juan P. Bellón, Arthur Ruiz & Alberto Sánchez show, the Spanish archaeologist Gómez-Moreno was preoccupied several decades later with broadly similar questions regarding Hispanic and Iberian identity. Quite obviously, questions of identity have also much to do with the individual archaeologists at work, their background and motivations. As convincingly shown by Visa Immonen & Jussi-Pekka Taavitsainen, it was J. Rinne's use of the Swedish language in 1920s Finland that stirred controversy and led to the cancellation of the professorial chair to which he was destined. Comparing the professional and political trajectories of Virchow and of Kossinna serves Sebastian Brather in his contribution to better contextualise the history of German archaeology, while in the final chapter of this volume Martijn Eickhoff assess the impact of national socialist ideas in Dutch pre- and protohistory of the 1930s and 40s, skirting between the creation of a putative Dutch 'national character' and the pursuit of objective scientific standards of research.

As can be gathered, many chapters in this volume could have been equally presented in a different sequence and in other thematic sections: Halbertsma's biographical study includes fascinating insights on archaeology in the field, Evans and his models bear as much on the visualisation of archaeology as on its practice, González Reyero and her photographs bear as much on the practice of archaeology as on its visualisation, Micale's discussion of architectural reconstructions touch also on questions of identity, Price's discussion of amateurs in archaeology could find its place next to Murray on the one hand and Sommer on the other, and likewise Barbanera's comments of archaeological exhibitions are closely linked to questions of identity – as is Platonova's reassessment of Soviet historiography. Be it as it may, and acknowledging many other permutations and possibilities, we will be satisfied as editors if we have conveyed the makeup of this particular volume, with its deliberate plurality and aspired coherence, as a more general characteristic of the histories we aim for. That, and the recognition that the history of archaeology can be a credible, enriching and indeed inspiring field of enquiry.

Part I
SOURCES AND METHODS FOR THE HISTORY OF ARCHAEOLOGY

Chapter 1
Biography as Microhistory

The Relevance of Private Archives for Writing the History of Archaeology

Marc-Antoine Kaeser

Abstract

Current interest in the history of archaeology is mainly due to theoretical, social, and political developments in contemporary archaeological research. This makes such historical undertakings particularly vulnerable to presentist biases. In this respect, this article underlines the preventive role of archival material, and especially of private archives (correspondence, diaries, etc.). Drawing on my recently published biography of Edouard Desor (1811–1882), I try to show that such sources can help to free us from present-day categories of analysis. By following the path of the historical subject under study, the biographer can grasp the internal logic of thought processes that are alien to current archaeology. Furthermore, writing history at the micro scale of a single scientist makes it possible to encompass all the social, political, intellectual, cultural and religious factors which interact in the construction of archaeological knowledge, to grasp the changing relations shared by these factors, and also to underscore the dynamics which sustain such relations. Understood as a kind of 'microhistory', this biography requires us to transcend the anecdotal. The subject of the biography is actually not the subject of the study, as much as a 'key' that leads to the wider reality of past archaeology. Microhistorical biography appreciates history in a realistic way, through the notions of an actor of the past – which have to be corrected through their confrontation with the pluri-individual data of contextualised prosopography.

Why Care about the History of Archaeology? Some Reflexive Considerations

Since the beginning of the 1990s, the history of archaeology has undergone a considerable expansion (cf. Trigger 2001, Murray 2002, Schlanger 2002). Being characterised by a formidable increase in the number of research projects, publications, meetings, and exhibitions relating to the past of the discipline throughout the world, this expansion is not merely quantitative: beyond the amount of scholarship carried out, one can also notice the growing theoretical awareness of its practitioners, as well as an increase in the general attention aroused. Thus, research into the history of the discipline can no longer be belittled as a 'hobby for retired archaeologists', a comfortable retreat for occasional, anecdotal papers, as it often used to be. In fact, until to the 1980s, few studies sought to raise above memorialist triviality, and most of these were rather considered as philosophical essays on the role and destiny of archaeology (e.g. Wahle 1950/51, Laming-Emperaire 1964, Daniel 1975, Trigger 1989, Malina & Vasicek 1990).

Gratifying as this historiographic trend might be, we ought to wonder on the possible causes of such an expansion. Broadly speaking, this trend fits in with the general blossoming of Science studies, insofar as historical reflections obviously benefit from the post-modern denial of the natural objectivity of science. And in our discipline, these historical undertakings have of course taken advantage of the reaction against the positivism or the scientism blamed on the New Archaeology, as well as from the globally relativist climate of post-processualist trends.

From a more specific point of view, it appears that the modes and forms of this expansion also stem from several interrelated factors peculiar to contemporary circumstances within archaeology. Indeed, most of the themes under focus in the present historic investigations appear to be connected to current conditions in the politics of archaeological research, as well as to epistemological, theoretical and ethical concerns which are the subject of current debates in our discipline.

If we take, for instance, research themes like colonial archaeology and its position within imperialist policies, gender aspects in the past of archaeological research, the role of archaeological interpretation in the construction of national identities, the more general relations between archaeological paradigms and contemporary philosophical trends (such as materialism or evolutionism) or ideological movements (like communism, fascism, national-socialism or liberalism), as well as the study of the development of techniques and methods in their relationship with the changing goals, aims and significance of archaeological research – all these themes feature an undoubted topicality, in one way or another. In the cases in point, we shall only mention postcolonial adjustments and the opposition to neo-imperialism, feminist commitments to the politics of cultural heritage and archaeological research, the development of communautarist claims, the building of Europe and the resurgence of nationalisms, the collapse of the Soviet model (or foil), German reunification and the retirement of the last generation of Third Reich professors' students, the calling into question of the role of the state in the 'management' of cultural heritage, the current crisis of preventive archaeology, etc.

In brief, the causes of the current interest in the history of archaeology rest mainly with theoretical, social and political developments in the contemporary practice of archaeology: the promptings of such historical undertakings appear to be embedded in present debates and questionings within the discipline.

Internalist Approaches and Presentist Biases

The close connection between historiographic inquiries and present concerns as well as contemporary circumstances in the field of archaeological research is easily understandable. As a general rule, within Science studies, it is a characteristic of historical investigations carried out by practitioners of the disciplines under study – investigations which are commonly termed 'internalist', as opposed to 'externalist' investigations carried out by professional historians, sociologists, or philosophers of science. It is precisely this connection which ensures their relevance and significance within current archaeological research.

If we consider the question from the standpoint of historical method, however, the important part played by such internal, archaeological designs may constitute a problem – or, to put it plainly, be a challenge for the scientific validity of these historical undertakings. For, on principle, historians are compelled to strive for detachment towards their subject of research: as far as possible, they should leave aside contemporary concerns in the course of their investigations.

From that point of view, it is worth remembering that for a long time, historians and sociologists of science have disparaged and categorically condemned internalist approaches. This question has been the subject of impassioned disputes. But eventually, after what constituted one of the classic debates of Science studies in the last quarter of the twentieth century, a more conciliatory position prevailed, acknowledging the effective and specific contribution of internalist research in the writing of the history of science – especially in view of the expert skills of the practitioners in the respective disciplines.

The acceptance of the heuristic worth of internalism is good reason for satisfaction, insofar as history of archaeology is almost exclusively written by archaeologists. In fact, it appears that the past of our discipline did not and still does not arouse much interest among professionals within Science studies.[1] Obviously, our histories of archaeology are basically addressing an audience of fellow archaeologists. But if we are in a way working 'in-house', the fact remains nonetheless that in order to ensure the soundness and efficiency of our research, we need to abide by the commonly accepted rules set by sociologists and historians of science following much reflection and theoretical debate. In this respect, the main obstacle to avoid appears to be 'presentism'. Being a characteristic of many internalist studies, presentism marks out an approach which analyses the past from a present, modern perspective, with a modern agenda, as well as with modern concepts and ways of thought.

As a matter of fact, presentism leads indirectly to a prejudicial splitting up of historical research. Since presentist studies are prompted by and meet concerns specific to very diverse specialities of archaeological research, they tend to become out of reach or useless to other historians of archaeology (Kaeser 2005) – let alone to historians of science in general. Now, this presentist splitting up dashes, or at least delays what precisely constitutes the purpose of projects such as AREA (Archives of European Archaeology) – that is, the setting-up of a real *research field* dedicated to the history of archaeology, where each researcher would not be compelled to define his own method and theoretical principles at every new study.

But the main defect of presentism remains that it somewhat naïvely searches in the past for unilateral answers to contemporary scientific problems. Aiming at an immediate 'usefulness' of historiographic inquiries,[2] presentism does not worry of course about anachronisms; it has therefore been subjected to eloquent criticism (e.g. Stocking 1968, Blanckaert 1988) that need not be repeated here. It is certainly more useful to go into the possible causes of presentism's surprising persistence in many histories of archaeology, despite the devastating indictment of professional historians.

The resistance of presentism is probably due to a misunderstanding of the nature and signification of so-called 'historicism' which is set against it as the path to be followed (Di Brizio 1995, Blondiaux & Richard 1999, Mucchielli 2000: 175–76). While putting forward relativist claims contending that nobody can really cut themselves off from the present, some believe this undermines the very basis of historicism's axiomatic legitimacy. Such claims are not unfounded; but they are used improperly. For historicism is not a formula: it is *a methodological principle serving an ideal purpose on the theoretical level.* Thus, if the aims of historical research always remain in a sense presentist, the achievement of these aims calls for an approach that respects, as far as possible, the principles of historicist methodology.

Historicism, Microhistory and Scientific Biography

For the application of historicism, the main difficulty lies in the reification of the categories of analysis. In the course of their work, historians necessarily resort to categories which are obviously constructions, conceptual tools which they shape to apprehend reality. From that standpoint, microhistory constitutes the best answer, insofar as it strives to avoid the reduction of reality through a reduction of its own field of analysis.

Microhistory (Ginzburg 1982, Levi 1989a, 1992, Revel 1996) is a rather loose and varied historical movement born as a reaction against structuralism and quantitative history, which is characterised by its focus on the unique experience of social 'actors'. At a very small scale and from fine traces in the archive material scrutinised intensively, it endeavours to reconstruct the complex web of past actions, relations and social networks. Being influenced by ethnology and cultural anthropology, it aims at the understanding of the past from the functioning of the cogs in the wheel rather than from a reconstitution of the global system or the general structure. In Science studies, furthermore, microhistory is felicitously able to put to use the respective assets of the history, the philosophy, and the sociology of science, beyond all quarrels between factions.

As the title of this chapter indicates, I consider that scientific biography can be implemented as a kind of microhistory. This is what I attempted to do in the biography to be discussed here as a case study,[3] that of Edouard Desor (Kaeser 2004). The German-born Swiss geologist and palaeontologist Edouard Desor (1811–1882) was one of the main instigators of prehistoric archaeology as a scientific discipline during the 1860s and 1870s (Kaeser 2002). As such, Desor is not the real subject of the analysis, but rather a 'key' opening to a life-scale study of emerging prehistory. Following Desor's path with his own testimony, I endeavoured to relate the birth and early development of prehistoric science *from the interior* (Fig. 1.1).

Fig. 1.1 Edouard Desor (1811–1882). Bibliothèque Publique et Universitaire, Neuchâtel (Switzerland).

For the history of science, such a microhistorical biography actually has the advantage of calling on conceptual tools which are not constructed by the historian: the categories are inferred from the perceptions of the subject of the biography, whose subjectivity paradoxically forms an absolutely objective historical fact. While using terms like 'the clerical party', 'amateur antiquarians', or putting forward the difference between nineteenth-century 'anté-histoire' and the modern sense of 'prehistory', the biographer can rely on notions and concepts actually employed by the person under study. Now, basing on the individual perceptions of one archaeologist among many, grasping the social representations he shared with a number of colleagues, comprehending the meaning they gave to the world they were living in, we most certainly better understand their actions and motives (Chartier 1989, 1997a, 1997b) – and thus, the archaeology they practised.

In this respect, scientific biography seems to be the best way to approach the ideal goal of historicism in the history of science: plunging into the life experience of a scientist forces the historian to submit himself to the otherness of the past, instead of imposing, knowingly or not, his own perspectives onto it. The biography of an archaeologist makes it possible to beyond present-day categories and concepts of modern research, in order to grasp some internal logics of thought processes characteristic of past science. All the more so, since writing the history of archaeology at the small scale of a single scientist helps to transversely encompass all the social, political, intellectual, cultural, and religious factors which interacted in the construction of archaeological knowledge, to detail the changing relations which these factors shared, and to underscore the dynamics which sustained such relations. In short, such a microhistorical biography proposes a multicontextualised reconstruction of the scientific, social, cultural, intellectual, political, ideological and religious grounds in which prehistoric archaeology was bred and grew as a new science.

The Relevance and Teachings of Private Archives

Just as microhistory does not amount to the mere adoption of a small scale of analysis, so are biographical accounts not necessarily microhistorical. But beyond the adoption of a microhistorical approach, the interest of biography already lies in the nature of the potential sources. Thanks to the limited range of his starting point, the biographer can cut his dependence on second-hand historiography, and rely above all on archival material. Besides, biographic subjects often allow for

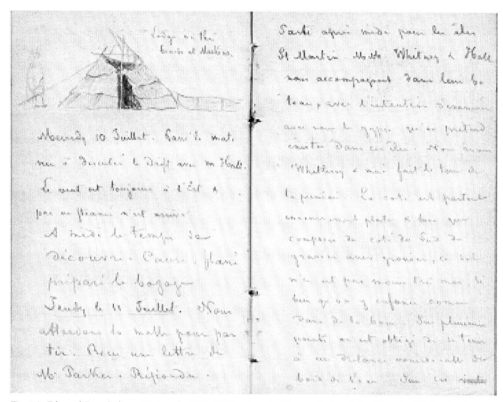

Fig. 1.2 Edouard Desor's diary, 10–11 July 1850. Bibliothèque Publique et Universitaire, Neuchâtel (Switzerland). During his participation to the the US Geological Survey of Michigan, Desor noted down his scientific observations, as well as the turns taken by the exploration. From the angle of a 'human geography', he also reported comments on the customs of the Chippewa, Cotarais and Menomones native communities.

an abundant and varied body of documentation – especially those male scientists of the middle classes who formed the overwhelming majority of the archaeologists' community, up to the middle of the twentieth century.

The case of Edouard Desor is a perfect illustration of such a wealth of archival material (quantitatively as well as qualitatively). Apart from the books and the offprints of his personal library,[4] most of his scientific papers (corrected proofs, drafts and original manuscripts of articles and lectures) have been preserved. Particular attention will be paid to his correspondence and private diary. While the circumstances of their composition and their tone vary considerably, such documents nevertheless place the historian straight into the scientist's daily activity. The spontaneity characteristic of many of these pieces of writing dispenses the historian with *a posteriori* reconstructions; and the collation of these different documents gives a qualified vision of the objectives, ambitions, attitudes and acts of their author.

What is left of Desor's ample correspondence (both letters received and copies of letters sent) amounts to no less than 30,000 items, which do not seem to be the result of a selection. This fond consists of business and private, as well as scientific or political mail, thus giving access to all the facets of Desor's life and personality. The combining of comparisons between the letters assesses the relevance and significance of their respective content. To that purpose, a prosopography taking each correspondent's personality, as well as the nature and the strength of his (or her) ties with Desor, is needed.

In the diary he kept for almost forty years (spanning more than 70 notebooks), Desor wrote down very concise comments, amounting basically to a daily account of business done. But despite its outward triviality, this document is highly informative on his activities and social network; and the words used attest to their author's thoughts.[5] As we shall see below, the diary also reveals surprising connections between concerns which the historian would otherwise have ordered in quite distinct spheres (Fig. 1.2).

However, the biographer should not be content with those sources directly related to the character under study. I thus had to turn to 'tertiary sources', which put the exchanges between Desor and the respective individuals in perspective. This cross-analysis of testimonies from individuals or institutions having themselves direct relations with Desor (a kind of 'triangulation') proved most fruitful. Through converse checking, such a triangulation shows the functioning of an environment among which Desor is only a component, and enables us to assess the specificity or representativity of his thoughts, works and actions.

Desor as a Key to the Broader Context of Emerging Prehistoric Archaeology

Apart from the issue of appropriate documentation, some individuals are better suited than others to microhistorical biography. As we shall see, Desor actually presents certain features which make him a most relevant figure on all significant problematics of the birth and first development of prehistoric science. Besides, the scientist Desor offers the interest of having been equally active in industrial and financial business, politics, and religion – characteristics which make him a ideal mediator for the above-mentioned 'multicontextualisation'. And in all these different spheres, his personal path has been both original and turbulent, thus offering clearly contrasting viewpoints and enhanced contours to the historian.

Fig. 1.3 Combe-Varin, Desor's second home in the Jura Mountains. Engraving by Auguste Bachelin, 1860. Edouard Desor turned this summer house into a kind of pastoral academy dedicated to the worshipping of Science, welcoming scientists, politicians, theologians, writers and artists willing to share their ideals and knowledge beyond all social, professional or ideological boundaries (Vogt 1879, De Beer 1950).

An orphan of the lower middle class reduced to social assistance, Desor lead a bohemian life up to his 40s, when he suddenly became a prosperous millionaire, who could exploit his fortune in favour of philanthropic works and social issues, as well as scientific and political initiatives. A young revolutionary German student, he had had to move to France as a political refugee; settling later in the United States, where he campaigned for the abolition of slavery, he finally established himself in Switzerland. There, he managed an outstanding political career which he completed with his election to the presidency of the national House of Representatives. In the matter of religion, he rejected the pietistic education of his youth and professed atheism for a long time. Awakening to spiritualism as a consequence of his American experience, Desor rallied rationalism, and even took a prominent part in the foundation in Switzerland of Liberal Protestantism, a church 'without priests nor catechism'.

During his life, he travelled through every corner of the European continent; his scientific research lead him to all kinds of terrains, from the Sahara Desert to the virgin forests of the American Great Lakes, climbing as well the main Alpine summits on the occasion of his work with his master and former friend Louis Agassiz, the 'inventor' of the Ice Age. Being German by birth, French by education and naturalised Swiss citizen, mastering English and Italian languages as well, this sociable-natured man shared contacts throughout Europe and the United States, building scientific and business networks of a considerable extent and density (Fig. 1.3).

On the scientific level, one can note that being a self-taught man did not prevent him from reaching the heights of academic hierarchy, even after a serious setback, when the whole American establishment strove to ostracise him, as a result of a private dispute with Louis Agassiz, who had become the figurehead of United States science. In this respect, his uneven path makes him a textbook case for a sociological study of the requirements of the construction of a scientific career, as well as of the limits of the status of 'professional scientist' in the nineteenth century.

Above all, his work covers a very broad spectrum, for he did not undertake research in prehistoric archaeology and anthropology only. Trained as a geologist and a palaeontologist specialised in the study of Tertiary and Quaternary terrains, he was also a complete naturalist in the largest meaning of the word, dealing from ethnography to oceanography or botany. Furthermore, his scientific activity took very diverse ways: beside his basic and applied research, Desor actually operated as a publicist and a populariser of science who became deeply involved in the promotion and politics of science – thus bringing to light the social functioning of scientific research.

In brief, thanks to the abundance of archival material, as well as to the diversity of his activities and personal commitments, Desor's life and works give precious insights into numerous historical and epistemological issues. In the scope of this paper, I will now concentrate on some general and theoretical lessons from such a microhistorical biography regarding our historicist 'multicontextualisation'.

Prehistoric Archaeology and its Original Relations with Other Sciences

Internalist approaches always tend to deal with the past of archaeology regardless of the scientific context in which it developed. This proves particularly prejudicial for the study of the period prior to the first decades of the twentieth-century, when archaeological research did not yet exist as a discipline, and was undertaken within very varied scientific settings, by people with very different backgrounds and heuristic promptings, covering an extraordinarily broad spectrum, from the humanities to the natural or physical sciences (Kaeser 2006).

Of course, also conventional histories of ideas draw some connections with issues and debates external to archaeology. Unfortunately, such connections are usually restricted to questions explicitly called upon in past archaeological literature. In the case in point, Darwinism can serve as a typical example: most histories of archaeology referred and continue to refer to the alleged decisive influence of Darwinism in the setting up of evolutionary archaeology. Now, it has been clearly established (e.g. Freeland 1983, Bowler 1987, Richard 1992, Delisle 1998) that Darwinism had virtually no role to play in this process. This process actually dates back to the ideology of Progress, long before the publication of Darwin's *Origin of Species* in 1859; and as far as biological analogies were concerned, transformism was more appropriate than natural selection (Bowler 1989). In a way, Darwinism was actually to have some influence on archaeology; but this influence did not act upon research and epistemology: it only applied to the subsequent popularisation of archaeological work and to the ideological uses of prehistoric knowledge.

From that point of view, it can be quite instructive to examine, from the interior, the setting up of the archaeological debates. In Desor's case, when one considers the practice of prehistoric research at its very beginnings, it appears that there was absolutely no solution of continuity with other sciences. This might indeed not be a real surprise for the historians of science. It is easy, for instance, to imagine that there have been strong connections between vertebrate palaeontology and the study of the Upper Palaeolithic, which was actually termed the 'Reindeer Age'. The same may apply to the relations between Quaternary geology and the stratigraphical analysis of paleolithic sites. But it proves more interesting, when one takes into account that on a far more general plane, prehistoric archaeology was combined with palaeontology, geology and botany in the development and the strengthening of a holistic 'progressionism' (Bowler 1976, Blanckaert 2000). Here, archaeology has not merely been subjected to influences from other fields of knowledge: through a game of mutual backing-up, it also played an active part in the epistemological shaping of these disciplines.

Lastly, the analysis of Desor's works shows that such an absence of compartmentalisation also applied between spheres and notions without obvious ontological or cognitive proximity. His notion of 'archaeological cultures', for example, did not derive from ethnography or cultural anthropology, but was directly inspired from the geological 'facies' – a concept which had been characterised by a geologist colleague in his study of the sedimentary rocks in the Jura Mountains (Gressly 1838). Likewise, it is apparently from botany that he drew the inspiration of a theoretical pattern allowing for a conciliation between the synchronic diversity of archaeological cultures and the diachronic progress of human society, technology and morals. Desor based himself on Moritz Wagner's theory (1868) regarding the central role of migrations in the process of speciation in the vegetable kingdom.[6] Now, such inspirations, analogies and connections were never stated explicitly in Desor's published works. Probably because they were considered to be compromising, conflicting with the necessities of positive and reasoned scientific method, these inspirations can in fact only be detected in private archives.

'Science' and 'Society' in the Construction of Knowledge

A similar continuity can be traced between the so-called 'intrinsic' and 'extrinsic' factors in the construction of knowledge. As it happens, Desor systematically took advantage of his political, commercial, financial and theological competence and power in his scientific work. Conversely, he constantly resorted to his scientific knowledge in the choice of his financial investments, as well as in the definition and assertion of his political or religious positions.

From the choice of his subjects of research up to their treatment, to the definition of the interpretative models, and to the gathering of facts, his practice of science was widely governed by promptings and questionings ensuing from other spheres. As an example, his archaeological work in Northern Africa primarily suited a desire to solve some problems regarding the hermeneutics of the Old Testament; and the data brought to the fore, as well as their archaeological and anthropological interpretation, lie and can only really be understood in the scope of this theological question. Similarly, on the occasion of a sojourn in Scandinavia in the summer of

1846, it was a geological problem relating to the dating of various glacial phenomena which lead him to take an interest in (and to join) the prehistoric studies of Nordic antiquarians. To give a last example, it was a social and economic analysis of contemporary Italian underdevelopment (a criticism whose motivations resided in theological concerns) which strengthened Desor's understanding of prehistoric technological and cultural evolution.

Eventually, it proves impossible to make any clear-cut and objective distinction between 'science' and the 'social' (Latour 1997). In truth, there is nothing revolutionary about such a conclusion: it is even a favourite refrain of post-modern analysis in recent Science studies. But this interconnection gains under biographical and microhistorical scrutiny a concrete expression which profitably compensates for its comfortable abstraction in theoretical discourse. Viewed in a realistic way, such a continuity does not reduce past scientific undertakings to a shapeless jumble. In the case of Desor's biography, it has to be stressed that the lack of boundary between science and society is not simply a deconstructionist interpretation; for it is based on the representations of the historical subjects themselves as, quite simply, Desor did not consider 'science' and 'society' to be distinct entities.

This becomes clearer when one takes into account the meaning that Desor gave to his own scientific undertakings. To him, the mission of science applied all over: scientific Truth was actually to be the basis of spiritual principles, political progress, social justice, and economic welfare as well. Now, since science was to exert its authority over all spheres, it sustained, and at the same time benefited from all the other activities of the scientist. In Desor's viewpoint, as in that of most of his contemporaries, the 'social' thus *dissolved* into science (Kaeser 2004: 466–69).

'Context' and the Representativity of the Biographical Subject

The details of such a biography show that the personal path of the scientist, his commitments in other matters (scientific, political, commercial, or religious) can notably influence upon his archaeological research and epistemology. One should not, however, interpret such influences as a kind of social determinism affecting the production and diffusion of science. It should rather lead us to question the meaning of what we call the 'context' of scientific research. The 'context' in question does in no way constitute a rigid determinant: scrutinised at the scale of a singular life, it turns out to be extraordinary flexible. In Desor's case, we could not content ourselves with drawing parallels between his political liberalism, his theological progressivism, his biological transformism and his cultural evolutionism. For none of these elements are given, positive data: they gradually developed under reciprocal influences which depended upon particular contingencies, where ideas, patterns or concepts could temporarily pass from one sphere to the other.

Thus, it is only through the subjective perception and the uncertain awareness of the historical actors that the 'context' can exert its influence. As a construction, the context is composed of all the elements (intellectual as well as institutional) which the scientist chooses to make use of within his wider environment (Latour 1994: 148). In brief, context does not steer science, and does not either impose insuperable constraints on scientific research. On the contrary: through the multiplicity of its impulses and the almost infinite variety of their combinations, this flexible 'context' constitutes an inexhaustible source of inspiration for each scientist – according to his nature, to his former experiences, and to his personal inclination. Eventually, this notion of 'context' also offers an elegant solution to the tricky problem of the representativity of the subject of the biography. For it shows that individual specificities alone allow for a realistic reconstruction of the social context. Indeed, uses and practice are the best illustration of the varying elasticity of the norm.[7] Assuming that the slits are part of the system, it is pointless to contrast individual liberty with supposedly rigid and pre-existing social contingencies: in reality, both share a dynamic relation.

Conclusion

Considering the teachings of such a biography within the broad scope of the origins of prehistoric archaeology, it appears that the heuristic orientations which Desor and his contemporaries followed when they settled the epistemology and the principles of prehistoric archaeology were of an extremely contingent nature. Social, political, spiritual, and economic circumstances and concerns specific to their time, as well as now long forgotten and often invalidated debates in other sciences, played a considerable role in the shaping of *our* prehistoric archaeology. Thus, many concepts and analytical categories of present-day research are a legacy of an outdated and often forgotten past. In brief, some of the frameworks we are still moving in have been shaped for uses (social and intellectual) that are no more. All in all, modern prehistory can be considered as a prisoner of its own past.

Here lies the strength of the history of archaeology. Thanks to the underscoring of the forms, the characteristics, and the motives of this constraining legacy, historiographic inquiry can help us to free our discipline from the weight of the past, to clear archaeology from certain epistemological automatisms and from hitherto obsolete heuristic conventions. But this can only be reached when these historical undertakings refrain from presentism, and follow a historicist approach.

Resorting to archival documentation is essential in that respect. And as I have tried to show, private archives and biography are certainly most appropriate for such approaches, since they offer unique insights into the concrete realities of science in the making. Eventually, the biographer adopting a microhistorical method might be in the best position in order to set aside present-day categories and modern preconceptions. Studying it from the inside, with contemporary words and concepts, he can grasp the underlying, intrinsic logics of past archaeology – and, ensuing, deconstruct it afterwards, in order to bring its persistent weaknesses to light.

Notes

1. This is quite worrying, in my view. As Alain Schnapp points out (personal communication), this lack of concern on the part of Science studies actually seems to testify to an epistemological flimsiness of archaeology. As a matter of fact, among sociologists of science in particular, demonstrations based upon the analysis of a discipline lacking a solid core and coherent structures can hardly prove very conclusive. In this respect, and in order to draw the historians' attention to archaeology, we probably ought to stress two important facts. Firstly, that our discipline stands at the merging of the sciences of Life, of the Earth and of Man, between natural and human sciences, making it thus a potentially strategic field of study. And secondly, that as a result of its extreme dependence upon material sources, archaeology may open quite promising prospects on the study of the role of such sources in the construction of natural and cultural history.

2. Coye 1997: 295–97 contrasts 'useful' (and instrumentalised) historiography with 'efficient' historiography.

3. For the theoretical and methodological principles which governed this biography, see Kaeser 2003. Generally speaking, the use of biography in the writing of the history of archaeology has not given rise to much theoretical thought. In my opinion, Givens 1992, Murray 1999, and Nordbladh 2002, are setting excessively modest goals to the exercise of biography (see also Gillberg 1998). And despite its sensible resorting to the philosophy and sociology of science, Baudou 1998 illustrates the limits of internalism (see also Nordbladh 1998's comments).

4. This is not to overlook contemporary scientific publications, whose importance needs no demonstration. In Desor's case, his works need always to be confronted to those of his colleagues, with whom they interacted. I have been anxious to collect Desor's exhaustive bibliography (some 1100 books, articles, offprints, and published transcriptions of oral contributions at learned societies' sessions); it has been of crucial importance to illustrate the construction of various fields of research, and the analysis of their editorial scope (Kaeser 2004: 483–532).

5. On the conscious and unconscious sincerity of private diaries, and the value of such testimonies, see Lejeune 1975; regarding Desor, see Kaeser 2003.
6. Similarly, it is noteworthy that Wagner exerted a strong influence on Friedrich Ratzel's study of the movements of material culture, which in turn opened the way for his disciple Leo Frobenius' anthropological concept of 'Kulturkreis' – not to mention Kossinna's later paradigm.
7. See Levi 1989b, Loriga 1996 (as a reply to Bourdieu 1986). In this respect, the apparently paradoxical role of social history in the revival of biography has to be underlined. Within the history of science, the sociological articles of Shapin & Thackray 1974 and of Hankins 1979 had a considerable impact.

References

Baudou, E. 1998. 'The Problem-Orientated Scientific Biography as a Research Method', *Norwegian Archaeological Review* 31/2: 79–96 [Reply to comments: 113–18].

Blanckaert, C. 1988. '"Story" et "History" de l'ethnologie', *Revue de synthèse* 109: 451–67.

———. 2000. 'Avant Adam. Les représentations analogiques de l'homme fossile dans la première moitié du XIXe siècle', in A. & J. Ducros (ed.), *L'homme préhistorique: Images et imaginaire*. Paris: L'Harmattan, pp. 23–61.

Blondiaux, L. & N. Richard. 1999. 'A quoi sert l'histoire des sciences de l'homme?', in C. Blanckaert & al. (ed.), *L'histoire des sciences de l'homme. Trajectoire, enjeux et questions vives*. Paris: L'Harmattan, pp. 109–30.

Bourdieu, P. 1986. 'L'illusion biographique', *Actes de la recherche en sciences sociales* 62/63: 69–72.

Bowler, P.J. 1976. *Fossils and Progress: Palaeontology and the idea of progressive evolution in the nineteenth century*. New York: Science History Publications.

———. 1987. *Theories of Human Evolution. A Century of Debate, 1844–1944*. Oxford: Basil Blackwell.

———. 1989. *The Invention of Progress. The Victorians and the Past*. Oxford: Basil Blackwell.

Chartier, R. 1989. 'Le monde comme représentation', *Annales E.S.C.* 6: 1505–20.

———. 1997a. 'Introduction générale', in *Au bord de la falaise. L'histoire entre certitudes et inquiétude*. Paris: Albin Michel, pp. 9–21.

———. 1997b. 'L'histoire entre récit et connaissance', in *Au bord de la falaise. L'histoire entre certitudes et inquiétude*. Paris: Albin Michel, pp. 87–107.

Coye, N. 1997. *La préhistoire en parole et en acte. Méthodes et enjeux de la pratique archéologique, 1830–1950*. Paris: L'Harmattan.

Daniel, G. 1975. *A Hundred and Fifty Years of Archaeology*. London: Duckworth.

Darwin, Ch. 1859. *The Origin of Species by Means of Natural Selection or the Preservation of Favoured Races in the Struggle for Life*. London: Murray.

De Beer, G.R. 1950. 'Combe-Varin', *Annals of Science* 6: 215–29.

Delisle, R. 1998. 'Les origines de la paléontologie humaine: essai de réinterprétation', *L'Anthropologie* 102: 3–19.

Di Brizio, M.B. 1995. '"Présentisme" et "Historicisme" dans l'historiographie de G.W. Stocking', *Gradhiva* 18: 77–89.

Freeland, G. 1983. 'Evolutionism and Arch(a)eology', in D.R. Oldroyd & I. Langham (ed.), *The Wider Domain of Evolutionary Thought*. Dordrecht: Reidel, pp. 175–219.

Gillberg, A. 1998. 'Biography in the History of Archaeology', in A.-C. Andersson & al. (ed.), *The Kaleidoscopic Past. Proceedings of the 5th Nordic TAG Conference*. Göteborg: Göteborg University Press, pp. 323–32.

Ginzburg, C. 1982. *The Cheese and the Worms: the Cosmos of a Sixteenth-Century Miller*. Harmondsworth: Penguin Books [Original Italian edition 1976].

Givens, D.R. 1992. 'The Role of Biography in Writing the History of Archaeology', in J. E. Reyman (ed.), *Rediscovering our past: Essays on the History of American Archaeology*. Avebury: Ashgate, pp. 51–66.

Gressly, A. 1838. 'Observations géologiques sur le Jura soleurois', *Mémoires de la Société helvétique des sciences naturelles* 1838/2: 1–112.

Hankins, Th. L. 1979. 'In Defence of Biography: The Use of Biography in the History of Science', *History of science* 17: 1–16.

Kaeser, M.-A. 2002. 'On the International Roots of Prehistory', *Antiquity* 76: 170–7.

————. 2003. 'La science vécue. Les potentialités de la biographie en histoire des sciences', *Revue d'Histoire des Sciences Humaines* 8: 139–60.

————. 2004. *L'univers du préhistorien. Science, foi et politique dans l'œuvre et la vie d'Edouard Desor (1811–1882)*. Paris: L'Harmattan.

————. 2006. 'The First Establishment of Prehistoric Science. The Shortcomings of Autonomy', in J. Callmer et al. (ed.), *Die Anfänge der ur- und frühgeschichtlichen Archäologie als archäologisches Fach (1890–1930) im europäischen Vergleich / The Beginnings of Academic Pre- and Protohistoric Archaeology in a European Perspective*. Rahden: M. Leidorf (Berliner Archäologische Forschungen 2), pp. 149–60.

————. 2005. 'L'histoire des recherches lacustres. De l'instrument disciplinaire à un historicisme réflexif', in Ph. Della Casa and M. Trachsel (ed.), *WES'04: Wetland Economies and Societies. Proceedings of the International Conference. Zurich, 10–13 March 2004*. Zurich: Swiss National Museum, Chronos, pp. 17–24.

Laming-Emperaire, A. 1964. *Origines de l'archéologie préhistorique en France*. Paris: Picard.

Latour, B. 1994. *Pasteur, une science, un style, un siècle*. Paris: Perrin.

————. 1997. *Nous n'avons jamais été modernes. Essai d'anthropologie symétrique*. Paris: La Découverte.

Lejeune, Ph. 1975. *Le pacte autobiographique*. Paris: Seuil.

Levi, G. 1989a. *Le pouvoir au village. Histoire d'un exorciste dans le Piémont du XVIIe siècle*. Paris: Gallimard.

————. 1989b. 'Les usages de la biographie', *Annales E.S.C.* 6: 1325–36.

————. 1992. 'On Microhistory', in P. Burke (ed.), *New Perspectives on Historical Writing*. Oxford: Polity Press, pp. 93–113.

Loriga, S. 1996. 'La biographie comme problème', in J. Revel (ed.), *Jeux d'échelles. La micro-analyse à l'expérience*. Paris: EHESS-Gallimard-Seuil, pp. 209–31.

Malina, J. and Z. Vasicek. 1990. *Archaeology Yesterday and Today. The Development of Archaeology in the Sciences and Humanities*. Cambridge: Cambridge University Press.

Mucchielli, L. 2000. 'Review of C. Blanckaert et al. (ed.), L'histoire des sciences de l'homme. Trajectoire, enjeux et questions vives, Paris: L'Harmattan', *Revue d'Histoire des Sciences Humaines* 2: 171–76.

Murray, T. 1999. 'Epilogue: the Art of Archaeological Biography', in T. Murray (ed.), *Encyclopedia of Archaeology. The Great Archaeologists*. Oxford/Santa Barbara (CA): ABC-Clio, pp. 869–83.

————. 2002. 'Epilogue: Why the History of Archaeology Matters', *Antiquity* 76: 234–38.

Nordbladh, J. 1998. 'Comments on Baudou (1998)', *Norwegian Archaeological Review* 31/2: 109–11.

————. 2002. 'How to Organize Oneself Within History: Pehr Tham and His Relation to Antiquity at the End of the 18th Century', *Antiquity* 76: 141–50.

Revel, J. 1996. 'Micro-analyse et construction du social', in J. Revel (ed.), *Jeux d'échelles. La microanalyse à l'expérience*. Paris: EHESS-Gallimard-Seuil, pp. 15–36.

Richard, N. 1992. *La préhistoire en France dans la seconde moitié du dix-neuvième siècle (1859–1904)*. Unpublished PhD dissertation, Université de Paris-I Panthéon-Sorbonne.

Schlanger, N. 2002. 'Ancestral Archives: Explorations in the History of Archaeology', *Antiquity* 76: 127–31.

Shapin, S. and A. Thackray. 1974. 'Prosopography as a Research Tool in History of Science: the British Scientific Community 1700–1900', *History of Science* 12: 1–28.

Stocking, G.W. 1968. 'On the limits of presentism and Historicism in the Historiography of Behavioral Sciences', in *Race, Culture and Evolution. Essays in the History of Anthropology*. New York: Free Press, pp. 1–12.

Trigger, B. 1989. *A History of Archaeological Thought*. Cambridge: Cambridge University Press.

————. 2001. Historiography, in T. Murray (ed.), *Encyclopedia of Archaeology. History and Discoveries*. Oxford/Santa Barbara (CA): ABC-Clio, pp. 630–39.

Vogt, C. 1879. 'Eine Naturforscherallee im Hoch-Jura', *Nord und Süd* 9: 127–40.

Wagner, M. 1868. *Die Darwin'sche Theorie und das Migrationsgesetz der Organismen*. Leipzig: Duncker & Humblot.

Wahle, E. 1950/51. 'Geschichte der prähistorischen Forschung', *Anthropos* 45: 497–538, 46: 49–112.

Chapter 2

From Distant Shores

Nineteenth-Century Dutch Archaeology in European Perspective

Ruurd B. Halbertsma

Abstract

This paper deals with the pioneer years of Dutch archaeology, which can be reconstructed only following extensive research drawing on a range of archives throughout Europe. The first professor of archaeology in the Netherlands, Caspar J.C. Reuvens (1793–1835) aimed to establish archaeology as a fully accepted branch of academia, and to instruct his contemporaries on the importance of ancient art by creating a National Museum of Antiquities. To achieve these goals, he followed the example of England, France and Germany by organising archaeological expeditions in the Mediterranean, resulting in an enormous growth in Dutch collections. The Dutch archaeological agents in the field – in Italy, Greece and Tunisia – came in contact with various other European explorers and collectors, for example with Champollion le Jeune (collecting for the Louvre) and the Danish explorer Christian Tuxen Falbe (active in Tunisia). Reconstructing these activities, the provenance of the collections and the legality of their actions can be achieved only through the Dutch National Archives and in comparison with other archives across Europe. Archaeological collections often ended up divided between different museums, and archival studies can help us trace the original provenance or even reconstruct the original archaeological context from which these finds were extracted. Focusing on Reuvens, this article exemplifies archival work at a European archaeological scale.

Introduction

The history of museums is the history of people: the men and women involved in creating museums, collecting objects, raising funds, organising expeditions, publishing the collection and permanently making decisions. On a higher level these actions are fostered (or thwarted) by local officials or government institutions, often with their own cultural agenda in mind. Thus, the history of a museum might be a story about local collecting and antiquarian interest within its own region, but it can also grow into a cultural chapter in national or even international history. The history of the Dutch National Museum of Antiquities falls into this latter category, as its activities and contacts extended to countries like England, France, Germany, Denmark, Greece, Italy and Tunisia.[1]

The origin of the National Museum of Antiquities lies in a collection of Greek and Roman sculptures, which were donated to the University of Leiden in 1744 by the Amsterdam gentleman Gerard van Papenbroek (1673–1743).[2] His collection consisted of 150 Greek and Roman antiquities, mostly sculptures, which he had acquired by buying at auctions and by trading with other collectors. Some of the pieces in his collection can be traced back to such collectors as Gerard Reynst and Peter Paul Rubens. The university placed the sculptures in the central hall of the

Fig. 2.1 The Marmora Papenburgica in the orangery of the botanical garden. Drawing by J. van Werven, *ca.* 1745, Leiden City Archive.

orangery in the botanical garden, where they could be admired by both the academic community and the inhabitants of Leiden (Fig. 2.1). Although the collection was open to the public, it could not be called a museum, as curators were not appointed and the collection played no role in education or academic teaching. The task of publishing the antiquities was given to the history professor Franciscus Oudendorp, who wrote a Latin eulogy on Van Papenbroek's generosity and published a catalogue of the sculptures, with special attention to the inscriptions.[3] Oudendorp especially stressed the importance of the collection for the academic youth:

> In the meantime, youngsters, enjoy your good luck, dear pupils of the academy, chained by love for the free arts, and be happy with merry excitement. You have received a basket with all kinds of antiquities, which might contain the sweetest nourishment for your studies. If it is pleasant for you to stand eye to eye with Roman generals, laurelled emperors and young caesars, commanders of the youth, then it will now be possible to see a number of them with your own eyes. If you find pleasure in seeing queens and empresses, then the female portraits and representations, carved with utmost skill, will leave you astonished. If you prefer men of learning, you will not find them absent. Or do you prefer to look at the hollow gods and demigods of the pagans, and treat them with a smile? Then look! Jupiter, Sarapis, Apollo and Bacchus in different attire and ornamented with their own attributes,

CASPARUS IACOBUS CHRISTIANUS REUVENS, HAGANUS.

LITER. HUM. PROF. IN ATHENAEO HARDEROVIC. Aº 1816,
ARCHAEOLOGIAE IN ACAD. LUGD. BAT. PROFESSOR
EXTRAORD. Aº 1818. PROFESSOR ORDIN. Aº 1826.
NATUS D. 22 M. IAN. Aº 1793, OBIIT D. 26 M. IULIO Aº 1835.

Fig. 2.2 Portrait of Professor C.J.C. Reuvens (1793–1835), anonymous, *ca.* 1819. University History Museum, Leiden.

naked Venuses, beautiful Cupids, Silenus, Pan, Fauns, remarkable in their attitudes, Hercules struggling with Antaeus, or proud with the golden apples of the Hesperides, and finally the goddesses Domina Urbs, Fortuna, Salus, Abundantia and Nehalennia, and the frightful head of Oceanus with his fishermen: the Papenbroekiana Marmora, now the Leydensia Marmora, present them all to your judgment.[4]

Oudendorp's excitation did not meet with success. The general lack of interest for the sculptures and the climatic conditions in the greenhouse led to a severe deterioration of the physical condition of the collection. This state of affairs ended in 1818 when a young classical scholar, Caspar Jacob Christiaan Reuvens, was appointed as professor of archaeology at Leiden University (Fig. 2.2).[5] Reuvens, born in 1793, had been destined by his father to a career in the study of Law. His sharp intellect and his love for the classics led to a combination of studies: Law and Classics at the universities of Amsterdam, Leiden and Paris. Reuvens spent three years in the French capital, where his father was appointed as one of the judges at the Court of Cassation. Reuvens junior finished his doctoral degree in Law in 1813 with a dissertation on the juridical aspects of loan contracts. In Paris the young Reuvens also read classics with Jean François Boissonade and encountered the richness of the archaeological collections of the Louvre and the ideas of creating a National Museum, as formulated by Dominique Vivant-Denon, the first director of the Musée Napoléon. After the fall of the emperor Napoleon, father and son returned to the Netherlands, where Reuvens applied for a professorship at the Athenaeum of Harderwijk, the start of his academic career. After three years of teaching Classics, the Athenaeum was closed due to university reforms. Reuvens went to Leiden, where a new chair was created for him, dedicated to the study of archaeology, 'the knowledge of antiquity, elucidated by remaining monuments' as the profession was described by the Dutch Minister of Education. Before Reuvens, scholars and antiquarians had studied the past of the Netherlands, sometimes making use of finds from the earth, but these activities had been isolated sparks of scholarship, which had expired when the investigators passed away. In 1818 Leiden was given the chance to start with a new branch of academia, exclusively devoted to the study of the past through the artefacts themselves.

Reuvens can be described as a pioneer: he had to establish archaeology at the university and to start teaching a new discipline. He had to transform a small, neglected collection of antiquities into a modern museum and to start collecting on a grand scale. For Reuvens archaeology comprised all ancient cultures which were known, or influenced by the world of the Greeks and Romans. This definition included Egyptian, Persian and even Indian and Indonesian ancient artefacts, and the general archaeology of Europe. It excluded the archaeology of the New World: when a collection of objects from Mexico was offered to the museum, Reuvens declined the objects as not belonging to the classical world:

> I would not cut off the possibility of enlarging our Dutch museum collections with the so unknown objects from Mexico, but these objects should not be placed in a Museum of Antiquities, which should confine itself to classical antiquities and to those regions, which were known by the Greeks and Romans and which were influenced by their civilisation, e.g. India.[6]

Reuvens also had to deal with antiquities in other Dutch museums. With more or less success he succeeded in acquiring prehistoric stone artefacts from the Museum of Natural History and Roman antiquities from the Cabinet of Curiosities. More difficult was the question where engraved ancient stones had to be placed. As "carved stones" these objects had always been kept in the Royal Coin Cabinet in The Hague. But when Egyptian scarabs were sent to the new archaeological museum, these were also claimed by the director of the Royal Coin Cabinet. Reuvens disagreed and sent his protests to his colleague, but he blaimed especially the ministry for not having set clear-cut rules about collecting policies:

> Indeed you cannot blame me for having doubts from time to time: I have never received any information about the right boundaries between museums, for reasons that I do not know. If a *strictum jus* can be alleged against me, then this rule must come forward from a clear governmental decision. If this decision is not shown to me, then it is natural that I bring back the question to its prior state. If I were summoned to give my opinion on neutral ground, for example in a foreign country, about the dividing lines between museums, then in a cabinet of coins and carved stones I would place only objects which belonged there according to the most rigid rules, from fear 1) that nowhere else a natural borderline could be found, and 2) that too many objects would be lost for serious study.
>
> Firstly, as far as the so-called carved stones are concerned, I would consider only the precious stones engraved with images, from Greek and Roman craftmanship, and the ancient glass pastes to be part of such a cabinet. Persian, Egyptian and Gnostic stones do not belong to the fine arts, but simply to scholarship and I would not consider placing them in that cabinet. The Egyptian ones are not even made of precious stones, but of hard, rocky materials like granite, syenite, basalt and the like. When in doubt I would always decide in favour of scholarship and to the detriment of a collection, which has beauty as its principal aim.
>
> I repeat that I absolutely do not know the government's definition of engraved stones, let alone – if it exists – the quality of this definition. [...] Egyptian scarabs are neither precious stones, nor seal stones: has someone made a separate classification for these objects? And is the definition extended to all carving in hard stone? But then by consequence all Egyptian objects with relief, sarcophagi, cippi, statues etc. are included: they are all made of hard stone, the same stone as the scarabs, and all covered with the same representations and carvings. If the cabinet claims all scarabs, then also the items of earthenware have to go there, which the ministry has always placed in the Museum of Antiquities. And finally, if one desires all small objects with hieroglyphs, which were used as amulets, in the coin cabinet, then no Egyptian statuette of earthenware will be left in the collection of antiquities. And if we were to acquire a scarab with a diameter of five feet, like the one of Lord Elgin, or of one foot, like the one of Denon, would you consider also those 'carved stones'? Or a gemstone?[7]

During the first years of his directorate Reuvens travelled to England, France and Germany to see archaeological collections and their ways of display, and to meet colleagues in his field. In England he bought a number of casts of the so-called Elgin Marbles, which had recently been put on display in the British Museum. He published articles in which he stressed the importance of the acquisition and discussed the legality of Elgin's activities; he treated also the supposed damage done to the Parthenon and the reliability of the eyewitnesses concerned.[8] He began to develop himself as a European archaeologist, trying to propagate new ideas about archaeology in the Netherlands, and to accustome the public with the latest finds and developments.

Reuvens first had to take care of the dilapidated statues in the botanical garden. About the state of affairs he wrote to the Trustees:

> Exposed to the insults of air and people, and without custody, many pieces have suffered: the rusting of the iron, with which they were restored, has deformed and broken the

attached pieces. Subsequently the marble have also been damaged deliberately. I will do my utmost best to cure these deficiencies, as much as my feeble abilities and the finances of the Academy will allow.[9]

Reuvens managed to move the collection to a new building, where he was allowed to occupy the ground floor. Here he also started his courses of archaeology with lectures on numismatics and ancient sculpture. Lessons were open to the general public (artists especially were invited). To accommodate these newcomers to academia Reuvens was permitted by the university's Trustees to drop the use of the Latin language and to speak in the native tongue instead. He also started field-archaeology in the Netherlands. With two students, two draughtsmen and an army of workmen he unearthed parts of the Roman town of Forum Hadriani, the westernmost Roman city of the province Germania Inferior and capital of the tribe of the Cananefates (Plate 1). These archaeological drawings are masterpieces of artistry, and they also testify to the accuracy of the fieldwork (Plate 2). In his diaries a beginning is made of teaching how to read the soil and its hidden meanings:

> A long trench is often needed to start the research, but there is the danger of losing the coherence. When workmen find a few stones in a trench, they often throw them out, because the foundation is so weak that they do not recognise it as such. Continuing a trench to pursue a foundation is not advisable because you miss all kinds of small peculiarities. Thus we would never have noticed the foundations of columns and the wells. [...] Foundations of one and the same building do not appear at the same level everywhere. The workmen must be instructed not to throw the stones away which they find in the upper layers. [...] However, much is lost by the investigation itself, before one recognises what is in front of him.
>
> The deep traces of black ground, which one can see sharply against the untouched soil, are without doubt the result of human activities, and nearly always foundations. If those have been dug out, they are still recognisable by small remaining pieces of stone. If small stones are missing, then they are probably conducts for water, for example for leaden pipes.[10]

Greece

The world of collecting antiquities in the early nineteenth century was largely populated by amateurs: artists, gentlemen at leisure, officers, diplomats, princes and clergymen. The birth of the National Museum of Antiquities attracted two of these antiquarians to Leiden, who offered their collections for sale to Reuvens in the year 1820. Both of them were subsequently trained by Reuvens as archaeological agents on different missions in the Mediterranean. The first was the retired Flemish colonel Bernard Rottiers from Antwerp (1771–1857).[11] During the years of the Napoleonic occupation of the Netherlands, he joined the army of the Russian czar and saw active duty in the southern part of the Russian empire. He led military campaigns against Persian and Turkish armies. In 1818 he travelled back to the Netherlands via the Black Sea, Turkey, Greece, Italy, France and England. In Athens he made the acquaintance of the French diplomat Louis Fauvel and the Austrian consul Georg Gropius, both of them old hands in the antiquities' trade. With Rottiers' money and the influence of the diplomats, excavations were organised in the surroundings of Athens (Aixone). Also the Dutch consul C. Origone and his chancellor, Paul Giuracich, were part of the excavation team. The data about where and by whom excavations were carried out are very confused. The finds of Rottiers, Fauvel and Gropius were divided, exchanged and resold according to now untraceable arrangements. Rottiers came home with some superb fourth-century BC Greek grave reliefs, which were sold to the museum after a painstaking evaluation of their pecuniary value by Reuvens.

A year after this successful purchase a second collection was offered for sale. Jean Rottiers, a son of the colonel, provided the museum with a collection of Greek ceramics, which he had acquired during a trip to Greece in 1821. They were the first Greek ceramics to arrive in the Netherlands with an assured provenance, which was important in this period with its discussions about their provenance and place of production.

In 1824 Rottiers entered negotiations with the Minister of the Interior (under which the museum resided) about a journey to Greece. It was Rottiers' intention to organise an expedition lasting two years, during which he offered to collect antiquities for the archaeological museum. In exchange for his services to archaeology, he asked money for his travelling costs to Minorca (where the Dutch fleet was stationed), an increase in his pension and a sum of 2,000 guilders for minor purchases. For larger acquisitions he had to ask permission first. Furthermore he asked permission to use one of the Dutch warships for his travels and the transport of the antiquities. All his demands were granted by the ministry, even before Reuvens heard of this expedition. When the professor was informed, he compiled a list of instructions, fearing that without help Rottiers would not meet the standards of archaeological investigation. The list has been preserved and gives a good insight into Reuvens' ideas of an archaeological expedition:

A. It is important to receive: plans, sections, elevations, perspectives, details and orientation of buildings. No so-called restoration on paper, or only with exact indications which part is antique, and which part is guessed. Samples of the stone of which the building is made. The drawings do not gain value by their number, but by their use for archaeology, completeness and accurate design. If in a funerary monument vases or other antiquities are found and taken away, I desire a precise indication where each piece came from and how it was placed.

B. Concerning removable antiquities it will be useful (if possible) to investigate empty Turkish fortresses and mosques, especially those in which they have never allowed foreigners. In these buildings very beautiful reliefs and other pieces have often been used as building stones.

C. Concerning the acquisition of vases it is requested not to look for small and ordinary objects, which the museum now owns in considerable measure. But the desired ones are specifically:

a) large vases with important drawings as the ones found in Aulis and owned by Gianachi Logotheti, primate of Levadia, and published by Millin, Vases, tom. II, pl. 55–56. Confer Dodwell Travels I, p. 301.

b) vases with figures or floral patterns in relief, some of which come from Milo (if I remember correctly) and owned by Mr Durand in Paris.

c) vases with white ground and red figures; but not washed with any liquid. The only means to discover if there is a drawing beneath the dirty crust is to remove the crust with utmost care using a sharp pen or razor. But this should be done only on a small part and only inasmuch is necessary to see if a decoration is hidden.

D. Greek, Latin and old Eastern manuscripts, especially to be found in Greek monasteries. Of course those of classical authors are highly valued. But old books, the Church Fathers, homilies, missals etc. should be inspected to see if they were copied (*palimpsesti*): if the parchment, on which an older writer had written, was scraped off to write the later text across it. In that case they have much value.

E. Samples of the different varieties of stone and especially marble in the quarries on the isles, with notes from where the samples have been taken.

F. Specific astronomical measurements of all locations, if time allows it. Detailed maps of those places, where antiquities have been found, will be most welcome.

G. Botanical information, drawings, etc. as much as is possible for the traveller.

H. Buying medals and gemstones need not be mentioned: this goes without saying. But one should take notes about the places where certain types of medals occur frequently, because such notes can be useful for tracing the origin of questionable coins.

P.S. Clearing the ruins of collapsed temples, digging in and around them and also digging in old wells seem to promise good results.[12]

The expedition was not a great success: due to the hostilities during the War of Independence Rottiers had to change his itinerary more than once. Furthermore, his main point of interest lied in a six month's stay on Rhodes, where he worked on a publication of the medieval architecture of the city, and hardly acquired any antiquities.[13] With every report of Rottiers about failed opportunities, Reuvens' irritation grew. Nevertheless Rottiers managed to excavate for a few days on the island of Milos, where he discovered a Roman mosaic floor, an altar and a late-Hellenistic head of a priest. Other purchases during this expedition included a head of a kouros from Thera, marble cycladic vessels and architectural drawings from Athens. Greek antiquities with a certain provenance thus came to the museum in Leiden.

Tunisia

Another retired officer returned to the Netherlands at the same time as Rottiers: mayor Jean Emile Humbert, who had left the Netherlands in 1795, as a result of the French invasion and the proclamation of the Batavian Republic.[14] Together with two other officers, Humbert was enlisted by Hamouda Pacha, Bey of Tunisia, to design and construct the harbour of La Goulette in the neighbourhood of Tunis. Between the years 1796 and 1806 the three officers worked on a modern harbour in front of the Lake of Tunis with a canal, sluices and an arsenal. Humbert became very interested in Tunisian life, languages and customs. He began to assemble notes on the history of Tunisia, especially on the topography of ancient Carthage, the ruins of which were to be found only a few miles from La Goulette. As engineer of the Bey he had permission to make detailed drawings of the peninsula. He even carried out some excavations. He is mentioned in every travel journal of the period as the authority on the location of Punic Carthage, with its romantic memories of Dido and Aeneas, Sophonisbe and the Punic Wars. Het met with the French writer Chateaubriand, with the Danish antiquarian A.C. Gierlew, with Caroline Princess of Wales and with the German historian B.G. Niebuhr, the author of the *Römische Geschichte*, who consulted Humbert about the topography of Carthage. In the years 1815–1816 Humbert worked together with the Italian count Camillo Borgia, a refugee from post-Napoleonic Europe, who intended to publish a travel account of Tunisia with chapters on its earlier history.[15] Together they made three long expeditions through the interior of the country, recording inscriptions, architecture, landscapes and ruins (Fig. 2.3). Borgia returned to Naples in 1817, the year in which he died as a result of a malaria infection he had caught when excavating at Utica. His unpublished manuscripts were sold to the French writer Alexandre de Laborde, but were eventually bought by the Dutch government and placed in the National Museum of Antiquities.

Fig. 2.3 Camillio Borgia and Jean Emile Humbert on horseback in the interior of Tunisia (*ca.* 1816). Anonymous etching. Archive, National Museum of Antiquities.

Humbert was the first explorer of Carthage to find Punic antiquities on the site of the peninsula: in 1817 he unearthed four stelae and two fragments, inscribed with words in the yet undeciphered Punic language, which he published in a monograph dedicated to the Dutch king. Together with these finds and a voluminous portfolio with plans and drawings, he returned to the Netherlands in 1820, where he soon met with Reuvens. The young professor was amazed by the richness of Humbert's material about Carthage and suddenly saw his academic star rising with the prospect to be the first scholar to publish the topography of ancient Carthage, with the aid of Humbert and the manuscripts of count Borgia. To realise this publication Reuvens organised two archaeological expeditions to Tunisia. Humbert was promoted to the honorary rank of Lieutenant-Colonel and received a knighthood for his archaeological investigations and his willingness to sell his important collection to the Dutch government.

The first expedition to Tunisia lasted two years (1822–1824). The instructions of Reuvens were twofold: to organise excavations with the aim of finding the boundaries of Punic Carthage and the later Roman Colonia Julia Carthago, and to acquire antiquities for the museum, for example more Punic inscriptions. In exchange for lavish gifts and his willingness to work partly on the harbour of La Goulette, Humbert received permission from the authorities to investigate the Carthaginian peninsula by means of excavations. He succeeded in finding more Punic inscriptions and made detailed drawings of the topographical excavations while searching for Punic and Roman architectural remains (Fig. 2.4).

In the archives of the National Museum of Antiquities a document is kept, which records the organisation and permission of excavations in Tunisia in the early nineteenth century. It gives the conditions under which count Borgia was granted permission to dig at Utica. Although the rules are simple, it becomes clear that the Tunisian government did not allow uncontrolled theft of cultural property:

[Borgia] paid the workmen in the excavations 8 to 10 caroubes each day, which amounts to about 45 Dutch cents;

The overseers who managed the excavations and paid attention that no objects were stolen by the workmen were paid 80 cents each day; the number of overseers was calculated on the number of workmen;

A Mamelouk, or officer of the Bey, needed for keeping order, was paid one guilder and 60 cents each day;

The gold and silver objects which were discovered in whatever form, were estimated and the countervalue of the metal was paid by Count Borgia to the Bey;

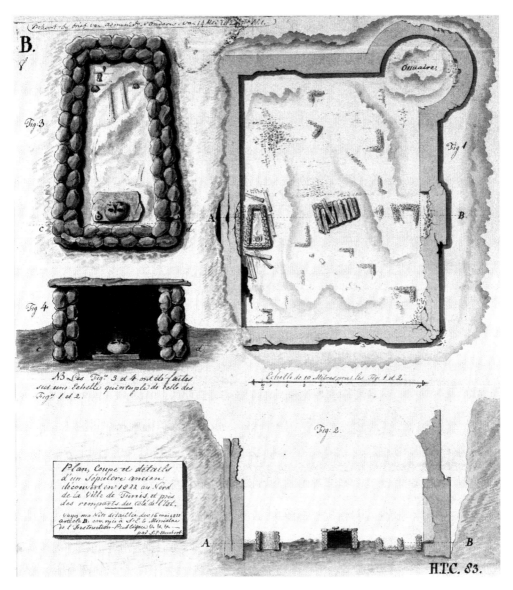

Fig. 2.4 Plan, sections and details of a Roman mausoleum, discovered in 1822 near Tunis. Drawing by J.E. Humbert. Archive, National Museum of Antiquities.

Copper, bronze and all terracotta objects could by law be kept by Count Borgia. But when statues were discovered, their value had to be estimated by an artist and half of their value was paid to the Bey.[16]

The antiquarian endeavours brought Humbert in conflict with the Danish consul and antiquarian Christian Tuxen Falbe, who was also preparing a study on the topography of Carthage. The first incident involved a collection of Roman statues, which had been found in Utica some 20 years earlier. The statues belonged to the Governor of La Goulette and were on display near the harbour. When Humbert started negotiations with the Governor, he noticed that one statue of a draped woman (the most beautiful female statue of the collection) was missing: it had been bought by Falbe during Humbert's absence and send to Copenhagen as a gift to the Danish king. Humbert retaliated by destroying part of Falbe's excavations at Carthage. A well placed rumour about a treasure chest hidden beneath a Roman mosaic floor launched a group of Tunisian soldiers to pillage the site and destroy all visible remains before the eyes of the consul.[17]

During his Tunisian years, Humbert called himself 'le solitaire des ruines', and wrote romantically about his life amidst the ruins of the past:

> When one passes most of the time between the ruined remains of temples and palaces, when one is constantly busy reading rusted coins and grave inscriptions, is it then surprising that one's mood gets a bit lugubrious? Every step I take and every object I touch reminds me of the transience and futility of human endeavours. These sad examples of the past are serious lessons for the future. From what has been, I learn what shall be: ambition, fanatism, intolerance, despotism and prejudice will continuously injure, harm and shame the human race![18]

In 1824 Humbert sailed home with his collection of Punic monuments, Roman statues and notes and drawings on the topography of Carthage. A second expedition was mounted for the years 1826–1830, but this time Humbert did not cross the Mediterranean but remained in Italy, where he acquired considerable collections for the museum in Leiden.

Italy

With Livorno as his home base, Humbert made extensive travels in Italy, searching for collections on sale. During these activities he frequently met with Champollion le Jeune, who was active as a collector for the Musée Charles X. In the summer of 1826 Humbert managed to buy six Etruscan urns from the Giorgi collection in Volterra, to the displeasure of Champollion, who had wanted to acquire the objects but had not received authorisation from Paris in time. Later in 1826 he acquired the complete Museo Corazzi in Cortona, a private collection of mostly Etruscan bronzes, which comprised some extraordinary pieces. From Malta he bought Punic and Roman artefacts, which had belonged to the British consul Alexander Tulin. In Livorno he acquired Egyptian antiquities from Maria Cimba, the widow of Henry Salt's physician. The crown on his activities was the purchase of the complete collection d'Anastasy, bought in Livorno in 1828. This collection, owned by Jean d'Anastasy, consul-general of various countries in Alexandria, comprised more than 5000 Egyptian antiquities: monuments, statues, reliefs, papyrus scrolls and a very large amount of human and animal mummies. With the collections in Paris, London and Turin, Leiden now ranked among the most important Egyptian collections in Europe. After the (very costly) d'Anastasy purchase no other collections were bought in Italy, although Humbert started negotiations in Venice (collection Nani-Tiepolo of Greek and Roman sculptures) and in Naples (collection Pacileo of Greek and South Italian vases). Documents and catalogues about these collections were send to Leiden and placed in the archives.

A year later the Borgia manuscripts were bought in Paris which were necessary for Reuvens' publication on Carthage, although the refusal of Humbert to travel to Tunisia had hindered the progress of the work considerably. This promising start for Dutch archaeology suffered a very serious setback in 1830 when the Belgian provinces revolted against King Willem I. As is often the case in times of need, the department of culture suffered considerably, resulting in a serious cut-down of the budgets. Leiden became a silent city, with splendid collections but no museum building (Reuvens realised his new museum only on paper), with very rich archives, but no final publication on the topography of Carthage. Reuvens met an untimely death in 1835, only 42 years old. Humbert died in Livorno in 1839. The egyptologist Conrad Leemans succeeded Reuvens as director of the museum in 1839. A year earlier the museum had opened its doors to the public in an improvised building in the centre of town.

Nationalism and Collecting Policy

As has been described above, Reuvens had developed himself as an archaeologist with an international view. He had studied in Paris and had extended his scholarly network across Europe. His correspondence and publications earned him the membership of learned societies in the Netherlands, Denmark, England, Germany and Italy. The model for a National Museum of Antiquities he found abroad, although the size and influence of the Netherlands were, of course, not comparable to countries like France and England.

When trying to convince the Ministry of Education to spend money on buying antiquities in the Mediterrean area, Reuvens more than once used feelings of national pride: the Netherlands had to compete with other European nations, if the nation had serious plans for a National Museum of Antiquities. A kind of litmus test occured in 1826, when a collection of Etruscan antiquities was on sale in the Tuscan city of Cortona. The price for the Corazzi collection was considerable. Reuvens argued that a small museum of antiquities could do without such an amount of Etruscan material (a few samples would suffice), but a serious National Museum certainly could not. Reuvens asked the Department explicitly in which direction the national collection of antiquities had to develop itself:

> It is a question which I am not allowed to answer: is the Government willing to spend such an amount of money on a branch of archaeology, which cannot be considered indispensable for a good museum? If I am allowed to express my feelings straightforward without taking sides, then I would let the decision of this question depend on another one: does the Government have in view to expand the Museum of Antiquities in such a direction that it does not only foster archaeology among our compatriots, but also nourishes and extends it generally to achieve honour and foreign glory for our country? And does the museum have to have only enough antiquities to cultivate an *elementary* knowledge of archaeology for the natives? In this last case, although the possession of some Etruscan artefacts as *examples* is indispensable, the purchase of this collection would be too heavy for the use and pleasure it could give; these kinds of objects will not be held in high artistic esteem, and will not be used as subjects of scholarly investigations by most students. But in the first case a good Etruscan collection (which as I have said cannot be found on this side of the Alps) will increase the renown of the museum considerably, and the richness of the whole museum will encourage and foster the study of each separate subject, also the less known and abstract ones like the Etruscan antiquities. The study of Etruscan artefacts will specifically stimulate the interest in Roman antiquities and the study of older history in a considerable way.[19]

The collection was eventually bought 'in consideration of the benefit of Ancient History and in consideration of the renown which will be awarded to the collection in Leiden' as the Minister of the Interior suggested to king Willem I.

A second occasion when foreign politics became involved in archaeological activities occurred in 1827, when Reuvens was making preparations for the first scientific excavations in the Netherlands. He had suggested the Ministry buy the country seat 'Arentsburg' (in the village of Voorburg, near The Hague). In the gardens and meadows of this house numerous Roman finds had been made in previous centuries, and it was suggested that the Roman town of Forum Hadriani, known only from the *Tabula Peutingeriana*, might be located on this spot. When the country seat was put on sale in 1826, Reuvens urged the Ministry to purchase the house and its surroundings for archaeological investigations, which would take at least two years. After this period the Ministry could sell the house again, with the costs of excavations limited to annual summer campaigns. At first the Ministry was in favour of the project, but when the annual costs were estimated at some 5,000 guilders per campaign, sentiments towards fieldwork changed. For such an amount of money a nice collection could be bought, instead of searching the soil with 'a very uncertain chance of finding something substantial'. Moreover, the excavations would keep Reuvens away from 'more useful studies'. These considerations forced the professor to write a long letter, in which he explained the importance of archaeological excavations, and the loss of face of the Dutch government, if this chance for academic glory was left unused. The decision could even destabilise the fragile unity of the newly created Dutch kingdom, which since 1815 comprised The Netherlands, Belgium and Luxemburg. The most elucidating passage runs as follows:

> I cannot say it often enough, although I have to repeat it every time when the shipments of Rottiers and Humbert arrive: archaeology is not benefitted by a single pot, a coin or even a statue, but by the consequences of these finds for the study of ancient topography and history. The question of Voorburg, about its possible identification with Forum Hadriani, is one of the main issues in the debate about the ancient topography of our country. Will the foreigners not say that the Dutch Government speaks a lot about fostering archaeology, but when things get serious steps back with the usual economy? I believe with quiet conviction that not starting the excavations would be a major scholarly and administrative lapse. It would set back the budding profession more than acquiring many collections has made it grow, and it would generate a general distrust about the government's sincerity towards scholarly endeavours. All the absolute sovereigns in Italy, France, Austria, Prussia and Russia spend money on such enterprises. Is a constitutional state unwilling to give funds for such things? Will not all ultra-monarchicals in and outside our country say that indeed such endeavours are unthinkable in a constitutional state, and will not the Belgians, who have more feelings for such things than the Dutch, have one more reason to wish back the French or Austrian government? I will spend my time on this subject, as well as on others. I am able to treat one subject without neglecting others. This opportunity is unique, and will not return for the country and for me.[20]

Eventually the Arentsburg estate was bought, and excavations continued there for more than five years. Apparently the ministry and the king (who had to give his approval to all projects) showed themselves sensitive to Reuvens' arguments. This general sense of honour and the longing for foreign glory helped to build the collections and to undertake excavations. Reuvens made good use of these sentiments to realise his ideas about a National Museum of Antiquities.

When we try to summarise the early years of Dutch archaeology, it is obvious that the growth of the museum must be seen in a European context. Collections were gathered on the distant shores of Greece and Tunisia. Collectors sold their antiquities to the museum in cities like Volterra, Cortona and Livorno. Negotiations took place in Venice and Naples. Competing collectors like Christian Tuxen Falbe and Champollion le Jeune were active with the result that collections were divided between, for example, Paris, Leiden and Copenhagen. Italian manuscripts about the history of Tunisia travelled from Naples to Paris, were bought by the Dutch government but never published. For anyone who is trying to reconstruct the events of these early years of Dutch archaeology, it is necessary to combine data from different European archives. Apart from the inventory books and letters in the museum's archive, valuable information is to be found in other sources: the Dutch National Archives, where a huge amount of information is kept: political deliberations about the role of archaeology, involvement of the Foreign Office in acquiring collections in the Mediterranean, the role of the king and his advisors, and even logbooks of ships, which transported the antiquities to the Netherlands.

But anyone who wants to study the history of the Etruscan collection of Corazzi in Cortona, for example, has to have access to the archives of the Accademia Etrusca. For the connections between the Danish and Dutch antiquarians in Tunisia a research trip to Copenhagen is necessary. To reconstruct the wanderings of the Borgia manuscripts one needs to consult archives in Leiden, Naples, Velletri and Paris. In many museums valuable archives rest, without a proper description and with an accessability which can only be guaranteed by a curator or librarian with some predilection for the history of his or her collection: an awkward situation, as the availability of the material for study depends on the presence and personal interests of individual employees.

It would be an important promotion for the history of archaeology if all archaeological museums would publish the entries of their archives on the Internet. The AREA database of archaeological archival funds could play an important role in unearthing the archival treasures hidden in museum's vaults. On the other hand, many museums already have websites with information on their collections: it would be useful to add information about the contents and availability of the museum's archive. Thus the quest for documents related to, say, Corazzi, Borgia or Falbe would take only a few seconds, whereas writing, telephoning and e-mailing looking for the right person to ask questions to sometimes resembles an Odyssean pilgrimage. The AREA network, following the norms set out by the International Council of Archives for the description of archival funds, could provide formats and examples for the museums and other cultural institutions, which are willing to participate in such a promising project.

Notes

1. On the early history of the National Museum of Antiquities (Rijksmuseum van Oudheden), see Halbertsma (2003).
2. For a biography of Gerard van Papenbroek and his collection of paintings, see Van Regteren Altena and Van Thiel (1964).
3. Oudendorp (1745).
4. Oudendorp (1745, p. 39).
5. For a biography of Reuvens see Brongers (2002).
6. From a letter by Reuvens to the ministry of Education, 17–02–1828, Museum Archive, 17.1.1/3.
7. Reuvens to De Jonge, 24–11–1824, Museum Archive, 17.1.1/1.
8. Reuvens (1823).
9. From a letter of Reuvens to the Ministry of education, 25–11–1820, Museum Archive, 17.1.1/1.
10. Diary excavations Arentsburg, Museum Archive, 19.1.2/53.
11. A biography and a description of his archaeological activities can be found in Bastet (1987) and Halbertsma (2003, pp. 49–70).

12. Reuvens to the Ministry of Education, 3 August 1824, Museum Archive, 17.1.1/1.
13. He published his monograph a few years later with superb engravings of the medieval architecture by P.J. Witdoek, see Rottiers (1830).
14. A biography of J.E. Humbert and his archaeological activities can be found in Halbertsma (1995) and Halbertsma (2003, pp. 71–111).
15. On Borgia and his antiquarian activities, see Ciccotti (1999, 2000).
16. Humbert to Reuvens, 03–06–1822, Museum Archive, 17.1.1/2.
17. Years later Falbe made the incident known to the scholarly world. See Falbe (1833, p. 43).
18. Humbert to his friend Falchi, 22 October 1823, Museum Archive, 19.3.1/21.
19. Reuvens to Van Ewijck, 23 October 1826, Museum Archive, 17.1.1/2.
20. Reuvens to Van Ewijck, 11 January 1827, Museum Archive, 19.2.1/57.

References

Bastet, F.L. 1987. *De drie collecties Rottiers te Leiden.* Leiden.
Brongers, J.A. 2002. 'Een vroeg begin van de moderne archeologie: leven en werken van Cas Reuvens (1793–1835).' *Nederlandse Archeologische Rapporten,* 23, Amersfoort: Rijksdienst voor het Oudheidkundig Bodemonderzoek.
Ciccotti, V. 1999. *Camillo Borgia (1773–1817), soldato ed archeologo.* Velletri.
Ciccotti, V. 2000, ed. *Atti del convegno internazionale di studi Camillo Borgia (1773–1817).* Velletri.
Falbe, C.T. 1833. *Recherches sur l'emplacement de Carthage.* Paris.
Halbertsma, R.B. 1995. *Le solitaire des ruines – de archeologische reizen van Jean Emile Humbert (1771–1839) in dienst van het Koninkrijk der Nederlanden.* Leiden.
Halbertsma, R.B. 2003. *Scholars, Travellers and Trade. The Pioneer Years of the National Museum of Antiquities in Leiden.* London: Routledge.
Reuvens, C.J.C. 1823. 'Disputatio de simulacris quibusdam tympanorum Parthenonis, ad Taylorem Combium, Musei Britannici Antiquitatibus Praefectum', *The Classical Journal* 55: 175–83; 56: 273–87.
Rottiers, B.E.A. 1830. *Description des monumens de Rhodes.* Brussels.
Van Regteren Altena, I.Q. and P.J.J. Van Thiel 1964. *De portretgalerij van de Universiteit van Amsterdam en haar stichter Gerard van Papenbroek, 1673–1743.* Amsterdam.

Chapter 3

The Hemenway Southwestern Archaeological Expedition, 1886–1889

A Model of Inquiry for the History of Archaeology

Curtis M. Hinsley and David R. Wilcox

Abstract

The Hemenway Southwestern Archaeological Expedition (1886–1889), led by anthropologist Frank Hamilton Cushing, was the first major archaeological expedition to the American Southwest. Cushing became ill and never finished a final report, and for more than a century his reputation has suffered accordingly. Over the past ten years the authors of the present chapter – an American cultural historian and a south western archaeologist – have unearthed the archival records of Cushing's expedition, including his original but fragmentary report, as well as diaries and field notes of the participants. The Hemenway Project is gradually publishing this multivoiced documentary history, in the hope that it will provide a model for the history of archaeology that gives immediacy to the actors and relevant, contemporary meaning to their intentions and actions.

The Hemenway Expedition and its Reputation

In the fall of 1886 Mary Tileston Hemenway, a wealthy Boston widow and philanthropist, agreed to sponsor the Hemenway Southwestern Archaeological Expedition under the direction of anthropologist Frank Hamilton Cushing.[1] Mrs Hemenway supported many worthy causes in the years following the American Civil War (1861–1865), concerned chiefly with education and American history, and she was intrigued by Cushing, his five years' sojourn among the Zuñi Indians in northwestern New Mexico, and his visions for American anthropology (Hinsley 2002: 5–18). Together they dreamed of founding a private 'Pueblo Museum' in Salem, Massachusetts, and the artifact collections from Arizona and New Mexico were intended to form the nucleus of its collections (Cushing to Hemenway 1887). Accordingly she appointed a board of directors, and in late 1886 Cushing outfitted the Expedition and left for the field in southern Arizona, intending to conduct a reconnaissance in search of the ancestors of the Zuñi Indians – and perhaps, he hoped, to solve larger problems of prehistoric migration through the American hemisphere.[2] Cushing saw his expedition as a 'rock of ages … the foundation of something good and great' for archaeology and the sciences of humanity (Cushing to Baxter 1887).

The first significant archaeological expedition to the American Southwest, the Hemenway Expedition was a deliberately multidisciplinary undertaking. Cushing gathered together a remarkable group: Adolph Bandelier (1840–1914), the Swiss-American historian and anthropologist; Frederick Webb Hodge (1864–1956), who began a long anthropological career as Cushing's personal secretary; U.S. Army surgeon and Navajo ethnologist Washington Matthews (1843–1905); Herman F.C. ten Kate (1858–1931), the Dutch world traveller, linguist, and anthropologist;[3] Cushing's wife Emily and her younger sister, Margaret Whitehead Magill (1863–1935), who was an accomplished artist; and many others, including two Zuñi companions, Mexican labourers, Pima Indian guides, and various temporary visitors and helpers (cf. Magill 1995).4 For nearly two years the expedition laboured in the deserts of southern Arizona and the piñon country of northwestern New Mexico near Zuñi, but within three years Cushing's persistent and debilitating illnesses, growing doubts about his methods and reliability, and concern over Mrs Hemenway's declining health led her son, Augustus Hemenway, and the expedition board of directors to fire Cushing in the summer of 1889. They appointed Jesse Walter Fewkes, a Harvard-trained naturalist with no archaeological experience, in his place. Although Fewkes would officially conduct a 'second Hemenway Expedition' for several more years (Wade and McChesney 1980), the Hemenway Southwestern Archaeological Expedition effectively ended with Cushing's departure.[5]

Returning eastward to Washington and upstate New York, for two years Cushing withdrew into serious illness and depression. Without access to most of his records, at the prompting of the Hemenway board he nonetheless attempted to write an account – an 'Itinerary' – of the expedition as he recalled it; but after two years of intermittent effort he turned to other interests.[6] He never returned to the Southwest or the Hemenway Expedition, and he never again saw the artifact collections, field maps, catalogues, or other expedition materials; and he also never again saw Mary Hemenway, who died of diabetes in 1894. Several fragmentary studies from the expedition were published (Baxter 1888, Cushing 1890, Matthews 1900, Matthews *et al.* 1895), but Cushing's own notes and partial reports still lay in manuscript form at his own sudden death, at age 43, in 1900. Later that year the southwestern publicist and author Charles Lummis expressed the general opinion of the Hemenway Expedition when he called it 'a cruel disappointment to Mrs. Hemenway,' a 'crash of doom' to Cushing, and 'a scattered and uncoordinated wreckage' for archaeology (Lummis 1900: 9).

The boxes and crates of artifacts from the expedition were donated by the Hemenway family to Harvard's Peabody Museum in 1895. Here they remained untouched and unstudied until the 1930s, when Alfred Tozzer suggested to a young archaeology graduate student, Emil Haury, that he should write his dissertation on the Hemenway collections. Haury did so, and he produced a classic study of late Hohokam ceramics and material culture – thereby also establishing the Hemenway Expedition as the founding moment of Hohokam archaeology (Haury 1945).[7] Searching for the ancestral Zuñis, it turned out, Cushing had found the prehistoric Hohokam.[8]

But Haury found that the written records of the Hemenway Expedition were more elusive. They had had an interesting itinerary of their own, as it turned out. During the expedition Cushing's sister-in-law and the expedition artist, Margaret Magill, and Cushing's secretary, Fred Hodge, fell in love. As the expedition was collapsing Cushing obtained a position for Hodge, his future brother-in-law, in the Smithsonian Institution's Bureau of American Ethnology. In 1891 Fred and Margaret were married, and after Cushing's death in 1900, Hodge eventually came into possession of most of Cushing's papers. Over the first half of the twentieth century, as his own career in archaeology and museum anthropology took him from the Smithsonian in Washington (1889–1916) to the Museum of the American Indian in New York (1916–1930) to the Southwest Museum in Los Angeles (1930–1955), Hodge carried the textual record of the Hemenway Expedition with him, leaving a trail of archival deposits along the way. He also portrayed to Emil Haury and others a highly negative view of Cushing as an archaeologist and expedition leader. For example, in 1931 Hodge told Haury that most of the written archives of the Expedition he had were 'bunk'; in his foreword to Haury's monograph Hodge publicly belittled Cushing's accomplishments as an archaeologist (Hodge 1945).[9]

The Hemenway Documentary Project

Hodge's negative representations of Cushing and the Hemenway enterprise prevailed for three decades beyond his death in 1956, but gradually new archival sources and information began to emerge. In 1979 archaeologist Wilcox excavated a large portion of a site in Tempe, Arizona, which Cushing had examined in 1887 and had named La Ciudad de los Hornos (Wilcox *et al.* 1990). Curious to know what Cushing had seen there nearly a century before, he began to follow the archival and artifactual trail of the Hemenway Expedition, now spread across American museums and libraries. At about the same time, Hinsley was doing research on the history of anthropology at Harvard's Peabody Museum and, since the Hemenway artifacts were housed at the Museum, he began to explore the cultural roots of the Expedition. In 1983 we first met at Harvard and began talking about a joint project; but it was only in 1992, after we had both moved coincidentally to Flagstaff, Arizona, that we seriously began collaborating on a multi-volume history of the Hemenway enterprise.

Having become aware of the Hemenway Expedition and discovered some of the corpus of materials – archives, data and artifacts – we agreed that a collaboration would be mutually advantageous. For some time we imagined a very large documentary publication project, but we realized that while we had many interesting pieces, we lacked a contemporaneous set of records on which to build a core narrative. We then focused more narrowly on Cushing's unfinished and unpublished account of the Expedition's roots and early months, a text which was itself divided in several parts and in various archives. But one day in 1991, Mary Davis, librarian at the Huntington Free Library in Bronx, New York, was inventorying materials in the library's vaults, and she discovered on a high shelf a set of nine bound volumes. Taking them down and opening them, she immediately recognized Cushing's distinctive handwriting: these were Cushing's letterbooks of the Hemenway Expedition (and his later Florida work), about 4500 pages in all. Knowing of our interest, she contacted us, and in a memorable trip to New York we quickly realized that the other pieces of the Expedition puzzle could now be viewed coherently. We returned to the original, large-scope documentary history – of which we have thus far produced three volumes. In the remainder of this essay we would like to discuss some of our purposes, philosophies and methods in this project in the history of science.

American Archaeology, Then and Now: Institutional and Intellectual Contexts

Our first purpose has been to create a baseline conception of American archaeology in North America in a period just before professionalization of the discipline in the United States, and to indicate what it might have become – in other words, to consider roads ultimately not taken, and to suggest why. By the 1880s archaeology in the United States was still overwhelmingly a local endeavour. The few institutions with national scope were either government-based – specifically the Smithsonian Institution (National Museum and Bureau of Ethnology), and military and geological expeditions (Hinsley 1981, 1994) – or they were connected to universities. The latter were very few in 1885 (one thinks chiefly of the Peabody Museum associated with Harvard) but university-museum collaborations in archaeology would increase significantly after the Chicago World's Fair of 1893, which was a powerful stimulus to the popularity, professionalization, and support of archaeology in the United States. Even so, institutions with national scope and interests often ran into jealousy and resistance from local individuals and archaeological societies. Beyond the government and the university, the remaining option for an ambitious, visionary young archaeologist was to obtain private patronage of some sort. But this involved its own limits and risks (Snead 2001).

Thus, the first frame for understanding this case in the history of archaeology is the institutional framework of time and place, in its possibilities and limits – the situation in which a man like Cushing inevitably found himself. But the institutional context is always tightly bound to a second set of factors, namely the dominant intellectual and political concerns of the cultural moment. In the case of the Hemenway Expedition we have found ourselves engaged with the values and concerns of the oldest, most wealthy and established urban centre of America – Boston (and by extension New England) – and simultaneously the mostly unsettled and unknown American Southwest of the 1880s. To further complicate matters, regional matters tended frequently to overflow nationally and even internationally.

For example, the rapidly developing southwestern territories (New Mexico, Arizona, southern California) of the 1880s were in the process of being incorporated imaginatively, economically and politically into the U.S. nation through increasingly effective means of communication, and in this process (which was particularly powerful between 1880 and 1920) portrayals of the living Indian peoples and the material ruins of their presumed predecessors became essential elements of the public perception of the American Southwest and its preparation for White settlement and tourist consumption (Hinsley 1992, Dilworth 1996, Padget 2004). Specifically, the Arizona desert country was being quickly redefined from a land of wild and dangerous Indians to a land ready for speculative transformation into green orchards and peaceful communal life. Irrigation was a central part of this scenario of transformation, and the exploration of prehistoric irrigation canals, such as Cushing was finding on the Expedition (Hodge 1893), added great weight to a set of highly desirable images for investment. Similarly, evidence of settled agricultural communities in the distant past seemed to confirm and project future possibilities for settlement and economic growth. As the deserts had once bloomed under the hands of the prehistoric indigenes, so they would bloom again under the hands of industrious American farmers. At least, this was the vision and promise.

Apart from the constructions and preoccupations of the new southwestern territories, New England cultural concerns, especially those of Mary Hemenway's wealthy social circles, also played critical roles in the formation and the expectations of her Expedition. These concerns are best described in terms of recovery: the recovery of national purpose and identity after a devastating civil war. To that end, the 'salvaging' and recording of American Indian cultural legacies – linguistic, archaeological, ethnological, or folkloric – on the assumption that they would soon disappear, were parts of the project of gathering and collecting the Indian past. These ethnological, linguistic and archaeological materials were ultimately intended to serve an important cultural and political function: to provide the deep human history that the American nation so desperately needed for balance and direction, a belonging in the land and the landscape so obvious among European peoples but lacking in a recently disrupted but rapidly industrializing American nation. To be sure, this was an old concern in American culture, traceable in the writings of Washington Irving, James Fenimore Cooper, and Nathaniel Hawthorne, among others; but it acquired new urgency after the civil war, with the ongoing destruction of trans-Mississippi Indian cultures and the apparently free-for-all economic expansion released by the triumph of northern industrial and financial interests during the recent civil war.

The regional concerns of New England and the Southwest blended and mixed into questions of national growth and purpose. The doubts, though, usually took the form of strong assertions of the evolutionary superiority of European-Americans and the inevitable, perhaps divinely ordained manifest destiny of the American nation to prosper, succeed and expand. American history, accordingly, was read not as conditional and ambiguous but as unquestionably progressive and teleological – even the costly and ghastly Civil War could be seen in such terms. When added to the dominant mode of knowledge inquiry at the time – a virulent strain of rather simplistic positivism – these powerful political and intellectual currents left little room for serious second thoughts or mental meandering.

For all their focus on American society and its destiny, regional and national preoccupations also played on the larger field of international relations, especially with European centres of learning and debate. Simply stated, European opinions mattered greatly. For evidence of this we need go no further than the Hemenway Expedition itself: in 1888 Mary Hemenway paid for two representatives of the Expedition to attend the International Congress of Americanists (ICA) in Berlin in order to present Cushing's paper on his theory and fieldwork.[10] The title of the paper was: 'Preliminary Notes on the Origin, Working Hypothesis, and Primary Researches of the Hemenway Southwestern Archaeological Expedition'. As described in that paper, Cushing's central hypothesis, which concerned the persistence of the 'essential thoughts' or *Elementargedanken* of a people, was almost certainly borrowed from Adolph Bastian (1826–1905). Cushing's paper was one of the first ever contributed by an American to the ICA; it was published in the *Proceedings* two years later.

Cushing's own essential thoughts, too, extended beyond the U.S. to the American hemisphere. He participated in an intellectual tradition – from Alexander von Humboldt and including such Americans as Albert Gallatin, John Lloyd Stephens, and Daniel Brinton – that persisted strongly through the nineteenth century but faded by its end, and which saw the western hemisphere as a single entity and a proper sphere of inquiry from pole to pole (Fowler 2000, Fowler and Wilcox 1999, Wilcox and Fowler 2002). During the expedition Cushing's imagination travelled beyond the Southwest as he toyed repeatedly with theories of hemispheric migration. He claimed to see, for instance, evidence of llama-like creatures ('guanacos') in petroglyphs and on the figurative ceramics he was unearthing; he even made plans for further explorations along the South American coast (Cushing 1890) in order to pursue 'Peruvian connections' with the American Southwest.

While our first purposes have been to understand intellectual and institutional contexts in order to place the archaeological expedition as firmly as possible in its time and place, these historicist concerns are complemented by the concerns of the disciplinary present: How can materials gathered a century ago be made to contribute to our archaeological understanding today? Accordingly we have been concerned to 'bring them back to life,' as Emil Haury did in the 1930s, but as must be done again now that our knowledge of the prehistoric Southwest grows and deepens. Cushing excavated and gathered at a time prior to serious settlement in what is now the second-fastest growing urban centre in North America. Most of the landscape has been radically altered or obliterated in the past century; Cushing thus not only collected tons of material that would have been lost, but also saw and recorded mounds and surface features that no longer exist. Indeed, for some of them Cushing's is the only observation we have.[11] As early after the expedition as 1906, Dutch anthropologist Herman ten Kate returned briefly to the campsite and nostalgically noted:

At the foot of the hill lies the Salado [River], dusty as ever, and the little town [Tempe], now remarkably larger, changed beyond recognition. Around me, solitude and silence. Only the rustling of the bushes and a roadrunner searching for food.

I look far and wide across the land. That has also changed beyond recognition, except for the mountains. The white man has turned the sandy desert plain into green fields, many with alfalfa, and orchards with orange trees. A new life has developed on the ruins of the gray past. In the distance I search for the location where Los Muertos, the City of the Dead, was situated and where we were camped, but I only see an ocean of green (Hovens 1995: 699).

Support Systems and Networks in Archaeology

We have also been concerned to explore in some detail the persistent question of support in archaeology, and the nature of support systems under various historical conditions. For both of us this has been a long-standing interest, about which we have written separately on various occasions.[12] What kinds of support do various types of individuals require, what kinds of support are available in specific situations – and with what restrictions – and how does the match or mismatch determine the 'success' or 'failure' of an archaeological enterprise?

In the case of Cushing, his entire career could be approached through these questions. Even when he worked for the Smithsonian, Cushing's relationships were always intensely personal, and he relied on private understandings – or what he took to be personal arrangements and understandings – for his own functional balance. In the case of the Hemenway Expedition, Cushing assumed that he and Mary Hemenway shared a set of values and visions to a greater degree, we believe, than was actually true. When his health and her health both failed and the bond of trust between them became strained and finally broken, the results were devastating for him.

To put this in perspective, it is important to emphasize that Cushing's generation of young men was the first to have to adjust to new, large-scale organizations of government and business in the industrializing American society, and thus the first to experience the routines, or routinization, of daily work life. Expressed in Max Weber's familiar terms, Cushing was much more a figure of charisma than a man of bureaucratic routine (Weber 1947; cf. Hinsley 1983). Unlike his brother-in-law Hodge, who began as a secretary and spent his entire adulthood happily embedded in organizational life, Cushing revolted against institutional constraints. He required almost unconditional personal support for his research style, wide latitude for his irregularities and eccentricities, and largely unquestioning acceptance of his expenditures. Indeed, his career is best understood as a series of personal relationships with patrons, no matter where he actually worked.

The Problem of Failure and Motivation in Archaeology

The issues of support systems and client/patron relations have led to yet another set of questions in our project: Why did the Hemenway Expedition fall apart? What did it mean for this enterprise to fail, and what do we mean by – how do we define – success or failure in the history of archaeology, anyway? We are engaged in a case study of historical failure, but mainly in order to inquire into the category of 'failure'. All of the contextual factors discussed above conspired in this collapse: the intellectual, the institutional, and the personal. But at the same time careers grew from it; valuable collections were preserved; and, many years later, they were examined with significant results. Indeed, a new field of Hohokam studies is based upon the Hemenway work.[13] So what, really, do we mean by such judgemental terms as 'failure'? A failure for whom, and when?

Finally, on a more philosophical level, our explorations of the Hemenway Expedition present an opportunity to probe into the basic motivations for archaeology, and science more broadly. We both came to graduate work in the 1960s – Wilcox in archaeology/anthropology and Hinsley in cultural history. It was the heyday of Lewis Binford's New Archaeology, but Wilcox found himself at crosscurrents with the new wave, more influenced by archaeologist K.C. Chang's *Rethinking Archaeology* (Chang 1961), the method of multiple working hypotheses proposed by the nineteenth-century geologist T.C. Chamberlin (Chamberlin 1965), and Robert Merton's reminder from Newton that, after all, we only stand *On the Shoulders of Giants* (Merton 1993). Well, how do you climb up on those shoulders? Assuredly not by dismissing all archaeology that has gone before, but by taking seriously the words and actions of those who have preceded us, and this is possible only by embracing a scholarly and historical understanding that is as intimate as possible – and, methodologically, we both agree, by permitting those who have struggled before us to speak in their own words. Above all, we are both convinced of the need for a stance of humility in the presence of our predecessors, in the recognition that fallibility is the foundation of tolerance (Kamen 1967) and that, as English historian and philosopher R.G. Collingwood observed many years ago (Collingwood 1939), our questions are the contexts for our answers, and we must seek first to understand the questions that were asked, and that we would ask, before seeking answers.

We must often be satisfied, if only in some instances temporarily, with uncertainties and ambiguity, for definitive answers to our questions elude us – as they also eluded our predecessors. History and science alike, then, are always an unfinished business, ever calling upon us to engage in an unending quest.

Of course, knowledge and data sometimes appear where we least expect them, and serendipitous discoveries of things hidden on high shelves may ultimately alter our interpretations of events. As several papers in this volume demonstrate, with closer attention to what are often surprisingly complete archival records of previous archaeologists and their work, we are beginning to realize that more nuanced social and cultural understanding of the conditions, praxis, and results of our archaeological predecessors may be open to us, an understanding that takes into account the purposes and dilemmas of their times, and their struggles for support and stability. While they may not precisely match the conditions and issues of today, our predecessors' challenges and solutions may nonetheless alert us to the particularities of our own moment and thereby, one hopes, instill in us a certain humility.

Notes

1. Remarkably little has been written about Mary Hemenway, even though her contributions to American life were profound (Hinsley and McChesney 1984; McChesney 1988, 2003). Cushing's life has been more extensively explored (see recently Green 1979, 1990, McFeely 2001, and Wilcox 2003).
2. Cushing's mentor, John Wesley Powell, suggested that he begin the expedition as a reconnaissance. For Cushing's conceptions of what he called the 'Aridian' culture, see Cushing (1890 and 1896, and Lyman (1982).
3. Ten Kate first met Cushing in 1883 at Zuñi, and their friendship helped to inform Cushing about European conceptions of anthropology, including the work of Adolph Bastian (see Hovens 1988, 1989, 1995).
4. Siwaititsailu and Weta accompanied Cushing on his reconnaissance from December, 1886 to August 1887. Prior to the expedition three important Zuñi leaders (governor of the pueblo Palowahtiwa, Waihusiwa, and Heluta) visited Mrs Hemenway's summer home on the north shore of Massachusetts, where Cushing worked with them translating Zuñi oral traditions. It was a magical time that led one of Mrs Hemenway's friends (Dewey 1995: 564) to remark that 'It was like hearing the Homeric songs at first hand'. The experience helped to persuade Hemenway to sponsor the expedition (Goddard 1995; Hinsley and Wilcox 2002).
5. Unlike Cushing, Fewkes promptly published a series of brief descriptive reports in the *Journal of American Ethnology*, which he founded and edited with Hemenway support. At first Fewkes attempted to continue Cushing's field efforts, but after his first publication (Fewkes 1891) he was accused by Cushing of plagiarism. Fewkes wisely moved his focus to Hopi (Adams and Zedeño 1999).
6. At the Chicago World's Fair in 1893 Cushing received lavish recognition for his contributions to anthropology. Zelia Nutall and Alice Fletcher called him the 'sun of anthropology' (Cushing 1893), and his friendship with Philadelphian Stewart Culin eventually led to an expedition to Florida for the University Museum of Pennsylvania (Cushing 1897; Gilliland 1975, 1989; Wilcox 2003; Kolianos and Weisman 2005a, 2005b).
7. For Haury's reminiscences of his Harvard experiences, see Haury (1995). His work on the Hemenway collections became the cornerstone of a long career in southwestern archaeology (Thompson 1995, Haury 2004).
8. Connections between the Hohokam and Zuñi have recently again been postulated (Shaul and Hill 1998). The explanation for the data cited, however, may mainly result from intermediary relationships with populations in the Safford Valley of present-day Arizona (Gregory and Wilcox 2007).

9. For recent analysis and evaluation of some of Hodge's charges, see Wilcox (2003).
10. Adolph Bandelier also contributed a paper (Bandelier 1890), as did physical anthropologist Jacob Wortman and Herman F.C. ten Kate (1890).
11. Wilcox has incorporated many of those observations in studies of the Los Hornos site (Wilcox et al. 1990), Casa Grande Ruins (Cushing 1995; Hinsley and Wilcox 2001; Wilcox and Sternberg 1981), and Pueblo Grande (Wilcox 1993a).
12. See Wilcox 1987, 1988, 1993b.
13. In addition to work cited above, the collections at the Peabody Museum continue to be studied with new results (Brunson 1989) and are currently being made more accessible.

Archival Sources

HFL CLB: Huntington Free Library, Cushing Letter Books, Bronx, New York
SWM CC: Southwest Museum, Cushing Collection, Los Angeles, California

References

Adams, E. and M. Zedeño. 1999. 'BAE Scholars as Documenters of Diversity and Change at Hopi, 1870–1895', in M. Zedeño (ed.), *Scholars of the Bureau of American Ethnology: Exploring the Roots of American Anthropology. Journal of the Southwest* 41(3): 311–34.

Bandelier, A. 1890. 'The Historical Archives of the Hemenway Southwestern Archaeological Expedition', in *Congrès International des Américanistes, Berlin, 1888*, Berlin: W.H. Kühl, pp. 151–94.

Baxter, S. 1888. *The Old New World: An Account of the Explorations of the Hemenway Southwestern Archaeological Expedition in 1887–88, under the direction of Frank Hamilton Cushing.* Salem, Massachusetts: Salem Press.

Brunson, J. 1989. 'The Social Organization of the Los Muertos Hohokam: A Reanalysis of Cushing's Hemenway Expedition Data', Ph.D. dissertation, Tempe, Arizona: Arizona State University.

Chamberlin, T. 1965. 'The Method of Multiple Working Hypotheses', *Science* 148: 754–59.

Chang, K. 1961. *Rethinking Archaeology.* New Haven: Yale University Press.

Collingwood, R. 1939. *An Autobiography.* London: Oxford University Press.

Cushing, F. to S. Baxter, 5 March 1887, HFL CLB 1: 205–14.

Cushing, F. to M. Hemenway, August, 1887. HFL CLB 2: 169–212.

Cushing, F. 1890. 'Preliminary Notes on the Origin, Working Hypothesis and Primary Researches of the Hemenway Southwestern Archaeological Expedition', in *Congrès International des Américanistes*, Berlin, 1888, Berlin, W.H. Kühl, pp. 151–94.

———. 1893. Diaries. [Transcribed by D. Wilcox, Museum of Northern Arizona.] National Anthropological Archives, Washington D.C.

———. 1896. 'Exploration of Ancient Key-Dweller Remains on the Gulf Coast of Florida', in *Proceedings of the American Philosophical Society* 35. Philadelphia, Pennsylvania, pp. 329–448.

———. 1995. 'Itinerary of Reconnaissance to Casa Grande Ruins, December 31, 1887 to January 4, 1888', *Journal of the Southwest* 37(4): 590–604.

Dewey, M. 1995. 'Visit of the Zuni Indians to the Summer House of Mrs. Mary Hemenway in 1886', *Journal of the Southwest* 37(4): 551–65.

Dilworth, L. 1996. *Imagining Indians in the Southwest: Persistent Visions of a Primitive Past.* Washington: Smithsonian Institution Press.

Fewkes, J. 1891. 'A Few Summer Ceremonials at Zuñi Pueblo', *Journal of American Ethnology and Archaeology* 1: 1–160.

Fowler, D. 2000. *A Laboratory for Anthropology: Science and Romanticism in the North American Southwest, 1846–1930.* Albuquerque: University of New Mexico Press.

——— and D. Wilcox. 1999. 'From Thomas Jefferson to the Pecos Conference: Changing Anthropological Agendas in the North American Southwest', in E. Carter (ed.), *Surveying the Record: North American Scientific Exploration to 1930.* Philadelphia: American Philosophical Society Memoirs 231, pp. 197–224.

Gilliland, M. 1975. *The Material Culture of Key Marco, Florida*. Gainesville: University Press of Florida.

———. 1989. *Key Marco's Buried Treasure: Archaeology and Adventure in the Nineteenth Century*. Gainesville: University Press of Florida.

Goddard, M. 1995. 'A Zuni Religious Service at Manchester-By-The-Sea', *Journal of the Southwest* 37(4): 566–70.

Green, J. 1979. *Zuni: Selected Writings of Frank Hamilton Cushing*. Lincoln: University of Nebraska Press.

———. 1990. *Cushing at Zuni: The Correspondence and Journals of Frank Hamilton Cushing, 1879–1884*. Albuquerque: University of New Mexico Press.

Gregory, D. and Wilcox, D. 2007. 'A New Research Design for Studying Zuni Origins and Similar Anthropological Problems.' In D. Gregory and D. Wilcox (eds), *Zuni Origins: Toward a New Synthesis of Southwestern Archaeology*. Tucson: The University of Arizona Press.

Haury, E. 1945. *The Excavations of Los Muertos and Neighboring Ruins in the Salt River Valley, Southern Arizona*. Cambridge, Massachusetts: Peabody Museum of American Archaeology and Ethnology.

———. 1995. 'Wherefore a Harvard PhD?', *Journal of the Southwest* 37(4): 710–33.

Haury, L. 2004. *Emil Haury Centennial*, Special Issue of *Journal of the Southwest* (46: 1).

Hinsley, C. 1981. *Savages and Scientists: The Smithsonian Institution and the Development of American Anthropology, 1846–1910*. Washington: Smithsonian Institution Press.

———. 1983. 'Ethnographic Charisma and Scientific Routine: Cushing and Fewkes in the American Southwest, 1879–1893', in G. Stocking (ed.), *Observers Observed: Essays on Ethnographic Fieldwork*. Madison: University of Wisconsin Press, pp. 53–69.

———. 1992. 'Collecting Cultures and Cultures of Collecting: The Lure of the American Southwest, 1880–1915', *Museum Anthropology* 16(1): 12–20.

———. 1994. *The Smithsonian and the American Indian: Making a Moral Anthropology in Victorian America*. Washington: Smithsonian Institution Press.

———. 1999. 'Life on the Margins: The Ethnographic Poetics of Frank Hamilton Cushing', *Journal of the Southwest* 41(3): 371–82.

———. 2002. 'The Lost Itinerary of Frank Hamilton Cushing', in C. Hinsley and D. Wilcox (eds), *The Lost Itinerary of Frank Hamilton Cushing*. Tucson: University of Arizona Press, pp. 3–37.

——— . and L. McChesney. 1984. 'Anthropology as Cultural Exchange: The Shared Vision of Mary Hemenway and Frank Cushing', *American Ethnological Society and the Southwestern Anthropological Association, March, 1984*. Phoenix, Arizona.

——— . and D. Wilcox. 2001. 'Arizona's First Sacred Site: The Mystique of the Casa Grande, 1848–1889', *Bilingual Review/La Revista Bilingüe* 25(2): 1–17.

———. and D. Wilcox.1995. *A Hemenway Portfolio*. Special Issue of *Journal of the Southwest* 37(4): 517–744.

——— . and ——— . 1996. *The Southwest in the American Imagination: The Writings of Sylvester Baxter, 1881–1889*. Tucson: University of Arizona Press.

——— . and ——— . 2002. *The Lost Itinerary of Frank Hamilton Cushing*. Tucson: University of Arizona Press.

Hodge, F. 1893. 'Prehistoric Irrigation in Arizona', *American Anthropologist* 6: 323–30.

———. 1945. 'Foreword', in E. Haury, *The Excavation of Los Muertos and Neighboring Ruins in the Salt River Valley, Southern Arizona*. Cambridge, Massachusetts: Peabody Museum of American Archaeology and Ethnology.

Hovens, P. 1988. 'The Anthropologist as Enigma. Frank Hamilton Cushing', *European Review of Native American Studies* 2(1): 1–5.

———. 1989. *Herman F. C. ten Kate, Jr. (1858–1931) en de Antropologie der Noord-Amerikaanse Indianen*. Meppel, Netherlands: Krips Repro.

——— . 1995. 'Ten Kate's Hemenway Expedition Diary, 1887–1888', *Journal of the Southwest* 37(4): 635–700.

——— . W. Orr, and L. Hieb (eds). 2002. *Travels and Researches in Native North America, 1882–1883, by Herman ten Kate*. Albuquerque: University of New Mexico Press.

Kamen, H. 1967. *The Rise of Toleration*. New York: McGraw-Hill.

Kolianos, P. and B. Weisman. 2005a. *The Florida Journals of Frank Hamilton Cushing*. Gainesville: University Press of Florida.

———. and ———. 2005b. *The Lost Florida Manuscript of Frank Hamilton Cushing*. Gainesville: University Press of Florida.

Lummis, C. 1900. 'The White Indian', *Land of Sunshine* 13: 8–17.

Lyman, S. 1982. 'Two Neglected Pioneers of Civilizational Analysis: Perspectives of R. Stewart Culin and Frank Hamilton Cushing', *Social Research* 694–729.

McChesney, L. 1988. 'Appropriation for Cultural Reproduction: The Vision of Mary Hemenway', *American Anthropological Association, November, 1988*. Phoenix, Arizona.

———. 2003. 'The American Indian and the (Re-)Production of the Primitive: Hopi Pottery and Potters', Ph.D. dissertation. New York: New York University.

McFeely, E. 2001. *Zuni and the American Imagination*. New York: Hill and Wang.

Magill, M. 1995. 'Margaret Magill's Zuni Diary', *Journal of the Southwest* 37(4): 535–50.

Matthews, W. 1900. 'The Cities of the Dead', *Land of Sunshine* 12: 213–21.

———. J. Wortman and J. Billings. 1895. *Human Bones in the Hemenway Collection in the U.S. Army Medical Museum*. Washington: Memoirs of the National Academy of Sciences No. 6.

Merton, R. 1993. *On the Shoulders of Giants: The Post-Italianate Edition*. Chicago: University of Chicago Press.

Padget, M. 2004. *Indian Country: Travels in the American Southwest*. Albuquerque: The University of New Mexico Press.

Shaul, D. and J. Hill. 1998. 'Tepimans, Yumans, and other Hohokam', *American Antiquity* 63(3): 375–96.

Snead, J. 2001. *Ruins and Rivals: The Making of Southwest Archaeology*. Tucson: University of Arizona Press.

Thompson, R. 1995. 'Emil W. Haury and the Definition of Southwestern Archaeology', *American Antiquity* 60(4): 640–60.

Wade, E. and L. McChesney. 1980. *America's Great Lost Expedition: The Thomas Keam Collection of Hopi Pottery from the Second Hemenway Expedition, 1890–1894*. Phoenix: The Heard Museum.

Weber, M. 1947. *The Theory of Social and Economic Organization*. New York: Free Press.

Wilcox, D. 1987. *Frank Midvale's Investigation of the Site of La Ciudad*. Tempe: Arizona State University Archaeological Field Studies No. 19.

———. 1988. 'The Changing Context of Support for Archaeology and the Work of Erich F. Schmidt', in J. Hohmann and L. Kelley (eds), *Erich F. Schmidt's Investigations of Salado Sites in Central Arizona*. Flagstaff: Museum of Northern Arizona Bulletin 56, pp. 11–28.

———. 1993a. 'Pueblo Grande in the Nineteenth Century', in C. Downum and T. Bostwick (eds), *Archaeology of the Pueblo Grande Platform Mound and Surrounding Features, Volume 1: Introduction to the Archival Project and History of Research*. Phoenix: Pueblo Grande Museum Anthropological Papers No. 1, pp. 43–72.

———. 1993b. 'Pueblo Grande as Phoenix: Odd Halseth's Vision of a City Museum', in C. Downum and T. Bostwick (eds), *Archaeology of the Pueblo Grande Platform Mound and Surrounding Features, Volume 1: Introduction to the Archival Project and History of Research*. Phoenix: Pueblo Grande Museum Anthropological Papers No. 1., pp. 97–138.

———. 2003. 'Restoring Authenticity: Judging Frank Hamilton Cushing's Veracity', in D. Fowler and D. Wilcox (eds), *Philadelphia and the Development of Americanist Archaeology*. Tuscaloosa: University of Alabama Press, pp. 88–112.

———. and D. Fowler. 2002. 'The Beginnings of Anthropological Archaeology in the North American Southwest: From Thomas Jefferson to the Pecos Conference', *Journal of the Southwest* 44(2): 121–234.

———. and D. Gregory. 2005. 'Introductory Essay II', in D. Gregory and D. Wilcox (eds), *Zuñi Origins: Anthropological Approaches on Multiple Americanist and Southwestern Scales*. Tucson: University of Arizona Press.

———. and C. Sternberg. 1981. *Additional Studies of the Architecture of the Casa Grande and Its Interpretation*. Tucson: Arizona State Museum Archaeological Series 146.

Wilcox, D., J. Howard and R. Nelson. 1990. *One Hundred Years of Archaeology at La Ciudad de los Hornos*. Phoenix: Soil Systems Publications in Archaeology 16.

Wortman, J. and H. ten Kate. 1890. 'On an Anatomical Characteristic of the Hyoid Bone of Pre-Columbian Pueblo Indians of Arizona, U.S.A.', *Congrès International des Américanistes*. Berlin, 1888, Berlin: W.H. Kühl, p. 263.

Chapter 4
The Phenomenon of Pre-Soviet Archaeology

Archival Studies in the History of Russian Archaeology – Methods and Results[1]

Nadezhda I. Platonova

Abstract

From the 1930s onward, official Soviet historiography displayed a critical attitude towards the Russian archaeology of the first third of the twentieth-century, singling it out for its empiricism, eclecticism and absence of theoretical or methodological approaches. This idea, first set out by V.I. Ravdonikas in his 'For a Marxist History of Material Culture' (1930) was for more than half a century the mainstream view enforced upon successive generations of archaeologists. L. Klejn (1993) undertook a shrewd and witty analysis of 'The Phenomenon of Soviet archaeology' from the 1930s to the 1980s, but the same ideological demystification remains to be done for 'the phenomenon of Pre-Soviet archaeology'. Besides using published sources, it is also essential to draw on archival material. These confirm the considerable activities of Russian archaeology in the 1920s, notably those associated with V.A. Gorodtsov, and those belonging to the 'Paleoethnological' school, including the pioneering use of statistics, ethnographic analogies and other methods. Altogether, this re-evaluation confirms that it is our role as historians to take on board relevant socio-political conditions and to seek to overcome the stereotypes and myths inherited from the recent past.

The official Soviet historiography of the period lasting from the 1930s to the 1980s tends toward a rather critical view of Russian archaeology during the first third of the twentieth century. Invariably stressed were its empiricism, eclecticism and absence of theoretical or methodological approaches. The tone was set by V.I. Ravdonikas in 'For a Marxist History of Material Culture' (1930). Its trenchant style was suggestive of a political objective – to discredit the 'old archaeology' and lay a theoretical foundation for the crackdown that began in 1929 with mass purges, dismissals and arrests of prominent specialists. Despite the evidence of his political connections, Ravdonikas' views proved extremely durable and post-Stalin Soviet historiography has reiterated most of them with few if any modifications (Gening 1982). For more than half a century the idea that Russian archaeology in the years 1900 to 1930 was highly empirical and methodologically impotent was a mainstream view, forced upon successive generations of archaeologists. L. Klein's works (1977; 1993) contain a shrewd and witty analysis of 'the Phenomenon of Soviet Archaeology' from the 1930s to the 1980s, but it is not until recently that we have began to understand also 'the phenomenon of Pre-Soviet archaeology'.

For more than half a century the idea that Russian archaeology between 1900 and 1930 was highly empirical and methodologically impotent appeared self-evident. Eventually Western scholars accepted the idea as well. A chapter in Bruce Trigger's excellent book on the history of archaeological thought is devoted to Russian archaeology and written much in the official Soviet vein (Trigger 1989). Unlike their Soviet colleagues, archaeologists in the West cannot be blamed for their mistake. The unpublished legacy of the 1920s, preserved in Russia's archives, was unavailable and unknown to them. Western views of this period echoed the same condemnations that Soviet Marxists aimed against 'old science' in early 1930s (e.g., Bykovskii 1931; Ravdonikas 1930, 1932: 49–60).

The views of the Leningrad-based Vladislav Iosifovich Ravdonikas (1894–1976) may have become official doctrine and defined the Western view of Russian archaeology, but they were simply a version of an ideological myth that was popular under the totalitarian regime (see Platonova 2002: 261–78). This was the only perspective from which the development of virtually all the humanities and natural sciences that had been crushed in the late 1920s and early 1930s and subsequently transplanted to the 'one and only' fertile soil of Marxism could be viewed. Not in a single instance, however, are these views supported by facts.

Attempts at analysing the history of Soviet archaeology in the 1920s and early 1930s have been based almost exclusively on published sources, and even these have not been used to their fullest extent. Only isolated aspects of the history have been reconstructed with the help of archival materials (the present author was among the first to use them) (Platonova 1989, 1995; Tikhonov 1993, 1995, 2003). And yet, in the few cases where these materials have been used, they have led to a radical revision of existing interpretation.

The principal problems with which the researcher is faced concern the methodology underlying the use of the vast archival materials, their order of priority, the informative potential of various sets of archival data, and the way in which the same events are reflected in different categories of documents such as shorthand reports, newspaper publications, and letters. At present, top priority should be accorded to complete sets of materials representing a single category of archival sources and reflecting specific historical processes over the time period in question. These materials include series of shorthand reports of general meetings of the Academy for the Study of the History of Material Culture (AIMK) and those of the meetings of its board and council throughout the entire period of its existence. A review of the complete set of documents preserved at the IIMK archives concerning graduate studies at AIMK, as well as a series of instructions issued by Glavnauka (the Ministry of Science) and RANION (Russian Association of Institutes of Social Studies), also proved highly informative.

Not the least important category of documents are manuscripts of articles and books, their summaries, programs of university courses and abstracts of papers – in short, everything that was not published but was highly relevant to the issue. Finally, published sources also were widely used in the present study. Those pertaining to the period from the late 1910s to the late 1920s are highly informative and many of them had not been previously employed although some contain unique information.

The history of archaeology in the U.S.S.R. falls into two principal stages separated by the year 1930, which was officially termed 'the Year of the Great Breakthrough'. During the first stage (1917–1929), we see a relatively straightforward archaeology comprising a variety of diverse views, competing trends, the formation of local schools, and an emphasis on regional studies. This archaeology was an inherent part of culture and cultural education that, in contrast to the situation in later years, was practiced not only in the major cities but also in the provinces.

The structure of archaeology at that time was radically different from that of the pre-revolutionary period. Immediately after the Revolution, the discipline underwent radical changes.

However, this restructuring was not directed by the central authorities. Before 1924, the leadership of the People's Commissariat of Education merely approved the structural changes in archaeology rather than initiating them. The idea of transformation was rooted in pre-revolutionary Russian science and culture (Platonova 1989: 5–16). In fact, the process itself started before the October Revolution. The changes began after the February Revolution (e.g., Znamenskii 1988: 185–91, 322–324). The traditions of Russian archaeology of 1917–1929 are inseparable from those of the so-called 'Silver Age' (a term used with reference to early twentieth-century Russian culture).

Within the first stage, four sub-periods may be distinguished, and each of them is characterized by specific historical conditions and tendencies in the development of archaeology.

Between 1917 and 1924, the organizational structure of Russian/Soviet archaeology was defined. The key events in the process were these:

(a) The establishment during the summer of 1917 of KIPS (The Academy of Sciences Commission for the Study of Russia's Tribal Structure) for the purpose of a multidisciplinary ethnological, linguistic, and archaeological study of the entire nation, and the organization (in the Caucasus) of the first institute for historical and archaeological studies.

(b) The abolition of the Archaeological Commission and the foundation of the Petrograd Academy of Archaeology, which was named AIMK (Academy for the Study of History of Material Culture). This was the first institution aimed at a methodological integration of research conducted in prehistoric, Oriental, classical and 'historic' (or 'domestic') archaeology. Also, it stressed the importance of scientific methods for studying archaeological sites regardless of age. The practical result of the latter was the foundation in 1919 of a separate institute within AIMK: The Institute of Archaeological Technology.

(c) The foundation of archaeological sub-departments within the departments of humanities and social sciences at Petrograd and Moscow universities (1922).

(d) The establishment of separate sections specializing in paleoethnological and paleoethnographical (essentially archaeological) studies within all large museums, and the foundation of new centres, including the State Museum of the Central Industrial Region (1919) and the Central Museum of Ethnography in Moscow (1924).

(e) The foundation of the Moscow Institute of Archaeology and Art Studies within RANION (1923).

(f) The formation of a broad network of provincial museums and societies whose responsibilities included the protection and study of archaeological sites. At the same time, the Central Bureau of Regional Studies was established within the Academy of Sciences for the purpose of supervising the work of provincial bodies.

By the middle of 1924, this new organization of archaeological institutions had been created. It included two major research institutes (AIMK in Leningrad and IAI RANION in Moscow), about a dozen large central museums having archaeological divisions, and over a hundred provincial museums. Formally, both the museum network and the research institutions were subject to the Central Committee for the Museums and the Protection of Sites (a body associated with the People's Commissariat of Education). However, at that time, the authorities refrained from interference in scientific affairs. Future archaeologists were being educated at the universities, specifically at the archaeological subdivisions of the departments for humanities and social sciences (FONs). Also, in accordance with pre-revolutionary tradition, archaeology was being taught at university departments of geography and physics. Tensions between science and the regime became evident between 1925 and 1927. They concerned archaeological methodology and infrastructure, as well as the education of future specialists. The principal methodological issue was that archaeologists of the 1920s searched for regularities in the development of extant, or ethnographic, cultures with the intent of using them to interpret extinct, or archaeological, cultures (see below).

By this time, moreover, a radical and potentially dangerous doctrine had made its appearance, through the Leningrad-based philologist, archaeologist and linguist Nikolaj Yakovlevich Marr (1864–1934). Already in the 1900s, Marr had formulated a 'Japhetic doctrine' on the cultural and linguistic history of the Caucasian tribes. Professional linguists (then and today) thought it erroneous (cf. Thomas 1957), but some historians remain interested in Marr's original ideas on the evolution of human culture (see Vasil'kov 2000; Platonova 2002a). N. Ya. Marr was indeed a great philologist and well-known archaeologist in pre-revolutionary Russia. He served as director of a large-scale archaeological expedition in Turkish Armenia for 17 years. Then he succeeded in organizing the Archaeological Institute of the Caucasus (1917) (Platonova 1998).

The 'new theory of language' (or 'marrism') appeared in the mid-1920s. Marr was no more than a dilettante in linguistics (see Alpatov 1991). Prevented by his neurotic disease from working with concrete philological or archaeological data, but still he attempted to address the question of the universal laws of cultural and linguistic evolution. Marr's 'new theory' may be seen as an original and unique phenomenon of Russian cultural life, subsequently warped by the Revolution and dictatorship. Marr believed that every period is characterized by a specific type of language and its own 'linguistic thinking'. After a social revolution, the structure of language remains the same as before, but social changes may cause people to alter their 'linguistic thinking'. In this way, people may deform or destroy their inherited language. Those who speak a language do not understand its old forms and create new ones. So Marr's basic principle was that all deformations of society (and of language and culture) were natural. This view was of great value for ideological propaganda.

The style of Marr's works published in the 1920s and 1930s exposed his neurological disease. He was able to suggest some ideas at that time but could not articulate them on paper or even think logically. Marr's own works were incomprehensible to Communist readers, but interpreters of his ideas quickly appeared. Marr saw the key to all the problems of interpreting archaeological data in the so-called 'paleontology of language'. He believed that this method could be applied universally in archaeology and would permit the reconstruction of ancient thinking. Although the 'method' was based on Marr's fantasy and had no base in the real (not 'marrist') linguistics, it was approved as a Marxist one in 1929. Indeed, Marr's Soviet interpreters asserted that 'Marr's theory was a materialistic one' and that 'Marr studied the process of cultural change in a dynamic way'. They emphasised the fact that Marr had: (a) nearly rejected the importance of geographic and 'race' factors, (b) stressed evolution and 'revolutionary changes' of language, and (c) linked these changes of linguistic structures with the social and economic changes in society. On the basis of these, they declared that Marr's theory was 'close to Marxism' and had to be 'united with Marxism'. In the early 1930s this 'Japhetology' gave rise to the stadialist doctrine in archaeology.

Supported by the Soviet power, Marrism became a real 'false doctrine' and an instrument of ideological repression. In the early 1930s it started replacing the really progressive methods of archaeological and ethnological study. Certainly marrism seemed to be more beneficial for the needs of contemporary politics. This 'method' really permitted the reconstruction of the past in any way the authorities required.

In spite of this fact N. Ya. Marr had earned respect during the 1920s (especially in Leningrad), but only as an administrator and leader. He was the leading figure in protecting archaeological and cultural institutions and societies in Petrograd during the period of 'War Communism' (1918–1921). He had undertaken the reconstruction of the central state archaeological institution of Russia (Archaeological Commission) in 1918 and became one of the founders of the AIMK in 1919 (Platonova 1989). The Leningrad colleagues remembered all these and were grateful to Marr. Some of them could understand even at that time that the sick old man had become a puppet ruled by the authorities.

Apart from such theoretical orientations, also the institutional infrastructure was affected by changes. In 1925–1927, most archaeological work was being done under ethno-anthropological projects associated with interdisciplinary economic studies in various regions. Because of this, archaeology became part of research conducted by VSNKh (Council of National Economy) and Gosplan (Planning Committee) in order to assess the nation's productive forces. Archaeology was thus officially considered 'useful' for socialist construction and received ample financial support. However, this also made it possible for Soviet planning bodies to interfere in the affairs of archaeology. In 1925–1926, archaeological institutions were instructed to comply with current policies.

Also, there were problems with the educational process. In 1925, postgraduate training of archaeologists began. Again, on the one hand, the effect was positive, but the step was ideologically motivated. People in charge of People's Commissariat of Education did not conceal the fact that after their postgraduate studies, the new generation of Marxist scholars was expected to become 'grave-diggers.' Their political task was to bury the 'old' archaeology. Although the heyday of the NEP (New Economic Policy, 1925–1927) was marked by conflicting trends, the scholarly atmosphere was generally favourable, and intense research was being undertaken.

In 1928, radical changes in the government's attitude toward science became apparent and cooperation with specialists who had been trained before the revolution gave way to sharp confrontation. After the NEP had been halted, several large-scale projects concerned with interdisciplinary regional studies were curtailed. At the same time, the first in a series of the so-called 'methodological discussions' took part. The true purpose of these campaigns was not to discuss scholarly matters, but to crack down publicly on certain schools and ideas. 'Free theorizing' was thereby banned, and it was only half a century later that the ban was lifted.

The next stage of Russian archaeology was one of extreme politicization. Between late 1929 and 1933, the new 'Soviet' archaeology broke away from the preceding tradition in a number of respects. Regional archaeology was completely crushed, as was the wide network of provincial institutions, and prominent archaeologists working in Moscow and Leningrad were arrested. Archaeological and ethnographic sub-departments at the universities were closed down. The formerly decentralized archaeological infrastructure was subjected to radical change. The Moscow IAI RANION was disbanded. The AIMK became a monopolist institution – an ideological monster whose responsibility was to propagate Marxism and the stadialist doctrine.

Gorodtsov's School

The Moscow-based Vasilii Aleksejevich Gorodtsov (1860–1945) was perhaps the only archaeological theorist of the 1920s who managed to articulate all his views before the advent of the 'Great Breakthrough'. It was during these years that his theoretical ideas took shape, and several of his works focusing on archaeological classification and the typological method were published (Gorodtsov 1923a,b, 1927). Gorodtsov's intense teaching created a school that regarded archaeology as an independent discipline with its own objects and methods. According to Gorodtsov, archaeology was a study of artifacts and their evolution. In opposition to the ethnological paradigm, which was the predominant trend in that period, he claimed that archaeology was not merely an independent discipline, but a science that could apply its own methods for discovering the laws underlying the function and evolution of sites and artifacts.

The attitudes of the authorities to Gorodtsov in the 1920s were quite positive. Immediately after the Revolution, he was appointed Head of the Archaeological Subdivision of Glavmuzey (the

Chief Administration of the Museums). He was surrounded by influential Marxist historians of the older generation, such as V.M. Friche, V.K. Nikol'skii, and others. They actively popularized his ideas and publicly claimed that he had become much closer to Marxism. In 1923, V.K. Nikol'skii used Gorodtsov's chronological scheme as a basis for the construction of a Marxist history of material culture. The reason was that the creator of this 'exceptionally elegant and harmonious' system had placed the main emphasis on "the most important cultural indicators, the tools" (Nikol'skii 1923: 314). Gorodtsov, in turn, wrote an approving preface to Nikol'skii's book, urging readers to 'discard the old views when their fallacy has been demonstrated, and accept the new ones if they have proven more accurate" (Gorodtsov 1923: 7–20).

Indeed, none of Gorodtsov's writings was really influenced by Marxist theory. Quite independently, even before the Revolution, he had formulated certain universal regularities in the evolution of culture and used archaeological materials for the study of mechanisms whereby cultural phenomena appear and evolve. Elements of the evolutionary approach were combined in his works with diffusionist ideas, although on the whole his approach was closer to diffusionism. Gorodtsov implemented the idea of regional cultural stratigraphy using specific materials. He developed a stringent methodological approach to the study of materials at all levels, from excavations to a complete classification resulting in a sequence of cultures. This was the foundation on which all later Russian and Soviet studies were based, regardless of the tendency they represented (see Lebedev 1992: 353–55).

The last version of the "laws of evolution of archaeological phenomena and their relationships,' published by Gorodtsov in 1923–1927, sounded quite 'progressive' to a 'Marxist' ear. These 'laws' bore a certain resemblance to attempts at a direct application of the laws of dialectics to specific disciplines, a practice that was becoming more and more fashionable. A deeper penetration of Marxism into prehistoric studies was postponed until the new generation of specialists completed their university training.

Understandably, Gorodtsov's search for general regularities in cultural evolution was received favourably by Russian Marxists in the first post-Revolutionary years. At that time, the Marxist classics had not yet become an unquestionable dogma. But the ideological myth of a Soviet science equipped with the best theory in the world had already been created and was forced on the younger generation of archaeologists who, some time later, attacked both their predecessors and the 'old' Marxists.

The Paleoethnological School

The most influential trend in archaeology in the 1920s was the so-called paleoethnological school. Its theoretical positions warrant special attention because of certain erroneous views that remain popular among archaeologists today. The paleoethnological school was the one that was subjected to the most severe repressions. Its methodological platform must be reconstructed piece by piece using a variety of information sources. The leaders were physically destroyed and their ideas were either forgotten or grossly distorted. Those who survived had to summarize their ideas at a time when vulgar Marxism had been proclaimed the only true theory. Only recently, after the legacy had been revisited, has it become clear that some ideas of this school anticipated modern archaeological thought (Vasil'ev 1994: 202–204).

The paleoethnologists' views diverged from Gorodtsov's school with its view of archaeology as an independent science and the belief that certain universal laws might be discovered solely on the basis of archaeological materials. Indeed, typology, as seen by Gorodtsov, was an accurate and universal method allowing one to 'read' sites as one might read hieroglyphic inscriptions, to understand their contents, and to draw historical conclusions thereby. By contrast, the paleoethnologists did not believe that archaeological data alone might provide a basis for adequate reconstruction of the past. Archaeological sites, in their view, should be interpreted with the help of relevant patterns brought to light by ethnography. To rule out the possibility that parallels were due to chance, both categories of data – ethnographic and archaeological – had to be analysed thoroughly using modern methods. Hence the principal requirement put forward by paleoethnology: each specific region must be studied with regard to both archaeology and ethnography. Artifacts cannot be interpreted from a modern common-sense standpoint, nor can they be interpreted with the use of isolated and randomly selected ethnographic parallels. Rather, in the words of Aleksandr Aleksandrovich Miller (1875–1935), the final integration must be preceded by observations concerning 'the very nature and mechanism of changes occurring in material culture' (Miller 1927: 15–19).

Clearly, museum collections that had been obtained by excavations conducted over a long time span with differing methods, could not serve this purpose. Given the nature of their 'initial accumulation', most of them were unable to meet even 'elementary demands made with regard to the sources' (Miller 1927: 15). In other words, as new objectives and problems were being formulated with regard to archaeological materials, a practical problem arose – that of creating and analysing a new database, both ethnographic and archaeological. This new material had to provide a basis for the study of processes such as diffusion, borrowing, ethnic admixture, and migration, with a view to discovering their laws and tracing the ways in which they were reflected in material culture (see Platonova 1997a: 147–51, 1997b, 2004).

The parallel undertaking of complex geographic, anthropological and ethnological (including paleoethnological = archaeological) studies of each region became one of the principal ideas of the 1920s. The State Planning Committee of the U.S.S.R. began holding conferences devoted to the complex study of production forces in the country at that time. The population of the Soviet Union was also considered to be a production force, and it required special investigation. Anthropological and ethnological works were included in programmes devoted to these economic studies (Bunak 1927: 81–82). Archaeological field projects were also considered a component part ('the present and future of each region can be understand only after the past is known' [Rudenko 1928: 78–79]), and they were recognized as necessary and useful for the future cultural and economic construction of the U.S.S.R. The expeditions were well financed and archaeologists began receiving more money for their field research than before the Revolution (e.g. Miller 1926, Rudenko 1927, 1928: 77–78; Materialy o S.I. Rudenko: 7–7 ob.).

Sergej Ivanovich Rudenko (1885–1969) from Leningrad was the first to publish his own program of such complex field investigations. He planned to study the diffusion of culture, adoption of cultural elements, migration of ethnic groups, and their extinction. The laws of cultural development studied empirically had to be extrapolated for the interpretation of archaeological data (Rudenko 1928: 78–79; see also Platonova 1997a: 147–51).

The creation of a standard database was possible provided that field methods were improved and more attention was paid to this aspect of study. The legacy of the 'old' pre-revolutionary paleoethnology (the schools of D.N. Anuchin and F.K. Volkov) proved quite useful here. Indeed, one of its first demands was that of rigor ('complexity') in the use of scientific methods for reconstructing the prehistoric geographical environment, analysis of raw materials, and the study of human and animal skeletal remains. In the 1920s, this tradition had not yet been lost. Indeed, the scope of studies carried out by expeditions that lacked adequate financial support and occasionally suffered from food shortages is impressive (Bonch-Osmolovskii 1932; see also Platonova 1995: 135–37). Most paleoecological reconstructions made at that time were largely complete. Paleoethnologists of the 1920s introduced methods such as measuring the position of each artifact relative to the permanent benchmark, dividing unstratified deposits into horizons, and using the arrangement of finds in the deposits to locate dwellings. The Leningrad-based archaeologist and ethnologist Gleb Anatolievich Bonch-Osmolovskii (1890–1943) noted that the precision of excavations on Russian Palaeolithic expeditions surpassed that observed by him in 1926 in 'the cradle of the Palaeolithic' – France (Tageyeva: Materialy: 41).

Publications of the late 1920s indicate a significant breakthrough in the methodology of analysis and classification. In a paper that antedated F. Bordes' works by 20 years, Bonch-Osmolovskii attempted a statistical analysis of a stone industry for the first time, and stressed the importance of studying flint-knapping techniques (Bonch-Osmolovskii 1928: 147–86; see also 1940: 71–98). Large-scale field studies of the 1920s were not carried out for their own sake, but were a means of creating a standardized database. This was an organized programme aimed at bringing archaeology to a new level. Works by A.A. Miller (e.g. 1926), S.I. Rudenko, B.A. Kuftin (e.g. 1929), B.S. Zhukov, G.A. Bonch-Osmolovskii, and others were a considerable step in that direction.

There are many similarities between Russian ethnology and paleoethnology of the 1920s, on the one hand, and Boas' 'American school of historical ethnology' on the other. These parallels are evidently not accidental. People who inculcated Russian scholars with Boas' ideas were prominent Russian early twentieth-century ethnologists such as V.I. Jochelson, V.G. Bogoraz-Tan and L.J. Shternberg (see Bogoraz-Tan 1928). What they found especially promising was Boas' plan 'to study diffusion within a clearly delimited area in order to understand the dynamics of the very process of diffusion' (Shternberg 1926: 29–31). This plan was implemented in interdisciplinary projects of the 1920s by Rudenko, who regarded "cultural dynamics" traced in extant cultures as a clue to the major problems of archaeology (Rudenko 1928: 78). Proof of Boas' impact on Russian ethnology is the fact that early twentieth-century 'regional monographs' – the first to focus on peoples inhabiting specific areas – resulted from a direct cooperation with Boas and were financially supported by U.S. foundations.

The complex study of national regions and autonomic republics was aimed at giving some practical advice in the field of social and cultural politics. The situation in this field in the 1920s was similar to that of Great Britain in the same period. In those years the British government began to give generous financial support to 'social anthropology'. The same conditions existed in the U.S.S.R., but only briefly. Russian scientists occupied the same position as their British colleagues. They were ready to support the government and assist the formulation of a sensible policy, but in exchange for independence in their own field.

During the NEP period, Russian paleoethnologists began successful studies of large units of archaeological data (Zhukov 1929: 54–77). They introduced the concept of a complete set into the scientific literature, and developed the method of tracing cultural-stratigraphic sequences on the basis of guiding archaeological complexes (e.g. Bonch-Osmolvskii 1928; Petri 1926; Teploukhov 1929; Zhukov 1929). The first efforts at the application of mathematical methods to archaeological materials were made (e.g. Efimenko 1926: 59–84; Bonch-Osmolovskii 1928: 150–51). In 1929 a work applying (for the first time anywhere) the combinatorial statistic method to archaeological materials was completed and sent to press in Leningrad. Nevertheless, owing to the political situation in the country, this article written by M. P. Gryaznov was published only much later – in 1941 (Gryaznov 1941: 237–271; see also Sher 1992: 88–91; Platonova 2002: 269).

The huge part of the data collected by the large expeditions of the 1920s remained unpublished in the 1930s and 1940s. After the abolition of NEP, this trend in archaeology was promptly destroyed.

Why was paleoethnology considered dangerous? Clearly, it was too closely connected with the progressive Russian ethnology of the 1920s in its attempt to study the laws of cultural change empirically with the help of ethnographic data. By the end of the 1920s, this work was in full swing. But in 1929 the political situation and the attitude of the government to research changed dramatically. After that time, the Soviet regime saw no need for the recommendations of scientists.

Mass repressions and deportations began all over the U.S.S.R. (Maksudov 1991: 66–67). Ethnologists had no right to study these new changes in society. All free investigations in this field were abolished. The attempt to study the laws of cultural development empirically without using the Marxist dogma a priori was considered to be one of the deadly sins, and the paleoethnologists had to pay for it. The more precise and rigorous their methods, the more dangerous they seemed.

The destruction of Russian paleoethnology began in April 1929 during the first of the 'methodological discussions' (Soveshchanie etnografov 1929: 111–44), where it was termed 'the bourgeois substitute of social science raised to the second power'. In the period between 1929 and 1933 almost all the leading figures of this trend were arrested. Among them were A.A. Miller, S.I. Rudenko, G.A. Bonch-Osmolovskii, S.A. Teploukhov, B.S. Zhukov, B.A. Kuftin and many others. As a result, the succession of traditions of different generations of archaeologists was broken in the U.S.S.R. As soon as the results of ethnological research became useless and even dangerous to the Soviet regime, the stadialist doctrine assumed control of the field (Platonova 1997a: 147–51; Vserossiiskoe arkheologo-etnografischeskoe soveshchanie 1932: 1–6).

Conclusion

The history of archaeology in the totalitarian age is littered with various myths reflecting contemporary views of the period. The creation of these myths affected all aspects of the discipline at that time. But modern specialists should not accept the inherited stereotypes at face value. Accepting the myths, we are unable either to adequately assess the past of our archaeology or to see its future. Overcoming the stereotypes is one of the historian's tasks. The history of science cannot be understood without knowledge of socio-political conditions under which the researchers concerned were living. This is why a rigorous and accurate analysis of the archival evidence concerning our archaeology in the years 1917 to 1934 is so important.

Notes

1. This paper is based on research funded by Project RSS No.755/1997 (1998–1999).

Archival sources

Materialy o S. I. Rudenko: Materialy (protokoly, dokladnye zapiski) o S. I. Rudenko i ego vliyanii na ekspozitsionnuyu deyatel'nost' muzeya 1931–1932. *Arkhiv Rossiiskogo etnograficheskogo muzeya*, F. 2 Op. 1, No. 362.
Tageeva. Materialy: Tageeva N.V. Gleb Anatol'evich Bonch-Osmolovskii kak arkheolog- doistorik. Materialy. vol. 1, RA IIMK RAN, F. 71, No. 61.

References

Alpatov, V.M. 1991. *Istoriya odnogo mifa: Marr i marrizm.* Moscow: Nauka. Glavnaya redaktsiya vostochnoi literatury.
Bogoraz-Tan, V.G. 1928. *Rasprostranenie kul'tury po zemle. Osnovy etnografiii.* Moscow: Gosizdat.
Bonch-Osmolovskii, G.A. 1928. K voprosu ob evolyutsii drevnepaleoliticheskikh industrii. *Chelovek* 2/4: 147–86.
——. 1932. 'K probleme kompleksnogo izucheniya chetvertichnogo perioda'. *Soobshcheniya GAIMK* 3/4: 44–49.
——. 1940. *Grot Kiik-Koba.* Moscow: Akademiya nauk SSSR.

Bunak, V.V. 1927. *Zadachi izucheniya natsional'nykh meh'shinstv. Byulleten' Orgkomiteta Vtoroi Vsesoyuznoi Konferentsii po Izucheniyu Proizvoditel'nykh Sil SSSR.* February 3–4 (6–7): 81–82.

Bykovskii, S.N. 1931. 'O klassovykh kornyakh staroi arkheologii'. *Soobshcheniya GAIMK* 9/10: 2–5.

Efimenko, P.P. 1926. Ryanazanskijen mogil'niki: opyt kul'turno-stratigraficheskogo analiza mogil'nikov massovogo tipa. *Materialy po etnografii* 3(1): 59–84. Leningrad: Russian Museum.

Gening, V.F. 1982. *Ocherki po istorii sovetskoi arkheologii. U istokov formirovaniya marksistskikh teoreticheskikh osnov sovetskoi arkheologii. 20–e pervaya polovina 30–kh godov.* Kiev: Naukova dumka.

Gorodtsov, V.A. 1923a. *Arkheologiya vol. 1, Kamennyi Period.* Moscow: Gosudarstvennoe Izdatel'stvo.

———. 1923b. Vvedenie: Nikol'skii, V.K. 'Ocherk Pervobytnoi Kul'tury', pp. 7–20. Moscow: izdatel'stvo L.D. Frenkel'.

———. 1927. *Tipologicheskii Metod v Arkheologii.* Ryazan': Obschestvo issledovaniya Riazanskogo kraia. Seriya metodologicheskaya. 6.

Gryaznov, M. P. 1941. 'Drevnyaya bronza Minusinskikh stepei. Bronzovye kel'ty'. *Trudy Otdela Istorii Pervobytnoi Kul'tury Gosudarstvennogo Ermitazha* 1: 237–71.

Klein, L.S. 1977. 'A panorama of theoretical archaeology'. *Current Anthropology* 18: 1–42.

———. 1993. *Fenomen sovetskoi arkheologii.* St. Petersburg: FARN.

Kuftin, B.A. 1929. *Zadachi i metody polevoi etnologii.* Etnografiya 2: 125–28.

Lebedev, G.S. 1992. *Istoriya otechestvennoi arkheologii 1700–1917.* St. Petersburg: St. Petersburgskii Gosudarstvenny universitet.

Maksudov, S. 1991. 'Poteri naseleniya SSSR v gody kollektivizatsii'. *Zven'ya. Istoricheskii al'manakh* 1: 66–96.

Miller, A.A. 1926. Kratkii otchet o rabotakh Severo-Kavkazskoi ekspeditsii GAIMK v 1924 i 1925 godakh. *Soobshcheniya GAIMK* 1: 71–142.

———. 1927. 'Drevnie formy v material'noi kul'ture sovremennogo naseleniya Dagestana'. *Materialy po etnografii* 4(1): 15–76. Leningrad: Russian Museum.

Miller, M.A. 1958. 'Aleksandr Aleksandrovich Miller 1875–1935'. *Vestnik instituta po izucheniyu SSSR.* 3(28): 127–30.

Nikol'skii, V.K. 1923. 'Kompleksnyi metod v doistorii'. *Vestnik Sotsialisticheskoi akademii* 4: 309–344.

Petri, B.E. 1926. 'Sibirskii neolit'. *Izvestiya biologo-geograficheskogo NII pri Irkutskom universitete* 3(1): 39–75.

Platonova, N.I. 1989. 'Rossiiskaya Akademiya istorii material'noi kul'tury. Etapy stanovleniya'. *Sovetskaya Arkheologiya* (4): 5–16.

———. 1995. 'Gleb Anatolievich Bonch-Osmolovskii. Etapy tvorcheskoi biografii,' in Sankt-Peterburg i otechestvennaya arkheologiya. Istoriograficheskie ocherki, pp. 121–44. St. Petersburg: St. Petersburgskii Gosudarstvennyi universitet. S. 121–44.

———. 1997a. 'Ob odnoi popytke utochneniya metodov v pusskoi arkheologii (po materialam zhurnala 'Chelovek' za 1928 god)', in *Pamyatniki stariny. Kontseptsii. Otkrytiya. Versii*, vol. 2, pp. 147–51. St. Petersburg-Pskov: Institut Istorii Material'noi Kul'turi RAN. Pskovskii Gosudarstvenny obiedininny musei-zapovednik. S. 147–51.

———. 1997b. 'Paleoetnologicheskaya shkola v russkoi arkheologii 1920–kh godov', in *Traditsii otechestvennoi paleoetnologii*, pp. 52–55. St. Petersburg: St. Petersburgskii Gosudarstvenny universitet. S. 52–55.

———. 1998. 'Nikolai Yakovlevich Marr – arkheolog i organizator arkheologicheskoi nauki'. *Arkheologicheskie vesti.* 5. St.-Petersburg. S. 371–82.

———. 2002a. 'Panorama otechestvennoi arkheologii na "Velikom perelome" (po stranitsam knigi V. I. Ravdonikasa 'Za marksistskuyu istroriyu material "noi kul'tury")'. *Arkheologicheskie vesti* 9: 261–78.

———. 2003. 'Bezzakonnaya kometa na nautchnom nebosklone'. N.Ya. Marr. *Znamenityje universanty.* 1. St.-Petersburgskii Gosudarstvenny universitet. S. 156–78.

Ravodonikas, V.I. 1930. 'Za marksistskuyu istroriyu material'noi kul'tury'. *Izvestiya GAIMK* 7(3–4).

———. 1932. 'Na novyi etap'. *Soobshcheniya GAIMK* 1–2: 49–60.

Rudenko, S.I. 1927. 'Ocherk byta kazakov basseinov rek Uila i Sagyza', in *Kazaki. Antropologicheskie ocherki.* Leningrad: Akademiya nauk SSSR.

———. 1928. 'Antropologicheskie issledovaniya v ekspeditsiyakh Osobogo komiteta Akademii nauk po issledovaniyu soyuznykh i avtonomnykh respublik'. *Chelovek* 2–4: 77–79.

Sher, YA.A. 1992. 'K voprosu o prioritetakh', in *Voprosy istorii arkheologicheskikh issledovanii Sibiri*, pp. 86–92. Omsk: Omsk University.

Shternberg, L.YA. 1926. 'Sovremennaya etnologiya. Noveishie uspekhi, nauchnye techeniya i metody'. *Etnografiya* 1–2.

Soveshchanie etnografov. 1929. 'Soveshchanie etnografov Leningrada i Moskvy (5–11 aprelya 1929)'. *Etnografiya* 8(2): 111–44.

Teploukhov, S.A. 1929. 'Opyt klassifikatsii drevnikh metallicheskikh kul'tur Minusinskogo kraya'. *Materialy po etnografii* 4(2): 41–62.

Thomas, L.L. 1957. *The Linguistic Theories of N. Ya. Marr.* Berkeley – Los-Angeles: University of California Press.

Tikhonov, I.L. 1993. *Razvitie arkheologii v Sankt-Peterburgskom-Leningradskom universitete (1724–1936).* Dissertation, Candidate of Historical Science, St. Petersburg.

———. 1995. 'Peterburgskaya paleoetnologicheskaya shkola. Etapy formirovaniya', in *Sankt-Peterburg i otechestvennaya arkheologiya. Istoriograficheskie ocherki*, pp. 100–20. St. Petersburg: St. Petersburgskii Gosudarstvenny universitet.

———. 2003. *Archaeology at St. Petersburg University: Historiographical Essays.* St. Petersburg: St. Petersburg University Press.

Trigger, B. 1989. *A History of Archaeological Thought.* Cambridge: Cambridge University Press.

Vasil'ev, S.A. 1994. 'G.A. Bonch-Osmolovskii i sovremennoe paleolitovedenie'. *Rossiiskaya Arkheologiya* (1): 202–7.

Vasil'kov, Ya.V. 2000. 'Tragediya akademika Marra // Khristianskii Vostok. 2 (VIII)'. *Novaya seriya.* St.-Petersburg. S. 390–421.

Vserossiiskoe Arkheologo-Etnograficheskoe Soveshchaniya Gaimk 1932. *Soobscheniya GAIMK* 7–8: 1–6.

Zhukov, B.S. 1929. 'Teoriya khronologicheskikh i territorial'nykh modifikatsii nekotorykh neoliticheskikh kul'tur Vostochnoi Evropy po dannym izucheniya keramiki'. *Etnografiya* 1: 56–57.

Znamenskii O.N. 1988. *Intelligentsiya nakanune Velikogo Oktyabrya.* Leningrad: Nauka. Leningradskoe otdelenie.

Chapter 5
Prehistoric Archaeology in the 'Parliament of Science', 1845–1900

Tim Murray

Abstract

My account of the development of prehistoric archaeology in nineteenth-century England stresses that conflicts between anthropology and ethnology (primarily over which discipline could claim that its database and questions were the more general and fundamental), provided the critical context for the development of archaeological questions, archaeological interpretations and archaeological explanations. In essence this conflict, which raged for much of the nineteenth century, was over which discipline (ethnology or anthropology) could claim to properly define human nature, and the terms under which it was to be understood (Kuklick 1991; Rapport 2002; Stepan 1982; Urry 1993). Significantly, the systems developed by Lubbock, Tylor and Morgan, which were to become the theoretical foundations for evolutionary archaeology and anthropology, couched the interpretation of the deep prehistoric past within classic ethnological issues of unity and diversity, mind and body, nature and culture. Archaeological data were thought to illustrate the material consequences of the development of human rationality, the genesis of human physical and cultural variability due to adaptation to external environmental conditions, and the connectedness of peoples.

In this chapter, which is part of a much larger work on the history of prehistoric archaeology in England, I will very briefly exemplify the complex interplay between ethnology and the emergent disciplines of anthropology and prehistoric archaeology, through the medium of The British Association for the Advancement of Science. Although my primary purpose is to understand the history of prehistoric archaeology in England, we will see that it is impossible to abstract debates in England from those happening elsewhere in Britain, particularly in Scotland. Indeed, while the two rival societies where much of these debates unfolded – the Anthropological Society and the Ethnological Society – were London-based, the fact that they both chose the British Association as one of their prime battlegrounds demonstrates that prehistoric archaeology in England was not only of national significance, but also considerably open to wider influences.

In any case, there are three reasons why the British Association provides the ideal forum through which to pursue this analysis. To begin with, the conflicts between ethnology and anthropology were played out on the national stage within the British Association, as well as in direct conflict primarily occurring in London (see Burrow 1966; Hodgen 1973; Stocking 1968, 1987; Weber 1974). As well, the British Association became a regular contributor to the costs of archaeological excavations (notably at Kent's Cavern), it acted as a clearing-house for archaeological information and promoted the popularity of interdisciplinary excavation teams, and aided the development of anthropological methodology through its series of questionnaires – *Notes and Queries* (see Fowler 1975; Stocking 1983; Urry 1972). Lastly, as the 'Parliament of British Science', the British Association provides a focal point for a continued discussion of the ramifications of the differences between methodological rhetoric and performance in prehistoric archaeology. Historians of science (see e.g. MacLeod 1981a, 1981b; Morrell and Thackray 1981; Orange 1972, 1981; Yeo 1979, 1981) have indicated that inductivism formed the central plank of the scientific method accepted by its proponents, and that the scientific method was absolutely crucial to the aims and objectives of the Association (see also McGee 1897; von Gizycki 1979).

I will take the response of the British Association to the debates raging between anthropology and ethnology, and about the interpretation of archaeological data, as critical support for another argument, made by me in connection with the passage of the first Ancient Monuments Protection Act in England (Murray 1989), that the discrepancies between methodological rhetoric and practical performance in English prehistoric archaeology were ignored both by the disputants and by the general public. My previous arguments have stressed the fact that the meanings and values of anthropological, ethnological and archaeological interpretation and explanation justified, and were in turn justified by, common-sense understandings abroad in England during the nineteenth century.

The uncertain positions of both anthropology and ethnology on the cognitive map of nineteenth century British science is demonstrated by their slow acceptance into the British Association, and for several decades their virtually constant movement through its committees and sections, as the managers of the Association struggled to deal with unceasing conflict between the adherents of either discipline. There were three crucial reasons for this state of affairs: First, as Morrell and Thackray have observed: 'the career of ethnology shows another science being excluded from the British Association so long as it appeared to be a political, social and religious tinderbox, and then being reluctantly incorporated when it had been stripped of dangerous features' (1981: 283–84). Second, the Association had little experience with generalizing sciences that spanned many pre-existing disciplines. Third, the heated debates between ethnology and anthropology as to which science was the most general necessitated numerous attempts at finding a formula of relationship that would suit the parties.

Briefly, there were four phases of movement for the sciences of man within the committee and sectional structure of the Association during the nineteenth century, and I outline them here.

Phase 1, spanning the period from the foundation of the Association (in 1831) to 1846, when James Cowles Prichard found formal recognition for the science of ethnology as a sub-section of section D – Zoology, Botany, Physiology and Anatomy. Prior to this, papers of relevance to ethnology had appeared in other sections such as geology and in section D itself. Indeed, although there was only one ethnological paper published in the first and second reports of 1831 and 1832 (bound as one volume), by 1838 when Prichard's highly influential 'On the Extinction of the Human Races' had stung the Association into contributing £15 towards the cost of producing an ethnological questionnaire (Fowler 1975; Urry 1972), the number of ethnological papers submitted to the Annual Meetings of the Association began to skyrocket. Consequently the failures of this arrangement had become embarrassing as a number of ludicrous juxtapositions between zoological and ethnological papers occurred, reinforcing the claim that ethnology was best located somewhere else. Prichard (1847: 230) outlined the history of ethnology's lack of independence within the BAAS structure and discussed the pitfalls of its formal association with physiology and anatomy, even though the majority of early papers had been read to the zoology section:

It may be remembered that in the series of reports on the progress of science in its different departments, comprised in the first volume of the *Transactions of the British Association*, there was one memoir on the contributions afforded by physical and philological researches to ethnology and the history of the human species. The admission of that paper by the editors of the *Transactions*, gave those persons who had made ethnology their favorite pursuit some ground for hope, that this would for the future be among the recognized branches of knowledge, for the cultivation of which provision would be made at the meetings of the Association. It is almost needless to say that this hope was disappointed, and that no arrangements having been adopted for the discussion of ethnological questions, some very elaborate memoirs having been sent to the meetings of the Association, by distinguished scholars, were returned without having obtained a hearing. It was not until after several meetings having taken place, that it was determined to afford an opportunity for the pursuit of ethnological inquiries by making for that purpose a subdivision of one of the sections devoted to natural history or physiology.

Though he was President of the new sub-section, Prichard was not entirely happy with the arrangement, recognizing that the new science was of a different order to the sciences already admitted to the Association and that the ruling parties of the Association would therefore have trouble classifying it. The struggle to establish the particularly broad nature of such a generalizing science could only be won by indicating that whatever decisions were made as to its location within the sectional structure of the Association, the sum of ethnology was greater than its parts, even though important elements of its database might be scientifically dubious by the standards of the times. Referring to the new arrangement Prichard (1847: 230–31) remarked:

> There seemed to be an obvious propriety of systematic arrangement in contemplating the natural history of man as forming but a part of the study of living nature in general ... If, therefore, the real scope of ethnology was merely an inquiry into the physical constitution of human tribes in comparison with each other, as it appears to have been supposed, there would be an obvious propriety in making this study a subdivision of physiology or of the science of human nature. But those who have devoted their attention to that pursuit are well-aware that the objects of ethnology are very distinct from the study of organic nature or physiology. Ethnology is, in fact, more nearly allied to history than to natural science.

Given Prichard's conceptualization of the composition of ethnology, it is hardly surprising that he could defend ethnology as a science on two grounds. First, its clear links with established inductive sciences such as geology and anatomy. Second, the use of the scientific method in ethnography, philology, and archaeology. Despite the power of Prichard's advocacy, the controllers of the British Association – ever careful to avoid public controversy that would lead to a loss of public confidence in the objectivity of science, were equally impressed by the contentious nature of ethnological researches (Yeo 1981). True, the geologists flouted the Bible, but the facts were on their side, however uncomfortable they might be. Further, who knew where ethnology would lead? In time the new generalizing science of anthropology would become the locus of conflict, and the Councillors and committees of the Association would offer much stiffer opposition to a science that seemed to be 'about everything and about nothing'.

Phase 2, spans the period between 1847 and the admission of Ethnology into the newly created Section D (Geography and Ethnology) in 1852. During this time aspects of what was later to become prehistoric archaeology were more frequently found in the geological section than in Section D. The tradition of viewing human antiquity as being primarily a geological problem was to continue through to the end of the century, although after 1865 relevant papers were also presented to anthropology and ethnology.

Phase 3 (1852–1869) is in many respects the crucial period for ethnology and anthropology in the British Association. It was during this time that ethnology obtained its divorce from section D, was incorporated with geography (itself divorced from geology and physical geography) in section E, and was later returned as a department of section D (newly renovated as Biology).

Phase 4 (1870–1884) refers to the development of the constituent disciplines of anthropology, and its final divorce from section D by being established as a separate section (H) of the Association. The formal links between anthropology and biology were never to be restored.

The Peregrinations of the 'Sciences of Man'

The hard-fought debates between ethnology and anthropology that took place within the rival societies of the Anthropological Society of London (ASL) and the Ethnological Society of London (ESL) have been extensively discussed (Burrow 1966; Harris 1968; Stocking 1971, 1987; Urry 1972; Weber 1974). Stocking and others have stressed that since the late eighteenth century discussions in England about the natural history of human beings (especially those focusing on race, language, culture and physical form) have been very closely linked to Continental perspectives. The debates between ethnology and anthropology in London were no exception being very strongly influenced by researchers such as Paul Broca and Carl Vogt. Indeed, one of James Hunt's great innovations was to organize translations of some of the more significant Continental texts (see e.g. Pouchet 1864; Vogt 1864; Waitz 1863). However they were not the only external influences, with both sides paying particular attention to the work of American race theorists such as Nott and Gliddon (1854), that had gained special relevance as a result of the American Civil War.

On the surface the difference between the two disciplines – ethnography and anthropology – can be readily established. The concerns of ethnology were largely confined to documenting and understanding the causes of cultural, social, linguistic and physical differences between human beings, and to charting the relationships between different human groups. Anthropology, on the other hand, was conceived of as being a broader discipline incorporating the concerns of ethnology, but doing so within a framework that included all aspects of humanity past and present. Yet there was more to the conflict than the simple issue of which discipline effectively incorporated the other. Historians of anthropology have stressed that the acrimonious debates were in fact based as much on contemporary political and social issues as on the litigious personalities of the disputants. On this basis we already have grounds for creating a fairly clear division between the supporters of ethnology (such as Lyell, Lubbock, Huxley), and the supporters of anthropology (Hunt, Beddoe, Broca, Quatrefages, Pouchet and Vogt), on the basis of their religious affiliation and their stance on such matters as equality between the sexes, slavery, imperialism and above all, whether they were monogenists or polygenists – that is, whether they believed in a single or a multiple origin for humanity. Inevitably, there were people who managed to belong to both societies and to hold what appear to be conflicting opinions.

In the hail of invective that characterized relationships between the two London Societies, the disputants regularly accused each other of being unscientific, because they sought motivation from subjective and implicit political or religious agendas. One major area of conflict was the rights and wrongs of the Darwinian hypothesis, another was the admission of anthropology to the British Association. Like it or not, the British Association had to find a way of dealing with anthropology, and as its most prominent members were implacably opposed to the implicit (sometimes explicit) polygenism of the anthropologicals, the battle was to be to the death. In the process, the name anthropology survived, but much of its programme as defined by Paul Broca (and his disciple the ASL president James Hunt) did not.

My analysis is based on a close reading of all British Association records, particularly the Proceedings and Transactions of the Annual Meetings, and of course the records and publications of the two London societies. Together they comprise a very large storehouse of examples of scientific politics, exhibiting all the nuances of political chicanery and bad behaviour that occurred over 40 years of conflict. Excerpts from a few of the more celebrated confrontations exemplify the nature and tone of the confrontation.

The 1863 meetings of the BAAS mark the opening round of a conflict which was to prove both acrimonious and publicly damaging. It is no coincidence that these were the first meetings attended by James Hunt in his guise as an activist for anthropology (having previously been an active member of the Ethnological Society of London). He and the other 'anthropologicals' demanded a hearing, but the problem for the British Association stemmed, in part, from the breadth of anthropological researches. Papers considered to be of vital importance to anthropologists, especially those dealing with physical anthropology and the evidences of high human antiquity, were being rejected by section E as being more appropriate for zoology or geology. The other significant problem was that one generalizing science of man already held the field, and its supporters were extremely reluctant to relinquish the spoils of their hard-won battle with the central committee of the Association that had occurred some years before.

The opening shot was fired in the *Anthropological Review* (a publication of the ASL), and from the start the language used had that peculiarly intemperate flavour so beloved by James Hunt (its founder and President). Hunt's rhetorical tactics were clear enough; an attempted acquisition of ethnology by anthropology, the use of non-British authorities to support his argument, and the reported resistance of the ethnologists to plain reason:

> Anthropology in name is not yet recognized in theory; but it is to some extent in practice. It is not a little remarkable, that some of those who are most opposed to the recognition of Anthropology as a recognized branch of science into the Association, are the very men who, in practice at least, admit the claims of Anthropology, and who read papers which are entirely anthropological. For instance, Mr Crawfurd, one of England's most consistent and venerable ethnographers, lost no opportunity of protesting against the introduction of anthropological papers into Section E; and yet, with that inconsistency for which he is occasionally distinguished, was one of the very first men in the section to read a paper on a purely anthropological subject. Mr Crawfurd's paper, entitled 'Notes on Sir Charles Lyell's Antiquity of Man', was from the beginning to the end a paper on Man or Mankind, as distinguished from Ethnology, or the science of the Races of Man. No writer of any authority, either English, American, or continental, will now call the question of the antiquity of man an ethnological question. It is pure and simple an anthropological question. Other papers bearing on the same subject, we understand, were rejected by the Committee of Section E, because they were anthropological! and could not be read because Anthropology was not recognized by Section E, which was entirely confined to Geography and Ethnology (Anon., probably James Hunt, 1863: 379).

This article established a pattern of reporting which was to continue through to the time when the Anthropological and Ethnological Societies amalgamated. Its salient features, apart from combative tone, were the classification of all papers (regardless of who presented them, or of their allegiances) into anthropological or ethnological (prehistoric archaeology of all kinds being firmly anthropological), an enumeration of the anthropological and ethnological papers (usually a strict correspondence between the paper and the speaker's institutional loyalties), and the indication of which papers were entirely new, or had been presented elsewhere. These were all aspects of the tactics of the inter-society disputes that formed the backdrop to the events at the British Association, the objects being to exclude certain data sets from inclusion into ethnology (prehistoric archaeological data in particular), to demonstrate which society was the most active, and which construal of the proper study of man the most fruitful for research. In Hunt's view there could never be any doubt that the points would go to anthropology, if only because ethnology was manifestly a branch of anthropology. Again, the rhetoric is clear. Anthropology is the coming wave of human science, ordained by the nature of the subject matter itself. For example:

> We feel sure, therefore, that it only requires a little more time to remove any jealousy that may exist in the breasts of some ethnologists, respecting the success attending the labours of anthropologists. Let them learn not to quarrel with the decrees of Nature. Astronomy was not arrested in her progress by the clamours of the astrologers; nor will anthropologists cease to develop the extent, magnitude, and importance of their science by the invectives of ethnologists. Rather let them develop their own subject, and look with rejoicing on the beneficent wave which will ere long raise them from their present state of isolation, and raise them to their place as one of the branches of light which will illuminate the great system of organic light (Anon., probably James Hunt, 1863: 381).

The battle lines were drawn, and a conflict which had hitherto been confined to London, was now poised to ride into the provinces on the back of the British Association. By the end of the 1870s one would probably have had to be living in the outer Hebrides to have avoided hearing the case of both or either of the parties. Significantly, the battle was to be engaged within the sectional structure of the Association. The editor of the *Anthropological Review* intoned:

> Everything bids fair to make the next meeting in Bath successful. We trust that during the time that will elapse before the meeting, Anthropologists will bestir themselves to bring all their forces together, and thus help to secure the formal recognition of Anthropological science by the Association. We understand that notice has been given by Dr Hunt, that Section E shall for the future be devoted to 'Geography, Ethnology, and Anthropology'. A general rumour prevailed that there was to be a sub-section especially devoted to Anthropology. We think, however, that an increase in the number of sections is objectionable, and we see no necessity for such a division. As an independent journal, devoted to Anthropological science, we shall feel it our duty to advocate a union of Anthropology with the present Geographical and Ethnological section (Anon., probably James Hunt, 1863: 464).

Therefore anthropology was not to be made marginal by its inclusion in a special 'quarantine' section, but on whose terms was it to be incorporated into Section E? There could only be one satisfactory solution, the eclipse of ethnology, and Hunt gathered his forces to achieve this. Things did not go as planned.

The discomfiture of anthropology at Bath gives some idea of the forces ranged against the 'lunatic polygenists and free-thinkers' from the Anthropological Society. Perhaps this explains why Sir Roderick Murchison, who seemed to have a virtual mortgage on the Presidency of Section E during this period could constantly serve up a listing of annual 'triumphs of exploration' masquerading as a presidential address, rather than pursuing a defense of the idea of ethnology against the attacks of the anthropologists (see for example Murchison 1864).

The report of the state of anthropology at the British Association published in the *Anthropological Review* of 1864 is a tale of lost battles and fighting spirit. The anthropologists had begun with high hopes and a sense of wounded dignity. In 1863 the Section E committee had allowed anthropological papers to be read only on sufferance, and, in response, Carter Blake moved a motion before the General Committee of the Association should recognize anthropology and allow the presentation of papers written under its aegis. Blake also offered the threat that if such recognition was not granted then the papers submitted to the Association in the name of the Anthropological Society of London would be withdrawn from the meeting. Blake spoke as the representative of the Anthropological Society, and claimed a fair hearing on the basis of the Society's strength and popularity:

> I may state, sir, that this Society now numbers more than 430 members, exclusive of more than 100 honorary and corresponding members. I feel convinced that the good sense of the Committee will not allow them to refuse the claims of such a Society, which is founded, like the British Association itself, for the advancement of truth. I have been informed that there are some here, who, for reasons best known to themselves, will oppose such a resolution; but I beg the Committee to pause before they commit themselves by a step which would thus estrange a large scientific society from this Association (Blake 1864: 294).

Murchison rose to give the first line of defence against the claims of the anthropologists. Section E was already overburdened with work, and nobody really had much of an idea of, or a sympathy for, the anthropological programme:

> He told them [Dr Hunt and Mr Carter Blake] then that their science was one-half – or to a great extent – ethnological, and to a great extent anatomical. Anthropology, in the sense in which is was treated by those gentlemen, or one-half of it, was a science of which he was profoundly ignorant. Almost all the gentlemen associated with him – his vice-presidents, his secretary, and his friends right and left of him, thirty or forty in all – were unacquainted with anthropology, with the exception of Mr Blake (Blake 1864: 295).

The simple solution to the problem was to place the 'ethnological' papers with Section E, and the other works with physiology or geology. This view was generally supported, especially by Crawfurd a former President of Section E and of the Ethnological Society of London. Sir John Lubbock, this time in his role as President of the ESL, also rejected Blake's motion, making plain his view that ethnology and anthropology were one and the same: 'he looked upon anthropology as an ugly name for ethnology' (Lubbock quoted in Blake 1864: 296). Accordingly, if the anthropologists didn't like it in Section E, then the best solution was to transfer them to Section D. Needless to say, Blake's motion was lost by a large majority, and the anthropological papers were withdrawn. The *Anthropological Review* of 1864 counted the cost:

> The scientific congress of England has thus passed away, and with it the hopes which many confidently entertained of the recognition of anthropological science at the British Association in the year of 1864 (Blake 1864: 297).

Carter Blake advanced a number of reasons for the failure of the motion, among the most significant being the fact that the ASL had no official representation on the Committee for Section E. However, Hunt and his associates were still capable of a point-by-point refutation of the arguments which had been used against them at Bath. On Murchison's characterization of anthropology as being one-half ethnological and to a great extent anatomical (Blake 1864: 297):

> ... [he] fails to see that although anthropology is certainly ethnological to a great extent, yet it is a science which *comprises* ethnology, ethnography, archaeology, philology, but only trespasses on anatomical grounds so far as anthropotomy (the science of *human* anatomy alone) is legitimately included in it [original emphasis].

However, it was Lubbock's assertion that anthropology was an ugly name for ethnology that really stirred an outraged response:

> That a serious scientific assembly, like the General Committee of the British Association, should consider which two names were the 'prettier' can hardly be imagined. We doubt if anthropology is really an ugly word; we think it glides as musically over the tongue as 'kjokkenmodding,' and that, although neither word may be very euphonious, each is an exponent of a scientific fact, and must therefore be necessarily maintained in the British language (Lubbock quoted in Blake 1864: 298).

It was to go on like this for years, rising to fever pitch at the Annual Meeting for 1868 in Dundee. In the previous Annual Meeting at Nottingham in 1867 the Anthropologists felt that they had begun to dominate their rival Ethnologists in the Association. Time was allowed for the reading of Anthropological papers (whereas previously this had been very difficult to organize), and many of the papers were read in the same section (therefore to the same audience) and not spread around through Geology, Anatomy, Ethnology and Geography, as had previously been the case. These tactics, of restricting 'air space' and of diluting the impact of anthropology by rejecting any notion of disciplinary integrity, had been very successfully used by the managers of the Association before Nottingham.

There were early indications of trouble, always anathema to the Council of the British Association, and the *Anthropological Review* was not slow to heed the signs:

> BRITISH ASSOCIATION, DUNDEE – The *Dundee Advertiser* of August 24th, says: 'A considerable degree of alarm has been, and is still, prevalent about the Anthropological section of the British Association, and what may be said and done there ... Some jokes, too, good, or bad, have been cracked on the subject. Some have called the British the 'Brutish' Association. One lady is said to have remarked, that she could not believe that apes had been turned into men; but she would not have wondered though some men, for their sins should be turned into apes! Under all this outside cachinnation there runs on, however, a deeper current of vague fear, which we must, if possible, try to modify, if not to check' (Anthropological Review 1867: 376).

It did not work. At Dundee things returned to pre-Nottingham days. Anthropology completely disappeared from Section D, but Ethnology remained. The ethnologists paid a high price for their association with the Geographers. Sir Samuel Baker, Nile explorer, gave an extraordinarily tedious resume of the latest adventures in heathen lands, and prematurely consigned Livingstone to his grave into the bargain! Throughout what must have seemed an interminable ramble the delegates were warned to keep watch on Russian movements near the Afghan border (!), and to uphold the Christian and Anglo-Saxon values in their dealings with the natives. Given the fuss and furore that was breaking over the conference due to the exclusion of anthropology, even the ethnologists must have thought Baker's address to be at least peripheral.

What had gone wrong? James Hunt and Carter Blake were, for once, at a loss for words. C.W. Devis from the Anthropological Society of Manchester wrote the report for the *Journal of the Anthropological Society of London*.

> It had been apprehended that the British Association would not on this occasion renew
> the welcome which it had extended to anthropology as a specific science at its previous
> meeting. The expectation was unfortunately realized ... (1868: iv).

It was clear to the anthropologists that once again their science had been the subject of
humiliation. At Dundee Hunt declined to accept an arrangement that separated the papers
submitted as Anthropological from those marked as Ethnological and he accordingly withdrew the
papers brought up under the auspices of the Anthropological Society. Victory for the forces of
opposition seemed complete with the Anthropologicals being cast as being uncompromising.
Indeed the Local Committee for the reception of the anthropologists reacted with indignation, but
Hunt quickly showed his political mettle by turning the resulting public and professional
disapproval of anthropology back onto the British Association.

> At a general meeting of anthropologists, subsequently held, there was entire unanimity in
> the opinion that they would be wanting, both to themselves and to the common interests
> of science, if they allowed the non-appointment of their department to pass without an
> earnest protest (Devis 1868: iv).

However, the protests were not directed against the Association itself, but at those opponents of
anthropology who had misused their political power within it. Hunt was also alive to the need for
a public reading of anthropological papers, and, as a result, an alternative Anthropological
Congress was held while the Annual Meeting went on. There was a public outcry that
anthropology had been unfairly treated and the British Association, ever on guard against adverse
publicity which could lead to questioning about the objectivity of science, renounced the tactics
of previous years and promised that justice would be done. That signal victory achieved, Hunt
wound up the proceedings of the Congress.

Part of the settlement reached between the anthropologists and the Association was that
anthropological papers would be read in Section E (where the Ethnologists were) for the remainder
of the Dundee meeting. However, only one paper was ever read under these conditions. This was
the result of an oversubscription to Section E, and this turn of events added further weight to the
demand that Geography and Ethnology be separated at future meetings:

> Anthropology must either be conducted apart from Geography or ignored altogether;
> which of these issues is to become final now rests with its students; if they be true to
> themselves, they will in future be received into the Association in a respectful, if not a
> cordial, spirit; other wise, a renewed display of the inveterate hostility banded against
> them will be encouraged, almost justified (Devis 1868: vi–vii).

A further demonstration of the damaging classification of anthropological papers within the
Association was provided by the fact that Pengelly's report on excavations in Kent's Cavern
(undertaken for the Association) was read to the geological section, and Lubbock's paper on 'The
Early Condition of Man' was read to Section E.

But what caused the British Association to court the charge of unfairly restricting scientific
discussion? It appeared to the anthropologists at Dundee that the Association had attempted to
please what it took to be Scots' public opinion by excluding anthropology from the meeting. It
sadly backfired. The Scots rejected outright that they were too benighted to cope with the
revelations of the new science, and the Dundee press had such a field day whipping up the
wounded feelings of the inhabitants that the Council of the Anthropological Society later passed

a vote of thanks to the press and people of Dundee (*Journal of the Anthropological Society* 1868: lxxv). Thus what looked to be a major defeat for anthropology resulted in a signal victory. The difficulties of anthropology at the British Association had been well and truly publicly aired, and for all the distaste held by the Scots for anthropology, it was widely perceived by them that the Association had acted against the interests of science generally, rather than for its advancement. The alarms and disturbances of Dundee marked a turning point for anthropology.

In the following year at Norwich, all was comparatively quiet, and prehistoric archaeology provided ample reason: at the late meeting of the British Association at Norwich, the science of Anthropology was almost wholly unrepresented. This was due not to the falling off in the general interest of the science, but to two causes that presented themselves, one depending upon the other. The chief of these was the annual meeting of the Congress of Archaic Anthropology, the name of which was there changed to that of Prehistoric Archaeology. Mainly because this meeting occurred at the same time and place as that of the British Association, no Anthropological department was nominated in Section D, and papers that would have been brought before the latter, were read before the Congress (Gibb 1869: xxiv). The change of name from Archaic Anthropology to Prehistoric Archaeology, in the light of the preceding contests between ethnology and anthropology over its control, and given that the Presidency of the Congress was held by Lubbock, raises the possibility of further political chicanery – this time in an international scientific body. Strangely, the Anthropological Society made no protest, perhaps believing that whatever it was called, it was still a constituent discipline of anthropology. Yet the name change appeared to signify the development of specialism inimical to the overall programme of anthropology. Be that as it may, prehistoric archaeology it was, and prehistoric archaeology it was to remain.

By 1870 much had changed, possibly due in part to the death of that most prominent of the Anthropologicals, James Hunt. The events at the Liverpool meeting in 1870 confirmed the feelings of mutual goodwill between anthropologist and ethnologist. From this point of accommodation, the object of agitation since 1863, the triumph of anthropology was shortly to become complete. In 1871, at the Edinburgh meeting of the British Association, anthropology at last stood alone as a department within Section D. Ethnology had been absorbed. Professor Turner's Presidential Address of 1871 made it clear that in those years since Prichard had gained entry for ethnology into the British Association, the real reason for trouble and strife had been the fact that ethnology had been excised from Section D. It was a strange, yet comfortable reading of events:

> Again, if a separate Ethnological Department or subsection were formed, as has been suggested, or even if ethnological papers were read, as was for so many years the case in the Geographical Section, not only would all these communications on the characteristics of the different varieties of man, or of their distribution over the globe, but even papers on comparative philology, and on questions appertaining to the early history of man, and to his primitive culture, in all probability be subtracted from our proceeding. Without doubt, all ethnic questions form an integral part of anthropological study, for ethnology is one of those subjects which form the groundwork for our science; and it is an axiom that the whole is greater than and includes the part, all these questions naturally fall to be discussed in this department, and should not be divorced from their natural allies. The decision of the General Committee that the ethnological papers should be transmitted to this department was but to restore them to the place they originally occupied in the proceedings of the Association, for in its early years ethnology was a subdivision of Section D. The brief history of this department teaches us that its struggle for existence has been a severe one (Turner 1871: 147).

Anthropology only stayed in its temporary haven until 1884, when the final phase of the programme instituted by Hunt over thirty years before was complete. Even though the Anthropological Institute of Great Britain and Ireland continued the publication of reports of the British Association meetings, they became very much an extension of new sources of strife that arose within the Institute itself. These sources, although to a limited degree cast in the terms of the great contests of the past, found their cause in the relations between the constituent disciplines of anthropology itself. Such conflicts, in the light of the clash between anthropology and ethnology for control over archaeology, physical anthropology and philology, were inevitable.

Even in the first number of the Institute's Journal, a clear division can be found between General Anthropology (read physical anthropology), Ethnology, and Prehistoric Archaeology. The specialisms of anthropology continued to lie together under a general integrative rubric, but this remained a potential, a possibility, rather than an actuality. As the specialisms developed from the 1870s onwards, the departments of anthropology, particularly ethnology, found less and less in common. A succession of presidents of the Anthropological Department at the British Association, indeed, of the Institute itself, found it increasingly difficult to emulate Lubbock's achievement of spanning all the fields of anthropology. In recognition of this state of affairs, succeeding presidents delivered annual addresses from their pet perspective, admitting their limited range but uttering the increasingly ritual integrative incantations. The prospects of a general anthropology (as envisaged by Hunt and by Broca) receded further from view.

It is indeed an irony that Lubbock, the most bitter opponent of anthropology, was, with the possible exception of Tylor, the quintessential British anthropologist (in the most general sense of the term) of the nineteenth century. Yet, much in anthropology had been beyond even him. Hunt, ever true to the breadth of the Continental construal of anthropology – especially its wariness of Darwinian theory, and the loudly-proclaimed intention to subject all aspects of society, mental, moral and political, to questioning – would no doubt have chosen such as Broca, Quatrefages, Topinard or Waitz as his candidate.

Conclusions

Readers of this brief history of invective and internecine strife could be forgiven for thinking that the anthropology of James Hunt and Paul Broca had triumphed over the restricted reading given of it by the ethnologists in Britain. It did, but only partially. As the promoters of the new science were fond of reminding just about anyone who would listen, the fate of anthropology in Britain was very different from that experienced by the new, vital, discipline on the Continent. What Hunt failed to mention was, that in comparison to the political restriction in France, anthropology in Britain was largely free from direct government interference.

But interference there was, and in the British tradition, the checks and balances were provided by the Parliament of Science rather than by the Mother of Parliaments. Clearly, the Councillors of the British Association had been seriously alarmed by the free-thinking attitudes of the anthropologists, their willingness to discuss issues of morals and politics that most members of the physical, earth and life sciences studiously (but not always successfully) managed to avoid. True, there were contentious figures such as Huxley and Spencer, but the ideal for science was a kind of timeless objectivity separated from the subjective concerns of the everyday. Anthropology offended against these principles (so, incidentally did ethnology), it was therefore to be reined-in before it called into question the value and pristine methodology of science.

The Anthropology that survived to full-blown recognition in 1871 had, possibly because of the death of Hunt, gradually been stripped of its power to disturb the British political balance. Certain of its hobby horses such as its anti-Irish leanings, and its advocacy of the manifest political destiny of the Anglo-Saxon, were widely held outside the discipline itself. They occasioned no general revulsion. On the other hand, its barely concealed polygenist tendencies, with their implied support for a non-relativist interpretation of physical and moral differences between the Anglo-Saxon and the 'ethnographic other', found little support.

Although from the 1880s perceptions of human diversity made a forceful return to the ranks of anthropology, this diversity was clearly to be located in ethnic and cultural, rather than purely physical differences. Explanation for diversity and similarity was increasingly to be sought in cultural historical factors, rather than by appealing to the doctrine of independent inventions and the psychic unity of mankind. Clearly the universalist programme which was supposedly at the heart of two competing forms of anthropology – that of Tylor, Lubbock and Morgan, and that of de Quatrefages, Waitz and Topinard – was replaced by historicism. Real historical forces acting on real (different) groups of people, past and present, could explain the peculiar differences between human beings far more convincingly than generalized uniformitarian forces. The revolutionary science of anthropology became the tool of imperialists and nationalists, the universal programme was at an end.

In discussing these events at the British Association, one of my goals has been to establish the manner in which anthropology fought ethnology to enroll archaeology into its programme during the nineteenth century. Briefly put, there were both liberating and constraining effects of this enrolment. On the one hand archaeological data expanded in significance, and this was to further increase during the period to the end of the Second World War. On the other, the terms of archaeology's contribution to anthropology were frozen by contemporary views of what it was meaningful and valuable to know about human beings. Archaeology was very slow to free itself from the agenda given it by both Hunt and Lubbock (as well as by the Continental anthropologists). Alone among the constituent disciplines of anthropology so defined, archaeology went on holding to an empty shell – mistaking what are effectively institutional structures and integrative rubrics for theoretical substance.

References

Anonymous (probably James Hunt). 1863. 'Anthropology at the British Association', *Anthropological Review* 1: 379–464.

Anthropological Review. 1867. 'Anthropological News'. *Anthropological Review* 5: 369–76.

Anthropological Society of London. 1868. 'Annual Meeting of January 14, 1868', *Journal of the Anthropological Society of London* VI: lxv–lxxvi.

Blake, C. 1864, 'Anthropology at the British Association', *Anthropological Review* 2: 294–335.

Burrow, J.W. 1966. *Evolution and Society*. Cambridge, Cambridge University Press.

Devis, C.W. 1868. 'Report on Anthropology at the British Association', 1868. *Journal of the Anthropological Society of London* VI: iii–xiii.

Fowler, D. 1975. 'Notes on Inquiries in Anthropology: A Bibliographic Essay', in T.H.H. Thoresen (ed.), *Toward a Science of Man: Essays in the History of Anthropology*. The Hague: Mouton, pp. 15–32.

Gibb, D. 1869. 'Report on the State of Anthropology at the Meeting of the BAAS at Norwich', *Journal of the Anthropological Society of London* VII: xxiii–xxvi.

Harris, M. 1968. *The Rise of Anthropological Theory*. New York: Crowell.

Hodgen, M. 1973. 'Anthropology in the BAAS, its inception', *Scientia: Rivista di Scienza* cviii: 803–11.

Kuklick, H. 1991. *The Savage Within: The Social History of British Anthropology, 1885–1945*. Cambridge, Cambridge University Press.

MacLeod, R. 1981a. 'Retrospect: The British Association and Its Historians', in R. MacLeod and P. Collins (eds), *The Parliament of Science*. Northwood, Middx.: Science Reviews Limited. pp. 1–16.

———. 1981b. 'Introduction: On the Advancement of Science', in R. MacLeod and P. Collins (eds), *The Parliament of Science*. Northwood, Middx.: Science Reviews Limited. pp. 17–42.

———. and P. Collins (eds) 1981. *The Parliament of Science*. Northwood, Middx.: Science Reviews Limited.

McGee, A. 1897. 'Anthropology at the American Association for the Advancement of Science', *Science* 6: 508–513.

Morrell, J. and A. Thackray. 1981. *Gentlemen of Science: Early Years of the British Association for the Advancement of Science*. Oxford: Clarendon Press.

Murchison, R. 1864. 'Section E Address', *British Association Reports* 33: 130–35.

Murray, T. 1989 'The History, Philosophy and Sociology of Archaeology: The Case of the Ancient Monuments Protection Act (1882)', in V. Pinsky and A. Wylie (eds), *Critical Directions in Contemporary Archaeology*. Cambridge: Cambridge University Press, pp. 55–67.

Nott, J.C. and G.R. Gliddon. 1854. *Types of Mankind or, Ethnological Researches: based on the ancient monuments, paintings, sculptures, and crania of races, and upon their natural, geographical, philological and biblical history, illustrated by selections from the inedited papers of Samuel George Morton and by additional contributions from L. Agassiz; W. Usher; and H.S. Patterson*. Philadelphia: Lippincott, Grambo.

Orange, A.D. 1972. 'The Origins of the British Association for the Advancement of Science', *British Journal for the History of Science* 6: 152–76.

———. 1981. 'The Beginnings of the British Association, 1831–1851', in R. MacLeod and P. Collins (eds), *The Parliament of Science*. Northwood, Middx.: Science Reviews Limited. pp. 43–64.

Pouchet, G. 1864. *Plurality of the Human Race*, trans. H.J.C. Beavan, London: Longman, Green, Longman and Roberts for the Anthropological Society of London.

Prichard, J.C. 1847. 'On the Various Methods of Research Which Contribute to the Advancement of Ethnology and the Relations of that Science to Other Branches of Knowledge', *British Association Reports* 16: 230–53.

Rapport, N. (ed.) 2002. *British Subjects: An Anthropology of Britain*. Oxford: Berg.

Stepan, N. 1982. *The Idea of Race in Science: Great Britain, 1800–1960*. Hamden, Conn.: Archon Books.

Stocking, G.W. Jr. 1968. *Race, Culture, and Evolution*. New York: The Free Press.

———. 1971. 'What's in a Name? The Origins of the Royal Anthropological Institute (1837–71)', *Man* (ns) 6: 369–90.

———. 1983. 'The Ethnographer's Magic. Fieldwork in British Anthropology from Tylor to Malinowski', in G.W. Stocking Jr. (ed), *Observers Observed. Essays on Ethnographic Fieldwork*. Madison: University of Wisconsin Press, pp. 70–120.

———. 1987. *Victorian Anthropology*. London: Collier Macmillan.

Turner, G. 1871. 'Professor Turner's Address to the Department of Anthropology', *British Association Reports* 50: 144–47.

Urry, J. 1972. 'Notes and Queries on Anthropology and the development of field methods in British anthropology, 1870–1920', *Proceedings of the Royal Anthropological Institute* 45–57.

———. 1984. 'Englishmen, Celts and Iberians: The Ethnographic Survey of the United Kingdom 1892–1899', in G.W. Stocking Jr. (ed.), *Functionalism Historicized*, Madison: University of Wisconsin Press, pp. 83–105.

———. 1993. *Before Social Anthropology: Essays in the History of British Anthropology*, Philadelphia: Harwood Academic Publishers.

Vogt, K. 1864. , trans. J. Hunt, London: Longman, Green, Longman and Roberts for the Anthropological Society of London.

Von Gizycki, R. 1979. '*Lectures on Man: His Place in Creation, and in the History of the Earth* The Associations for the Advancement of Science: An international comparative study', Zeitschrift für Sociologie viii: 28–49.

Waitz, T. 1863. I*ntroduction to Anthropology*, trans. J.F. Collingwood, London: Longman, Green, Longman and Roberts for the Anthropological Society of London.

Weber, G. 1974. 'Science and Society in Nineteenth Century Anthropology', *History of Science* XV: 260–83.

Yeo, R. 1979. 'William Whewell, Natural Theology and the Philosophy of Science in Mid Nineteenth Century Britain', *Annals of Science* 36: 493–516.

———. 1981. 'Scientific Method and the Image of Science 1831–1891', in R. MacLeod and P. Collins (eds), *The Parliament of Science*. Northwood, Middx.: Science Reviews Limited. pp. 65–88.

Part II
ARCHAEOLOGICAL PRACTICE

Chapter 6
Wilamowitz and Stratigraphy in 1873

A Case Study in the History of Archaeology's 'Great Divide'

Giovanna Ceserani

Abstract

Aforgotten late ninteenth-century episode serves me in this paper to illustrate the power, and limits, of archives in approaching the ways classical archaeology conceives its disciplinary genealogies and boundaries. Ulrich von Wilamowitz published a stratigraphical report on the Campanian site of Capua in the 1873 *Bullettino of the Instituto di Corrispondenza Archeologica* (now German Institute of Archaeology in Rome – DAI). Whatever the value of his interpretation, Wilamowitz is not normally associated with stratigraphy: the 'Prince' of German Classical philology' is a central figure for classics, but not for archaeology. Moreover, the 1873 Capua report was also strikingly unique in the pages of the classically oriented *Bullettino*, from which the language and use of stratigraphy were to be absent for many years to come – as if confirming the 'great divide' between classical and World archaeology. How can one explore this episode further and explain its uniqueness? How can it be related to the 1870s explosion of new methodologies and practices that were to deeply change the scholarly landscape of archaeology? These questions are addressed here through published sources, but mainly through archives (notably those of the DAI). Archives might not provide all the answers and they leave gaps, just like narratives do. But the discrepancies revealed by comparison between published histories of past scholarship and archival records prove a good starting point for unmasking accepted genealogies and for showing that disciplinary boundaries are always in the making, rather than naturally given.

Introduction

A previously unnoticed episode in 1873 reveals the illustrious philologist Ulrich von Wilamowitz (1848–1931) discussing the stratigraphy of the site of Capua, near Naples. Wilamowitz and stratigraphy make a surprising couple: on the one hand, the most representative figure of classical philology in the prestigious German tradition; on the other, one of the defining practices of archaeology. Moreover, while stratigraphy is widely used in all archaeological enterprises, it has long been the hallmark of prehistory, or world archaeology, rather than classical archaeology. The Great Divide – as the difference between classical and other archaeologies has been called – is indeed evident in the little interest taken by classical archaeologists in theoretical and explicitly methodological questions at the very moment when these issues became crucial to the nineteenth-century coming of age of prehistory as a modern and respectable academic discipline. Wilamowitz's dip into stratigraphy – almost unprecedented among classical archaeologists of his times – takes us straight to the incisive moment when this divide opens up and allows us to explore further the role played by the tight relationship between classical archaeology and classical philology.

When Colin Renfrew made use of the very effective expression 'Great Divide', he explained it with reference to differences in objects of study. He noted that 'prehistory, and with it many techniques of field excavation, originally developed most vigorously in lands lacking the elaborate and well preserved monuments' (1980: 288) of classical antiquity. He argued that classical archaeology, in contrast, delves into details and description because of its great tradition of spectacular finds, in the same way that classical philology focuses on great, canonical texts. More recently, Ian Morris (1994 and 2000) took issue with this explanation, which he criticized for being object-driven and for proposing a timeless picture. Rather he sees the insulation of classical archaeology from other archaeologies as the result of active policing that in the 1870s created a de-peopled archaeology as an auxiliary discipline to texts-dominated Classics and one that would avoid asking historical questions troubling to the ideal of Hellenism (1994: 28). Clearly interpretations of the Great Divide are neither self-evident nor innocent. Institutionally the divide exists: classical archaeology alternatively finds itself lodged in art history, classics, or, more rarely, archaeology departments. But histories of archaeology that reiterate these firm, commonly accepted disciplinary boundaries, miss the chance to ask historical questions crucial to the development of modern archaeology. Morris, as well as Michael Shanks (1996: 118), have argued powerfully for the importance of historicizing the peculiar development of classical archaeology within the contexts of its tight relation to the practices of philology and the ideology of Hellenism. Wilamowitz's report on Capua offers the opportunity to focus further this approach from the perspective of philology.

Wilamowitz occupies a special place in the history of classical scholarship: he is often referred to as 'the most influential Hellenist of modern times'. The volume of his work is staggering: in more than seventy books he covered what no one else managed, or dared to, by dealing with many ancient authors. He envisioned the goal of classical studies to be the recovery and study of the Graeco-Roman world in its totality, as a unique, indivisible whole, an effort to be spearheaded by textual criticism with its various allied disciplines. His vision gained special authority as Wilamowitz embodied this ideal by the extraordinary coverage of his own work: he believed that one should look at the classical world in its entirety, and he appeared to be the one scholar who could still do it. He has indeed been a powerful model of scholarship to many classicists up to today: *Wilamowitz and no end* is the title of a recent edited volume (Mülke 2003) and not so long ago a brief autobiography that he wrote in the first, lonely months at boarding school was published in a professional classical journal (Calder 1971). Even classicists who support very different directions and aims for the discipline recognize his immense influence: Stephen Nimis (1984) has coined the term 'the Wilamowitz footnote' to describe the most recurrent strategy for classicists to bestow academic authority on their papers. Wilamowitz himself asserted his stake for posterity in two works published in his last years: the *History of classical scholarship* (1921) and the autobiography *My Recollections* (1928), in which he promoted his vision of the study of classical antiquity and his life in its service. Both his writings and their reception by later classicists have often transformed Wilamowitz's life into an iconic representation of the history of the discipline. This is precisely the reason why one needs to treat with caution this very rich but multi-layered historical material.

How much classical scholarship is invested in Wilamowitz is revealed by a famous episode from his early years when, fresh out of University, he wrote a ferocious review of Nietzsche's 1872 *The Birth of the Tragedy*. The review dismantled Nietzsche's arguments by careful philological references, displaying plenty of Greek sentences in contrast to Nietzsche's avoidance of any Greek word, and concluded 'let him step down from the lectern from which he is supposed to teach knowledge' (2000: 24). Nietzsche did indeed retire from his professorship of classical philology in 1879. He has since been perceived as an outsider in the history of philology and is mainly remembered for his philosophical writings. In *My Recollections*, Wilamowitz attributes Nietzsche's stepping down to his review, 'boyish as much my work in question, with the conclusion I hit the bull's eye' (1930: 152). The debate surrounding Nietzsche's work certainly shaped the study of classical antiquity, and it still does, but Wilamowitz's claim – often taken at face value – is probably groundless. Recent research has also offered careful analysis showing how much in fact Nietzsche and Wilamowitz shared and how Nietzsche's influence on classical philology goes well beyond his dismissal (see Porter 2000: 16 and 265–73).

In contrast to this debate, the episode of Capua is forgotten in the otherwise extensively explored life of Wilamowitz. Just after writing the review of *The Birth of Greek Tragedy*, Wilamowitz left for a two-year journey in the classical lands: he spent much time at the *Instituto di Corrispondenza Archeologica* – Institute of Archaeological Correspondence – and it was in its *Bullettino* that he published the report on Capua. His name, however, does not figure even once in the 1879 history of the first fifty years of the *Institute* that otherwise lists most of its visitors, established scholars and young researchers alike, many of whom held official archaeological scholarships (Michaelis 1879: 130). Wilamowitz himself seems to respond to this oversight when in his autobiography he explains that it was suggested to him to 'apply for the archaeological travelling scholarship', but he declined because his mother had already put aside money for his travels South (1930: 148). In order to understand what Wilamowitz was doing in Rome and his attraction to archaeology, one needs to take a step back, turning to the wider developments in archaeological studies.

Archaeologies in the Nineteenth Century: From Antiquarians to 'Big-Digs'

The deepest time-perspective brought to bear on the historical context of the Great Divide is Alain Schnapp's work (1997) on the origins of archaeological enquiry. Paying attention to both the development of practices, including stratigraphy, and the shaping of professional and academic institutions, Schnapp showed the differences between classical archaeology and prehistory emerging in the course of the nineteenth century from what used to be, with all its regional variations, a much more unified antiquarian tradition. Since the Renaissance antiquarian curiosity cabinets had collected and studied varieties of material culture from different times and places, ranging from *naturalia*, to classical and prehistoric objects (Schnapp 1997: 121–218). During the nineteenth-century process of academic specialization, the definition of professionally shared practices and objects of study created different disciplines. Schnapp demonstrates that prehistoric archaeology's scientific status and academic credibility became tightly connected to the debate on the long antiquity of man; prehistory's professional recognition developed in parallel to the acceptance of Darwinism (1997: 275–303). With no texts to turn to, typology, technology and stratigraphy were established as the defining methods of the new science of prehistoric man: chairs in this discipline were established starting in the middle of the nineteenth century (for example at Prague in 1850, Paris in 1853, Copenhagen in 1855, Berlin in 1856 and Rome in 1877).

The professionalization of classical archaeology took a very different route and one that, from the start, shared much with classical literary studies. The acknowledged founder of classical archaeology is J.J. Winckelmann who presented his 1764 *History of Ancient Art* as a revolutionary departure, from the works of his antiquarian predecessors. In this book, he combined close examination of Rome's antiquity collections with the concept of style to organize for the first time ancient works of art within the framework of a historical narrative that celebrated the perfection of the unsurpassed beauty of Greek classical art (Schnapp 1997: 258–66 and Marchand 1996: 7–16). Winckelmann owed to antiquarian knowledge and practices more than he admitted (see most recently Kaufmann 2001), but his influence was tremendous, shaping modern Philhellenism, art history and classical archaeology. But in Winckelmann's times not even the word 'archaeology' was in common use and its academic establishment was not a straightforward and linear process. In the academy, German students of ancient classical texts first turned to Winckelmann's *History of Ancient Art.* His work contributed to the turn that made classical philology into an independent academic discipline: as F.A. Wolf's foundational *Prolegomena to Homer* illustrates (see Grafton 1981), the new philologists established the methods of textual criticism as their practices, but found in Winckelmann's formulation of the Greek ideal the justification for their subjects of research. By the late eighteenth century, seminars of *Altertumwissenschaft* were a prestigious component of German universities and acquired the cultural prestige to make classical studies central to the early nineteenth-century reform of secondary school education.

When scholars of classical archaeology sought professional and institutional status they took as a model the success of German classical philology. In 1828 an international group of lovers of antiquity, travellers, diplomats, dealers and also university scholars of many European nationalities established in Rome the Institute of Archaeological Correspondence that brought together corresponding members throughout Europe (Schnapp 1997: 305–307 and Marchand 1996: 51–65). The project was to promote and publish in the Institute's publications – the *Bullettino* and the *Annali* – systematic information on archaeological discoveries gathered through the capillary presence in classical lands of the Institute's members. A living encyclopaedia, as Schnapp defined it, the Institute soon became a meeting point, with its own library and, starting in 1859, official archaeological fellowships for research students: it set in place the model for all modern institutes of archaeology to come. Its main promoter and indefatigable activist, the German scholar Eduard Gerhard (1795–1867), had a clear vision of how classical archaeology should become a respectable, scientific academic discipline. Focusing on the remains of Graeco-Roman antiquity, classical archaeology should become the 'philology of monuments'. At its core should be systematic observation of ancient remains; Gerhard's famous motto was: 'he who sees one art monument sees none; he who sees thousands, sees one.' The approach was to be modelled on philology and based in literary knowledge: the archaeologist's

> explication of art [should stand] beside the criticism and explanation of philological texts; his art history [should stand] beside the literary history of antiquity; his other research, especially on religious and individual relics, [should stand] beside the real representation of ancient life (Gerhard 2004: 174).

Gerhard's approach was successful: he went back to Berlin first as Museum archaeologist (1837), but soon as one of the first professors of archaeology at the university (1844). Some of the greatest nineteenth-century *Altertumwissenschaft* scholars practised this style of archaeology alongside history and philology. Karl Ottfried Müller (1797–1840) wrote a book on the Etruscans and one on the Dorians, a history of Greek literature and a handbook for archaeology. Otto Jahn (1813–1869) both edited Latin texts and published works of iconography, especially on Greek painted vases. Jahn had been introduced to archaeology by Gerhard's lectures at the Berlin Museum: he later took issue with Gerhard's 'philology of monuments', but only because he wanted archaeology to be an independent science of art with closer ties to philology. This philology of monuments, however, ignored the methodology and interpretation of excavation – so crucial in those same years to establishing the prehistoric antiquity of man by way of stratigraphy. Excavation never figures in Gerhard's programmatic archaeological theses. He did call for the importance of reporting the original location of statuettes or vases in tombs: he thought that, while weapons or jewels could be readily identified, the location would be crucial in helping to decide whether other objects were, for example, tutelary deities rather than items beloved in life (Gerhard 1829b: 184). But he viewed excavation mainly as a means to produce objects ready to study, as if off the shelves of a museum. Revealing is his 1829 description of the unearthing of the Etruscan necropolis of Vulci from where thousands of painted vases were recovered: 'the countryside has become a museum of noble monuments of the happiest centuries in the history of art' (Gerhard 1829a: 2).

Yet, this very desire to recover more objects for museums changed the face of classical archaeology from the 1870s onwards (Marchand 1996: 75–115). European countries began sponsoring excavations in sites of Greece and Asia Minor. In 1875 the German excavation of Olympia started, while Schliemann was already privately at work at Troy in 1871. These large enterprises – the so-called 'big digs' – faced unprecedented tasks in classical archaeology: the quantity of material to be interpreted was immense and highly confusing, in comparison with earlier cases of recovery of monumental sculptures or tombs. The teams began to include specialized personnel who introduced stratigraphy and seriation, like Wilhelm Dörpfeld, who was called first at Olympia and then at Troy to help make sense of the evidence. Important questions were at stake and methods were discussed. Anthony Snodgrass has highlighted how pioneering for modern archaeology were Dörpfeld's achievements in Ithaca and Adolf Furtwängler's catalogues of gems and vases (Snodgrass 1987: 16–24). But these were also the years when the Great Divide crystallized. How did this happen? Morris points to several factors that constituted the active policing that insulated classical archaeology from world archaeologies. He identifies the submission of Greek archaeology to an aesthetic ideal and nationalist ideologies, accompanied by the perception of the threat it would pose to Hellenism if left free to ask socio-historical questions and to tighten its ties to world archaeology (Morris 2000: 48–52). But how exactly did these factors work?

Suzanne Marchand's recent study (2002) of Furtwängler's academic trajectory exemplifies how to answer such questions. She shows that, after his university education in ancient Greek art criticism, when joining Olympia's excavation team in 1778 he was faced with the unexpected task of organizing thousands of excavated bronzes. He resorted to methodologies of antiquarian origin that prehistory was also using and developing, like typology, seriation and stratigraphy, and produced very impressive studies. But it was not this work that promoted him in academia: what finally gained him a chair was his book on the masterpieces of Greek classical sculpture. My case study of Wilamowitz is a further exploration of, and contribution to, understanding how the 1870s challenge to the philology of monuments resulted in the Great Divide. Individuals' practices and experiences can indeed reveal the working of wider trends that characterized the unique relationship between classical archaeology and philology at the end of the nineteenth century.

The Making of a Classicist

Born to a family of Prussian nobility, Wilamowitz was first educated at home and then attended the excellent boarding school Schulpforte that counted among its pupils many other future professors, including Jahn and Nietzsche (The choice of an academic career was odd in his aristocratic family – his brother followed the more usual path of service in the army before turning to manage the family's land properties. Wilamowitz first enrolled at the University of Bonn: his favourite teacher was Jahn who infused him with enthusiasm for philology and archaeology (Calder 1991). Jahn commissioned him to write an essay comparing satiric drama to vase paintings, a project that combined philology and archaeology and that Wilamowitz still hoped to carry out in Italy but never did (Wilamowitz 1930: 106). He also followed Kekule's lectures on ancient art history and wrote for him on Roman sarcophagi. After Jahn's death in 1869 Wilamowitz moved to Berlin where he was allowed to graduate early on account of his impressive

Fig. 6.1 Picture of Wilamowitz as a young man.

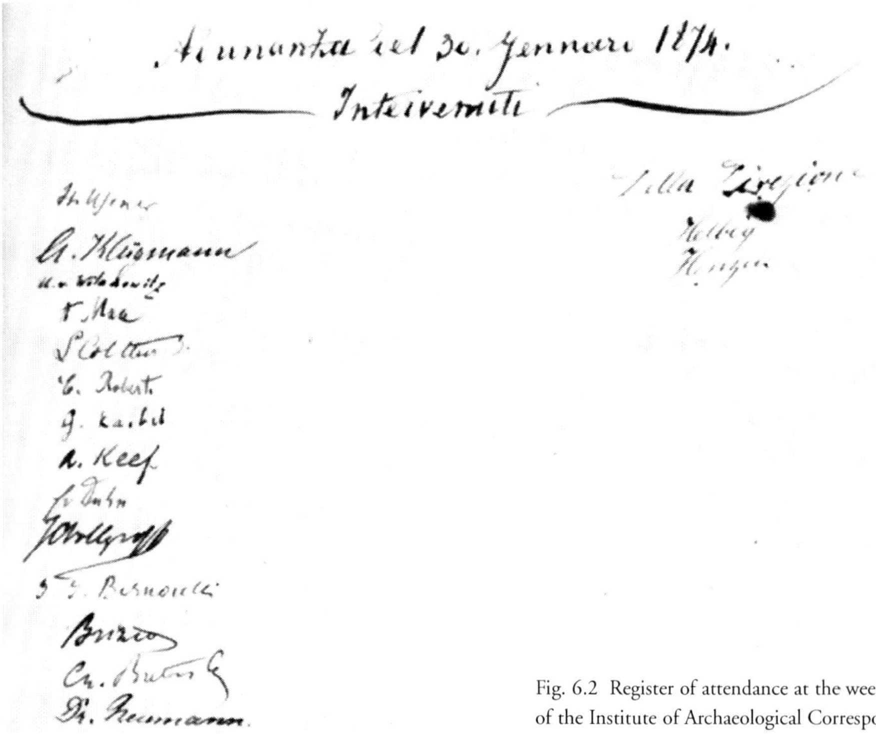

Fig. 6.2 Register of attendance at the weekly meetings of the Institute of Archaeological Correspondence.

academic record. There he met Mommsen but only briefly, as most of the time the famous historian was travelling out of the country for the Corpus of Latin Inscriptions. Both Jahn and Mommsen shaped his plan to spend time in the classical lands: Jahn had travelled extensively through Italy including Sicily in 1838–1839 and Mommsen recommended Wilamowitz to the Institute of Archaeological Correspondence in Rome (see Mommsen to Henzen, 9 May 1872, in DAI Rome) and offered him the opportunity to work for the Corpus of Latin Inscriptions while in Italy. After a few months' service as a grenadier at the end of the Franco-Prussian war, Wilamowitz left for Italy in August 1872 to return in April 1874: he based himself at the Institute in the winters and travelled to Greece from March to May 1873. It was during this Italian period that he visited the archaeological excavation at Capua.

The chapter of Wilamowitz's autobiography dedicated to his time in the classical countries reads pleasantly like a travel narrative. There are plenty of amusing travel incidents and encounters, colourful representations of the locals and anecdotes that are retrospectively bestowed with meaning. For example, Wilamowitz recounts that the epiphany of Renaissance culture in Florence revealed to him 'the unity of historical life' that 'is impressed on everybody who follows the buildings and their decoration, the great art and its irradiations into the life of every citizen family' – history, poetry, art, 'it is all a stream of life.' He claimed that it was 'to this insight that [he] then saw clearly the task of historical-philological science, which [he] advocated all [his] life' (1930: 158) and that was to guide his life-long study of the ancient world. The narrative is also punctuated by academic visits to libraries and museums to collate manuscripts and record inscriptions. From Florence in October 1872 Wilamowitz wrote a letter to the director of the Institute, announcing his arrival and his desire to make himself a useful guest (Wilamowitz to Henzen, 4 October 1872, in DAI Rome). And eager he certainly was in the exciting scene of the capital of the newly established Italian state (Dyson 2006: 94–110). If not in Michaelis' 1879 history, Wilamowitz was

Fig. 6.3 Drawing of an Etruscan engraved mirror-case of the same type as the one discussed by Wilamowitz. From the archives of the Institute of Archaeological Correspondence.

much present in the Institute's activities, his signature well visible in the registers for every weekly meetings during the years 1872–74 (see IKA Registers 1872–74 in DAI Rome; Fig. 6.2). Following his traces in the Institute's archives and publications, while comparing them with his autobiography, allows us to reconstruct episodes of Wilamowitz's sojourn, including that of Capua, and gives us a privileged insight into the 1870s practices of the archaeological institute.

Exegesis of Archaeological Monuments

The weekly seminars of the Institute offered the major meeting venue for archaeologists in Rome to discuss and circulate archaeological news and objects. The monthly *Bullettino* published the minutes of these seminars. It is here that one can follow the unfolding of the discussions and find Wilamowitz's voice on various occasions. On 17 January 1873 he discussed an Etruscan mirror-case from Tarquinia owned by a prominent Roman collector. Likewise in following meetings, he presented an inscribed tablet from the collection of a Polish count, a marble inscription from the Florence Museum, and a small sculpture of an ancient girl head that he had purchased during his trip to Greece (*Bullettino dell'Instituto* 1873: 10–11, 34 and 1874: 50). The relations between collectors and scholars were tight, as illustrated by Wilamowitz presenting objects from private collections and acquiring some for himself.

Wilamowitz moved comfortably in this world of objects already excavated and de-contextualized. Objects, be they inscriptions or sculptures or paintings, were mostly looked at in relation to written culture and read for their figurative representations. Wilamowitz could thus display and put to use his knowledge of ancient culture and texts. A good example is Wilamowitz's discussion of the Etruscan engraved mirror-case from the Roman collection. Figure 6.3 depicts not the piece that Wilamowitz discussed, but a copy of the same type, which circulated at the Institute four years later (Fig 6.3). Four copies of this particular type of mirror-case survive, while the one that Wilamowitz saw is now lost. Wilamowitz first presented and described the object, then interpreted it. In the Institute's minutes one reads that Wilamowitz explained that the 'myth here depicted should be explained by the stories of heroic education, that is to say of an hero exposed by his parents and fed by an eagle in the desert, later on found by a shepherd or farmer' (*Bullettino dell'Instituto* 1873: 11). Today the accepted interpretation of the image is rather that it depicts a specific episode of Greek mythology: the god Bacchus as a child being raised by a nymph with Hermes standing by them. Apparently one of the reasons for Wilamowitz's misinterpretation is that the copy he saw was damaged so that one could not see the caduceus which clearly identifies Hermes. How in keeping this 'figurative exegesis' approach was with Wilamowitz's career as a philologist, as well as how much he invested in it, is shown by the fact that he went back to the same object in his *Analecta Euripidea* (1875: 188). There he attempts a new interpretation of the image and explains it as Hercules finding Telephus.

What is most interesting for us is the practice behind Wilamowitz's interpretation. The object is read for what it depicts, while there is no stylistic analysis, nor any typological or functional interpretation, nor certainly any interest in context and excavation. It is a clear example of Wilamowitz engaging in the tradition of philology of monuments sponsored by Gerhard and elaborated further by Jahn. Objects are connected to texts by iconographic reading: Wilamowitz's exercise on the mirror-case shows that he keenly respected Jahn's wish that young classicists learn to interpret the 'language of artworks', using the same care and rigour that philologists applied to texts (Marchand 1996: 41–42).

Visit to an Excavation Site

The case of Capua is different. Wilamowitz was not reporting at the Institute's meetings, but was asked to inspect the site of an excavation and to write about it for the *Bullettino*. At the time Wilamowitz was in Naples visiting museums and Pompeii and carrying on research for Mommsen: his task was to browse through local publications, old and new, to find references to ancient inscriptions. When news of the discovery of a temple in the private garden of a local small landowner reached Rome, Wilamowitz happened to be on hand. He arrived on the site when excavations were already over. In his report he expressed regret for this: because 'only while excavations are taking place one can solve important problems, before most revealing traces are lost' (1873: 145). But he promised the readers to make the most of the trusted information kindly offered to him by the excavators themselves.

Wilamowitz spends most of the report discussing the tuff statues – the famous votive sculptures of women figures holding children, the *'matres matutae'* of the Capua sanctuary – and describing some painted vases that the excavator happened to have collected. But a few paragraphs strike a different note. Wilamowitz attempts a history of the building: he explains that the temple was already destroyed in antiquity by a fire in the 2nd century BC and was never rebuilt, that in fact some time later the level of the soil was elevated by 3 meters using ruins from the temple and clay vessels (some of which were so well preserved that he thought there must have been a production centre nearby) and that finally, in late imperial times, the area became a cemetery, as some tombs and Alexander Severus' coins attest. Wilamowitz put forward this interpretation on the basis of the soil layers that he reconstructed from the excavators' description. This is how he describes the 'prospectus of the layers': 'at two-meter deep begins a stratum in which tuff sculptures lie in no order, in all possible positions, something that can be explained only if they were buried together with much soft soil'. Wilamowitz interpreted this as the refill subsequent to the ancient destruction of the building. 'Deeper down', he writes, 'one tells me that also some stairs were found … and underneath a 0.25 cm stratum of cinder and other remains of a fire. Further down nothing … at 4 meters deep the virgin soil' (1873: 147).

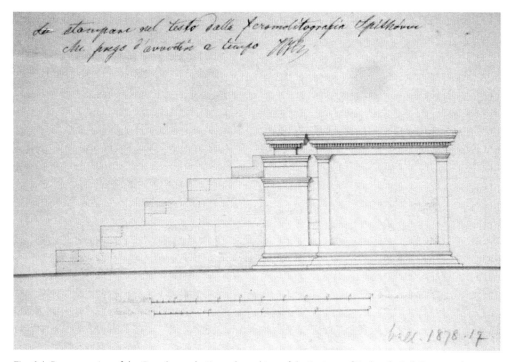

Fig. 6.4 Reconstruction of the Capua's temple. From the archives of the Institute of Archaeological Correspondence.

Wilamowitz, however, was missing crucial information: what he identified as a refill layer was not ancient but only 25 years old, made by that same landowner who had then found the temple, took out some of its decorative elements and concealed his excavation. What Wilamowitz interpreted as the stratum of the ancient destruction was actually the result of this clandestine excavation. This information came to light a few years later, in the midst of a controversy about what this temple must have looked like, when scholars sought the original excavator and scrutinized his memory (see Fig. 6.4). This debate can also be traced in the *Bullettino* and the Institute's archives. By then, however, Wilamowitz was back in Germany in his first university position.

Wilamowitz and the Great Divide

Despite the significant mistake, Wilamowitz's report on Capua is remarkable for its unusual and early reference to stratigraphy. It certainly reads differently from Gerhard's type of excavation report that presented objects as the products of discovery, but independently from any excavation process or technique. Nor is it about reading the language of artworks according to Jahn's model, but rather it reads and reconstructs a story from the soil. The language and concepts introduced by Wilamowitz in his reference to stratigraphy never figured in the work of Gerhard, Müller and Jahn. They also stand out among other reports on excavations published in the *Bullettino* in those same years. Wilamowitz's reference to stratigraphy is also earlier than the successful work of Dörpfeld who made use of stratigraphy first at Olympia in 1877 and then at Troy, where he joined Schliemann in 1882. At the time of Wilamowitz's visit to Capua the excavations of Troy were still the occasion, within the classicists' community, for suspicions and ridicule of Schliemann. At the Institute's 1873 Christmas celebrations, Wilamowitz had even dressed up as a woman to impersonate Schliemann's wife hiding antiquities in her petticoat to the great amusement of all present (Wilamowitz 1930: 175–76).

What, then, inspired Wilamowitz to make stratigraphy an important component of his Capua report? The archives do not tell us how Wilamowitz familiarized himself with stratigraphy's language and concepts, nor does he talk about this in his autobiography. One can only speculate. Was it because of conversations with the exciting circles of Italian prehistory? In the 1870s Luigi Pigorini (1842–1925) was organizing the official establishment of Italian prehistory, coming a long way since his publication of Bolognese *Terramare*'s stratigraphic excavations when still a high school student. In 1870 he was elected to the new national *Direzione Generale dei Musei e degli Scavi*, in 1871 the fifth international meeting of prehistoric archaeology and anthropology was held in Bologna, in 1875 he founded the *Bullettino di Paletnologia Italiana*, in 1876 the *Museo Nazionale Preistorico ed Etnografico* was instituted and in 1877 Pigorini was called to the first chair of prehistory at the University of Rome (Guidi 1988 and for earlier developments Toracca 1993). Pigorini and some of his closest associates like Edoardo Brizio had been members of the Institute of Archaeological Correspondence since the late 1860s, presented some talks there and attended a few meetings together with Wilamowitz, as attested by the signatures in the Institute's registers (see IKA Registers 1872–1874 in DAI Rome and Fig. 6.2, Wilamowitz 1930 [1928]: 171 and Michaelis 1879: 132).

Another possible source of information and excitement about stratigraphy could have been Wilamowitz's visit to Pompeii. It was, in fact, from Pompeii that Wilamowitz sent back to Rome his report on Capua (Wilamowitz to Helbig, 11 July 1873, in DAI Rome). In *My Recollections* Wilamowitz remembers fondly the days in Pompeii, where, thanks to Mommsen's introduction, Giuseppe Fiorelli let him wander freely by day and night. Wilamowitz praises Fiorelli for beginning the 'scientific study of Pompeii' and mentions 'the house in Pompeii reserved for scientific work which contained some books' (Wilamowitz 1930: 192–93). That was the archaeological school where Fiorelli was at the time institutionalizing the teaching of excavation techniques applied at Pompeii, among which was stratigraphy (Barbanera 1998: 64–70, Manacorda 1982: 94–95). While it is impossible to know for certain what inspired Wilamowitz's application of stratigraphy at Capua, it is likely that these experiences played a role. Certainly it might appear a superficial effort: lacking experience of field-work himself, Wilamowitz ventured his interpretation on the basis of reports that turned out to be biased. But in this episode one catches a glimpse of the 1870s explosion of new methodologies and practices that were to change profoundly the scholarly landscape of archaeology.

In the Roman archaeological scene of the 1870s, moreover, contacts between the developing modern archaeologies and the classical one, as well as between local and foreign scholars, figure prominently, more than they do in more recent histories of archaeology that set sharp disciplinary or national boundaries. Yet, however much it was judged excellent by the directors of the Institute (Helbig to Henzen, July 1873 in DAI Rome), Wilamowitz's piece on stratigraphy remained unique for a long time in the *Bullettino* that rather continued to focus on art objects and monuments out of their archaeological context, while just in the same years the *Bullettino di Paletnologia Italiana* started publishing stratigraphic prospecti (Manacorda 1982: 86). What, then, does the report of the young philologist Wilamowitz, with its early use of a new archaeological methodology, tells us about the Great Divide?

There is an individual level of the story, in which the young, ambitious and extremely capable Wilamowitz hits a wall. He left for Italy with many expectations, very well read and following in the footsteps of compelling models. But the trip presented many surprises. One episode aptly symbolizes the discrepancy between the books he had read and the reality of classical lands and sites. In Greece Wilamowitz was asked to accompany the hereditary prince Bernard of Meiningen in a tour of the Peloponnesus. When they arrived in Olympia – three years before Curtius' excavations took off – Wilamowitz, the philologist of the group, was to take the lead for an excursion in the surrounding area on the basis of Pausanias, VI 21.3–22.5. It was a great disappointment with long term consequences. He could not relate what he read to the landscape – 'nothing would agree' (Wilamowitz 1930: 185) – as he had not realized that Pausanias described the site moving from the opposite direction, Wilamowitz's ensuing low appreciation of Pausanias had a negative effect on this Greek author's modern critical reception (Habicht 1985: 165–75). The experience with the new developments in stratigraphy can be seen as another surprise. Wilamowitz certainly shows himself to be more perceptive than most of his colleagues in realizing that 'reading the soil' – be it archaeological survey or stratigraphy – was a new exciting development in the practices for the study of antiquity. But he could not get it right. While for the exegesis of figurative material the knowledge of ancient texts was a great help, these new archaeological methodologies and practices required specialization and experience. The inspiring scene of the making of modern archaeology confronted a scholar as capable as Wilamowitz with unexpected limitations. The most illustrious scholars of the previous generation, like Wilamowitz's favourite teacher Jahn, seemed easily to master the classical world in its entirety as well as the several practices necessary to its study, but such mastery was not possible any more.

Yet Wilamowitz is remembered precisely for his adamant view of Graeco-Roman antiquity as an indivisible, historical whole – as he learned in Florence – and for his insistence on the unity of the practices and aims of its study. The unusual perspective offered by Wilamowitz's interest in archaeology, however, well reveals the vested idealism of these programmatic positions (on which see also Porter 2000: 269–70). Archaeology indeed always remained an important component of Wilamowitz's vision: his flattering words at the conclusion of his official visit to the newly inaugurated Pergamon Museum in Berlin – 'you people of the spade won!' – are often quoted. Archaeology also plays an important role in Wilamowitz's history of scholarship, in fact gaining a large share in what he calls the 'nineteenth-century conquest of the ancient world by science' (1982: 105). This conquest is indeed symbolized by a sort of bird's-eye view of the archaeological illustration of antiquity: 'excavation of ancient sites and the scrutiny of every scrap of evidence brought up from the earth have been so prevalent that the shortest way to describe the progress achieved is to glance briefly at the territories of the former Roman Empire' (1982: 160). But a closer reading shows that in the *History of Classical Scholarship* the origin and backbone of the study of antiquity remains philology: the narrative begins with Hellenistic grammarians and it dedicates detailed discussion to various developments and debates of textual criticism, while the study of material culture appears as narrative departures into antiquarians, travellers, art history and excavations that helped to reveal antiquity. Schliemann's name does not appear, but Furtwängler, the excavations of Olympia, of Crete and others, are well praised. Yet, it remains a view of material culture as complementing written sources on papyrus, stone or parchment; there is never a reference to archaeological methodology or theories per se. The way archaeology is made to fit in Wilamowitz's history of scholarship exposes how its unity held together: archaeology is easily incorporated because it is represented as pursuing the same object of reconstructing ancient life, at the expense of distinctively archaeological scholarship.

The success of this projected ideal unity of objectives in the study of Graeco-Roman antiquity was, explains, for example, why Furtwängler put his effort in compiling catalogues of bronzes and vases and in writing on Greek sculptural masterpieces, rather than proposing innovative interpretations of the past or seeking further contacts with contemporary prehistoric archaeologists, as Marchand has shown (2002). This peculiar development of classical archaeology owes much to the powerful grip that the classical ideal continued to hold on nineteenth-century study of antiquity: as Grafton writes (1992: 239), 'from Wolf at the beginning of the century to Wilamowitz at the end, influential scholars set out research programs that called for a rigorous historicism, but insisted on their personal allegiance to the unique superiority of Hellenism.' One thing that did change between the times of Wolf and Wilamowitz, however, was the dramatic increase in scale and sophistication of archaeological fieldwork (Marchand 1996: 75–115). In defence of the classical ideal Wilamowitz enlists scientific positivism in the guise of professional specialisation, by way of emphasising the ideal unity of the various disciplinary efforts employed in studying the ancient world. But how archaeology figures in Wilamowitz's history of scholarship again exposes the contradictory nature of this project. The book opens by declaring that 'Graeco-Roman civilization in its essence and every facet of its existence … is a unity' and that 'the task of scholarship is to bring the dead world to life by power of science' (1982: 1). Yet in the final pages one reads that 'the soil of southern Italy and Sicily has yielded little that adds to our knowledge of the Greek past, but it has provided a great deal of information about the earlier inhabitants'; one learns of the prehistoric Terramare, their excavation 'reduced to a fine art by the Italians', that will provide 'solution to the ethnological problems involved' (1982: 163). That in Wilamowitz's own work such tensions emerge and remain unresolved, shows how the Great Divide's history is imbricated together with the development of classical studies. Wilamowitz's own experience with archaeology, as explored in this chapter, on the other hand, reminds us that to understand the making of the Great Divide, the history of classical archaeology needs to abandon accepted disciplinary boundaries and genealogies. Rather one should begin by questioning such narratives, looking for their inconsistencies and exploring the marks quietly but revealingly left by scholars' practices, whether or not successfully put to work, both in published sources and archives.

Acknowledgements

The author wishes to thanks Dr Blanck and Dr Frölich at the DAI Rome, and M. Beard, A. Grafton, S. Marchand, A. Schnapp, S. Settis and A. Snodgrass.

References

Barbanera, M. 1998. *L'archeologia degli italiani*. Rome: Editori Riuniti.

Calder, W. III 1971. 'Ulrich von Wilamowitz-Moellendorf. An Unpublished Autobiography', *Greek, Roman and Byzantine Studies* 12: 561–77.

____. 1991. 'What did Ulrich von Wilamowitz-Moellendorf learn from Otto Jahn?', in W. Calder III, H. Cancik and B. Kytzler (eds), *Otto Jahn (1813–1868)*. Stuttgart: Franz Steiner, pp. 195–203.

Deutsches Archäologisches Institute Archive in Rome: DAI Rome.

Dyson, S. 2006. *In Pursuit of Ancient Pasts. A History of Classiccal Archaeology in the Nineteeth and Twentieth-Centuries*. Yale and London: Yale University Press.

Gerhard, E. 1829a. 'Scavi Etruschi', *Bullettino dell' Instituto di Corrispondenza Archeologica*, 1: 1–18.

____. 1829b. 'Cenni Topografici intorno i Vasi Italo-Greci', *Bullettino dell' Instituto di Corrispondenza Archeologica*,1: 161–76.

____. 2004 (first pub. 1850). 'Archaeological Theses', trans. M. Tiews and N. Roken, in *Modernism/modernity*, 11(1): 173.

Grafton, A. 1981. 'Prolegomena to Friedrich August Wolf', *Journal of the Warburg and Courtault Institutes*, 44: 101–29.

____. 1992. 'Germany and the West 1830–1900', in K.J. Dover (ed.), *Perceptions of the Ancient Greeks*. London: Blackwell.

Guidi, A. 1988. *Storia della Paletnologia*. Bari: Laterza.

Habicht, C. 1985. *Pausanias' Guide to Ancient Greece*. Berkeley: University of California Press.

Kaufmann, T. 2001. 'Antiquarianism, the History of Objects, and the History of Art before Winckelmann', *Journal of the History of Ideas*, 62(3): 523–41.

Manacorda D. 1982. 'Cento anni di ricerche archeologiche italiane: il dibattito sul metodo', *Quaderni di Storia*, 16: 85–119.

Marchand, S. 1996. *Down from Olympus: Classical Archaeology and Philhellenism in Germany 1750–1970*. Princeton: Princeton University Press.

___. 2002. 'Adolf Furtwängler in Olympia', in H. Kyrieleis (ed.), *Olympia 1875–2000. 125 Jahre Deutsche Ausgrabungen*, Mainz am Rehm: Philipp von Zabern, pp. 147–62.

Michaelis, A. 1879. *Storia dell'instituto archeologico germanico*. Rome.

Morris, I. 1994. 'Archaeologies of Greece', in I. Morris (ed.) *Classical Greece: Ancient Histories and Modern Archaeologies*. Cambridge: Cambridge University Press, 8–47.

___. 2000. *Archaeology as Cultural History: Words and Things in Iron Age Greece*. Oxford: Blackwell.

Mülke, M. 2003. *Wilamowitz und keine Ende. Wissenschaftsgeschichtechtliches Kolloquium Fondation Hardt*. Hildesheim: Olms.

Nimis, S. 1984. 'Fussnoten: das Fundament der Wissenschaft', *Arethusa*, 17(2): 105–35.

Porter, J. 2000. *Nietzsche and the Philology of the Future*. Stanford: Stanford University Press.

Renfrew, C. 1980. 'The Great Tradition versus the Great Divide: Archaeology as Anthropology?', *American Journal of Archaeology*, 84, 287–98.

Schnapp, A. 1997 (first published 1993). *The Discovery of the Past*, trans. I. Kinnes and G. Varndell. New York: Harry N. Abrams.

Shanks, M. 1996. *Classical Archaeology of Greece. Experiences of the Discipline*. Routledge: London.

Snodgrass, A. 1987. *Archaeology of Greece: The Present State and the Future Scope of a Discipline*. Berkeley: University of California Press.

Toracca, D. 1993. 'Giovanni Capellini: gli albori dell'archeologia preistorica in Italia', *Ricerche di Storia dell'Arte*, 50: 27–34.

Wilamowitz von, U. 1873. 'Scavi nelle Curte vicino a S. Maria di Capua', *Bullettino dell'Instituto di Corrispondenza Archeologica*, 35: 145–52.

___. 1875. *Analecta Euripidea*. Berlin: Borntraeger.

___. 1982 (first pub. 1921). *History of Classical Scholarship*, trans. by A. Harris, Baltimore: Johns Hopkins University Press.

___. 1930 (first pub. 1928). *My Recollections: 1848–1914*, trans. by G.C. Richards, London: Chatto & Windus.

___. 2000 (first pub. 1872). 'Future Philology! A Reply to the Birth of Tragedy by Friedrich Nietszche', *New Nietzsche Studies*, 4(1/2): 1–32.

Chapter 7

Methodological Reflections on the History of Excavation Techniques

Gisela Eberhardt

Abstract

The historiography of archaeological fieldwork has been dominated by tales of constant success and name-dropping. In contrast, I am going to look at the objectives of a contemporary approach to the history of excavation techniques. First, the article outlines two possible aims of such historical explorations: the recognition of past scientific patterns and, as a more intra-archaeological approach, the assessment of early excavation data. Secondly, it identifies aspects central to the investigation of procedural developments in archaeological fieldwork. These include, for example, the different ways in which specific ideas or material remains become objects of scientific interest, or the factors that shape and determine excavation methods.

Introduction

An important change in the perspective of the history of science came about in the 1980s with the so-called 'experimental turn', when the focus of study was extended from theories and ideas to experimental practice (Hagner 2001). Looking at the practical side of the discipline, archaeology was among the branches which sought to get to the bottom of their 'science in action' (Latour 1987). Yet, apart from a few exceptions, for a long time such reflections have usually been mere by-products of excavation manuals or reports (e.g. Echt 1984; Harris 1989; Roskams 2001). On the other hand, the development of archaeological methods in general has been presented as a story of linear success, a progression towards an ever better practice (e.g. Daniel 1981). Such stories sometimes even identify specific points in time when core elements of 'correct' digging were introduced or are set out as monuments to the memory of 'great archaeologists'.

However, to understand how excavation techniques have evolved and in what way these developments have shaped the disciplines of archaeology, it is necessary to develop a novel methodological framework for the study of the history of excavation procedures. Therefore, both objectives and possible routes of investigation need to be discussed. To bring the research on the history of archaeological practice up to date we need to consider first the aims that such a history could, and should, pursue. Secondly, we have to find out how to achieve these aims, i.e. how to investigate the issues that are considered important. In order to do this, it is necessary to look at the conditions which excavation techniques depend on in general. That means identifying the key factors that shape excavation methods and techniques, or rather identifying the factors that influence the decisions in favour of or against them. In a third step, the sources available for such research, for example excavation reports, will be reviewed.

As I will show in this chapter, it proves useful to adopt methodological approaches and questions from the historiography of other scientific fields, such as natural-scientific experimental systems, in order to write a valid history of archaeological practice.

Aims of a History of Excavation Techniques

Two crucial aims need to be addressed in this context.

Firstly, from a more general viewpoint as taken by the current history of science, the recognition of patterns in the production of scientific knowledge should be considered. According to the idea that every historical period has its specific variety of scientific alternatives, an appropriate science history ought to ask why and how specific solutions or procedures gain general acceptance while others do not. Or, in the words of Gavin Lucas (2001: 195): 'Is it simply a case of better techniques and knowledge today compared with a hundred years ago or is there perhaps something a little more complex occurring, a question of different ways of seeing?'.

One basic issue in this context is the question of how features or things gain attention which have either not been recognized before or have been regarded as being something different. Scandinavian shell-middens and Swiss lake dwellings had been identified at certain moments in time as being relics of human settlement activities. They had existed before and their contents in part been noted. Apparently change of perspective altered specific findings from being regarded as worthless rubbish into artefacts worth excavating, collecting and analysing. With the scientific establishment of geological stratification at the beginning of the nineteenth century 'the object' in general had become a chronologically independent source of information and had subsequently changed its historical relevance. Another example of 'discovery' in fieldwork took place at the end of the nineteenth century, when the significance of posthole structures was recognized. Again the question arises, how and why this happened at that specific point in time, what was it that made features suddenly 'observable' that had been seen but not identified before.

Apparently, there are certain changes in perspective that allow observations which could not have been made before. In the research on scientific experimental systems a similar phenomenon is called the 'transformation of natural objects into scientific model objects' (Hagner and Rheinberger 1998: 364). It has been shown for instance that particular organisms became reference points for biological 'problem packages' (and in turn began to shape these packages), such as in the early nineteenth-century investigations of bioelectricity and of nerve and muscle physiology which were centred around the frog. The crucial observation (in this case) is the change in the definition of the 'scientific objects': what happens is not simply the 'discovery' of something existent, but that a re-description of objects occurs. Even though archaeological practice differs markedly as there are no 'manipulated objects' like frog muscles involved, such transformations can still be observed. The discovery of animal bones and nut shells as evidence of human settlement or the identification of particular circular features as posthole structures represent a re-description of plant and animal remains or of soil discolorations into objects of scientific focus: the transformation of objects (one certainly could not call them natural) into scientific objects.

The second aim addresses a specifically archaeological question, the assessment of early excavation results: One feature peculiar to archaeology is, after all, that archaeologists cannot but draw on scientific results produced many decades ago, results produced using techniques we today regard as outdated.

While other scientific disciplines are able to re-examine and re-check earlier results by using new techniques and instruments, archaeologists have to rely on data that has been retrieved from a particular location site that cannot be examined anew. 'Since no two archaeological sites are the same, either in the whole or in detail, it is never possible to verify conclusively the results of one excavation by another, even on part of the same site, except in the broadest terms and sometimes not even in these' (Barker 1993: 13f.). Barker's idea of excavation as a strictly 'unrepeatable experiment' might, however, be questioned. Sites have occasionally been re-excavated to investigate digging strategies of former excavators, suggesting a way of reconstructing those aspects which excavators paid special attention to, what kinds of archaeological remains or features had not been considered in a previous excavation and are therefore left on the site (Lucas 2001: 201f.). One might even contradict the statement that no two sites are the same. Tilley (1989: 276) stated that the lack of unique sites leads to the very repetitiveness of archaeological data at a regional level: 'In many respects one Bronze Age grave or Roman villa reproduces many features of another.' He came to the conclusion that in terms of data collection, many excavations are unnecessary. In the present context, one could also deduce something else from that statement: due to the regularity of specific data, the value of results produced in earlier excavations might – up to a certain extent – be estimated by excavation of comparable sites.

Even if the two solutions described permit an easy yet comprehensive assessment of early excavation results, they would be impracticable on a larger scale for obvious reasons. It is necessary therefore to find other ways of assessing reports and stated results of past excavations.

It is by now widely agreed that, to a certain extent, we will 'find only what [we] expect to find' (Reynolds and Barber quoted in Roskams 2001: 35), or rather that we 'dig and 'see' in relationship to what has been recognized and written' (Evans 1989: 447). This seems to be an inevitable phenomenon of the excavation procedure. The selective nature of archaeological excavations implies that 'missing' data have to be taken into account ever since excavations have been carried out. The significance of posthole structures, as already mentioned, had not been recognized until the end of the nineteenth century and therefore these features were previously ignored. One may also cite the known fact that it used to be common practice by classical archaeologists to ignore or poorly document features from other epochs on their excavations (Lang 2002: 80, n. 74). Other examples demonstrate the decidedly selective recording of features on a site, e.g. leaving out those features that did not show sharp contours and could therefore not be measured precisely (Kiekebusch 1910: 416 and plates). Understanding the patterns which archaeological excavations followed at different moments in time may possibly help us to analyse what might be missing or misleading in early excavation results.

Factors Shaping Excavation Procedures

To investigate the two aims discussed above it is necessary to understand the conditions on which excavation techniques depend. Therefore, I will take a closer look at the key factors shaping excavation techniques, i.e. what influences the decisions in favour of or against specific techniques and procedures.

What does 'technique' mean precisely in this context? As Ferdière stated already in 1980, techniques of excavation, or the 'tools', as he calls them, are innumerable. Of course 'technique' does not signify specific tools or the way tools are, or should be, used. Rather, the term 'excavation technique' or 'excavation procedure' describes the variety of practical solutions to choose from, in order to capture as much as possible of the data considered important on a site (Ferdière 1980: 37; Roskams 2001: 34). Therefore it is obvious that besides technical factors like material conditions or size of the area to be excavated, the procedure of digging is shaped by the data that is considered to be important.

Four factors responsible for the choice of excavation procedures can be distinguished. First, *administrative aspects*, including conditions of manpower and material like size and composition of the team as well as financial resources, time frames, etc.

Secondly, the *physical characteristics of the site or feature* (or rather assumptions about the physical characteristics of the site), for example its size and topography, the structure of the soil, or the different kinds of archaeological features likely to be encountered.

Thirdly, *preconceptions regarding the character of the site or feature under excavation.* As is generally known, the assumptions made by excavators as to what they are dealing with have a considerable influence on the excavation procedure. Obviously the procedure would differ greatly for a site assumed to be a cemetery from one assumed to be a settlement. Specific details of such preconceptions either draw on information from historical sources or emerge from the comparison with supposedly similar sites. This is illustrated by the German excavations at Olympia in the 1870s, which relied on the descriptions of the classical author Pausanias. As early as 1852, Ernst Curtius had drawn a ground plan of ancient Olympia according to Pausanias' portrayal (Curtius 1852). Twenty years later, in excavating the site, the primary intention was to uncover the buildings and objects of art which Pausanias had depicted (Borbein 2002: 167). The excavation strategy was laid out accordingly: trenches were dug leading out from the temple of Zeus.

In connection with the preconceptions that emerge from the comparison with supposedly similar sites, the appearance of regular 'feature fashions' can be observed following exciting new discoveries, as in the search for lake dwellings in Northern Germany. These excavations were carried out in the nineteenth century in the wake of the identification of Swiss lake dwellings as settlement relics. A 'lake-dwelling-fever' set in, and lakes in north-east Germany were surveyed to find the self-same relics as in Switzerland in order to prove the existence of Prussian lake dwellings (Lisch 1862). Having found the sought-after pieces of evidence, the connection between the 'prototype feature' and the local feature was satisfactorily stated. Many of the reports and statements published at that time show that the main objective was not the examination of identified locations or sites, rather, the aim was actually to locate that specific kind of site. Potential areas, like lakes, were checked for initial evidence – usually wooden posts on the lakebeds (Lisch 1864: 120; Virchow 1869: 404). A closer investigation only took place if additional corresponding discoveries were made. Organic relics (such as the bones of specific animals, or hazelnuts) were selectively analysed, whereupon one concluded that the result – the feature observed – was the same that had been found in Switzerland. As a consequence of this procedure, each and every trace of an earlier human presence in lake areas was thought to have originated with or at least be connected to prehistoric lake-dwelling people of the Swiss mould. Only a few years later, most of the sites thus interpreted were identified as being of Slavic age.

Fourthly, *professional and intellectual backgrounds of the excavators or executive staff.* Education, individual interests and academic relations as well as individual aspects such as skilfullness or personal discipline strongly influence how particular excavations are carried out. They also influence the development and spread of digging methods. Different professional backgrounds may decisively influence the researchers main focus or documentary style. Contacts between archaeologists further the mutual exchange of insights and processes. Therefore, the patterns of communications and the flow of informations between individuals and institutions should be investigated.

As seen above, archaeological features considered to be exceptional or even sensational help to give rise to scientific paradigms. This takes place by personal contact between excavators all over Europe, especially in the early years. Famous sites, such as the lake dwellings or the Scandinavian shell-middens already mentioned were very popular within specialist circles and thereby fostered the implementation of specific stratigraphic or scientific views which were linked to corresponding excavation techniques.

To cite an example: Rudolf Virchow, the German physician and prehistorian, was very much influenced by the idea of the stratigraphy of archaeological deposits ever since the construction of a shell-midden had been explained to him by Thomsen at Copenhagen. Virchow wrote: 'At the Museum of Antiquities at Copenhagen in 1859 Thomsen in his old age showed me the section of such an old kitchen deposit [...]. Layer lies above layer, just as in a natural deposit of the earth's crust, but scattered in between lie tools from the Stone Age made of horn, bone, flint, ceramics as well as coal and ashes. Therefore, one cannot help but conclude, that tribes of the stone age have lived here [...] and have thrown the captured material, the kill of hunting and fishing into huge heaps, heaps which have finally [...] taken on a nearly geological appearance.' (Virchow 1866: 19f., author's translation)

Virchow wrote this in 1866. As early as 1870 he himself started to carry out excavations with regard to stratigraphical analyses in the areas surrounding Berlin (Virchow 1870). His early short reports on domestic archaeology correspond to his statements on Troy concerning stratigraphical order and the chronological assignment of layers by artefacts, giving the impression that it was he who first recognized the usefulness of stratigraphical observations for settlement exploration and strongly influenced the intense stratigraphical work carried out at Troy (Virchow 1881; see also Herrmann 1992: 96; Jähne 2001: 332).

It is obvious and illustrated by the examples given that the factors listed above cannot be viewed separately. Along the lines of the historical approach to practices in physics, all the elements being in any way part of an experimental system – such as research objects, theories, instruments, social contexts etc. – are seen to 'add up to amalgams of every conceivable gradation' (Hagner and Rheinberger 1998: 359). However, the problem of exactly how to investigate particular elements and the extent of their activity within the working process seems to remain unresolved, if these elements are not be sorted out of the 'amalgams' just mentioned.

In addition, it became evident that research on disciplinary practices has to be framed within a specific time and its context (ibid. 358; Gillberg and Jensen 2004: 3f.). In particular with regard to its more abstract contents, such a history of technique would be worthless without an historical contextualisation. For it does not simply aim at the reconstruction of technical details, but the better understanding of scientific practical work and its patterns. Jensen (2000) for example, has argued that a significant change in the attitude towards objects occurred in the mid-nineteenth century due to a new attitude towards the human body, while Roskams (2001: 19), in treating another question, views the increase of geological and archaeological data during that epoch as a consequence of the Industrial Revolution and major drainage schemes.

Primary Sources of Data

The primary sources of data for a historical investigation of excavation techniques are undoubtedly all kinds of documents from past excavations, like published excavation reports and user's manuals on excavation procedures as well as fieldnotes in books, on context sheets, in letters, etc. Here we again cite the investigation of scientific experiments, where unpublished sources such as laboratory notebooks, letters and interviews are increasingly regarded as suitable sources in reconstructing past procedures (Hagner and Rheinberger 1998: 358). The historiography of archaeological practice also seems to tend in that direction (e.g. Easton 1990: 435).

Still, the question of how to treat the source material is open to discussion. The two aims discussed, i.e. the patterns of knowledge production on the one hand and the assessment of data from past excavations on the other, require slightly different approaches to the source material. Or, rather, they require that the investigation of particular elements be given different significances.

On the second of the two issues, the assessment of excavation results, efforts have been made in several archaeological fields to meticulously re-examine early excavation reports or even reconstruct processes set out in early reports with a view to assessing given data (e.g. Easton 2002; Wanzek 2001). The documents consulted in such studies are supposed mainly to help in examining techniques and procedures that are either explained explicitly or can be reconstructed from given images and descriptions.

Turning to the investigation of knowledge patterns in a more general sense, the formal structure of excavation documents itself should also be explored. Viewed as objects of inquiry in their own right, the forms and rhetorics of texts and the structure of images, i.e. of drawings and photographs, will provide substantial insight into fieldwork processes from a historical perspective.

Yet only few examples of such structural analyses of excavation documents can be found. Language and style of reports have been analysed in order to distinguish the 'contextualized and contingent' early reports from the 'dry description of a self-evident' of today (Hodder 1989). Idiosyncratic representations of plans and sections executed by nineteenth- and early twentieth-century excavators and the disciplinary consequences of individual differences have also been discussed (Piggott 1965, 1978; Lucas 2001: 43f., 208, 210).

Returning to investigations of other discipline's practices, we will again find stimulating approaches to the issue. Concerning geological illustrations, for example, it has been stated that artistic representation is a visual language, which 'has to be learned and which changes over time' (Rudwick 1976: 151). Rudwick has shown in this context that mineralogical maps were merely structural in the eighteenth century. In the nineteenth century the necessity to illustrate causal explanations produced more and more visual expressions of geological *processes* (ibid. 160–62), which had a lasting and significant influence on geological representations. Another inspiring example for a deeper understanding of documentary modes concerns the increasing use of technical equipment in order to avoid human impact in the representation of scientific results. The camera has been identified as a characteristic of that idea of 'mechanical objectivity' in the nineteenth century. In conflict with the generally accepted view, Daston (2001) showed that the significant preference of photography to drawing was due to the authenticity of the images rather than to their exactness. Colour drawings could be much more natural and rich in detail than the occasionally blurred photographs. But the way the camera works was more compatible with the idea of mechanical objectivity, as it created the illusion of an image produced without human influence. This could even extend to the point where a higher level of accuracy was sacrificed to objectivity (ibid: 154).

Conclusions

As I have shown, two aims can be distinguished for the historical exploration of excavation techniques. On the one hand, we can pursue the investigation of procedural developments as a historical phenomenon. On the other hand, a mainly technical approach is possible in order to assess the outcome of past excavations. While the latter kind of investigation is limited to intra-disciplinary interest, the first kind represents an extensive historiographical view and therefore requires more complex modes of research, including broader historical contextualisation as well as formal analyses of documents. I have suggested the adoption of methodological approaches and questions from the historiography of other scientific fields to meet these specific challenges. In both cases, several factors determining the decisions for specific procedures in archaeological excavations must be considered, such as aspects of material resources and characteristics of the site as well as of pre-existing concepts and the biographies of excavators. Yet it remains to be explored whether the cited demand for an investigation of such elements of practical work as a compound, as an inseparable combination, also applies to the research of the history of excavation techniques, and if so, by what means could the influence of particular elements be properly assessed.

References

Barker, P. 1993. *Techniques of Archaeological Excavation*, 2nd edn. London: Batsford.

Borbein, A.H. 2002. 'Olympia als Experimentierfeld archäologischer Methoden', in H. Kyrieleis (ed.), *Olympia 1875–2000. 125 Jahre Deutsche Ausgrabungen. Internationales Symposium, Berlin 9.-11. November 2000.* Mainz/Rhein: Philipp von Zabern, pp. 163–76.

Curtius, E. 1852. *Olympia. Ein Vortrag im wissenschaftlichen Vereine zu Berlin am 10. Januar gehalten.* Berlin: Hertz.

Daniel, G. 1981. *A Short History of Archaeology.* London: Thames and Hudson.

Daston, L. 2001. 'Die Kultur der wissenschaftlichen Objektivität', in M. Hagner (ed.), *Ansichten der Wissenschaftsgeschichte.* Frankfurt/Main: Fischer, pp. 137–58.

Easton, D.F. 1990. 'Reconstructing Schliemann's Troy', in W.M. Calder and J. Cobet (eds), *Heinrich Schliemann nach hundert Jahren.* Frankfurt/Main: Klostermann.

——— . 2002. *Schliemann's Excavations at Troia 1870–1873.* Mainz/Rhein: Philipp von Zabern.

Echt, R. 1984. *Kamid el-Loz. 5: Die Stratigraphie.* Bonn: Habelt.

Evans, C. 1989. 'Archaeology and Modern Times: Bersu's Woodbury 1938 & 1939', *Antiquity* 63: 436–50.

Ferdière, A. 1980. 'La fouille, pour quoi faire?', in A. Schnapp (ed.), *L'archéologie aujourd'hui.* Paris: Hachette.

Gillberg, A. and Jensen, O.W. 2004. *Five Hundred Years of Archaeological Practice in Sweden.* Gotarc Serie D: Arkeologiska Rapporter 54. Presented at the conference 'Histories of Archaeology', Göteborg, 17–19 June 2004.

Hagner, M. 2001. 'Ansichten der Wissenschaftsgeschichte', in M. Hagner (ed.), *Ansichten der Wissenschaftsgeschichte.* Frankfurt/Main: Fischer, pp. 7–39.

——— . and H.-J. Rheinberger. 1998. 'Experimental Systems, Objects of Investigation, and Spaces of Representation', in M. Heidelberger and F. Steinle (eds), *Experimental Essays – Versuche zum Experiment.* Baden-Baden: Nomos-Verlags-Gesellschaft, pp. 355–73.

Harris, E.C. 1989. *Principles of Archaeological Stratigraphy*, 2nd edn. London: Academic Press.

Herrmann, J. 1992. 'Fragestellungen und Forschungsprobleme Schliemanns und die zeitgenössische Archäologie' in J. Herrmann (ed.), *Heinrich Schliemann. Grundlagen und Ergebnisse moderner Archäologie 100 Jahre nach Schliemanns Tod.* Berlin: Akademie-Verlag, pp. 93–102.

Hodder, I. 1989. 'Writing Archaeology: Site Reports in Context', *Antiquity* 63: 268–74.

Jähne, A., 'Heinrich Schliemann. Troiaausgräber wider Willen', in Archäologisches Landesmuseum Baden-Württemberg et al. (eds): *Troia. Traum und Wirklichkeit. [Begleitband zur Ausstellung, Troia – Traum und Wirklichkeit'. 17. März – 17. Juni 2001, Stuttgart].* Stuttgart: Theiss, pp. 330–37.

Jensen, O.W. 2000. 'Between Body and Artefacts. Merleau-Ponty and Archaeology', in C. Holtorf and H. Karlsson (eds), *Philosophy and Archaeological Practice. Perspectives for the 21st Century.* Göteborg: Bricoleur Press, pp. 53–62.

Kiekebusch, A. 1910. 'Das vorgeschichtliche Wohnhaus von Buch bei Berlin', *Brandenburgia* 18: 409–30.

Lang, F. 2002. *Klassische Archäologie. Eine Einführung in Methode, Theorie und Praxis.* Basel: Francke.

Latour, B. 1987. *Science in Action.* Cambridge: Harvard University Press.

Lisch, F. 1862. 'Pfahlbauten in Meklenburg', *Jahrbücher des Vereins für meklenburgische Geschichte und Alterthumskunde* 27: 171–72.

——— . 1864. 'Höhlenwohnungen und Pfahlbauten in Meklenburg', *Jahrbücher des Vereins für meklenburgische Geschichte und Alterthumskunde* 29: 115–33.

Lucas, G. 2001. *Critical Approaches to Archaeological Fieldwork.* New York: Routledge.

Piggott, S. 1965. 'Archaeological Draughtmanship. Part 1. Principles and Prospectives', *Antiquity* 39: 165–76.

——— . 1976. *Ruins in a Landscape: Essays in Antiquarianism.* Edinburgh: Edinburgh University Press.

Roskams, S. 2001. *Excavation.* Cambridge: Cambridge University Press.

Rudwick, M.J.S. 1976. 'The Emergence of a Visual Language for Geological Science 1760–1840', *History of Science* 14: 149–95.

Tilley, C. 1989. 'Excavation of a Theatre', *Antiquity* 63: 275–80.

Virchow, R. 1866. 'Ueber Hünengräber und Pfahlbauten', in R. Virchow and Fr. von Holtzendorff (eds), *Sammlung gemeinverständlicher wissenschaftlicher Vorträge.* Berlin: Lüderitz, pp. 1–36.

——— . 1869. 'Die Pfahlbauten im nördlichen Deutschland', *Zeitschrift für Ethnologie, Anthropologie und Urgeschichte* 1: 401–16.

———— . 1870. 'Über alte Höhlenwohnungen auf der Bischofsinsel bei Königswalde', *Zeitschrift für Ethnologie, Anthropologie und Urgeschichte* 2: 470–80.

———— . 1881. 'Vorrede', in Schliemann, H. *Ilios. Stadt und Land der Trojaner.* Leipzig: F.A. Brockhaus, pp. 11–19.

Wanzek, B. 2001. *Die bronzezeitliche Siedlung in Berlin-Buch. Geschichte einer Ausgrabung und Ausstellung.* Berlin: Staatliche Museen zu Berlin – Preußischer Kulturbesitz.

Chapter 8
'More than a Village'

On the Medieval Countryside as an Archaeological Field of Study

Emma Bentz

Abstract

This paper discusses the emergence, establishment and further development of the medieval countryside as a field of archaeological research, with the aid of examples and case studies drawn from different parts of Europe. The case studies all date from the high and late Middle Ages (ca. tenth to fifteenth centuries AD) and were excavated intermittently between 1930 and 1990. The excavation of the deserted medieval village of Hohenrode, Germany (in 1935– 1937), will serve here as an example of the work undertaken thus far. Original field documentation as well as published material is used in order to discuss the changing technical, disciplinary and ideological conditions. These three conditions form the basis of the analysis conducted here: the technical conditions aim at discussing the development of excavation methods, and notably the relationship between medieval and prehistoric settlement archaeology. The disciplinary conditions address how and why did medieval rural settlements became part of the archaeological agenda in different countries. The last ideological condition relates to the perception of the (medieval) countryside in the surrounding society: how did the Zeitgeist at certain times influence the interest politics and people showed in these remains? It is argued that only by studying the three mentioned aspects all together, can one understand the dynamics of medieval rural settlement archaeology as a field of study, from the early days up to the present.

Introduction

Since the first half of the twentieth century there has been an increasing interest in the archaeological study of medieval rural settlements in different parts of Europe, resulting in a steadily growing amount of excavations and publications. At present, the archaeology of medieval rural settlements is considered an established field of study, represented both at conferences and in the university teaching of medieval archaeology. However, the interest in these remains has fluctuated over time and place. From the first glimpses of an antiquarian interest, seen through written reports and maps of deserted medieval settlements in late medieval and early post-medieval times to today's large-scale excavations, the field has undergone considerable changes. These changes include the establishment of the field as such, as well as the development of excavation techniques suitable for this category of sites. This chapter seeks to discuss an approach to the study of this field of research, with the aid of examples and case studies. It is argued that by studying the technical, disciplinary and ideological conditions prevailing at different times, it is possible to explain and understand the emergence of and further changes to this field of research. Sweden serves as a point of departure, but the wider context is of importance to the study, including other European countries, such as Denmark, Germany, England and the Czech Republic.

A broad, main question for this study, which also forms part of an ongoing Ph.D.,[1] could be formulated as follows: in what terms is it possible to explain and understand the emergence, further development and establishment of the medieval countryside as an archaeological field of research, and further, what consequences does this have for practice and research today? Does the archaeology of the medieval countryside follow the beaten track, or are there any visible tendencies towards disintegration or a reorientation? The overall aim of the study is to understand and visualize when, how and why the medieval rural settlements received the attention of archaeologists and how this interest changed further. By looking back on the history of the field in a time of expansion, it is hoped that the ongoing study will lead to a better understanding of today's premises for the practice of medieval rural archaeology, and that this will lead to the formulation of new questions based on the archaeological material.

Chronological and Spatial Frameworks

The period under study encompasses the twentieth century up to the present day, with some deviation back in time, which I consider necessary in order to discuss the roots of an interest in the medieval rural settlements. In order to discuss and exemplify the emergence and development of an archaeological interest in these remains, case studies have been selected. Material for the case studies comes from Sweden, Denmark and Germany, but some more are to be added. In this paper the deserted medieval village of Hohenrode (Germany), excavated by Paul Grimm, will serve as an example (Fig. 8.1).

The time frames constructed for medieval archaeology as a subject result in different chronological boundaries which vary from country to country. In order to overcome these problems I have chosen to work with a wider definition of the medieval period, from c. 500 to c. 1700 AD, partly corresponding to Jacques Le Goff's extended definition of the Middle Ages (Le Goff 1988). From a Swedish perspective, this means including also remains that according to the Swedish definition of the Middle Ages (c. 1050–1550 AD) would belong to the younger Iron Age. The main emphasis of the study does, however, lay within the centuries 1000–1500 AD. It is important to stress, though, that – as in the case of the sites selected for case studies – it is not primarily the dating of these remains that are of importance for the ongoing work, but rather *how* these remains have been treated scientifically within the frames of medieval rural archaeology.

When speaking of *medieval rural settlements* and *medieval rural archaeology*, I primarily include the different types of settlements connected with the peasant's dwellings that can be identified archaeologically and related to the medieval period. This means focusing primarily on different types of villages as well as on single farmsteads. Other features of the medieval countryside, such as field systems, manors, moted sites and castles, have been to a large extent excluded from the study. However, the definition of what can be said to make up the field of medieval rural archaeology has changed over the years. The initial focus on the single deserted farmstead at the beginning of the century has been partly replaced by the study of whole landscapes and interconnections between different features in the landscape. This broadening perspective emphasizes the dynamic and constant renegotiations of the field, and it shows that in order to fully understand what can be said to have constituted the field at different times, sometimes one also has to take into account other features in the landscape. From this it also becomes clear that when speaking of medieval rural archaeology as a field of research today, one of its main characteristics is its diversity. This is emphasized by the fact that the study of medieval rural settlements is also conducted within other subjects, such as history or geography. This is a fact that should not be forgotten in the kind of analysis presented here.

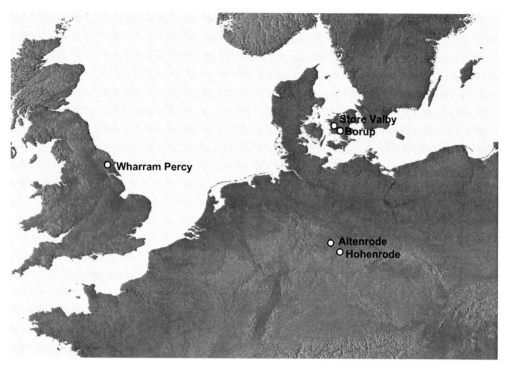

Fig. 8.1 Map showing the location of the sites mentioned in the text.

Three Conditions: Technical, Disciplinary and Ideological

In order to discuss the main questions posed in the work presented here, a qualitative approach has been chosen. The aim of working with a limited number of case studies is to understand and illustrate which processes together contribute to the formation of the field under discussion. The basic source material for answering these questions consists of documentation from the fieldwork, as well as from the post-excavation work (i.e. field plans, photographs, drawings, field diaries, correspondence, newspaper articles and publications). The case studies are considered in the light of three conditions, namely technical, disciplinary and ideological, as presented below. With the aid of sub-questions connected with the three conditions, it is hoped that they will contribute to answering the overall questions posed in the thesis. Together the three conditions cover both internal and external factors, both of which have played a role in the emergence and establishment of the field under discussion. In the next section preliminary results from the case study of Hohenrode will be presented in order to give an example of how work has been conducted so far.

Technical Conditions

The *technical* conditions relate primarily to the fieldwork and the process of excavation at certain times. Which technical approaches have been applied on the rural settlements, and how does this practice change over the decades? What makes practice change? In connection with these questions, I would like to mention the importance of networks for the spread of ideas. The meeting between Danish ethnologist Axel Steensberg and British researchers in 1948 can serve as an example. As a guest of the British Council, invited by the economic historian M. M. Postan, Steensberg spent a one-month study visit in England. At a meeting in Cambridge, where some of the persons who were later to form the Deserted Medieval Village Research Group[2] were present,

Steensberg presented his methods of excavation. With experiences gained during excavations in Denmark (e.g. Store Valby, Zealand), Steensberg introduced the British colleagues to the technique of open area excavation on rural medieval sites (Fig. 8.1). Similar techniques had been practised in the British Isles before, but never to that extent on medieval rural sites.[3] The meeting in Cambridge resulted in British-Danish collaboration, including several study visits by British archaeologists to sites excavated by Steensberg in Denmark. Among others, archaeologist Jack Golson went to Denmark in 1952 to try out the open area method, before it was gradually introduced at the Wharram Percy excavations in Britain. Later, archaeologist John Hurst joined Steensberg for field work in Borup (Fig. 8.1).

This episode is a good illustration of what Richard Bradley has called *craft traditions* within field archaeology (Bradley 1997: 66). A certain way of seeing, in this specific case equal to Steensberg's ability to formulate an excavation technique suitable to the thin and compact cultural layers of the medieval countryside settlements, is introduced and taken over by other archaeologists as a result of personal contacts. In this specific case, the contacts resulted in study visits to Denmark, where British archaeologists took part in Steensberg's excavations in order to gain insight in the methods applied. Finally, the method was introduced in a new context: medieval rural sites in England. Although one can question the almost 'sacred' status given to the Danish-British meeting and its aftermath in existing publications, it cannot be denied that these and other personal contacts were of a major importance for the spread of ideas, and through this, for the formation of the field as a whole. Interestingly enough, it is not only later generations of researchers that emphasize the importance of these contacts, but also those directly involved (see for example Hurst 1971: 77; Hurst 1986: 8; Steensberg Østergaard 1974: 188). Their frequent mentioning of this episode in different publications does illustrate well how the history of an archaeological field is actively created, and how certain episodes can after a while acquire mythical qualities.

Furthermore, one can ask which traces of the medieval settlements are visible to the archaeologist at different times, and how does this relate to the excavation techniques in use? The relation between the techniques being used and the questions that one wishes to answer is also being discussed. This also relates to the disciplinary conditions, since in the early days of medieval rural archaeology the questions were often formulated by people other than archaeologists, such as historians or geographers. This is a pattern visible also within other branches of medieval archaeology. What does the relation between prehistoric settlement archaeology and the archaeology of medieval rural settlements look like? For the study of the early days it is important to relate the investigation of deserted medieval villages to the prehistoric settlement archaeology in general, studying similarities and distinctions. Where can you draw the line between settlement archaeology for prehistoric and medieval times? In which way do they differ? Is it the amount of written sources or the absence or presence of cultural layers that have motivated a distinction, or is it simply an unnatural border, existing as a result of university discipline specialization? For the later decades the impact of machine-stripping, advanced digital documentation, contextual methods of excavation and the so-called reflexive field archaeology are discussed in my work. In which way have these changes affected our idea of the medieval countryside? Finally, one should not forget that investigating medieval rural sites does not only include the moment of excavation. Surveying whole landscapes and mapping deserted medieval villages was an early practice, and still is, in all of the studied countries. Further, aerial photographs played an important role in the early days, perhaps most notably in England. These different approaches to the deserted villages also reflect the broad spectra of subjects that have had, and have, an interest in these remains.

Disciplinary Conditions

The second condition is the *disciplinary*. Here the focus is on the main figures in the field as well as on the discipline of medieval archaeology itself. Who were the early archaeologists within this subject area? What did their networks and contacts look like? What background did they have, and what were their motives for excavating these remains? As already mentioned, several of the early excavators had backgrounds other than a strictly archaeological one. How did this fact influence the way they viewed the archaeological material? When the questions are formulated by, for example, historians, what does this mean for the relation between the source material of the historian and the archaeologist? Underlying this question is a discussion on the relationship between material culture and the written word, a much debated topic within medieval archaeology today (see, for example, Austin 1990; Andrén 1998; Moreland 2001).

A concrete example of how the relation between written sources and archaeological material can lead to biased conclusions is the case of Wharram Percy in England (Fig. 8.1). This project, initiated in the 1950s and finished in 1990, has been one of the standard textbook examples of the archaeological investigation of deserted medieval settlements. Furthermore, it has played a fundamental role in the formation of this field of study as well as for the establishment of British medieval archaeology as a whole (Beresford and Hurst 1990). During the decades, interpretations of the quality of the buildings have changed remarkably. Until the 1980s, John Hurst argued, on the basis of what he interpreted as flimsy and non-durable remains of dwellings and other buildings, for the impermanence of these medieval buildings (Hurst 1971: 96, 122, Hurst 1984: 97–98). His interpretations were influenced by written sources and coloured by a common picture of the peasants as a group exposed to non-secure and quickly changing conditions, resulting in impermanent constructed dwellings (e. g. Hurst 1984: 98). Later reinterpretations made by Stuart Wrathmell in the late 1980s has shown that the dwellings in Wharram Percy were durable cruck constructions, easy to maintain and therefore likely to survive over generations (Wrathmell 1989). In fairness, it should be added that John Hurst and Maurice Beresford were convinced by Wrathmell's arguments. This is illustrated in the popular publication on the excavations, where several pictures show houses in Wharram Percy reconstructed as cruck buildings (Beresford and Hurst 1990). The changing opinions over time regarding the quality of the buildings illustrate the importance that a field of study is confident enough to formulate its own questions. Only with an insight into the possibilities and limitations of its own source material, is it possible to cooperate successfully with other disciplines. In the case of Wharram Percy, one circumstance contributing to the inaccuracy of the early interpretations could also be explained by the lack of comparative material, leading to insecurity about the potential of the archaeological remains. But the fact remains that the archaeological study of the medieval countryside has been heavily influenced by other disciplines, and that this sometimes has led to a lack of independent questions from an archaeological point of view.

This imbalance has been commented upon by Grenville Astill, among others (Astill 1993: 131). In a retrospective article on medieval rural archaeology in Britain, Astill states that the development within this field seems to have had more to do with the changing relationships over time between archaeologists and representatives from other disciplines, than with developments within the archaeological field itself (Astill 1993: 131). It is clear that the field under discussion has many diverse roots and spheres of influence, the situation varying from country to country. Today, the archaeological study of medieval rural settlements may have its tightest connection with the discipline of medieval archaeology, but this has not always been the case. One obvious point to make is that at the time of the earliest excavations, medieval archaeology did not exist as an independent university discipline. Archaeological excavations were conducted within the frames of other subjects. Therefore, in order to understand how the field was shaped and changed gradually over time, it is of vital importance to take other disciplines, such as human geography, economic history, history and ethnology, into account when trying to formulate how the study of medieval rural settlements later became a part of the archaeological research agenda.

When discussing disciplinary conditions, again the notion of networks is of importance. Not only changes in excavation techniques can be studied by the reconstruction of networks, but also other aspects. By studying dedications, acknowledgements, references, conference and excursion participation and much more, an insight is gained in what contacts looked like at certain times and, thus, gives information about who and what could be said to constitute a field at a certain time. Bonds between persons, institutes and countries become visible and can contribute to the reconstruction of the field as a whole. There are numerous examples of these kinds of interconnections within the early phase of medieval rural archaeology. John Hurst contributing to Paul Grimm's festschrift in 1969 and the frequent mentioning in the British literature of Steensberg and his excavation techniques, already commented on above, are only two examples out of many (Hurst 1969).

Ideological Conditions

The *ideological* conditions constitute the last perspective. Here the socio-economic factors are incorporated, such as legislation as well as more mental aspects on perception of the (medieval) countryside at different times. When and why did it become important to protect the remains under discussion? What were the arguments and who were the actors? Concerning the more personal, intellectual aspects, it is of interest to examine which image people in general had of the countryside at a certain time (as seen in books, art – and later on – television). In Sweden, as well as in other parts of Europe, an image of the farmer as something very ancient and national emerged around the turn of the nineteenth century. How was this used in the construction of an identity and self-image in different countries? Are these ideas and notions also visible in the archaeological interpretations? Is it, for example, a coincidence that an interest in the medieval settlement remains arose at the same time as the countryside in many parts of Europe became depopulated, and the countryside of times long gone is being looked back upon with a touch of nostalgia and romanticism?

Working with Case Studies: The Hohenrode Example

Today Hohenrode is a quiet place where the medieval village remains are visible as conserved stone fundaments in the middle of the forest, but it was the subject of intense activity in three excavation campaigns between 1935 and 1937 (Figs. 8.2 and 8.3). The excavations were conducted by archaeologist Paul Grimm and local day-labourers, on behalf of the *Landesanstalt für Volkheitskunde* in Halle (today: *Landesmuseum für Vorgeschichte*). During the excavation seasons, remains dating from the tenth to fourteenth century AD were uncovered (Grimm 1939) (Fig. 8.3). Hohenrode frequently occurs in various historiographical texts of mainly introductory and overviewing nature, in Germany as well is in other countries. In these texts, Hohenrode is often mentioned in the context of the earliest excavations of this kind of remains or as representing the beginning or starting point for this field of study in Central Europe (Hurst 1971: 77; Janssen 1988: 14; Gerrard 2003: 77). Going through Grimm's documentation of the site as well as written statements made by him, it is clear that Grimm himself viewed his own work as an extension of prehistoric settlement archaeology (Grimm 1939: introduction). He was well aware of the fact that he did something new (i.e. conducting the first large-scale excavation of medieval remains with prehistoric methods), but it obviously did not cross his mind at that time that this would contribute to the emergence of a new archaeological field. Only much later he was given the epithet as one of the 'founding fathers' of medieval archaeology in Germany, an image that is still being reproduced today, and which – it should be added – holds some truth.

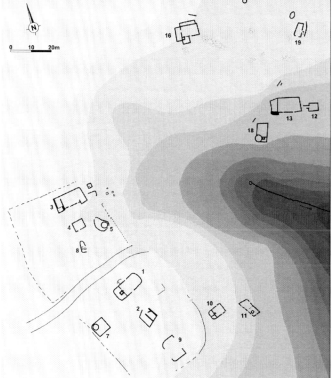

Fig. 8.2 Photo showing dwelling house number 1 in Hohenrode, as seen from the west. Photo by the author (May 2004).

Fig. 8.3 Plan of the deserted medieval village at Hohenrode, Germany. After Grimm (1939) with modifications.

From my point of view, Grimm's main contribution in Hohenrode is not so much that he conducted one of the earliest excavations of a high- and late medieval deserted village. This is in fact also not entirely true. One year before the excavations in Hohenrode – 1934 – Grimm himself made a small-scale investigation of Altenrode, another deserted medieval village site in the vicinity of Hohenrode (Fig. 8. 1) (Grimm 1934, 1935). Although the excavation in Altenrode was conducted by much the same methods and with the same aims as later in Hohenrode, this excavation has never reached the same status, and has – as far as I know – never been mentioned in any research oriented texts. The part of Grimm's work that nowadays seems visionary to me, when it comes to Altenrode and Hohenrode, is the fact that he realised the possible contribution of archaeology in the discussion of these abandoned settlements, a field of study traditionally dominated by historians and geographers and their questions.

An analysis of Grimm's work in Hohenrode, using the previously discussed three conditions as a starting point, is in progress elsewhere. Here I would only like to put forward a few points that can be made at this stage of the analysis. Relating to the disciplinary conditions it can be said that Grimm did not solely commit his career to the archaeological investigation of *Wüstungen* (German: deserted, mainly medieval, settlements). The excavations in Hohenrode rather should be regarded as expressions of a general interest in settlement archaeology, independently of the archaeological period to which the excavated remains belonged. This interest is mirrored in Grimm's dissertation, which is a study dedicated to the settlement history of the Unterharz region (Grimm 1930). Even if the results of the excavations in Hohenrode were encouraging, Grimm himself never again excavated any medieval village sites. After the Second World War he came to focus on early medieval castles and fortifications, parallel to his interest in the Neolithic period, which had been the topic of his *Habilitation* in 1938 (Grimm 1938a).

Turning to the ideological conditions, the fact that the excavations in Hohenrode were conducted during the Nazi era in Germany has to be investigated further. How did these circumstances influence Grimm's work? What was his personal standpoint, and is this something that can be seen in his interpretations? Grimm became a member of the Nazi party in 1933 (Eberle 2002: 373). How should one interpret this fact? Furthermore, the results of the excavations in Hohenrode were published in the popular monthly magazine *Germanen-Erbe* (Grimm 1938b). This magazine was edited by archaeologist Hans Reinerth on behalf of the *Reichsbund für Deutsche Vorgeschichte*, and can be considered a propaganda tool, supporting the Nazi ideology (Hassmann 2000: 79, 92). It is an interesting fact that this reference does not appear in the bibliography of Grimm's publications, compiled at the time of his 70th birthday in 1978 (Heinrich 1978). Neither does this article occur in an extended bibliography published after his death in 1993 (Heinrich 1994). This situation, as well as other aspects of the excavation of Hohenrode in fascist times, will require further investigation. Only upon this can unambiguous conclusions be reached on how ideological conditions might have influenced Grimm's work in the 1930s.

I have chosen to work solely with published, large-scale excavations where coherent structures are visible and documented, as in the case of Hohenrode. In this context I would like to comment on the use of case studies for studying a field of research. As others have already pointed out, even in younger publications of historiographical character, it is the same persons and places that tend to occur as examples (Gillberg 1995: 20). At first it might seem like a contradiction to criticize earlier writers of historiographical texts for constantly using, and thereby reproducing, the same excavations and persons in their texts, and thus creating an image of a coherent and united past – only then to use them oneself. I would argue, that looking at these excavations is in fact necessary, in order to revise and understand a field and its historiography. By asking why some excavations have been selected to represent the field's or a discipline's past while others have not, you can gain insight into how a field is created and the structures of power within a certain subject area. It then becomes very clear how the history of research and the research itself tend to produce and reproduce each other. Since every generation of researchers are acquainted with these rather homogenous representations on the history of a field (often written by authorities within the field), they all have to relate to this image in one way or another. The way they choose to interpret these texts is important for the future directions of the field. I would argue, therefore, that there is a point in selecting some of these frequently occurring excavations and persons, even in a new study of this kind.

The main focus of the study presented here lies on the constant interaction between the archaeological study of the medieval countryside and contemporary society, as well as on the events within the archaeological discipline. These interplays could be said to construct both the frames and conditions for this field, which is studied with the three above mentioned conditions as a methodological starting point. A discussion underlying this analysis concerns questions about what could be said to make up a field, the possibilities to trace some kind of origin for a field, and when it is possible to regard a field as established in different countries. These questions also relate to how the histories of a field should be viewed and presented. Writing the history of a discipline, a person or a field was little problematized in earlier days, but since the late 1980s, the traditional way of writing historiographical texts has been the subject of criticism within the archaeological discipline (Scandinavian examples are, among others, Brattli 1993; Svestad 1995). The main objections concern the traditional way of presenting complex and often unpredictable events as coherent and straightforward phenomena. The underlying perspective is in these cases an evolutionary one, assuming constant progress and improvements on the way to complete the puzzle of prehistory.

I sympathise with the notion of a field or a discipline as something more complex than just following a straight and unquestionable development, and will try to approach the archaeology of medieval settlements in these terms. This perspective can be applied from the 'beginning' and onwards. When discussing the first signs of an interest in the remains under discussion, it is important to accept that there cannot be one single root or origin to the field. This means being aware of the fact that studying a field or a discipline can never mean that you have formulated the final version of it. It is important to realise that a field or a discipline is something very complex, which makes it the subject of constant revisions and therefore can never be regarded as a closed chapter (cf. Nordbladh 1998).

By naming this paper 'More than a village ...' I wish to emphasize the dynamic in the archaeological study of medieval rural settlements. Since the first attempts were made to understand these remains, the range of questions and incorporated aspects have broadened. It is no longer only about the single farmstead and its most immediate surroundings, but also about the outland and the landscape as a whole. Perhaps it is a healthy sign for a dynamic field of study, or maybe it signals a reorientation and disintegration? A second connotation concerns how the village over time has become much more than simply the archaeological remains of times long gone. Instead, the physical traces are just as much a reflector of the time when the different investigations were conducted and the prevailing ideas of theses times, as simply the material traces of past centuries.

Notes

1. This Ph.D. is conducted at the Department of Archaeology and Ancient History, Lund University, and is expected to be completed in 2008.
2. The Deserted Medieval Village Research Group was established in England 1952 as a forum for addressing issues related to the medieval countryside. From the beginning it has been characterised by its multidisciplinary approach.
3. Perhaps the best known example in the history of research comes from the Iron Age site of Little Woodbury, excavated by the German immigrant Gerhard Bersu in the late 30s. Although his method was not strioctly that of open area excavation, Little Woodbury has been identified with the introduction of open area excavation techniques into British prehistoric archaeology (cf. Evans 1989; Krämer 2001: 64 ff).

References

Andrén, A. 1998. *Between Artifacts and Text: Historical Archaeology in Global Perspective*. New York: Plenum Press.

Astill, G.G. 1993. 'The Archaeology of the Medieval Countryside – a Forty-year Perspective from Britain', in H. Andersson and J. Wienberg (eds), *The Study of Medieval Archaeology. European Symposium for Teachers of Medieval Archaeology, Lund 11–15 June 1990*. Lund Studies in Medieval Archaeology 13. Stockholm: Almqvist & Wiksell International, pp. 131–47.

Austin, D. 1990. 'The "Proper Study" of Medieval Archaeology', in D. Austin and L. Alcock (eds), *From the Baltic to the Black Sea: Studies in Medieval Archaeology*. London: Unwin Hyman, pp. 9–42.

Beresford, M. and J. Hurst. 1990. *English Heritage Book of Wharram Percy: Deserted Medieval Village*. London: Batsford.

Bradley, R. 1997. '"To see is to have seen". Craft Traditions in British Field Archaeology', in B. Leigh Molyneaux (ed.), *The Cultural Life of Images: Visual Representations in Archaeology*. London: Routledge, pp. 62–72.

Brattli, T. 1993. *Evolusjonismen og det moderne: ein analyse av tilkomsten av arkeologien som vitskaplig disiplin*. Tromsö: Universitetet i Tromsö.

Eberle, H. 2002. *Die Martin-Luther-Universität in der Zeit des Nationalsozialismus 1933–1945*. Halle: Mitteldeutscher Verlag.

Evans, C. 1989. 'Archaeology and Modern Times: Bersu's Woodbury 1938 & 1939', *Antiquity* 63(240): 436–50.

Gerrard, C. 2003. *Medieval Archaeology. Understanding Traditions and Contemporary Approaches*. London: Routledge.

Gillberg, Å. 1995. 'Anmälan av Alain Schnapps bok "La conquête du passé"', *Arkeologen* 3: 20–24.

Grimm, P. 1930. 'Die vor- und frühgeschichtliche Besiedlung des Unterharzes und seines Vorlandes auf Grund der Bodenfunde', *Jahresschrift für die Vorgeschichte der sächsisch-thüringischen Länder* 18.

——— . 1934. 'Ein mittelalterliches Gehöft bei Altenrode, Kreis Wernigerode', *Zeitschrift des Harz-Vereins für Geschichte und Altertumskunde* 1: 23–37.

——— . 1935. 'Ein mittelalterliches Gehöft von Altenrode bei Wernigerode', *Mitteldeutsche Volkheit. Hefte für Vorgeschichte und Volkskunde* 2: 51–52.

——— . 1938a. 'Die Salzmünder Kultur in Mitteldeutschland', *Jahresschriften für die Vorgeschichte der sächsisch-thüringischen Länder* 29: 1–104.

——— . 1938b. 'Die mittelalterliche Bauernsiedlung Hohenrode im Südharz', *Germanen-Erbe. Monatsschrift für Deutsche Vorgeschichte* 8: 234–41.

——— . 1939. *Hohenrode – eine mittelalterliche Siedlung im Südharz*, Veröffentlichungen der Landesanstalt für Volkheitskunde zu Halle 11. Halle (Saale).

Hassmann, H. 2000. 'Archaeology in the "Third Reich"', in H. Härke (ed.), *Archaeology, Ideology and Society. The German Experience*. Gesellschaften und Staaten im Epochenwandel 7. Frankfurt am Main: Peter Lang Verlag, pp. 65–139.

Heinrich, H. 1978. 'Verzeichnis der Schriften von Paul Grimm', *Jahresschrift für mitteldeutsche Vorgeschichte* 62: 15–25.

——— . 1994. 'Zum Schriftenverzeichnis von Paul Grimm', *Ausgrabungen und Funde* 39(4): 163–64.

Hurst, J. 1969. 'Medieval Village Excavation in England', in K-H. Otto and J. Herrmann, (eds), *Siedlung, Burg und Stadt: Studien zu ihren Anfängen [Paul Grimm zum 60. Geburtstag]*. Schriften der Sektion für Vor- und Frühgeschichte/Deutsche Akademie der Wissenschaften Berlin 25, Berlin: Akademie-Verlag, pp. 258–70.

———. 1971. 'A Review of Archaeological Research (to 1968)', in M. Beresford and J. Hurst (eds), *Deserted Medieval Villages: Studies*. London: Lutterworth Press, pp. 76–144.

———. 1984. 'The Wharram Research Project: Results to 1983', *Medieval Archaeology* 28: 77–111.

———. 1986. 'The Work of the Medieval Village Research Group 1952–1986', *Medieval Settlement Research Group Annual Report* 1: 8–13.

Janssen, W. 1988. 'Die Stellung der Archäologie des Mittelalters im Gefüge der historischen Wissenschaften', *Beiträge zur Mittelalterarchäologie in Österreich* 4/5: 9–18.

Krämer, W. 2001. '*Gerhard Bersu – ein deutscher Prähistoriker 1889–1964*', Bericht der Römisch-Germanischen Kommission 82: 5–101.

Le Goff, J. 1988. 'Den långa medeltiden', *Res Publica* 11: 34–42.

Moreland, J. 2001. *Archaeology and Text*. London: Duckworth.

Nordbladh, J. 1998. 'Försök till en arkeologisk självsyn', in O.W. Jensen and H. Karlsson (eds), *Arkeologiska horisonter*. Stehag/Stockhom: Symposion, pp. 236–41.

Steensberg, A. and Østergaard, J.L. 1974. *Store Valby: Historisk-arkæologisk undersøgelse af en nedlagt landsby på Sjælland*. Historisk-filosofiske skrifter. Det Kongelige Danske Videnskabernes Selskab 8, Copenhagen.

Svestad, A. 1995. *Oldsakenes orden. Om tilkomsten av arkeologi*. Oslo: Universitetsforlaget.

Wrathmell, S. 1989. 'Peasant Houses, Farmsteads and Villages in North-East England', in M. Aston, D. Austin and C. Dyer (eds), *The Rural Settlements of Medieval England: Studies Dedicated to Maurice Beresford and John Hurst*. Oxford: Basil Blackwell, pp. 247–67.

Chapter 9
Amateurs and Professionals in Nineteenth-Century Archaeology

The Case of the Oxford 'Antiquarian and Grocer' H.M.J. Underhill (1855–1920)

Megan Price

Abstract

This research concerns the formal and informal links between amateur and professionals, and the contributions they made to the development of the study of British prehistory during the late nineteenth century. The City and University of Oxford provide valuable archival resources, including records of the formation and membership of local 'scientific' societies. The thread I follow through this research is the work of H.M.J. Underhill. A significant contributor to local intellectual societies in Oxford, Underhill was also a talented artist. He came from an old Oxford family and spent his life running the family shop, 'Suppliers of High Quality Provisions to the Gentlemen of the University'. Between 1880 and 1897 Underhill created over 600 hand-painted coloured lanternslides covering natural history, archaeology and folktales. An examination of the range of Underhill's work provides a insight into the world of an amateur and autodidact who circulated within the milieu of growing academic professionalism during the late nineteenth century.

Introduction

A plain wooden box stored in the basement of Oxford University Institute of Archaeology, labelled 'Underhill Slides: The Great Stone Circles of Britain' led to a discovery of an unexplored network of social and intellectual connections between amateurs and academics of 'town and gown' in late nineteenth-century Oxford. Many of those individuals became involved in a new scientific society, the Oxfordshire Natural History Society and Field Club, a society 'open to all interested in science' which was formed in the 1880s (Bellamy 1908: 14). In this chapter, I identify how various social and intellectual relationships emerged between amateurs and professionals in Oxford from the 1870s through their membership of this society. I will examine the consequences of the professionalization of the study of the past during the second half of the nineteenth century, through a case study of the intellectual work of an eclectic amateur, Henry Underhill (1855–1920), an Oxford resident and proprietor of a 'High Class Provision Merchant to the Gentlemen of the University'.[1] Through the work of Underhill and like minded individuals, it is possible to trace the gradual separation of the spheres of amateurs and professionals as advances in knowledge in all fields of the human sciences led to the foundation of discrete academic disciplines. The gradual demise of the antiquarian by the end of the nineteenth century was a consequence of the redefining and reshaping of intellectual boundaries.

Nineteenth-Century Britain

By the middle of the nineteenth century, the growth of scientific knowledge in Britain had, by and large begun to replace religious explanations of human origins. Important social and cultural advances had been made in medical care, education, air and land travel, and entertainment for the benefit of all levels of society. This was a period of great optimism in Britain: colonial expansion and industrial prosperity brought with them a new class of wealthy industrial manufacturers, generating a demand for more and more material goods. John Evans, for example, was able to profit from this economic growth, during the 1850s as partner in the family firm of John Dickinson, paper manufacturers. This enabled him to pursue his archaeological studies and to ensure that his eldest son Arthur Evans would benefit from an education at public school and Oxford (Evans 1943: 81).

Oxford provides a unique case study for urban social, cultural and intellectual life in late Victorian Britain. The City and University displayed a long historical and traditional division between 'town and gown', which had often led to confrontations between citizens and students (Brock and Curthoys 1997: 281, Howe 1993). By the nineteenth century the permanent population, 'the town', included the upper and middle classes, tradesmen and servants. The 'gown' consisted mainly of members from the upper middle classes, dons in permanent residence at their college and students who came 'up' to University for the three-terms.

In the 1850s, the University was composed of 20 or so self-governing colleges founded from medieval times, with a resident population of unmarried dons who, as well as teaching their subject, natural theology, and classics, were also ordained as Anglican Clergymen. From the 1860s, the city of Oxford began to grow both economically and geographically (Day 1983, Brock and Curthoys 1997). The University student population was steadily increasing and by the 1870s, dons were permitted to marry and live outside their colleges (Engel, 1983: 156–61). This caused a demand for new houses in Oxford and the services to go with them. The city continued to rely on the Colleges for much of its income and employment, but other industries and trades, like publishing and the railways, were beginning to flourish (Sephton 2001).

During this period of change, the traditional University ways of teaching and learning at Oxford were transformed. Until the 1850s, students resided at their particular college, which provided their social life, and all their teaching from a syllabus, which concentrated on the classics and theology (Brock and Curthoys 1997: 149). Time spent at University often served as a temporary occupation for young Anglican clergymen, awaiting an appointment as a parish priest. In contrast, by the end of the century, University dons were no longer trained in holy orders, nor required to remain celibate, and were appointed to professional teaching posts in separate disciplines with structured careers. Engel argued that by the 1890s 'The traditional clerical Oxford had been destroyed to make way for a new secular profession' (Engel 1983). In terms of function, status, and the new academic faculties that developed, these events determined the shape of many of today's disciplines. By 1914, many academic disciplines at Oxford had more or less assumed their present form.

Amateur Societies

In nineteenth-century Britain, antiquarian, historical and archaeological studies of the past attracted a wide body of enthusiastic and committed devotees. Whether they were able to involve themselves full-time or only part-time in these pursuits, these individuals formed a highly motivated self-taught group of people, on familiar and friendly terms with one another and sharing a common body of knowledge (cf. in particular Levine 1986).

During the 1840s and 1850s, Mechanics Institutes had been formed in many towns and cities in Britain to educate the 'labouring classes'. Recently there has been much interest in this issue and its valuable contribution within the history of science (e.g. Secord 1994). In Oxford, a series of public lectures was founded in 1848; these were well attended and lasted for many years. They took place in the Town Hall and were on 'scientific and literary subjects only'.

By the mid-nineteenth century, Oxford had become a venue for meetings between devotees of science from London and the provinces. The Oxford contingent was headed by one of the founder members of the Ashmolean Society, William Buckland who was Reader in Mineralogy from 1813 and in Geology from 1818. Oxford scholars including Samuel Wilberforce, Bishop of Oxford from 1844 and Baden Powell, Savilian Professor of Geometry founded the society on 11th December 1828 at an inaugural dinner. It was decided at the meeting that membership should be limited to fifty individuals, by election and ballot to gentlemen, not under the Degree of M.A. from Oxford, Cambridge and 'other Universities'.[2] Two or three meetings were held each term at which papers were read, all the officials and the committee being required to read papers in turn. By the mid-nineteenth century attendance at meetings averaged about eighty members in the crowded conditions of the Ashmolean Museum in Broad Street (the original Ashmolean Museum and now the Museum for the History of Science).

From 1860, the Society met in the North Oxford building of the 'New Museum' for the Natural Sciences (now The University Museum), which had been planned and encouraged by Sir Henry Acland (Brock and Curthoys 1997: 664). Nevertheless, by 1866 membership was declining. It was felt that, 'particularly in winter, the isolated position in an imperfectly lighted district of the city was a disadvantage' (Simcock 1985). Having initially encouraged and nurtured the popular sciences and making a bid for their recognition alongside the more ancient and acceptable disciplines, the society had outlived its purpose.

A new, more egalitarian society was founded in the 1870s, The Oxfordshire Natural History Society and Field Club. Weekly meetings were held in the new University Museum, opened in 1860 and followed the same pattern as other local and national societies. A typical annual programme consisted of talks on natural history, geology and archaeology. Members came from both the University and the City of Oxford and, in contrast to many exclusive 'Gentlemen's societies,' no election for membership was necessary. This was the society in which many non-University members such as Henry Underhill were able to flourish.

By 1895, the Ashmolean Society had only 34 members, most of them in arrears with their subscriptions (Bellamy 1908: 48). It made an unsuccessful attempt to amalgamate within University, with the Junior Scientific Club (est. 1882), but in 1901 the committees of the Ashmolean Society and the Oxfordshire Natural History Society and Field Club agreed to amalgamate their societies to form the current Ashmolean Natural History Society (see Bellamy 1908, Parry-Jones 1983).

The 1860 Oxford Meeting of the British Association for the Advancement of Science

The committee members of the Ashmolean Society were instrumental in inviting the British Association for the Advancement of Science to Oxford for their 1860 meeting. It was here that the 'notorious' exchange of views concerning human origins between Thomas Huxley, the 'new' scientist, and Samuel Wilberforce, the theologian heralded a new era for the role of science in Britain, and also left its mark on intellectual Oxford itself (Lucas 1979, Brooke 2001, and see also Turner 1979, 1983 on debates between science and religion).

In the 1860s the question of human antiquity and the revelation of the existence of earlier human societies was still unresolved. The recent discoveries of the Abbeville jaw, and the contentious comparisons of human and Gorilla brains, were already public knowledge, and formalised teaching or research on human origins would eventually appear as the disciplines of Anthropology and Archaeology. The public setting of this debate at the Meeting of the British Association in Oxford not only secured an audience for Huxley's ideas of the 'new science', the event also revolutionized the fundamental organisation and practices of many amateur approaches to research by demanding new standards of professionalism.

I would suggest that the encounter acted as a marker for the emergence of scientific professionalism producing a radical shift from amateur approaches in the human sciences to those based on methodical investigation and scientific laws. The work of Henry Underhill acts as a case in point.

Tracing Henry Underhill

From the 1870s in Oxford, many social and intellectual relationships between amateurs and professionals were nurtured through their membership of a new scientific society, *The Oxfordshire Natural History Society*. On 12th February 1896 Henry Underhill gave a lantern lecture called *'The Great Stone Circles of Britain'* using lantern slides before an audience of members, which included the archaeologist Arthur Evans.[3] Underhill's forty exquisitely hand-painted lanternslides showed prehistoric sites of Britain and included Wayland's Smithy (Plate 3), The Rollright Stones, Stonehenge and Avebury.

The slides had been stored among unused equipment in the basement of Oxford's Institute of Archaeology and were discovered during departmental re-organisation. Nothing was known of their history or creator. Each slide measured three and a half inches square and had the initials *'H.M.J.U. 1895'* painted on the glass with the date and details of the sources used by the artist on the corner of each mount.

Using an 1895 street directory of Oxford residents, I identified 'H.M.J.U' as the grocer, Henry Michael John Underhill, who lived at his shop in central Oxford. Further investigation revealed that he was one of many, individuals owning businesses in the town, or employed as non-professionals at the University, who shared wide scientific and intellectual interests, and whose contribution to various disciplines has so far been overlooked. Examples are listed Frank Bellamy, an amateur astronomer was employed as a technician at the University Observatory, and George Claridge Druce, a botanist who owned a Chemist's shop in Oxford's High Street (see Bellamy 1908).

So far, three strands of evidence for Underhill's academic work and interests have emerged. First, the visual artefacts: a large collection of hand painted lanternslides of natural history, folklore and British prehistory.[4] Second, his hand written accounts of natural history observations; his sketchbook and photograph albums and journals kept whilst a schoolboy at Christ Church Cathedral School from 1869.[5] Third, in these accounts he refers to various contributions to amateur scientific journals (sometimes with his cousin Frank Allen, another antiquarian) such as *Microscopy, Magic Lantern, The Midland Naturalist*. There, he was writing on such topics as the diptera (microscopic creatures) (Underhill and Allen 1875), microscopic animals (Underhill 1890), and, of course, lantern slides (Underhill 1888). Further evidence of the breadth of Underhill's activities were found in the weekly newspapers, *Jackson's Oxford Journal* and *The Oxford Chronicle* which reported regularly on the activities of all the local societies. These publications summarised the social and intellectual events that had occurred in both the city and University during the previous week. Though time-consuming to research, they contain valuable social and intellectual 'micro-histories'.

Assuming that Henry Underhill's wider civic and intellectual interests would have begun in his mid-20s, I searched through the newspaper microfilms from the 1880s. The first reference to Underhill's intellectual activities was an announcement in 1887 that he had become a founder member of the newly formed *Oxfordshire Natural History Society* (Jackson's Oxford Journal 1887 June 18). From these newspaper reports, I traced collections of lecture lists, minutes of meetings, letters, term-cards and illustrated posters of the society that have been preserved in various archives at the Bodleian Library. One particularly valuable collection of material had been donated to the Library by another amateur, Frank Bellamy (1864–1936). His unique contribution to the *Oxford Natural History Society* is his privately published account of the growth of this local amateur society (Bellamy 1908).

The 'Antiquarian, Entomologist and Grocer' Henry Underhill lived through the social and cultural changes of the Victorian and Edwardian periods. He experienced the evolution of the camera, the moving picture and the advent of the petrol engine and of flight. He was known for his intellectual work only to a local group of colleagues, and as a 'tradesman', was not able to become a member of the growing society of professional University teachers in Oxford.

Today Underhill's contribution to this knowledge may be of minor importance; his work and illustrations have received little attention since his death in 1920. The significance of his work, nevertheless, lies in the evidence it offers for intellectual relationships between town and gown, during the growth and dissemination of new scientific knowledge and ideas.

If we examine Underhill's interests chronologically, they reveal significant changes in direction, evolving from an antiquarian view of 'Natural theology' to a scientific specialization. Many of the changes in interpretation of the human past during the latter half of the nineteenth century are reflected through Henry Underhill's eclectic interests. His papers for local scientific societies and journals appear to follow a pattern, also echoing contemporary discoveries and research in the natural sciences.

Underhill: Antiquarian and Grocer

Henry Underhill was born above the family grocer's shop at 7 High Street, Oxford, in 1855. That year marked a point half-way between two significant and very different Victorian events: the Great Exhibition of 1851 – celebrating the British Empire and the pursuit of consumerism – and the publication of Darwin's *Origin of the Species* in 1859 – culminating decades of scholarship of the evolution of life. As a schoolboy, Underhill kept a record of the natural history books he read, at the Radcliffe Camera, the new science library opened in 1861. From the mid 1870s, the University Museum became the focus of Henry Underhill's intellectual and cultural pursuits. Here he copied drawings and made notes of specimens to research or collect later. The library books appear to be the standard reference material of the day, often written by clergymen-naturalists, for example, *Microscopic Fungi* by M.C. Cook, and *Objects of the Microscope* by Dr Lane (cf. Lightman 1997: 187–211). As Underhill dated all his work, it is possible to form a chronology of his intellectual involvements in Oxford. His diaries, now held at the History of Science Museum show, for example, that he exchanged information on local entomological finds and specimens with friends and contributed to two amateur science journals, *Hardwicke's Science Gossip* and *Postal Microscopy*.

In the mid-nineteenth century, many well-known scientists of natural history, such as Charles Darwin and his neighbour, John Lubbock, spent time together, 'botanising'. Natural history was a traditional pursuit, a science that could be done at home, by amateur naturalists, geologists and archaeologists. Many of these amateurs were part of 'the clerisy', a term adopted to describe the phenomenon of the parson-naturalist and 'gentleman-amateur' (Wetherall 1998: 22). Many of these naturalists were Anglican clergy by default; all students at university were trained in holy orders until the 1871 University Test Act abolished religious tests, and Oxford became a non-denominational, 'free-thinking' educational institution (Brock and Curthoys 1997: 3). Darwin, himself, was from the clergy-naturalist background and had originally intended to enter the priesthood. These Anglican clergymen were members of a relatively tightly knit social group, often related to one another by kinship and marriage; a man's clerical colleagues were also his scientific colleagues his Oxbridge contemporaries and his kinsfolk (Armstrong 2000: 15). The phenomenon is also noticeable among British archaeologists of the time: Canon William Greenwell regularly corresponded and worked with Oxford men such as William Boyd Dawkins and George Rolleston as well as with active members of national archaeological societies, such as John Evans and George Lane Fox (later Pitt Rivers).[6]

In contrast, Underhill's case displays an expansion of intellectual interests and activities between people from different and wider social classes during the late nineteenth century. Many of these interests were possibly stimulated by Victorian popularisers of science, including such books as such *Vestiges of the Natural History of Creation* published anonymously in the 1840S and later revealed to be by Robert Chambers. By the 1860s, scientists such as Huxley and John Lubbock had also begun writing for the non-specialist audience (Lightman 1997).

Amateurs like Underhill felt able to contribute to this growing field of scholarship and his work provides us with examples of the ways in which knowledge was being transmitted, not only through popular publications, but also through the medium of public lectures. In the 1880s he was using the technique of hand-painting lantern slides on glass, a process in which he seems to have been a leading expert. His natural history notebooks in the Museum of the History of Science in Oxford contain drawings and watercolours of microscopic animals from his own entomological collections, which were the first he transferred to lantern slides for lectures. According to the present Curator of Entomology at the University Museum, these are a scientific collection worthy of further study (George McGavin, pers. comm. 2003).

In the 1890s, Henry Underhill developed an interest in folklore and folktales. Possibly this academic interest was inspired by anthropologists such as Edward Burnett Tylor (1832–1917), the first Professor of Anthropology at Oxford who was also an active member of *The Oxfordshire Natural History Society*. Tylor examined 'survivals' of social and cultural life from earlier societies and compared them to existing rural customs in both British and world folklore. Archaeologists such as Arthur Evans (Evans 1895) and other anthropologists, classicists and philologists such as Andrew Lang and James Frazer also pursued this intellectual and scientific interest in folklore and myth.

Underhill's folktale slides, illustrating stories from Northern Europe and Japan, appear to have been prepared before 1893. This 'folktale period' coincided with the growing academic interest in British and European prehistory and the search for national identity. Underhill used the texts of recently translated European folktales collected by Andrew Lang and the brothers Grimm, whilst his characters reflected the pre-Raphaelite genre of storybook illustrations, notably those of H.J. Ford. It is simple to identify Underhill's placing of British archaeological landscapes in the background of many of these hand-pained slides. The landscape for the Irish tale of *Guleesh*, for example, is identical to the Romano-British earthworks at Alfred's Castle on the Berkshire Ridgeway. In another tale the scene has echoes of Silbury Hill, near Avebury, and in another, we can see megaliths, possibly those at Stonehenge.

Underhill painted the set of lantern slides showing *Ancient Stone Circles of Britain* between 1894 and 1895. They show the sites and the plans of the British megalithic monuments of Stonehenge and Avebury, in Wiltshire, the Rollright Stones in Oxfordshire and Wayland's Smithy, in Berkshire. On the slides he scrupulously acknowledged information taken from earlier antiquarians, noting when he had copied diagrams from William Stukeley at Stonehenge and Avebury. He painted them all from sketches and notes made on site during the summer. On each slide he noted the date of sketching, 'Aug. 24th, 1895', and the date of painting, 'Nov. 4th to 6th 1895'. It is interesting to note that most of the watercolours and photographs for these slides were prepared between July and September, during the University's Long Vacation. During term-time he was obliged to work long hours in the shop, and could only work on his personal interests after the shop had closed at nine oclock, or on Bank Holidays (see Whittaker 1973 on contemporary shopkeepers) .

By the 1890s, as well as being proprietor of the grocery shop, which employed over twenty people, Underhill had become a leading member of various local intellectual societies, such as the *Oxford Camera Club* and in particular the *Oxfordshire Natural History Society*, of which he was a founding member, first secretary and subsequently president in 1893. He resigned in 1902 citing 'pressure of business'. Between 1887 and 1900, he gave eleven lectures on natural history and archaeology to the society (Bellamy 1908: 96).

On 8 February 1896 Underhill gave a lecture entitled *'Great Stone Circles'*, which accompanied his slides to the *Oxfordshire Natural History Society* in the University Museum. According to the report in *The Oxford Chronicle*, Mr Arthur Evans, Keeper of Antiquities at the Ashmolean Museum, and Professor Poulton, the Hope Professor of Entomology (actually Zoology), were both in attendance and 'a long and interesting discussion' subsequently took place. This event provides significant evidence for the social and cultural links between amateurs and professionals during this period of mutual interest in the 're-discovery' and reinterpretation of British prehistoric sites. Such 'discussions' between the non-academic amateur and the university professional suggests that the study of British prehistory had not yet become enclosed within its present professional disciplinary boundaries.

Underhill's slides of *The Great Stone Circles* appear to be among the last he created. The remains of one further set *Buried Roman Cities in England* have recently been discovered, fourteen hand-painted and photographic slides showing the mosaics at the Roman Villa of North Leigh in Oxfordshire and excavations at the Roman towns of Silchester and Cirencester. Underhill's photographic slide of the North Leigh mosaic has recently been used to verify the original design for a forthcoming publication on Roman Mosaics (Grahame Soffe, pers. comm.).

In 1895, Underhill gave an illustrated talk on the Roman sites to the Annual Conference of the Midland Union of Natural History Societies, which was hosted by the members of the Oxfordshire Natural History Society. This event included a field trip for all members and friends organised by Underhill. Two years later, he repeated this lecture to *The Oxfordshire Natural History Society*, in preparation for another afternoon excursion (*Oxford Chronicle*, 22 May 1897). The Field Trip played an important social and cultural part in the annual programme of local history societies. Geologists, botanists and archaeologists could collaborate on these multidisciplinary occasions; a party of thirty or so would travel by rail or carriages, partaking in the obligatory, lunch and tea en route, which was often commented upon in the following *Proceedings* of the society (*Nature*, 30 November 1873).

It seems that after 1895, Underhill concentrated entirely on photographic work, developing and mounting his own pictures. In 1907, he compiled a collection of over sixty Windmills from Southern Britain, as part of the O*xford Camera Club*'s contribution to a national photographic archive of Prehistoric, Roman and Anglo-Saxon remains. It is unclear how successful this project was nationally, but Underhill's collection of slides, notes and photographs of Windmills at the Museum for the History of Science in Oxford provide a valuable reference for industrial archaeologists, as many of these structures no longer exist.

Underhill's intellectual activities between 1907, when he completed his photographic collection of windmills, and his death in 1920, seem uncertain. His last photographs were taken in 1918 and 1919 during outings to sites around Oxford when he revisited Wayland's Smithy and the Uffington White Horse. These photographs of Wayland's Smithy and the earlier hand-painted slides from 1894 show the site as it was before 'restoration' in the 1920s (Aitkinson 1965). As an archaeological record, they present us with a valuable representation of the 'past within the past' and provide a unique example of the sensitive and meticulous work of a dedicated antiquarian, amateur naturalist and archaeologist. Indeed, Professor Barry Cunliffe was still using some of Underhill's slides to illustrate his own lectures on prehistory during the 1970s (Barry Cunliffe, pers. comm. 2003).

The Growth of Academic Prehistoric Archaeology at Oxford

Until the First World War, interest in prehistoric archaeology in Britain was almost entirely a private pursuit largely in the hands of a relatively small class (Clark 1989: 2). It was a leisure interest for a comparatively few individuals, some of whom were also obliged to earn their living. John Evans, for example was involved in paper manufacture (Evans 1943), John Lubbock was a banker and politician and George Rolleston was teaching anatomy at Oxford until 1875, when promotion enabled him to 'devote his time wholly to anthropology'.[7] Most archaeological excavations were done privately as a congenial and 'gentlemanly' summer break, and the reports were prepared in the winter months, often for presentation to members of intellectual societies.

The teaching of archaeology as an academic discipline did not enter the university curriculum in Oxford until the late nineteenth century. In 1883 when Arthur Evans heard rumours that Oxford might appoint a Professor of Archaeology, he assumed 'bitterly' but correctly that it intended to do so in the sphere of literary studies, rather than 'real' archaeology, though there is no evidence that he ever applied for the post (Evans 1943: 361–62).

In 1887, Percy Gardner was appointed as Professor of Classical Archaeology and Art. From 1890, Classical Greek Archaeology was taught at Oxford as an optional course to undergraduates as part of their degree in classics, the teaching centred on the collections of casts and vases at the Ashmolean Museum. Already Gardner in his time noted Oxford's 'antiquated machinery' for innovation and change (Boardman 1985: 50).

In 1909, Arthur Evans retired from the Ashmolean Museum, and was accorded the title of Extraordinary Professor of Prehistoric Archaeology, at a nominal salary and with few duties. He was by that time fully involved with his excavations on Crete. Through this appointment the University acknowledged Evans' eminence as a prehistoric archaeologist without committing itself to the academic advancement of the subject, still less to making it a subject for examination by undergraduates. This was an example of what Clark terms 'a vicious circle'; until archaeology was pursued professionally, it could not qualify for academic recognition and until universities brought themselves to teach and engage in research in archaeology, it was hard to see where the professionals were to come from' (Clark 1989: 10).

The first teaching in prehistoric archaeology began in Oxford as it had in Cambridge under the aegis of anthropology. Efforts had been made by Edward Tylor to include anthropology for undergraduate examination in the Honours School of Natural Science in 1895, but his proposal lacked the necessary support. Ten years later anthropology was accepted, though only as a post-graduate diploma. Under Edward Tylor, the syllabus recognized two main spheres, physical anthropology, the study of man and his fossil remains, and cultural anthropology, which dealt with prehistoric archaeology, cultural ethnology and sociology. As at Cambridge, one of the reasons for accepting the diploma was the recognition that it might have practical value for training colonial administrators (Marett 1941: 168). This inclusion of prehistory, even if as only a small part of the Diploma, played a significant part in the future development of the subject.

In 1946, Oxford appointed Christopher Hawkes to the Chair of European Archaeology; his teaching was intended to 'throw light on the barbarian antecedents, post-Roman as well as pre-Roman, of European civilization'. By confining its range in this way, the University ensured that the new professor would not embark on any large view of world prehistory. In 1972, when Barry Cunliffe moved to the chair of European Archaeology at Oxford, prehistory was still not an undergraduate subject and The Institute of Archaeology was a graduate department (Clark 1989: 148). As late as 1986, Andrew Sherratt could note that the organizational and conceptual framework of archaeology as a subject had hardly changed since the nineteenth century, that archaeology was only erratically represented in undergraduate courses in other disciplines and that the tradition was still entirely literary.

Clark's (1989) comprehensive survey of the growth of the discipline of prehistory at Cambridge embraces its academic connection with Oxford. In 1989, he noted that when a supervisor was chosen for a candidate in prehistory, the Board of Anthropology and Geography would call upon one of three lecturers at Oxford, namely Ray Inskeep, Dennis Briton and Derek Roe, or the professor of European Archaeology Barry Cunliffe, and Andrew Sherratt of the Ashmolean

Museum. As it happens, all five were products of the Cambridge Faculty of Archaeology and Anthropology: a study of the social, cultural and intellectual kinships and descent within the university system is obviously called for. In oxford, in any case, it was not until 1991 that a joint honours degree in Archaeology and Anthropology was finally offered to undergraduate students.

Conclusions: Points for Further Research

The case of H.M.J. Underhill, antiquarian and grocer, opens up several avenues for further research.

Amateurs in Archaeology

A crucial factor in any research into the history of an academic discipline is the contribution made by members of amateur societies, where much of the early scientific investigation was shared and disseminated in related journals and proceedings. There has been relatively little research on the impact and contribution made by local societies, though much of their work was a foundation for contemporary academic and theoretical approaches. The annual programmes of these societies covered an eclectic range of subjects, an inter- and multi-disciplinary dimension reflecting a time before professionalization or disciplinization at higher academic levels (Allen 1978: 120). Levine (1986) has addressed the links between archaeological and historical societies in her invaluable study covering the years between 1840 and 1886, and has focused on those from the classes or professions where education and leisure were an accepted factor.

In the latter part of the nineteenth century, local scientific societies like The Oxfordshire Natural History Society were increasing in city and county in both scope and breadth of membership. They actcd as a conduit for amateurs from outside the intellectual circles of the larger prestigious societies such as The Royal Society and The Athenaeum, which not only required nomination and election procedures but possessed power and recognition within the upper-class social networks in steering scientific policy and politics (for example The X-Club; Barton 1998, Desmond 2001).

Recent theoretical work in the History of Science is beginning to address the issues of the provincial and artisan amateurs from the 'working' classes in natural history (Allen 1976, Alberti 2003). In archaeology, however, the work of individual members of local societies and their publications has yet to be examined. At present, apart from the work of Levine, historians of archaeology are obliged to draw on the scholarship of theoretical approaches from other disciplines. The contribution made by amateurs and workers in discovering and uncovering evidence from British prehistory, whether through their employment or through an individual and personal interest could provide a valuable field of study.

The Value of Visual Images

During the 1880s Henry Underhill was applying his artistic gifts to the technique of handpainting lantern slides on glass, his interest in microscopy appeared to have diminish during the late 1880s and by 1892 he was writing for *The Optical Magic Lantern Journal* on 'the techniques of painting lantern slides' (reprinted in *The New Magic Lantern Journal* 5:1, January 1987). While the lantern was the major device for visual presentations for both public education and entertainment at that time, little research has been carried out on its uses. Before the general accessibility of photography, the magic lantern served as an effective means of social and cultural communication to all levels of society. Today, many collections of lantern slides remain to be salvaged or recovered from archives and stores. The equipment and the vast subject-range of slides produced should be considered as part of the material culture of the nineteenth century. The early uses of photography as anthropological or archaeological records are for their part now receiving academic attention, notably with the work of Elizabeth Edwards (2000) in conjunction with the Pitt Rivers Museum in Oxford.

Henry Underhill's distinctively visual contributions to archaeology have helped to increase our knowledge of the work of people from outside the formal academic communities and societies. The world of nineteenth-century Oxford consisted of many whose work has now been forgotten or ignored. Tracing the evidence of their activities provides a poignant and often moving account of one individual's enthusiasm and passion for new discoveries in natural history and the prehistoric past. By the end of the nineteenth century, a liberal agenda and intellectual progress in Britain was providing more educational opportunities for different sections of the community, regardless of their class, gender or age. At the same time, however, this was accompanied by a more professionalized control of knowledge and the creation of academic boundaries. The rise of the professional was a characteristic development of late nineteenth century Britain and antiquarians and amateurs found themselves caught in a grey area between the interests of the professional scientist, historian and archaeologist as bodies catering for narrower and less general interests grew (Levine 1986: 59). Henry Underhill's resignation from the Oxford Natural History Society in 1902 suggests that he was aware of this factor.

The intellectual identity and social and cultural position of amateurs, academics, and their role in the pursuit of knowledge of the past is a crucial element in the history of prehistoric archaeology. The discipline is now entering its second century and it is vital to ensure that every facet of its ancestral composition is considered.

Notes

1. Shop brochure,1885, John Johnson Collection, Bodleian Library.
2. Ashmolean Society Papers, 1876–1905, Bodleian Library.
3. As reported in the Oxford Chronicle February 26th 1896.
4. Held at the Institute of Archaeology in Oxford and at the Folklore Society London, donated by his sister Maud after his death in 1920.
5. Mss Underhill, Museum of the History of Science, Oxford, donated by Maud in 1935. Some fifteen years ago the archivist at the Museum of the History of Science found and entered this collection into The National Record of Archives, describing Henry Underhill as an 'Oxford Antiquarian, Entomologist and Grocer' (pers.comm).
6. Rolleston Letters, John Evans Correspondence Ashmolean Museum.
7. Letter to Greenwell, March 1875, Rolleston Archive, Ashmolean Museum.

References

Armstrong, P. 2000. The English Parson-Naturalist: A Companionship between Science and Religion. Leominster, Herefordshire: Gracewing.

Alberti, S. 2003. 'Natural History and the Philosophical Societies of Late Victorian Yorkshire', Archives of Natural History 30(2): 342–58.

Allen, D.E. 1978. The Naturalist in Britain: A Social History. London: A. Lane.

Atkinson, R. 1965. 'Wayland's Smithy', Antiquity 39: 126–33.

Barton, R. 1998. 'Huxley, Lubbock, and Half a Dozen Others': Professionals and Gentlemen in the Formation of the X Club, 1851–1864', Isis 89(3): 410–44.

Bellamy, F.A. 1908. A Historical Account of The Ashmolean Natural History Society of Oxfordshire, 1880–1905. Oxford, J. Vincent.

Boardman, J. 1985. '100 Years of Classical Archaeology at Oxford', in Beazley and Oxford, D. Kurtz (ed.) pp. 43–55. Oxford: Oxford University Committee for Archaeology.

Brock, M.G. and Curthoys, M.C. (eds) 1997, Nineteenth-Century Oxford. Oxford: Oxford University Press.

Brooke, J.H. 2001. *The Wilberforce-Huxley Debate: Why Did it Happen?* Oxford: Farmington Institute for Christian Studies.

Clark, G. 1989. *Prehistory at Cambridge and Beyond.* Cambridge: Cambridge University Press.

Cordeaux, E.H. and Merry, D.H. 1976. *A Bibliography of Printed Works Relating to the City of Oxford.* Oxford: Clarendon Press.

Engel, A.J. 1983. *From Clergyman to Don: The Rise of the Academic Profession in Nineteenth-Century Oxford.* Oxford: Clarendon Press.

Evans, A. 1895. 'The Rollright Stones and Their Folklore', *Folklore* 6: 7–51.

Evans, J. 1943. *Time and Chance: The Story of Arthur Evans and his Forbears.* London: Longmans, Green and co.

Howe, A. (ed.) 1993. *Oxford: Studies in the History of a University Town.* Manchester: Manchester University Press.

Levine, P. 1986. *The Amateur and the Professional.* Cambridge, Cambridge University Press.

Lightman, B. 1997. *Victorian Science in Context.* Chicago and London: The University of Chicago Press.

Lucas, J.R. 1979. 'Wilberforce and Huxley: A Legendary Encounter'. *The Historical Journal* 22: 313–30.

Marett, R. 1941. *A Jerseyman at Oxford.* Oxford: Oxford University Press.

Parry-Jones, B. 1983. 'The Ashmolean Society', *The Ashmolean* 8–10.

Secord, J. 1994. 'Science in the Pub', *History of Science* 32: 269–315.

Sephton, R. 2001. *The Oxford of J.J. Faulkner, 1798–1857: Grocer, Chartist and Temperance Advocate.* Oxford: The Author.

Simcock, A. (ed.) 1985. *Robert T. Gunther and the Old Ashmolean.* Oxford: Museum of the History of Science

Turner, F. 1979. 'The Victorian Conflict between Science and Religion: A Professional Dimension', *Isis* 69: 356–76.

———. 1993. *Contesting Cultural Authority: Essays in Victorian intellectual life.* Cambridge: Cambridge University Press

Underhill, H.M.J. 1888. 'Artistic Lantern Slides' *The Optical Magic Lantern Journal*, 14–15.

———. 1890. 'Microscopic Animals', *The Midland Naturalist* 13: 224–29.

———. and Allen, F.J. 1875. 'Notes on the Diptera', in *Hardwicke's Science Gossip*, pp. 147–50.

Whittaker, W. 1973. Victorian and Edwardian Shopkeepers. Newton Abbot: David and Charles.

Wetherall, D. 1998. 'The Growth of Archaeological Societies', in Brand, V. (ed.) *The Study of the Past in the Victorian Age,* pp. 21–34, Oxbow Monograph 73.

See also http://web.arch.ox.ac.uk/archives/underhill/

Chapter 10

Revisiting the 'Invisible College'

José Ramón Mélida in Early Twentieth-Century Spain

Margarita Díaz-Andreu

Abstract

This chapter revisits the concept of the 'invisible college', defined within the field of the History of Science in the 1960s as the informal power groups formed in academia. It is argued that the concept of the 'invisible college' is still valid but should integrate new developments within the social sciences. Thus, the networks formed in the invisible colleges should be understood as fluid and contingent and even as overlapping. These ideas are tested in the case of José Ramón Mélida y Alinari (1856–1933), an archaeologist who was at the centre of a number of important networks in early twentieth-century century Spanish archaeology.

Towards a Flexible 'Invisible College'

Academic life is, and has always been, not only about ideas but also about daily practices such as letters (emails nowadays), conversations, encounters, conferences, committees, institutions and so on. All these are the media through which essential information is passed on and key alliances are formed. Scholars do not work in isolation, but in a complex network in which social interactions change the scene at every moment. Strategic movements are essential to achieve notoriety, if this is what the individual has decided to accomplish. In the 1960s historians of science came up with a term – 'invisible college' – to define the informal power groups formed in academia. As understood then, these communities of interest (cf. Allen 1978) were formed by individuals within the same area who were considered to be fairly frequently in contact with all the other members of the group. They met regularly through conferences, circulated pre-prints of their work, kept in touch and cooperated in research. Moreover, some of these groups were able to define who was important in the field, and even control the administration of research funds. Finally, they could be fundamental in influencing the acceptance or rejection of new ideas in the field, as well as the general strategy for future research (Price and Beaver 1966: 1011). The concept of 'invisible colleges' proved to be a useful analytical tool in the external analyses of the history of ideas in the natural and social sciences undertaken by several scholars from the 1960s to the 1980s (Goldstein 1983; Price 1965; Price and Beaver 1966; Rudwick 1985). Archaeology, however, has been relatively slow to assess the extent to which knowledge production is constrained by the interaction between scholars and the circumstances in which they operate.

As first defined, however, the concept of 'invisible college' included a high degree of inflexibility that is at odds with daily scientific practice. In the present article, the term will be understood in a much more open fashion. The study of the Spanish archaeologist José Ramón Mélida will show that although each researcher strategically develops strong links with others, these links are not unchanging. On the contrary, they are characterized by being in continuous flux. Membership to the college is not fixed. Indeed, each college member would include a different number of scholars in it. To a certain extent the 'invisible college' is very much an 'imagined college', to borrow a term normally used in the field of the study of nationalism (cf. Anderson 1991). Not only that, if we focus our attention on a pair of scholars – let us say Mélida and Gómez-Moreno[1] – the strength of the relationship (or the antagonism) between them will vary throughout their lifetime, not only because of the initiation of new projects that may need other partners, but also because established partners may also change alliances or projects. Invisible colleges are therefore continuously mutating networks of an ever changing number of scholars. This loose definition is not to imply that they do not exist – they do, but not as monolithic groups of individuals, despite being perceived as units by some scholars. Finally, I would contend that it is not essential to have a shared theoretical perspective within the invisible college: some allegiances are more related to power within academia and control of its resources than to academic ideas and convictions.

Scene 0: Accessing the Network (1876–1898)

José Ramón Mélida y Alinari was born in Madrid in 1856. He studied in the *Escuela Superior de Diplomática* (ESD, Higher School of Diplomatics, a school mirroring the French *École de Chartes*), in which archaeology, epigraphy and numismatics were taught. At the ESD he established good contact with one of the lecturers at the institution and keeper of the National Archaeological Museum (MAN, Museo Arqueológico Nacional), Juan de la Rada, and immediately after graduation he was given a post as unpaid assistant to work at the museum.[2] He managed to become a fully-paid civil servant in 1881, but he remained in a relatively low position until 1901.

Mélida's slow promotion should be seen in the light of his initial lack of direction in his attempt to enter any of the existing networks. Although he had been successfully accepted as an assistant in the MAN thanks to the protection of Rada, his lack of tact in hiding their differences in political ideology seems to have been influential in a drop of interest on the part of his protector. While Rada was very conservative in his outlook, Mélida became involved during his first years working for the MAN (1881–1883) with two of the most liberal institutions in Spain at the time: the Free Institution for Teaching (Institución Libre de Enseñaza) and the Ateneum of Madrid. Mélida tried twice (1878 and 1880), to become a civil servant before finally succeeding in 1881 (AGA, FE, 31/6535). His application was backed up by the then director of the museum, and not by Rada, which may or may not be significant.

In 1885 Mélida applied without success for a chair in the Higher School of Diplomatics (AGA, FC, 31/6535; AGA, FC; MAN, exp. Mélida, 1987/114 (II)). His lack of success did not come as a surprise to him. Before the competition, Mélida had written to a friend who was also thinking of entering the competition, telling him that the chair was already intended for someone else. The selected candidate was Juan Catalina García López (whose name is usually shortened to his second family name, Catalina). Mélida explained that 'there will be no scarcity of methods, more or less legal' to favour the candidate (Mélida personal letter to Llabrés, 11 November 1884 in Peiró Martín and Pasamar Alzuria 1996: 90–91). Both Catalina and Rada were actively engaged in Catholic right-wing politics.

Mélida learned the lesson. From the mid-1880s, perhaps in connection with changes in his personal life (in 1885 he started to court the woman whom he would marry in 1889 (MAN, exp. Mélida, 1987/114 (I) and1987/114 (II)), he abandoned his previous left-wing liberalism and adopted instead a form of patriotic conservatism. State administration was dominated by the latter and the only means to get promotion was to be seen favourably in the eyes of the networks that the conservatives had formed, with a marked aristocratic presence. The number in positions of responsibility related to culture – as well as other fields – is staggering. Mélida had his first opportunity to show his political transformation when, between 1888 and 1905, he took as an extra job a position as librarian for the Duchess of Villahermosa (MAN, exp. Mélida, 1987/114 (II)). In this he was following the steps of the very conservative Marcelino Menéndez Pelayo. His second opportunity came when he joined a study trip to Greece and Turkey organised by the Parisian *Revue Générale des Sciences* in 1898, in which he met Antonio Vives (Mélida 1899). Vives was another of Rada's protégés; he had a close relationship with the Count Valencia de don Juan, who was the organiser of weekly cultural meetings (*tertulias*) where invited individuals had the opportunity to further strengthen their links with particular networks (Gómez-Moreno 1995: passim). Both Menéndez Pelayo and Vives would be key figures in the raising of Mélida's profile within their network.

Scene 1: Rising in the Network (1898–1910) (RABM)

From 1898 to 1911 Mélida sent the highest percentage of his articles to the journal of the professional body of archivists, librarians and archaeologists (CFABA, *Cuerpo Facultativo de Archiveros, Bibliotecarios y Anticuarios* (from 1900 *'y Arqueólogos*) (Díaz-Andreu 2004: table 2, lxvi). This body had been formed in 1858, two years after the opening of the ESD. School graduates would form the workforce of civil servants in the increasingly organised network of national and regional archives, libraries and museums. These civil servants were managed by the CFABA which published the journal, the *Revista de Archivos, Bibliotecas y Museos* (RABM), as a form of creating an institutional identity. After some difficulties the journal restarted in 1896. Menéndez Pelayo was one of the main organisers behind the initiative and in 1898 stood in as director (a post made official in 1900 after the actual director's death). Mélida was given the post of chair of the editorial board (Peiró Martín and Pasamar Alzuria 1996: 187n). The main period of Mélida's contribution to the RABM lasted from 1896 to 1909. From 1910, however, Mélida's efforts would turn to another journal, the *Bulletin of the Royal Academy of History* (BRAH).

The change of emphasis from the RABM to the BRAH can be seen as the result of the strategies organised by Mélida for his academic promotion. From 1898 to 1910 many things would change in his position. After 1898 and his study trip to Greece and Turkey everything changed. In March 1899 he was elected to the Royal Academy of Fine Arts. Fellowship to this academy was essential in order to be considered as a candidate for the directorship of the Museum of Casts (*Museo de Reproducciones Artísticas*), briefly directed by Rada in 1901. After Rada's death, the post was inherited by Mélida and he directed the institution from 1901 to 1916.

From his entrance to the RABASF Mélida's power continued to increase. After his selection as the director of the Museum of Casts, he was commissioned to write the Provincial Monumental Catalogues for Cáceres and Badajoz in 1906. This had been an initiative organised by both the RABASF and the RAH to make an inventory of the main monuments from prehistory to the modern period in each province as a way to protect them (Gómez-Moreno 1995: passim). He was also selected to represent the RABASF in the Commission for the Excavation of Numantia in 1906. The excavation of Numantia was very significant for Spanish nationalism (Díaz-Andreu 1995: 44–45). Numantia had been a pre-Roman town located in central Spain, in Castille, where the fight against the Romans had led its inhabitants towards a collective suicide, as at Massada. Excavating Numantia was therefore a prestigious affair. The Commission was granted an annual sum of 15,000 pts by the Parliament, the highest amount provided by the state for an archaeological excavation for several years (see Díaz-Andreu 2003: table I). Mélida explained that with such a gesture the parliament had 'renewed the memorable page that with its blood Numantia wrote in [the history of] our race'. He saw the government's decision as an inspiration originating from the national conscience (Mélida 1906: 4). Mélida found as colleagues in the commission the director of the RAH, Eduardo Saavedra, and his old enemy, Catalina. Somehow these contacts – this new network – did the trick: in December 1906 he would be elected a Fellow of the RAH. Mélida also actively participated in the development of national tourism as early as 1908 through his collaboration with the Marquis of La Vega Inclán, from 1911 the director of the Royal Commissary of Tourism, an institution created in that year to organise tourism in Spain. Tourism had been pronounced by King Alfonso XIII to be of public interest as a source of income for the nation (www 2004).

Scene 2: At the Height of Power (1910–1922) (BRAH)

Mélida's position of authority would continue to increase, especially after Catalina's death in 1911. Following the customary rules the person who had substituted his teaching would have obtained the chair. This, however, did not happen, despite a long legal battle (Encyclopaedia 1908: T30, 945–6) to try and prevent what eventually occured: the chair of Archaeology was divided into two, one for Archaeology and the other one for Epigraphy and Numismatics. No examinations were held, as the prestige of the two official candidates was such that the legislation was changed to allow them access without competition. Mélida obtained the chair of Archaeology (Royal Order 26 December 1911) and his friend Vives that of Epigraphy and Numismatics. As a university professor Mélida would be able to promote positivism in Spain, through his teaching and especially through his handbook *La arqueología española* (Mélida 1929) (see Díaz-Andreu 2004).

From 1910 to 1922 Mélida focused his attention to the Bulletin of the RAH. This may be related mainly to his post of antiquarian of the RAH from 1913. During this period he became the best funded archaeologist in Spain for excavations, a situation that lasted until 1922 when he moved to second place in the list. In 1911 the law of archaeological excavations was passed (7 July 1911) and in the regulations published in 1912 (1 March 1912) the Higher Council for Excavations and Antiquities (JSEA, *Junta Superior de Excavaciones y Antigüedades*) was created to manage archaeological work. An analysis of the excavations that received most funding from 1915 to 1934 clearly shows that one of the main aims of the JSEA was to make archaeological sites and monuments interesting and suitable for tourism. No wonder that one of the members of the governing body of the JSEA was the Marquis of La Vega Inclán. Of the other members (Díaz-Andreu 2004: table 5, cxxxv), most had an institutional link with Mélida: they were either Fellows of the RAH, or/and the RABASF (most members), and/or they were professors at the university of Madrid. This perhaps explains the high subsidy he received from the JSEA: about 25% of the total. Mélida was in charge of two major archaeological sites: in addition to Numantia (he chaired the commission of excavations after Catalina's death), he became the director of the excavations of the spectacular remains of the Roman town of Merida.

In 1916 Mélida was invited to return to the National Archaeological Museum (MAN) as director (AGA, FE, 31/6535; MAN year 1916, box 13, numbers 18, 23). He may have been organising his return for a few years. The name of Vives again turns out to be relevant in this context, as in 1912 Mélida organised the purchase of one of Vives' collections for the museum (Mélida 1912, García-Bellido 1993a).

The beginning of the end of Mélida's dominance, however, started in this period and was partly connected to the rise to power of Manuel Gómez-Moreno. This Andalusian had arrived in Madrid at the start of the century, protected by another Andalusian, Juan Facundo Riaño (1829–1901), the then director of the Museum of Casts, and Fellow both of the RAH and RABASF. He arranged for Gómez-Moreno to elaborate all the Provincial Catalogues of Monuments, but his death in 1901 meant that others were able to change the plans and he was only commissioned the provinces of Avila, León, Salamanca and Zamora. After Riaño's death Gómez-Moreno would find his main ally in the professor of Fine Arts at the University of Madrid, Elías Tormo. The first step in climbing the power ladder for Gómez-Moreno was to become a professor. Tormo managed to convince the authorities to create a third chair from that of Catalina vacated in 1911, originally divided in 1912, as explained above, into those for Vives (Epigraphy and Numismatics) and for Mélida (Archaeology). However, Gómez-Moreno was not even a doctor in 1911. In order to fulfil the requirements he had to complete his masters and his thesis all in one year. This he managed, obtaining the chair of Arabic Archaeology in 1913 (Gómez-Moreno 1995).

Through Elías Tormo, Manuel Gómez-Moreno also became one of the key figures in the newly founded Centre for Historical Studies (CEH – *Centro de Estudios Históricos*) of the Council for the Enhancement of Studies and Scientific Research (JAE – *Junta para la Ampliación de Estudios e Investigaciones Científicas*). The JAE had been created in 1907 in the aftermath of the reaction to the loss of the last colonies (Cuba, Puerto Rico and the Philippines) in 1898. It followed the model of the Collège de France (Rodríguez de Lecea 1988: 526) and aimed to provide an alternative to the teaching and research undertaken in the university, considered to be in decline. Yet, it failed in its attempt to have its teaching approved as an alternative to the state university, and therefore most of its staff, in addition to their affiliation to the JAE, were also university professors. This created a two-tier system by which a few scholars exclusively located in Madrid received an additional salary and facilities, a channelling of money denied at that time to the university. While the JAE and its institutions was a problem for those living outside Madrid, within the capital itself a dual system was created in which some of the professors at the university were doubly paid and had alternative, brand new places to work in the centre of Madrid, whereas the others received lower salary and only had the facilities at the university. The JAE clearly achieved good results that are still celebrated nowadays (Sánchez Ron 1988), but they were put in danger because the institution was not able to break with perhaps the most damaging disease in the Spanish university: the patronage system. As we saw, appointments were often made not solely on the basis of merit, but also following friendship, political convictions and regional origins.

In the case of Gómez-Moreno, his integration into the CEH meant that students perceived him as an attractive option to work with. In contrast to the high number of students taught by Gómez-Moreno, Mélida had only one student, Blas Taracena, at the start of his university career. Mélida helped him to pass the examinations for entry in the CFABA and put him in charge of the Museum of Numantia. Mélida also organised his inclusion in the Commission for the Excavation of Numantia in 1917. Taracena wrote his thesis under Mélida's supervision on the pottery found in Numantia, a subject Mélida had published in an article when Taracena met him as an undergraduate (Mélida 1913). However, from the moment he became a doctor in 1924 he started to collaborate with Gómez-Moreno and published in the journal controlled by the Andalusian (Taracena 1924a, 1924b). Gómez-Moreno's success may have been linked with other factors we ignore today – special charm and dedication to students, for example – but in any case it seems to show the use of strategies on the part of the students. They deliberately chose the professor with whom they thought it would be of greater benefit to be associated.

Strategy also seems to be the reason why years later the young man who followed Mélida in the chair, Antonio García y Bellido, claimed to be his disciple (García-Bellido 1993b: 13). He was not. He had written his thesis in the field of History of Art on the early modern artist family of Churriguera under Tormo's supervision. Yet, he had been successful in obtaining the chair against one of Gómez-Moreno's disciples who had been failed by Mélida, who was a member of the examination panel in the competition for the chair. García y Bellido, as the professor of Classical Archaeology could not say that he was Tormo's disciple and given that Mélida was already dead and could not dispute this, he created a strategic scholarly kinship, re-inventing himself as one of Mélida's students.

Scene 3: Mélida's Role in the Protection of Antiquities: 1923–1933 (BRABASF)

From 1923 Mélida turned his attention from the Bulletin of the RAH to that of the RABASF. Though he should have retired in 1923, Mélida did not want to go. Only in exceptional circumstances were civil servants allowed to keep their jobs, and a petition was therefore made by the director of the RABASF, the Count of Romanones (in AGA, FE, 31/6535, dated 23 October 1923). It was addressed to the dictator General Primo de Rivera (gov. 1923–1930) and in it Mélida's figure was described as irreplaceable as the director of the MAN. Permission granted (Royal Decree 31 October 1923), he continued as university professor until November 1928 (AGA, FE, 32/29–40) and as the director of the MAN until June 1931. His gratitude to the RABASF may explain why he focused his efforts in this institution in the last decade of his life, until his death in 1933.

His special links with the RABASF explain why Mélida was the first to have his Provincial Catalogues of Monuments published, although it was probably no accident that those by Gómez-Moreno soon followed. From 1923 to 1933 Mélida concentrated his energies on the protection of archaeological and monumental heritage, a task linked to the RABASF. His earlier efforts in this field had been made within the framework of the RAH. Until 1911 he published there seven reports on the declaration of National Monuments – a list of special monuments to be protected in Spain conceived in 1836 (Ordieres Díez 1995: 25–35). The first monument on the list – the Cathedral of Leon – had been included in 1844 (Hernández-Gil 1983: 27). Yet, for some reason, from 1914 he chose the Bulletin of the RABASF to publish these reports, writing thirteen altogether (see Díaz-Andreu 2004).

In 1915 the concept of 'Historic-Artistic Monument' had been created (Act of 4 March 1915). This was a legal protection of lesser status than that of 'National Monument'. From the RABASF Mélida processed reports dealing with applications for permission to carry out work in monuments such as the Roman theatre of Sagunto, the Roman forum of Tarragona, the Upper Palaeolithic painted cave of Altamira, and other prehistoric, classical and medieval sites. He also wrote reports on the acquisition by the State of several archaeological and artistic objects. Many articles written in the Bulletin of the RABASF were related to the law for the Protection of the Monumental and Artistic Monuments of Spain of 9 August 1926. The committee formed to set the law included Mélida, as well as Tormo, Gómez-Moreno, and several aristocrats – the Count of Las Infantas, the Count of Cedillo, the Duke of Alba, the Marquis of La Vega Inclán (Ordieres Díez 1995: 39). After the law was passed, they all also formed part of the committee to implement it. Yet, in order to accommodate other friends, in some cases the institution represented by each member changed. Mélida, for example, represented the RAH in the first committee, but was included as the director of the MAN in the second. He may also have been member of a special committee of the State Council of the National Artistic Treasure (*Junta Central del Tesoro Artístico Nacional*), as president of the Evaluating Committee for the Artistic Objects for Export (*Comisión valoradora de objetos artísticos a exportar*) (see Díaz-Andreu 2004: table 4, cxxx). All the other colleagues mentioned in the two first committees were included in this third one. This clearly illustrates that it was not the institution represented which was important, but the individuals. In this case they were not of the same college or network but belonged to two different ones which collaborated – or were impelled to collaborate – together in the project.

Testing the Fluidity of Invisible Colleges

In this article the study of José Ramón Mélida y Alinari has been used to test the concept of fluid invisible colleges. It has been argued that networks – crystallized in intangible relationships such as friendships, for which we have details in letters and comments in articles – were essential in Mélida's rise to power and in the opposition evinced by others. The point of this article, however, is not to focus on one individual, but to use his biography as a way to assess whether such academic networks had their impact on the processes of knowledge formation, and on the institutionalisation of the discipline. The first aspect has not been fully developed in this article, but it is clear that only when Mélida was ready to communicate a conservative message did the dominant intellectual networks (represented by Vives and Menéndez Pelayo as well as members of the intellectual aristocracy) allow him to rise to power. From this position Mélida was able to convey a vision of the archaeological past in tune with the most traditional Spanish nationalism. He did this through many conferences, articles in high circulation newspapers such as *ABC*, and about 600 academic publications including two handbooks (Mélida 1923, 1929) of key importance for generations of students and even for other intellectuals in Spain (Díaz-Andreu 2004: clxix–cxcix).

Networks had a definite impact on the institutionalisation of the discipline, on how the administration and protection of heritage was organised through legislation and how museums and higher education were structured. Thanks to his friends (mainly people belonging to or connected with the politically powerful aristocracy), Mélida could access a range of institutions (Royal Academies of Fine Arts and History, the Museum of Casts, the National Archaeological Museum and the University of Madrid). Nationalist outrage at the export of antiquities to foreign countries may explain why the cultural elite, formed in large measure by aristocrats, allowed administrators (Mélida and others) to recommend tough legislation sanctioned to regulate heritage (Acts of 1911 and 1926). Surprisingly, this resulted in a stricter legislative framework than in Britain (Breeze 1996, Champion 1996) and France (Schnapp 1996).

Institutionalisation and knowledge formation are not two separate spheres. This can be seen by looking at the excavations that received funding –and what amount. The huge funding that Mélida should have received to excavate the site of Numantia, one of the most recognizable symbols of Spanish nationalism, can be seen as a result of the ability of the cultural elite in power to promote a very specific understanding of Spanish prehistory.

One of the issues that has come up on several occasions in the article has been that of how individuals and/or networks use strategies to obtain something they desire. This is something that should not surprise anyone, as it forms part of our daily experience. However, its impact on the development of the institutionalisation and knowledge-base in our discipline in general, and of Spanish archaeology in particular, is poorly understood. It explains processes in the transmission of knowledge such as why certain professors stop being directly influential when close to the age of retirement (as happened to Mélida). It also accounts for the purchase of particular collections by museums (the Vives collection bought by the MAN in 1912) as well as the composition of particular committees (all of those related to the Act of 1926).

Networks are in continuous flux, not least because their membership is formed by living beings who retire and at some point unfortunately die. Rada died in 1901, the Duchess of Villahermosa in 1905, Menéndez Pelayo in 1912, Vives in 1925. Mélida retired in 1923 although he managed to retain power for several years at least in the MAN and the royal academies. Friendships also change. Mélida was at one time a participant at one of the weekly cultural meetings (*tertulias*) in which Gómez-Moreno was a protagonist, and presumably on good terms with him. Later on, however, all data seem to point to an increasing antagonism between the two, which had an impact on students and schools of thought. Mélida's network had a sympathy for French archaeology that would later be substituted by those closer to German archaeology, the dominant paradigm from the 1920s. Networks are also overlapping, some of those who assisted Mélida were also involved in other cultural fields, so that, for example, together with the image of Numantia other elements, such as the figures of the sixteenth-century painter El Greco and writer Cervantes, were promoted for the formation of a cultural base for Spanish nationalism.

The case of José Ramón Mélida y Alinari has been used in this article to revisit the concept of the invisible college. First proposed in the 1960s in the field of History of Science, I have argued that its definition should be changed to allow fluidity and contingency in their nature. The analysis undertaken in the previous pages has shed new light on the history of late nineteenth- and early twentieth- century Spanish archaeology, by looking at how theories and institutions are influenced by personal relations within academia. This study demonstrates the benefit history of archaeology (not only of Spain, but also of elsewhere in the world) may obtain from looking not at particular data in isolation, but at processes occurring in the development of our discipline.

Notes

1. For further information about the biographies and institutions mentioned in this article see (Díaz-Andreu *et al.* forthcoming 2008).
2. The information provided in this chapter is based on a wide range of archival sources. For this study of Mélida three archives were consulted: the General Archive for the Administration (*Archivo General de la Administración*, shortened as AGA), the National Archaeological Museum (*Museo Arqueológico Nacional*, shortened as MAN), and the Archive of Retired Civil Servants (*Archivo de Clases Pasivas*). Research for this article was undertaken between the years 2001 and 2003. All documentary sources are detailed in Díaz-Andreu (2004). FE refers to 'fondo de educación' and FC 'fondo de cultura'. *Expediente* (group of documents in an archive) is shortened as 'exp.'

References

Allen, D.E. (ed) 1978. *The Naturalist in Britain: A Social History*. London: Allen Lane.

Anderson, B. 1991. *Imagined Communities. Reflections on the Origin and Spread of Nationalism*, 2nd edition. London: Verso.

Breeze, D.J. 1996. 'Archaeological Nationalism as Defined by Law in Britain', in J.A. Atkinson, I. Banks and J. O'Sullivan (eds), *Nationalism and Archaeology*. Glasgow: Cruithne Press, 95–103.

Champion, T. 1996. 'Three Nations or One? Britain and the National Use of the Past', in M. Díaz-Andreu and T. Champion (eds), *Archaeology and Nationalism in Europe*. London: UCL Press, 119–45.

Díaz-Andreu, M. 1995. 'Nationalism and Archaeology. Spanish Archaeology in the Europe of Nationalities', in P.L. Kohl and C. Fawcett (eds), *Nationalism, Politics, and the Practice of Archaeology*. Cambridge: Cambridge University Press, 39–56.

———. 2003. 'Arqueología y Dictaduras: Italia, Alemania y España', in F. Wulff and M. Alvarez Martí-Aguilar (eds), *Antigüedad y Franquismo (1936–75)*. Málaga: Diputación Provincial de Málaga, 33–74.

———. 2004. 'Mélida: Génesis, Pensamiento y Obra de un Maestro', in J.R. Mélida *La Arqueología Española*. Clásicos de la Historiografía Española. Pamplona: Urgoiti : I-CXCIX.

———. (with the collaboration of) G. Mora and J. Cortadella (ed.) 2007. *Diccionario Histórico de la Arqueología en Espa.*, Madrid: Marcial Pons, forthcoming.

Encyclopedia 1908–. *Enciclopedia Universal Ilustrada Europeo-Americana*. Madrid, Barcelona: Espasa-Calpe.

García-Bellido, M.P. 1993a. 'Prólogo', in A. García y Bellido and M.P. García-Bellido (eds), *Album de Dibujos de la Colección de Bronces Antiguos de Antonio Vives Escudero*. Anejos de Archivo Español de Arqueología XIII. Madrid: Consejo Superio de Investigaciones Científicas.

García-Bellido, M.P. 1993b 'Prólogo', in A. García y Bellido (ed), *España y los Españoles Hace Dos Mil Años Según la Geografía de Strábon*. Madrid: Espasa-Calpe, 9–53.

Goldstein, D.S. 1983. 'The Professionalisation of History in Britain in the Late Nineteenth and Early Twentieth Centuries', *Storia della Storiografia* 3: 3–26.

Gómez-Moreno, M.E. 1995. *Manuel Gómez-Moreno Martínez*. Madrid: Centro de Estudios Ramón Areces.

Hernández-Gil, D. 1983. 'Datos Históricos Sobre la Restauración de Monumentos', *50 Años de Protección del Patrimonio Histórico Artístico 1933–1983.* Madrid: Ministerio de Cultura, 25–31.

Mélida, J.R. 1899. *Viaje a Grecia y Turquía. Memoria que presenta al Ministerio de Fomento don José Ramón Mélida. Jefe de la sección de "Protohistoria y Edad Antigua" en el Museo Arqueológico Nacional y en tal concepto comisionado para efectuar dicho viaje.* Madrid: Imp. del Colegio Nacional de Sordomudos y de Ciegos.

——— . 1906. *Las excavaciones de Numancia. Publicado en la Revista 'Cultura Española'.* Madrid: Imprenta Ibérica.

——— . 1912. *Los Bronces Ibéricos y Visigodos de la Colección Vives. Suscripción Pública para Adquirirlos.* Madrid: Tipografía de la Revista de Archivos, Bibliotecas y Museos.

——— . 1913. 'Cerámica Numantina', *Arte Español* 5: 216–19.

——— . 1923. *Arqueología Clásica*, 1st edition. Barcelona: Labor, taller gráfico iberoamericano.

——— . 1929. *Arqueología Española*, 1st edition, Colección Labor, Sección IV Artes Plásticas nº 189–90. Barcelona: Labor [Talleres Gráficos Ibero-americanos].

Ordieres Díez, I. 1995. *Historia de la Restauración Monumental en España (1835–1936).* Madrid: Ministerio de Cultura.

Peiró Martín, I. and G. Pasamar Alzuria. 1996. *La Escuela Superior de Diplomática (los Archiveros en la Historiografía Española Contemporánea).* Madrid: Asociación Española de Archiveros, Bibliotecarios, Museólogos y Documentalistas (ANABAD).

Price, D. De Solla 1965. *Little Science, Big Science.* New York: Columbia University Press.

——— . 1966. 'Collaboration in an Invisible College', *American Psychologist* 21: 1011–18.

Rodríguez de Lecea, T. 1988. 'La Enseñanza de la Historia en el Centro de Estudios Históricos: Hinojosa y Altamira', in J.M. Sánchez Ron (ed), *1907–1987. La Junta para la Ampliación de Estudios e Investigaciones Científicas Ochenta Años Después vol. II.* Madrid: Consejo Superior de Investigaciones Científicas, 519–34.

Rudwick, M.J.S. 1985. *The Great Devonian Controversy.* Chicago: Chicago University Press.

Sánchez Ron, J.M. 1988. 'La Junta para la Ampliación de Estudios e Investigaciones Científicas ochenta años después', in J.M. Sánchez Ron (ed), *1907–1987. La Junta para la Ampliación de Estudios e Investigaciones Científicas Ochenta Años Después vol. I.* Madrid: Consejo Superior de Investigaciones Científicas, 1–61.

Schnapp, A. 1996. 'French Archaeology: Between National Identity and Cultural Identity', in M. Díaz-Andreu and T. Champion (eds), *Archaeology and Nationalism in Europe.* London: UCL Press, 48–67.

Taracena, B. 1924. *La Cerámica Ibérica de Numancia. Tesis Doctoral.* Madrid: Impr. Samarán y Cía.

——— . and M. Gómez-Moreno. 1924. 'Epigrafía Soriana', *Boletín de la Real Academia de la Historia* 85: 23.

www 2004. 'Fundamentos de la Intervención Administrativa Turística [No Author Specified]', www turismoenred.webcindario.com/deadminis/ administrativo1.doc: (January 2004).

Chapter 11

Between Sweden and Central Asia

Practising Archaeology in the 1920s and 1930s

Jan Bergman

Abstract

This paper concerns the archaeological practices of the Swedish archaeologist, Folke Bergman (1902–1946), first around Uppsala in Sweden and later in the north-western parts of China. It is based mainly on published and unpublished reports of excavations and other field activities as well as private diaries and letters from the actual time period. The circumstances were different in the two areas, with considerable impact on archaeological practice. Sweden was at that time a stable society with fairly good public services, reasonable accommodation opportunities and decent climate (at least for a Swede). Folke Bergman could obtain the scientific backing of various disciplines from his Alma Mater, Uppsala University. China, on the other hand, was characterised by political unrest among warlords. People were poor, roads were in bad condition and communication facilities extremely slow. The climate of the western provinces was harsh, with very hot summers and cold winters, with dust and sand storms. Folke Bergman worked in a vast, insufficiently mapped area which necessitated not only surveying sites, but also extensive route-mapping, with long-distance transport of equipment and antiquities by camels, horses and donkeys. As a member of the so-called Sino-Swedish Expedition led by Sven Hedin, Folke Bergman had occasional access to medical care and scientific support, but for long periods he was accompanied only by servants and beasts of burden. Other factors strongly affecting scientific practice were the nationalism of Chinese authorities and academics, as well as the religious conceptions of the local people.

Introduction

Archaeological practice as a theme in the history of archaeology can, of course, be approached in a number of ways. My approach is based on the fact that a couple of years ago, I came across a bunch of private letters and diaries written by a Swedish archaeologist in the 1920s and early 1930s that contain a wealth of information on his daily work in two completely different areas of the world, namely in Uppland, Sweden and in the western provinces of China. This means that I am only going to describe the practice of a single professional during a fairly short period of time. I will by no means try to address issues of archaeological practice in general, in either of these countries.

An important source of inspiration for me to publish on this subject is Åsa Gillberg's dissertation, in which she elaborates on the role of biographies of researchers as a part of the history of a scientific discipline and on the fact that most writing of this kind is about so-called Great Men and their achievements (Gillberg 2001: 38). She believes that researchers in the history of archaeology should pay attention not only to the prominent figures but also to the unnoticed servants to the discipline. After all, the bulk of archaeology is and has been created by less prominent individuals. To describe the achievements of these people can of course be a difficult task since many of them have not cared or been able to leave any informative documents behind. With this perspective, I think it is worthwhile to extract relevant information from the above mentioned letters and diaries and try, not to produce a biography but to describe the practice of a rather unnoticed archaeologist as well as possible.

By archaeological practice, the layperson will no doubt understand primarily archaeological excavation, and perhaps also the treatment and analysis of finds from ancient times. The professional on the other hand will be well aware of all the numerous preparatory steps involved, such as permits, funding, organising, etc., that have to be undertaken before any fieldwork can begin, as well as of the laborious registration of finds, writing of reports, distribution of results, etc., all constituting necessary parts of any archaeological investigation. However, in a country like Sweden, it is taken for granted that things like transportation, food and lodging, medical care and communication will not present any problems that have to be considered as part of archaeological practice, and this was also generally the case in the 1920s. In China, on the other hand, matters were then very different. This is the reason why I have chosen in the following account to regard such circumstances as forming part of archaeological practice. Other influencing factors include the professional and social relations between different researchers, and I have paid some attention to such matters as well.

Method

In addition to private letters (henceforth PL) and diaries (henceforth PD), I have consulted official reports, correspondence and newspaper articles written in western languages. It has not been possible to make use of reports published in Chinese, which would have been desirable. As far as the practice in Sweden is concerned, the letters tell about a number of parishes in which Folke Bergman was active as an archaeologist. Reports concerning this work are in most cases available at ATA in Stockholm and so is relevant correspondence with the Swedish authorities on antiquarian matters. Regarding the Chinese area, a number of reports have been published in English including an official diary. Background information has been collected from various books and periodicals published mainly during the first half of the twentieth century. For the Romanisation of Chinese names, I have used the Wade-Giles system.

The Subject

The archaeologist I am writing about here is Folke Bergman (1902–1946). He was born in Stockholm and graduated from the senior high school in natural sciences intending to become a military officer. After a few months at the military college, he changed his mind, however, and went to Uppsala where he began studying archaeology at the university in 1923. One source of inspiration to become an archaeologist may have been a book written by Otto Hauser (Hauser 1917), which Folke Bergman acquired in Swedish translation in 1922.

The professor of archaeology, Oscar Almgren, was the first of that discipline in Uppsala and the number of his students was still rather limited, maybe a dozen. Other teachers of the discipline were Gunnar Ekholm, Nils Åberg and Bengt Thordeman. The students were soon commissioned with archaeological fieldwork, primarily in Uppland, and did a lot of inventory and excavations, especially during the summer months. In the spring of 1924, Folke Bergman was employed as temporary amanuensis by the University Museum for Nordic Antiquities in Uppsala (the Museum) with an hourly compensation of less than 3 Sw.Crowns (PL 8 November 1926).

In the beginning of 1927 and before he had obtained any academic degree, Folke Bergman was given the opportunity to join an expedition to Central Asia organised by Sven Hedin for one and a half years. Hedin had been asked by the German airline company, Lufthansa, to establish a number of temporary meteorological observation stations in the western provinces of China in order to make airline connection between Europe and China possible. Hedin had accepted, provided that he also could bring a number of researchers of other disciplines than meteorology with him, the cost of which should be borne by Lufthansa as well. Hedin had not thought of archaeology in the first place but was convinced by J.G. Andersson, the Swedish geologist and archaeologist, who had been active in China since 1914, to do so. Hedin turned to the King's Custodian of Antiquities, Sigurd Curman (the Custodian), who recommended Folke Bergman for the task. As also Oscar Almgren strongly supported the idea, Folke Bergman accepted the assignment after a few days to think it over (PL 4 January 1927). His monthly salary would be 885 Swedish Crowns (PL 26 January 1928). Already at the end of January, he was on his way to Peking via Berlin and the Trans-Siberian railway. The original commission was later successively prolonged and did not end until the autumn of 1934.

Folke Bergman returned twice for short visits to Sweden, the first time to marry and the second to bring his family to Peking where he stayed and served as the local representative of the expedition for two years. The rest of the time he spent in the field or waiting for permission to go there in some godforsaken hole in China or Russia. Not always was the scientific work in the field devoted to archaeology. He also had to occupy himself with anthropometry, meteorology and route mapping.

Practice in Sweden

Archaeological practice in Uppsala in the 1920s was theoretically based on a culture-historical approach. Style of artefacts, ethnic group, race and language belonged together and culture was thought to be spread by migration of large groups of people. Simultaneously, great importance was attached to ancient authors like Tacitus, Jordanes and Snorre Sturlasson, whose writing was used to explain and construe the existence of prehistoric monuments, kingdoms and political deeds (Nerman 1913, Wessén 1927). Lauritz Weibull's source-critical questioning of ancient chronicles and narratives (Weibull 1925) was opposed and nationalism and national romanticism were still favoured by many academics in Uppsala in the 1920s. Independent of this, there existed in Uppland, like in many other parts of Sweden, a genuine interest in ancient remains by common people, manifested by the formation of regional antiquarian associations, e.g. Upplands fornminnesförening or local folklore societies, but legislation regarding ancient remains was lagging behind. Accelerating road and building construction caused increased damage to prehistoric graves and cemeteries, and a state committee was appointed 1913 to analyse the need for new rules regarding the protection of antiquities. Their conclusions, published in 1922 (SOU 1922: 12) proposed a number of changes to existing legislation as well as a new organisation of the central authorities. However, none of this was accomplished until much later. The highest state official, the Custodian, as well as the Royal Swedish Academy of Letters, History and Antiquities (the Academy) had only limited financial means to carry out any archaeological fieldwork. No entire inventory of Sweden's ancient remains had yet been started, except for some local areas. For fieldwork the Central Board of Antiquities (RAÄ) had to rely on the local associations and private donors. It was, however, prepared to carry the cost of management, inspections, photographs and material as well as written reports (ATA, RAÄ-letter in the file of Orkesta parish). From 1925, annual funds for creating and maintaining a general register of all archaeological remains found by the inventory were appropriated by the Swedish parliament (Gustawsson 1930: 197).

The study of archaeology at the university included seminars in the field and Folke Bergman was evidently fairly well trained in the fieldwork when in the summer of 1925 he was charged by the regional antiquarian association, which would bear the cost, with the inventory of remains from the pre-Roman Iron Age in a number of parishes of eastern Uppland. In his report, which was delivered in November, he writes that his method in the first place had been to visit all known pre-Roman, Iron Age cemeteries i.e. those with menhirs, triangular or quadratic stone settings. Furthermore, many other cemeteries, both shown and not shown on the geological map, were visited. Great help in the search for previously unnoticed remains was received from local representatives, appointed by the Custodian. He described the geographical position, counted and measured the menhirs and graves and classified the latter according to their geometrical shape and composition and noticed any existing damages. No excavations were made but nevertheless some prehistoric artefacts were found. He also obtained information regarding privately owned antiquities that had been found in the respective area and about observations that had been made at previous diggings for sand and gravel in and close to the cemeteries. No maps were drawn. It took Folke Bergman 25 days to go almost completely through six parishes whereas his investigation had not been completed in four. His original report is available in the Museum of Uppland and a copy was also sent to the Custodian (Bergman 1925). In a letter to Upplands fornminnesförening, dated 9 February 1926, the Custodian expresses his satisfaction with the report and urges the inventory work to continue (ATA, file of Funbo parish).

In 1925, Folke Bergman also worked for a period of time in Gotland, leading some excavations within the town of Visby (Fig. 11.1). These were almost entirely financed by private donors. The chief investigator, John Nihlén, has given an expressive account of how he and his staff had to spend as much time in fund-raising as in digging. When they were running out of money and threatened to discontinue the work, the local people started subscriptions and also single donors appeared (Nihlén 1982: 52)

The following year, Folke Bergman was entrusted with a large number of archaeological tasks by his teachers and the Custodian: not only inventory work but also excavations which sometimes were carried out together with other students (PL 3 March 1926, 6 October 1926) (Fig. 11.2).

Fig. 11.1 Folke Bergman in Visby, Gotland (Nihlén 1982).

Fig. 11.2 Excavation at Gödåker, Uppland, 1925. Photo Pär Olsén.

This time he also made maps of the sites. About 20 parishes were visited, most of them in the summer. For this work, Folke Bergman had applied for financial support by the Academy with 350 Swedish Crowns but received only 200. From Upplands fornminnesförening he received 300 Swedish Crowns plus help with typewriting of his final report (ATA, file of Knutby parish). For documentation of the inventory, special forms were filled out. The remains documented included mounds, cairns, stone settings, cup marks, menhirs, stone and metal artefacts, rock carvings and runic stones, seals of resin, ceramic shards, carbon lumps, burned and unburned bones. Neither bones nor carbon lumps were taken care of but drawings were made of human skeletons if they were undisturbed and small artefacts were taken to the Museum provided they had not already become private property. Some runic stones were also repaired and put in an upright position (PL 27 July 1926).

A major assignment that Folke Bergman was entrusted with was the inventory of the parish of Vendel. This attracted the attention of the local newspaper and one article (UNT 22 June 1926) illustrates something of the ideological basis for the investigation of the Uppland countryside. The article reads, for instance, that this investigation will supply 'a clear picture of how the nucleus of the Swedish State had emerged and developed ...'.

Part of archaeological practice in Uppsala were the weekly seminars where students and teachers from other disciplines often participated. These seminars were often followed by supper in a restaurant and night-caps in for instance the flat of Gunnar Ekholm. We can imagine that various ideas of what life in prehistory was like were aired and exchanged on those occasions (PL 1, 6, 25 November 1926, 11 December 1926).

Working Conditions in Sweden

Conditions for archaeological fieldwork in Uppland in the 1920s were quite favourable. Travel was by train, car, motorbike or bike and accommodations were found in private homes or inns. The most frustrating incidents seem to have related to a bed that was too short or in poor condition, or again a flat tyre. Often entertainment was offered by wealthy landowners, and labourers with their digging tools was available everywhere. Many tasks could be finished in a single day and a more extensive investigation by Folke Bergman could take a week. The only larger equipment that he had to bring with him from Uppsala seems to have been a plane table for the mapping, which was borrowed from the geographical institution of the University. The most troublesome experiences in the archaeological work were evidently the wet weather, or a case of split trousers and on one occasion the breakdown of the plane table. To repair it, it was necessary to go to Stockholm since there were no qualified shops in Uppsala (PL 17 June 1926).

Practice in China

The reason why the Hedin expedition required an archaeologist was that in the 1920's J.G. Andersson had made unique discoveries of remains from the stone and bronze ages in the Chinise provinces of Honan, Kansu and Kuku-nor (Andersson 1943). His finds of Neolithic painted pottery of a kind similar to European wares attracted particular attention, and the question was whether similar items could also be found in the area in between, thus proving early cultural connections between the Yellow and the Black Sea. Previous archaeological investigations in this area had dealt almost entirely with historical periods and prehistory was regarded as a completely unwritten chapter, as far as the planned route of the Hedin expedition was concerned (Bergman 1945: 4). Hedin himself was interested in establishing the exact location of the ancient so-called Silk Road and thought the archaeological investigations might be helpful in doing this (Hedin 1944: 303).

China in 1927 was a country in great disorder. It was ruled by a number of so-called warlords who frequently fought each other. Simultaneously, Japanese imperialism had made a thrust against

Fig. 11.3 Folke Bergman's practice areas in Asia.

the northern part of the country, and some European states also tried to strengthen their position. At the same time, Chinese nationalism was growing, especially in the academic world. Hedin thus met many practical obstacles and intellectual resistance when he tried to organise his great expedition to Inner Mongolia and Sinkiang. It was only thanks to Sven Hedin's eminent diplomatic talent and after tiresome negotiations that on 20 May the expedition could leave the starting point, Pao-t'ou, and head westward. However, Hedin had been forced to make considerable concessions to the Chinese to get the necessary permits, the most important of which was that he had to bring with him and support ten additional Chinese members, five educated researchers and five students, elected by the scientific institutions of China. One of them was an archaeologist, Huang Wen-pi. Another stipulation in the contract that Hedin had to sign was that all archaeological collections should be brought to Peking for further treatment. To begin with, the complete expedition would thus consist of 18 Europeans, 10 Chinese scholars, 22 Mongolian and 12 Chinese servants and about 300 camels (Hedin 1943a: 76).

As the scientific results from the expedition became known to the public, it was possible to successively extend its duration until the spring of 1935. When the original funding by the German Lufthansa corporation ended, Hedin was able to raise funds from the Swedish state, from some American and Swedish private donors and finally also from the Chinese national government of Chiang Kai-shek.

It was only during the first weeks that the expedition operated as one body. Pretty soon it was found more practical to split up into a number of smaller, independently operating units. During most of the time, Folke Bergman had to lead his own unit through the deserts and mountains of western China. He thus travelled between the longitudes 85° E and 115° E, a distance of about 2500 km, and between latitudes 38° N and 44° N, a distance of about 650 km (Fig. 11.3). He worked in three of the western provinces of China, namely Inner Mongolia, Kansu and Sinkiang. He climbed as high as 4,314 metres above sea level, and also visited the town of Turfan, some 150 metres below sea level.

As it turned out, Folke Bergman hardly ever co-operated with Huang Wen-pi in the field or elsewhere and they went mostly on different routes (PD 11 October 1927, 1 January 1934; PL 30 October 1927). On the other hand, Chinese diggers or collectors (Folke Bergman used both words) were put at his disposal. As time went on, the other researchers and also the servants gained experience in looking for ancient artefacts, and a considerable number of objects were brought to Folke Bergman's collections this way. Furthermore, the geologists of the expedition gave him valuable information regarding mineralogy, petrography, geomorphology and hydrology.

Equipment and Planning

The technical equipment that Folke Bergman brought with him for his professional work was not too complicated. It consisted of spades, archaeological sieves (which, incidentally, were also used for fishing), alidade and plane table, measuring tape, wrapping paper for the finds and a camera with film processing equipment.

Folke Bergman quite evidently tried to use the same methods for inventory, collecting and documentation of artefacts as he had applied in Sweden. He had received valuable information from J.G. Andersson (PL 15 February 1927) but his general surveying strategy remains unclear. Maybe, like later researchers (Bettinger, Madsen and Elston 1994: 74), he had found that so few data were available at the time that it was difficult to actually design a research programme of survey and excavation. However, it seems that the Edsen-gol and Lop-nor basins were considered the most interesting areas of investigation. He had in his baggage books by previous explorers of those areas, e.g. Aurel Stein's *'Innermost Asia'* (Stein 1928) as well as excerpts from Chinese annals. Because of the political conditions, plans had to be changed several times and as the results of the investigations became known to the public, questions of priority of discovery also came to play a role in the selection of working areas (Bergman 1945: 131).

Inner Mongolia and Kansu

Already outside Pao-t'ou, the starting point of the expedition, Folke Bergman made his first prehistoric discovery, a Stone Age site, yielding flint points and painted potsherds which seemed to him a promising start. It was not long before he found that the area he was going to investigate was almost free of cultural deposits. All fine soil material had been removed by wind erosion and now most finds lay on or just under the surface of sand or gravel. This of course simplified collection but rendered dating difficult, not to say impossible. Very inspiring, however, was the fact that prehistoric finds could be discovered in many, now desolate areas which indicated that climate change and desertification had probably put an end to ancient nomadic and maybe also farming cultures there. Stone Age sites were found at wells, rivers, lakes and dry river beds. Graves in the form of stone settings (Fig. 11.4), some of which were connected with long rows of stones, were also found but only sketching and not excavation was possible because of the beliefs of the local people (Bergman 1945: 7). Close to outcrops of suitable rocks, large numbers of flakes, nuclei and half-finished stone artefacts were found, indicating the location of ancient tool workshops. Some rock carvings were found and then sketched and photographed after they had been filled in with chalk or gypsum. Less positive was the fact that many of the archaeological sites had to be left prematurely because the caravan itself was forced to move on, for example because pasturage and water were scarce (PD 25 October 1930).

Fig. 11.4 Stone setting in Inner Mongolia. Photo: F. Bergman.

As Folke Bergman entered the river system of Edsen-gol, it was inevitable that he should find remains from historical periods as well. In this area lies a ruined city called Khara-khoto (The Black Town) which is thought to be the remains of the ancient city of Edzina mentioned by Marco Polo and destroyed in 1372 (Norin 1966). The Edsen-gol region had however been inhabited by Chinese farmers already during the Han dynasty (206 BCE–221 CE) who had watered their fields by irrigation. The Han emperors had also built walls, fortresses and rows of watchtowers along the river as a protection against the Huns. Previous explorers like P.K. Kozloff (Kozloff 1909) and Aurel Stein (Stein 1928) had worked in the area but Folke Bergman soon discovered that they had not visited many sites and also that the documentation they had published was in part incorrect.

Following his first visit in 1927 he returned in 1929 and then spent more than one year in the Edsen-gol and Khara-khoto region making maps, investigating a large number of ruined watchtowers and fortresses and also establishing the position of ancient defence walls. In old refuse heaps at some of the watchtowers, he dug up a very large number of manuscripts on wood of a kind that was used in China before paper was invented. The dating of many of these manuscripts could be done simply by reading of the ideographs written on them. Other objects found in the ruins were textiles, artefacts of bronze and wood, ancient grains of millet, ceramic vessels, well preserved bamboo arrows, a writing brush and spindle-whorls (Bergman 1945).

Folke Bergman passed the region between Edsen-gol and Sinkiang twice and both times at an accelerated rate because of the scarcity of provisions in this so-called Black Gobi. Nevertheless, archaeological finds were made on the ground near the springs where his party had to pitch its camps (Bergman 1945: 19; PD 31 January 1934).

Sinkiang

In Sinkiang the number of prehistoric objects collected was more limited. The reason for this may have been the political conditions, which did not allow free travelling, and staying in the province (Hedin 1943b: 36; Bergman 1945: 26). Folke Bergman's major archaeological finds there were from historical times and mainly made in the so-called Lop-desert. This is an area that was fairly densely populated 2000 years ago but was abandoned at about 300 CE when the river, Qum-darya, feeding the terminal lake, Lop-nor, changed direction and became the river Tarim. The lake found another position in the south (Hörner and Chen 1935: 147). At the time of Folke Bergman's visit the river and the lake had returned to its former position but the living conditions were still very inhospitable. Also here wind erosion had removed the cultural deposits, but left sand forming huge dunes. The dry climate, however, had been favourable for the preservation of ancient human material remains. Even though most of the archaeological sites had been disturbed by treasure hunters, there were plenty of objects to pick up or excavate from the ground including mummified human corpses, bones, textiles and hides, wooden sculptures, pillars, coffins and tools, stone and metal implements, coins, glassware and ceramics. Only a selection of the items could be brought to civilised places for further investigation. The richest site was a cemetery called 'Ördek's necropolis' and the discovery of this was the result of a combination of lucky circumstances and hard work. It was based on information given by Ördek, a 72–year-old former Turki servant to Hedin in 1900, who said he knew about a hill in the desert covered with 'a thousand' coffins. Hedin and Folke Bergman decided to investigate the matter further. Even though Ördek himself participated in the search, it took almost a month before they could find the place (Bergman 1939: 53).

Some artefacts of prehistoric age were also found in Sinkiang, even shards of painted ceramic vessels. The most spectacular item, however, was a vase acquired for Folke Bergman by the digger Chin in a town at the southern rim of the Tarim basin, Charchan. It was similar to the pottery found by J.G. Andersson and was said to have been excavated locally. When the seller of the vase heard about Folke Bergman's delight at this object, he sent a messenger demanding the purchase to go back or the price to be increased. When this had been refused, the seller himself arrived together with another person who pleaded for the purchase to go back, otherwise the seller's father would beat his son and stab him with a knife. Folke Bergman, who held this for a typical Chinese negotiation procedure refused again and told them to bring in the father so he could negotiate with him directly. He felt pretty sure that the father would never come and so was also the case (PD 12 August 1928).

Folke Bergman paid a visit, as a tourist, to the Bezeklik grottoes close to Turfan with their Buddhist paintings, and he saw there the ugly traces of previous explorers who had sawn away part of the mural paintings (Bergman 1945: 26).

Working Conditions in China

Political Conditions and Security

Even though a central government was gradually established in Nanking, China remained in the 1920s and 1930s a weak nation, with different parts of the country governed by various warlords with their more or less private armies of soldiers of fortune or compulsory recruits. From time to time the men did not get their payment and therefore turned to robbery, badly harassing the local farmers, merchants and herdsmen. For this reason, the expedition members had to bring arms and sometimes also to carry them. However, these never came to be used except for the rifles, used for hunting. Now and then they took night watch in turn and on one occasion they even hired a gang of what they thought were robbers to protect them. Mongolian robbers knew how to behave if they were sufficiently well paid (PL 24 May 1927). Paper money was seldom accepted in Central Asia so the expedition had to bring its financial resources in the form of silver coins. The currency used was Mexican silver dollars – a widely available and reliable currency at that time – and the exchange rate was about 1.80 Swedish Crowns. In Sinkiang, however, paper money was sometimes useful (Hedin 1943a: 230; PD 29 May 1928).

In addition to the warlord system, there were also struggles for autonomy from both Inner Mongolia by the lamaistic Mongols and from Sinkiang by the Mohammedan Uighurs. In both cases there was also a not always unwelcome influence from the communist north. Matters were even more complicated by the political and military activities of Chinese Mohammedans, the so-called Tungans. It had been planned that Folke Bergman should return to Sinkiang after his visit to Sweden in 1929. However, he was denied entrance at the border and had therefore to change his plans. Instead he went to Inner Mongolia where he stayed for one and a half year, most of the time in the Edsen-gol area. (Bergman 1945)

As regards security, the most serious incident occurred in Sinkiang in 1934 when the expedition, which was then travelling by car, ran into a civil war between uprising Mohammedan forces and the Chinese provincial government forces. For a couple of weeks the expedition was deprived of its trucks with their drivers and the other members were imprisoned in the town of Korla. Ironically, Folke Bergman found himself, contrary to his normal practice, actually burying their silver money under the floor of their temporary prison (Hedin 1935: 198).

Travelling and Transportation

The Chinese railway system in 1927 ended at the town of Pao-t'ou and the Trans-Siberian railway was available in the city of Sergiopol in Russia. Between these two places, Folke Bergman had to walk or ride a camel, horse, donkey or mule or enter a two-wheel cart except during the last period of the expedition (1933–1934), when motor cars were used. Equipment and provisions and, after a while, also the archaeological finds carefully packed in cases, were loaded on beasts of burden, mostly on camels who could carry up to 200 kg each. These animals were normally obliged to feed on the local vegetation, which could be scarce especially in wintertime. Since drinking water was often also scarce, many of the animals died and new ones had to be purchased or hired from the local population. When Folke Bergman felt sorry for the dying animals and wanted to put an end to their suffering with a rifle shot, he was stopped by the Mongolian camel-men who had other beliefs (PD 8 October 1927). On the other hand, when the camels were well fed after a period with good pasture, they became reluctant to carry any load and it happened many times that they ran away, throwing off their loads (Hedin 1943a: 101).

Folke Bergman could not bring all the archaeological collections with him all the time but had to organise separate storage in local villages and caravans solely for transportation of the goods. This seems to have worked well in the countryside but when the goods were sent by rail from Russia to Peking, many cases were lost and never retrieved (Bergman 1945: 55).

Helpers and Servants

Unlike in Sweden, Folke Bergman could not expect to recruit locally for manual labour in Central Asia. So beside the scholars, the expedition therefore comprised a crew of caravan leaders, diggers, camel tenders, cooks and other servants. The crew was a mixture of Europeans, Chinese, Mongols and Turkis. Guides were hired locally. In his diary, Folke Bergman delivers both positive and negative judgements on the different members of the crew but generally, the relations seem to have been satisfactory. Three diggers or collectors are mentioned. Chin and Chang, who both had previous archaeological experience (Hedin 1943a: 48; PD 7 September 1929), receive only positive mentions (PL 22 March 1930), whereas Wang, a former lieutenant of one of the warlords' armies with no collection experience, at the beginning was considered too careless for an archaeologist (PD 5 Mai 1930).

Food, Lodging and Health Care

Tinned food was brought along but the staple food was rice, flour, dried milk and fresh meat: the latter was obtained by purchase of livestock from local people. When the stocks of purchased meat were low, Folke Bergman and his fellow travellers had to try hunting for wild game (Fig. 11.5). The game available was ducks, geese, pheasants and antelopes but the supply was variable and sometimes, he had to endure weeks of meatlessness. Along the main caravan routes, Chinese merchants had established shops where provisions could be bought but when the research took place in more desolate areas, it was necessary to bring along considerable quantities of provisions. The meals were prepared by the servant cooks, normally twice a day, using a portable stove (PL 20 October 1929).

The climate of Inner Mongolia and Sinkiang is arid with low winter and moderate to high summer temperatures. The difference between day and night can be considerable. Rain and snowfalls occur but mainly in mountain areas. Since Folke Bergman worked year round, he had to adapt to very varying weather conditions and was temporarily prevented from doing any archaeology both by heat and snowy or hard-frozen ground. He normally slept in a tent which in wintertime could be heated by a small oven fired with the standard fuel of the region, camel dung (*argel*). The tent provided good protection against rain and snow but when storms occurred, the fine dust penetrated small openings and everything inside became covered with a thick layer of silt. Sometimes snakes, frogs, rats and once a scorpion took refuge in his tent. In wintertime, the temperature plummeted in the night, once to below -40°C, and it happened that his ink was frozen in the morning (Bergman 1945: 147).

In the very beginning Folke Bergman tried to uphold his European habits in hygienic matters including shaving, bathing and changing of clothes but quite soon he, as well as his European colleagues, abandoned most of those procedures and let his beard grow, used water almost only for

Fig. 11.5 Meat supply guaranteed. Photo: F. Bergman.

drinking and slept in his working outfit (PL 270524, 270530). The main hygienic effort became the fight against fleas (PD 2 October 1927). Nevertheless, he fell seriously ill only once when he had jaundice. Fortunately, he happened to be travelling together with Hedin's personal physician, and was taken good care of (PD 30 November 1933). When travelling with his own caravan, however, Folke Bergman actually had to practise medical care himself, including light surgery, for the local population. One morning, when he had 25 visiting 'patients', he complained in his diary that the supply of medicine was running low (PD 5 August 1928).

Local Peoples and Languages

Central Asia consists in large parts of steppes and deserts. Mongolian nomads sparsely populated the steppes, and in the 1920s only the oases in the deserts contained any human settlements. The population in general was of mixed Chinese, Mongolian and Turkish ethnicity. As soon as he arrived in Peking, Folke Bergman started learning Chinese and could passably communicate with the Chinese in simple matters (PL 5 February 1927). Many of the Chinese in service to the expedition, however, knew some English and even French. Soon after meeting with the Mongols, Folke Bergman started to pick up some of their language. This language was easier and I have the impression that he had fewer problems communicating with the Mongols than with the Chinese in their language (PL 20 Oct. 1929). He never learnt the Turkish language except for the local place names. The Romanisation of place names presented a particular problem. Explorers with various mother tongues had produced the available maps and they had expressed the phonetics of place names as used by the local population in different ways. Many places also had different names in Chinese and Mongolian or Chinese and Turkish languages (Bergman 1945).

Telegraph and Mail Service

There was a telegraph line between Peking and Sinkiang and when Folke Bergman passed any of the telegraph stations, he took the opportunity to communicate with Sweden. However, the line was often broken and when open, only short messages were possible to transmit so it was used almost only in matters of deaths and births. In fact, the telegraph service in Kansu was said to be slower than a camel (Bergman 1945: 151). Radio was only available as receiver and battery use had to be rationed (PL 30 May 1927). Surprisingly, mail service actually worked but was extremely slow. A letter to Sweden could take three months or more. This was partly due to the fact that letters most often were sent with and received by means of merchants travelling with commercial camel caravans with a maximum speed of 60 km per day. Chinese censorship could also be a delaying factor. It was certainly a strange experience for Folke Bergman as well as for his family in Sweden to ask questions and receive the answer after six months. Communication with Hedin and the other members of the expeditions, when the parties were separated, suffered similar delays. Decisions regarding working area and organisation of his own caravan had in most cases to be made by him. This worked well as long as his supply of money was ensured and the local authorities did not put a spoke in his wheel (PD 12 May 1929, 20 July 1930; PL 14 August 1930, 21 January 1931).

Huang Wen-pi

The Chinese archaeologist Huang Wen-pi was a member of the Hedin expedition following the contract signed by Hedin in 1927. When Hedin made a new contract in 1933, this time with the government in Nanking, the main assignment was to investigate the possibilities for road-building to Sinkiang, possibly along the ancient so-called Silk Roads. It was not planned to undertake any archaeological investigations but Hedin was prepared to ignore this, so he employed Folke Bergman to join the venture which this time should use motor vehicles instead of beasts of burden for transport. Officially, in order not to violate the terms of contract, Folke Bergman was hired for topographical matters. In reality, as on the previous expedition, he spent much of his time route mapping. However, at the last moment, when Hedin had everything settled with his counterpart at the Ministry of Railways, Huang Wen-pi appeared with an assignment from the Ministry of Education to join the party. Hedin was very annoyed that a Chinese archaeologist should be allowed to follow him but officially Huang Wen-pi's mission was to inspect the school system of the western provinces (Hedin 1943b: 213).

Folke Bergman and Huang Wen-pi never actually worked together and their co-operation was limited to avoiding going into the investigation areas of each other. I think the main reason for this must have been pure personal relations (PD 10 November 1933, 23 December 1933; PL 11 May 1927, 22 September 1927; Bergman 1945: 174). Another reason may have been the fact that Huang Wen-pi did not speak any foreign language (Hedin 1943a: 92). Hedin seems to have taken a negative attitude towards him. This is obvious from the rare mentions of his name in Hedin's writings on the expedition. I have only found one published picture in which Huang Wen-pi is visible, and even then without his name in print, unlike the other persons on the picture (Fig. 11.6). In the last chapter of his history of the expedition (Hedin 1944: 306), Hedin is very outspoken about the behaviour of Huang Wen-pi 'who had been indefatigable in his endeavours

Fig. 11.6 Second from left: Huang Wen-pi. In the middle, with stick: Sven Hedin.
Extreme right: Folke Bergman (Hedin 1935).

to put obstacles in the way of the expedition and its work'. In his own official documentation,
Folke Bergman cites three of Huang Wen-pi's publications. He expresses a different opinion on
some of the conclusions, but in general I think he respected Huang Wen-pi's professional capacity
(Bergman 1939). Evidently Huang Wen-pi's ability to endure hardship in the field was not
questioned. It would certainly be interesting to learn what Huang Wen-pi himself thought about
Hedin and Folke Bergman. It is furthermore possible that this controversy of the 1920s and 1930s
might have influenced other Chinese scholars later on. In a book about Peking Man (Huang
Weiwen and Jia Lanpo 1990: 28) one can read that 'Sven Hedin ... in the spring of 1927, (without
permission) was shipping cultural relics found in Sinkiang Province out of China'. This is actually
quite erroneous since the expedition did not arrive in Sinkiang until the beginning of 1928, and
furthermore as later shipments were sent in full agreement with the Chinese representatives.

Analysis of the Finds

According to the agreement with the Chinese, all collected items were brought to Peking. The
prehistoric material collected by Folke Bergman and his colleagues was then allowed to be sent to
Sweden since similar collections by Huang Wen-pi would stay in China. Part of the collections
from historical time was allowed to go to Sweden as a loan for scientific investigation but had to
be, and was, returned afterwards. The wooden manuscripts, however, had to stay in China for
analysis by Chinese scholars. Because of Folke Bergman's death in 1946, his only published,
complete report was about objects found in Sinkiang. Others have treated different parts of the
other collections and documented their work in the publication series of the expedition.

Summary and Discussion

I have tried to give a brief account of the practice of a Swedish archaeologist, Folke Bergman, in
the 1920s and 1930s with special emphasis on the various conditions under which he worked. He
had the opportunity early in his life to undertake archaeological fieldwork in two very different
areas of the world, Sweden and Central Asia, where in the latter case prehistory was almost
unknown at that time. In Sweden he participated in the beginning of the organised inventory and
excavations of archaeological remains in Uppland and Gotland. In Central Asia he reconnoitred
vast areas of the Chinese western provinces.

Both the range of finds and the sites investigated were of course very different. In Asia, almost all cultural deposits had been affected by erosion and the human material remains were lying on bare ground or covered by drift sand. A very large amount of stone and metal artefacts were found but the prevailing dryness had also preserved more of the organic remains than is usually the case in Sweden. In Sweden there is also an upper limit to the age of archaeological objects set by the melting of the inland ice. In Central Asia there is no such limit except in the southern mountains and there are indications that climate might have been more favourable to humans during the Palaeolithic and Neolithic times than it is now.

It is quite clear that luck played an important, not to say decisive, role in Folke Bergman's practice in China. The initial plans of trying to find evidence of Stone Age connections between China and Europe could only be followed to a minor extent. On the other hand, his research among the Han ruins in the Edsen-gol area yielded conspicuous objects, above all the wooden manuscripts, which received great medial interest. This was, of course, exploited by Hedin when he applied for additional financing of his expedition with Swedish institutions and elsewhere.

The conditions including the hardship that Folke Bergman had to endure in Asia were certainly of the kind that would influence the analysis and documentation of the finds. Bjørnar Olsen has elaborated on this theme in one of his books (Olsen 1997). The road from 'Things to Text' would be winding and have many pitfalls not to say dead ends. These problems were certainly not less evident as most of the reports had to be written by others, partly because of Folke Bergman's untimely death.

In general my conclusion is that archaeology as science in the 1920s was still at a premature stage so that aims and decisions by a few individuals were highly influential on the practice according to which it was performed. Research in foreign and 'exotic' countries was not induced by scientific objectives only, but also to a great extent by aspiration for glory. Previous explorers like Nordenskiöld and Nansen, not to mention Sven Hedin, were held in high esteem for their achievements, gained in harsh environments. Even though he had an adventurous touch, I think that the major driving force for Folke Bergman himself was to improve his career opportunities in Sweden. He had no intention of specialising in Asian archaeology but rather to enter into the antiquarian organisation of the Swedish State (PL 4 January 1927, 24 May 1927). This was prevented by his death by cancer at the age of 44. This cancer may well, in my lay medical knowledge, have been the combined effect of heavy smoking and inhalation of eolian dust during the years in Asia (PD 20 July 1928, 29 July 1928; PL 17 May 1929).

References

Andersson, J.G. 1943. Researches into the prehistory of the Chinese. *The Museum of Far Eastern Antiquities Stockholm, Bulletin* No 15. Göteborg, Elanders boktryckeri AB.

Bergman, F. 1925. *Berättelse över en antikvarisk-topografisk undersökning i östra Upland sommaren 1925*. Uppsala, Upplands Museum.

———. 1939. *Archaeological researches in Sinkiang*. Reports from the Scientific Expedition to the North-Western Provinces of China under the Leadership of Dr Sven Hedin, Publication 7. Stockholm, Bokförlags AB Thule.

———. 1945. *Travels and Archaeological Field Work in Mongolia and Sinkiang – A Diary of the Years 1927–1934*. Reports from the Scientific Expedition to the North-Western Provinces of China under the Leadership of Dr Sven Hedin, Publication 26. Göteborg, Elanders boktryckeri AB.

Bettinger, R.L., D.B. Madsen and R.G. Elston. 1994. Prehistoric Settlement Categories and Settlement Systems in the Alashan Desert of Inner Mongolia, PRC. *Journal of Anthropological Archaeology, 13:* *74–101*. Elsevier, Academic Press.

Gillberg, Å. 2001. *En plats i historien. Nils Niklassons liv och arbete.* GOTARC Serie B. Gothenburg Archaeological Theses no 18. Göteborg, Novum Grafiska.

Gustawsson, K-A. 1930. Inventarisierung der vorgeschichtlichen Denkmäler in Schweden. *Acta Archaeologica.* I(2): 197–204. J. Brøndsted, København, (ed.) Levin & Munksgaard.

Hauser, O. 1917. *Der Mensch vor 100000 Jahren.* Leipzig.

Hedin, S. 1935. *Stora hästens flykt. Stockholm*, Alb. Bonniers boktryckeri.

———. 1943a. *History of the Expedition in Asia 1927–1935. Part I*, Reports from the Scientific Expedition to the North-Western Provinces of China under the Leadership of Dr Sven Hedin, Publication 23. Göteborg , Elanders boktryckeri AB.

———. 1943b. *History of the Expedition in Asia 1927–1935. Part II*, Reports from the Scientific Expedition to the North-Western Provinces of China under the Leadership of Dr Sven Hedin, Publication 24. Göteborg, Elanders boktryckeri AB.

———. 1944. *History of the Expedition in Asia 1927–1935. Part III.* Reports from the Scientific Expedition to the North-Western Provinces of China under the Leadership of Dr Sven Hedin, Publication 25. Göteborg, Elanders boktryckeri AB.

Hörner, N.G. and P.C. Chen. 1935. 'Alternating lakes. Some River Changes and Lake Displacements in Central Asia.' In 'Hyllningsskrift till Sven Hedin …' *Geografiska annaler.* Stockholm, Svenska sällskapet för antropologi och geografi.

Huang Weiwen and Jia Lanpo 1990. *The Story of Peking Man.* Grimes: Foreign Languages Press.

Kozloff, P.K. 1909. 'The Mongolia-sze-chuan Expedition of the Imperial Russian Geographical Society.' *Geographical Journal*, 34: 4, October.London.

Nerman, B. 1913. *Vilka konungar ligga i Uppsala högar?* Uppsala, K.W. Appelbergs boktryckeri.

Nihlén, J. 1982. *Utgrävningarna på Stora Torget i Visby 1924–1926. En berättelse om ett arkeologiskt äventyr.* Gunnar Svahnström (ed.), Burgsvik, Förlag: Hanseproduktion AB.

Norin, E. 1966. Edsengol-oasen i Gobiöknen. *Geologiska Föreningens i Stockholm Förhandlingar* 88: 340–50. Stockholm, Kungl. Boktr.

Olsen, B. 1997. *Fra ting til tekst. Teoretiske perspektiv i arkeologisk forskning.* Oslo, Universitetsforlaget.

Stein, A. 1928. *Innermost Asia.* Oxford.

Weibull, L. 1925. Jordanes' framställning av Scandza och dess folk. *Vetenskaps-Societetens i Lund Årsbok.* 39–69. Lund, C.W.K. Gleerup.

Wessén, E. 1927. *De nordiska folkstammarna i Beowulf.* Kungl Vitterhets- Historie- och Antikvitets-Akademiens handlingar. Stockholm, Akademiens förlag.

Abbreviations

ATA: The Antiquarian-Topographic Archives. Stockholm.

SOU: Statens offentliga utredningar (Official reports of the Swedish State).

UNT: *Uppsala Nya Tidning* (Newspaper in Uppsala, Sweden).

PL: Private letters to Folke Bergman's family. In the author's possession.

PD: Folke Bergman's private diaries. Kept by the National Museum of Ethnography in Stockholm.

Chapter 12
Model Excavations

'Performance' and the Three-Dimensional Display of Knowledge

Christopher Evans

Abstract

This study is concerned with nineteenth-century modes of archaeological representation and the performance of the past; primarily the rendering of sites and monuments in various model-based formats. This was a crucial, if now neglected, facet of the subject's visualisation. It is argued that, originally reflecting the quasi-architectural orientation of much practice, model depictions subsequently influenced the conceptualisation of excavations and archaeology's methodologies, and ultimately related to an ethos of 'complete' or a totalising representation.

Introduction

In May 1857 Stephen Stone delivered an 'Account of Certain (supposed) British and Saxon Remains, recently discovered at Standlake in the County of Oxford' to the Society of Antiquaries of London:

> On removing the soil, the workmen first came to a circular pit whose diameter was 5 feet 6 inches. The pit, marked *a* in the sketch I have prepared, I subsequently cleaned out, the gravel diggers not choosing to be at the trouble themselves… Having prepared *a model*, as well as a ground plan, of the whole from measurements carefully made and repeated, I need not enter into a minute description of each excavation (1857: 93, 95; emphasis added).

By today's conventions the accompanying plan in the published text is abstract and highly stylised (Fig. 12.1). Shaded, its features appear almost sculptural, like floating geometric solids. Typical of the time, Stone's text is difficult to follow and is a disjointed chronicle of discovery with many 'We next came to's … . Although evidently lacking a magic lantern, he clearly refers to a model somewhere in the room, which remarkably in this instance survives (Fig. 12.1). It is a scale reproduction of all the features open at the end of excavation and is, in effect, a three-dimensional base plan. Display models lurk behind a number of nineteenth-century site reports (many of which were published as direct communications; see Evans forthcoming), and it is with these that this paper is concerned.

During the eighteenth and nineteenth centuries various types of models were a major means of technical demonstration, and for popular amusement, edification and professional display were a common form of representation (e.g. Wilton-Ely 1965, Barker 2004, Schaffer 2004). They featured in international exhibitions, with more than 70 displayed in the Great Exhibition

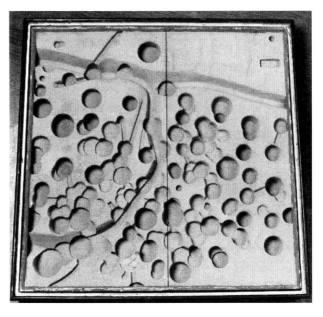

Fig. 12.1 Left, Standlake excavation plan (Stone 1857 : 94); right, the plaster with sand coating model (85 x 84 x 10 cm, scale 1/2" to 1'. Published with permission of Oxfordshire County Museums).

(Physick and Darby 1973: 13). When Lucas' models of the Parthenon first went on show in the British Museum in 1846, they apparently drew much public attention and their appreciation would have been comparable with Siborne's vast model of the Battle of Waterloo (drawing over 100,000 fee-paying visitors when exhibited 1838–1841; Siborne 1838 and Hofschröer 2004) or the great tableaux of Jerusalem and the Holy Land that were also then popular (see Altick 1978: 213). Together with London's many cork model, wax effigy and various automata displays, this led Horace Warpole to remark that by 1770 'The rage for exhibitions is so great that sometimes one cannot pass through the streets where they are' (in Barker 2004: 34–35).

It is the visual directness of models that still makes them an appropriate means of presentation to a broader public as they do not require disciplinary initiation. They are usually not symbolic in the way that the archaeology's technical illustrations have developed, and do not, for example, require a hachured line in order to render the slope of a ditch or the sides of a pit. In them features can be appreciated without conventions, and specialised graphic codes need not stand between the viewer and object. This appeal would have been all the greater prior to the twentieth century, as literacy in general – and probably with it the ability to read complex map-based information – could not then be presumed for the population at large.

What few archaeological models of the period that survive today have an anachronistic charm akin to battered model railway sets. Easily overlooked and with many having succumbed to the vestiges of wear and museum discard policies (i.e. they no longer exist), they have not featured in histories of the discipline. Yet it is crucial to recognise that, along with various forms of magic lantern shows and mechanical panoramas (and later dioramas), models were amongst the premier display tools of their day and, in their time, were distinctly 'modern'. As vehicles of 'mobile knowledge' they were a key accompaniment to presentation and a factor of antiquarian performance. Colour slide film did not come into common usage until the 1920s and 1930s and magic lanterns were evidently rare in academic circles (the Society of Antiquaries of London only acquired one in the 1890s; Evans 1956: 364; see Price this volume for further discussion). Illustrations could either be pinned up or held aloft by assistants, but otherwise how were lectures to be illustrated?[1] Accordingly, models were an integral part of archaeological congresses and conferences until well into the last century, at which time they were also a key component of museum displays. As such, the changing context of their exhibition – from private collections to society meeting rooms and eventually museums – relates to the development of the subject's domains and reflects upon its institutionalisation and professional specialism (Levine 1986). Yet, beyond this it will be argued that the use of models within the subject influenced its own visualisation and interpretation, particularly promoting an architectonic emphasis and modes of 'mechanical' analogy.

Having elsewhere more fully sketched out a history of this theme within British archaeology (Evans 2004), in this paper only key aspects of model appreciation will be explored. Its thrust is with later eighteenth- and nineteenth-century 'antiquarian' and demonstration models. Aside from depicting monuments *per se*, these include various renderings of sites which to a greater or less degree illustrate processes or principles of excavation itself. Sharing affinities with the period's scientific models (as opposed to full reconstructions which were primarily a phenomenon of twentieth-century museum display), they relate to the establishment of the discipline's methodological procedures and tell of different ways of *seeing the past*.[2]

First Architectures – Affecting Monuments

Amongst the most renowned model collections of nineteenth-century London was that of the architect Sir John Soane (Richardson 1989). Aside from those of his own buildings, these were largely of classical ruins but also included a Stonehenge and a model of the generic prehistoric house (Wilton-Ely 1969). Apart from his personal interest and inspiration as an architect and collector, these served to illustrate his public lectures and appropriate examples could be viewed in his house on the days preceding and after their delivery (Thornton and Dorey 1992: 38, Watkin 1996).

Pride of place in Soane's collection was an enormous model of the structures excavated at Pompeii (Evans 2004: fig. 5.1), that arguably influenced Soane's representation of his own buildings (e.g. Gandy's 'The Bank of England' of 1830; see Evans 2000: fig. 1). Although probably acquiring this piece directly from Neapolitan model builders, it may alternatively have been obtained from Dubourg's fee-charging museum of cork models. Established in Pall Mall in 1778, Soane is known to have visited the museum and apparently his model room duplicated a number of its exhibits.[3]

Amongst the earliest surviving archaeological models in Britain is that of the megalith at Mont St Helier, Jersey in the collection of the Society of Antiquaries of London (Fig. 12.2). The extraordinary history of this monument has been fully described (Hibbs 1985). Discovered during levelling operations for a military parade ground in 1785, the Island's Assembly presented it to its retiring Governor, Field Marshall Conway, who by 1788 had it re-erected within the grounds of his estate at Park Place, Henley-on-Thames. Dubbed the 'Little Master's Stonehenge', this gave rise to considerable public interest and was, for example, reported in the *Gentleman's Magazine* (Dec. 1788). Conway donated a scale wooden model of his 'Druidical Temple' to the Society of Antiquaries, to whom he also communicated a description of its discovery (1787; see also Molesworth in the same volume of *Archaeologia*). Three, possibly four, other early models are known to have been made of the monument.

Probably intended to illustrate the architect's public lectures, there is a large watercolour of the same site in the Soane archives (24/9/8; Evans 2000: fig. 4). Given the megalith's displacement,

Fig. 12.2 Top, the Society of Antiquaries of London model of the 'Druidical Temple' at Mont St Helier, Jersey (Cat no. 57); below, Tongue's 1832 model of the double 'Cromlech' megalith at Plas Newydd (scale 1" to 1'; British Museum).

what is remarkable about this illustration is its rendering as from life. It obviously cannot show the monument *in situ* at St Helier, as it had left Jersey some 20–30 years earlier. Nor is this the landscape of Park Place; much simplified, the site is seen from a slight bird's-eye perspective and shown perfect without the clutter of fallen stones, bushes or humans. In short, the setting is fabricated and this begs the question from what source the watercolour was itself taken. Whilst one cannot be absolutely certain that it does not derive from an engraving, it most likely was taken from one of its models.

Regardless of its exact source, this potential interrelationship between a model and apparently as-if-from-life figures has ramifications for other seemingly 'topographic' site renderings. How many of these might derive from models? This is especially true of overtly rusticated bird's-eye renderings, as Stonehenge was often portrayed (e.g. Piggott 1978: figs. 5 and 7). Could not the 'imagined' perspective of at least some come from looking down upon models and, rather than *style*, the gnarled rustication of their stones be the result of depicting cork-built depictions?

Stonehenge itself was an obvious choice for model rendering. William Stukeley recorded the making of a model in 1716, describing another chain of convoluted translations between three- and two-dimensional media (i.e. a 'view' to a model to plans) which raises basic questions concerning the veracity of sources:

Happening to fall into a set of thoughts about Stonehenge in Wiltshire, by a prospect of Loggan's which I met withall, I undertook to make an exact Model of that most noble and stupendous piece of Antiquity, which I have accomplish'd, and from thence drawn a groundplot of its present ruins, and the view of it in its pristine State ... and propose from thence to find out ... its design, use, Founders etc ... (in Piggott 1989: 125).

Later in the century the natural philosopher and polymath, John Waltire, apparently toured with cork models of the site to accompany his popular lectures (Higgins 1827: xviii; Peck and Wilkinson 1950: 160–61) and Henry Browne, the first 'guardian' of the great henge, is known to have produced models of it since 1807.[4] Although, as discussed below, Browne later became involved in London-based 'model networks', these are unlikely to have been his original source of inspiration. While other unknown eighteenth-century exemplars must lurk in the background, it is conceivable that Waltire provided its impetus as both he and Browne shared similarly extraordinary theories concerning Stonehenge's antediluvian origins (Chippindale 1985: 128, Piggott 1989: 146).

The most renowned of Browne's models accompany John Britton's Celtic Cabinet in Devizes Museum (Evans 2004: fig. 5.3; Chippindale 1985). Believed to date to c. 1824, the Cabinet is thought to have been assembled on commission for a gentlemen antiquarian to house his collections (who subsequently refused it). Topped by 'As it is' and '... was' cork models of Stonehenge (and in the drawer below, Avebury), the front of this heavy furnishing carried framed watercolours of the most renowned megaliths of the era; a large Stonehenge roundel being matched by an aerial view of Avebury. A friend of Soane's, the antiquarian, topographer and church historian associated with the Gothic Revival, Britton was the author of both the *Beauties of England and Wales Series* and the first published account of Soane's collections, *The Union of Architecture, Sculpture and Painting* of 1827. The closeness of the shaded-plan perspective style of the Cabinet's stonehenge roundel with the surveys of Soane's students indicates that either the architect must have given a version of the illustration to Britton (which was then subsequently cut down) or that Britton commissioned the piece in the manner of Soane's studio (Evans 2000: figs. 7 and 8).

The Stonehenge models which top the Cabinet were set within a glass box whose variously tinted sides could affect the monuments' lighting at different times of day.[5] As demand for Browne's models increased, Britton explored the idea of establishing a 'Druidical Antiquarian Company' to promote their sale and, too, for a display in London exhibiting the monument in pictures and models with accompanying magic lantern effects (Chippindale 1985: 129). In archaeological circles this venture and the Britton Cabinet itself have been considered as highly eccentric. However, recognising the linkage between Britton and Soane re-casts the context of these enterprises, relating them to model exhibitions such as Dubourg's and the very arrangement of Soane's Lincoln's Inn Fields collection. What, after all, is Britton's Cabinet itself but a 'union of architecture' (at least furniture), 'sculpture' (models) and painting involving the main display media for both amusement and edification of the time.

The assembly of the Britton Cabinet also has parallels in the mixed media genre of Richard Tongue of Bath – 'painter and modeller of megaliths' – and is evident in his donations to the British Museum (Evans 1994). As in the Cabinet, Tongue rendered monuments in both modelled and painted form. Akin to the effect of the tinted panes atop the furnishing, he also shared an interest in the 'atmospheric' presentation of sites. The pictures the artist/antiquarian gave to the Museum were respectively rendered to show three times of the day – dawn, noon and dusk: the megalith at *Plas Newydd*, *Stonehenge* and *The Tolmen*, a great 'druidic' balanced stone. Signing himself the 'Honorary Curator of Models of the Bath Scientific and Literary Institute', in a letter announcing his presentation of six models to the Museum in 1834 (Fig. 12.2) Tongue declared that he had shown his models to Britton; the earliest examples by him date from eight years before. In his correspondence to the Museum it is clear that Tongue envisaged the paintings and models to be exhibited together as a unified group, with the latter to be shown below the three canvases. Although never realised, this clearly was intended as a multi-media display in a manner reminiscent of Britton's Cabinet or the unfulfilled ambitions of the Druidical Antiquarian Company.

Whilst also relating to traditions of architectural and craft-based model construction (e.g. ship-building), the specific context of these early efforts can be further appreciated by considered what other such holdings were in the collection of the Society of Antiquaries of London. Aside from a plaster model of the amphitheatre at Dorchester given in 1854 (Cat No. 433), these were of classical ruins. Catalogue entry 8, presented by Capt. W.H. Smyth in 1830, is 'A Model of the Ancient Thermal Baths Discovered in the Island of Lipari' (Smyth 1830) and, in 1767, they received a cork model of the Temple of the Sibyl at Tivoli (Cat. No. 16). As is the case with many pieces in the Soane model collection, these Italianate benefactions – variously mementos of travel and testimonials to 'taste' – attest to the appreciation of classical prototypes and the impact of Grand Tour travel.[6]

Depicting monuments and not excavations, the early models of 'rude stone' megaliths are similarly architectonic and, it has been argued, are essentially expositions of megalithic 'first architectures' rather than sites *per se* (Evans 2000). Excavation was then very much in its infancy and largely restricted to barrows; as in the case of Tongue, in part, these renderings reflect upon the constitution of antiquarianism, for which the illustration of monuments alone was considered a defining activity. Yet these depictions did not just relate to developments within the discipline itself. Demonstrated by Soane's interest in Stonehenge and that, for example, both Turner and Constable painted the great henge (e.g. Chippindale 1983; Edmonds and Evans 1991), and reflective of the intellectual eclecticism and 'open' networks of the time, it equally marks archaeology's participation in a broad cultural discourse. Engendered by the unification of the United Kingdom and the further forging of national identity through the Napoleonic Wars (e.g. Colley 1992) – the war itself promoting 'local' interests and discouraging Continental travel – ancient monuments increasingly began to contribute to a 'new' national cultural landscape.

Site Workings – Conceiving Sequences

Dating to the mid-nineteenth century, it has not proven possible to account for the direct influence behind Stone's Standlake base-plan model (Fig. 12.1). Be this as it may, its rendering appears itself to have fostered other efforts. As discussed in the President's Address for 1869, P. Stevens' delivery of a paper concerning Highfield settlement at Fisherton, Salisbury to a meeting of the Wiltshire Archaeological and Natural History Society had been accompanied by an 'occupation' model (Awdry 1870: 148). Apparently unextant, this was not cited when the excavations were finally published some 60 years later (Stevens 1934).

In both cases these settlements were conceived of in relationship to that renowned red herring of nineteenth- and early twentieth-century practice, the ubiquitous pit dwelling, and a comparable ethos (and means of presentation) still pervaded, for example, Clay's account of the Fifield Bavant Down settlement excavated some 70 years later:

> A series of models of the more interesting pits, made to scale, to illustrate the various types, communicating pits, pits with recesses in their walls, pits with steps in their walls, pits with seats, and pits with flint shaft, have been made (1924: 462; see Evans 2004: fig. 5.8).

Employing a markedly different 'grammar' of excavation, this is not how sites are envisaged today; the subtle interrelationship of negative form, horizontal strata and the context of finds was little appreciated. Their determination was greatly influenced by the scale of excavation. This was to prove a drawback until the 1940s and 1950s, at which time earthmoving machinery was regularly employed allowing for large-scale exposure and the detection of posthole buildings (see Evans 1988 for overview). Nevertheless, modelling clearly influenced the perception of such sites as they granted architectural solidity to negative features. Non-analogous to the excavator's experience (when compared, for example, to villas) and lacking visibly upstanding expression in the manner of megaliths, models gave a sense of tactile reality to this rogue settlement construction.

Lt-General Pitt Rivers – Britain's first Inspector of Ancient Monuments and a great innovator of fieldwork technique (Thompson 1977, Bowden 1991) – is the figure most closely associated with archaeological models in Britain. There were more than a hundred of both solid wood and 'hollow' (plaster on wire frame) construction in his museum at Farnham, where they were arranged centrally down rooms along whose sides artefacts were displayed (Thompson 1977: fig. 14 and Dudley Buxton 1929: pl. VIII; see also Gray 1929: 36–37 concerning their construction). Made by his estate carpenters under strict instruction, he considered them the culmination of a site's record:

> Since the models of my excavations were exhibited at the Society of Antiquaries, the excavators at Silchester have pursued the same course with very great success, and *I think the use of such models promises to become general. There is nothing that conveys such a correct idea of the work done in investigations of this nature* (Pitt Rivers 1892: 298; emphasis added; see also 1898: 23–24; Thompson 1977: 99).

His models fall into several main types. Relating to his tenure as Inspector of Ancient Monuments, a number simply document megaliths in a manner not dissimilar to earlier antiquarian efforts (e.g. Bowden 1991: fig. 26; there are also a number of Celtic crosses). Most, however, are of his excavations. While some only record individual pits or burials, many were remarkably sophisticated. Hawkes' reassessment and publication of the Iwerne villa site 50 years after its excavation (Pitt Rivers' one unpublished Cranborne Chase site), evidently owed much to the survival of its model (Hawkes 1947; Dudley Buxton 1929: pl. XI). Equally, in their recent Cranborne Chase investigations Barrett *et al.* note that the South Lodge Camp contour model so accurately reproduced the original mapping that it shows earthwork features that went unrecognised by the General and which were only identified in the later excavations (1991: 14–15; R. Bradley pers. comm.).

In Pitt Rivers' model of the Neolithic Wor Barrow the location of finds within the ditches flanking the mound are shown by pins (Evans 2004: fig. 5.6). The height of each indicates the depth of the artefact and the different colours of their heads denote their period (Roman and Neolithic); drawings of skeletons, accordingly elevated on small pedestals, depict the position of secondary interments. The model, therefore, contains an enormous amount of information, interrelating the evidence of his finds tables, sections, contour maps and base-plans (*cf.* Pitt Rivers 1898: pl. 249–52). It is actually conventionalised in the symbolism of its plotting as the viewer must be able to 'read' a pin (and its colour) to attribute artefacts and appreciate that their length is representative of depth. Equally, in other of his models, while the ground slope is moulded, painted contours have also been applied.

Although, as another example, the Cissbury model seems superficially less detailed as it does not portray the location of artefacts, it is complicated in its demonstration of stratigraphic sequence (Plate 4). Carved from wood, it is 'mechanical' insofar as it is hinged and allows for viewing of galleries of the Neolithic flint mine beneath the ramparts of the Iron Age hillfort. Models of this ilk have marked affinities to scientific demonstration pieces of the age. Thomas Sopwith's series of geological models of 1841 provides a ready instance. Employing laminated woods, these variously show basic principles of stratigraphic tilting, folding and faults (Fig. 12.4; see Sopwith 1841).[7] Here it is relevant that the General's use of models was not confined to archaeology alone. In its spirit of public edification his Farnham Museum also included agricultural collections, amongst which were miniature farming implements (Bowden 1991: fig. 47).[8]

Through his military background the General would obviously have been familiar with a range of fortification tableaux and topographic models, and indeed is known to have constructed one to demonstrate the projection of ordnance (1861). Interesting enough, when writing of his models in Volume III of the Cranborne Chase publications, he failed to acknowledge any archaeological precursors (Pitt Rivers 1892: 297–98). However, in the first of that series he admits to having seen Stone's Standlake model (1887: 20). Though the Silchester models which Pitt Rivers inspired were much more detailed than that of the Standlake site, they were basically just a record of excavated features. Made between 1890 and 1893 by the site's excavators, St John Hope and George Fox (and housed today in Reading Museum), these straightforwardly depict building foundations exposed within the Roman town (Evans 2004: fig. 5.7). 'Peopled' by archaeologists (and labourers), they are remarkably accurate and even show the ragged trench edges produced through a 'wall-chasing' excavation technique (see Wheeler 1954: 127). Although applauded by the General and, while certainly demonstrative of the *appearance* of excavation, they lack the sophistication of Pitt Rivers' more complicated pieces. In effect, the Silchester tableaux reconstruct site-work without demonstrating principles of excavation (e.g. distribution or sequence) or interpretation.[9]

In many respects, it was Harold St George Gray, an assistant of Pitt Rivers from 1888 until 1900, who most directly continued his legacy of model construction. Thereafter excavating a number of important sites in his own right and co-directing others, upon leaving the General's service he went on to dig the stone circle and henge at Arbor Low, Derbyshire. He duly made a model of the site and was commissioned by *MAN* to provide a description of its manufacture. Estimating that it involved 450 hours' labour, the note is illustrated with photographs of the sequence of its construction. The resultant piece is essentially an unremarkable relief model showing the circle as an earthwork onto which the outline of the excavation trenches was painted (Gray 1903: fig. 1). It tells of the effort that went into it (and the 'proclamation' of detail) that its scaled standing stones were apparently carved in soapstone *in-situ* on the site. Dorset Museum also holds a similar relief model of Gray's later excavations of the Neolithic henge and Roman amphitheatre at Maumbury Rings, Dorchester (1903–1913; Bradley 1975), the dug features and trenches being moulded white to mimic chalk.

The construction of such site models presupposes the existence of scale plans and, therefore, their interrelationship with graphics must be acknowledged. Although sympathetic to the conventions of engraved reproduction, the almost lunar-like abstraction of the Standlake plan could suggest that it was itself influenced by the site's model (Fig. 12.1). Standlake is held to be amongst the first 'proper' excavation of a settlement site of this type; how pits and ditches were to be depicted was not then conventionalised and model representations may well have been influential. Hope and Fox's Silchester plans are equally simplistic and essentially consist of hard-edged renderings of building foundations. While in both sites artefacts would have been attributed to discrete features, finds were not individually plotted.

Appropriate to his advocation of a 'fuller' and more nuanced archaeology, Pitt Rivers brought a wider range of evidence to bear in his excavations and practised more detailed recording. Consequently, many of his graphics are complicated. The stylised ditch sections from Wor Barrow or South Lodge show the vertical plotting of differential artefact types; with section figures impinging on plans, some of his published Cissbury illustrations are, in fact, overloaded with information. The General was producing a dense and multi-faceted record, and his figures strive to incorporate more than one aspect of the data. In effect, portraying the 'workings' of sites, his more dynamic archaeology was, in many respects, better suited to the more 'mechanical' means of model-based depiction. It is, in fact, likely that his ability to solidly model such complex interrelationships did itself abet his conceptualisation of fieldwork and its possibilities.

Modelling Space – Abstracting Excavation

The majority of extant archaeological models date to the first half of the twentieth century, and excavation models *per se* continued to be built up until the Second World War. When compared to those discussed in the previous section, the difference of many from this time is that they often seem to be specially built for museums and usually not by the excavators themselves, and it tells of the growing public interest in archaeology at the time that museums felt the need to document local fieldwork. There are, however, exceptions to this, most notably Stuart Piggott, who made base-plan models of sites he was engaged with. These include a Neolithic 'pit dwelling' from a ditch segment of Curwen's Trundle excavations (in the Barbican House, Lewis Collections) and a portion of Bersu's renowned Little Woodbury Iron Age settlement (see Acknowledgements in Bersu 1940 and Stone 1958: pl. 68).[10] Stylistically the latter closely matches the Standlake model and one suspects that it may have been the source of its inspiration. Equally, variants of demonstration models continued to be constructed and amongst these must be assigned Clay's casting mould-like, Iron Age pit 'trays' of the Fifield site and Devizes Museum's 'Woodhenge

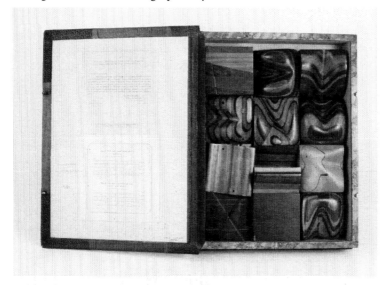

Fig. 12.3 Sopwith's boxed set of wooden geological models of 1841 (Whipple Museum, Cambridge Cat no. 1581).

Reconstructed'; the latter site was excavated by the Cunningtons in 1926–1928 and its model was built in the following year for the museum by the husband of that team (Evans 2004: fig. 5.8).[11]

Over the course of the century full reconstruction modelling came increasingly to the fore. Bringing to 'life' the results of excavations, this not only involved the reconstruction of sites as a whole or in part, but also generic scenes of, for example, typical prehistoric flint mines or houses. Frequently 'peopled', it is these reconstructions that captured attention in the museums of our youths. They have an endearing quality and certainly their appeal is markedly different from that of the 'lifeless' demonstration models of the Standlake or Pitt Rivers' excavations. Almost akin to dolls' houses, and involving the pleasures of a 'miniaturist phenomenology', these 'worlds shown small' conceptually straddle a divide between play and instruction. This emphasis upon 'as lived' scenes obviously has parallels in the development of museum habitat dioramas (see e.g. Moser 1999). Museums themselves increasingly aspired to a 'totalising' experience, with reconstruction models displayed cheek-by-jowl with artefacts of the relevant period; looking up, their upper walls would carry paintings depicting generic scenes of life at that time.

The specific genealogy of such modelling need not unduly concern us in this context (see, however, Evans 2004: 129–30), but rather what was the impetus behind such efforts. Perhaps foremost is a totalising vision of archaeology and the past. This would be common to nineteenth-century 'atmospheric' display tableaux and earlier twentieth-century artefact/model/mural museum displays. Yet, beyond this is also a striving for a complete or 'total' archaeological record. Such aspirations are very much at odds with declarations of 'fragmentation' that pervades so much current fieldwork. Yet, as stressed by Kockel, it was a driving force behind the 'official' later eighteenth- to earlier nineteenth-century models of Pompeii – a sense that 'full' modelling could compensate for the inadequacies of the excavations' publication (Kockel 2004). At least some of Pitt Rivers' excavation models equally seem motivated by an ethos of 'complete' representation.

The modelling of excavation practice arguably influenced the 'possibilities' of fieldwork. Stone's Standlake model helped realise base-plan representation, just as Pitt Rivers' more complex pieces furthered the conceptualisation of three-dimensional artefact distributions and vertical sequences. In short, physical modelling abetted paper-based abstraction of excavation procedures. Modelling of this type found little expression in twentieth-century practice. Yes, continuing an architectural tradition, miniature versions of excavated buildings were constructed (see Note 9), but the possibilities of modelling excavation procedures were not really explored further. This seems to

Fig. 12.4 The site as model. Left, John Alexander's employment of the Wheeler box-excavation technique at the Arbury Villa site, Cambridge (1970; see also Wheeler 1954). Right, the senior staff of the Feddersen Wierde excavations analyse the Roman Iron Age *terpen* settlement's sequence, having put their section illustrations onto interconnecting white card mounts above a same-scale plan of the site (Wilhelmshaven Museum).

relate largely to the imposition of more abstract modes of site 'modelling' (i.e. conceptual); primarily *the grid*, with its most extreme expression being Wheeler's box techniques intended to maximise section exposure (e.g. 1954). Ultimately deriving from military and engineering surveying, this became a dominant 'model' of excavation space, which when carried to its full logic (e.g. Fig. 12.4) was underpinned by the possibility of a fully scaled/miniature excavation framework, which today, of course, sees even more nuanced expression in computer graphics.

The capture of data, and how the nature of representation and its media itself influences thought – the extent to which that which is portrayable and conceivable are interlinked – are themes that have underlain this study. Archaeology's experimentation with models in the nineteenth and earlier twentieth century essentially related to the discipline exploring its own visualisation. Yet, it also occurred within a broader milieu, involving both the representation of the past to the public at large and the employment of models as a means of technical demonstration within the sciences as a whole. Just as with the advent of off-set lithography or colour slide film (or now interactive computer visuals), what this legacy attests to is that the 'archaeology' of archaeology is not just a matter of its intellectual history, but also the technologies and media of its reproduction – the materiality of its own production and domains of presentation. Models were an integral part of the practical discourse of its representation, which has always involved the *seeing*, as much as a 'reading', of the past.

Notes

1. Amongst its collections the Ashmolean Museum has a nineteenth-century cranked roller blind system on which illustrations could be advanced to accompany lectures (A. Sherratt, pers. comm.). The 1877 engraving of Schliemann's evidently slide-less, audience-packed lecture concerning his work at Mycenae to the Society of Antiquaries of London in the *Illustrated London News* in March of that year (reproduced in Bacon 1976: 55, fig. 30) conveys a sense of the circumstances of these early 'performances'. A colleague experienced what must be comparable lecture conditions whilst attending an archaeological symposium in the final years of the Soviet Union. Lacking slides and with only limited publication opportunities, the speakers hung their figures around the hall. When referred to, members of the audience would cross the room to examine these, interjecting comments and queries. In short, a state of theatrical pandemonium (M.L.S. Sørensen, pers. comm.).

2. See Bradley (1997) concerning archaeology's visualisation and 'learning to see' in fieldwork.

3. See Kockel (2004) concerning early Italian model production. In London, Dubourg's exhibits apparently succumbed to fire in 1785 upon an overly successful demonstration of the Vesuvius effect; later re-opened in Duke St, it moved to Lower Grosvenor St in 1801 where it continued to operate until 1819 (Altick 1978: 392–96, fig. 140; Richardson 1989: 225–26; Thornton and Dorey 1992: 67). Legrand (1806: 158–59) relates that 'Monuments Celtiques ou Druidiques' featured in the model collection of the architect, L.-F. Cassas, shown in Paris in 1806 (and later sold to the Academy). Aside from a Stonehenge, this included a 'druid temple' from Dewinwater, Cumberland. See also Vogt (1998) concerning how exposure to models of the Pantheon cut in half in order to show its interior provided the inspiration for Gondouin's demonstration hall for surgery at the Sorbonne of 1767 – literally a half-Pantheon (262–64, figs. 195 and 196).

4. Aside from the Cabinet models, Browne is known to have sold at least four other 'Before and After' Stonehenge pairs. These apparently were sold for seven guineas each and, anticipating greater demand, he even had moulds made so that plaster copies of the stones could be produced quickly (Chippindale 1985: 128–29). Conveying a sense of a 'heavy' architectonic record and an almost geological solidity of representation, the Ashmolean Museum's versions of Browne's Avebury and Stonehenge models were respectively accompanied by specimens of 'earth from its centre' and 'stones from the circles and altar' (1824; Cat. No. 329–31).

5. See Edmonds (2004: 13 (Note 2)) concerning later eighteenth-century 'Claude glasses', hand-held viewing frames that allowed observers to frame and tint (*'in situ'*) landscape views in a picturesque manner.

6. Goethe wrote that on first arriving in Rome in 1786 his 'imagining' of the city had been tempered by exposure to paintings, prints and *various models of its ruins* (in Vogt 1998: 263).

7. Pitt Rivers most certainly would have been familiar with Sopwith's models as they were advertised for sale (at £5.00 a set) on the back cover pages of the same volume of *The Proceedings of the Geological Society* as his 1872 'Palaeolithic Implements' paper appeared. See Freeman (2004) concerning geological models generally, the production of which was often announced in the *Reports of the British Association for the Advancement of Science*.

8. Upon his return to Britain from Java, Sir Stamford Raffles (the founder of Singapore) brought back a series of doll-like figures illustrative of local 'social types', and also miniature sets of contemporary weapons and the instruments for gamelan orchestras. Used as the basis for as 'if-from-life' illustrations in his *History of Java* of 1817, these were commissioned as a means to transmit *information*; this being held to be the prime goal rather than any intrinsic value of the original object (Barley 1999; ethnography was, of course, to develop its own range of reconstruction models – *the* African or South Pacific village, etc.: O'Hanlon, per comm.). Although not involving miniaturisation, to some extent the archaeological equivalent of Raffles' pieces are casts of individual artefacts. Ranging from flint axes to Bronze Age swords, the British Museum, for example, has some 90 of these in its stores. Pitt Rivers also commissioned cast artefact copies; the only extant record of the West Buckland Bronze Age hoard is, for example, from a set of these (Taylor 1982). Mounted on sticks like giant lollipops, the General also casted excavated stakeholes.

9. Generally having much more tangible 'formal building' remains (and often closer professional architectural ties) than prehistory, there has been a strong tradition of architectural reconstruction modelling in the archaeology of the classical and ancient worlds. On a similar scale to Soane's Pompeii model, in the Roman Baths Museum, Bath, there is a large wooden model showing the base of the ground storey walls, etc., of the great baths complex. Although the precise date of its construction is unknown, it was part of the City of Bath's displays in the British Empire Exhibition of 1923 (illustrated in Fletcher 1945: 143). London, Colchester and St Albans Museums also have a number of models reconstructing their respective Roman towns. See Bernbeck (2000) for models in the Pergamon Museum, Berlin and Kemp (2000) on the large model of Tell el-Amarna, Akhenaten's ancient Egyptian capital, recently commissioned for the Boston Museum of Fine Arts.

10. Bersu himself was great exponent of model building reconstruction as a test of their engineering qualities and 'completeness' of the interpretation of structure-related features (1940 and 1977: 23, pl. iii). Despite this, archaeology never really developed a variant of the experimental model *viz.* building reconstruction/destruction or general depositional principles. 'Miniaturisation', instead, predominantly related to visualisation processes; there was no sense of trying to scale down the operation of building stresses (e.g. duplicate materials) or weathering/decay processes. It is only really in the landscape-scale projects since the 1960s – the Overton Down Earthwork or the Buster Experimental Farm – that, focusing much more on long-term processes rather than structural form alone, an experimental component was incorporated into (full-scale) reconstruction.

11. Bullied, the director of the Glastonbury excavations (perhaps encouraged by his assistant, Gray in his post-Pitt Rivers career), had two 'unpopulated' models made showing the portions of the settlement as reconstructed (see Coles *et al.* 1992: fig. 21). Vogt (1998) discusses the broader social and architectural impact of the prehistoric Swiss Lake Village discoveries and its models during the later nineteenth century (1998: 260, figs. 192–194). Featuring in that Country's school curriculum of the period, he in fact argues that the espoused egalitarianism and raised stilt-style construction of the Lake Village settlements were a formative influence on the 'modernist' architect, Le Corbusier, who was then educated in its system.

Acknowledgements

Although seeing further development, specific detailing and re-emphasis, this paper is essentially an abridged version of that which appeared in S. de Chadarevian and N. Hopwood's 2004 edited volume, *Models: The Third Dimension of Science*, and in which full source acknowledgements are provided. Beyond these, however, for long-term discussions and the provision of crucial information certain individuals must be singled out: R. Boast, R. Bradley, C. Chippindale, M. Edmonds, V. Kockel, T. Murray, M. O'Hanlon and M.L.S. Sørensen. I am also grateful for the tried patience and encouragement of Jarl Nordbladh and Nathan Schlanger.

References

Alexander, J. 1970. *The Directing of Archaeological Excavations*. London: John Baker Ltd.

Altick, R. 1978. *The Shows of London*. London: Belknap Press.

Awdry, J.W. 1870. 'President's Address', *Wiltshire Archaeological and Natural History Magazine* 12: 133–52.

Bacon, E. (ed.). 1976. *The Great Archaeologists*. London: Secker & Warburg.

Barley, N. 1999. 'Introduction', in N. Barley (ed.), *The Golden Sword: Stamford Raffles and the East*. London: British Museum Press, pp. 11–15.

Barker, M. 2004. 'Representing Invention, Viewing Models', in S. de Chadarevian and N. Hopwood (eds), *Models: The Third Dimension of Science*. Stanford, Calif.: Stanford University Press (Writing Science Series), pp. 19–42.

Barrett, J., R. Bradley and M. Green. 1991. *Landscape, Monuments and Society*. Cambridge: Cambridge University Press.

Bernbeck, R. 2000. 'The Exhibition of Architecture and the Architecture of an Exhibition', *Archaeological Dialogues* 7: 98–145.

Bersu, G. 1940. 'Excavations at Little Woodbury, Wiltshire. Part I, The Settlement as revealed by Excavation', *Proceedings of the Prehistoric Society* 6: 30–111.

——— . 1977. *Three Iron Age Round Houses in the Isle of Man*. The Manx Museum and National Trust.

Bowden, M. 1991. *Pitt Rivers: The Life and Archaeological Work of Lieutenant-General Augustus Henry Lane Fox Pitt Rivers, DCL, FRS, FSA*. Cambridge: Cambridge University Press.

Bradley, R. 1975. 'Maumbury Rings, Dorchester: The Excavations of 1908–1913', *Archaeologia* 105: 1–97.

——— . 1997. '"To see is to have seen": Craft Traditions in British Field Archaeology', in B.L. Molyneaux (ed.), *The Cultural Life of Images: Visual Representation in Archaeology*. London: Routledge, pp. 62–72.

Chippindale, C. 1983. *Stonehenge Complete*. London: Thames & Hudson.

——— . 1985. 'John Britton's "Celtic Cabinet" in Devizes Museum and its Context', *Antiquaries Journal* 65: 121–38.

Clay, R.C.C. 1924. 'An Early Iron Age site on Fyfield Bavant Down', *Wiltshire Archaeological Magazine* 42: 457–96.

Coles, J., A. Goodall and S. Minnitt. 1992. *Arthur Bulleid and the Glastonbury Lake Village, 1892–1992*. Somerset County Museums Services.

Colley, L. 1992. *Britons: Forging the Nation 1707–1837*. London: Yale University Press.

Conway, H.S. 1787. 'Description of a Druidical Monument in the Island of Jersey', *Archaeologia* 8: 386–88.

Dudley Buxton, L.H. (ed.). 1929. *The Pitt Rivers Museum: General Handbook*. Farnham Museum.

Edmonds, M. 2004. *The Langdales: Landscape and Prehistory in a Lakeland Valley*. Stroud: Tempus.

——— . and C. Evans. 1991. 'The Place of the Past: Art and Archaeology in Britain', in *Excavating the Present* 2: History. Cambridge: Kettle's Yard.

Evans, C. 1988. 'Monuments and Analogy: The Interpretation of Causewayed Enclosures', in C. Burgess, P. Topping, C. Mordant and M. Maddison (eds), *Enclosures and Defences in the Neolithic of Western Europe*. Oxford: British Archaeological Reports (International Series 403), pp. 47–73.

——— . 1994. 'Natural Wonders and National Monuments: A Meditation upon the Fate of The Tolmen', *Antiquity* 68: 200–208.

——— . 1998. 'Constructing Houses and Building Context: Bersu's Manx Roundhouse Campaign', *Proceedings of the Prehistoric Society* 64: 183–201.

———. 2000. 'Megalithic Follies: Soane's "Druidic Remains" and the Display of Monuments', *Journal of Material Culture* 5: 347–66.

———. 2004. 'Modelling Monuments and Excavations', in S. de Chadarevian and N. Hopwood (eds), *Models: The Third Dimension of Science*. Stanford, Calif.: Stanford University Press (Writing Science Series), pp. 109–37.

———. Forthcoming. '"Delineating Objects": Nineteenth Century Antiquarian Culture and the Project of Archaeology', in S. Pearce (ed.), *Visions of Antiquity: A Tri-centenary Celebration of the Society of Antiquaries of London*. London: Society of Antiquaries.

Evans, J. 1956. *A History of the Society of Antiquaries*. Oxford: University Press.

Fletcher, B. 1945. *A History of Architecture on the Comparative Method*. London: Batsford.

Freeman, M. 2004. *Victorians and the Prehistoric*. London: Yale University Press.

Gray, H.St G. 1903. 'Relief Model of Arbor Low Stone Circle, Derbyshire', *Man* 3 (84): 145–46.

———. 1929. 'Models of Ancient Sites in Farnham Museum', in L.H. Dudley Buxton (ed.), *The Pitt Rivers Museum: General Handbook*: 36–37. Farnham Museum.

Hawkes, C.F.C. 1947. 'Britons, Romans and Saxons Round Salisbury and in Cranborne Chase', *Archaeological Journal* 104: 27–81.

Hibbs, J. 1985. 'Little Master Stonehenge: A Study of the Megalithic Monument from Le Mont de la Ville, Saint Helier', *Annual Bulletin of the Society Jeriaise* 110: 49–74.

Higgins, G. 1827. *The Celtic Druids*. London: R. Hunter.

Hodder, I. 1989. 'Writing Archaeology: The Site Report in Context', *Antiquity* 63: 268–74.

Hofschröer, P. 2004. *Wellington's Smallest Victory: The Duke, the Model Maker and the Secret of Waterloo*. London: Faber & Faber.

Kemp, B. 2000. 'A Model of Tell el-Amarna', *Antiquity* 74: 15–16.

Kockel, V. 2004. 'Towns and Tombs: Three-dimensional Documentation of Archaeological Sites in the Kingdom of Naples in the Late Eighteenth and Early Nineteenth Centuries', in I. Bignamini (ed.), *Archives & Excavations: Essays on the History of Archaeological Excavations in Roman and Southern Italy from the Renaissance to the Nineteenth Century*. London.

Legrand, L.-G. 1806. *Collection des Chefs-d'oeuvre de l'Architecture des différents Peuples exécutés en Modèles*, Paris.

Levine, P. 1986. *The Amateur and the Professional: Antiquarians, Historians and Archaeologists in Victorian England, 1838–1886*. Cambridge: Cambridge University Press.

Molesworth, R. 1787. 'Description of the Druid Temple Lately Discovered on the Top of the Hill Near St Hillary in Jersey', *Archaeologia* 8: 384–85.

Moser, S. 1999. 'The Dilemma of Didactic Displays: Habitat Dioramas, Life-groups and Reconstructions of the Past', in N. Merriman (ed.), *Making Early Histories in Museums*. Leicester: Leicester University Press, pp. 95–116.

Peck, T.W. and K.D. Wilkinson. 1950. *William Withering of Birmingham, M.D., F.R.S., F.L.S.* Bristol: John Wright & Sons Ltd.

Physick, J. and M. Darby. 1973. '*Marble Halls*': *Drawings and Models for Victorian Secular Buildings*. London: Victorian and Albert Museum.

Piggott, S. 1978. *Antiquity Depicted: Aspects of Archaeological Illustration*. London: Thames & Hudson.

———. 1989. *Ancient Britons and the Antiquarian Imagination*. London: Thames & Hudson.

Pitt Rivers, Lt-Gen. A.H.L.F. 1861. 'On a Model Illustrating the Parabolic Theory of the Projection for Ranges in Vacuo', *Journal of the Royal United Service Institution* 5: 497–501.

———. 1872. 'On the Discovery of Palaeolithic Implements in Association with *Elephas Primigenius* in the Gravels of the Thames Valley at Acton', *Proceedings of the Geological Society of London* 28: 449–66.

———. 1887. *Excavations in Cranborne Chase* (I). Privately Printed.

———. 1892. *Excavations in Cranborne Chase* (III). Privately Printed.

———. 1897. 'Presidential Address to the Dorchester Meeting of the Archaeological Institute', *Archaeological Journal* 54: 311–39.

———. 1898. *Excavations in Cranborne Chase* (IV). Privately Printed.

Richardson, M. 1989. 'Model Architecture', *Country Life* 183 (Sept. 21): 224–27.

Schaffer, S. 2004. 'Fish and Ships: Models in the Age of Reason', in S. de Chadarevian and N. Hopwood (eds), *Models: The Third Dimension of Science*. Stanford, Calif.: Stanford University Press (Writing Science Series), pp. 71–105.

Siborne, W. c. 1838. *Guide to the Model of the Battle of Waterloo*. London: P. Dixon.

Smyth, W.H. 1830. 'Account of an Ancient Bath in the Island of Lipari', *Archaeologia* 23: 98–102.

Sopwith, T. 1841. *Description of a Series of Geological Models*. Newcastle upon Tyne.

Stevens, F. 1934. 'The Highfield Pit Dwellings, Fisherton, Salisbury', *Wiltshire Archaeological Magazine* 46: 579–624.

Stone, J.F.S. 1958. *Wessex before the Celts*. London: Thames & Hudson.

Stone, S. 1857. 'Account of Certain (supposed) British and Saxon remains ... , *Proceedings of the Society of Antiquaries of London*, 1st series, 4 (1856–9): 92–100.

Taylor, R.J. 1982. 'The Hoard from West Buckland, Somerset', *Antiquaries Journal* 62: 13–17.

Thompson, M.W. 1977. *General Pitt-Rivers: Evolution and Archaeology in the Nineteenth Century*. Bradford-on-Avon: Moonraker Press.

Thornton, P. and H. Dorey. 1992. *A Miscellany of Objects from Sir John Soane's Museum*. London: Laurence King.

Vogt, A.M. 1998. *Le Corbusier, the Noble Savage: Toward an Archaeology of Modernism*. Cambridge, Mass.: MIT Press.

Watkin, D. 1996. *Sir John Soane: Enlightenment Thought and the Royal Academy Lectures*. Cambridge: Cambridge University Press.

Wheeler, M. 1954. *Archaeology from the Earth*. Oxford: Clarendon Press.

Wilton-Ely, J. 1965. *The Architect's Vision: Historic and Modern Architectural Models*. Nottingham: University of Nottingham.

——— . 1969. 'The Architectural Models of Sir John Soane: A Catalogue', *Architectural History* 12: 5–38.

1. C.J.C. Reuvens and Conrad Leemans at the excavations at Arentsburg. Drawing by T. Hooiberg, ca. 1829. Archive, National Museum of Antiquities.

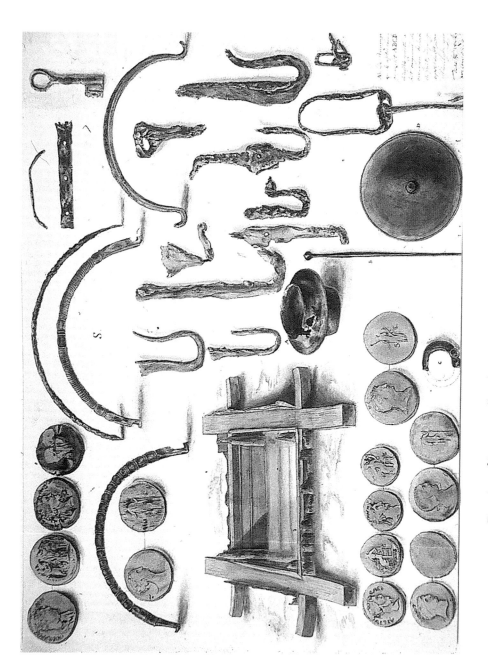

2. Drawing of Roman well and its contents. Drawing with watercolour by
   T. Hooiberg, ca. 1829. Archive, National Museum of Antiquities.

May.14 1894

H.M.J.U
Aug 24 1895

3. Two views of Wayland Smith' Cave, Berkshire. Lantern slide by H.M.J. Underhill, 1895.

4. Pitt Rivers' hinged model of the Cissbury hillfort with flint mines below. The upper portion longitudinally divides to allow its halves to be raised separately; lifting one portion exposes a central sction through the rampart indicating the relationship of its upcast upon the geological strata and, too, the upper profiles of the earlier mines (47.5 x 32.5cm; scale 6'6" to 1"; reproduced with permission of Sailsbury and South Wiltshire Museum).

5. Vatican Museums: Rotunda of the Museum Pio-Clementino.

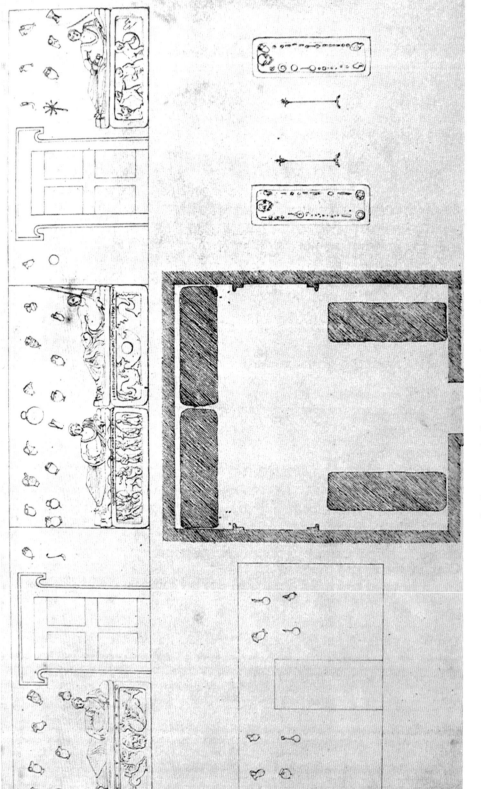

6. Campanari's Plan of the Tomb in London.

7. Vatican Museums: Museum Gregoriano Etrusco, view before 1920–22.

8. Jean-Léon Gérome, Sculpturae Vitam insufflat Pictura, 1893. Toronto, Art Gallery of Ontario.

9. Drawing of several Attic black-figure amphorae held in Munich (after Brunn, H., Krell, P. F. and Lau, G.T., 1877, pl. XII).

10. Nimrud: fantastic reconstruction (Layard 1849, II: Pl. 1).

11. Joseph Déchelette during his visit to Santa María de Huerta in 1912
(Soria, Spain). © Aguilera y Gamboa (1916: 78–79, pl. XIV).

12. The excavation of supposed sunken huts at Uddelermeer in 1908.

13. During a study tour through Germany, Holwerda documented these urns in the Landesmuseum in Trier.

14. Early representation of Torriani Indigenes. Torriani, I, L., 1978 (1592). *Descripción e Historia del reino de las Islas Canarias, antes Afortunadas, con el parecer de sus fortificaciones.* Santa Cruz de Tenerife: Goya Ediciones.

15. Spectacular and symbolic cover showing an entrance to the great Civilización Chaco Santiagueña. Painted by Duncan Wagner for the Wagners' book (originally published by Wagner and Wagner 1934).

16. Excavations in the bombed city centre of Middelburg by the
National Museum of Antiquities (1941) (fotocollection RMO).

Part III
VISUALISING ARCHAEOLOGY

Chapter 13

The Impossible Museum

Exhibitions of Archaeology as Reflections of Contemporary Ideologies

Marcello Barbanera

Abstract

While exhibitions of Renaissance or Modern art have a long history behind them, those dedicated to archaeology have only gradually grown in the last decades. Looking for the earliest traces of this phenomenon leads us back to the beginning of the nineteenth century, when public exhibitions of archaeological material were rare and often tied to contemporary cultural debates – or, in the twentieth century, to political moments. The question is: how much can these events be read as a reflection of contemporary cultural trends or governing ideologies? Or, inversely, did these exhibitions have influence on the contemporary culture, society and politics in a broader sense? I will focus here on the exhibition of Etruscan objects organised in London by the Campanari brothers in 1837, on the reconstruction of the Athena Parthenos for the Exposition Universelle in Paris of 1855, and on the Mostra Archeologica organised in Rome in 1911. In these initiatives we can trace strong aesthetic and ideological ties to a society at a given moment, and also glimpse at models for some ideal though unrealised museums. At their origin, archaeological exhibitions have represented an opportunity for an experimental and innovative museography that remained for long unfulfilled in European museums. Therefore, the impetus to conceive them bears examination. Archaeological exhibitions may thus be an index for understanding the uses of archaeology by political powers and the value that ancient traditions have upon the modern conscience. Through these examples, my aim is draw attention to the wider importance of such archaeological exhibitions.

Introduction

The curious visitor to the Museo Nazionale Romano, with its impressive displays of incomparable masterpieces and exhaustive explanatory panels, would emerge nonetheless with a rather disconnected feeling whereby the meanings of the ancient world were forever relegated to the past, and the exhibition just experienced was designed more for our facile contemplation rather than our profound comprehension (Fig. 13.1). The cold, a-contextual nature of the installation is in part the consequence of the specialisation in the study of antiquity, but also the loss of a relevant role that ancient art played in society (Borbein 2004, 35–36). Eighteenth-century Europe constructed a dialogue with ancient Greece and Rome in a holistic fashion, in a way that would not have been possible neither in the Renaissance (Seznec 1976: 2033–47) nor later in the nineteenth century with its greater philological rigour but diminished vitality (Marchand 1996: 36–51). The antiquity of the Enlightenment did not represent – as was the case in later centuries – merely a universe to explore and reconstruct through the study of ancient texts, but an ethical and aesthetic exemplum, 'like a lost Eden in which everything yearns to return' (Assunto 1973: 57). The discovery of Herculaneum and Pompeii or, a little later, the rediscovery of Paestum, provided the concrete and vibrant image of a world that up to that time was found in literary texts or haphazard objects selected for their decorative aesthetic value.

Alongside a growing culture of collecting, the increase of available material brought about a change in the relationship with ancient objects: the Recuéil d'antiquités of the Comte de Caylus published from 1752 to 1767, and the Geschichte der Kunst des Alterthums by Winckelmann of 1764 reflect the need to incorporate the evidence of the ancient world into an epistemological

Fig. 13.1 A visitor in Museo Nazionale Romano.

Fig. 13.2 Vatican Museums: Cortile of Belvedere, general view.

system – be it that of Caylus, merely tied to experimental antiquarianism (Aghion 2002), or that of Winckelmann which became a powerful interpretive model (Potts 1994).

These systems were translated into institutional models through the creation of the museum (Ferretti 1980), a place where the works of art are classified and exhibited according to style and provenance, having by now outgrown entirely the passionate albeit also rather confusing container of the Kunstkammer (Findlen 1996: 93–4).

The museum of the Enlightenment, beyond its role as a place to conserve art objects, also aimed at educating the populace in the cult of beauty, in the history of ancient times as an ethical example and to enliven in the visitor the sensation of living among the gods and their muses. Allusions to Olympus and Parnassus were explicit on the part of contemporary architects and their consultant archaeologists. One of the most successful examples and paradigm is the Museo Pio-Clementino in the Vatican, finished under Pope Pius VI Braschi to the designs of Michelangelo Simonetti and the installation supervised by Winckelmann's successor, Giovanni Battista Visconti and his ingenious son Ennio Quirino (Consoli 1996, 1994, 2000). The museum, inaugurated in 1784, represents the most ardent institutional reflection of a modern science of antiquity: the domed chapels (Fig. 13.2) designed by Simonetti to display the masterpieces of ancient sculpture in the Cortile del Belvedere stimulate a private sense of encounter between the visitor and the work, the basis of Winckelmann's aesthetic principles and tourist guides still today that transform the visit to museums into an almost theatrical experience (Chevallier 1976: 344). The reconstruction of the mosaic from Otricoli in the grandiose Rotunda (Plate 5) which recalls the architectonic forms of the original edifice in which they were found serves to recreate a context for the statues placed in the niches that seem to give life to a conversation on Mount Olympus. The museum aspires to become not simply a container of antique sculpture but a place that reflects the society and its times, and, at the same time, searches to direct it in its taste, proposing a global aesthetic experience where not only one contemplates the past but receives models for the present. Here, for the first time, a public museum proposes to unite time – that is history – with the spirit of the place (Collins 1994: 249–315).

In the nineteenth century, the 'museums of reason' were supplanted by what we might call 'museums of guilt', that is the institutions created after the Restoration to house the works of art extracted from their original contexts (Mottola Molfino 1998: 11–60). These museums were configured more as a 'refuge of wrecks of the past' or 'a gallery of fine examples for artists', thereby losing the vital connection between history, space and place. It is, however, still possible to retrace the close adherence between object and context, or the immediate reception of a scientific debate in the concrete initiatives we could call with a felicitous expression, 'ephemeral museums' (Haskell 2000): temporary exhibitions independent of institutions that reveal a vital indication of the discussions at the heart of archaeology, or of the ideologies connected to it.

I will present three examples: an exhibition of Etruscan objects organised in London in 1837, the reconstruction of the Athena Parthenos for the Exposition Universelle in Paris of 1855, and the Mostra Archeologica organised in Rome in 1911. These are three initiatives where, on the one hand, we can trace the strong aesthetic and ideological ties to a specific society and moment, and, on the other hand, we can glimpse at models for ideal albeit unrealised museums.

1. The Campanari Exhibition

It is known that interest in the Etruscans begun at least in the sixteenth century, when discoveries in Tuscany and northern Lazio initiated a certain fashion that was felt in numerous social environments (Cristofani 1983, 1992). But it is at the beginning of the nineteenth century that numerous discoveries at Tarquinia, Vulci and other locations widened the historical perspective and allowed for the posing of the problem of the Etruscans in new terms (Heurgon 1973). Among

Fig. 13.3 Wall paintings reconstructed in the Campanari Tomb in London.

those first attracted to the site of ancient Vulci was Vincenzo Campanari, a Tuscany landowner who at the end of the 1820s obtained permission to excavate an area of the ancient Etruscan city of Vulci. These excavations generated considerable interest, and they also brought to light an enormous quantity of objects, immediately fed to the avid market for antiquities across Europe (Buranelli 1992).

The name of Vincenzo Campanari and his sons became known in Europe through the principal antiquities dealers, in particular for the close ties that they developed with London and the local collectors market. It was the Campanari, in the 1830s, who bore witness to an advanced museography with their initiative on the fringes of the academic and museological world, but that presented perhaps the first real attempt to exhibit Etruscan materials according to a contextual conception. Their exhibition opened in London at 121 Pall Mall at the end of January 1837 (Plate 6) (Colonna 1978, 1986, 1992, 1999) at the centre of the great interest in antiquities, fuelled by the display of the 'Elgin Marbles' in 1808. Artistic exhibitions and a vibrant art market gravitated to London where one could find the Royal Academy, Christies' auction house and the British Gallery.

Archaeological exhibitions there at the beginning of the century were far from unusual. In 1824, for example, William Bullock organised the first archaeological exhibition of artefacts from Mexico in the so-called 'Egyptian Hall' (Locke 2003). The Campanari exhibition will help us to understand the development of museology of the era and the consequences for European culture and the cognisance of Etruscan antiquity.

The Campanari designed the exhibition according to their experience of the real excavation sites, enriched in ways unknown to the antiquarian: the materials in the context of their original deposition. The exhibition featured eleven tombs (Colonna 1999: 39 ff.) reconstructed to actual scale containing assortments of the original artifacts, sarcophagi, vases and funerary implements and gems, down to copies on canvas of the original fresco wall paintings. (Fig. 13.3) (Colonna 1984; Pittura etrusca 1986; Weber-Lehman 1992; Haynes 1992). The objects were mostly strewn about in a scenographic fashion; even skeletal remains were shown with armor still attached. The visit to the exhibition was given by torchlight, perhaps to relive the atmosphere of their rediscovery descending underground (Colonna 1978: 85 ff.). The organisation of the objects in their presumed original locations, the reproduction of the frescoes down to the details of the faded or damaged parts, denotes a will to stimulate in the visitor an emotive reaction half way between the aesthetic of the picturesque of the romantic era and the necessity to adhere to some archaeological facts.

The success of the exhibition demonstrates how the Campanari had perfectly met public taste. It received a positive review in the Times, and one visitor – Lady Hamilton Gray – became so enamoured with Etruscan things that she planned her Grand Tour accordingly, and recorded it in her diary (Hamilton Gray 1841; Colonna 1978: 86 ff.). This popular and critical success drove the British Museum to acquire the exhibited sarcophagi at the close of the exhibition, as well as the copies of the wall paintings, the plaster casts and many other materials that formed the nucleus of the museum's Etruscan collection (Price 1931: 148).

The pioneering nature of the exhibition in Pall Mall can be grasped by the fact that at the time the antiquarian market was interested in so-called Etruscan vases (in reality they were Greek), but had little interest in sarcophagi which were considered rather crudely made and of no real value in contrast to Roman ones. In fact, it was only by the late nineteenth century that the principal museums abroad begun to acquire this type of object, although cautiously at first. On a wider view, the exhibition in Pall Mall can be considered the first 'Etruscan exhibition' which has come down to us, and one of the best of the time that was ever installed. Not only the common visitor but also the scholar could extract something valuable from this show, given that there was gathered a vast documentation of the major discoveries from Etruria from the preceding decade that gave an entirely new configuration to the archaeological face of the region.

The importance of the Campanari Pall Mall exhibition becomes clearer when contrasted with two contemporaneous museographic initiatives: the institution of the Museo Etrusco Gregoriano at the Vatican and the installation of the large part of the objects from the Pall Mall exhibition in the British Museum. The Museo Etrusco Gregoriano was installed soon after the London exhibition and inaugurated on 2 February, 1837 (Magi 1963, Roncalli 1983, Pietrangeli 1985: 157 ff.). The installation demonstrates, however, that the spirit of the Campanari exhibition was not followed: the objects, deprived of their context of provenance, were exhibited rather haphazardly along the walls, not unlike eighteenth-century collections (Pietrangeli 1985: figs. 147, 149, 152).

The copies of the Campanari frescoes had a similar fate. They were installed in the Vatican in an anodyne manner, hanging like so many picture frames without any contextual accompaniment for the objects (Plate 7). It was Lady Gray, visiting Rome, who gives us this report: 'There we recognized Campanari's representations, but the exhibition of them altogether, in broad daylight, and with none of the divisions, was not half so pleasing, natural or imposing, as what we had seen in London' (Hamilton Gray 1841: 65; Colonna 1978: 90–1). On her return to London Lady Gray went straight to the British Museum to admire the Campanari collection, but here also a disappointment awaited her: the objects were set up in the rooms between the 'Elgin Marbles' and Egyptian antiquities, 'ranged along the wall', as she noted, 'in melancholy confusion and neglect, without a place in the catalogue, nor any indication to the curious of what they were. Our Etruscan friends lay in silence. They looked indeed as if they felt they were in a strange country, cold, comfortless and far from home' (Hamilton Gray 1841: 65; Colonna 1978). The Campanari brothers' Etruscan exhibition thus remained an isolated experiment. No museum followed, in whole or even in part, the suggestive ideas and system of the Pall Mall exhibition, whose architectural environment was specifically designed to highlight the coherence of the objects.

2. The Reconstruction of the Athena Parthenos by Charles Simart

Let us turn to a second example, moving to Paris in the middle of the nineteenth century, to the Athena Parthenos of Charles Simart. The French aristocrat, Honore Theodoric Paul Joseph d'Albert, duke of Luynes, nurtured a strong interest in antiquities since his childhood (Aghion and Avisseau-Broustet 1994: 12 ff.; Gran-Aymerich 2001: 426). In 1825, at 23 years of age, he became

Fig. 13.4 Charles Simart,
Athena Parthenos, 1846–
1855. Château de
Dampierre.

director of the Musée Charles X at the Louvre for Greek and Egyptian antiquities. Among the
founders of the Instituto di Corrispondenza archeologica, he undertook from 1828 onwards trips
to southern Italy to complete his study of ancient monuments. Attracted to Magna Graecia, he
joined an excavation at Metaponto with the architect F.J. Debacq who executed drawings and site
plans. Together, they studied fragments of architectural decorations in terracotta still with strong
traces of polychromy (De Luynes and Debacq 1833).

The experience at Metaponto stimulated de Luynes's interest in the question of polychromy in the ancient Greek world – a widely debated question among scholars of antiquity and artists of the early nineteenth century. This interest blossomed in the commissioning of a reconstruction of the Athena Parthenos from the sculptor Charles Simart (Fig. 13.4). This reconstruction was exhibited at the Exposition Universelle in Paris in 1855, and gave rise to strong reactions (Shedd 1986).

Pierre Charles Simart (1806–1857) was at the time an established academic sculptor, convinced that the art of his times needed to draw inspiration from the antique, insuperable as it was in the observation of nature and in its rendering in art. It is not surprising then that the choice to reconstruct the Athena fell to him. At that time the principal sources upon which the Parthenos is reconstructed today were still unknown. Only texts were used, as Quatremère de Quincy had done in 1825, Flaxman in 1838, Gerhard in 1844 and Paccard and Lucas in the following year (Shedd 1986: 124). Simart, however, was inspired by carefully selected elements: a relief and a coin from Athens, a gem in the Cabinet des Medailles, and the famous Aspasios gem on which the reconstruction of the helmet and jewels were based, while by some bronzes from Siris bought by the British Museum inspired the decoration of the armature. For the battle scene between the Centaurs and the Lapiths, painted in miniature relief on the deity's sandals, Simart used the sculptures of the temple of Hephaestus at Athens and of Apollo at Bassae, while the fighting deities and the giants represented on the shield were taken from a vase discovered at Vulci and published by Gerhard in 1848. For the Nike, a coin from the collection of the Duke was used as well as his reliefs of the Temple of Nike Apteros discovered in Athens in 1830. It is not improbable that the reconstruction proposed by Simart and de Luynes was also based on the so-called Athena Medici, the torso at the Villa Medici which was later sent by Ingres to the Ecole des Beaux Arts as an example of a fifth-century BC sculpture. This is suggested by the request by the Duke de Luynes for a plaster cast of this piece.

The exhibition of the statue provoked strong reactions that found an immediate echo in the contemporary Parisian press; some objected that it was not a matter of an artistic creation but a hybrid work that mixed art and craft; others noted the coldness of the work declaring it a failed attempt to revive the ancient masterpiece. The archaeologist Beulé, who had already proposed his own reconstruction of the statue the previous year (Beulé 1854), criticised Simart's work on several grounds: for mixing the styles of various epochs, for basing his reconstruction more on visual sources than on textual, but above all for creating a monochromatic sculpture, and not a polychromatic one. Simart had, in fact, carefully reconstructed a prevalent bi-chromatic coloration throughout the entire piece, evoking the white of the ivory and the brilliance of the gold. This lead us to question what was actually known at that time of polychromy in the ancient world. While the presence of colour on ancient sculpture had been noted since the time of Winckelmann and Caylus, the founding study on polychromy in sculpture is *Le Jupiter Olympien* by Quatremère de Quincy in 1814. This study paved the way for a vast debate among scholars. The question was closely related to the relevance of colour in the practice of contemporary art, so it is not surprising that the debate may have been triggered in the first instance by artists who sought to reconstruct polychromatic works. The neoclassical sculptors, basing their taste on white works, found themselves incapable of imagining the sculptures of antiquity as multicoloured. Similarly, their aesthetic conception resisted works of art assembled and composed from diverse materials, as was, effectively, the Phidian Athena. Quatremère contributed to liberate ancient art from the vision of current aesthetics, and the first to follow him were artists like Simart. Gérôme's painting entitled *Sculpturae insufflat vitam pictura* (Painting infuses life into sculpture) (Plate 8), shows an allegory of painting represented as intent on applying colour on a Tanagrina – at the time a kind of popular statuette figure – clearly with the aim of giving it life (Tanagra 2003: 53, fig. 5; Shedd 1986: 131).

With Romanticism, artists abandoned pure form for a journey into the new unity of the arts in which they also discovered the life of colour. The museography of the time did not react to the experiments of the dilettante archaeologists and artists. It took until the end of the nineteenth century for professional archeologists like Georg Treu to carry out experiments in the Skulturensammlung of Dresden, collaborating with artists like Max Klinger (Knoll 1994). Otherwise, only towards the end of the century did some isolated European museums dare to present to the public polychromatic reconstructions of ancient sculpture – an aspect for which there is nowadays a renewal of scientific interest (Bunte Götter 2003; Liverani 2003; Prater 2003).

3. The Mostra Archeologica of 1911 in Rome

One of the clearest examples of the intersection of political ideology with the celebration of antiquity was the exhibition organised in Rome in 1937. The occasion was the celebration of the bi-millennium of the birth of Augustus, founder of the Empire, of which Mussolini fashioned himself a direct descendent. This exhibition, by now thoroughly researched (Scriba 1995), had as a precedent the Mostra Archeologica in 1911 in Rome organised by Rodolfo Lanciani on the occasion of the fiftieth anniversary of Italian national autonomy (Lanciani 1911, Mancioli 1984, Mancioli 1984a, 1984b) (Fig. 13.5). This exhibition took place in the same year that Italy conquered Libya, is in a climate of strong nationalism and a celebration of Italian civilisation (Scriba 1995: 308 ff.). The Baths of Diocletian were chosen for the exhibition site. Lanciani and his collaborators must have had in mind the programme developed by Pietro Rosa as early as the 1880s for a new archaeological museum for the Italian state in the Baths of Diocletian, where the installation was based exclusively on aesthetic criteria (Scriba 1995: 320 ff.). Lanciani proposed to organise the objects according to style, school, and epoch, aiming in this way to document not only the history of Rome but also of those peoples that were conquered and then absorbed by the *Urbs* (1995: 320–29).

Fig. 13.5 Rome, Baths of Diocletian: *Mostra Archeologica* of 1911.

Lanciani wanted the objects to be exhibited in a scientific and didactic manner. The idea of a contrast between the diverse ancient cultures, scientifically correct, was not seen as counterproductive to the propagandistic function of the ancient Romans as civilisers. All of this had to be expressed by the works of art, and this was achieved by the use of originals and plaster casts. The exhibition begun with the *Dea Roma*, followed immediately by a room entirely dedicated to Augustus, giving to the founder of the Empire an honor denied all other emperors. There was exhibited the Augustus *capite velato* from the Via Labicana, encircled by models of monuments from around the empire: La Turbie, Susa, Pola, Aquileia, fragments of the *Ara Pacis* recomposed for the first time, and, at the end, the pronaos of the *Monumentum Ancyranum* at actual scale (Scriba 1995: 320–29; Strong 1911). The subsequent rooms included objects arranged according to their provenance in the ancient provinces, with works from the palace of Diocletian at Split, the trophy of *Adamklissi*, and the theater at Orange. At the end, however, the Roman civilisation did not remain unchallenged in its superiority: for example, the Greek government sent hundreds of plaster casts, including the sarcophagus of Hagia Triada. However, these were all exhibited to better document the accomplishments of Italian archaeologists abroad than the diffusion of ancient Roman culture (Kavvadias 1911).

Fig. 13.6 Rome, view of the former Museo dell'Impero.

The principal message of propaganda remained that of Rome's pre-eminent civilising mission in overcoming barbarism, and the founding role of Augustus. The show did represent barbarian culture alongside the Roman, but it was taken for granted that the Latins dominated. All of this linked with the political climate of colonial expansion promoted by the government of Giovanni Giolitti. However, the civilising message and the geographic organisation of the materials were not strictly connected. The message only became clear to the observer on the basis of single objects that could lead back to the thematic context. In the exhibition's inaugural address, Lanciani expressed the hope that the objects might find a definitive installation, but this came about only in 1927 with the creation of the Museo dell'Impero (Giglioli 1927–28, 1928, 1929; Scriba 1995: 330 ff.; Liberati Silverio 1984a, 1984b (Fig. 13.6). The political climate between 1911 and 1927 had changed decisively: from 1926 onwards the Fascist regime had effectively taken authoritarian control, and there was no longer place for comparisons between Romans and non-Romans.

Indeed, in the 1927 museum only Roman objects were exhibited, so that the visitor could no longer contrast the Roman civilisation with others, or trace the non-Roman roots of other cultures whose origins were absorbed into a pan-Roman vision of cultural diversity. The display was amplified with the scientific ambition to exhibit reproductions of all works of Roman art from the Empire. The scope for comparison was thereby annulled in the attempt to eliminate any dissenting voice within the historical framework of the Roman Empire, even if at the detriment of the cognitive value of archaeology.

The *Museo dell'Impero*, a bellwether in the climate of *Romanità*, did not preserve any of the spirit of comparison and contrast of the 1911 exhibition. The curator of the later exhibition, Giulio Quirino Giglioli, who also was the organiser of the Mostra Augustea, indeed sought to diminish Greek art, above all Hellenistic art, in comparison with Roman (Scriba 1995: 330–338). Once again, the transfer from the ephemeral experience of the archaeological exhibition to the permanence of a museum resulted in a loss. And as in other cases, it is precisely in this loss that resides the idea of the impossible museum.

Discussion

The three cases of an archetypal archaeological exhibition under consideration in this brief presentation were selected from among a vast array of examples. The aim is to offer an extended diachronic view of the inter-relation – or, more exactly, the lack of inter-relations – between the temporary exhibition of archaeological objects and the criteria adopted, at the same time, for the installation of some new museums.

My goal was not to research the genesis of the archaeological exposition as such and follow its development to the present; this line of inquiry would rightly merit a more in-depth investigation. My interest here is double; to examine the lack of reception of certain contextual principles demonstrated by these (admittedly ephemeral) exhibitions, and also to understand modern archaeological museums as the unavoidable products of a narrow specialisation, an inheritance of the nineteenth century and of the Restoration rather than of the eighteenth-century Enlightenment. State archaeological museums across Europe have been guided by the scientific spirit of nineteenth-century Positivism and also influenced by Idealism. Its curators often worried about corrupting a supposedly unrepeatable aura of the artistic creation. For this and other reasons, our state museums have become increasingly remote from the curiosity of the greater part of the modern urban public. The case of Rome is emblematic: its incomparable archaeological museums actually suffer from a serious lack of visitors (Zanker 2003: 5–122).

Let us return to the central case of the Museo Nazionale Romano from where we began. The intention to renew and re-open it are praiseworthy (as would any re-opening of a long-closed museum), but one has the impression that behind this initiative there is no real progressive museological project, one open and receptive to lively intellectual and cultural stimuli, either provocative or even didactic in intention. This is not really surprising, insofar as museum studies (museography and museology) have never been considered worthy of being taught in Italian universities, and they remain today, after the recent reforms, the prerogative of art historians. In Italy, the art of improvisation predominates – as in the cinema, in theatre and in the politics of the country – and the director of the archaeological museum is called on to create the installation himself, a bit like decorating his own home.

This principle might have been justified in times when the understanding of archaeological objects was directly related to the exquisite taste of a refined collector or his consultant (Pius VI and the Visconti, Cardinal Albani and Winckelmann, just to cite the more emblematic examples). But what is the result when the modern museum director conceives the installation according to some unrefined bourgeois conceptions?

Like other modern museums, archaeological museums are often the outcome of a tentative recontextualisation of objects from the past which have been filtered through numerous experiences. Nevertheless it is not sufficient to dismantle or reassemble according to presumed original conditions, as has happened at Palazzo Altemps, with the result already lucidly prefigured by Massimo Ferretti much earlier: 'It proves to be impossible to 'disassemble' a collection derived from excavations conducted still according to the selective and classicising intentions, in order to have emerge through a different arrangement the methodological or didactic concerns of a more modern and equilibrated discipline of archaeology, attuned to the totality of the social and material life that an excavation can, today, restitute. In this type of intention there is nothing progressive, but it is still the same cultural paternalism that is often hidden behind museographic efficiencies' (Ferretti 1980: 47).

Let us return for a moment to our examples: visitors to the Museo Pio-Clementino took away from the experience a vivifying encounter with antiquity. The Campanari brothers succeeded in investing enthusiasm into the snobbish Londoners, giving them the impression that the rooms at Pall Mall were real Etruscan tombs. The Parisian intelligentsia in 1855 discussed animatedly the question of the polychromy of the Parthenos, a theme that still today some scholars hesitate to consider relevant. Lanciani knew how to conceive an exhibition that, despite evident nationalistic spirit of exalting Roman Empire and by analogy the Italian monarchy, still could include reference to the non-Roman elements upon which the Empire was built, as distinct from Giglioli who did the opposite in installations of the Museo dell'Impero.

There are traces of a vital relationship between modern culture and the fragments of antiquity that we have chosen to preserve over the course of time. One needs to be sure that archaeological fragments are no longer merely abandoned remnants of a classical world stranded negligently in museums, institutions no longer culturally justified by the bourgeois class which they originally addressed. Museums are cultural spaces that must offer to the community a kind of comfort to the spirit and thus to be attractive, not repugnant, welcoming not cold, pulsing with activity not giving off an impression of torpor inexorably reflected in the expression of absent visitors, indeed to be something entirely different than 'cemeteries of art', as Théophile Thoré lamented as long ago as 1861 (Bürger 1901: 84). This is not necessarily a difficult process; one needs to look beyond the narrow confines of one's own country, and sometimes indeed it is sufficient also just to look to disciplines other than the sciences of antiquity.

References

Aghion, I. (ed.) 2002. *Caylus mécène du roi. Collectionner les antiquités au XVIIIᵉ siècle*, Paris.

Aghion, I. and M. Avisseau-Broustet 1994. 'Le duc de Luynes, archéologue, historien, homme de sciences et collectioneur', *Revue de la Bibliothèque Nationale de France*, 3: 12–20.

Assunto, R. 1973. *L'antichità come futuro. Studio sull'estetica del neoclassicismo europeo*, Milano.

Beulé, Ch. H. 1854. *L'Acropole d'Athènes*, Paris.

Borbein, A.H. 2004. 'Scultura antica. Retrospettiva e prospettiva su un campo dell'archeologia classica caduto in discredito', in M. Barbanera (ed.), *Storie dell'arte antica. Atti del Convegno La storia dell'arte antica nell'ultima generazione: tendenze e prospettive, Roma 19–20 febbraio 2001*, Roma: pp. 33–38.

Bunte Götter. Die Farbigkeit antiker Skulptur 2003, München.

Buranelli, F. 1992. *Gli scavi a Vulci della Società Vincenzo Campanari – Governo Pontificio (1835–1837)*, Roma.

Bürger, W. 1901. *Salon de 1861*, Paris.

Chevallier, E. 1976. 'L'oeuvre d'art dans le temps. Comment on a vu le Laocoon et l'Apollon du Belvédère à la fin du XVIIIe siècle, d'après la relation d'un voyageur allemand venu à Rome en 1783', in *Aiôn. Le temps chez les Romains*, Paris: pp. 344.

Collins, J. L. 1994. 'Arsenal of Art: the Patronage of Pope Pius VI and the End of the Ancien Régime', Ph.D. dissertation, New Haven: Yale University Press.

Collins, J. L. 2000. 'The God's abode: Pius VI and the Invention of the Vatican Museum', in C. Hornsby (ed.), *The Impact of Italy. The Grand Tour and Beyond*, London: pp. 173–194.

Colonna G. 1992. 'L'aventure romantique', in *Les Etrusques et l'Europe*, Paris: pp. 322–339.

Colonna, G. 1999. 'Ancora sulla mostra dei Campanari a Londra', in Mandolesi, A. and A. Naso (eds.), *Ricerche Archeologiche in Etruria Meridionale nel XIX secolo. Atti dell'Incontro di studio. Tarquinia 6–7 luglio 1996*, Firenze: pp. 37–62.

Colonna, G. 1978. 'Archeologia dell'età romantica in Etruria: I Campanari di Toscanella e la Tomba dei Vipinana', *Studi Etruschi* 46: 81–117.

Colonna, G. 1984. 'Le copie ottocentesche delle pitture etrusche e l'opera di Carlo Ruspi', in C. Morigi Govi, G. Sassatelli (eds.), *Dalla Stanza delle Antichità al Museo Civico*, Bologna: pp. 375–79.

Colonna, G. 1986 (ed.), Dennis, G. and E. C. Hamilton Gray, *Tuscania*, Siena.

Consoli, G. P. 1996. *Il Museo Pio-Clementino. La scena dell'antico in Vaticano*, Modena.

Cristofani, M. 1983. *La scoperta degli Etruschi. Archeologia e antiquaria nel '700*, Roma.

Cristofani, M. 1992. 'Le mythe étrusque en Europe entre le XVIe et le XVIIIe siècle', in *Les Etrusques et l'Europe*, Paris: pp. 276–291.

De Luynes, H. and F. J. Debacq 1833. *Métaponte*, Paris.

Ferretti, M. 1980. 'La forma del Museo', in *Capire l'Italia. I Musei*, Milano: pp. 46–79.

Findlen, P. 1996. *Possessing Nature. Museums, Collecting, and scientific Culture in early modern Italy*, Berkeley.

Giglioli, G.Q. 1927–28. 'Il Museo dell'Impero Romano', *Capitolium* 3: 8–14.

Giglioli, G.Q. 1928. 'Origine e sviluppo del Museo dell'Impero', *Capitolium* 4: 303–312.

Giglioli, G.Q. 1929. *Museo dell'Impero Romano*, Roma.

Gran-Aymerich, E. 2001. *Dictionnaire Biographie d'Archéologie, 1798–1945*, Paris.

Greenhalgh, P. 1988. *Ephemeral Vistas: the expositions universelles, great exhibitions and world's fairs 1851–1939*, Manchester.

Hamilton Gray, E.C. 1841. *Tour to the Sepulchres of Etruria in 1839*, London.

Haskell, F. 2000. *The Ephemeral Museum: Old Master Paintings and the Rise of the Art Exhibition*, New Haven.

Haynes, S. 1992. 'La Grande-Bretagne et les Etrusques', in *Les Etrusques et l'Europe*, Paris: 310–20.

Heurgon, J. 1973. 'La découverte des Etrusques au début du XIX siècle', *Comptes Rendus Academie des Inscriptions*, 1973: 591–600.

Kavvadias, P. 1911. *Marbres des Musées de Grèce. Catalogue de la collection de moulages exposés à Rome*, Athènes.

Knoll, K. 1994. 'Treus Versuche zur antiken Polychromie und Ankäufe farbiger Plastik', in *Das Albertinum vor 100 Jahren – Die Skulpturensammlung Georg Treus*, Dresden: pp. 164–79.

Lanciani, R. 1911. *Mostra Archeologica nelle Terme di Diocleziano*, Bergamo.

Liberati Silverio, A.M. 1984. 'Il Museo dell'Impero Romano 1927–1929', in *Dalla mostra al museo*, Venezia: pp. 65–67.

Liberati Silverio, A.M. 1984a. 'Il Museo dell'Impero Romano 1929', in *Dalla mostra al museo*, Venezia: pp. 68–73.

Liverani, P. 2003. 'Der Augustus von Prima Porta', in *Bunte Götter. Die Farbigkeit antiker Skulptur*, München: pp. 186–91.

Locke, A. 2003. 'Ausstellungen und Sammlungen altmexikanischer Artefakte in Grossbritannien', in *Azteken*, Berlin: pp. 80–91.

Magi, F. 1963. 'Il Museo Gregoriano Etrusco nella storia degli scavi e degli studi etruschi', in *Etudes Etrusco-Italiques, Recueil de travaux d'histoire et de philologie* 31: Louvain: pp. 119–30

Mancioli, D. 1984. 'La Mostra Archeologica del 1911 e le Terme di Diocleziano', in *Dalla mostra al museo*, Venezia: pp. 29–32.

Mancioli, D. 1984a. 'La Mostra archeologica', in *Dalla mostra al museo*, Venezia: pp. 52–61.

Marchand, S.L. 1996. *Down from Olympus. Archaeology and Philellenism in Germany* 1750–1970, Princeton.

Mottola Molfino, A. 1998. *Il libro dei Musei*, Torino.

Müller-Scheessel, N. 2001. 'Fair Prehistory: archaeological exhibits at French Expositions Universelles', *Antiquity* 75(287): 391–401.

Pietrangeli, C. 1985. *I Musei Vaticani. Cinque secoli di storia*, Roma.

Pittura etrusca, disegni e documenti del XIX secolo dall'Archivio dell'Istituto Archeologico Germanico 1986, Roma.

Potts, A. 1994. *Flesh and the Ideal. Winckelmann and the Origins of Art History*, New Haven.

Prater, A. 2003. 'Streit um die Farbe. Die Wiederentdeckung der Polychromie in der griechischen Architektur und Plastik im 18. und 19. Jahrhundert', in *Bunte Götter. Die Farbigkeit antiker Skulptur*, München: pp. 256–67.

Price, F.N. 1931. *British Museum. Sculptures*, I.2. London.

Roncalli, F. 1983. 'I Musei Gregoriano Etrusco ed Egizio', in *Musei Vaticani Egizi ed Etruschi*, Firenze.

Rydell, R.W. and N. Gwinn 1994. *Fair representations*, Amsterdam.

Scriba, F. 1995. *Augustus im Schwarzhemd? Die "Mostra Augustea della Romanità" in Rom 1937/38*, Frankfurt a. Main.

Seznec, J. 1976. 'L'invention de l'Antiquité', in *Studies on Voltaire and the Eighteenth Century* 155: 2033–2047.

Shedd, M. 1986. 'Phidias at the Universal Exposition of 1855: the Duc de Luynes and the Athena Parthenos', *Gazette des Beaux Arts* 1986: 123–33.

Strong, E. 1911. 'The Exhibition Illustrative of the Provinces of the Roman Empire at the Baths of Diocletian Rome', *Journal of Roman Studies* 1: 1–49.

Tanagra. Mythe et archéologie 2003, Paris.

Weber Lehman, C. 1992. 'Les reproductions des peintures étrusques', in *Les Etrusques et l'Europe*, Paris: pp. 414–31.

Zanker, P. 2003. 'I nuovi musei archeologici e la mancanza di visitatori', *Bollettino Museo Comunali Roma* 17: 5–12.

Chapter 14

Towards a More 'Scientific' Archaeological Tool

The Accurate Drawing of Greek Vases between the End of the Nineteenth and the First Half of the Twentieth Centuries

Christine Walter

Abstract

First studied essentially for their iconographic representations, Greek vases were increasingly studied for their style when issues of artistic individualities and stylistic affinities became reachable. The bases for stylistic analysis were laid down by the Italian Giovanni Morelli in a series of articles on Italian paintings published between 1874 and 1876. Adolf Furtwängler and Paul Hartwig adapted this method in the field of archaeology and John Beazley applied it systematically to the entire production of Greek Attic vases from the sixth to fourth centuries BC. This desire to classify all vases and their painters chronologically meant paying greater attention to methods and 'tools' for studying and recording these 'hands' with more fidelity. Consequently, special attention was paid to the accurate drawing (copying) of the figures on Greek vases. Old illustrations not always equal to the ambitions of contemporary archaeologists because of their considerable variations from the originals. Furtwängler was the first to insist on the need for a more scientific drawing of Greek vases, which would be clear of modern artistic distortions or copyist peculiarities. He was persuaded that a good knowledge of Greek vases depended entirely on their faithful reproduction, and this conviction influenced all subsequent generations of specialists.

Ancient Greek vases were initially studied for their iconography. Over time, they were scrutinised also for the style of their drawing, and this made it necessary to elaborate a classification of individual artists and their workshops. It is generally acknowledged that the bases for a more accurate method of stylistic analysis were laid down by the Italian Giovanni Morelli, from 1874 to 1876, in a series of articles on Italian paintings housed in the Borghese Gallery in Roma (published under the pseudonym of Lermolieff; see Lermolieff 1874–1876 and particularly Lermolieff 1891, the chapter entitled 'Princip und Methode'). This method allows the style (or graphism) of certain unsigned artistic personalities to be used to distinguish them various works in order to form a corpus. It was later rediscovered by the archaeologists Adolf Furtwängler (Reinach 1907: 310; Stewart 1990: 30)[1] and Paul Hartwig in the last quarter of the nineteenth century, before being adapted and applied systematically by John Beazley, at the beginning of the twentieth century, to the whole Attic production from the sixth to fourth centuries BC. The aim to track down the graphic peculiarities of each painter or group of painters drew wider attention, and generated further study. Interest was apparent in archaeological drawings which copied the figures or decorative designs on these vases, drawings which would have to be as accurate as they possibly could. The aim of this chapter, which derives from my Ph.D. research (Walter 2001), is to explain, by specific examples, the emergence and the evolution of a 'scientific' drawing of Greek vases between the end of the nineteenth and the first half of the twentieth centuries, in order to understand clearly its real sources, its objectives, and its limitations.

The German archaeologist Adolf Furtwängler (1853–1907) was one of the first scholars to draw official attention to the need of scientific drawings of Greek ceramics, in order to determine the characteristics of each painter (Furtwängler 1990: 84–92; Flashar 2003). As early as 1885, he planned to publish a book on ancient painting in which he could give a scientific basis to his stylistic observations using individual descriptions (Furtwängler 1885: V). The emergence of this study of Greek-style vases required an entirely faithful drawing, a drawing with a quasi-botanical accuracy.

For this reason, Furtwängler had to reject the drawings of contemporary artists or copyists, who borrowed fashions, had idiosyncratic habits and made mistakes. Indeed, since the question of style had not been essential in the past, the illustrations of the figures did not have to be entirely exact and they often reflected neo-classical influences, as in some of the plates of Tischbein, Clener or Politi (Chamay and Aufrère 1996: 40; Tischbein 1791–1795; Woodford 2001: 1; Millin 1808; Fiorentini 1988: 41–62). Usually, vases were drawn to illustrate the beauty of some private collections (Schnapp and Jeanneney 2002: 7) and to provide inspiration and models for artists (Denoyelle 2002: 33–42; Woodford 2001: 1; Picard-Cajan 1992: 279–95; Picard-Cajan 2003: 299–314) or for copists (Hofter 2002: 693, no. 548 a-b). Furtwängler however was persuaded that the good knowledge of Greek vases depended entirely on their faithful reproduction, notably because Greek vases are so elaborate and complex that variations in just one element by the copyist could upset the entire unity.

A methodical individual, endowed with a classificatory mind, Adolf Furtwängler published these observations in 1883, in a book entitled *Griechische Keramik* in collaboration with Genick (Furtwängler 1883: 3–4). This book marks a decisive change in the history of the drawing of

Fig. 14.1 Drawing of three cups held in Berlin (after Furtwängler, A., 1883, pl. XXVIII).

Greek vases because it was the first to lay down some scientific principles for a reliable 'tool' for drawing Greek vases. The high-quality drawings produced by Genick (Fig. 14.1) enabled Furtwängler to show the vases in profile, with details of the form and ornaments presented with remarkable rigour and accuracy.

It can be assumed that Furtwängler took as his model if not his starting point the work of Heinrich Brunn (1822–1894), his teacher at the University of Munich, whom he would succeed in 1894. Indeed the *Griechischen Vasen* by Brunn, Krell and Lau (1877) included a thought-provoking discussion of the form and decoration of the vases. This book offered an overview of the form of many vases (Plate 9), as well as their profile – then still an uncommon practice – and especially a reproduction of their decoration through a fairly elaborate system, in which Brunn presented together on the same plate samples of patterns or elements found on different vases so as to stimulate stylistic comparisons and connections between them. Despite the evident overloading of the plates that resulted, the system is ingenious and the quality and accuracy of the drawings undeniable. Nevertheless, as Furtwängler's book, the figures and ornaments are still dependent on the form of the pottery and are sometimes illegible.

Already by the end of the century, the example and standards set by these first two books let to two types of 'scientific' drawings, the complete drawing and the line drawing, both fulfilling Furtwängler's 'stylistic' requirements:

I. The complete drawing (with a black background) was a direct outcome of Furtwängler's research (Fig. 14.2). It appears for example on the large plates of Furtwängler's *Griechische Vasenmalerei*, published in three volumes between 1904 and 1932 (Furtwängler and Reichhold 1904–1932) drawn by the German artist Karl Reichhold (1856–1919) (Ohly-Dumm and Hamdorf 1981: 8–10). Here the decoration is set entirely free from the actual form of the vase, and is presented as a kind of unrolled scene. This *Griechische Vasenmalerei* represents a complete stylistic synthesis and also a real model of illustration because Reichhold's drawings were very

Fig. 14.2 Drawing of a part of a red-Figure cup signed by Euphronios and held in Munich (after Furtwängler, A. and K. Reichhold 1904–1932, n°2620).

Fig. 56 a.

Fig. 14.3 Illustration of part of an Attic red-Figure cup (after Hartwig, 1893: 416, fig. 56a).

frequently chosen to illustrate ceramologists' books – including very recently (e.g. Boardman 1988: ill. 29, 33.2, 129, 281, 350). These drawings with black background effectively represented the main method of 'scientific' reproduction of Greek vases between the end of the nineteenth century and the first quarter of the twentieth. We find such drawings, for example, in museum catalogues, in monographs dedicated to vase painters or in periodicals (see, for example, Pfuhl 1924: ill. 47 and Hoppin 1917: 313). They are either ordered from professional draughtsmen like Karl Reichhold for Adolf Furtwängler (Furtwängler and Reichhold 1904–1932), Ernst Eichler for Paul Hartwig (Hartwig 1893), Guido Gatto for Giuseppe Pellegrini (Pellegrini 1900), Lindsay Hall for Gisela Richter (Richter 1936), or produced by archaeologists themselves such as John Beazley at the beginning of his career.

II.   The second type of drawing, the line drawing, privileges the structure of the figures and of the secondary decorations (Fig. 14.3). It allows better emphasis of the graphic line of the painters since the picture is deprived of all superflous elements. This type of drawing has long existed (see Politi's drawings), but it only gained its scientific qualities through the work of Paul Hartwig (1859–1919) and especially that of John Beazley (1885–1970) whose method of analysis seems to derive directly from Hartwig (Williams 1996: 241; Bothmer 1983: 4).[2]

There are several reasons for these developments in the representations of Greek vases. First, the reproduction processes used in books had gradually evolved from engraving (the most popular process for archaeological publications from the mid- nineteenth century) to photography – which meant that drawing was never again handled by the engraver. Previously, engravings or lithographs were obtained by redrawing the original tracings which were the printed at a reduced scale. Already in the eighteenth century, Caylus had emphasised that the drawings in the different plates of his *Recueil d'Antiquités* did not always correspond to the reality, the artist and the engraver having difficult technical problems to deal with in the visual and cultural environment of their time

(Aghion 2002: 22). Therefore, the new processes of reproduction allowed the avoidance of these kinds of modifications or changes.

Second, the precision of such drawings could be increased through the use of an ingenious medium: the tracing paper. This allows the draughtsman to produce his drawing in direct contact with the vase, to copy the figures faithfully down to the tiniest details. This practice was not totally new, and it is known, for example, that the French artist Ingres used some tracing paper on vases in his own collection at the beginning of the nineteenth century (Picard-Cajan 1992: 283, 285; Picard-Cajan 2003). A century later, in 1908, Beazley discovered this perfect medium while visiting Karl Reichhold in Munich (Bothmer 1983: 6). But the aim and practice were different and, in order to fix its principles, the method was described in detail in 1936 by Lindsay Hall in the introduction to Gisela Richter's book, *Red-Figured Athenian Vases in the Metropolitan Museum of Art* (Richter 1936: vii-x). The drawing was first traced off the curved surface of the vases, and then redrawn in a final version. Where a black background was to be used, the last final stage was the inking.

The third factor in this development is related to Hartwig and Beazley's proposal of a more accurate method of presenting the different parts of the painted figures, especially the different thicknesses of lines in the drawings (Fig. 14.4). Beazley used at least three pencils in order to draw

Fig. 14.4 Drawing by Beazley after an Attic red-Figure stamnos held in Castle Ashby and attributed to the Berlin Painter. Oxford, Beazley Archive.

with fidelity the diversity of lines, the colours or incisions (for black figures) obtained in antiquity on the vases (Kurtz 1983). However, he did not find any solution to the problem of transcribing white touches in the drawings, with the result that he used photographs in parallel, in order to show the exact location of these white touches (Bothmer 1983: 7).

It was one of his students, Humphry Payne (1902–1936), who found the best solution for the transcription of colours and white in archaeological drawings. A student at the British School in Athens from 1924, and its director from 1929 to 1936, Payne published during these few years three substantial works on Corinthian Art (*British Archaeological Discoveries in Greece and Crete (1836–1936)*, 1936: 80–81), whose pottery was particularly colourful. This made it all the more important for Payne to develop an effective way of rendering the colours and the white. A comparison between two drawings of the same fragment of attic black figure made at the beginning of his career shows that he chose to indicate white with the letter 'w' on his first drawing (for example Rumpf 1937: 24), but that in the final drawing he replaced the letters into real touches of white (Fig. 14.5). In his numerous final drawings, held in the archive of the British School in Athens,[3] Payne nearly always followed this choice for white and for colours in his Corinthian studies.

Indication of colours, indication of the different thicknesses of lines, indication of missing areas were thus among the desired characteristics of a good 'scientific' drawing. The development of such drawings offered numerous advantages for archaeologists, since they could render more clearly scenes which could not be fully appreciated through photography. They made it possible to overcome distortions caused by the spherical shape of the vase, to show more clearly the variations of lines between two vases or between two series of vases in the case of poorly preserved figures, and to transcribe those parts that were physically missing. Readily transportable, these drawings made is possible to bring the scenes and figures of one or of several vases – sometimes held in very distant locations – together in front of the scholar who could then easily compare the style and details. However, photography remained a valuable medium thanks to its speed and precision for the study

Fig. 14.5 Drawing realised by Humphry Payne after an Attic black-Figure fragment of Crater. Athens, British School Archive.

of the whole vase, its shape and the disposition of the figure decoration. All in all, scholars most frequently used a combination of finished drawings and photographs in their studies.

With regards to fragments of vases, drawings were a perfect means for reconstructing scattered ensembles. Indeed, Payne often drew fragments of Corinthian vases in order to find connections with others pieces (Dunbabin 1951: 63–69, and see the Payne archives). In the same way, Beazley published in 1931 in the *Journal of Hellenic Studies*, a setting of a drawing produced from a fragment (perhaps of neck-amphora) held in Vienna, together with a photograph of another

Fig. 14.6 Drawings realised by Beazley after 'mantle figures' on reverses of vases attributed to the Achilles Painter (after Beazley, 1914: 185).

fragment held in Florence (Beazley 1931: 50, no.39 and 51, fig. 7). The use of such a 'tool' at a scale of 1/1 allowed him to bring easily together, on the same plan, drawings and originals (or photographs of originals), even if the pieces were physically very far from each other. Scholars have always noted Beazley's extraordinary eye, but what was really the importance of his 'tool' in all his most famous discoveries? What was, for example, the role of his drawings in his reconstitution and setting of an Oltos' cup, published in the frontispiece of his *Campana Fragments in Florence* in 1933 – a cup whose fragments are held in six different museums (Rome, Villa Giulia; Florence; Heidelberg; Brunswick; Baltimore; and Bowdoin College) (Beazley 1933)? It has already been shown that the production of the drawings and the experience of the eye were the guarantee of success in Beazley's works (Schnapp 1985: 74). Indeed, the drawings allowed him to become immersed in the artist's personality, to recall each detail of the iconography and style. Finally, they played a primary role in his method because they served to shore up his reasoning in his publications. The most revealing example is his presentation in the same plate – like botanical or anatomical comparatives plates of the nineteenth century – of his so-called 'mantle figures', these male figures standing in recurrent positions on the reverse of many Attic red-figured vases of the first half of the fifth century BC. This plate (Fig. 14.6; Beazley 1914: 185), with men drawn following vases all attributed to the same hand (the Achilles Painter), shows well the importance of a rigorous observation of the evolution of figurative types on vases – an importance revealed by Franz Winter a few decades earlier (Winter 1885: 21) – and also indicates the necessity of a rigorous choice in the figures or elements to draw. In a conference in 1943 about the future of archaeology, Beazley explained why it was so precious for him to draw and what it was necessary for him to draw:

> If you wish to learn to distinguish one style from another, my advice will be one word: draw: draw freehand; make sketches of the shape, of the general composition, and of separate details (for details, not despising the magnifying glass): and draw the details larger than the original. Draw the details separately, and do not try to fit them in on top of your rough general sketch. [Another] time, make a more or less finished drawing of a vase-picture: you will find that you have to take notice of many details that you would pass by if you had not decided to draw everything, and you will have continually to be making up your mind on small questions that might not present themselves to you: Just how much of this is genuine? Are there traces of anything ancient between this point and that? Is this mark original, or a chance addition? Don't say you can't draw. If you can't, you will be learning to draw. For the finished drawing, trace the original, if necessary in bits. Transfer the tracings, and work on the paper freehand; or work up the tracing itself freehand, following the several firm lines, noting where each line begins and ends [...] The working-up will take a long time; but when you have drawn one vase you know it well, and you have learned a great deal about all vases. Draw: the hand remembers as well as the eye (Beazley 1943: 101–102).

In this quotation, Beazley made a clear distinction between a 'finished' drawing (with tracing) and details drawn freehand. As a matter of fact, the assiduous application of Morelli's method and the production of the finished drawings – unless it was its exceedingly laborious process (Kurtz 1985: 249) – prompted the appearance of another type of drawing in Greek pottery: the detail. We can find it in personal notes of archaeologists – such as Beazley or Payne – and also in publications. These details were developed in archaeological works at the beginning of the twentieth century, alone or in series – for example in Pottier's plates of eyes and ears (Pottier 1906: 839, ill. 3, 4) – and sometimes directly inserted in the text. We can distinguish details of patterns, like meanders or palmettes, or anatomical details, sometimes presented with elements of drapery. They persisted during the whole first half of the twentieth century, for example in Reichhold's *Skizzenbuch* published in 1919, in Banks article of 1926 about the Painter Euthymides and his tradition, or in Richter's book in 1946 (Reichhold 1919: pl. 11, 16 and 60; Banks 1926: pl. III–IV; Richter 1946: 63, 92).

The drawing of detail is a kind of polarisation on a specific element that reveals the painter's style. But it is not usually sufficient to reveal 'the system of renderings', that is to say, according to Beazley, the whole principal characteristics of one painter's style on a vase (Beazley 1914: 207–22; Beazley 1922: 82–85). This 'system of renderings' includes also the material aspect of the vase, 'the shape, features and proportions of the vessel itself, the arrangement of dark and light, and of line with line, to form a pattern (design in the narrower sense), and to represent something in nature (theme, movement, ethos and pathos)' (Beazley 1922: 85). But as the detail falls more into the background than in the complete drawing, it allows to bring more objectivity and more experimental verification to the archaeologist.

The detail is not born in the field of archaeology but in History of Art, in the famous publications of Morelli. Indeed, Morelli was one of the first scholars – if not the very first – to insert illustrations of anatomical details in order to support his theories on the attribution of Italian paintings. He defined his method as the first real 'scientific' method in the study of paintings, because it was based on schemes used in anatomy, and particularly on Cuvier's theories and Spix's demonstrations on the evolution and classification of animal species (Cuvier 1992; Spix 1815), theories he had studied carefully in Germany and Paris. We know that he copied plates from Spix's book on the development of animal skulls (Pau 1993: 305, 309). At the end of the nineteenth century and later, the influence of research into anatomy was not negligible and went beyond the field of Italian paintings or Greek vases: at the same period (in 1890), when Morelli was using plates of eyes and ears for his research, the French Alphonse Bertillon, chief of the *Service de l'Identité Judiciaire* in the police prefecture in Paris, was producing his 'synoptic plates' of ears belonging to suspects or criminals (Madlener 2002: 234). We also know that the German architect Gottfried Semper, was so impressed by Cuvier's demonstrations in Paris that he swore to become himself a 'Cuvier de l'Art' in his own field of architecture (Oesterle 1994: 64).

Indeed, all of this shows that the research undertaken in the study of Greek vases and their iconography followed a wider movement of classification which reflected a positivist, nineteenth century attitude. The reference to sciences like anatomy in the field of artistic productions was a sign of modernity and acted as a confirmation of the validity of the tools employed. The success of Cuvier's principles of classification results from an agreement between a model based on the analysis of external elements to be ordered with a logical precision, and the attempts of archaeology (or those of the history of art) to achieve a similar logical organisation related to the problems of style. The faithful reproduction of Greek vases emerged from a study of styles. However, as we have seen in the case of Adolf Furtwängler and Heinrich Brunn, initially such drawings were not just concerned with the study of figures and their representation, but included also a study of form, of composition, of space and a presentation of different connections between form and decoration. Drawings which concentrated only on figures, without reference to any elements of form or shape would re-appear in the work of Beazley. Although such drawings first appeared in publications with a pedagogical aim, archaeologists gradually set up their own archives of drawings – which often remained unpublished – as a support for their own research. Drawings of Greek vases thus rapidly evolved from entirely decontextualised scenes to single figures, to finally only characteristic details of these figures. These archives are very precious now for helping us understand how we approach Greek vases, and it is hoped that in the future numerous descriptions of these drawings will reappear and be published, thus preserving in memory the important work of our archaeological predecessors.

Notes

1. On Morelli's influence on Furtwängler's works, Reinach wrote: 'A côté de l'influence de Winckelmann et de Brunn, Furtwaengler subit celle de Morelli; sans avoir connu personnellement le grand critique italien, non seulement il prit l'habitude de regarder les originaux avec patience, avec intensité, mais de chercher, dans des détails de facture insignifiante en apparence, la marque, et comme la signature d'une école d'art ou d'un ouvrier'. Reinach 1907: 310

2. According to Williams, the analysis of Beazley's article 'Kleophrades' (in *JHS*, 1910) reveals that Beazley's method derived directly from Hartwig's: the language is identical, the use of drawings is the same and the acknowledgement addressed to his predecessor is evident. Bothmer also noted that the famous collector E. Perry Warren gave Beazley some of Hartwig's drawings.

3. Thanks are due to the British School in Athens and to its archivist Amalia Kakissis for allowing me to study Humphry Payne's archive and especially his precious drawings, photographs and notes.

References

Aghion, I. 2002. 'Le Comte de Caylus (1692–1765), Gentilhomme et Antiquaire', in *Caylus, Mécène du Roi. Collectionner les Antiquités au XVIIIe Siècle*. Paris: Institut National d'Histoire de l'Art.

Banks, M.A. 1926. 'The Survival of the Euthymidean Tradition in Later Greek Vase-Painting', *American Journal of Archaeology* 30: 58–69 and pl. III–IV.

Beazley, J.D. 1914. 'The Master of the Achille's Amphora in the Vatican', Journal of Hellenic Studies 34: 179–226 and pl. XIII-XVI.

———. 1922. 'Citharoedus', *Journal of Hellenic Studies* 42: 70–98 and pl. II–V.

———. 1931. 'Disjecta Membra', *Journal of Hellenic Studies* 51: 39–56.

———. 1933. *Campana Fragments in Florence*. Oxford: Oxford University Press and London: Humphrey Milford.

———. 1943. 'The Training of Archaeologists. *University Training*', in D.C. Kurtz (ed.) 1989. *Greek Vases. Lectures by J.D. Beazley*. Oxford: Clarendon Press, pp. 98–102.

Boardman, J. 1988. *Athenian Red Figure Vases – The Archaic Period*. London: Thames & Hudson.

Bothmer, D. (von). 1983. 'The Publication of the Drawings' (3–5) and 'The Execution of the Drawings' (6–8), in D.C. Kurtz, *The Berlin Painter*. Oxford Monographs on Classical Archaeology, Oxford: Clarendon Press.

British Archaeological Discoveries in Greece and Crete (1836–1936), 1936. Catalogue of the exhibition arranged to commemorate the fiftieth anniversary of the British School at Athens, London: Royal Academy of Arts, pp. 80–81.

Brunn, H., Krell, P.F. and Lau, G.T. 1877. *Die Griechischen Vasen. Ihr Formen- und Decorationssystem. Historische Einleitung und Erläuternder Text von Heinr. Brunn und P. F. Krell*. Leipzig: E.A. Seemann.

Chamay, J. and S.H. Aufrère. 1996. 'Peiresc (1580–1637). Un Précurseur de l'Etude des Vases Grecs', *Antike Kunst* 39: 38–51 and pl. 5–9.

Cuvier, G. 1992 (1st ed. 1812). *Recherches sur les Ossements Fossiles de Quadrupèdes. Discours Préliminaire*. Paris: Flammarion.

Denoyelle, M. 2002. 'Naturalisme et Illusion: les *Vases Grecs et Etrusques*, une Œuvre d'Alexandre-Isidore Leroy de Barde (1777–1828)', *Revue du Louvre* 2: 33–42.

Dunbabin, T.J. 1951. 'Humfry Payne's Drawings of Corinthian Vases', *Journal of Hellenic Studies* 71: 63–69 and pl. XXVIII–XXX.

Fiorentini, G. 1988. 'Le Necropoli di Agrigento e i Viaggiatori e Antiquari del XVIII e XIX Secolo', in *Veder Greco – Le Necropoli di Agrigento*, Mostra Internazionale. Agrigento, 2 maggio–31 luglio, Rome: «L'erma» di Bretschneider.

Flashar, M. 2003. *Adolf Furtwängler. Der Archäologe*. Catalogue of the exhibition of the archaeological collection of University of Freiburg, 1 July–5 October 2003, Freiburg.

Furtwängler, A. 1883. (Einleitung und Beschreibung), *Griechische Keramick. XL Tafeln*. Ausgewählt und Aufgenommen von A. Genick, Zweite Auflage, Berlin.

———. 1885. *Beschreibung der Vasensammlung im Antiquariium, I.* Berlin : W. Spemann.

Furtwängler, A. and K. Reichhold. 1904–1932. *Griechische Vasenmalerei. Auswahl hervorragender Vasenbilder.* Munich: Bruckmann.

Furtwängler, A.E. 1990. 'Adolf Furtwängler', in W.W. Briggs and W.M. Calder II (eds), *Classical Scholarship. A Biographical Encyclopedia.* New York, Garland Pub.

Hartwig, P. 1893. *Die Griechischen Meisterschalen der Blüthezeit des Strengen Rothfigurigen Stiles.* Stuttgart and Berlin: Spemann.

Hofter, M.R. 2002. 'Die Unerkannten Griechen. Griechische Originalmonumente im Humanismus der Frühen Neuzeit', in *Die Griechische Klassik. Idee oder Wirklichkeit*, catalogue of the exhibition in Martin-Gropius-Bau, Berlin, and in the Kunst-und Austellungshalle, Bonn, 2002. Mainz: Philipp von Zabern, pp. 689–707.

Hoppin, J.C. 1917. *Euthymides and His Fellows.* Cambridge: Harvard University Press.

Kurtz, D.C. 1983. *The Berlin Painter, Oxford Monographs on Classical Archaeology.* Oxford: Clarendon Press.

———. 1985. 'Beazley and the Connoisseurship of Greek Vases', *Greek Vases in the J. Paul Getty Museum* 2: 237–50.

Lermolieff, I. 1874–1876. 'Die Galerien Roms. Ein Kritischer Versuch von Iwan Lermolieff. I. Die Galerie Borghese. Aus dem Russischen Übersetz von Dr Johannes Schwarze mit Illustrationen', *Zeitschrift für Bildende Kunst*, IX, 1874: 1–11, 73–81, 171–78, 249–53 ; X, 1875: 97–106, 207–11, 264–73, 329–34 ; XI, 1876: 132–37, 168–73.

———. 1891. *Kunstkritische Studien über Italienische Malerei. Die Galerien Borghese und Doria Panfili in Rom. Von Ivan Lermolieff.* Leipzig: F.A. Brockhaus.

Madlener, E. 2002. 'L'Exploration Physiognomonique de l'Âme', in *L'Âme au Corps. Arts et Sciences, 1793–1993*, 2nd ed, Paris: RMN.

Millin, A.-L. 1808. *Peintures de Vases Antiques, vulgairement appelés étrusques.* Paris: P. Didot.

Oesterle, G. 1994. 'Gottfried Semper: la Destruction et la Réactualisation du Classicisme', *Revue Germanique Internationale* 2: 59–72.

Ohly-Dumm, M. and F.W. Hamdorf. 1981. *Attische Vasenbilder der Antikensammlungen in München nach Zeichnungen von Karl Reichhold.* Munich.

Pau, R. 1993. 'Le Origini Scientifiche del Metodo Morelliano', in *Giovanni Morelli e la Cultura dei Conoscitori*, II, atti del convegno internazionale, Bergamo, 4–7 giugno 1987, Bergamo: Pierluigi Lubrina Editore, pp. 301–19.

Pellegrini, G. 1900. *Catalogo dei Vasi Antichi Dipinti delle Collezioni Palagi ed Universitaria.* Bologna.

Pfuhl, E. 1924. *Meisterwerke Griechischer Zeichnung und Malerei.* Munich: F. Brückmann.

Picard-Cajan, P. 1992. 'Ingres et le «Vase Etrusque» ', in A.F. Laurens and K. Pomian, *L'Anticomanie. La Collection d'Antiquités aux 18e et 19e Siècles.* Paris: Editions de l'Ecole des Hautes Etudes en Sciences Sociales, Paris, pp. 279–95.

———. 2003. 'Le Vase Grec dans l'Imaginaire d'Ingres', in P. Rouillard and A. Verbanck-Pierard (eds), *Le Vase Grec et ses Destins*, catalogue of the exhibition in the Royal Museum of Mariémont and in the Calvet Museum in Avignon, 2003, Munich : Biering & Brinkmann, pp. 299–314.

Pottier, E. 1906. *Catalogue des Vases Antiques du musée du Louvre*, III.

Reichhold, K. 1919. *Skizzenbuch Griechischer Meister. Ein Einblick in das Griechische Kunststudium auf Grund der Vasenbilder.* Munich: Bruckmann.

Reinach, S. 1907. 'Adolphe Furtwängler', *Chronique des Arts*.

Richter, G.M.A. 1936. *Red-Figured Athenian Vases in the Metropolitan Museum of Art.* New Haven: Yale University Press.

———. 1946. *Attic Red-figured Vases.* New Haven: Yale University Press.

Rumpf, A. 1937. *Sakonides.* Leipzig: H. Keller.

Schnapp, A. 1985. 'Des Vases, des Images et de quelques uns de leurs Usages Sociaux', *Dialoghi di Archeologia* 3(1): 69–75.

Schnapp, A. and J.N. Jeanneney. 2002. 'Avant-propos: Caylus Redécouvert? ', in *Caylus, Mécène du Roi. Collectionner les Antiquités au XVIIIe Siècle.* Paris: Institut National d'Histoire de l'Art, 7.

Spix, J.B. (von) 1815. *Cephalogenesis.* Munich.

Stewart, A. 1990. *Greek Sculpture. An Exploration*. New Haven: Yale University Press.

Tischbein, W. 1791–1795. *Collection of Engravings from Ancient Vases Mostly of Pure Greek Workmanship Discovered in the Sepulchres in the Kingdom of the Two Sicilies but chiefly in the Neighbourhood of Naples during the Course of the Years MDCCLXXIX and MDCCLXXX. Now in the Possession of Sir Wm. Hamilton, His Britannic Majestaty's Envoy Extr.y and Plenipotentiary at the Court of Naples*, I–V, Naples.

Walter, C. 2001. *La Méthode 'Morelli' et son Application aux Vases Grecs et aux Dessins Florentins*, Mémoire de 3ème cycle, Paris: Ecole du Louvre (unpublished but consultation is possible in Ecole du Louvre).

Williams, D. 1996. 'Refiguring Attic Red-Figure: A Review Article', *Revue Archéologique* 2: 227–52.

Winter, F. 1885. *Die Jüngeren Attischen Vasen und ihr Verhältnis zur Grossen Kunst*. Berlin-Stuttgart: W. Spemann.

Woodford, S. 2001. 'Tischbein and the Fragments of Vases Recovered from HMS Colossus', *Source. Notes in the History of Art* 20(2): 1–7.

Chapter 15

European Images of the Ancient Near East at the Beginnings of the Twentieth Century

Maria Gabriella Micale

Abstract

The image of Near Eastern architecture held by modern scholars is based mainly on the architectural conception expressed in the reconstructions of Ashur and Babylon made by the two German archaeologists Walter Andrae and Robert Koldewey during the first decades of the twentieth century. Even though the architecture depicted in the reconstructions sometimes seems to be chronologically and geographically incongruous, the images impacted the shared imagery as if they were the real shape of the Mesopotamian architecture. As a result, these reconstructions lead to a process of image 'materialisation' and they also provide the source for the modern *in situ* restoration of some important Mesopotamian buildings. This chapter focuses on the image of Near Eastern architecture as expressed in architectural reconstructions by European archaeologists, in the light of history, culture and research.

Introduction

Developments in both the study of antiquities and in European antiquarian research following the Middle Ages are well known (Schnapp 1993; Trigger 1996: 37–42). Works of art were often recognised from their descriptions by classical authors, and their study led to an interest in collecting antiquities and to the recognition of the ideological value of possessing them. Thus, the palaces, the temples, the houses, and in some cases the ruins that had been visible during the centuries gradually completed the 'material' picture of the ancient world. In order to put this material culture to a visible environment and to give it a material image, objects from the past were collected and set side by side with modern ones. This made it possible to re-create scenes, backgrounds, perspectives and landscapes.

So far as the Near East is concerned, however, and despite the fact that its populations always lived surrounded by impressive ruins, there do not seem to have emerged much interest in local antiquarian studies (Trigger 1996: 46). The approach to antiquities is a recent phenomenon in the Near East and, as previously in Europe, it is strongly related to the propagandistic national politics of the local rulers and dynasties. As a case in point (and see later in this chapter), the reconstruction of ancient Mesopotamian monuments in Iraq was part of a government programme which depended on the strong secularism of the State. In terms of foreign policy, it was promoted as an opposition to the neighbouring Islamic Countries (Trigger 1996: 194). Moreover, also in terms of internal politics, the current rulers aspired to be the heirs of ancient Mesopotamian dynasties, and they therefore made continuous references to these ancient political structures to establish their secularism. Such an attitude towards pre-Islamic antiquities was already manifest in the 'cultural politics' of the neighbouring Persian monarchy: in 1971, it commemorated the supposed 2500th anniversary of the ancient Persian monarchy in the ruins of Persepolis (Strika 2000: 1583–84).

The Western world for its part originally paid attention to Near Eastern antiquities in direct relation to the Christian focus on the Holy Land. At the same time, the presence of many religious missions and the growing role of this region as a trading crossroads between the colonial powers on the one hand and the Far East on the other brought several Europeans to discover the cultures of ancient Mesopotamia.[1] While this European interest had several reasons and motivations behind it, it led to the production of essentially idealised representations of ancient Near Eastern scenes.

The growth of archaeological research in this field brought with it increasing knowledge of the material culture of ancient Mesopotamian civilisations. This new knowledge did not necessarily help to rectify commonly held conceptions, but archaeologists and scholars did turn to the archaeological evidence as an informative device to spread and increase awareness of their research. The integration of the architectural structures, the location of the decorative apparatus, the construction of an environment as well as the location of human figures within it, all represented the beginning of a process that aimed to transform an idealised 'intellectual' image into a 'visual' image. All these events together are of paramount importance for the global reconstruction of contexts: this approach to the re-creation of the past was not only an artistic description of some places and events, but it also served to explain the archaeological and architectural features of the ancient Near East in both words and images.

Walter Andrae and Robert Koldewey: The Ancient Near East Rises Again

Handbooks on history or archaeology provide an image of ancient Near Eastern architectural contexts based mainly on reconstructions of Babylon and Ashur made by the German archaeologists and architects Robert Koldewey (1855–1925) and Walter Andrae (1875–1956).[2] Collected into two legendary syntheses that meaningfully go by the name of *Das wiedererstehende Babylon and Das wiedererstandene Assur*,[3] their reconstructions are usually, and maybe even subconsciously, accepted as reproductions of the original state of the buildings depicted. This means that the mere mention of either these cities or their important monuments will bring to mind these famous images, but also that only those images and no others will be evoked (Fig. 15.1).

Opening the season of 'Babylonian' excavations, Robert Koldewey reached Mesopotamia during March 1899 (Koldewey 1913: iii),[4] and laid the foundations for the so-called 'German school' of archaeology. Some years later, Walter Andrae, a member of the Babylonian expedition,[5] begun excavations at Qala'at Sherqat, the ancient Ashur.[6] On both methods and results, the revolutionary impact of the German excavations can be summarised in the words of some local workers who took part in the German expedition. Several years after the Babylonian excavations had begun, they reported to the American archaeologist Edgar James Banks that they had employed 'new methods' under the direction of the Germans (Liverani 2000: 1). These new methods consisted of a rudimentary version of stratigraphical excavation, which in this case is 'stripping off' each artificial mound or *tell*, the typical result of stratified urban settlements in the Near East. While the main aim of archaeological excavations had hitherto been the collection of tablets, seals and reliefs – that is objects suitable for museums and exhibitions – for the first time in Near Eastern archaeology it became possible to clarify the historical meaning of the stratification of a *tell*, and to give each uncovered object its topographical and stratigraphical context (Micale and Nadali, in press).

As a consequence, the first ever detailed two-dimensional image of Mesopotamian architecture carried with it a three-dimensional representation. In fact, the German architects gave a perspective reconstruction to each building and every single building stage they excavated.

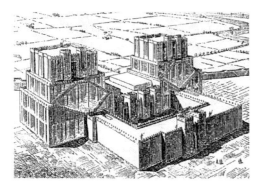

Fig. 15.1 Ashur, Temple of Anu and Adad: perspective reconstruction. Drawing by Walter Andrae, 1924 (Andrae 1977: 189, fig. 168).

Fig. 15.2 Babylon, Emakh: perspective reconstruction. Drawing by Robert Koldewey, 1907 (Koldewey 1911: 4, fig. 1).

Fig. 15.3 Ashur: panoramic view from North. Drawing by Walter Andrae, 1937 (Andrae 1977: 54, fig. 37).

Fig. 15.4 Ashur, Tabira Gate: perspective reconstruction. Drawing by Walter Andrae, 1937 (Andrae 1977: 22, fig. 5).

Moreover, not only did the reconstruction affect each single building, but it also specified its location in the urban plan, thus becoming part of a larger and more complex process of reconstruction within a more comprehensive human context (Fig. 15.3). Furthermore, the recurring presence of the human figure was a device that not only aimed at the immediate perception of the size of the building, but also at the representation of urban life itself. Thus, the reconstructions by Andrae and Koldewey are once an informative architectural image and a visual narrative of ancient city life.

At the beginning of the twentieth century, then, the two German architects with their new historical and scientific consciousness, brought to life the ancient cities and the civilisations that conceived them. These images represent much of what we know and think about the architectonic culture of ancient Mesopotamia (Figs 15.2, 15.4).

Victor Place - England and France in the Near East during the Nineteenth Century

Observing the images of Ashur and Babylon, we may wonder to what extent they arise from the evaluation of architectural and archaeological data.[7] Thus, let us suppose that the conceptual scheme underlying the reconstructing process is 'what I have + what I see = what I imagine', where

Fig. 15.5 Khorsabad, the Citadel: bird's eye view from south-east (Place 1867–1870).

the third factor is the overall completed reconstruction, the first is the whole of the archaeological and structural data of the building reconstructed and the second is the architectural image (Micale 2005: 135–39). Analysing both this scheme and the reconstructions, it is possible to infer that factors which do not belong to the archaeological field take part in the reconstruction process as well. In fact, bearing in mind both the perspective reconstructions and probable iconographic sources (the second factor, 'what I see'), it seems possible that the sources for the architectural image are not exclusively based on archaeological accounts. By contrast, these sources might belong to a shared imagery, in which the reconstructions are part of a common way of visualising a building. When looking for indications resulting from these 'intellective' sources in the perspective reconstructions, it is necessary to bear in mind the architectural images, which are already a result of a reconstructing process. The employment of the reconstructed images by scholars is usually never mentioned. Concerning the perspective reconstructions of Ashur and Babylon, only rarely do Andrae and Koldewey admit they were inspired by already existing images. When they do, they refer to the perspective reconstructions of Khorsabad made at the middle of the nineteenth century by Victor Place (Andrae 1909: 82; Koldewey 1911: 52).[8]

Indeed, the architectural reconstructions of Khorsabad published by Victor Place in the nineteenth century are the basic source for the architectural image of Ashur and Babylon (Fig. 15.5). These need not however be considered as a source of iconography as of imagery. This raises the question as to why these French images were chosen as a model in the first place? And why, at the same time, were the celebrated images published by the English Sir A.H. Layard in nineteenth century ignored (e.g. Lloyd 1976: 28)?[9] In part, this was because the ideas expressed by Place in his reconstructions were the only credible image of Assyrian architecture available at that time. In fact, these images were the first that were broadly consistent with both the archaeological data and the iconographic sources and, thus, with the earliest architectural conception concerning these monuments (cf. Place 1867–1870, III: Pls. 3, 6, 40–41).

The reconstructions made by Place represented a real revolution in the perception of Mesopotamian architecture for the first time, the European notion of Near Eastern architecture changed and became an 'archaeological' image. This revolution remained silent however, possibly because of the discredit of Victor Place following the shipwreck of the Khorsabad findings in the Tigris River.[10] In fact, his archaeological research was more systematic than others, and he made clearly precocious advances for his times. Comparing Place's drawings with those published by Layard, we can understand the distance that separates them, and appreciate Place's reconstructions as the first credible images of the Assyrian architecture (Plate 10). The architecture described by Layard seems to be a combination of suggestions coming from other ancient cities and the generalised use of some ancient architectural representations (Layard 1854: 521–23). These representations were not very consistent with the available evidence regarding Assyrian architecture.[11] Although the cause of this change is not wholly clear, there appears between the two researchers a transformation in the image of architecture, from 'sumptuous' (Layard) to 'powerful' (Place). Regarding the factors affecting the reconstruction process, it is noteworthy that from Victor Place onwards the idea of architecture as reflecting strength and power was transmitted and used (possibly even unconsciously) in the iconographic sources, even in the reconstruction of non-Assyrian cities such as Babylon.

Following the English policy of controlling its eastern affairs, Claudius Rich represented the first real English contact with Mesopotamian archaeology (see Larsen 1996: 9–12; Díaz-Andreu 2004). Rich was a casual collector of Babylonian objects and tablets, and from 1825 onwards his collections became the first significant western collection of ancient Mesopotamian objects at the British Museum (Bohrer 1998: 341). In 1807 Rich was Resident of the British East India Company in Baghdad and he had the important task of simplifying the English 'traffic' towards India.[12] However, his presence in Mesopotamia was not the only 'by-product' (Ibidem) of colonial promotion.[13] At the same time, other interests in the past arose; even if they did not seem to share anything with colonial policies as such, they were undoubtedly by products of the same circumstances.

Bearing in mind this cultural context, little distinguishes the images published by Layard from the 'biblical' paintings then made by famous artists such as the English John Martin and the French Eugène Delacroix. Both express the same feeling about Assyria; they show an image of sensuality, licentiousness and immorality (Delacroix) that was the cause of its own doom (represented by Martin) – the whole contrasting with the integrity of Europe itself. However, in the case of both Layard and the painters, representations of Mesopotamia were a personal translation in image of the common ideas held in France and England on the Orient, namely a 'place picturesque, violent, sensual, and, perhaps most significant, doomed […]' (Bohrer 1998: 340; cf. Said 2001). This kind of art seems to be a further colonialist 'by-product'. The painter Martin himself confirmed this, when he asserted that the architecture of his painting 'The Fall of Nineveh' was consistently invented for a city situated between Egypt and India (Bohrer 1998: 338). He unconsciously emphasised the same central position Mesopotamia had in the English trades. In a century when the Old Testament dominated much of European culture (Larsen 1996: xi), the discovery of Assyria intensified the public interest in Eastern antiquities (Silberman 1989). However, these archaeological discoveries did not affect images of Assyria in either France or England, and they also failed to make them more correct.[14] In fact, even though between the two centuries some paintings represented scenes and backgrounds in which many features depended on knowledge of Assyrian material culture,[15] this archaeological knowledge was reproduced in a context in which Sardanaplus still represented the dominated Orient, and where the Europeans, and not the Arabs, were depicted as the heirs of the ancient Mesopotamian civilisations.

Andrae and Koldewey – Germany in the Near East

During the second half of the nineteenth century, the development of prehistoric studies and some of their conclusions had considerable impact in France and England. In particular, the theories of the Swedish archaeologist Oscar Montelius contributed substantially to the current conservative opinions regarding the origins of Western culture (for the context of Montelius's work, see Trigger 1996: 164–71). For Montelius, the most important cultural progress in prehistoric times was realised in the Near East, and spread from Mesopotamia to Europe in migratory waves (*ex oriente lux*). Montelius's hypotheses were also supported by non-scientific evidence: to consider the Near East as the birthplace of Western civilisation is to confirm both the biblical point of view about world history and its medieval interpretations, according to which the power and the creativity moved from East to West with the alternation of the Empires. This historical conception was of course not unrelated to the direct French and English presence in Mesopotamia.

Fig. 15.6 Stage setting for the opera Sardanapal: Court of an Assyrian temple. Draft by Walter Andrae, 1907 (Andrae – Boehmer 1992: fig. 132).

Taking account of the historical and cultural background of archaeological research in Mesopotamia, and of the context in which Koldewey and Andrae worked, is undoubtedly crucial to a complete understanding of their reconstructions and their influence. German archaeological research in the Near East was strongly supported by Wilhelm II, a major actor in the promotion of German interests in the Near East (see Marchand 1996: 192–208; Hauser 2001: 211–20; Crüsemann 2003: 35–44). Chancellor Bismarck's resignation in 1890 gave birth to the *Neue Kurs*, a process of 'modernising' that involved institutions, industry and production. This process had a significant effect on the cultural life and the intellectual directions of the country as well. Whereas at the beginning of the nineteenth century ancient Greece was a 'Romantic' ideal for young Germans, at the end of the century a strong connection between university-research and industry arose[16] and 'modernity' and industrialisation changed attitudes towards ancient civilisations (Hauser 2001: 215). The hegemony of classical culture decreased due to the rise a nationalism that was independent of ancient Greek culture,[17] and also due to contemporary interest in local history, as exhibited by Kossinna (see Brather, this volume).[18] In addition, an apparently inconsistent interest in 'exotic' culture was born.

Thus, the beginning of the *Neue Kurs* coincided, on the one hand, with the development of the cultural interest in non-classical civilisations,[19] and on the other, with the consolidation of the relationships between Germany and the Ottoman Empire. With time, the bond between the two powers became increasingly stronger following financial arrangements, such as concessions to the *Deutsche Bank* for the realisation of the 'Baghdad Railway'; and the resulting economic and industrial growth of Germany itself (Earle 1966: 35–37; Strika 1993: 28; Marchand 1996: 190 ff). Since Germans conducted the geological survey along the railway's layout, they held all rights over a stretch of 20 kilometres on either side of it (Strika 1993: 28–29). Thus, across the two centuries, this circumstance led to two exceptional results: first, the determination of numerous ancient settlements and, second, the exact location of a substantial number of oil prospects (Strika 1993: 26–29).[20] The geological and topographic survey, the direct control over what was inside the 40 km and the promotion of the interest in archaeological research, could hypothetically be related to each other.[21]

It was the Emperor's opinion that attention to Mesopotamian cultures and the support given to the Near Eastern studies represented the best way to transform classical German culture into an 'open-minded', non-classical culture (Hauser 2001: 218). As a result, on the one hand, Wilhelm II supported industry by the construction of the Baghdad Railway and promoted research financing the *Deutsche Orient-Gesellschaft*.[22] On the other hand, he improved the diffusion of the Assyrian image, for instance, by organising the performance of the historical opera *Sardanapal* at the Royal Opera House in Berlin, for which Andrae himself designed the stage (Andrae and Boehmer 1992: 21, 125; Bohrer 2003: 300) (Fig.15.6). Koldewey and Andrae interrupted their research in Mesopotamia at the beginning of the First World War.[23] During the Weimar Republic, the discoveries in the ancient Near East were no longer of public interest (Hauser 2001: 222).

Considered as a representation of objects, each architectural reconstruction can uncover a tangle of thoughts and images strongly linked to its creator. In fact, if we assume that everyone puts their ghosts, secrets and more or less consciously held desires in the image, it is possible to realise that the archaeological reconstructions will also hold the 'ghosts' or the 'desires' contained in the architectural image itself. Thus, the reconstructions of Ashur and Babylon hold more than Koldewey and Andrae's image of Ashur and Babylon and more than Place's idea of the Assyrian architecture as well.

Instead, since the two Germans were originally architects, the contribution of their technical and artistic personal education is perceptible in their reconstructions.[24] Both of them switched among different techniques and styles, even though it is possible to distinguish more frequently used methods and maybe several techniques chosen according to the destination of the drawing itself.[25] For instance, many of Koldewey's reconstructions are characterised by the almost absolute lack of details. The amplification of quadrangular volumes, which are given by the contrasts of light and shadow, on the one hand, and the lack of any decorative element on the other seem to reveal Koldewey's conformity to the principles that anticipate the later results of the Rationalist Movement, of which at the beginning of the century Germany was one of the most productive centres.[26] Conversely, Andrae used any device to make the city's image spectacular, such as either the lower or the panoramic point of view. The propensity to a regular use of decorative elements, the composite landscape rendering and the adoption of a specific point of view seem to reveal the employment of both the principles and the techniques that Andrae learnt at university at the end of the nineteenth century thanks to some of the most important representatives of the *Jugendstil*.[27]

The more Andrae and Koldewey write about Mesopotamia the more their drawings show more monumental and magnificent cities. Certainly, this is a result of their will to make this ancient architectonic culture worthy of the attention of their contemporary colleagues. Despite that, they never surrendered to the cultural demand of the time, namely to falsify the features of the identity of the cities and to adapt them according to the notion of European and German identity.[28]

Conclusion: The Reconstructions as a Vehicle of the Architectural Image through the Centuries: From Ancient Mesopotamia to Modern Iraq

Reconstructions of the buildings of Ashur and Babylon could in principle take into account new interpretations of archaeological and architectural data, but these images remained extremely effective, being impressed in the shared imagery as the only believable reproduction of the original architecture. The perspective reconstructions produced by Andrae and Koldewey are not simply images printed on paper. Although they are mere interpretations of buildings, some images were actually 'translated' and fixed in a physical and material condition that seems to be unsuitable for an essentially graphic representation. Such a 'material' reconstruction of the buildings of Ashur and Babylon was indeed carried out under the auspices of the Iraqi government, in line with its secularist policy (Trigger 1996: 194). The first reconstruction works of an archaeological site begun in Babylon in 1931, and went on much more systematically from 1956 onwards (Voet 1986: 43).

The reconstruction of the *Emakh* of Babylon represents one of the most sensational instances of translation from graphic image to material reality. As a model and symbol for Babylonian architecture, the Iraqi Department of Antiquity selected to show it foreign visitors (Damerji 1981: 32; Voet 1986: 42). The evident conflict between the needs of preservation and those of fulfilling the original objectives of an ancient monument does not prevent the building's reconstruction, purported to let the temple live again (Cavigneaux 1986: 48). The perspective reconstruction made by Koldewey in 1907 was employed to this aim as well. In spite of the restoration of the Tabira Gate of Ashur (Madhloom 1981: 58), the adoption of the German drawings as iconographic source for the restoration of the *Emakh* is explicit. Bearing in mind both Koldewey's drawing and the material reconstruction *in situ*, it seems that the Iraqi Department reproduced the image without any evaluation of the hypothetical value of the drawing itself.

Cavigneaux is probably right to believe that many scholars would shiver before such an oversimplified reconstruction (Cavigneaux 1986: 48). However, the simple appearance of the building is not the real problem: it is the adoption of the German drawings as a model for the material reconstruction of the temple, without any critical evaluation. This means that an image including choices, mistakes and hypotheses all together was fixed and exposed as a symbol of neo-Babylonian architecture. The material reconstruction of the Tabira Gate of Assur represents the best example of the use of a reconstructed image as a model, even if this image seems to be the result of non-archaeological-based interpretations. In fact, the architectural analysis of the ruins of the Gate emphasised that it could be different from what Andrae had hypothesised, since nothing of the frontage reconstructed was in reality preserved (Andrae 1913: 22). The reconstruction of the Gate with original materials and the adoption of traditional methods are not enough to suggest a verisimilar copy of the original Gate.[29] This is especially true given that the two imposing towers flanking the Gate in the perspective reconstruction were never found, and that Andrae only hypothesised their existence on the basis of their occurrence in some contemporary Assyrian urban gates.

According to Aby Warburg's definition of the image, the architectural reconstruction is a tangle of *mnemischen Wellen*. In this case, the archaeological data, the common places surrounding the interpretation of these data, the common idea regarding the cultural context to which the reconstructed buildings belong, together with the techniques and the styles used in the reconstruction drawings, all add up and contribute to the perspective reconstruction unconsciously as well as consciously. For this reason, even though they shared the same idea, Andrae and Koldewey represented their own world in the reconstructions. They shaped both buildings and cities according to what they were more familiar with and maybe according to what they wanted the architectural reality to be.

Andrae wrote: 'Only when we will see in it men move and walk anew […] will Ashur rise again' (my translation), expressing thus the whole meaning of its reconstructions (Andrae 1977: 7). The time of the perspective reconstruction is also the time of the rebirth of a building. It is conceived for the second time, showing both the signs of what it was in the past and the features of its new condition of simple image. Sometimes a building grows up physically for the third time, taking both the 'lives' it had before. In this case, the perspective reconstructions function to transport the architectural image from antiquity to modern times. Temples and palaces take shape again thanks to these images, and this is why all those who have used Andrae and Koldewey's drawings as iconographical sources have been able to see ancient Babylonians live and walk again inside these monuments.

Notes

1. Pietro Della Valle was one of the first Italian travellers and explorers of ancient settlements in the Orient (travelling from 1614 to 1652). His narratives might be considered as 'scientific' reports, since he was very interested in the structure of the ruins and in recording graphically the archaeological evidence in several regions (Invernizzi 2000: 643–46. For the first contacts between Europe and the Mesopotamian world, see also Lloyd 1980: 7–12).

2. For biographical details about Walter Andrae and Robert Koldewey, see Andrae (1952), Heinrich (1957), Andrae (1961) and Andrae and Boehmer (1989, 1992).

3. The publication of these reconstructions occurred over a long period, from 1909 (W. Andrae, *Die Anu-Adad-Tempel in Assur*) to 1955 (A. Haller, W. Andrae, *Die Heiligtümer des Gottes Assur und der Sin-Šamaš-Tempel in Assur*). In this period, many monographs on Ashur and volumes on Babylon were published.

4. The main expedition was preceded by a preliminary expedition from 1897 to 1898 (Andrae 1952: 82–89; Crüsemann 2003: 38). The excavations of Ashur and Babylon, the archaeologists that undertook them and all the events related to the destination of the findings are discussed by Suzanne Marchand (1996: 188–227), whose reconstruction of the historical context is based mainly on archival sources.

5. For the Babylonian period of Andrae, see Andrae-Boehmer (1992: 6–17, 111–22).

6. For Andrae in Ashur, see Andrae (1903: 9–30; 1952: 180–91; 1977: 273–81; Andrae-Boehmer 1992: 17–25, 122–30).

7. Although the scientific publications show several images and drawings in which the hypothetical shape of the excavated buildings is reconstructed, the various steps leading to the actual reconstructions – from the excavation, through documentation, to hypotetical reconstruction (in graphic form) – are generally not divulged.

8. For the history of French archaeological research in the Orient, see Chevalier (2002). For a narrative of the work of Victor Place in Mesopotamia, see Place (1867–1870); Pillet (1918).

9. Lloyd's words underline to what extent Place's work was underestimated as well.

10. For the counting of both the recovered and lost cases, see Pillet (1918: 53–54).

11. Note that the plan of the Palace S/O of Quyunjiq published by Layard shows a building with projecting towers (Layard 1853: 67), and that no towers characterise the reconstructed buildings.

12. Politically, the region of the Persian/Arabic Gulf was an appendix to British India. In fact, since the Suez Canal did not exist at that time, Indian authorities pressed the use of Mesopotamia as the shortest way between the motherland and the colonies (Strika 1993: 23–24).

13. See Bahrani's (2000, 2001) interesting narrative of the relationship between archaeology and colonialist culture.

14. Some French scholars have argued that the translation of ancient Semitic languages and the increasingly sound historical knowledge of the Near East was of greater importace to contemporary culture than the archaeological discoveries themselves. Orientalism could be considered a cultural area of studies rather than a sub-field of archaeology (Schnapp *et al.* 1991: 93).

15. For instance, 'The Dream of Sardanaplus' by F. M. Brown (1871), and 'The Queen of Saba' by E. Dulac (1911). Furthermore, in the second half of the nineteenth century, a generalised use of 'Assyrian' collection of details, together with features of other Eastern cultures, seems to characterise the illustrations made by Gustave Doré for an edition of the Old Testament (Pedde 2000). For the transmission of Sardanaplus's image in the classical sources, see Frahm (2003: 21).

16. The field of art was also invaded by the 'useful'. For instance, Cornelius Gurlitt, art critic in the period of the *Jugendstil* and Andrae's teacher in Dresden (Andrae and Boehmer 1989: 4, 110), affirmed that 'an object belongs to the Art industry when its author thought about it as both a practical tool and an item expressing its aim artistically' (own translation) (Cremona 1984: 109).

17. In the opinion of Wilhelm II it was necessary to '[…] educate young Germans, not young Greeks or Romans' (Härke 1991: 204; Hassmann 2000: 66).

18. For Kossinna and the influence of its theories on contemporary nationalistic currents, see Härke (1991: 204–208; Trigger 1996: 173–77).

19. To be sure, Mesopotamian civilisations were not the only non-classical civilisations. Interest in 'other' cultures as a sign of the colonialist aims of Germany at the end of the nineteenth century was also turned

to the Central Asian regions. Studies and research on Indian art, and the archaeological expeditions in Turfan (Chinese Turkestan) between 1902 and 1914, are significant examples of this (See Marchand 2000).

20. The search for oil had already begun many decades before (Earle 1966: 14).

21. The relationship between the works concerning the construction of the 'Baghdad Railway' and the growth of the German 'archaeological' presence in the Near East still needs to be confirmed. However, some coincidences seem to be particularly significant, even if they do not always attest to direct correlation. For instance, between 1896 and 1899 (the years of Koldewey's preliminary Babylonian expedition) a German commission of evaluation of the whole railway's work was prepared; this commission consisted of some officers of the State Railway (Strika 1993: 33–34), in which Andrae's father himself worked (Andrae and Boehmer 1992: 109). In Crüsemann's opinion, interest in Mesopotamian antiquities was based on German ambition and the search for international prestige (Crüsemann 2003: 36–37). However, also raw materials and oil gained paramount importance for a strongly industrialised country: 'The securing of sources of raw materials may involve the acquisition of a colonial Empire; it may require the establishment of a protectorate over, or a 'sphere of interest' in, an economically backward or a politically weak nation' (Earle 1966: 46). Thus, it is possible that archaeology represented one of these spheres of interest. On the relationships between archaeological research and such interests, see also Liverani (1994: 6–12; 1999a, 1999b) and Crüsemann (2000).

22. On the foundation of this society, see Moortgat (1976), Matthes (1997, 1998, 1999), Wilhelm (1998) and Crüsemann (2000; 2003: 38–39).

23. In 1914, even though the excavations were officially declared completed, the question of the findings from Ashur was still unsolved (Marchand 1996: 217).

24. Cf. 'In those early days, styles of drawing and techniques of reproduction were naturally of a sort which today would be regarded as unsuitable or even primitive' (Lloyd 1976: 28).

25. In fact, all the drawings published in the two syntheses about the excavations both in Babylon and Ashur (Koldewey 1913; Andrae 1977) were realized in ink.

26. See, in particular, *Ornament und Verbrechen* by Adolf Loos. For trends in German architecture between the nineteenth and twentieth centuries, see Frampton (1993).

27. In fact, some clouds seem to be those 'voluptuous clouds' belonging to the repertory of the typical sensual elements of the *Art nouveau* (Cremona 1984: 88); whereas a low perspective point of view calls to mind the trends of the *Gothic revival* of the 1920s expressed in both architecture and figurative arts; see Masini (1991).

28. J. Jordan remained in Iraq until 1939. Once in Germany, he wrote an article about Hatra and devoted the last paragraph to explain that its ruins seem to reflect an Aryan spirit (Hauser 2001: 228). For the opinion of F. Delitzsch, the central promoter of Germany's Mesopotamia, about the Aryanness of the Assyrians, see Bohrer (2003: 286–97).

29. This is contrary to Madhloom's opinion (1981: 58).

Abbreviations

AOAT	Alt Orient und Alt Testament
ARID	Analecta Romana Instituti Danici
BaM	Baghdader Mitteilungen
CMAO	Contributi e Materiali di Archeologia Orientale, Roma
DossAParis	Dosssier Archéologique, Paris
ICAANE	International Congress on Archaeology of Ancient Near East
ISIMU	Revista Sobre Oriente Próximo y Egypto en la Antigüedad
MDOG	Mitteilungen der Deutschen Orient-Gesellschaft zu Berlin
WVDOG	Wissenschaftliche Veröffentlichungen der Deutschen Orientgesellschaft

References

Andrae, W. 1903. Reise von Damaskus nach Mosul, in *MDOG* XX: 9–30.

———. 1909. *Die Anu-Adad-Tempel in Assur* (= WVDOG 10), Leipzig: J.C. Hinrichs.

———. 1913. *Die Festungswerke von Assur* (=WVDOG 23), Leipzig: J.C. Hinrichs.

———. 1952. *Babylon. Die versunkene Weltstadt und ihr Ausgräber Robert Koldewey.* Berlin: Mann.

———. 1961. *Lebenserinnerungen eines Ausgräbers.* Berlin: Mann.

———. 1977. *Das wiedererstandene Assur.* Zweite, durchgesehene und erweiterte Auflage herausgeeben von Barthel Hrouda, 2. Aufl. München: CH. Beck.

——— and Boehmer, R.M. 1989. Die Orientbilder von Walter Andrae, in *BaM* 20: 1–89.

——— and ———. 1992. *Bilder eines Ausgräbers / Sketchs by an Excavator. Walter Andrae im Orient 1898–1919.* Berlin: Gebr. Mann Verlag.

Bahrani, Z. 2000. 'The Extraterrestrial Orient: Colonizing Mesopotamia in Space and Time', in L. Milano, S. de Martino, F.M. Fales and G.B. Lanfranchi (eds), *Proceedings of the XLIVe Rencontre Assyriologique Internationale, Venezia, 7–11 July.* Padova: Sargon Srl, pp. 5–10.

———. 2001. 'History in Reverse: Archaeological Illustration and the Invention of Assyria', in T. Abusch, P.A. Beaulieu, J. Huehnergard, P. Machinist and P. Steinkeller (eds), *Proceedings of the XLVe Rencontre Assyriologique Internationale, Part I.* Bethesda: CDL Press, pp. 15–28.

Bohrer, F.N. 1998. 'Inventing Assyria: Exoticism and Reception in Nineteenth-Century England and France', *The Art Bulletin* LXXX (2), June: 336–56.

———. 2003. *Orientalism and Visual Culture*, Cambridge: Cambridge University Press.

Cavigneaux, A. 1986, 'Babylone. Les monuments et la vie', *DossAParis*, 103: 48–51.

Chevalier, N. 2002. *La recherche archéologique française au moyen-orient, 1842–1947.* Paris: Éditions recherches sur les civilisations.

Cremona, I. 1984. *Il tempo dell'Art Nouveau.* Torino: U. Allemandi.

Crüsemann, N. 2000. *Vom Zweistromland zum Kupfergraben* (=Jahrbuch der Berliner Museen 42), Berlin.

———. 2003. '"Ja! Wir werden das Licht des deutschen Genius auch dorthin tragen". Der Beginn der Ausgrabungen in Assur im Spiegel preussisch-deutscher Orientpolitik unter Wilhem II', in J. Marzahn, B. Salje (eds), *Wiedererstehendes Assur. 100 Jahre deutsche Ausgrabungen in Assyrien.* Mainz am Rhein: Philipp von Zabern, pp. 35–44.

Damerji, M.S.B. 1981. 'Babylone. Les fouilles nouvelles et les travaux de restauration'. *DossAParis* 51: 26–31.

Díaz-Andreu, M. 2004. 'Britain and the Other: the Archaeology of Imperialism', in H. Brocklehurst and R. Phillips (eds), *History, Nationhood and the Question of Britain.* London: Palgrave Macmillan, pp. 227–45.

Earle, E.M. 1966. *Turkey, The Great Powers, and The Bagdad Railway. A Study in Imperialism.* New York: Russell an Russel.

Frahm, E. 2003. 'Zwischen Dichtung und Wahrheit. Assur und Assyrien in den Augen der Nachwelt', in J. Marzahn and B. Salje (eds), *Wiedererstehendes Assur. 100 Jahre deutsche Ausgrabungen in Assyrien.* Mainz am Rhein: Philipp von Zabern, pp. 19–28.

Frampton, K. 1993. *Storia dell'architettura moderna*, trans. M. De Benedetti and R. Poletti, Bologna: Zanichelli.

Haller, A. and W. Andrae 1955. *Die Heiligtümer des Gottes Assur und der Sin-Šamaš-Tempel in Assur.* Leipzig: Mann.

Härke, H. 1991. 'All Quiet on the Western Front? Paradigms, Methods and Approaches in West German Archaeology', in I. Hodder (ed.), *Archaeological Theory in Europe.* London/New York: Routledge, pp. 187–222.

Hassmann, H. 2000. 'Archaeology in the "Third Reich"', in H. Härke (ed.), *Archaeology, Ideology and Society. The German Experience.* Frankfurt am Main: Peter Lang, pp. 65–139.

Hauser, S.R. 2001. 'Not out of Babylon? The Development of Ancient Near Eastern Studies in Germany and its Current Significance', in T. Abusch, P.A. Beaulieu, J. Huehnergard, P. Machinist and P. Steinkeller (eds), *Proceedings of the XLVe Rencontre Assyriologique Internationale, Part I, Harvard and Yale Universities.* Bethesda: CDL Press, pp. 211–37.

Heinrich, E. 1957. 'Leben und Wirken Walter Andraes', in *Neue Ausgrabungen in Nahen Osten, Mittelmeerraum und in Deutschland. Bericht über die Tagung der Koldewey Gesellschaft in Regensburg vom 23. bis 27. April 1957*, pp. 7–13.

Invernizzi, A. 2000. 'Discovering Babylon with Pietro Della Valle', in P. Matthiae, A. Enea, L. Peyronel and F. Pinnock (eds), *Proceedings of the Ist ICAANE, Rome, 18–23 May, 1998*. Roma: Università degli Studi di Roma 'La Sapienza', pp. 643–649.

Koldewey, R. 1911. *Die Tempel von Babylon und Borsippa* (= WVDOG 15). Leipzig: J.C. Hinrichs.

———. 1913. *Das wieder erstehende Babylon*. Leipzig: J.C. Hinrichs.

Larsen, M.T. 1996. *The Conquest of Assyria. Excavations in an Antique Land*. London: Routledge.

Layard, A.H. 1849. *Monuments of Nineveh, from Drawings Made on the Spot*. London: J. Murray.

———. 1853. *Discoveries in the Ruins of Niniveh and Babylon; with Travels in Armenia, Kurdistan and the Desert: Being the Result of a Second Expedition Undertaken for the Trustees of the British Museum*. London: J. Murray.

———. 1854. *Discoveries among the Ruins of Niniveh and Babylon*. New York: Barnes.

Liverani, M. 1994. '"Voyage en Orient": The Origins of Archaeological Surveying in the Near East', in *The Near East and the Meaning of History. International Conference (23–27 November 1992)* (= Studi Orientali XIII). Roma: Bardi, pp. 1–16.

———. 1999a. 'Ancient Near Eastern History from Euro-centrism to an "Open" World', in J.J. Ayán and J.M. Córdoba (eds), Estudios sobre las culturas de Oriente y Egipto. Homenaje al Prof. Angel R. Garrido Herrero (= ISIMU II), Madrid: Univ. Autónoma, Centro Superiore de Est. De Asiriología y Egiptología, pp. 3–9.

———. 1999b. 'History and Archaeology in the Ancient Near East: 150 Years of a Difficult Relationship', in H. Kühne, R. Bernbeck and K. Bartl (eds), *Fluchtpunkt Uruk. Archäologische Einheit aus methodischer Vielfalt. Schriften für Hans Jorg Nissen*. Rahden: Leidorf, pp. 1–11.

———. 2000. 'La scoperta del mattone. Muri e archivi nell'archeologia mesopotamica', *Vicino Oriente* 12: 1–17.

Lloyd, S. 1976. 'Illustrating Monuments: Drawn Reconstructions of Architecture', in J.V.S. Megaw (ed.), *To Illustrate the Monument. Essays on Archaeology Presented to Stuart Piggott*. London: Thames and Hudson, pp. 27–34.

———. 1980. *Foundations in the Dust. The Story of Mesopotamian Exploration*. London: Thames and Hudson.

Madhloom, T.A.W. 1981. 'Assur : la résurrection d'une capitale', *DossAParis* 51: 54–61.

Marchand, S.L. 1996. *Down from Olympus. Archaeology and Philhellenism in Germany, 1750–1970*. Princeton: Princeton University Press.

———. 2000. 'Down from Olympus? The Turfan Expedition. Between Classicism and Colonialism', *Bericht über die 40. Tagung für Ausgrabungswissenschaft und Bauforschung. Vom 20. bis 23. Mai 1998 in Wien*, pp. 31–40.

Masini, L.V. 1991. *Art Nouveau*. Firenze: Giunti.

Matthes, O. 1997. 'Zur Vorgeschichte der Ausgrabungen in Assur 1898–1903/1905', *MDOG* 129: 9–27.

———. 1998. 'Der Aufruf zur Gründung der Deutschen Orient-Gesellschaft vom November 1897', *MDOG* 130: 9–16.

———. 1999. 'Zur Vorgeschichte der Deutschen Ausgrabungen in Babylon', in J. Renger (ed.), *Babylon: Focus mesopotamischer Geschichte, Wiege früher Gelehrsamkeit, Mythos in der Moderne. 2. Internationales Colloquium der Deutschen Orient-Gesellschaft 24–26. März 1998 in Berlin*. Saarbrücken: Saarbrücken Druckerei Verlag, pp. 33–45.

Micale, M.G. 2005. 'Immaginni d'architettura. Struttura e forma dell'architettura mesopotamica attraverso le ricostruzioni moderne' in D. Nadali e A. Di Ludovico (eds), *Contributi e Materiali di Archeologia Orientale. Studi in onore di Paolo Matthiae*, (=CMAO X): 121–166.

——— and D. Nadali in press. '"Layer by layer ... " Of Digging and Drawing: the Genealogy of an Idea', in R. Biggs, J. Mayer and M. Roth (eds), *Proceedings of the LI Rencontre Assyriologique Internationale*. Chicago, 18–22 July 2005.

Moortgat, A. 1976. 'Die Deutsche Orient-Gesellschaft: Rückblick 1976', *MDOG* 108: 53–71.

Pedde, B. 2000., Altorientalische Motive in den Illustrationen zum Alten Testament von Gustave Doré', in R. Dittmann, B. Hrouda, U. Low, P. Matthiae, R. Mayer-Opificius and S. Thürwächter (eds), *Variatio Delectat. Iran und Westen. Gedenkschrift für Peter Calmeyer* (= AOAT 272). Munster: Ugarit-Verlag, pp. 567–591.

Pillet, M. 1918. *Khorsabad. Les découvertes de V. Place en Assyrie*. Paris: Éditions Ernest Leroux.

Place, V. 1867–1870. *Ninive et l'Assyrie, avec des essais de restitution par F. Thomas*, vols I–III, Paris: Imprimerie impériale.

Said, E. W. 2001. *Orientalismo. L'immagine europea dell'Oriente*, trans. S. Galli, Milano: Feltrinelli.

Schnapp, A. 1993. *La conquête du passé. Aux origines de l'archéologie*. Paris: Carré.

———, S. Cleziou, A. Coudart and J.-P. Demoule 1991. 'The Use of Theory in French Archaelogy, in I. Hodder (ed.), *Archaeological Theory in Europe*. London/New York: Routledge, pp. 91–128.

Silberman, N.A. 1989. *Between Past and Present: Archaelogy, Ideology, and Nationalism in the Modern Near East*. New York: H. Holte.

Strika, V. 1993. *La guerra Iran-Iraq e la guerra del Golfo*. Napoli: Liquori.

——— . 2000. 'The Perception of the Past in the Near East. Two Case-Studies: Iraq and Saudi Arabia', in P. Matthiae, A. Enea, L. Peyronel and F. Pinnock (eds), *Proceedings of the Ist ICAANE, Rome, 18–23 May, 1998*. Roma: Università degli Studi di Roma 'La Sapienza', pp. 1579–86.

Trigger, B.G. 1996. *Storia del pensiero archeologico*, trans. G. Scandone Matthiae, Firenze: La Nuova Italia.

Voet, G. 1986. 'Babylone. Où sont les fouilles?', *DossAParis* 103: 42–43.

Wilhelm, G. 1998. Zwischen Tigris und Nil. 100 Jahren Ausgrabungen der Deutschen Orient-Gesellschaft in Vorderasien und Ägypten, Mainz am Rhein: Philipp von Zabern.

Chapter 16

Weaving Images

Juan Cabré and Spanish Archaeology in the First Half of the Twentieth Century

Susana González Reyero

'Photographs are never evidence of history: they are themselves the historical.'
(Trachtenberg 1989)

Abstract

El presente trabajo supone una reflexión sobre el papel que la fotografía ha desempeñado en la investigación arqueológica. Nos centramos en el caso español y, en concreto, en la documentación fotográfica de Juan Cabré Aguiló (1882–1947), uno de los investigadores españoles más importantes de la primera mitad del s. XX. Este análisis nos lleva a considerar el largo proceso por el que se descubrió y caracterizó la cultura ibérica a partir de finales del s. XIX y las repercusiones que la generalización del discurso visual –fotografías y dibujos- tuvo en las teorías y acercamientos a lo largo de este proceso.

This chapter aims to present a reflection on the role that photography has played in archaeological investigation. The focus here is on the Spanish case and, in particular, on the photographic documentation produced by Juan Cabré Aguiló (1882–1947), one of the most important researchers in Spain in the first half of the twentieth century. This analysis considers the process by which the Iberian culture was discovered and characterised from the end of the nineteenth century, and the impact that visual media – photographs and drawings – had on the theories and approaches developed throughout this process.

The Artificial Retina. On Photography in Archaeology

Photography has transformed the practices of historians and archaeologists. Together with drawings and casts, these three forms of appropriation and substitution of objects for the analysis of reality have modified our approach to the cultures of the past. As Walter Benjamin has pointed out (1971), they have even transformed the original object of study.

In the following pages I would like to address several issues arising from the adoption of photography in archaeology in Spain. The technique of photography was incorporated into a scientific discipline that was, at that time, in its process of formation. Applied to the study of the past and its remains, photography introduced hitherto new visual perspectives, while providing archaeologists with a new instrument that had multiple applications and purposes. But it must be recalled that, rather than a reflection of reality, photography implies an elaboration, a historical construction that has to be analysed and decoded. In this respect, the rate of adoption and the uses of photography can inform us on the state of archaeological science. The increasing use of photographic images made possible the creation of types, the systematisation, the stylistic analysis, the comparisons and the argumentation of parallelisms, the elaboration of *corpora*. Indeed, besides affecting archaeological methodology, as we will see below, the use of photography also greatly facilitated communication and exchange among researchers.

The invention of photography took place, and is comprehensible, in a nineteenth-century society fascinated by scientific and industrial progress. In this context of total confidence in progress, photography was enthusiastically received. While manual reproduction –drawings – was receiving increasing suspicion, mechanical reproduction transmitted great confidence: photography allowed the emphasis of certain aspects of the original object that were only accessible to a lens and not to the human eye (Benjamin 1971: 21).

Despite the fact that our discipline often takes photography as a working document, as a substitute for the object itself, there is a lack of deep reflection on the consequences of its generalisation, on the fact that, as Malraux pointed out, the history of art, during the last hundred years, is mainly the history of what we are able to photograph (Malraux 1949: 32). Archaeologists keep considering photographs as objective documents, and this axiom is very seldom questioned. We can build, however, on the reflections that have been made in other fields, including philosophy, semiotics, anthropology or cultural history, with pioneering works from authors such as Benjamin (1971), Freitag (1979, 1997), Hamber (1990, 2003), Burke (2001), Fawcett (1983, 1995), Edwards (2001) or Crary (1990, 1999).

Photography was applied very rapidly to archaeological studies in countries like France, Great Britain and Germany. Its arrival was simultaneous with the demand for more trustworthy sources, which, as already someone like Champollion had claimed, would be able to avoid errors induced by inexact drawings. Photography revolutionised all aspects of modern life. With respect to history of art, then still a relatively new discipline, the invention of photography effectively determined its future course (Freitag 1997: 257). In Spain the new technique was adopted with an enthusiasm similar to that of the rest of the western world (Naranjo 1997: 73; Riego 2003). The perception of its exactitude seems to have been equal, although its adoption rates depended on the Spanish socio-political situation. Monlau, who would eventually become the first director of the National Archaeological Museum, communicated the discovery of photography to the Academy of Barcelona on 24 February 1839. In his opinion, the daguerreotype was the great discovery of the century, and added: 'It is a pity that the huge drama of industrial and scientific progress sees the Spaniards, by circumstances independent of their capacity, condemned to the dark role of spectators' (López Mondéjar 1989: 15).

To evaluate the influence of photography on nineteenth century science, the commonplace belief that photographic recording reproduced reality turns out to be fundamental. Its mechanical registry was believed to reproduce reality without any intervention from the photographer. What was seen in the daguerreotype was 'reality' (Clarke 1997: 45). This apparent objectivity fostered the interest of scientists and scholars in this mechanism of reproduction, and photographs were soon attributed such virtues as constituting a 'témoin incorruptible' that offered representations that were 'irrécusables' and 'mathématiquement exactes' (Feyler 1993: 189).

The adequacy of photography to the needs of science was already pointed out by Arago in the speech he made at the time of its invention in 1839. As he emphasised 'chacun songera à l'immense parti qu'on aurait tiré, pendant l'expédition d'Égypte, d'un moyen de reproduction si exact et si prompt' (Arago 1839; Brunet 2000: 111). In fact, it dominated engravings and drawings, thanks to its qualities of fidelity with respect to the original, as well as its instantaneity and suitability for multiple reproductions. Both in the spirit of those who took them, as in the one of those who used them, there was certainty about them being true documents. This belief relied on the credibility that was granted to mechanical procedures.

In the twentieth century, the confidence of archaeologists in the photographic medium continued to increase, especially in the favourable scientific atmosphere of the new century (López-Ocón 1999: 40). Deonna indicated in the 1920s how photography provided the scholar with the possibility of contemplating, in the tranquillity of his cabinet, the results of the on-site investigations (Deonna 1922: 85). Taking this perception into account, it is not surprising that many archaeologists considered that its use allowed 'que l'archéologue puisse emporter avec lui à loisir une représentation absolument exacte du sujet douteux' (Foliot 1986: 131). However, as Trachtenberg pointed out: 'a photographer does not have to convince the spectator to adopt his point of view, because the reader does not have any option; in the photo we see the world from the partial angle of view of the camera, from the position it had at the moment in which the shutter was released' (Trachtenberg 1989: 251–52).

The fact is that photography facilitated the spread of a more accurate knowledge of the material and architectonic culture of past civilisations, particularly their classification, characterisation and progressive definition. However, the support and the corroboration that it has provided in this process of knowledge have not been innocent. The essence of photography depends on selection. Contrary to reality, to the total of the excavation site, it can show us only a fragment. Frequently, this fragment is presented, interpreted and evaluated as if it were universal, whereas in fact its contents depend on a multitude of factors. Like any other act of selection, it always implies the prioritisation of several aspects over others, it is indeed a construction of reality. From this perspective my work tries to raise awareness of the consequences that the arrival of photography had on the construction of the guidelines and characteristics of one of the most important peninsular cultures: the Iberian culture.

Archaeology in Spain during the First Half of the Twentieth Century

In the first half of the twentieth century, Spanish archaeology experienced a slow and eventful process of institutionalisation and incorporation to occidental science. Throughout the first third of the century there was a scientific effervescence, which included the support of the often recently created official institutions. Unfortunately, many of the projects and efforts of that period were tragically cut short by the Spanish Civil War (1936–1939). Thereafter, many different historical constructions were put forward. It is in this context in which Juan Cabré Aguiló (1882–1947), one of the most relevant scholars in peninsular protohistory, would undertake his activity (Blánquez and Rodríguez 2004; Blánquez and González Reyero 2004; González Reyero 2004) (Fig.16.1).

Fig. 16.1 J. Cabré Aguilo (1882–1947). One of the main researchers of Spanish archaeology in the first half of the twentieth century. © Cabré's family.

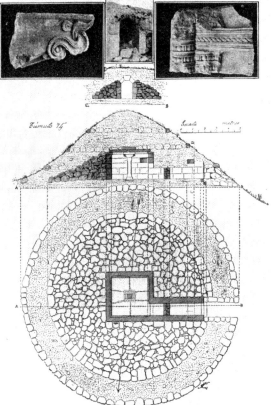

Fig. 16.2 Illustrious visitors to the Altamira cave, ca. 1912. From left to right Juan Cabré, the guide, Pascual Serrano, Henri Breuil, Louis Siret, Hugo Obermaier, H. Alcalde del Río and Henri Siret. © Museo Juan Cabré, Calaceite (Teruel).

Fig. 16.3 Photographs and drawings representing the Iberian burial mound no 74 from Galera (Granada). © Cabré and De Motos (1920: pl. XII).

Cabré's work has to be placed between two worlds, that of the antiquarian tradition and that of the new practices of the twentieth century, and was influenced by such great figures as Breuil, Gómez-Moreno, Bosch Gimpera, Mélida and Déchelette (Fig. 16.2, Plate 11). His activity, which spans the first half of the twentieth century, was fundamental in the definition of the protohistoric cultures. His excavations in key sites of the Iberian (Collado, Toya and Galera) and Celtiberian (Cogotas and Azaila) cultures made possible the first synthesis of the peninsular protohistory. These cultures were one of the focal points at that time, since they were fundamental to the different constructions of the unity or diversity – Spanish, Catalan or Basque – of Spain (Figs 16.3, 16.4).

At that time, the liberal state began to assume the task of discovering the past (Díaz-Andreu 2002; Díaz-Andreu and Champion 1997; Ruiz, Sánchez and Bellón 2002). Under its control there was a pretension to institutionalise and to professionalise its studies, to define its cultural and political roots. In the twentieth century the dominant interpretative guidelines in peninsular archaeology were historicism and historicist idealism. In this context of crisis and regeneration, the Centro de Estudios Históricos was the origin of interesting constructions. Their objectives, according to their foundational text of 1907, were centred on the accumulation of materials for investigation that were perceived as fundamental to reconstruct the history of the country.

From 1939 onwards, following the Civil War that brought to power the dictatorship of General Franco, a nationalistic historiography centred primarily in the modern age was harnessed. This period of the Spanish Empire was then conceived as the foundation and golden age of the Spanish nation. In the historiography of the 1940s positivism and nationalism were predominant. Particularly rooted in the fields of archaeology and medieval history, the basis of this tradition appeared even before 1936 and was consolidated later with prehistorians like Taracena and Santa-Olalla and, later on, García y Bellido, Luis Pericot and Martín Almagro (Jover 1999: 280). This continuity of positivism under

Fig. 16.4 Juan Cabré, his family and workers, in the Celtiberian site of Las Cogotas (Ávila) during the summer of 1931. © Cabré's family.

several re-elaborations throughout the first half of the twentieth century makes comprehensible the absence of a critical reflection on the unquestionable veracity of photography in Spain. The irresistible myth of its mechanical origins was still present (Snyder 1998: 30). This almost total absence of questioning of the reproduction mechanism meant that any photograph could still be used as a way of supporting the most diverse theories.

Appreciating this positivist conception is fundamental, I believe, for understanding the successive uses made of photography, and its continued appropriation for very different discourses. Well into twentieth century, photography continued being a safe means towards the acceptance of any theory, in spite of changes within the archaeological discipline. Photography was thus applied in Spain to a science that, in the middle of the twentieth century, continued being eminently positivist, idealistic and historicist. The isolationism that followed the Civil War promoted this continuity, as did difficulties in the renewal of Spanish science.

Towards the 'Photographic' Construction of the Iberian Culture (1860–1904)

The discovery and characterisation of the Iberian culture was a complex process in which photography became increasingly present. It was incorporated, at different levels, into the interesting succession of discoveries, synthesis, contradictions and debates concerning the ancient Iberian inhabitants. During the last third of the nineteenth century it was used in the sense of the 'photo of the finding', that is to say, like a mechanism to demonstrate the truthfulness of the discovery. From that moment, some of the most important peninsular discoveries, such as the Phoenician sarcophagus of Punta de Vaca (Cádiz) or the Venus of Itálica were accompanied by a photograph that immortalised the moment of the finding. Exceptionally its use as a substitute for drawings also began at that point: photography allowed a more exact reproduction of the details and considerable time savings. In a climate of constant discoveries, the fast and precise classification of remains seemed basic. Some of the first synthesis works in which photography was already indispensable would see the light shortly after. This was the case of the fundamental *Essai sur l'art et l'industrie de l'Espagne primitive* by Pierre Paris (1903–1904).

However, the above mentioned constitute exceptions in a panorama in which photography had only been incorporated in a punctual manner. With the second and third decades of the twentieth century, more and more archaeologists took their own pictures. The increasing ease of use of the camera, its more affordable price, the use of 35 mm film were among the factors which contributed without any doubt to the conversion of the archaeologist into a photographer. Several official projects, such as the *Monumental Catalogue of Spain* by Melida and the *Corpus Vasorum Antiquorum*, contributed to restore and to strengthen their use.

The Iberian culture was discovered in 1860, in a period when there was an obvious lack of a chronological and cultural scheme within which to insert the new findings. Photography immediately showed its usefulness in the inventory of the patrimony and the construction of the national memories and the collective identity (Brunet 2000: 102). The 'Iberian antiques' raised a particular interest given their possible occupation of all the peninsular territory; and thus they could be contemplated as the historical origin of contemporary Spanish unitarism.

The recognition of the Iberian culture was slow. It took decades and multiple discussions to agree and convene on the names and to establish the precise framework of the Iberians, to fix their location and their historical time. The discovery of the Lady of Elche in 1897 (see below) played a crucial role in this process, but the history of the Iberian culture had already begun with the 1860 discovery of numerous sculptures in the Cerro de los Santos (Montealegre, Albacete). These and other similar findings gave rise to different interpretations, relating to the Egyptians (Rada Delgado 1875) and to Visigoth martyrs, a fashionable culture back then (Amador de los Ríos 1889: 766). In fact, recognition of the sculptures from Cerro de los Santos required the existence of 'replacement' objects for European cabinets. In these years several forms of appropriation and substitution of the old pieces coexisted: casts, photographs and drawings. The studies made from these 'doubles' attest the credit that their contemporaries conferred on them. In the Universal Exhibition of 1873 in Vienna, casts of the main sculptures of the Cerro de los Santos were exposed. Shortly after, the casts and several originals were taken to the Exhibition of 1878 in Paris. The international scientific community had doubts about the veracity of the new findings in Spain. Moreover, several outstanding specialists, like Emile Cartailhac and Longpérier questioned the authenticity of the sculptures.

It was at that point that Léon Heuzey became interested in this debate. After a trip to Spain, the Frenchman defended the reality of what he called 'demi-civilisation gréco-phénicienne' (Heuzey 1897: 6). In his related works in the *Bulletin de Correspondance Hellénique* (1891a) and the *Revue d'Assyriologie et d'Archéologie Orientale* (1891b) Heuzey granted a considerable importance to the graphic section. The confusion generated around these sculptures was raised, in his opinion, due to the fact that its knowledge was based on inexact reproductions: 'Des reproductions, presque toutes également imparfaites, de plusieurs sculptures du *Cerro* ont été publiées par M. de la Rada, Cartailhac, Henzlmann et dans les Comptes Rendus du Congrès Archéologique de Valence' (Heuzey 1891a: 609, footnote 1). His stay in Madrid, in 1888, allowed him to conclude their authenticity: 'il a acquis la conviction qu'ils sont authentiques, qu'ils sont l'oeuvre d'un atelier local et indigène, formé sous la double influence des Grecs et des Phéniciens, mais gardant une originalité ibérique bien accusée' (Heuzey 1891a: 609). The exposed photographic plates served to verify and to discover affinities, to even point out comparisons with objects that were already known. This 'visual discovery' corroborated the idea that the new art 'avait reçu à son heure le lointain reflet des grands foyers de l'art antique' (Heuzey 1891b: 97). The graphic section was already indispensable to judge the pieces.

The discovery in 1897 of the Lady of Elche shocked the scientific world, and confirmed the existence of a true and original Iberian art. In his first study of the Lady, *Busto prerromano descubierto en Elche* (1897), Mélida included two photographs, showing its front and its back (pl. XVI). Apparently Mélida wanted to be cautious in his influences, indicating simply its pre-Roman character. The Spanish investigator did not know the original piece, which had been acquired by the Museum of Louvre soon after its discovery; he based his article only on the knowledge that the photographs provided him with, even stating how this 'precious sculpture is only known to us by two photographs' (Mélida 1897: 440). His conclusions were based, thus, on this substitute for the object, which was believed to be sufficient for the study of the piece.

Photography and Stylistic Studies: Oriental and Greek Explanations for Iberian Culture

Photography was increasingly relied on when a topic proved controversial. A paradigmatic case of this was that of Iberian ceramics, and the important debate surrounding the problem of its origins and chronology. The Mycenaean influence first, Punic and Greek later, were the main influences to which researchers resorted.

At the beginning of the twentieth century, and following the theories promoted by Pierre Paris in his *Essai sur l'art et l'industrie de l'Espagne primitive* (1903–1904), it was believed that Iberian ceramics were related to Minoan and Mycenaean pottery (cf. Mederos 1999: 12). The publication by A. and P. Gascón de Gotor, titled *Artistic, monumental and historical Zaragoza* (1890) was here of basic importance: it reproduced, in three phototypes of Thomas (Barcelona), diverse ceramics of Azaila that were described as 'Iberian'.

These phototypes were the 'materials' upon which the Mycenaean hypothesis was formulated. On their basis, A. Furtwängler and G. Perrot and Ch. Chipiez, in their *Histoire de l'art dans l'antiquité* (Perrot and Chipiez 1894), first suggested relations between Iberian and Mycenaean ceramics. The French indicated how they followed the interpretation of Furtwängler and how they

Fig. 16.5 Carpenter compares the 'Lady of Elche' with a Greek sculpture. From left to right: The Apollo Chatsworth and the 'Lady of Elche' (Carpenter 1925: pl. IX).

became aware of Iberian ceramics through a phototype published in Zaragoza: 'Furtwängler a bien voulu me signaler le vase auquel je fais allusion, c'est une boîte munie de son couvercle, qui appartient à la dernière époque de la fabrication mycénienne. Elle est figuré dans la planche III du tome I du livre de Gascón de Gotor, Saragossa' (Perrot and Chipiez 1894: 940, footnote 5). This Mycenaean interpretation was soon accepted by researchers such as Evans and Salomon, as well as Mélida and Vives. It was however rejected by Siret and also by Bosch Gimpera (Pereira 1987: 19).

Photography was also fundamental in the formulations of Carpenter, who was a strong defender of Greek influence in Iberian culture. His contribution in *The Greeks in Spain* (1925) consisted, fundamentally, in the differentiation of Greek elements among objects attributed to the Iberian culture. As he confessed: 'Being by training a Hellenic archaeologist, I can do no less'. This bias extended to the Lady of Elche, in which he found – through photography- a 'Greek strain'.

The numerical relations between canons observed in the Lady and other Greek sculptures were basic for the establishment of types and styles. To the original Lady of Elche, Carpenter substituted a photograph (Fig. 16.5). He took measurements, and established parallelisms and synchronies: 'But if one cares to apply a graduated ruler to the frontal photograph of the Lady of Elche on Plate XIII of Volume VI of the *Monuments Piot*, one will discover that the sculptor laid out the features by equal parts or units. And if one similarly measures the bronze head of the Chatsworth Apollo on plate I of Furtwängler's *Intermezzi*, one will discover an agreement with the Lady of Elche which is perfect except for a single item (the length of the nose and the consequent height of the eyebrows)' (Carpenter 1925: 64).

The photograph used had thus become the document under study, the basis of the theory or the interpretation. In order to shape these hypotheses Carpenter further resorted to put a mask over the original photograph published by the *Monuments Piot*, so that only the face appeared and not the hair. As he explained: 'If one covers with white sheets all the outstanding elements of the Lady of Elche on a photograph or blocks them out as I have done on plate X, much of the Iberian appearance will vanish' (Carpenter 1925: 68) – strengthening the hypothesis that the Lady of Elche had been made according to the Greek canon. It is noteworthy that Carpenter's Greek theories were almost unanimously accepted by the Spanish research community: by García y Bellido (1935), and after the Civil War by Dixon (1940) and Obermaier and García y Bellido (1947), among others.

The Photographic Documentation of Juan Cabré: Instruments and Corpora for the Definition of the Iberian Culture

Juan Cabré began his archaeological work in 1903, with the discovery of the cave paintings at Cretas (Teruel). His collaboration with the Marquis of Cerralbo allowed him to contact Joseph Déchelette, one of the most important European archaeologists of the time. Déchelette and Cabré met in 1912 during a trip that the Frenchman made (Cabré 1942: 340, note 1) to Santa María de Huerta (Guadalajara) (Déchelette 1962: 108). This was without doubt an opportunity to exchange diverse impressions and experiences on archaeology and on photography.[1]

Juan Cabré was of a generation that had learned the craft of photography. We can detect in his practice diverse manipulations of the negative that improved overexposed zones and allowed objects to be contrasted by means of photographic masks. His mastery of drawing and photography allowed him to take advantage of both disciplines and demonstrate for us the same differences between his works and those of his contemporaries. Cabré elaborated plates on which he reconstructed incomplete parts of the objects, so that the drawing showed his hypothesis. Photography became a working document on which the archaeologist wrote down data, measures and locations. These practices reveal the shortcomings and difficulties that photography entailed, the shortages of plates, the adjustments due to the impossibility to repeat the trip or the shot, etc. All of these differentiate Cabré's photographic practices from ours, and place them in their period.

Several trends can be identified in Cabré's photographs of various Iberian objects. First, there are images in which the objects are arranged to appear as in a pictorial still life. The archaeological object is thus inserted in a previous tradition of representation. The fundamental aspect here is the group, the global disposition. Following the appearance of photography, this still-life style was used by the majority of researchers, possibly due to this still dominant pictorial tradition, and also due to the fact that the high costs of publication made it necessary to accumulate several objects on a single plate. In this respect, we find that Cabré used photography in a way already defined by Petrie at the end of the nineteenth century. The famous British Egyptologist demonstrated the convenience of having the objects from the same group in a single plate, which allowed the observation of a 'whole class' at a single glance. Plates were instruments of comparison. In Petrie's opinion they had to be fundamentally 'self-contained and self-explanatory', eloquent in their own right and independently of the written text, of the contribution of the researcher (Petrie 1904: 116).

But photographs soon began to take on a different appearance. They showed how its centre and purpose was the object. Gradually photography of individual pieces began to appear. That was the form that was chosen for the systematisation of the findings, its rational disposition in the *corpora*. Paradigmatically Cabré carried it out, for example, in the accomplishment of the *Corpus Vasorum Hispanorum* dedicated to the finds at Azaila (Olmos 1999: 158–161).

The intention of the author is shaped, in particular, in the plates. They were not, on many occasions, an 'as is' transfer from the negative, but compositions between several of them. For example, two views that showed the same votive offering taken from the front and the side were put together. Thus one had, in a single view, two or more fundamental aspects by which to know the object. Photography thus followed the guidelines and conventions adopted years before by photography of anthropology and natural sciences. This type of photography demonstrates a will to obtain 'aseptic' data, and for that reason took the drawings from botanical specimens as a main point of reference.

This mosaic photography of specimens has been called 'floating objects' by Elizabeth Edwards. In these plates the photographer took part actively in the image. The objects seemed to be 'floating', without any resting point (Edwards 2001: 59). Its bottom could be retired, or kept, by means of masks. This scheme of representation of the objects as specimens did not come from the world of art, but from natural sciences. The influence of fields in which photography had had an earlier application, like medicine, allowed these existing guidelines to create models that sciences such as anthropology and archaeology adopted. Its relationship with scientific illustration was clear, following the convention that concentrated the data within a single plate as well as the assumption of its veracity. Thus photography could provide typological tables or orderings by 'species'.

This type of photography never became dominant in Spain, as attested by the predominance of other types of expositions such as those from antique dealers. However, Cabré did practise this type of disposition, especially in the publication of typologies. He elaborated comprehensible compositions with the objective of ordering and structuring a chronological and cultural framework in which the new Iberian findings could be inserted. This was the case with the publication of several Iberian votive offerings from the Collado de los Jardines (Jaén). They were grouped by types of 'Votive offerings of feminine, praying, figures of bronze' (Calvo and Cabré 1918: pl. XXIV, bronze XXV), the 'Bronze votive offerings of anthropomorphous figures' (Calvo and Cabré 1919: pl. V) and the 'Bronze votive offerings of soldiers with arms' (Calvo and Cabré 1919: pl. VI).

In addition, these plates were related to certain tendencies at the beginning of the twentieth century that tried to bring the methods of history closer to those of the sciences. The ceramics were thus studied as 'species', as would Castillo (Castillo 1943: fig. 51) and García y Bellido (García y Bellido 1956–1957: 100) still be doing years later. This influence or willingness to study the material culture as biological species was based upon the exemplary character of natural sciences. It also attested to a systematising eagerness, the necessity to elaborate tables: the juxtaposition of materials favoured the comparison of elements coming from very different contexts.

The development of comparative studies also had an influence on the appearance of photographs. The stylistic studies demanded a particular type of plate. Thus, the comparisons needed, for example, representations of different sculptures under a similar frame. This type of plate copied models from anthropology, which attempted to establish canons for different races. The disposition of the plates facilitated the conclusions. Therefore canons, volumes and dimensions were verified by means of the disposition of several profiles or views. In the Iberian sanctuary of Collado de los Jardines, Cabré used photographic sequences in his approach to the Iberian votive offerings. The plates were often formed by a composition of several trimmed original views (Calvo and Cabré 1918: pl. X, XII, XIII, XVI, XXI). Some votive offerings were reproduced by means of frontal and rear views (Calvo and Cabré 1917: plate I) or frontal and side views (pl. XII). Another significant novelty was the relation he established between the votive offerings and their place of appearance. In order to illustrate this context he included a plate with the 'Lot of votive offerings found together' (Calvo and Cabré 1917: pl. XXIA) and, next, the 'Crack in which they were found' (pl. XXIB). The importance and attention for the context seemed to be developing in his work.

The attention of the archaeologist was also addressed to the activity carried out in the excavation sites. Some showed a general view, where special care to portray workers, visitors, and infrastructure was taken (Fig. 16.6). They were, rather, illustrations of the daily life in the site. The main interest was not put in the structures, but in the activity, the campaign. They reflected, in fact, the success of the mission, its achievements. Once published, they showed the convenience of continuing those works. In many cases, these images constitute the only testimony of those works that we have today. Cabré frequently captured general views of his excavations in Las Cogotas, Azaila, La Osera, Recópolis, etc. With great testimonial value, the photographs of the excavation process that Cabré began to take illustrate structures that have already disappeared, as happened in the case of the questioned platforms of Collado de los Jardines (Jaén).

Fig. 16.6 A detail of the excavation process. Celtiberian necropolis at Aguilar de Anguita. © Aguilera y Gamboa (1916: 18–19, pl. II).

Like many other archaeologist-photographers, Cabré frequently placed workers or other people in his photographs of exteriors. This practice was quite usual until the appearance of other scales, like yardsticks or tugs, which are more characteristic of the archaeology of the second half of the twentieth century. The sensation of depth and global dimensions of the monument were provided this way.

It is crucial, in my view, to try and identify the conception that the author had of photography, and the credibility and value granted to it. Cabré made clear how photography could provide, in his opinion, a more complete and exact description than the written one: 'Whichever description we try to do on this particular weapon, no matter how tedious and faithful it might be, it will never be enough to give an exact idea of it; however by seeing plate 1 the reader will receive its right and true note' (Cabré 1916: 8). Photography could then replace the object of study.

The first years of the postwar period in Spain were characterised by a readjustment in the institutions, which implied changes of people and, therefore, changes in archaeological research and its priorities. In spite of the rupture that the war presupposes, a noticeable theoretical and epistemological continuity existed, in which two fundamental lines again dominated: positivism and nationalism. In fact, new elaborations of the roots of Spain were formulated, in which the protohistoric cultures, and in particular the Celt one, would become of central importance. The Iberian culture was even refused by hypotheses, a fact that has to be directly related to the political prestige that was associated with the Celtic artefacts, and the desire to grant a greater antiquity to them. The interpretation of the Iberian antiques changed until it became little less than an effect of the action of Rome.

Cabré's use of photography had remarkable repercussions on the archaeology of his time. Simultaneously, the use and presence of photography had been evolving: after initial sporadic use, it became a fundamental part of archaeological discourse. The two parts, text and graphic section, were irremediably intertwined. Cabré provided us with the best part of the visual materials we have today, and over which most of the questions that have been posed about the ceramics, the funeral and religious architecture of the Iberians, were raised. With his work in the *Corpus Vasorum Hispanorum* he undertook the accomplishment of one of the first systematisations of the Iberian ceramics (Cabré 1944).

The wealth and thematic amplitude of Cabré's photographs is today evident. The value of the ethnographic views is outstanding, including scenes of visits to the sites, portraits of the society of its time, archaeological materials, views of his family and the farmers and humbler people, found on his visits to many towns in Spain at the beginning of the century. That is, the people with whom Cabré worked, who were his guides on his exploration trips, with archaeological and photographic equipment. They show aspects of the context that surrounded and influenced his investigation, that turn the photographic set in testimony of the changes, in guardian of the memory. A rich world, which is that of the Spain of the first half of the twentieth century, is shown to us.

Conclusions. Photography and the Study of the Iberian Culture: Towards a Visual Discourse

When contemplating Cabré's photographic collections, questions arise on the role played by his images for the emerging discipline of archaeology. As we have seen, a photograph of a monument or an artefact is not only an object, it is also a subject: it contributes to define the elaborated intellectual construction of the historian (Recht 2003: 6). Photography emphasises several aspects and hides others; everything depends on the objectives and interests of whoever is behind the lens.

Since the late nineteenth century, photography has transformed archaeological practice in subtle but direct ways: photographs have been used daily as illustrations, mnemonic resources or substitutes for the objects (Gaskell 1993: 212). They have not been innocent in the process of interpretation and analysis of the finds, and they have often ended up replacing the object of study.

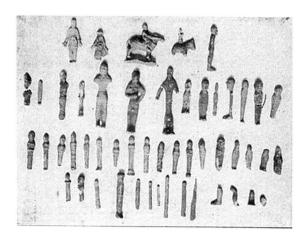
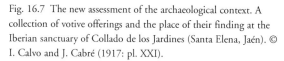

Fig. 16.7 The new assessment of the archaeological context. A collection of votive offerings and the place of their finding at the Iberian sanctuary of Collado de los Jardines (Santa Elena, Jaén). © I. Calvo and J. Cabré (1917: pl. XXI).

The incorporation of photography had important consequences on Iberian studies. We could say that its images, spread by photography, played an important role in its definition and cultural connection. To a large extent, questions of influences and possible origins were considered by virtue of these formal similarities. Comparison was the explanatory base of Iberian art: it was upon formal similarities with the Mediterranean that most researchers, such as Bosch Gimpera, Rhys Carpenter, García y Bellido and Ballester Tormo thought and formulated the Iberian culture.

Drawings, photography and, to a lesser extent, casts would conform what has been called the rhetoric of substitution of the objects. Together they made their appropriation, communication and study possible. Photography was adapted to several constant parameters of the investigation, such as classification and description. Cabré's work supposed in this context a substantial change in the use of the photography because, throughout his career, he transformed what had been its more common uses. Incorporated into his investigations, photography illustrated sequences that, following the excavation allowed knowledge of the *in situ* discovery of structures and materials. Little by little photography became increasingly present in the excavation process. These images gathered, among other things, the beginning of the works and unusual views of landscapes that today have disappeared. Its presence indicates also the increasing importance of the context. In fact, the findings began to be photographed in the position in which they were found. In this sense it is possible to emphasise the importance of the early photographs of Calvo and Cabré in the Iberian sanctuary of Collado de los Jardines. Several plates of the work testified the 'Position of the votive offerings in the cuts of the site' (Calvo and Cabré 1917: pl. V.A and V.B) (Fig. 16.7).

Photographs of the past are not, then, innocent. They contain histories, 'raw histories' as Edwards called them (Edwards 2001), hoping to be related, rescued, threaded. Cabré constitutes a paradigmatic example of the incorporation of photography, drawings and stratigraphic assessments in the early twentieth century. His photography appears doubly rich and evocative. It illustrates personal experiences, an investigating activity that hinged between two worlds: one more traditional, marked by its antique dealer and collector nineteenth-century origins, and the other advancing towards increasing professionalisation. Both worlds, mixed and confused, constituted and defined Spanish archaeology in the first half of the twentieth century. The thematic amplitude, the wealth that Cabré's photographs transmit, also informs us about a scientific activity whose progress and efforts would be truncated and undervalued after the Civil War. His photographic documentation constitutes an exceptional testimony, a window on the history of the discipline that illustrates its intrinsic features, its late and irregular history, and its difficult evolution in between wars and post-war periods.

Acknowledgements

This paper forms part of the research project 'La Historiografía de la Arqueología española a través de su imagen' (No. BHA 2003–02575). I would like to thank J. Blánquez for his help during the preparation of this article and F.J. Sarasola, C. Ramírez and M. Díaz-Andreu for the translation and comments.

Note

1. Cabré's photographic documentation is kept today at the *Instituto del Patrimonio Histórico Español* (IPHE), following its generous donation by the Cabré family to the Spanish State.

References

Aguilera y Gamboa, E. 1916. *Las Necrópolis Ibéricas*, Asociación Española para el Progreso de las Ciencias, 2. Madrid.

Amador de los Ríos, F. 1889. *España. Sus Monumentos y Artes. Su Naturaleza e Historia. Murcia y Albacete.* Barcelona: Daniel Cortezo y Cª Barcelona.

Arago, F. 1839. 'Rapport à la Chambre des Députés, Séance du 3 Juillet 1839', in *Historique et Description des Procédés du Daguerréotype et du Diorama.* Paris: Alphonse Giroux et Cie Paris.

Benjamin, W. 1971. *L'oeuvre d'art à l'ère de sa reproductivité technique*, first edition 1935. Paris: Denoël/Gonthier.

Blánquez Pérez, J. and L. Roldán Gómez (eds). 1999a. *La Cultura Ibérica a Través de la Fotografía de Principios de Siglo. Un Homenaje a la Memoria.* Madrid: Universidad Autónoma de Madrid.

——— . (eds). 1999b. *La Cultura Ibérica a Través de la Fotografía de Principios de Siglo. Las Colecciones Madrileñas.* Madrid: Universidad Autónoma de Madrid.

——— . (eds) 2000. *La Cultura Ibérica a Través de la Fotografía de Principios de Siglo. El Litoral Mediterráneo.* Madrid: Universidad Autónoma de Madrid.

Blánquez Pérez, J.J. and B. Rodríguez Nuere (eds). 2004. *El Arqueólogo Juan Cabré (1882–1947). La Fotografía como Técnica Documental*, Ministerio de Educación, Cultura y Deporte, Universidad Autónoma de Madrid. Madrid: Universidad Autónoma de Madrid, Ministerio de Cultura.

Blánquez Pérez, J.J. and S. González Reyero. 2004. 'D. Juan Cabré Aguiló (1882–1947). Comentarios Oportunos a una Biografía Inacabada', in J.J. Blánquez Pérez and B. Rodríguez Nuere (eds). *El Arqueólogo Juan Cabré (1882–1947). La Fotografía como Técnica Documental.* Madrid: Universidad Autónoma-Ministerio de Cultura, pp. 19–41.

Burke, P. 2001. *Eyewitnessing. The Uses of Images as Historical Evidence.* London: Reaktion Books.

Brunet, F. 2000. *La Naissance de l'Idée de Photographie.* Paris: Presses Universitaires de France.

Cabré Aguiló, J. 1916. 'Una Sepultura de Guerrero Ibérico de Miraveche (Burgos)', *Arte Español*, 1–16.

——— . 1942. 'El Rito Céltico de Incineración con Estelas Alineadas', *Archivo Español de Arqueología*, No. 15, 339–44.

——— . 1944. *Cerámica de Azaila: Museos Arqueológicos de Madrid, Barcelona y Zaragoza*, Consejo Superior de Investigaciones Científicas. Madrid.

Cabré Aguiló, J. and F. De Motos. 1920. *La necrópolis Ibérica de Tutugi (Galera, provincia de Granada)*, Memoria de la Junta Superior de Excavaciones y Antigüedades, nº 25. Madrid.

Calvo, I. and J. Cabré. 1917. *Excavaciones en la Cueva y el Collado de los Jardines (Santa Elena, Jaén). Memoria de los Trabajos Realizados en 1916*, Memorias de la Junta Superior de Excavaciones y Antigüedades, 8. Madrid.

———. 1918. *Excavaciones en la Cueva y el Collado de los Jardines (Santa Elena, Jaén). Memoria de los Trabajos Realizados en 1917*, Memorias de la Junta Superior de Excavaciones y Antigüedades, 16. Madrid.

———. 1919. *Excavaciones en la Cueva y el Collado de los Jardines (Santa Elena, Jaén). Memoria de los Trabajos Realizados en 1918*, Memorias de la Junta Superior de Excavaciones y Antigüedades, 22. Madrid.

Carpenter, R. 1925. *The Greeks in Spain*, VI. Pennsylvania: Bryn Mawr Notes and Monographs.

Castillo, A. del. 1943. 'La Cerámica Ibérica de Ampurias: Cerámica del Sudeste', *Archivo Español de Arqueología* 16(50): 1–48.

Clarke, G. 1997. *The Photograph*. Oxford, Oxford University Press.

Crary, J. 1990. *Techniques of the Observer*. Cambridge, Mass.; London: MIT Press.

———. 1999. *Suspensions of Perception. Attention, Spectacle, and Modern Culture*. Cambridge, Mass.; London: MIT.

Déchelette, F. 1962. *Livre d´Or de Joseph Déchelette, Centenaire 1862–1962*. Roanne: Sully.

Deonna, W. 1922. 'L´Archéologue et le Photographe', *Revue Archéologique* XVI : 85–110.

Díaz-Andreu, M. 2002. *Historia de la Arqueología. Estudios*. Madrid: Ediciones Clásicas.

———. and T. Champion (eds). 1997. *Nationalism and Archaeology in Europe*. London: UCL Press.

Dixon, P. 1940. *The Iberians of Spain and Their Relations with the Aegean World*. Oxford.

Edwards, E. 2001. *Raw Histories. Photographs, Anthropology and Museums*. Oxford: Berg.

Fawcett, T. 1983. 'Visual Facts and the Nineteenth-Century Art Lecture', *Art History*, 6: 443–60.

———. 1995. 'Plane Surfaces and Solid Bodies: Reproducing Three-Dimensional Art in the Nineteenth Century', in H.E. Roberts, *Art History Through the Camera´s Lens*. Australia, United States: Gordon and Breach, pp. 59–85.

Feyler, G. 1993. *Le Fonds de Photographies Anciennes de l´Institut d´Archéologie Classique de l´Université de Strasbourg (Fonds Michaelis)*, Ph.D. dissertation. Strasbourg: Strasbourg University.

Foliot, Ph. 1986. 'Histoire de l´image Archéologique depuis l´invention jusqu´à nos jours', in A. Chéné, Ph. Foliot and G. Réveillac, *De la Photographie en Archéologie*, Ph.D. dissertation. Aix-en-Provence: Provence University, pp. 14–215.

Freitag, W. M. 1979. 'Early Uses of Photography in the History of Art', *Art Journal* XXXIX/2, 117–23.

———. 1997. 'La servante et la séductrice. Histoire de la photographie et histoire de l´art', in VV.AA, *Histoire de l´Histoire de l´Art*, I and II, Louvre, Conférence et colloques. Paris: Louvre, pp. 257–91.

García y Bellido, A. 1935. 'Una Cabeza Ibérica, Arcaica, del Estilo de Korai Ática', *Archivo Español de Arte y Arqueología* 32: 165–78.

———. 1947. 'Estudios sobre Escultura Romana en los Museos de España y Portugal', *Revista de Archivos, Bibliotecas y Museos* 53: 537–67.

———. 1956–1957. 'Noticiario. Estado Actual del Problema Referente a la Expansión de la Cerámica Ibérica por la Cuenca Occidental del Mediterráneo', *Archivo Español de Arqueología* 95: 90–106.

Gascón de Gotor, A. and P. Gascón de Gotor. 1890. *Zaragoza Artística, Monumental e Histórica*. Zaragoza: C. Ariño.

Gaskell, I. 1993. 'Historia de las Imágenes' in Burke, P. (ed.) *Formas de Hacer la Historia*, 209–239. Madrid: Alianza editorial.

González Reyero, S. 2004. 'Fotografía y Arqueología en la Primera mitad del s. XX en España: la Obra Pionera de Juan Cabré Aguiló', in J.J. Blánquez Pérez and B. Rodríguez Nuere (eds). *El Arqueólogo Juan Cabré (1882–1947). La Fotografía como Técnica Documental*. Madrid: Universidad Autónoma-Ministerio de Cultura, pp. 43–69.

Hambcr, A. 1990. 'The Use of Photography by Nineteenth-Century Art Historians', *Visual Resources*, VII: 135–61.

———. 2003. 'Photography in Nineteenth-Century Art Publications' in R. Palmer, and Th. Frangenberg (eds), *The Rise of the Image. Essays on the History of the Illustrated Art Book*, pp. 215–44. Amsterdam: Ashgate Pub.

Heuzey, L. 1891a. 'Statues Espagnoles de Style Gréco-phénicien', *Bulletin de Correspondance Hellénique*, 608–25.

———. 1891b. 'Statues Espagnoles de Style Gréco-phénicien', *Revue d´Assyriologie et d´Archéologie Orientale* 3(2): 98–114.

————. 1897. 'Le Buste d´Elche et la Mission de M. Pierre Paris en Espagne', note de Léon Heuzey, Membre de l´Académie', *Académie des Inscriptions et Belles-Lettres. Comptes Rendus*: 505–9.

Jover Zamora, J.M. 1999. 'Corrientes Historiográficas en la España Contemporánea', in J.M. Jover Zamora, *Historiadores Españoles de Nuestro Siglo*, pp. 25–272. Madrid: Real Academia de la Historia.

López Mondéjar, P., 1989. *Las Fuentes de la Memoria. Fotografías y Sociedad en la España del s.XIX*. Barcelona: Lunwerg.

López-Ocón Cabrera, L. 1999. 'El Centro de Estudios Históricos: un Lugar de la Memoria', *Boletín de la Institución Libre de Enseñanza* 34/35: 27–48.

Malraux, A. 1949. *The Psychology of Art: the Museum without Walls*. London: Secker and Warburg.

Mederos Martín, A. 1999. 'El Joven Bosch Gimpera y la Primera Estructuración de la Prehistoria en España', *Boletín del Seminario de Arte y Arqueología* LXV: 9–28.

Mélida, J.R. 1897. 'Busto Prerromano Descubierto en Elche', *Revista de Archivos, Bibliotecas y Museos III*, 440–45.

Naranjo, J. 1997. 'Photography and Ethnography in Spain', *History of Photography* 21(1): 73–80.

Obermaier, H. and A. García y Bellido. 1947. *El hombre prehistórico y los orígenes de la humanidad*. Madrid: Revista de Occidente.

Olmos Romera, R. 1999. 'Una Utopía de Posguerra: El Corpus Vasorum Hispanorum' in J. Blánquez Pérez and L. Roldán Gómez (eds), *La Cultura Ibérica a Través de la Fotografía de Principios de Siglo. Vol. II, Las Colecciones Madrileñas*, pp. 155–66. Madrid: Universidad Autónoma de Madrid-Ministerio de Cultura.

Paris, P. 1903–1904. *Essai sur l´Art et l´Industrie de l´Espagne Primitive*. Paris: E. Lerona.

Pereira Sieso, J. 1987. *La Cerámica Pintada a Torno en Andalucía. Siglos VI-III a. C. Cuenca del Guadalquivir*. Madrid: Universidad Complutense.

Perrot, G. and Ch. Chipiez. 1894. *Histoire de l´Art dans l´Antiquité, Vol. VI Grèce primitive, l´Art Mycénien*. Paris: Typ. Georges Chamerot.

Petrie, W.F. 1904. *Methods and Aims in Archaeology*. London: Macmillan.

Rada y Delgado, J. de D. 1875. 'Antigüedades del Cerro de los Santos en término de Montealegre, conocidas vulgarmente bajo la denominación de antigüedades de Yecla', en *Museo Español de Antigüedades*, IV: 413-418.

Recht, R. 2003. 'Histoire de l´Art et Photographie', *Revue de l´art* 141: 5–8.

Riego, B. 2003. *Impresiones: la Fotografía en la Cultura del Siglo XIX (Antología de Textos)*. Girona: Centre de Recerca i Difusió de la Imatge.

Ruiz, A., A. Sánchez and J.P. Bellón. 2002. 'The History of Iberian Archaeology: One Archaeology for Two Spains', *Antiquity* 76 (291): 184–90.

Snyder, J. 1998. 'Nineteenth-Century Photography of Sculpture and the Rhetoric of Substitution', in G.A. Johnson (ed.), *Sculpture and Photography. Envisioning the Third Dimension*. Cambridge: Cambridge University Press, pp. 21–34.

Trachtenberg, A. 1989. *Reading American Photographs: Images as History, Matthew Brady to Walker Evans*. New York: Noonday Press.

VV.AA. 1889. *España Artística y Monumental*. Madrid: Viuda de Rodríguez.

Chapter 17

Frozen in Time

Photography and the Beginnings of Modern Archaeology in the Netherlands

Leo Verhart

Abstract

Photographs are an important source of information for the reconstruction of archaeological practice about 100 years ago. However, an excavation photograph provides a dual image of time. First, it is an image of archaeological research: an archaeological phenomenon sometimes thousands of years old. Second, it provides an image of the moment of exposure, as a result of the activities of an archaeologist. We are allowed a glimpse of life at that time. It is quite obvious that traces of the recent past can be discerned, where life a century ago comes into focus: the excavation itself, the small scale, simplicity, social relations, the countryside and, of course, the people themselves. All this can be found in the collection of nearly 4000 glass negatives, which are stored in the National Museum of Antiquities in Leiden, the Netherlands.

Introduction

Archaeology is a very strange scientific discipline. We as archaeologists study every detail of the remote past: soil traces, building constructions, art, pottery, flint, seeds, charcoal, use traces on flint tools, etc. But we know hardly anything of our own archaeological history. We are familiar with the history of the great discoveries. They are described in articles and books and we can even watch them on television. We know nearly all about the excavations of Troy and the opening of the burial chamber of Tutankamun. But what do we know about the history of archaeology in a country without such impressive finds? In the Netherlands no detailed records are available about how an excavation was conducted and organised, what exactly happened at a site, what kinds of methods were employed and how techniques and approaches in excavation were developed. We have to do our own archaeology, the archaeology of our discipline.

An important source of information is the photograph. A photographical image stops time. Time is captured in a single frame. The picture becomes a source of information showing us something of what happened at that particular moment. We study the picture and it raises any number of questions. What does it show, what does it represent, what is the meaning, what is the story behind the picture?

These are familiar questions an archaeologist faces in his investigation of the past. He – all archaeologists were male in the Netherlands 100 years ago – tries to paint a picture of the past, but with limited means. After all, there are no photographs from prehistory, just discolorations in the soil, sherds from pots, tools made of bone, stone and metal and remains of the humans themselves.

An excavation photograph of a century ago therefore provides a dual image of time. First, it is an image of archaeological research: an archaeological phenomenon sometimes thousands of years old. Second, it provides an image of the moment of exposure, as a result of the activities of an archaeologist. These photographs are an important source of information about excavations approximately 100 years ago. We are allowed a glimpse of life at that time. It is quite obvious that often it is not the centre of the picture that deserves most attention, but the edges. It is here that traces of the recent past can be discerned, where life a century ago comes into focus: the excavation itself, the small scale, simplicity, social relations, the countryside and, of course, the people themselves. All this can be found in the collection of nearly 4000 glass negatives, which are stored in the National Museum of Antiquities in Leiden (Verhart 2001).

A Very Short History of Dutch Archaeology

In the Netherlands archaeology is a relatively young science. Until the nineteenth century mainly art historians, practitioners of history and philologists were engaged in it. There were also amateurs, usually leading citizens, interested in the past of their immediate vicinity. Study was limited to objects found by accident in urban developments, construction of fortifications and canals or reclamation of wastelands.

That changed in 1818, when at the age of 25 Caspar Reuvens was made Professor Extraordinarius in archaeology at the University of Leiden, as well as Director of the National Museum of Antiquities (Brongers 2002; Halbertsma 2003, 2006). We are very proud to have the first professor in archaeology in the world, as is often claimed by us Dutchmen. He conducted several excavations, which were very sophisticated by modern standards. His premature death in 1835 brought an end to this promising scientific development in archaeology.

Not until 1905 would professional excavations return to the Netherlands. In the spring of 1905 the young Leiden archaeologist Jan Hendrik Holwerda (1873–1951) was trained in Germany at the Roman excavations at Halteren, led by the well-known Hans Dragendorff. There he learned to recognise all kinds of soil traces. The next summer he embarked on an impressive series of excavations. Fortifications, urnfields, megalithic monuments, barrows, churches and settlements were his objective. As a result of the activities of Holwerda, the National Museum of Antiquities became the leading excavating archaeological institution in the Netherlands.

Holwerda was the first to use a camera systematically in his archaeological investigations and his photographs provide a picture of his methods and what went on at an excavation site. He felt very strongly about popularisation of archaeology and must have understood at once the enormous potential of photographs. From that time onwards his excavation reports are lavishly decorated with pictures of the research in progress. There are no indications that he used the camera for exact scientific documentation purposes.

From 1917 onwards the Museum had a rival in Groningen. There, the young, ambitious archaeologist Albert Egges van Giffen (1884–1973) was active. He would finally dominate Dutch archaeology after the Second World War (Eickhoff 2003, 2006; Waterbolk 1976, 1989).

The development of pre-war Dutch archaeology was, in my opinion, linked to personal ambitions and had hardly any connection with the scientific development of archaeology in Europe at that time (Eickhoff 2003). What happened between Holwerda and Van Giffen?

The increasing field activities of Holwerda made it necessary to look for assistants. In 1911 a young biologist, Albert Egges van Giffen, was employed at the museum and he assisted Holwerda at his Roman excavation at Arentsburg near The Hague. In the summer of 1912 they both excavated in the province of Drenthe. Holwerda worked at the megalithic monument of Drouwen (Holwerda 1913) and Van Giffen excavated the Neolithic trackway of Buinen close by (Van Giffen

Fig. 17.1 The Dutch Society of Anthropology visits the excavation of the megalithic monument at Drouwen in 1912. Holwerda is the man with the beard between the stones, Van Giffen the man at the extreme right with his wife.

1913). When we look at the pictures from these excavations we see a striking difference. The excavation of Holwerda is rather old fashioned: a small excavation trench following the contour lines of the monument and soil heaps everywhere. In the background we see the portable hut from which Holwerda directed the excavation, where his wife served tea and were he could take a rest. In photographs for the publication we recognise also the romantic attitude of Holwerda. Very often labourers are used as scale bar.

Van Giffen had a totally different approach. His background as a biologist is clearly visible. His excavation is a combination of different levels and sections which provide a three-dimensional study of the archaeological phenomenon, similar to approaches in botany. There is a wide excavation trench and no romantic figures are visible.

During the period they conducted their excavations the Dutch Society of Anthropology visited the megalithic monument at Drouwen (Fig. 17.1). The gentlemen, some accompanied by their wives, posed on the monument in a way which is forbidden nowadays by our colleagues from cultural heritage. It is the only picture we have where we can see Holwerda and Van Giffen together.

Three months later the situation changed dramatically. In September 1912 Van Giffen accused Holwerda of scientific fraud and that became the start of a conflict that mushroomed out of control and even required intervention by the Prime Minister. The final result was that Van Giffen left for the University of Groningen. From that day onwards these scientists would sabotage each other for the rest of their lives, resulting in a 'Leiden' and 'Groningen' approach to archaeology. They never went to the same conferences, they never wrote letters to each other and as far as we now they never spoke to each other.

After the Second World War, archaeology experienced impressive developments in line with the vigorous economic growth in the Netherlands (Slofstra 1994; Van de Velde 2001). Excavations gained in scale and size and new methods, equipment, documentation and recording methods appeared as, for instance, at the Late Mesolithic settlement of Hardinxveld-Giessendam at a depth of 10 metres below groundwater table level (Louwe Kooijmans 2003).

The growth in archaeology was closely correlated with public support. This was one of the main differences with the pre-war period: no longer did archaeologists work in an ivory tower, they became community-based. The final result is that laws are made within a European context and large amounts of money become available. Managers with matching language and procedures run excavations like building projects. There is no resemblance at all between today's excavations and those of a century ago. Time goes on, even for archaeologists.

Why are Photographs Interesting?

When we look at the publications of excavations of one hundred years ago we will find hardly anything about the methods which were used. We get information about spoil traces and, of course, very detailed data on the finds. Very often we can read which landowner gave permission for the excavation, which well-known colleague scientist co-operated and which important citizens visited the excavation, but that is all. To know more about the people involved we have to search in the archives. If we are lucky, we find lists of labourers and what they earned. About excavation strategies we find nothing. So to reconstruct what happened at that time we have to do another kind of archaeology. Much of our information can be traced on the pictures of that time.

Making a picture during an excavation was not an easy undertaking at the beginning of the twentieth century. Of course, there were at that time relatively practical folding cameras that used small cassettes with glass negatives or flexible films, but for high-quality photographs large, heavy and unmanageable plate cameras were used. Glass negatives of various sizes could be used, but these would in general be 18 x 24 cm. The glass was covered with a layer of photosensitive emulsion. This emulsion was not very sensitive, necessitating relatively long exposure times. As a result people had to stand still for some time in order to provide a sharp picture. This is often visible in pictures where labourers are digging. These are always blurred due to their movements. When the work of labourers had to be recorded they all posed in more or less frozen postures.

We don't have any pictures of the photographer himself. The only glimpse of him is an occasional shadow at the edge of a photograph.

Excavation in Progress

The daily routine at an excavation can be traced on these pictures. Archaeologists love traditions. For a long time excavations were completely manual and small in scale. In the Netherlands approximately 10 labourers were employed per excavation, usually locally hired journeymen. They earned around 40 eurocents a day around 1910. Most excavations occurred in summer. This might be a single large, prolonged excavation or several smaller ones, often all over the country. These smaller excavations would take from a single day to several weeks. A barrow in a grave mound was investigated within a day. Only a long trench was dug to collect the finds and to draw the section.

The excavation leaders, almost always accompanied by their spouses, would stay in the better sort of hotel in the immediate vicinity and remain in contact with the rest of the world by letter and newspaper.

The tools that were used were simple: shovels and wheelbarrows and, when the investigation was sizeable, a narrow-gauge railway would be constructed that could carry a tipcart. The finds were packed in crates and shipped to the National Museum, until 1930 by cart and train, later in a special truck that was bought for that purpose by the museum. Finally the finds were cleaned, restored and exhibited in the museum.

Fig. 17.2 Holwerda's wheeled excavation hut at the excavation of Uddelermeer in 1910.

Fig. 17.3 The excavation of a grave mound at Vaassen in 1909.

Tents were erected as shelters from rain during the day and to store the excavation equipment. At first employees had to build their own accommodation. There were small tents for short stays and larger pavilions that would be erected for longer periods. These were visible from afar, more in particular because of the Dutch flag that would be flown as an indicator that the National Museum was excavating at that particular spot. Holwerda also had a wheeled excavation hut at his disposal that could be carted to the excavation area by horse (Fig. 17.2). The photographs are often of excellent quality. For instance in the picture of the wheeled excavation hut we can detect at Holwerda's feet a well-known Dutch quality newspaper, on the table stand a few cups of tea and at the back of the hut hangs a calendar on the wall indicating the second week of July 1910.

There was a clear hierarchy in the excavation. Labourers did all the work; the archaeologist watched and instructed, sometimes with a good cigar (Fig. 17.3). These differences are visible in everything: accommodation, clothes and activities. The labourers wear working clothes and old shoes or clogs. The archaeologist wears a suit and tie or cravat, hat and leather shoes. He is often sitting in a deckchair and lacks no comfort. Very seldom pictures were made in which the excavation leaders were portrayed together with the labourers. The only example is from one of Holwerda's first excavations in 1906. It is no surprise there are no photographs of an archaeologist actually wielding a shovel.

Finds and Traces

What is all this excavating really about? Of course about finds and treasures. Unfortunately no gold or royal tombs are found in the Netherlands, only everyday utensils and implements, some remains of foundations and lots and lots of soil traces. Even though this looks very normal and not so dramatic, yet archaeologists are excited when excavating. The remains of that dark past are eagerly sought. Beneath every scoop of soil something might lurk: important traces from a distant past.

Fig. 17.4 The discovery of the Roman sarcophagus at Simpelveld in 1930.

Fig. 17.5 Holwerda found soil traces beneath barrows, which he interpreted as the remnants of burned logs from a wooden superstructure, a primitive prehistoric translation of stone domed grave chambers from the Mediterranean.

And important finds do occur, although importance depends on its context. For some it is a sherd in their own backyard, for others a complete urn in an urnfield, an undamaged bell beaker or remnants of Roman cremations. Really dramatic is a find like the Roman sarcophagus from Simpelveld on 11 December 1930, which now occupies pride of place in the National Museum of Antiquities in Leiden (Fig. 17.4).

Soil discolorations on their own do not immediately provide a comprehensive picture of what went on in the past. Therefore reconstructions and models were manufactured and examples from the more recent past were used.

A famous misinterpretation is the reconstruction of the so-called domed tomb. Holwerda found soil traces beneath barrows, which he interpreted as the remnants of burned logs from a wooden superstructure (Fig. 17.5). These logs must have been the lower part of a wooden vaulted construction, which was covered by earth and sods (Holwerda 1910, 1912, 1918). A primitive prehistoric translation of stone domed grave chambers from the Mediterranean, as Holwerda thought. Shortly after the publication of his ideas his opponent Van Giffen demonstrated that these soil traces were in fact the relicts of an open ditch around the massive grave mound of soil and sods (Van Giffen 1922, 1924, 1930). There had never been a vault inside. Holwerda refused to believe it and for the rest of his life he held on to the idea of the domed tomb.

Visitors

The excavation usually occurred in the countryside or wastelands, what would nowadays be referred to as wildlife areas. Far from the centres of the civilised world traces and remains of our ancestors were searched for. As a result it was not easy to visit an excavation site, but apparently visitors enjoyed the outing. Colleagues would visit the excavation as a matter of course, but local dignitaries and members of learned societies and associations would appear as well. They must have announced their arrival, as often the photographer was present to record the important visitors for posterity.

Most important of course were members of the royal family. Early in Holwerda's career Queen Wilhelmina of Orange had become interested in archaeology and gave Holwerda an opportunity to investigate at her expense some barrows near her palace Het Loo at Apeldoorn (Van der Waals 1973). The Queen and her husband visited the excavation in 1907 and of course this had to be recorded, as Holwerda heeded royalty as well (Fig. 17.6). What should have been the climax for Holwerda turned into a disappointment: the picture was overexposed, due to the beautiful sunny weather and the

Fig. 17.6 Queen Wilhelmina of Orange visits the excavation of Niersen in 1907.

white dresses of the Queen and her lady-in-waiting. On a print he tried to retouch the picture, starting with the lady-in-waiting. The result was unsatisfactory and he relinquished his efforts. Finally he sent the original overexposed photograph to the Queen with a letter full of excuses.

Only one group of visitors has rarely been documented: the local people. They must have come often and in large numbers to visit these odd people, archaeologists from the big city. On the one hand with awe, on the other critical they will have followed the archaeologists' progress. Only rarely and by accident are they in a picture, their interest was obviously not important to the excavator. Local support for archaeology was not important at the time. Nowadays that has changed dramatically: the number of local people visiting an excavation site has become a measure of its success.

The Archaeologist as a Tourist

Archaeologists love to dig, but are observant as well. They enjoy the scenery, local customs and people. They travel a lot to visit sites and museums and document finds. In 1905 Holwerda made a tour through Germany. In the Landesmuseum in Trier he studied Iron Age pottery (Plate 13). He did not have time to draw all the pots so he took a photograph. Of course, and in accordance with the well-known frugality of Dutchmen, perhaps even more outstanding than the Scots, he tried to document as many pots as possible on one photograph.

In the immediate vicinity of the excavation the picturesque was recorded in particular, mostly farms, but terrain as well. Another reason for recording objects in the immediate vicinity is that these often are a source of inspiration when interpreting excavation data. There are, for instance, pictures of sod huts, derelict and primitive sheds and half-timbered houses where traditional construction techniques have been applied.

Notwithstanding his enthusiasm and fixation on archaeology – quite similar to us today – a social conscience was not absent in the archaeologist. On a trip to Drenthe the decline and poverty in the Netherlands were recorded: a derelict windmill and a sod hut with occupants (Fig. 17.7). In

Figure 17.7 A picture of a sod hut in the province of Drenthe around 1900.

front of the sod hut stands a mother with one child by the hand and two other children. The mother wears a dress that is black with dirt. The hut is dilapidated and made of old building materials. Outside are a chamber pot and a tin bath. A sorry, damp and muddy spectacle: an archaeologist's picture of society at that time.

Conclusion

Old photographs revealed unexpected aspects of the history of archaeology. They are a rich and valuable source of information. Apart from that we like them also for their picturesque aspects and sometimes we can smile about what we see from these long forgotten days.

We have to be very careful with these valuable documents. Glass plates are very breakable and the photosensitive emulsion is very vulnerable to light, in particular. They have to be kept in the dark but modern digitising techniques make it possible to access this important source of information. In the National Museum we are currently working on scanning, cataloguing and describing the glass plates so that they can be seen in the near future on the internet.

These photographs give us information about a time when not all was recorded in the way we are used to nowadays. But we have to be aware that the next generation will look and study our pictures probably in the same way. There will always be questions in the future that we do not think of today.

References

Brongers, J.A. 2002. Een vroeg begin van de moderne archeologie: leven en werken van Cas Reuvens (1793–1835). Nederlandse Archeologische Rapporten 23. Amersfoort.

Eickhoff, M. 2003. De oorsprong van het 'eigene'. *Nederlands vroegste verleden, archeologie en nationaal-socialisme*. Amsterdam.

——. 2006. This volume.

Giffen, A.E. van. 1913. 'De Buinerbrug en het Steenen voetpad aldaar.' *Oudheidkundige Mededeelingen van het Rijksmuseum van Oudheden te Leiden* 7, 51–90.

——. 1922. 'Een dubbele grafheuvel uit den steen- en bronstijd te Harendermolen bij Groningen.' *Verslag van den Toestand van het Museum van Oudheden voor Provincie en Stad Groningen*, 59–67.

——. 1924. 'Ein Neolithischer Grabhügel mit Holzkonstruktion in Harendermolen, Gem. Haren, Prov. Groningen, Niederlande.' *Prähistorische Zeitschrift* XV, 52–61.

——. 1930. *Die Bauart der Einzelgräber. Beitrag zur Kenntnis der älteren individuellen Grabhügelstrukturen in den Niederlanden*. Leipzig

Halbertsma, R.B. 2003. *Scholars, Travellers and Trade. The Pioneer Years of the National Museum of Antiquities in Leiden, 1818–1840*. London.

——. 2006. This volume.

Holwerda, J.H. 1910. 'Das alteuropäische Kuppelgrab. Eine Ausgrabung bei Vassen, Provinz Gelderland in den Niederlanden. Praehistorische nederzettingen aan het Uddelermeer.' *Prähistorische Zeitschrift* 3/4, 374–79.

——. 1912. 'Opgravingen aan het Uddelermeer.' *Oudheidkundige Mededeelingen van het Rijksmuseum van Oudheden te Leiden* 6, 1–16.

——. 1913. 'Zwei Riesenstuben bei Drouwen (Prov. Drenthe) in Holland.' *Prähistorische Zeitschrift* 5, 435–48.

——. 1918. *Nederland's Vroegste Geschiedenis*. Amsterdam.

Louwe Kooijmans, L.P. 2003. 'The Hardinxveld sites in the Rhine/Meuse Delta, the Netherlands, 5500–4500 cal BC.' In: L. Larsson, H. Kindgren, K. Knutsson, D. Loeffler and A. Åkerlund (eds.), *Mesolithic on the Move*. Papers presented at the Sixth International Conference on the Mesolithic in Europe, Stockholm 2000. Oxford, 608–24.

Slofstra, J. 1994. 'Recent Developments in Dutch Archaeology.' *Archaeological Dialogues* 1, 9–55.

Velde, P. van de. 2001. 'Netherlands.' In: T. Murray (ed.), *Encyclopidea of Archaeology*. Santa Barbara, 919–34.

Verhart, L. 2001. 'Dubbelfocus.' *Nederlandse opgravingsfoto's uit 1900–1940*. Abcoude.

Waals, J.D. van der. 1973. In Opdracht van hare Majesteit. In W.A. van Es, A.V.M. Hubrecht, P. Stuart, W.C. Mank and S.L. Wynia (eds.), *Archeologie en Historie. Bussum*, 509–20.

Waterbolk, H.T. 1976. 'Albert Egges van Giffen, Noordhorn 14 maart 1884–Zwolle 31 mei 1973.' *Jaarboek van de Maatschappij der Nederlandse letterkunde te Leiden 1975–1976*, 122–53.

——. 1989. 'Het was een mooie tijd en er viel veel te doen. De archeoloog A.E. van Giffen (1884–1973).' In G.A. van Gemert, J. Schuller tot Peursum-Meijer and A.J. Vanderjagt (eds.), *Om niet aan de onwetendheid n barbarij te bezwijken. Groningse geleerden 1614–1989*. Hilversum, 207–26.

Part IV
QUESTIONS OF IDENTITY

Chapter 18
Choosing Ancestors

The Mechanisms of Ethnic Ascription in the Age of Patriotic Antiquarianism (1815–1850)

Ulrike Sommer

Abstract

The years after the Vienna Congress (1815) saw the first systematic attempts at an ethnic ascription of archaeological finds in the German territories. A common 'patriotic' past was seen as an incentive to create a unified German national state. In the climate of political oppression and tight censorship after the Carlsbad Decrees, an idealised past served as a model for a more democratic future yet to be achieved. Numerous antiquarian and historical societies started a programme of enthusiastic if not very systematic excavations that were intended to illuminate the prehistoric past and to clarify the ethnic identity of the makers of the 'heathen urns' thus discovered. The criteria used for these ascriptions were ethnic stereotypes taken from historical and folkloristic sources. Folklore, linguistics, especially place-name studies, the history of law, history and personal empathy were seen as equally valid sources for a reconstruction of a 'heathen' past, the chronological depth of which had not yet been perceived. Contrary to common opinion, it was not always a Germanic past that was referred to. In the east of Germany, the industrious and cultured Slavs were preferred to the nomadic and uncouth Germanic tribes. While in South-West Germany, the Celts were often preferred as ancelors. It can be shown that the localised nature of many interpretations prevented the formation of a specific archaeological typology and terminology. This raises the question: did archaeology have to become nationalist in order to reach the status of an autonomous scholarly discipline?

Introduction

In 1825, three friends, the physician Julius Schmidt, Deacon Friedrich Alberti and the cleric M. Meißner, 'who had long since kept a vigilant eye on prehistoric remains in the area' decided to found an Antiquarian Society for the tiny Duchy of Reuß-Schleiz (316.7 km²) in Hohenleuben (fig. 18. 1). At that time, the town had about 1900 inhabitants. It was the seat of the local court of law, a 'decent cattle market' and of some textile mills (*Brockhaus* encyclopaedia for 1832: 374).

Thus, 'the Voigtland Antiquarian Society has joined the numerous societies and associations that have already united in all parts of Germany for research into the patriotic antiquity and for the preservation of its relics. It has obeyed the call of the times that everywhere reminds and exhorts to tend and honour the national history and to cultivate it carefully in the sure knowledge that a country will cease to exist if it does not hold its history in high regard.' (*Variscia* 1, 1829:

Fig. 18.1 Map of the Thuringian states, 1816–1848. Source: after Zentralinstitut für Geschichte der Akademie der Wissenschaften der DDR 1989.

99). It started its existence with 16 members, 'men united by their love of patriotic antiquities' (*Variscia* 1, 1829: 100). The founding members were predominantly clerics and public servants, with physicians and merchants making up the rest. The express aim of the society was to conduct research into patriotic antiquities and to work for their preservation. This 'Voigtländische Altertumsforschende Verein' is a good example of the work of German Antiquarian Societies in the period before 1848. It is, however, exceptional in that it conducted numerous excavations that had quite a high standard for the times, and started an extensive and well ordered antiquarian collection still extant today.[1]

In this paper I propose to examine in some detail the methods used by the early antiquarians in interpreting their finds, and more generally to assess the ways political and economic developments in Germany influenced the scope and aims of antiquarian research in the first half of the nineteenth century.

During the fight against Napoleon, the so-called 'Liberation Wars', German national feeling had surged. Volunteer regiments and a broad patriotic movement played an important part in the defeat of the 'foreign occupiers'. This was fuelled by hopes for a unified German state, constitutional monarchy, equal vote, the right of association and a free press. The new European order created at the Vienna Congress in 1815 put an end to these aspirations. While the plethora of often tiny and widely scattered statelets of the Old Empire had been significantly reduced, the new German Alliance (Deutscher Bund) still contained 41 sovereign territories and cities. The former members of the Rhenian Confederation, Bavaria, Württemberg, Baden and Saxony, together with Hanover, Hesse-Darmstadt and the Electorat Hesse formed middle-sized entities. Austria and Prussia were European powers, the territories of both including a sizeable proportion of non-German speaking peoples. Their rivalry precluded any attempt at further unification.

This impasse led to the specific German idea of a nation based on a spiritual, rather than political unity, the Cultural Nation (Kulturnation). National unity was based on the specific spirit of the people (Volksgeist). The philosopher of law Friedrich Karl von Savigny, for example, claimed in 1815 that it was less important to construct a unified civil code than to find the historical essence of the legal system and to design, or rather to rediscover and adapt laws which would conform to the German national genius (Jacobeit 1965, see also Heuer 1963).

The search for a genuine German culture could either entail a quietist escape from the pressures of the political reaction or an attempt to further political unity and to create a template for this future state. The years after the Vienna Congress thus saw both the systematic collection of medieval historical sources (*Monumenta Germaniae Historia*) and the first systematic attempts at ethnic ascriptions of archaeological finds in the German territories. A common 'patriotic past' was to be an incentive to create a unified German national state.

At this time, the nascent discipline of German Studies included linguistics, folklore, the history of law, comparative religion, history of art, history and antiquarian studies (Halub 1997). History was still dominated by culture history (see Schleier 2003 for an overview) or Romanticism and systematically incorporated antiquarian research. Many histories of this time start with a timeless, idealised prehistoric past encompassing everything that was known of pre-Roman times and collapsing it into one single picture of 'the' Germanic, Celtic or Slavonic life, based on classical and medieval sources, and allegedly prehistoric relics in folktales, medieval laws and romantic speculations. When strict press censorship, a ban on political associations, police supervision of suspect university teachers and students and a hunt for 'demagogues' were instituted according to the Carlsbad Decrees (1819), scholars looked for freedom in the dark Germanic (or Slavonic, as its was) forests.[2]

In this framework, history is only set in motion by the appearance of the Roman invaders in the West, conquering degenerate Franks, avaricious Christian missionaries or the Ottonic kings in the East. In a way, this was a cyclical history, and the Germans had to regain what they had lost when this history was set into motion – freedom, laws, nationhood, and a pure national language.

In Germany, the end of the Napoleonic Wars thus marked the transition from an universalist antiquarian tradition (Schnapp 2002) to a patriotic antiquarianism, where the main emphasis was placed on local finds. Even if patriotic antiquities had 'less pleasing forms' than finds from classical antiquity, they were evidence of the local past (*Heimathsgeschichte*), and the educated public was encouraged to be at home in German prehistory as well as in the temples and streets of Rome and Athens (Preusker 1841: v).

The Foundation of Antiquarian Societies in Germany

Before 1815, antiquarian research had mainly been the work of individuals. Most of the Humanistic societies had become defunct by the first half of the eighteenth century. Some Enlightenment societies, like the 'Churfürstlich Mayntzische Academie nützlicher Wissenschaften zu Erfurt' (founded in 1754, Döring and Nowak 2000), the 'Privatgesellschaft in der Lausitz' (1799, Homann 2004) or the 'Gesellschaft für nützliche Forschungen zu Trier' (1801, Merten 2000) did conduct archaeological research. But this was for them one activity among many, all directed at increasing knowledge in general and improving the common welfare.

After 1815, a new type of society came into being that was normally dominated by the bourgeoisie and directed at one specific goal only, like joint reading, music, social reform – or antiquarian research (Nipperdey 1972). Socialising was an important function as well, and the German governments often suspected political activities, as was certainly the case in many societies for physical education (*Turnvereine*). The 1820s saw a wave of new antiquarian societies (see Erhard 1835, Klüpfel 1844, and fig. 18.2). The 'Gesellschaft für ältere deutsche Geschichte', founded in 1819 in Frankfurt am Main by the Reichsfreiherr Karl Friedrich von Stein had a pan-German scope, but soon concentrated solely on editing Medieval sources. Most societies were confined to a single German state or a specific region within a state (Marwinski 1979). In some states, like the Kingdom of Bavaria and the Kingdom of Württemberg, historical societies were officially encouraged as a means to acquire local traditions for the newly formed territories (Heimpel 1963: 10); other governments viewed the activities of the societies with mistrust. When the 'Gesellschaft für Beförderung der Geschichtskunde' in Freiburg called for a national historical society, Metternich, the Austrian foreign secretary opposed it on the grounds that 'any congregation of scholars and writers in the historical and political disciplines will inevitably lead to dangerous and dubious activities, even if not intended as such originally' (Jacobeit 1965: 33f).

Membership of the Voigtland society was strictly local. A change of residence normally meant leaving the society, corresponding members were extremely rare. The monthly meetings in Hohenleuben formed the basis for the work of the society. As the town was difficult to reach

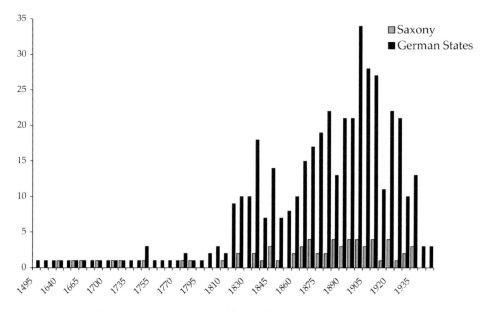

Fig. 18.2 Foundation dates of German antiquarian and historical societies.

(nearby Greiz received a railway connection in 1865, Hohenleuben itself only in 1883, cf. Maak 2000), especially in winter, branches were formed in other towns in the area. These rarely lasted long, as they either expired after a few years (Greiz) or dissented to form independent societies, like the Plauen branch, based in the biggest regional town. In some German countries, branch societies were actually forbidden, as the governments feared coordinated political activities.

As corporate memberships did not exist, a network of corresponding and honorary membership served to establish both national and international contacts. In special cases, the rulers of the territories in question were made honorary members. Thus, all rulers of the neighbouring Reuß principalities were honorary members of the Voigtland Society as well as Grand Duke Friedrich-Franz of Mecklenburg-Schwerin, Friedrich August of Saxony and Crown Prince Johann (later King Johann) of Saxony, while the King of Prussia is conspicuously absent. In turn, as was common practice, Prince Heinrich 62nd of Reuß-Schleiz was made honorary member of the Royal Nordic society in Copenhagen in 1833, 'as an ardent promoter of learning'. Scholars who had made important discoveries were sometimes made honorary members as well, in the hope of acquiring first-hand information and finds for the collection. This was the case, for example, with Friedrich Wagner, the excavator of a prehistoric 'sanctuary' at Schlieben, Brandenburg (e.g. Wagner 1828, 1833), and the influential antiquarian Benjamin Preusker in Lusatia.

The exchange of publications was the most important method for establishing a library and for keeping in contact with other societies. Publications and correspondence were read and discussed in the monthly meetings and sometimes published in the local newspapers as well. The number of exchange partners rose from seven in 1833 to 101 in 1876, and soon there were problems in housing the growing library (379 titles in 1833, 3,687 in 1874).

While the activities were local, their interest had a national, sometimes an international scope. When the members of the Voigtland society learnt that the Historical Society of America in Boston had discovered burial mounds at the Mississippi covered by trees at least 600 years old and containing skeletons 'in no way similar to those of the present-day savages', they decided to contact the American society in order to 'obtain antiquities or at least accurate drawings in exchange for Germanic antiquities' (*Variscia* 2 1830, 127). The merchant Heinrich Kretschmann was asked to pass a letter to the Boston Society to an American friend who was visiting the Leipzig fair. Unfortunately, the proceedings do not mention if contact was indeed established, and, as the society anticipated, 'a beam of light shed on the history of mankind by a comparison with German finds' (*Variscia* 1830: 128).

In the 1820s, numerous antiquarian and historical societies started enthusiastic if not very systematic excavations intended to illuminate the prehistoric past and to clarify the ethnic identity of the makers of the 'heathen urns' thus discovered. The criteria used for these ascriptions were ethnic stereotypes taken from historical and folkloristic sources. Folklore, linguistics, especially place-name studies, the history of law, history and personal empathy were seen as equally valid sources for a reconstruction of a pagan past whose chronological depth had not yet been realised.

Ethnic ascription was straightforward when the written sources mentioned only a single people. But this was the case in only some parts of northern Germany. The southwest and the Rhineland had been settled by Celts when the Romans first arrived, the area east of the River Elbe had been inhabited by Germanic tribes according to Tacitus, Ptolemy and Strabo, but had a Slavonic population by the time of the Carolingians and the Ottonic conquest. Further north-east, the Old Prussians, a people with a Baltic language, had settled in East Prussia when the Teutonic knights conquered the area in the late Middle Ages.

From the beginning, the members of the Voigtland society were keen on digging and exploring the remains of the past. When 'ancient skeletons' were discovered in a garden in Ranis in 1826, the society bought the lot in order to excavate it. Nine graves were excavated in 1826, 33 graves in the following year. In the remaining area bones and charcoal were discovered as well as "traces of former graves". This was taken as an indication that the graves had already been opened by 'earlier generations', and the excavation was stopped (Schmidt 1829: 82).

No plan of the cemetery was drawn, but the arrangement of the graves in orderly rows is described. Deacon Börner, who had conducted the excavation, provides a detailed description of each grave, containing the position of the skeleton, the position of the grave gifts, a description of their form and material. Sometimes the depth of a grave and its relation to other burials is mentioned as well. The descriptions are not standardised, but at this time it is rather unusual that the grave-inventories were kept separate at all. The finds from graves and the surrounding soil were kept separate as well, which indicates that an idea of context existed (Schmidt 1829).

The sex of the skeletons was identified, and juvenile and adults were distinguished. Julius Schmidt was a physician, and it can be assumed that the sexing was based on the skeletons, not on the grave goods. Indeed Schmidt had published an article, 'influence of climate, nutrition and race on size', in which he analysed size, pathology, race, robusticity and mental abilities of the former inhabitants of Germany, as deduced from the position of the foramen magnum and from phrenological traits (Schmidt 1829). Following this excavation report, the editor of the proceedings of the society, Deacon Friedrich Alberti (1796–1861) attempted to elucidate who had been buried at Ranis – even if the patriotic past was still hidden by dark veils, and the German antiquarian research too young to be able to explain everything (Alberti 1830a: 94). In the following section, I propose to examine his reasoning at some length (somewhat reorganising his arguments in the process), because they exemplify the methods used for ethnic ascription by the antiquarians of his day.

Finds from Ranis

Deacon Alberti identified the burials as pagan for the following reasons: they were not located near a church, the skeletons did not face eastwards but had various orientations, and some of the finds, such as sacrificial vessels, iron bird-figures and amulets 'obviously' indicated pagan beliefs. The preservation of the skeletons was good, not only of the solid bones of adults, but even the 'fragile, sponge-like bones of small children' (1830a: 97). Since the sandy soil was not conductive to the preservation of perishable objects, the burials were not expected to be of extremely high antiquity.

Alberti saw a number of indications that the people buried at Ranis had been peasants:

- The graves were numerous and had been dug in orderly rows, 'that ought to be exemplary for many Christian graveyards of our times' (1830a: 107)
- The cemetery was located in a fertile plain.
- Sheers for sheep had been found, a certain sign of husbandry.

All graves were inhumations. The question whether cremation was typical for Slavs or for Germani had already been discussed at some length in antiquarian circles, and Alberti cites parts of this discussion, finally deciding that the pagan German tribes of later antiquity commonly burnt their dead. Thus, the Ranis graves could not be Germanic.

Now Alberti turns to the finds:

- A piece of mummified substance had been found in one grave, and even put through a chemical analysis by the local apothecary. No ancient source gives indications that embalming was known to the Germani, but an early medieval source mentions that the Prussians tended to keep the bodies of the dead as long as possible. Embalming had been known in Bohemia as well, and Alberti cites two finds of mummies. Thus, 'these historical hints indicate that the Slavs were no strangers to the practice of embalming, and the mummy-like substance found in our graves makes them far more likely to be Slavonic.' (Alberti 1830a: 103).

- Sheep shears were known only from countries settled by Slavs. Alberti cites some parallels, showing a good knowledge of contemporary antiquarian sources.
- There are snake ornaments on the urns, and bracelets with snake-heads. Slavonic people were known to worship snakes, and Alberti cites a number of historical and folkloristic sources to strengthen his argument.

But it was the general furnishing of the graves that formed Alberti's central argument:

- The graves contained few weapons, but rich ornaments (Fig. 18.3), which indicates a people of a high degree of civilisation who 'preferred the arts of peace to the rough trade of war'.
- The female graves contained numerous ornaments. This was an unmistakable sign of some refinement, even luxury, and indicated a people 'among whom a higher degree of culture, industriousness and trade was to be found' (Alberti 1830a: 105), in contrast to 'true' savages, who mistreated their womenfolk.[3]

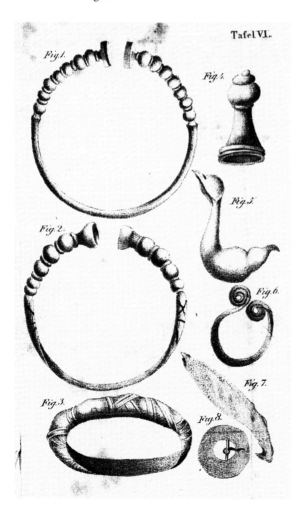

Both features indubitably pointed to a Slavonic origin of the finds, and Alberti gives a number of examples of the culturally advanced state of the Medieval Slavs. As Slavonic tribes had migrated into the Voigtland area during the fifth century and were at least partly pagan up to AD 1126, the Ranis cemetery was identified as Slavonic 'with complete certainty'.

Excavations on the Erisberg took place in the spring of 1827 (Alberti 1830b). Urns were found directly under the greensward. Several groups of urns were observed, placed in circles, the biggest always in the centre, filled with ash, horse's teeth and bird bones. Alberti gives a description of the raw material, the colour and the decoration of the urns; the shape is not mentioned. Only two pieces of 'composition', a metal not yet identified as bronze were found in the urns, one of which fell to dust when touched. Unfortunately,

Fig. 18.3 Finds from Ranis. Source: Alberti (1830: Table 4).

there are no illustrations. According to the description of the pottery the urns most probably belonged to the late Bronze Age (Lusatian Culture).

Friedrich Alberti identified the finds from the Erisberg as Germanic, probably Chattic, as there were place-names in the vicinity containing the element 'kat', like Katzenmühle, Katzenstein, Kattenloch). He gives the following reasons for this interpretation:

- The finds are of a 'noble simplicity' compared with those from Ranis and therefore had to be older.
- The dead had been cremated, the urns were covered with greensward, and teeth of horses were preserved. This was typically Germanic, the rite had been described by Tacitus in his Germania (27).

A barrow near Wernburg was excavated in 1829. The barrow seems to have been excavated completely, and not simply funnelled into from the top, as was often the case later on. At least five inhumations were found, one disturbed by a later burial. Again, the position of the individual graves and the respective grave gifts are described, though without a plan no really clear picture of the relative positions of the skeletons emerges. Two skeletons were buried exactly above each other, 'the long bones directly in contact, without any soil in between'. Deacon Börner, the excavator, discusses the position of the finds and the skeletons in details to elucidate which grave gifts belong to which burial, but in the end decides that the bigger vessel and the sword must belong to the bigger skeleton, 'whom nature had definitely formed as a hero' (Anon 1830: 90).

While emphasising his status as amateur, Börner reached a number of conclusions regarding the chronological relation between the different excavations:

- All graves are undoubtedly from the pagan period, as they include vessels (grave gifts).
- The Wernburg graves are partly contemporaneous with the Ranis burials, as some implements show a similar design (except the iron ones).
- The Wernburg graves are at least in part younger than the ones from Ranis, because iron is used more commonly and in a more refined way. Comparable objects are more frequently and more intensely decorated, there are for example brooches inlaid with enamel and vitreous sherds. Alberti (1830b: 106) in contrast, interpreted the burials from Wernburg as the family burial of a Sorabian chieftain (Župan), because of the similarity of the finds to those from Ranis, the isolated position of the burial and the quality of the grave gifts.

The excavation of a medieval cellar in Oepitz in 1833, interpreted by Alberti (1830b) as a Slavonic homestead, completed the picture of daily life in pagan antiquity. Numerous other excavations followed, but the members of the society were assured that the 'basic lines' of the patriotic past had been reconstructed. The ethnic ascription of these finds became the generally accepted framework for the classification of other finds from the area. The following general rules were deduced:

- Slavonic graves are always to be found in plains or river valleys, near settlements.
- Graves on hills or mountains are always Germanic.
- The Germani used single, haphazardly distributed barrows, the Slavs placed their graves in orderly rows.
- The Slavs never burned their dead.

As it happens, some of the methods employed by Alberti and his antiquarian co-workers are still in use today. A comparison with other finds of a seemingly secure attribution (for example, finds from 'purely Slavonic areas', like Bohemia) was commonly used. Scholars like Benjamin Preusker (1786–1851) in Saxony paid close attention to the association of finds and argued, for example, that finds occurring in graves with Roman objects had to be younger than those never found together with Roman material (Preusker 1840). Starting with Dobrowski (1786), burial customs were seen as important, and their ethnic nature was discussed using both classical authors, medieval and folklore sources. Foreseeably, no agreement was ever reached.

Other methods have fallen out of favour. Thus, the preservation of finds was taken as a sign of their age, even if the influence of the soil was acknowledged from early on.

But the most important clues for an ethnic ascription were the historically known traits and the mentality of a people. Johann Gottfried Herder (1784–1791) and other authors after him had described the Slavonic love for agriculture, and therefore all remains in fertile low-lying areas were Slavonic. Tacitus had described the warlike nature of the Germanic tribes, and therefore graves with weapons had to be Germanic. As the Germani were not inclined towards the cultivation of the fields, but enjoyed hunting instead, graves on hills were seen as Germanic as well. Some authors used the nomadic nature of the Germanic tribe of the Suevi, as described by Strabo (Geographica) to ascribe all finds to the Slavs, as the itinerant Germani were unlikely to leave any traces behind.

The sources used to determine these national characteristics were quite varied. Classical authors, medieval sources, modern folkloristic sources, ethnographic observations on the customs of the savages and 'common knowledge' were used. We can speak of 'dating by received wisdom' or dating by prejudice.

Even if 'modern' methods were used, they were often doomed to failure. Comparisons with other areas had to rely almost exclusively on descriptions, as illustrations were expensive and therefore rare. The undeveloped descriptive language meant that comparisons had to be limited to the occurrence of (undefined) general classes of artefacts, like shears or knifes, or the colour of pottery. Sometimes a description of the pottery-ornaments and striking features like deliberately bent weapons could be utilised. The emphasis on the burial rite (inhumation vs. cremation) should be understood in this context. As finds were few, and their interpretation was uncritically accepted, accidental discoveries, like the two Bohemian mummies mentioned above could seriously misdirect enquiries. The lack of chronological depth meant that two, at most three different peoples were assumed to have existed in a given territory, and oral tradition was expected to provide a tenuous connection to the most distant past. Chronological differences were simply not looked for.

Alain Schnapp (2002: 135) places the birth of archaeology as an independent discipline in the mid-nineteenth century, in the context of the emergence of a positivist science. In Germany, the failed revolution of 1848 and its aftermath of political repression and tight censorship led to a sharp decline in antiquarian activities and retarded the development of the nascent discipline.

Reinhold Resch (1859: 99) of the Voigtland Society lauded the politically benevolent nature of antiquarian research:

> While the intellectual trend that almost wholly ignored history and antiquarian studies has led to several dangerous deceptions both in private life and in the affairs of the government, antiquarians are mostly completely harmless people, who have quarrelled and fought over hypotheses, but have always cared for the preservation of all relics of the

242 | ARCHIVES, ANCESTORS, PRACTICES

past, even the tiniest, to give the present as well as future generations a solid foundation
for their endeavours.

This failed to impress his contemporaries. During the 1848 revolution, a number of societies failed
altogether, for example the formerly very active Sinsheim society in Baden. The overall number of
publications declined sharply.

Alberti and the other founders of the Hohenleuben Society never formally revoked their
interpretations. The late acceptance of Thomsen's three-age system in Germany meant that local
traditions persisted, especially in remote places like the Voigtland.

Rudolf Virchow (1821–1902), who travelled incessantly and seems to have visited not only
every major archaeological conference, but every German archaeological society as well (see Andree
1976: 17–48, Brather this volume), inspected the Hohenleuben collection in 1874 (*Festschrift zur
Feier des fünfzigjährigen Bestehens des vogtländischen Alterthumsforschenden Vereins in Hohenleuben
nebst dem 44. 45. und 46 Jahresbericht und Festbericht* 1876: 12). In the report of his visit to the
Congress at Jena, he mentioned a number of finds, among them from the cemetery of Ranis, where
he measured the skulls. Virchow did not try to date them, only identified them as 'pre-Frankish'. As
he had identified finds of the 'Burgwall type', that is, early medieval Slavonic pottery, with which he
was very familiar from the 1860s on, and remarked on the really curious pottery vessels from Ranis
with a 'delicate smooth surface and clean ornaments', they obviously had not rung a bell. With his
mainly east-German expertise, these La Tène (late Iron Age) vessels were unfamiliar to Virchow.

With the foundation of the German Society for Anthropology, Ethnology and Prehistory
(DAG) in 1870, influenced by the discoveries of Boucher de Perthes and the Swiss pile dwellings,
a positivist, universalist orientation became predominant in German archaeology. Rudolf Virchow,
the most influential prehistorian of the day, called for the abandonment of 'parochial attempts' to
ascribe finds to a historically attested people in favour of a 'scientific approach' that aimed at the
construction of a chronological and geographical framework on a national and international scale
(Virchow 1875). In his opinion, the era of local antiquarian societies was over.

It lay in the nature of these societies that the direction of research followed a certain
predestined direction. The historian will never abandon the idea that prehistory should
be understood in connection with the real history, and that the essential agents of history,
on which the antiquarian should primarily fix his attention should be the same. So in
Germany inevitably the great nationalities that had, one after the other, competed for the
rule of our territory, Celt, German and Slav, formed the central field of research as long
as it was in the hand of the societies. Even nowadays there is a certain predisposition to
connect to each work of art, each anthropological object, each settlement or fortification
an epitheton, not only as *ornans*, but as *significans*, and to say: these are Celtic
fortifications, Slavic weapons, Germanic buttons, etc. … This type of approach has
always retained a local character. (Virchow 1875: 6f.)

Virchow vigorously denied any connection between modern nation and prehistoric settlement. In
reaction to the claim of the French anthropologist Armand de Quatrefages that the 'Prussian race'
was not of Germanic, but of Finnish extraction, he refused to see any connection between the
modern German nation and 'long lost tribal characteristics' (Virchow 1872: 301).

This positivist prehistory, a part of the general science of man was quite influential (between
1880 and 1910, the DAG had between 2000 and 1600 members), there were numerous local
anthropological societies, periodicals and a steadily rising number of publications. But the nascent
discipline faced difficulties at getting established at the university level. Hermann Schaaffhausen

(1816–1893), now mainly known for the first scientific description of the Neanderthal skull, held an extraordinary chair at Bonn that gave him no say in university politics. He got a chair only shortly before his death, after which it remained vacant. Johannes Ranke (1836–1916) had to manoeuvre between the medical, the philosophical faculty and the Bavarian department of education for over twenty years until the Munich anthropological institute was founded in 1886 (Sommer and Struve 2006). The establishment of the new discipline was hampered by the understandable reluctance of the faculties to give up positions in her favour. The ambiguous position between the sciences and the humanities did not help, and the administration did not see any need for innovation. Only in rare cases did a combination of scientific brilliance and personal persistence result in a successful institutionalisation.

Normally, scientific brilliance was not enough to sway politicians. As the calls for anthropological and prehistoric chairs became more frequent from the 1890s onwards, two lines of argument emerged. The first, with an emphasis on ethnography, tried to utilise the colonial craze. In order to successfully expand trade-interests and to administer the newly acquired German 'protectorates', anthropological specialists were needed to accompany German administrators and German battleships (Waldeyer 1899, Buschan 1900, Weule 1902, Beltz 1919). The second line, represented mainly by Gustaf Kossinna (1858–1931) and connected to linuguistics and history, argued that German National consciousness should be bolstered by a discipline concerned with its prehistoric roots (Kossinna 1896: 605). While Kossinna received an extraordinary chair at Berlin in 1904, the full force of the argument did not develop until 1918. The loss of the colonies had cost the ethnological school its political impact. At the same time, the 'national catastrophe' created a perceived need for a glorious and ethnically homogeneous past, and this need was not filled by the universalist anthropology of Ranke and Virchow, but by the blatant nationalism and expansionism of Kossinna and his pupils. Richard (2002) has demonstrated for France how military defeat created an intellectual climate benevolent to the institutionaliation of prehistory. A similar development can be seen in Germany, where the first chair of prehistory was created in 1927 in Marburg.

It may seem strange that prehistoric archaeology did not develop methods for the identification of prehistoric people, a matter which had been the core problem of archaeology since its very emergence as a discipline. But the answers were always already there. The choice of ancestors followed political expediency, determined by forces exterior to archaeology, while the need for ancestors in general was rarely questioned. It was only in the positivist era, and then again in the 1960s that doubt was thrown on the timeless existence of peoples at all. In its formative period, archaeology developed around an empty core, as it were, and it still has not completely managed to perceive, let alone correct this blind spot.

Notes

1. There is no detailed history of the Society, http://home.t-online.de/home/museumreichenfels/vg71.htm offers a short summary.
2. This later on led Karl Marx to inquire in his famous 'Critique of Hegel's legal philosophy' (MEW 1, 380), what it was that differentiated this Germanic freedom from the freedom of a wild boar?
3. The idea of the females as drudges of the males among savage people was quite widespread at the time. It was derived, among others, from Georg Forster's (1777: 511) description of his journey around the World with Captain Cook: 'Among all savage nations the weaker sex is ill-treated, and the law of the strongest is put into force. Their women are mere drudges, who prepare raiment and provide dwellings, who cook and frequently collect their food, and are requited by blows and all kinds of severity. At New Zeeland it seems they carry this tyranny to excess, and the males are taught from their earliest age, to hold their mothers in contempt, contrary to all our principles of morality.'

References

Alberti, F. 1830a. 'Nachgrabungen in der Umgegend von Ranis, besonders auf dem von den voigtländischen Alterthumsforschenden Verein erkauften Gartengrundstücke daselbst. Nach den Berichten dortiger Alterthumsfreunde, insbesondere aber nach dem Diarium des Herrn Diac. Börner daselbst, bearbeitet von Diac. Fr. Alberti', *Variscia, Mitteilungen aus dem Archiv des Vogtländischen Altertumsforschenden Vereins* 2: 61–85.

———. 1830b. 'Vergleichender Ueberblick der in der Umgegend von Ranis und Wernburg angestellten Untersuchungen', *Variscia, Mitteilungen aus dem Archiv des Vogtländischen Altertumsforschenden Vereins* 2: 91–123.

Andree, C. 1976. *Rudolf Virchow als Prähistoriker*. Köln: Böhlau.

Anon. 1830 [Börner]. 'Tagesbericht über die in der Umgegend von Wernburg bey Pößneck veranstaltete Nachgrabungen', *Variscia, Mitteilungen aus dem Archiv des Vogtländischen Altertumsforschenden Vereins* 2: 86–90.

Beltz, R. 1919. 'Zur Vertretung der Vorgeschichte an den deutschen Universitäten', *Correspondenzblatt der Deutschen Gesellschaft für Anthropologie* 50: 39–40.

Buschan, G. 1900. 'Die Notwendigkeit von Lehrstühlen für eine "Lehre vom Menschen" auf deutschen Hochschulen', *Centralblatt für Anthropologie* 2: 65–72.

Dobrowski, J. 1786. 'Ueber die Begräbnißart der alten Slawen überhaupt, und der Böhmen insbesondere. Eine Abhandlung, veranlaßt durch die bei Horim im Jahr 1784. (!) auf einer ehemaligen heydnischen Grabstätte ausgegrabenen irdenen Geschirre', *Abhandlungen der böhmischen Akademie der Wissenschaften*: 333–59.

Döring, D. and K. Nowak (eds) 2000. 'Gelehrte Gesellschaften im mitteldeutschen Raum (1650–1820). Teil 1'. *Abhandlungen der Sächsischen Akademie der Wissenschaften zu Leipzig. Philologisch-historische Klasse* 76(2). Stuttgart: Hirzel.

Erhard, H.A. 1835. 'Ideen über den Zweck und die Wirksamkeit eines geschichtsforschenden Vereins'. *Westfälisches Archiv* 7: 278–310.

Foster, G. 1777. *A Voyage around the World in his Britannic Majesty's Sloop Resolution*. London: B. White.

Halub, M. 1997. *Johann Gustav Gottlieb Büsching 1783–1829; ein Beitrag zur Begründung der schlesischen Kulturgeschichte*, Wroclaw: Wydawn. Uniwersytetu Wroclawskiego.

Heimpel, H. 1963. *Geschichtsvereine einst und jetzt. Vortrag gehalten am Tag der 70. Wiederkehr der Gründung des Geschichtsvereins für Göttingen und Umgebung 19.11.1962*. Göttingen: Vandenhoek und Ruprecht.

Herder, J.G. 1784–1791 [1995]. *Ideen zur Philosophie der Geschichte der Menschheit*. Bodenheim: Syndikat.

Heuer, H.-U. 1963. 'Eichhorn und die historische Rechtsschule', in Streisand, J. (ed.), *Die deutsche Geschichtswissenschaft vom Beginn des 19. Jahrhunderts bis zur Reichseinigung von oben*. Berlin: Akademie-Verlag, pp. 121–33.

Homann, A. 2004. *Das bronzezeitliche Gräberfeld von Königswartha, Kreis Bautzen im forschungsgeschichtlichen Kontext*. M.A. Thesis. Leipzig: Universität Leipzig.

Jacobeit, W. 1965. 'Bäuerliche Arbeit und Wirtschaft. Ein Beitrag zur Wissenschaftsgeschichte der deutschen Volkskunde'. *Deutsche Akademie der Wissenschaften, Veröffentlichungen des Instituts für deutsche Volkskunde 39*. Berlin: Akademie.

Klüpfel, K.A. 1844. 'Die historischen Zeitschriften und Vereine Deutschlands', *Zeitschrift für Geschichtswissenschaft* 1: 518–559.

Kossinna, G. 1896. 'Professuren für deutsches Altertum'. *Grenzbote, Zeitschrift für Politik und Kultur* 2: 600–605.

Maak, S. 2000. 'Die Eisenbahnstrecke KBS 543 Greiz–Neumark'. Retrieved 13.9.2005 from http://www.mohlsdorf.de/geschichte/ge-3-1-8-4-eisenbahn.html.

Marwinski, K. 1979. 'Thüringische historische Vereine im 19. Jahrhundert'. *Jahrbuch für Regionalgeschichte* 7: 205–242.

Marx, K. 1976 [1844]. *Kritik der Hegelschen Rechtsphilosophie*, MEW 1. Berlin: Dietz-Verlag, pp. 378–91.

Merten, J. 2000. 'Vor 100 Jahren: Die Gesellschaft für nützliche Forschungen zu Trier 1901', *Funde und Ausgrabungen im Bezirk Trier* 32: 99–112.

Nipperdey, T. 1972. 'Verein als soziale Struktur in Deutschland im späten 18. und frühen 19. Jahrhundert', in Boockmann, H. et al. (eds), *Geschichtswissenschaft und Vereinswesen im 19. Jahrhundert, Beiträge zur Geschichte historischer Forschung*. Göttingen: Vandenhoeck und Ruprecht, pp. 1–44.

Preusker, K.B. 1840. 'Kleinigkeiten, 1. Abteilung. Über einige gegenseitige Verhältnisse der Slawen und Germanen'. *Neues Lausitzisches Magazin* 18: 250–261.

Preusker, K.B. 1841. *Blicke in die vaterländische Vorzeit: Sitten, Sagen, Bauwerke und Geräthe, zur Erläuterung des öffentlichen und häuslichen Volkslebens im heidnischen Alterthume und christlichen Mittelalter der sächsischen und angränzenden Lande, für gebildete Leser aller Stände*. Leipzig: Hinrichs.

Resch, F. 1859. 'Das allgemein verbreitete Interesse der Alterthumskunde, ein Zeichen der Zeit', *Jahresbericht Vogtländischer Alterumsverein*: 98–99.

Richard, N. 2002. 'Archaeological Arguments in National Debates in Late Nineteenth Century France: Gabriel de Mortillet's La Formation de la Nation Française (1897)', *Antiquity* 76: 177–84.

Schleier, H. 2003. *Geschichte der deutschen Kulturgeschichtsschreibung*. Waltrop: Hartmut Spenner.

Schmidt, J. 1829. 'Ueber die Körperbeschaffenheit der früheren Bewohner Deutschlands', *Variscia, Mitteilungen aus dem Archiv des Vogtländischen Altertumsforschenden Vereins* 1: 35–60.

Schnapp, A. 2002. 'Between Antiquarians and Archaeologists – Continuities and Ruptures'. *Antiquity* 76: 135–140.

Sommer, U. and R. Struve. 2006. 'Bemerkungen zur universitären 'Vor- und Frühgeschichte' in Deutschland vor Kossinna', in: J. Calmer et al. (eds), *Die Anfänge der ur- und frühgeschichtlichen Archäologie als akademisches Fach (1890–1930) im europäischen Vergleich*. Berlin.

Virchow, R. 1872. 'Ueber die Methode der wissenschaftlichen Anthropologie. Eine Antwort an Herrn de Quatrefages', *Zeitschrift für Ethnologie, Anthropologie und Urgeschichte* 4: 300–320.

——— . 1875. Eröffnungsrede der 6. allgemeinen Versammlung München. *Archiv für Anthropologie* 8: 5–14.

——— . 1876. 'Über den voigtländischen Verein in Hohenleuben'. *Correspondenz-Blatt der deutschen Gesellschaft für Anthropologie, Ethnologie und Urgeschichte*: 119–20.

Wagner, F.A. 1828. *Die Tempel und Pyramiden der Urbewohner auf dem rechten Elbufer unweit dem Ausfluß der schwarzen Elster*. Leipzig: Hartmann.

——— . 1833. *Ägypten in Deutschland, oder die Germanisch-slavischen wo nicht rein germanischen Altherthümer an der schwarzen Elster*. Leipzig.

Waldeyer, H.W.G. 1899. 'Universitäten und anthropologischer Unterricht', *Correspondenzblatt der Deutschen Gesellschaft für Anthropologie* 30(9): 70–75.

Weule, K. 1902. *Völkerkunde und Urgeschichte im 20. Jahrhundert*. Eisenach/Leipzig: Thüringische Verlags-Anstalt.

Zentralinstitut für Geschichte der Akademie der Wissenschaften der DDR (ed.) 1989. *Atlas zur Geschichte*. Berlin: VEB Hermann Haak geographisch-karthographische Anstalt Gotha.

Chapter 19

Archaeology, Politics and Identity

The Case of the Canary Islands in the Nineteenth Century

José Farrujia de la Rosa

Abstract

Late nineteenth-century archaeology in the Canary Islands was conditioned by the political and economic context, and also by the archaeology developed in Europe and in the north of Africa at that time, especially just after the Berlin Conference (1884–1885). In this chapter we analyse the case of the Canaries, its theoretical framework, and the different concepts of the identity of the first inhabitants of the islands as discussed by the German, French and Canarian archaeologists and anthropologists.

Introduction

The Canary Islands were rediscovered in the Middle Ages following the European expansion in the Atlantic by Portugal, Aragon and Italy in the fourteenth century, and later by Castile in the fifteenth century (Morales 1971).[1] The factors behind this European expansionism were: the efforts of mercantile capital to find direct access to African gold (Macías 2001: 131–32); pre-capitalist trade, which favoured colonisation abroad, as opposed to earlier concerns with frontier colonisation during the High Middle Ages; and the desire to incorporate new discoveries within the realms of Christianity before they were absorbed by Islam (Stevens 1997: 86).

A direct consequence of the contact between the indigenous Canarian people – who had been isolated on the islands for centuries – and the Europeans was the creation and elaboration, by the colonisers, of several hypotheses to explain the colonisation of the Canary Islands during 'primitive' times, from a European point of view. They were obviously interested in knowing who these 'barbaric' and 'savage' people were who had lived confined on an archipelago in the middle of the Atlantic Ocean and also where they had come from and what their traditions were. Nevertheless, opinions concerning the indigenous Canarian people were also conditioned by an entire series of interests which were not merely ethnographic (Farrujia 2005). However, this fact did not prevent the study of ancient colonisation from becoming a recurring discursive practice in many of the ethnographic sources, chronicles, memoirs and general histories written on the islands during the fourteenth, fifteenth, and sixteenth centuries.

These first written sources provide information about the autochthonous populations, who had not yet been wiped out; the first chroniclers were thus speaking about ethnographic populations, rather than extinct ones. This is why in the Canaries no medieval archaeology developed (Farrujia 2004), in contrast with the archaeology being practised at the time in Europe, where research into material remains supplemented studies based on written documentation (Trigger 1989, 1992: 22; Schnapp 1999).

Later, during the seventeenth and eighteenth centuries, the terms of the enquiry into the colonisation of the islands did not experience any substantial changes in relation to the former historiographical tradition. It was not until the middle of the nineteenth century – for reasons that will be explained later – that there was a complete break with the previous period, due to the development of evolutionism and imperialist archaeology in the Canary Islands. This marked the beginning of a second phase in the study of the colonisation of the islands, giving as a result a new concept of the indigenous Canarian people.

Having outlined these aspects, this chapter proceeds to analyse how the conception of the Canarian indigenous people was developed, from the archaeological point of view, by European archaeologists and anthropologists. It will also reflect on the repercussions of this type of studies (in terms of both theory and practice) on the study of the ancient colonisation of the islands, paying special attention to the European (French and German) imperialist archaeology developed at the end of the nineteenth century in the Canaries.

The Historical Context

The development of a European imperialist archaeology in the Canaries was directly related to the colonial partitioning of Africa at the end of the nineteenth century. Due to its geostrategic location in relation to the neighbouring continent and to expansion throughout the South Atlantic, the Archipelago became a 'key' piece in the imperialist politics of countries like France and Germany, which would eventually ensure French and German academic intervention in archaeological studies on Canarian prehistory[2] From the third quarter of the nineteenth century onwards the European powers (France, Great Britain, Portugal and Germany) acquired commercial interests and had begun developing their influence in different parts of Africa, although their direct political control was initially very limited (Uzoigwe 1987: 50).

In relation to 'formal' possession of the colonies, by 29th of April, 1885 an Anglo-German treaty had been signed which introduced the notion of spheres of influence and defined the areas of intervention of the two countries in specific parts of Africa (Miege 1975: 37; Uzoigwe 1987: 56). Subsequently in the 1870s these rough early calculations were developed further, whilst in the 1880s a new conceptual repertoire was introduced, involving agreements or partition treaties, ultimatums and guarantee treaties. From this point onwards, a tense and conflictual phase of international 'robbery' began, under the guise of the most cynical and pragmatic of military and diplomatic tasks. During these years, a series of treaties distributed the various areas amongst the European powers. Germany formally acquired Togo, Cameroon, South West Africa and East Africa. France, on the other hand, had already acquired Algeria in 1830 and occupied Tunisia in 1881, initially establishing a protectorate, but later on, in 1883, invading it militarily.

All the German possessions in Africa, with the exception of East Africa, were located on the western side of the African continent, so that accessing them by sea therefore implied sailing through the waters of the Canarian archipelago. Since the initial phase of European overseas expansion into the South Atlantic, the Canaries had undergone an undeniable strategic re-evaluation (Pérez Voituriez and Brito 1984: 37–39; Brito 1989: 81). It therefore seems evident that both German and French archaeologists would carry out their work with the aim of justifying their respective countries' interests in the islands, due to the significant geostrategic position of the archipelago itself.

German and French interests in controlling the Archipelago obviously followed the model for foreign presences developed in Atlantic Archipelagos by other European powers (Brito 1989: 53). They were considered territories lacking in fuel or mining resources and financially precarious, but possessing a favourable geostrategic location, especially from the Berlin Conference of 1883 onwards when the widespread use of steamships required frequent ports to supply coal and water,

Fig. 19.1 Tagoror or place for assemblies, related by Berthelot (1876) to the Celtic megalithic structures.

and consignee companies and financial middlemen to facilitate mercantile activities whose main theatres were the West African coast and Latin America (Macías and Rodríguez 1995: 387–88). This strategic location, within a complex intersection of traffic and international interests, meant that the islands were constantly influenced by international conflicts involving not only Germany, and France, but also the Spanish state and the ambitions of new rising powers (e.g. the USA's declaration of war against Spain in 1898, preceded by the British ultimatum to Portugal in 1890 and the failure of the political projection of the Zanjón Peace after 1893; cf. Brito 1989: 25).

However, in parallel to this geostrategic factor, it is also necessary to assess the actual commercial interests of Germany and France in the Canaries. In terms of the import trade at the time, developments in tourism had stimulated imports of all types of materials and supplies needed for the hotels and sanatoriums, including cotton cloth, coal and comestibles (biscuits, oil and grain). The German commercial presence in the Canaries, which had begun in the 1860s, doubled in size in just a few years. Thanks to the use of aggressive trading methods, by around 1860 German goods were able to displace imports from the rest of the national territory. Whilst in 1869 Germany had supplied 1.5 per cent of the goods imported into the Canaries, by 1890 its share had increased to 12 per cent. In the same period, the proportion held by Great Britain rose from 24.5 per cent to 50 per cent, whilst that of France dropped from 18 per cent to 12 per cent (Martín 1988: 265, 258–59). Thus, from 1885 onwards, the Canaries became another theatre for the intense British-German commercial rivalry that had extended across the entire world, acquiring special notoriety in the colonial territories.

This context enables us to understand the development in Africa of an imperialist archaeology with racist leanings by two of the main European powers: France and Germany. French anthropologists and archaeologists, as we will argue, would relate the blond African populations to the Celts, on the basis of the relationship they had established between Western European and North African Megalithism (Faidherbe 1873; Tissot 1876; Broca 1876). To validate this theory, that is to say, the idea of a population upsurge that would leave Celtica, reach the Straits of Gibraltar and Algeria and finally arrive at the frontiers of Egypt, the following arguments were sufficient: the archaeological argument (Megalithism) and the anthropological argument (the presence of blond people in Africa since the far distant past). The purpose of these claims was to legitimise and give precedence to the French occupation of these territories, and in this context the following fact is significant: the authors who developed the theory were directly linked to official French colonialist circles in Africa.

At the same time, German archaeologists and anthropologists were also developing their work. Nevertheless, whilst the French had related the blond populations of Africa to the Celts, the Germans established a nexus with the Aryan populations.

Nineteenth-Century European Archaeology

The development of nineteenth-century studies on the early colonisation of the Canary Islands was defined by the incorporation of evolutionist and positivist principles within the study of the indigenous Canarian world which, from then onwards, was essentially analysed on the basis of archaeology and physical anthropology. This qualitative turnabout, experienced from the second half of the nineteenth century onwards, cannot be understood without assessing the whole series of economic, political and social transformations that took place in Europe as a result of the Industrial Revolution, and affected – in their formation and development – the newly emerging archaeological and anthropological disciplines that were closely connected to the bourgeois sectors of society. In the case of the Canary Islands, economic factors (a crisis or boom in particular types of farming, the establishment of the Free Ports, the re-launching of mercantile activity, etc.) would configure and consolidate the capitalist economy, making the (commercial and landowning) bourgeoisie the dominant social group and, as in the rest of Europe, the sector of society most closely concerned with archaeological and anthropological studies. In this sense, it was the relationship forged between French anthropologists and Canarian authors, at first by a bourgeois author like Sabin Berthelot, and later by others, such as Gregorio Chil y Naranjo, that defined the development of emerging Canarian archaeology.

The beginning of this phase, coinciding with the development of European archaeology and physical anthropology, was to have a decisive effect on studies of the early colonisation of the Canary Islands, since it was just after 1848 that Canarian archaeological and anthropological studies began and the scientific institutions associated with both disciplines were founded: El Gabinete Científico (1877) and El Museo Canario (1880) (Farrujia 2004).

Theoretical Guidelines: Evolutionism and Diffusionism

The theory of evolution marked the birth of prehistoric archaeology and European physical anthropology. This theory, especially the biological evolution outlined by Darwin, questioned the medieval Christian world view that had survived until the middle of the nineteenth century. Moreover, the firm belief in progress, as a result of the innovations experienced during the Industrial Revolution, guaranteed that evolutionary ideas would be well received and would, in a certain sense, come to legitimise the advance of certain nations over others, and of European superiority and its consequent colonial dominion over Africa (Uzoigwe 1987: 44–45; Barros 1990: 160; Trigger 1992: 117; Zimmerman 2001: 174).

Nevertheless, as the years went by, evolutionist arguments began to lose status, basically from 1880 onwards, in consequence of the problems arising out of the Industrial Revolution, the political supremacy of the middle classes and the consequent rejection of the idea of progress. This led many authors to argue that change was contrary to human nature, and it also meant that the concept of independent development was discredited, since it was believed to be unlikely that certain inventions could take place more than once in human history. The main consequence of this series of transformations would be the emerging success of the diffusionist or migratory thesis to explain cultural change (Trigger 1992: 146–49). According to this theory, almost all cultural changes recorded in archaeology could be attributed to the diffusion of ideas from one group to another, or to migrations that had led to one human group and culture being replaced by another. Nevertheless, the transition from the evolutionary model to diffusionism was gradual, and diffusionist explanations frequently shared many evolutionist characteristics. In this sense, the nineteenth-century evolutionists considered there was no real opposition between evolutionism and diffusionism, as it was not necessary to distinguish between invented and diffused elements in order to demonstrate that similar cultural phases had been followed by others in a uniform way.

The only important thing was to verify the evolutionary uniformity of human groups. Consequently, nineteenth-century archaeology did not consider that the concepts of migration or diffusion were antithetical to evolution, but instead were two factors that contributed towards promoting evolutionary change (Trigger 1992: 146–49; Johnson 2000: 171).

In contrast, in the Canaries diffusionist theses had been part of historiography since the fourteenth century. This was due to several factors: first, almost all ethno-historical sources contained ethnographical comparisons between the islands and the African continent; second, all the authors had assimilated the Jewish-Christian world view and the Diaspora or migration concepts as an inherent part of it, and lastly, and most importantly of all, its status as an island meant that the first settlers had had to reach the archipelago by sea, and were thus foreign in origin (Farrujia 2004).

Nevertheless, the diffusionist arguments developed in the Canary Islands from the fourteenth century onwards were not articulated on the basis of archaeological data, which became available only by the second half of the nineteenth century. This theoretical and methodological change in Canarian archaeology was due to the influence of the European frame of reference (especially the French) on the Canarian authors, and the nature of the islands themselves, since this physical reality, according to the world view of the nineteenth-century archaeologists, had had a decisive influence on the gradual isolation of the primitive settlers of the Canary Islands. From a theoretical point of view, secular isolation only prevented evolutionist theories from being applied to explain cultural change, because it should be remembered, as Darwin had pointed out (1882: 190), that .... aborigines, who have long inhabited islands, and who must have been long exposed to nearly uniform conditions, should be specially affected by any change in their habits.

For this reason the foreign and Canarian intellectuals responsible for studying the indigenous Canarian people appealed to diffusionist and evolutionist theories when explaining cultural change. It was inexplicable that human groups who had lived in isolation could evolve at the same pace and in the same way as groups from Europe or the African continent had done, and that is why diffusionist theses, starting with the mechanism of migration, provided explanations for the similarities observed between the Archipelago and the place of origin (West Africa, the Near East, etc.)[3]. Another aspect that eventually influenced the theoretical basis of Canarian archaeological and anthropological studies was the exogenous nature of the different population theories. Basically, when defending the colonisation of the islands by certain foreign human groups that were racially and culturally defined (Celtic, Egyptian, Vandal, etc.), diffusionist positions were necessarily adopted, as they had been since the fourteenth century.

Imperialist Archaeology in the Canary Islands

The geo-strategic role of the Canaries Islands favoured the development within the islands of an imperialist archaeology, with clear racist leanings, in which some foreign authors engaged in Canarian studies were involved. This was the case with the French authors Jean-Baptiste Bory de Saint-Vincent, Sabin Berthelot, Cesar Faidherbe and René Verneau and the German authors Franz von Löher, Hans Meyer and Felix von Luschan. In this context, the theme of the early human colonisation of the Canary Islands was a recurring argument that served to legitimise the annexationist or imperialist aspirations of some European nations (Farrujia 2002, 2003). At the same time it was viewed by the island authors from another perspective, as a discursive practice used, amongst other things, to endorse the inherent class interests of certain Canarian political groups, as we will argue below. In other words, in spite of the more positivist character of archaeological and anthropological work during the second half of the nineteenth century, the close relationship between archaeology and politics in fact guaranteed that the scientific knowledge generated was sparse and precarious.

The Egyptian and Persian Hypothesis

Just a few decades before the partitioning of Africa, Jean-Baptiste Bory de Saint-Vincent linked the Guanches[4] with the Egyptians on the basis of archaeological evidence – effectively mummification and funerary goods (Bory de Saint-Vincent 1988 [1803]). It should be remembered that systematic investigations into ancient Egypt began at the end of the eighteenth century, with the first observations made by the French scholars who had accompanied Napoleon Bonaparte when he invaded Egypt (Gran-Aymerich 2001: 21). Involved as he was with the French military and scientific world, Bory de Saint-Vincent had been aware of this whole series of discoveries since the outset, so that in 1803, when he spoke about the colonisation of the Canaries, he had no hesitation in relating the Guanches to the Egyptians, by means of the mummies and their funeral goods. In parallel to the rediscovery of Egypt, the French campaigns in Syria had also allowed substantial knowledge of the Persian world to emerge following reciprocal interchanges between philology and archaeology (Gran-Aymerich 2001: 94–108). Thus Bory de Saint-Vincent, influenced by the research being carried out by his compatriots, did not hesitate to point out links between the Guanches and the Persians, since both worshipped the Sun God. In addition, *Mitra*, who was the *Guebro* God of the Sun, had a body of priests known as the *mages*, and *mag* and *magec* were the Canarian words for the sun (Bory 1988 [1803]: 284).

In Bory de Saint-Vincent's view, then, the Islands had been populated during primitive times by the ancestors of the two nations that France had tried to dominate at the end of the eighteenth century and the beginning of the nineteenth century: the Egyptians and the Persians. Did this imply that the Canary Islands could also be dominated by France? Did France have the right to occupy the islands that, in a certain sense, had been populated earlier on by Egyptians and Persians, two nations that it had temporarily subjugated at the end of eighteenth century? Was it possible to use history to justify the French presence in the Canary Islands? Was it pertinent to develop a scientific interventionism in the Canary Islands, behind which a clear political purpose could be hidden? We believe this is the case, and a good deal of evidence for this can be found in the words of Bory de Saint-Vincent himself, when in chapter IV, which was dedicated to commerce, he recognised that

> The European nation that managed to rule the Azores, Madeira, the Canary Islands, and even Cape Verde, and that did not neglect their agriculture and development, would find in these archipelagos an inexhaustible source of riches that would not have the disadvantage, unlike those we obtain from our distant colonies, of taking a considerable time to arrive [Bory 1988 (1803): 115].

He even went so far as to suggest a suitable colonial model for the Canary Islands based on the slave trade [Bory 1988 (1803): 116–17]. Archaeology clearly appeared as a device used to reinforce French influence in the Canary Islands, all the more so because French voyages, expeditions and archaeological missions were supported by public funding, and this gave them an official character, allying their development to the State's political perspectives. In fact the official nature of the missions, as well as the need for them to be undertaken, was recognised in 1842 with the creation of the Bureau des Missions Scientifiques et Littéraires (Gran-Aymerich 2001: 137–40).

In this light, the case of Bory de Saint-Vincent can be related to the use that England and France would make later on, at the end of the nineteenth century, of the diffusionist position of an author like the Swedish prehistorian Gustav Oscar Montelius (1843–1921). According to Montelius, the development of European civilisation could be explained by a series of innovations that had spread from the Near East to the periphery. On the basis of this argument Western

European nations intervened increasingly in political and economic matters in the Near East, since they could justify European colonial intervention in the region, and also the European colonisation of Africa, by claiming that they, rather than the Arab people, were the true heirs of the ancient Near Eastern civilisations (Trigger 1992: 154–55; Gran-Aymerich 2001: 111).

The Celtic Hypothesis and the Cro-Magnon Race

Coinciding with the French colonialist intervention in North Africa, another French author, Sabin Berthelot, argued for a Celtic presence in the Canary Islands, relating the indigenous Canarian people with the Celts (Berthelot 1879). The focal point for the origins of the first populations of the Archipelago was thus located in France. In this case, the archaeological argument used by Berthelot was the "presence" of Megaliths in the Canary Islands, specifically on the island of El Hierro. In relation to Berthelot's theory, we should not lose sight of the entire series of events that favoured the development of a national archaeology in France (Gran-Aymerich 2001), as well as the development of a French imperialist archaeology in North Africa (Farrujia 2004). All this scientific activity meant that the megalithic structures attributed to the Celts soon became mega defining factors in the national identity of France, its archaeological heritage and its past imperial achievements, as reflected in the works of Tissot (1876), Broca (1876) or Faidherbe (1873). Berthelot, who was the French Consul in Tenerife, limited himself, therefore, to arguing for the presence of megalithic structures in the Canaries, influenced by the nationalist and imperialistic academic literature he read and by the contemporary political interests he supported (Fig. 19.1).

The French anthropologist René Verneau also insisted on the link between the Canaries and France, but from an anthropological point of view: the presence of the Cro-Magnon race in the Canary Islands would be the result of prehistoric migrations to the Archipelago from the Dordogne (Verneau 1891). Verneau would also define the indigenous culture in terms of mega elements (dolmens or sepulchres in caves), which contributed towards creating an excessively simplistic vision of the cultures being studied (Fig. 19.2). In addition, the importance of the anthropological arguments themselves in his works overshadowed the role that socio-cultural factors might have played as defining elements of the societies being studied. A similar position

Fig. 19.2 René Verneau studying the Guanche skulls in El Museo Canario (Photo: El Museo Canario).

Fig. 19.3 Felix von Luschan.

was adopted by Louis Faidherbe (1870), when arguing for the presence of blond Celtic settlers in the Islands, related at the same time to the North African Lybic people.

The Aryan Hypothesis

In contrast to the French authors, German scholars argued for an Aryan presence in the Canary Islands, and therefore an ancient link between Germany and the Archipelago. Franz von Löher (1990 [1876]) insisted on the presence of Vandals in the islands (sixth century) partly on the basis of archaeological evidence (stone huts), but mainly through philological arguments (considering the Guanche or indigenous language as a German dialect). The source he used as a basis for his description of the Germanic people and their comparison with the Guanches was *De origine et situ Germanorum* by Cornelius Tacitus, in which the Latin author explained the customs in the Germanic towns at the time of the Varian disaster. In relation to this text, it should be remembered that German academic tradition had in fact built its national identity around the Germanic tribes, on the basis of classic texts such as the one by Tacitus.

Other German authors, such as Hans Meyer (1896) and Felix von Luschan (1896) also argued for Aryan invasions, but from an anthropological point of view (Fig. 19.3). According to them, the Armenian type, associated with Indo-Europeans (and therefore Aryans) was considered to be related to the indigenous Canarian people. In connection with the proposed relationship to the Armenian type, it is necessary to point out that the studies of Meyer and Luschan had in fact been developed at the same time as the rise of Germany in Egypt and Mesopotamia since, on the eve of the First World War, the Ottoman Empire had become a political and economic arena of the first order. After developing his studies on the anthropological materials obtained from the campaigns in the Near East, Luschan went on to argue that the first residents of Mesopotamia and Anatolia had been a brachycephalic Armenian type, with the Mediterranean dolichocephalics arriving after them. This justified the predominance of the Aryan presence in the territories of the Near East, and consequently legitimised the German right to occupy them.[5]

The Canarian Point of View

Canarian authors, as we have already pointed out, were directly influenced by imperialistic archaeology (especially the French version) and by the political situation of the Canary Islands themselves (regionalism). But the topic of the ancient colonisation was viewed by the island authors from another perspective, as a discursive practice used, amongst other things, to endorse the inherent class interests of certain Canarian political groups (Farrujia 2002).

The discovery of the Cro-Magnon race (1868), its anatomical similarities with the indigenous Canarian people, and therefore, with the early settlers of the Archipelago, implied their extrapolation within a historical evolution that would finally lead to the heights of European civilisation. This led to the Guanche material culture, morals and customs being overvalued, justifying their incorporation within the most progressive trends in the evolution of the human

Fig. 19.4 Rock engravings of Belmaco's cave (La Palma), related by Chil y Naranjo (1876) to those of the Dolmens of Morbihan (Brittany) (Photo: J. Farrujia).

races. It should not be forgotten that the French anthropologists, especially Paul Broca, conceived of the Cro-Magnon race as an intelligent and perfectible race that had developed art, a reflection of their fine cerebral organisation (Schiller 1979: 156).

In relation to the link established between French and Canarian prehistory, it is important to highlight that various factors influenced this situation: the contact between Canarian and French scholars, and the early relationship established between the Guanches and the Cro-Magnon type (just after 1868) and, consequently, with the French prehistoric environment. Regarding the scientific contact, remember that an author like Sabin Berthelot lived in the Canary Islands for more than 25 years, publishing some of his articles in Canarian magazines (*Revista Canaria*, for example). At the same time, René Verneau visited on several occasions the El Museo Canario, where he studied the anthropological and archaeological material of the ancient Canarian populations, publishing some of his articles in a local journal, *Revista de El Museo Canario*. At the same time, some Canarian authors, such as Gregorio Chil y Naranjo or Juan Bethencourt Alfonso, studied in France, where they participated in several congresses; and there was a high rate of circulation of French publications in the Canaries. The main consequence of all these aspects was the adoption of the French scientific premises by the Canarian authors, and therefore, the development of the ethnocentric concept of the early inhabitants of the islands (Fig. 19.4).

On the other hand, the German incidence was less important due to several factors: the language barrier, since hardly any Canarian intellectuals spoke German, or made reference to German publications; and also the absence of any sort of relationships between the German and Canarian academic worlds. Therefore, the theoretical and methodological guidelines developed in German archaeology and anthropology did not have such a deep effect on the Canarian academic world, which was more open and receptive to the French scientific environment. In this sense, the works of authors like Franz von Löher, Hans Meyer or Felix von Luschan on the Canaries were unknown to almost all Canarian academics. Only some authors from the islands referred to them but without developing a critical reading of their works, an aspect doubtless influenced by a lack of knowledge of the German language itself.

Anyway, the adoption of the premises of the imperialist archaeology (both French and German), however archaeologically unfounded, explains to a large extent the relationship that some Canarian authors (all of them bourgeois) proposed between the Guanche people (seen as their ancestors) and the major European cultures (Celtic or Iberian, and Aryan in last instance), since it was the only possible way to link the indigenous people of the islands with universal history. As Fernando Estévez has already pointed out (1987: 100, 163), this application, devoid of any traces of evolutionary theory as elaborated in Europe and therefore learned by Canarian intellectuals, placed non-Western societies outside history. Within these coordinates, only the great ancient civilizations could claim an honourable position in the history of humanity, and this goes a long way towards explaining the importance for Canarian authors of associating the ancient Canarians with the founding of the great civilizations (Celtic, Iberian, Egyptian, etc.). In connection with this, another fact should be borne in mind: the concept of race developed by Broca and his colleagues implied that other non-white races were unable to attain the same level of development in science, technology and art (Schiller 1979: 137–38). From the political point of view, the relation established between the ancient Canarian populations and the Celts or Iberians also justified their link, since prehistoric times, to the Spanish mainland, also populated since the far distant past by both human groups. According to the regionalist Canarian authors (such as M. de Ossuna or J. Bethencourt) the indigenous Canarian people were part of Europe, and of course of Spain (Farrujia 2002).

Conclusions

From the nineteenth century onwards, the whole series of evolutionist and diffusionist arguments that were developed in Europe and at the same time incorporated into Canarian archaeological and anthropological studies, led to the formation of new population theories, directly conditioned by imperialist purposes.

Evolutionary theories, even though positivist, contained important theoretical and methodological defects, in spite of the qualitative advance they represented in relation to Renaissance and Enlightenment approaches. When foreign approaches were applied, indigenous Canarian cultures were treated as if they shared the same evolutionary development as other parts of Africa or Europe. In this sense, the cultural evolutionist models simplified the indigenous Canarian societies, as they did other past societies. That is why the particular or specific features of a culture were not considered important elements. Second, the evolutionist cultural models took neither contingency nor historical accident into account. It seemed that all societies evolved inexorably towards the formation of a state. Another final point should be borne in mind: as I have argued, the evolutionist archaeology and anthropology developed in Africa after colonial partitioning (the Berlin Conference, 1884–1885) was a clear example of European imperialistic interventionism. In other words, the population theories developed in the Canaries at the end of the nineteenth century by European authors were influenced by imperialist interests and motivations rather than by science. This would explain the presence of the Cro-Magnon race, the Celts (French explanations), or the Armenian type, the Indo-European (German explanations), etc., in the Canaries. This would imply the French or German right to occupy islands that, in a certain sense, had been already populated by their early ancestors. It was pertinent to develop a scientific or pseudo-scientific interventionism in the Canary Islands, and therefore, it was also possible to adduce the historical right to justify the French and German presence in the Canary Islands.

On the contrary, the Canarian authors developed a vindictive conception of the indigenous people (seen as their ancestors), also conditioned by the local politics, and without a solid scientific base. But at the same time, the result was that the Guanches were also seen as Europeans, and not as Africans, being this way related to universal history. Therefore, both European and Canarian authors developed an ethnocentric conception of the indigenous Canarian people, but with completely different purposes (Plate 14).

In strictly anthropological terms, the adoption of the theoretical and methodological principles of that time made it impossible for the decisive importance of socio-cultural factors to be recognised. In this sense, the physical anthropology of the period did not contribute much towards an understanding of the culture and society of the indigenous Canarian people. The hotchpotch of classifications and typologies hardly helped clarify the enigmas posed by the history of the Guanche people. The firmly held belief that the level of civilisation depended unequivocally on the size of the cranium led anthropologists to ignore the decisive role of acculturation and, in general, the mechanisms of the economics, politics, religion, etc., of those they attempted to study.

At the same time, whereas archaeological studies were endorsed in Europe and the Near East by widespread archaeological excavations that aided the development of European archaeology, sponsored and protected by official organisations, there was no similar development in the Canary Islands. There, it would not be until the second half of the nineteenth century, partly due to the development of prehistoric studies in Western Europe and to the relationship established between the Cro-Magnon race and the Guanches, that archaeology, as a "science of objects", and fieldwork, began to take off. This did not imply, however, that the Canarian and foreign scholars who excavated on the islands understood and interpreted everything they found correctly.

In this context, however, it is important to stress that the cultural relationship between the Canary Islands and Egypt, the Near East, France or Germany, proposed by scholars, archaeologists or anthropologists, was traced through a subjective reading of written sources, without developing the relevant fieldwork and therefore without knowing the archaeology of the islands. The result was the development of a particular and ethnocentric concept of the indigenous people of the Canaries – whose Berber origins are nowadays well established.

Notes

1. Obviously, at that time the term 'European' did not have the same connotations that it has nowadays. In using it, following Stevens Arroyo (1997: 86), I am referring to a cultural concept of Europe which is synonymous with Christendom, without necessary geographical implications.

2. It is notable that a European power like Great Britain, with clear colonial interests in North Africa, did not develop an imperialist archaeology on the Canary Islands. While the British sphere of influence in Africa was essentially in the Eastern Mediterranean, this did not prevent them from maintaining interests and pseudo-colonial trade relations in the Canary Islands. The works of such British authors as the Marquis of Bute (1891) or John Abercromby (1917) on Canarian prehistory were conditioned by the European theoretical and methodological framework of the time (evolutionism, diffusionism, comparative linguistics, raciology, etc.), but they do not appear to have been subordinated to imperialist policy guidelines (Farrujia 2005).

3. A theoretical guideline evident amongst the European anti-evolutionists, consistent in the acceptance of the diffusionist postulates as the only possible explanatory model (Johnson 2000: 177), was also present amongst the anti-evolutionist Canarian authors (Farrujia 2005).

4. Although this is the indigenous name for the ancient inhabitants of Tenerife, in the nineteenth century the term 'Guanche' was used in a unifying sense to refer to the settlers of the Canarian archipelago as a whole. According to the chronicles and first written sources, every island was colonised by a defined ethnic group: Gran Canaria by the *Canarii*; Lanzarote and Fuerteventura by the *Mahos*; El Hierro by the *Bimbachos*; La Palma by the *Auaritas*; La Gomera by the *Gomeros*; and Tenerife by the *Guanches*. This ethnical distribution has been archaeologically confirmed only in Tenerife, Lanzarote and Fuerteventura. In any case, the Lybic-Berber origins of the first settlers of all the Canary Islands is not in doubt.

5. In the case of the Canary Islands, Luschan did not hold this view explicitly. Nevertheless, it should be recalled that he was a firm patriot, nationalist and imperialist who supported the need for a German overseas empire and defended the utility of imperialist competition. This was why he adopted a pro-belligerent position when defending the imperialist interests of Germany in Africa (Zimmerman 2001: 46), and why he defended the Aryan presence in the Canary Islands. In the case of Franz von Löher the imperialist ambitions were held explicitly, because as he wrote in the foreword to his book (Löher 1876: 4), if the Guanches were German, they should be liberated sooner or later from the Spanish yoke and incorporated into the great German empire.

References

Abercromby, J. 1917. 'A study of the ancient speech of the Canary slands'. *Harvard African Studies*, 1: 95–129.

Barros, P. de 1990. 'Changing Paradigms, Goals and Methods in the Archaeology of Francophone West Africa'. In P. Robertshaw (ed). *A history of African Archaeology* (pp. 155–72). London: James Currey Ltd.

Berthelot, S. 1876. 'Sur l'ethnologie canarienne'. *Bulletins de la Société d'Anthropologie de Paris*. Tome IX (2ª serie): 114–117.

——— . 1879. *Antiquités canariènnes, ou annotations sur l'origine des peuples qui occupèrent les îles Fortunées, depuis les premiers temps jusqu'à l'époque de leur conquète*. Paris: Plon et Cie.

Bory de Saint-Vincent, J.B. 1988 [1803]. *Ensayos sobre las Islas Afortunadas y la Antigua Atlántida o compendio de la historia general del Archipiélago Canario*. La Orotava: José A. Delgado Luis, Editor.

Brito, O. 1989. *Historia Contemporánea: Canarias, 1876–1931. La encrucijada internacional*. Colección Historia Popular de Canarias, 6. Centro de la Cultura Popular Canaria. Santa Cruz de Tenerife.

Broca, P. 1876. 'Les peuples blonds et les monuments mégalithiques dans l'Afrique septentrionale. Les Vandales en Afrique'. *Revue d'Anthropologie*. Volume V: 393–404.

Bute, J.C.S. 1891. 'On the Ancient Languague of the Natives of Tenerife'. A paper contributed to the Anthropological Section of the British Association for the Advancement of Science. Masters and Co. London.

Chil y Naranjo, G. 1876. *Estudios históricos, climatológicos y patológicos de las Islas Canarias.* Tomo I. D. Isidro Miranda Impresor-Editor. Las Palmas de Gran Canaria.

Darwin, C. 1882. *The Descent of Man and Selection in Relation to Sex,* 2nd edition. London: John Murray.

Estévez González, F. 1987. *Indigenismo, Raza y Evolución. El pensamiento antropológico canario, 1750–1900.* Publicaciones Científicas del Cabildo de Tenerife. Museo Etnográfico, 4. Aula de Cultura. Santa Cruz de Tenerife.

Faidherbe, L.L.C. 1870. *Collection complète des Inscriptions Numidiques (Libyques) avec des aperçus ethnographiques sur les Numides.* Libraire A. Franck. Paris.

———. 1873. 'Sur les dolmens d'Afrique'. *Bulletins de la Société d'Anthropologie de Paris*. Volume VIII (10ª serie): 118–22.

Farrujia de la Rosa, A.J. 2002. *El primitivo poblamiento humano de Canarias en la obra de Manuel de Ossuna y Van den Heede. La Piedra de Anaga y su inserción en las tendencias ideográficas sobre la primitiva colonización insular.* Estudios Prehispánicos, 12. Madrid. Dirección General de Patrimonio Histórico.

———. 2003. 'The Canary Islands under Franco's dictatorship: Archaeology, national unity and African aspirations'. *Journal of Iberian Archaeology*, 5: 209–222.

———. 2004. *Ab initio (1342–1969). Análisis historiográfico y arqueológico del primitivo poblamiento de Canarias.* Sevilla: Artemisa Ediciones.

———. 2005. *Imperialist archaeology in the Canary Islands. French and German studies on prehistoric colonization at the end of the nineteenth century.* British Archaeological Reports, International Series, 1333. Oxford.

Gran-Aymerich, E. 2001. *El nacimiento de la arqueología moderna, 1798–1945.* Zaragoza: Prensas Universitarias.

Guerrero Ayuso, V.M. 1997. *El pensamiento científico en la Prehistoria Balear. Fuentes bibliográficas para el estudio de la Prehistoria Balear.* Libres de la Nostra Terra, 30. Palma de Mallorca: Lleonard Muntaner Editor.

Johnson, M. 2000. *Teoría arqueológica. Una introducción.* Barcelona: Ariel Historia.

Löher, F. 1990 [1876]. *Los germanos en las Islas Canarias.* Viceconsejería de Cultura y Deportes del Gobierno de Canarias. Madrid.

Luschan, F. von 1896. Über eine Schädelsammlung von den Kanarischen Inseln. In H. Meyer. *Die Insel Teneriffe. Wanderungen im Canarischen Hoch-und Tiefland* (pp. 285–319). Leipzig: Hirzel.

Macías Hernández, A. 2001. 'La construcción de las sociedades insulares: el caso de las Islas Canarias'. *Anuario del Instituto de Estudios Canarios XLV*: 131–160.

Macías Hernández, A.M. and J.A. Rodríguez Martín. 1995. 'La economía contemporánea, 1820–1990'. In: A. Béthencourt Massieu (ed.). *Historia de Canarias*: 133–91. Las Palmas de Gran Canaria: Ediciones del Cabildo Insular de Gran Canaria.

Martín Hernández, U. 1988. *Tenerife y el expansionismo ultramarino europeo (1880–1919).* Aula de Cultura de Tenerife. Publicaciones científicas del Excmo. Cabildo de Tenerife. Arte e Historia, nº 5. Santa Cruz de Tenerife.

Meyer, H. 1896. *Die Insel Teneriffe. Wanderungen im Canarischen Hoch-und Tiefland.* Leipzig: Hirzel.

Miege, J.L. 1975. *Expansión europea y descolonización. De 1870 a nuestros días.* Colección Nueva Clio: la Historia y sus problemas. Barcelona: Editorial Labor.

Morales Padrón, F. 1971. 'Los descubrimientos en los siglos XIV y XV y los archipiélagos atlánticos'. *Anuario de Estudios Atlánticos* 17: 429–65.

Ortiz García, C. 2001. 'De los cráneos a las piedras. Arqueología y Antropología en España, 1847–1977'. *Complutum*, 12: 273–92.

Pérez Voituriez, A. and O. Brito González. 1984. *Canarias, encrucijada internacional.* Círculo de Estudios Sociales de Canarias. Ecotopía. Santa Cruz de Tenerife.

Schiller, F. 1979. *Paul Broca. Founder of French Anthropology, Explorer of the Brain*. Berkeley: University of California Press.

Schnapp, A. 1999. *The Discovery of the Past. The Origins of Archaeology*. Madrid: British Museum Press.

Stevens Arroyo, A.M. 1997. 'Canary Islands and the Antillian'. In A. Tejera Gaspar (ed). *La sorpresa de Europa. (El encuentro de culturas)* (pp. 83–107). La Laguna: Servicio de Publicaciones de la Universidad de La Laguna.

Tissot, Ch.J. 1876. 'Sur les monuments mégalithiques et les populations blondes du Maroc (avec une carte)'. *Revue d'Anthropologie*. Volume V: 385–92.

Torriani, I, L., 1978 (1592). *Descripción e Historia del reino de las Islas Canarias, antes Afortunadas, con el parecer de sus fortificaciones*. Santa Cruz de Tenerife: Goya Ediciones.

Trigger, B. 1989. *A History of Archaeological Thought*. Cambridge: Cambridge University Press.

———. 1992. *Historia del pensamiento arqueológico*. Barcelona: Editorial Crítica.

Uzoigwe, G.N. 1987. 'La división y conquista europeas de Africa: visión general'. In A. Adu Boahen (ed). *Historia General de Africa, VII. África bajo el dominio colonial (1880–1935)* (pp. 41–67). Editorial Tecnos. Madrid: UNESCO.

Verneau, R.P. 1891. *Cinq années de séjour aux Iles Canaries*. Paris: A. Hennuyer, Imprimeur.

Zimmerman, A. 2001. *Anthropology and Antihumanism in Imperial Germany*. Chicago: University of Chicago Press.

Chapter 20

The Wagner Brothers

French Archaeologists and Origin Myths in Early
Twentieth-Century Argentina

Ana Teresa Martínez, Constanza Taboada and Luis Alejandro Auat

Abstract

This chapter provides a brief overview of the work of the brothers Emilio and Duncan Wagner, archaeologists in 1920s and 1930s in an impoverished and remote of province Argentina. Sons of a French diplomat, they served as Ambassadors of Latinity in American lands. After undertaking several excavations in Santiago del Estero, where they uncovered thousands of ceramic pieces of rare beauty, they imagined a 'Chaco-Santiagueña Civilisation' that would have dominated the region in remote times. Elaborating a mythological epistemology around the opposition 'Civilization-Kultur' as an idealisation of German-French conflict, they claimed for archaeology a discourse closer to art than to science, expressed in a method they called 'visual and geographic'. This led them to link their 'Chaco-Santiagueña Civilisation' to Schliemann's Troy and to an imagined 'primordial culture' of humanity. While theses claims led to the tacit expulsion of the brothers from the field of Argentinean archaeology, they were nevertheless considered as wise founders by the elites of 'Santiagueña' province. At a time when identity discourse was being constructed in Argentina, the 'Chaco-Santiagueña Civilisation' gave a glorious past to the region and, at the same time, provided a link between the ancestral and contemporary indigenous populations, regarded both as problematic and atavistic. This origin myth served to install a historical division between the indigenous past and the present, and it also gave the province the status of 'identity reserve' for the whole nation.

Parents of the Chaco-Santiagueña Civilisation

Brothers Emilio Roger and Duncan Ladislao Wagner were born in the second half of the century to a French diplomat of Alsatian origins and a Polish noblewoman who had sought political asylum in Western Europe. Duncan (1864–1937) was born in Paris and Emilio (1868–1949) in Ormisten (by then a French territory) during the last phase of the Second Empire. Both brothers studied in the Jesuit College Saint Michele in Friburg (Switzerland) and, without specific academic training, they subsequently devoted themselves to archaeology and natural sciences, following the encyclopaedic model of the nineteenth century.

By the end of the century both brothers ventured to explore the New World. In doing so they returned to an environment that was familiar to them through their father's previous diplomatic travels. From 1892 onwards, the impressive Emilio's traveller life can be followed through forests and jungles in central South America, while his brother Duncan was launching unsuccessful commercial and industrial ventures in Brazil and Argentina, ending in bankruptcy. From 1904

Fig. 20.1 A very young Emilio Wagner, probably at the time of his arrival in the Santiagueña countryside (originally published by El Liberal, 25º Aniversario 1923: 81, Santiago del Estero).

they settled in Santiago del Estero. This Argentinean province had been ignoredm until then by local archaeologists, and the brothers dedicated the rest of their lives to the excavation and interpretation of the region's Prehispanic material, publishing in the process the best illustrated and printed book in the Argentinean archaeological literature. However, most controversial and debated were their interpretations of the material. Given their epistemology and formation, they proposed the existence of an ancient and fabulous 'Chaco-Santiagueña Civilisation' in the region. This proposal, as we shall see, generated a diversity of consequences both for regional archaeology and for the local image and discourse on the past of the region.

Germans, Frenchmen and an Epistemological Mythology

Emilio undertook his voyage through America at the time of colonial Empires, when European powers expanded not only to conquer and trade but also to 'civilise'. We can read in his texts the ambivalence of his position as 'European missionary of culture' (Fig. 20.1). A few ethnographic texts, regularly sent to French scientific societies, written and published in his mother tongue, are examples of an exquisite sensibility, not only towards the peasant narrations and practices recorded, but also for his attitude towards men and women that were its protagonists. At the same time, as conflicts and the interests of his country were at stake, America became a battleground between Latinism and Germanism: it was a space where American interests were assimilated to French interests, masked behind the ideology of Latinity. In this sense, all the beauty and profundity of perception that emerge from the brief ethnographic texts remain overshadowed by his three books (two travel stories and a novel – E. Wagner 1918, 1919b, and 1919a respectively) marked by the conflict of European War, and reduced to ideological propaganda. These three books were published in the Collection *Bibliothèque France-Amérique* at Alcan Editor, managed by the Alcan Committee, created in 1909 to 'work for the development of economic, intellectual and artistic relations' between American countries and France.

As a fact, we are not addressing here an ethnographer but an aristocratic 'naturalist', endowed with a keen eye for the natural world and a good humanistic culture, who resided in local aristocratic homes (where he felt at home and within his class), and with Europeans settled in America. With indigenous people, Emilio Wagner shared hunting adventures; with mongrel peasants, he shared stories of feats in battle; with the noblemen with whom he stayed, he talked of literature and politics. He was a conqueror, a missionary of culture, who had frequent diplomatic ambiences, and could count on his pertinence and social experience as his best weapons. In these no- archeological texts, Emilio is a propagandist for Latinity against the Germanic onslaught in South America. The opposition to the 'Civilisation-Kultur' is not for him only an opposition to political projects but the product of an unequal distribution of intellectual faculties among these two opposing 'races'. In his texts, in which Germans appear as the incarnation of evil, Wagner develops a well-known epistemological mythology: besides putting all their capacities to evil service, Germans are obscure, arrogant, deductive and narrow-minded. If they have any intellectual achievement, it is by dint of thorough work, imitative, repetitive, without 'creation'. The 'New', the 'Unknown' (habitually in capital letters) are hidden for them. By contrast, Frenchmen are lightweight, winged, brilliant, and because they are endowed with intuition, they can without any effort (namely, without soiling their hands at work, without sweat, as aristocrats of spirit), beat a path where narrow-minded people can follow. They are authentic 'creators'. The dichotomy between obscure and weighty versus winged and brilliant functions as an organising schema for the whole discourse.

This opposition, linked in different ways to his social origin and familiar experience, works for Emilio Wagner as an epistemological conceptual matrix, which also operates within his archaeological texts. It was at the core of the debate among the Argentine archaeological community in the 1930s, by then in process of scientific consolidation.

The Wagner Brothers: Civilisations and Origin Myths Builders

This opposition 'Civilisation-Kultur' made possible – and even convenient for the Wagners – to 'purge' their discourse of scientific communication from 'useless technicalities' and 'others obscurities from expert blindness' (Canal Feijóo and Paz 1934: XIV), as the archaeological technical language is called in the prologue of the book published by the brothers in order to disseminate their archaeological discoveries (Wagner and Wagner 1934). With a vision of archaeology nearer to art

Fig. 20.2 Archaeological vessels from Santiago del Estero, painted by Duncan Wagner (originally published by Wagner and Wagner 1934).

than to science, and applying a particular and peculiar comparative method, called 'geographical and visual', they postulate the discovery of the remains of a great civilisation.

Their method was simply to excavate an archaeological site, record its location, extract finds from it, and then search for formal analogies with archaeological material from other parts of the world. Besides functional considerations, each item of pottery was thought of as a piece of art (Fig. 20.2). After considering its technical condition but primarily its artistic sensitivity, it was possible to deduce the system of government, the religion or the role women played in society. From their point of view, the history of humankind was written in pottery, and was the clue to interpret and establish world-wide relationships (unlike the Diffusionists, the Wagner brothers did not presume direct historical links, but rather a common ancient antiquity). Bound by their European education and aristocratic roots, they tried to link their discoveries to the classical world. They searched and found stylistic similarities to classical archaeological material, notably from Troy. This method was useful to support an argument for the existence of a primordial cult, attested by ceramic representation of a unique 'anthropo-ornitho-snake' divinity. The major feature of this

Fig. 20.3 Map showing the routes and migratory waves that led to the colonisation of the world from a continent now disappeared, according to the Wagner brothers' final proposition (originally published in Wagner and Righetti 1946).

civilisation would be to have 'a symbolic art full of religious mysticism and fervour'. One of the main points of this theory is that of the perfection and homogeneity reached in ceramics. This origin, shared by all cultures and nations, served to demonstrate similarities and correlations that the Wagner brothers recognised all over the world at both material (representations, vessels, etc.) and non-material (worship to the same deity) levels (Fig. 20.3).

When the Wagner brothers wrote and publicised their texts – notably through a series of flowery conferences by Duncan Wagner – Argentine archaeology was not really prepared for loudly proclaimed proposal of this kind. The Argentine archaeological community was at that time in the process of defining boundaries around what and who would be considered scientific, and under what conditions they could be called archaeologists or anthropologists (cf. Martínez, Taboada and Auat 2003). The efforts of the authorities in Santiago del Estero (an impoverished province situated far from the political, cultural and commercial core of the country) in financing excavations and the publication of the lavish book were met with a disappointingly negative reaction by the nationally accepted scientific community. The Wagners were not part of that community, and they today rank in the official history of Argentine archaeology rather in the anecdotal section than in the annals. This exclusion was not gratuitous, but nor was it justified, for despite the important interpretative problems inherent in their work, the brothers had actually founded the archaeology of the territory of Santiago del Estero, performed important fieldwork and contributed with the first classifications of finds (cf. Martínez, Taboada and Auat 2003). At the same time as their work was being rejected by the scientific community, some members of the Santiagueña society (which saw itself as a preserver of national identity at the time of the construction of nationalism) continued to consider the Wagner brothers as eminent and wise scholars, as founding heroes who enabled local society to see itself as a cradle of a millenary civilisation. This is an important point which we want to develop.

Local Influences and Reactions

We can approach the issue of the influence of the archaeological work of the Wagner brothers on the identity construction processes of Santiago del Estero from many angles. One of them is the consequences of the de-historisation they made of the millenary 'Civilización Chaco-Santiagueña' and its consequent genetic diseugagement from the indigenous people at the time of the European conquest. The vagueness and absurdity of their temporal schema, that resulted in a-historicity, produced a real effect of de-historisation on the concrete indigenous world on which they claimed knowledge. These were not real indigenous people at the 'Civilización', but mysterious mythic heroes. And this was an origin myth not only for Santiago del Estero but with universal claims, due to its mysterious link with the primordial cradle of humanity. The resulting image, because of its projection into an infinite past, de-historicises the real past of the province.

The Wagner brothers imagined a Chaco-Santiagueña Civilisation emerging from an extra-American cradle, born out of a Magna Mater of all world civilisations: originating from an unknown continent it had scattered all around the planet through migratory waves, thus reaching America and the Chaco-Santiagueña prairie. With this framework they maintained the idea of an 'Empire of the Prairies' raised by mound builders from a disappeared civilised race, without any genetic link with indigenous people founded there by conquerors who arrived in the sixteenth century. Repeatedly they say it is a civilisation 'many thousand years old' although not temporal, not measurable, not contrastable, located in a heroic age, in a cradle of transcendent events. Lacking any absolute chronological timeline in an objective sense, it resides in a mythic chronological dimension, with no historical reference points.

A great antiquity, a great effort, a great size, a great spirit and originality were all characteristic traits found many times over within the Chaco-Santiagueña Civilisation by its discoverers. This civilisation lacked nothing, in the peculiar interpretation of the Wagner brothers, in order to represent its totemic, mythic, symbolic, distant and primitive origin. For them, nothing in direct historic continuity connected this civilisation with the state of savageness they saw in indigenous Santiago del Estero founded by the Spaniard conquerors. In their view, America as a whole had become impoverished in respect of former ages of glory:

> We agree with the words of archaeologist, Marquis of Nadailac: 'At every turn, South America displays vestiges of a disappeared race, from an eclipsed civilisation and always is necessary to come to the same conclusion, our absolute impossibility to know the origin or decadence of these races, represented today by a few poor savages, without past and without future' (Wagner and Righetti 1946: 99).

Despite the susequent cultural decline, the Chaco-Santiagueña Civilisation emerges as floating in time because of its extraordinary nature, losing itself ahistorically in the circumstances of a fantastic origin far away from any real context, only viable in a fabulous golden age.

Fusion between the archaeologist and the artist, often considered desirable by the brothers, and the application of their peculiar 'geographic and visual' method, favour this mix of myth and historiography traversing the texts. High antiquity expressions make sense as a support for the idea of a civilising heroic age, distant from so-called Hispanic-indigenous contact in barbarian times. This later period of the disappeared Civilisation constituted a time of 'peoples without history', of 'savages Indians', running around naked, impossible to identify with 'the great Civilisation' that had produced beautiful and significant ceramic pieces, as indicated by at the archaeological finds in Santiago del Estero, nor with the builders of multiples mound that furrowed Santiagueña land following an almost topographic plan, ascribed to a communal action mobilised by a theocratic power.

To mark a break with the moment of the contact Spanic–Indigenous seemed to be a goal of the exaggerated chronological expressions of the Wagner brothers. But these expressions, because of their vagueness and absurdity, contributed even more to de-historicise the indigenous world they claimed they were talking about. As the authors of the book's preface say: 'For now, the archaeology of the newly discovered "Chaco-Santiagueña Civilisation" introduces itself in a pure condition, away from any possible history, from any anecdote. It acquires an almost abstract value symbolism from the human spirit. Maybe it will escape forever any strict chronology, and glide in positive eternity' (Canal Feijóo and Paz 1934: XII). In fact, emerging as bearing a great antiquity added greater credibility to the discovery and to its discoverer, as had been the case with the 'Man of the Plata' and Ameghino (1881). The towering antiquity attributed to the archaeological finds appears repeatedly as important to Emilio Wagner, the discoverer, and to Santiago del Estero (and Santiagueños), the land that enabled the renaissance of the 'Chaco-Santiagueña Civilisation'. It is symptomatic, in turn, that the brothers dedicate 'the work of their lives' first to Santiago del Estero, and then to the Argentine Republic, their land of adoption that was good enough to receive them and profited from their work though the extraordinary claim to be the cradle of a disappeared empire.

This attempt to reconstruct through archaeology a past devoid of historicity has its parallels in the history of the discipline. The Wagner brothers regarded their hundreds of mounds as identical in many respects to those found in the west of the Appalachians, in the United States of America. These mounds made it possible for North Americans, also immigrants to new lands anxious 'to arrange [their] own history in order to compete with Europe' (Trigger 1992: 105), to forge themselves a past that would give them a local lineage but, at the same time, that would not contaminate them with the present indigenous population. Thus was constructed an origin myth and a glorious past for the North American nation that, as with the Wagners' Civilisation, was conceived without involving themselves with the 'wandering tribes' founded there by conquerors and settlers (Trigger 1992: 104). In a period of nationalism and ethnocentrism loaded with identity discourses, these racial myths served to justify the persecution of 'redskins', to deny them the possession of lands and to undermine their claims by reference to some mysterious 'mound builders'. In this manner myths for constructing great pasts for the new nations were developed, independently of any indigenous ancestors subsequently displaced from these lands.

As with the Chaco-Santiagueña Civilisation, many continued to believe in the myth of the mound builders even after it was discredited by the scientific community. As noted by Trigger (1992), refuting the myth of mound builders implied not only the total rejection of the glowing tributes it had always received from the public, but also a reappraisal of the genuine achievements of different group of builders. Lastly, it also implied the erasure of a past which, however constructed, had been chosen as legitimate. The Wagner brothers thus refused to accept the scientific proof and arguments that undermined the most significant and greatest features of their Chaco-Santiagueña Civilisation. It was made clear that there were no elements to support this proclaimed ancient antiquity, and that there was actually irrefutable evidence for Hispanic contact and cultural historic continuity with the indigenous population at the time of the conquest. In this same spirit we can consider the obstinate attempts to give pre-eminence to claimed influences or cultural dependencies from ancient civilisations of the Old World, expressed in 'correlations', over the local links to the indigenous culture.

The southeast North American mounds, like those of the Santiago del Estero, were the subject of a great scientific and extra-scientific debate, and provided important opportunities for mobilising interests and developing research work around the problem. The issue aroused such public interest that some books on the 'civilised' mound builders achieved significant commercial success (Fagan 1984). The press was gripped by sensationalism and by 'less sober authors', as in the case of the Wagner book (Martínez, Taboada and Auat. 2003). This mound-builders question (and that of Glacial man) was precisely the topic of the moment in North American archaeology when the brothers were in their youth. In fact, they seem to have ignored the decisive discoveries published at the end of the nineteenth century which debunked once and for all the myth: Wagner's text of 1934 maintains that the enigma of the mound builders has not yet been resolved.

What seems to us most significant here are the parallel attempts to give an antique and noble ascendancy to an American society overwhelmed by recent immigration and marked by some anguish regarding its origins. To achieve this it was necessary break down historical continuity, in order to dissociate those ancestors with the indigenous population at the moment of the European conquest, characterised by irremediable savageness and progenitors of the contemporary mestizo popular classes. For Chaco-Santiagueña Civilisation, culture nobility blurs in the enigma of the past, and reduplicates itself through another mysterious connection: the 'fusaiolas' (spindle whorls considered by the Wagner brothers to be identical to those found by Schliemann at Hissarlik) were connected with another distinguished past, that of the heroic Trojans of Homer's Iliad. This anguish for origins was of course spread all over Argentina; however, the 'Santiagueños' felt that they had a particular call and mission to respond to it.

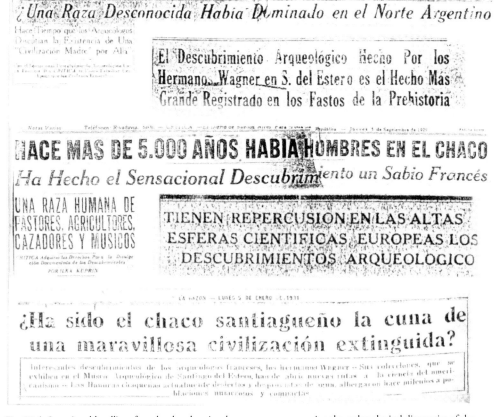

Fig. 20.4 Sensational headlines from local and national newspapers announcing the archaeological discoveries of the Wagner brothers in Santiago del Estero, and their international repercussions.

The Wagners' Work and the Building of Identity Discourses

Between 1927 (the date of the first Archaeological Missions financed by the province of Santiago del Estero) and 1934 (the date of the publication of the controversial book by the Wagner brothers), a significant part of the elite of Santiago del Estero blindly endorsed – in various ways – this popular work which tacitly build an image of the most remote past of the province: an elaborated discourse regarding what had occurred in this country before the arrival of the Spaniards. This was not isolated to the provincial level but extended to the whole country. Within the province it corresponded with the almost simultaneous emergence of an idea that constituted Santiago del Estero as the 'reserve' of the 'most authentic' of the country, expressed in dances, music and customs. In the context of national circumstances, as much from the point of view of literature as from the general social experience of the upper classes, the phenomenon was simultaneous with the impact of mass immigration and with the ensuing questions of national character, linked to early twentieth century nationalisms (Fig. 20.4).

A school inspector who had become a compiler of folklore, Andrés Chazarreta, begun performing at that time artistic tours around the country with a Native Arts Company. Likewise many intellectuals visited Santiago del Estero guided by Bernardo Canal Feijóo, a young friend, prefacist and translator of the Wagner brothers, and by other members of the Santiagueña Cultural Association 'La Brasa' (Fig. 20.5). These provided to the Santiagueños an image of their own making. Waldo Frank, a North American intellectual, was preparing 'a book of impressions and analysis around the Argentine Republic', in which – according to the local newspaper 'El Liberal' – 'a special place is reserved to Santiago, presented within the national panorama, with typical and unmistakable features'. Before departing from Santiago del Estero, Frank indicated that 'only in our province he found the pure art and noble spirituality he was searching for in Argentina'. And then, from Buenos Aires, before returning to his native country, he said that it was at Santiago del Estero where he found 'the most original', since here he could 'hear authentic music that attracts a great deal of my attention due to its rhythm and beauty. The society called La Brasa, formed by very intelligent boys, took it upon themselves to show me how much original features and scenary exist in that region'. The same general impressions would be repeated by Spanish poets Ramón Gómez de la Serna in 1931, Rafael Alberti in 1940 and Cordoba Iturburu in 1938.

'Patios' with guitars and geranium, warm hospitality, couplets and popular dances were, together with a tour of the Archaeological Museum, the obligatory trail for these visitors to Santiago del Estero, the province whose foreign population totalled just 3.7 per cent in 1914 compared with 30.3 per cent for the

BERNARDO CANAL FEIJÓO

◆

ENSAYO
SOBRE LA EXPRESION
POPULAR ARTISTICA
EN SANTIAGO

BUENOS AIRES
Compañía Impresora Argentina, S. A. Alsina, 2049
1937

Fig. 20.5 Canal Feijóo's book (1937) dedicated to the popular contemporary art of Santiago del Estero, but significantly illustrating a fragment of Santiagueña pottery on the cover.

whole country and 50 per cent in Buenos Aires. The original identity of Santiago Estero, linked to the origins of Argentina, has thus both a demographic and an historical basis. The impact caused by the established immigration in the 1930s, produced disdein for new national identity among the elites, and made them valorise 'criollismo' (Creole) as their title of nobility, validating those provinces that remained marginalised from the transformations. The process by which the provincial elites realised their 'originality' and then assigned themselves a mission of cultural 'reserve' for the nation is certainly a complex one, but it is difficult to exclude from this process the role undoubtedly played by the mirror of its prestigious visitors.

In this framework, it is possible to link the cultural effervescence that characterised the provincial capital of Santiago del Estero in those years – as expressed notably through archaeological research – with the broader questions of the Santiagueño and national identities and origins, and more generally with the collective construction of local traditions.

Despite the auspicious historic moment for the building of identity myths, the historical narrative of the Chaco-Santiagueña Civilisation does not provide a convincing starting point for an assertion of the original indigenous world of Santiago del Estero. The enormous (and mysterious) historic silence between 'The Civilisation' and the actual indigenous people led to exclude them and their descendants as actors in real history. Since there were only primitive 'Indians' when the conquerors arrived, these could only be considered as wombs for breeding, an indolent race that could not have helped Santiagueños descendants to build the future. Indeed, the indigenous people were frequently characterized as stupid and lazy in discourses of that period in Santiago del Estero. It follows from this thesis that civilised indigenous people are excluded from history, reduced to a symbol in order to feed the regional 'folklore'. In these circumstances, all that remains is the remarkable beautiful ceramic art, mute images from an unknown past: objects, with magnificent originality, hiding more than they reveal.

The image of an ancient 'great Chaco-Santiagueña Civilisation' continued in titles such as 'muy noble y leal' (very noble and loyal) and 'Madre de Ciudades' (Mother of Cities). These constituted important mythopoietic factors that, at the end, strengthened fatalist images of an identity anchored in the past and helpless to imagine a future, hardly an 'historical assertion' if talking about the mistreated 'mother of cities' and fundamentally hopeless if the reference was to the mysterious civilisation (Plate 15).

The concept of identity discourse, referring to a symbolic space floating in an indefinite past, can change over a *gesture*. Later works of Canal Feijóo, almost to the end, did not treat the Santiagueña identity issue in connection with ongoing archaeological discoveries, but rather they always showed photographs, drawings or vignettes extracted from the Wagners' great book of 1934. No less effective as a mythopoietic factor, the gesture assumes and maintains the hint of a past intended to make sense of the present. Santiago del Estero had a noble origin, even though marked by historical impotence. In return, that origin has left Santiago del Estero a legacy, perpetuated through tradition, to stand out through art, to reaffirm its singular personality through the higher forms of cultural expression.

References

Ameghino, F. 1881. *La Antigüedad del Hombre en el Plata*. Paris Buenos Aires: Imprenta Masson.

Canal Feijóo, B. 1937. *Ensayo sobre la Expresión Popular Artística en Santiago*. Buenos Aires: Compañía Impresora Argentina, S.A.

Canal Feijóo, B. and M. Paz. 1934. 'Prefacio de los Traductores', in E. Wagner and D. Wagner (eds), *La Civilización Chaco-Santiagueña y sus Correlaciones con las del Viejo y Nuevo Mundo*. Buenos Aires: Compañía Impresora Argentina, S.A, pp. XI–XV.

Fagan, B. 1984. *Precursores de la Arqueología en América*. México D.F.: Ediciones Fondo de Cultura Económica.

Martínez, A., C. Taboada and A. Auat. 2003. Los Hermanos Wagner: entre Ciencia, Mito y Poesía. *Arqueología, Campo Arqueológico Nacional y Construcción de Identidad en Santiago del Estero. 1920–1940*. Santiago del Estero: Ediciones Universidad Católica de Santiago del Estero.

Renfrew, C. and P. Bahn. 1993. *Arqueología. Teorías, Métodos y Práctica*. Madrid: Ediciones Akal.

Trigger, B. 1992. *Historia del Pensamiento Arqueológico*. Barcelona: Ediciones Crítica.

Wagner, E. 1918. *L'Allemagne et l'Amérique Latine (Souvenirs d'un Voyageur Naturaliste)*. Paris: Alcan Editions.

——— . 1919a. *A Travers la Forêt Brésilienne (De l'Amazone aux Andes)*. Paris: Alcan Editions.

——— . 1919b. *La Revanche de la Kultur (La Troisième Guerre Punique)*. Paris: Alcan Editions.

——— . and O. Righetti. 1946. Archéologie Comparée. Résumé de Préhistoire. Buenos Aires: Ediciones Peuser.

——— . and D. Wagner. 1934. *La Civilización Chaco-Santiagueña y sus Correlaciones con las del Viejo y Nuevo Mundo*. Buenos Aires: Compañía Impresora Argentina, S.A.

Chapter 21

Language, Nationalism and the Identity of Archaeologists

The Case of Juhani Rinne's Professorship in the 1920s

Visa Immonen and Jussi-Pekka Taavitsainen

Abstract

In the heat of the ethno-linguistic conflict between the Finnish-speaking and Swedish-speaking parties at the beginning of the 1920s, funding was given for a chair in medieval archaeology at the Finnish University of Turku. The professorship was actually specifically created for the archaeologist Juhani Rinne. However, his Swedish-speaking background was drawn to the centre of heated disputes over language, national identity and historical studies. The reasons why the professorship was not attained at the Finnish University of Turku are complex, combining many short- and long- term developments. Examining the reasons reveals the ways in which archaeology is intertwined with nationalist projects and university policies.

A New Professorship in a Newborn State

In the Nordic countries, archaeology was established as an academic discipline in the nineteenth century, but one aspect of archaeology, historical archaeology, remained outside academia until the mid-twentieth century. There were, however, unsuccessful attempts to introduce historical archaeology, or more precisely, medieval archaeology into the universities in Lund, Uppsala and Turku (Åbo). In this study, we concentrate on the case of historical archaeology at the Finnish University of Turku in the 1920s. The reasons why a professorship in the subject was never attained at the Finnish University of Turku are complex, combining many short- and long- term developments. Their examination reveals the ways in which archaeology is intertwined with the definitions of nationality and scholarly ideals. These issues culminated in a debate over the national identity of the archaeologist Juhani Rinne (1872–1950) (Fig. 21.1), who was intended to be the first holder of the chair. Although the dispute was fierce and often rhetorically crude, it should be noted that basically the same issues have become more and more topical at the beginnings of the twenty-first century, when the identities of archaeologists, the limits and definitions of objectivity, and scholarly ethics became central questions in archaeological discussion. Furthermore, the newly established interest in Finnish medieval archaeology in the 1990s has also been associated with the transformations of the Finnish nationalist project in the European Union (Ligi 1993: 31–32; Taavitsainen 1996; Fewster 2000: 108; Vilkuna 2001).

Before the colourful process of trying to create the new professorship and its ultimate failure can be scrutinised, it is crucial to understand the political situation of the 1920s. Finland was a young state; it had gained its independence in 1917. The following year saw a horrific civil war

Fig. 21.1 A portrait of the archaeologist Juhani Rinne. Photo courtesy of Johan Nikula.

between the socialists and conservatives, which shattered the illusions of a harmonious, unified Finnish people. Also Finnish academia was undergoing a fundamental transformation in the early 1920s. New universities were being founded in a country where there had previously been only one, in Helsinki. In Turku, a Swedish-speaking private university, the Åbo Akademi, opened in 1918, and its Finnish-speaking counterpart, the Finnish University of Turku, opened in 1920. The creation of new universities was to a large extent motivated by a need to create an academic community worthy of the new state. Another result of developing the academia was the founding of a chair in Finnish and Nordic archaeology at the University of Helsinki in 1921 (Salminen 1993: 32, 35–36). There were also rumours about and plans for a department of archaeology to be founded at the Åbo Akademi at the turn of the 1920s, but the initiatives came to nothing (Meinander 1991: 67–68).

Another important factor affecting the universities and the whole political and cultural life in Finland at the time was the so-called ethno-linguistic conflict (*kielitaistelu*) (Huttunen 1968: 507–26; Hämäläinen 1969: 73–96; Klinge 1964: 132–38). It was a wide-ranging debate over the position of Finnish and Swedish in building the nation and the dominance of the Swedish language among the intelligentsia. The pre-eminent status of Swedish in academia, business and administration was in marked contrast with that of Finnish, which was the language of the common people. In the centre of this socio-political conflict between conservative Swedish and radical Finnish-speakers was the relationship between the educational system and language policy. In academia, the battle concentrated on the state-funded University of Helsinki, whereas both the new universities in Turku were so tightly bonded to one linguistic faction or the other from the start that the conflict only rarely, if ever, raged inside them. Also the dispute over the professorship at the University of Turku mostly involved the various opinions within the Finnish-speaking lobby.

On the party political front, the most radical stance in the language issue was taken by the Centrist Agrarian Party, which pursued the Finnish-speaking cause in an uncompromising manner. The Agrarian Party even established some links with the radical Finnish nationalistic movement (*Aitosuomalaisuus*). The party strove to create a united, strong Finland by bridging the gap between the intelligentsia and the common people and conceived the demands of the Swedish-speaking minority as obstructing these aspirations (Klinge 1964: 133; Hämäläinen 1969: 97–135; Alanen 1976: 629–30). The ideological father of the party, Santeri Alkio (1862–1930), was a colossal figure in the ethno-linguistic conflict, and he eagerly expressed his influential opinions on the Rinne case (Alanen 1976: 222–26, 626). Alkio considered securing the position of the Finnish language to be the primary goal in academic and educational issues (Alanen 1976: 608–609; Salminen 1993: 35–36).

Two Donations

A characteristic means for pursuing the cause of a given faction in the ethno-linguistic conflict were various private associations and foundations. Also the functioning of the two universities in Turku depended on their respective foundations. However, the Finnish-speaking donors were, as a rule, from lower social classes than the Swedish-speaking ones, which raised anger in the Finnish-speaking lobby. In the heat of the language battle, on 11th March 1924, Anna von Rettig donated five million Finnish marks, a substantial sum, to the Åbo Akademi for founding a theological department. The donation infuriated the Finnish lobby, and the products of a tobacco company owned by the Rettig family were placed under a boycott. The right wing, nationalistic magazine *Aitosuomalainen* (3/1924: 45–47) claimed that the donation only supported the cultural aspirations of the minority using the profits made on the tobacco products bought by the majority of the people: 'News are coming in of enormous demonstrations in Karelia, Ostrobothnia and Central Finland, where businessmen are returning their cigarettes. Major wholesalers have ceased to supply these products. And, indeed, for an honest, genuine Finn the Rettig cigarettes will not do.'

The Finnish University of Turku was soon given its share when, a few weeks later, the Rettig company donated three million marks to be used for founding a chair in historical archaeology (Fig. 21.2). The total sum donated to the university that year was a little over four million marks. Although the timing of the donation could suggest that it was merely an attempt to quell the rage of the Finnish lobby, the idea was probably older, as was emphasised when the donation was made public. The Rettig family, especially Fredric von Rettig (1843–1914), had been the most important benefactor of urban archaeology in Turku at the turn of the century, and Fredric von Rettig had even supervised some early urban excavations (Bahne 1950: 203–205; Drake 1995).

Various administrative bodies of the Finnish University greeted the news with enthusiasm. The Consistory or the board of professors expressed its gratitude, and the Faculty of Humanities declared

Fig. 21.2 The representatives of the Rettig company have delivered the donation to the university for founding a chair in historical archaeology (Photo: The archive of the Otava Publishing Company).

that the new chair would complement the research done at the University of Helsinki and the National Museum and be a fruitful supplement to the curriculum. The faculty proceeded to officially assign the chair to 'Finnish historical archaeology and cultural history'. There are two important points to be made on the faculty's decision. First, the chair was not titled 'medieval archaeology', which was the case in other Nordic countries, but with the broader term 'historical archaeology'. Second, although the donors had expressed the wish to found a chair in historical archaeology only, the title has been supplemented with 'cultural history' (*sivistyshistoria*). The administration considered the donation important not only as making possible the new professorship but also as an inspiring model. It was hoped that a major donation would revitalise the flux of smaller donations which had been diminishing for some time. The founding of the chair was rushed through the administration and the existence of the new professorship was official by the end of May 1924.

The First Professor

The next step was to choose and install the first professor to the post. In June 1924, rector Artturi H. Virkkunen, who was a strong supporter of the new chair, presented to the faculty the discussions which he had had with State Archaeologist Hjalmar Appelgren-Kivalo, professor of Scandinavian history Väinö Voionmaa and Rinne. On the basis of these discussions Virkkunen suggested that Rinne should be appointed to the professorship. The faculty agreed and decided to install him directly without the usual application procedure, although three official evaluations

Fig. 21.3 Juhani Rinne at Turku Cathedral (Photo: The National Board of Antiquities).

were ordered. However, major problems emerged with the evaluations as one of the three evaluators died and the other two evaluations were delayed. At this point, the local newspaper *Turunmaa*, supporter of the Agrarian Party, voiced its concern over the delay and urged the Consistory to settle for two evaluations. Despite the plea, a third evaluation was ordered and all three evaluations were finally received by the end of January 1925. All three evaluators unanimously considered Rinne to be more than suitable for the post.

The new professorship was specifically tailored for Rinne from the beginning. Already in 1919, when the academic programme for the Finnish University was being designed, Rinne and the historian Kustavi Grotenfelt had suggested the creation of a chair in archaeology (Jäntere 1942: 293–94, 370). This suggestion, however, did not gain support and was rejected. A more substantial outcome of Rinne's efforts was the article 'Archaeological research tasks in Turku and its vicinity' (1922). It was widely quoted by rector Virkkunen when he advocated founding the chair in historical archaeology in 1924. In the article, Rinne presents in detail the results of the urban excavations in Turku and outlines objectives for future studies. He argues that the state of urban archaeology in Turku and Finland is weak, although its results would be crucial for a country 'so poor in written sources' (Rinne 1922: 65–72). Since the historical research done at the Åbo Akademi focused on written sources, Rinne concludes that it would be the task of the University of Turku to take historical archaeology into its programme.

Rinne was the most competent medieval archaeologist in Finland at the time (Cleve 1950: 5–8; Voionmaa 1950: 70–72). He was born in Finnish-speaking surroundings in Turku and also lived most of his life in the town. At the time of his graduation from the University of Helsinki in 1899, he worked as a temporary Finnish teacher, but left this work to become a trainee at the Historical Museum of the State in 1900. After this his career had an upward tendency, and by 1920 he was a departmental director at the State Archaeological Commission. In 1923, he took charge of the restoration of Turku Cathedral, which has been considered his most important accomplishment in historical archaeology in addition to his extensive fieldwork at Koroinen, a site of an early medieval bishop's see (Fig. 21.3). In addition to his studies on Finnish churches and urban excavations, Rinne studied medieval castles and fortifications. As a culmination of these studies, his dissertation, published in 1914, was a presentation of the Finnish medieval hill forts and castles. Rinne was also one of the first Finnish scholars to study medieval artefacts. Keeping all this in mind, it is not surprising that Rinne has been called the father of Finnish medieval archaeology (Sarvas 1977: 370, 376; Drake 1992: 578).

A Clash over Language

Everything seemed to run smoothly towards the establishment of the new professorship, and at the beginning of May 1925, the Consistory recommended appointing Rinne. This decision was made public in newspapers, and a week later, *Turunmaa* unexpectedly published a small article which was to be a prelude to a general attack on Rinne. Titled 'The Finnish University of Turku: a man who scorns Finnishness to be professor?', the article stated that Rinne, 'despite his academic merits, can hardly be a suitable man for a professorship in a Finnish university'. Based on an anonymous source, it argued that Rinne had 'forgotten his Finnish descent to the extent that he uses Swedish with his family; furthermore, his children go to Swedish schools.' The university cannot appoint Rinne, the article concludes, 'since it must be a requirement that professors of this academy, at least, are absolutely Finnish, saturated with nationalism.' It is not known what initially triggered the attack, but something probably happened behind the official scenes, since all the facts presented in the *Turunmaa* article had been largely known for years, and Rinne had not made public political statements and was not to make any. Furthermore, the debate over the professorship remained mainly at the local level.

The new development did not pass unnoticed by the university's administration. The newly appointed rector V.A. Koskenniemi considered the situation very harmful for the university. He was afraid of student demonstrations and, more importantly, the reactions of the donors, but he did not know how to answer the innuendo about Rinne's language use at home as Koskenniemi considered it to be true. He was not alone in the administration in seeing the accusations as having substance, although he, like many others, did not consider Rinne's use of Swedish language a proper reason to abstain from appointing him. Nevertheless, the situation was thought to be too harmful for the university. Members of the Consistory unofficially regarded it impossible for the appointment to proceed without a proper, public answer to the accusations, and Koskenniemi had hopes that Rinne would decline the post altogether. In a vote, the Consistory officially decided to recommend Rinne's appointment.

Newspapers played a pivotal role in the political life of the 1920s, and they also had a major impact on the professorship debate and its outcome. Rinne's pending professorship incited news, editorials and letters to the editor for almost two years from spring 1924 to spring 1926. In newspapers, the battle over the chair in historical archaeology raged between radicals and conservatives. The purpose and aims of research into the past came under scrutiny. Should scholars and scholarly institutions follow the requirements of objectivity or should they be faithful to nationalism? Or do these two aspirations exclude each other? Also the relationship of archaeologists' language identity with their research was debated. Can a scholar with 'improper identity' meet the requirements of research defined as proper?

The main supporter of the Agrarian Party was the newspaper *Ilkka*, founded by Alkio and subscribed to mainly by Ostrobothnian readers. It published extensive columns condemning the situation. In Turku, *Ilkka*'s local equivalent was *Turunmaa*, which after the initial attack continued criticising Rinne's appointment and expressed its disappointment over the university's policy. The appointment of a Swedish-speaking professor was considered a betrayal of the contract between Finnish-speaking donors and the university. In contrast, *Uusi Aura*, *Turunmaa*'s main competitor for the local agrarian readership and supporter of the right-wing Coalition Party, was more moderate. *Uusi Aura* reminded that one must not confuse the appointment policy with the relationship between the university and its benefactors. Only the independence of the university can guarantee the quality of its work. In terms of the number of subscribers, the most important of the local newspapers was *Turun Sanomat*. It had a liberal publication policy and supported the views of

Fig. 21.4 Political cartoon depicting the philosopher Eino Kaila. The caption accompanying the cartoon, where the tree represents the radical Finnish nationalistic movement: 'Damn, did I hit a rock after all? We philosophers don't seem to make good lumber-jacks...'

Fig. 21.5 Rinne walking in Turku (Photo courtesy of Johan Nikula).

the Progressive Party. Considering the paper's wide circulation and liberal policy, it is striking how little the incident and subsequent debate over the professorship was commented on, although the debate did not pass entirely without notice. *Turun Sanomat* remained somewhere between the polarities of *Turunmaa* and *Uusi Aura*, and saw the main problem in outsiders and political issues affecting the university policy. It abstained from pushing its point as drastically as the other newspaper involved. In addition to the local newspapers, the incident was reported in other newspapers, especially vigorously on the pages of the magazines *Aitosuomalainen* and *Suomen Heimo*. The former was the voice of the Finnish nationalistic movement and the latter of the equally radical Academic Society of Karelia.

The situation escalated when *Suomen Heimo* and *Ilkka* became involved, heavily criticising the university's appointment policy. Furthermore, they questioned the nationalist spirit of the university altogether, and saw the case of Rinne as only one indication among several others of 'bilingual theories' which infested the university. This fear of a compromised, Finnish-Swedish cultural hybrid was recurring theme in the rhetoric of the Finnish nationalistic movement (Alanen 1976: 628). Another often repeated argument stated that the university should appoint only the best, nationalistically minded Finnish academic talents (*Aitosuomalainen* 4/1925: 77–78; 5/1925: 91). Only that way would the university serve its purpose. According to the ideology of the Finnish nationalistic movement, only those men who spoke Finnish at home and in their office and who had a Finnish name and mind were suitable for posts which served the common good (Hämäläinen 1969: 104–106). The debate and openness on matters of appointment policy was claimed not to be harmful for the university but an opportunity to heal its infections and reinforce its nationalist spirit (Valkama 1977: 134–35).

The debate was fuelled when in the spring of 1925 the professor of philosophy Eino Kaila published an article analysing the Finnish nationalistic movement (*Valvoja-Aika* 4/1925). He described it as the symptom of a mass-psychological disorder. Using Rinne's case as just one example, Kaila concluded that the movement was chauvinistic, ultra-democratic and infused with primitive racism.[1] Kaila's article infuriated the supporters of the Finnish nationalistic movement and inspired articles and reader's comments for months (Fig. 21.4). The article and the fury it created deepened the crisis within the university administration drastically. As the situation threatened the funding of the university, the administration found the situation untenable. The Consistory did not see any other choice but to forcefully disengage itself from Kaila's opinions and express its support for the nationalist cause (Perälä 1970: 41). The announcement was met with satisfaction in the newspapers, and it became only the first in a series of actions which the university took in order to defend itself from the critics. One of these defensive moves was the appointment of Alkio into the administrative committee of the university and another was the cancellation of Rinne's appointment. After the Consistory's first decision to support Rinne's appointment, the Chancellor of the university had been postponing his formal approval and in the end did not sign the decision. Finally, in 1926 the chair in historical archaeology was replaced by a chair in sociology. Like historical archaeology, the discipline was new in Finland and the chair was in fact tailored for its first holder, Uno Harva.[2] As soon as this new plan had been devised, the new chair in sociology was hastily founded and its professor began his work in the spring of the same year (Anttonen 1987: 101–103).

While the professorship debate raged, Rinne was directing the restoration of Turku Cathedral and after finishing that in 1929, he started planning the restoration of the Turku Castle. Rinne was appointed State Archaeologist in 1929 and remained in the post until 1935 (Fig. 21.5) (Cleve 1950: 6). New plans for a chair in historical archaeology were not presented. In Turku, the teaching of prehistoric archaeology began in 1956, and a Department of Archaeology was, eventually, founded in 1964 (Perälä 1977: 187–88; Pihlman 1994: 2; cf. Taavitsainen 2003: 13).

Paradigms and Contracts

The opinions on Rinne's appointment expressed in newspapers and private letters orbited around nationalism. It was a point of gravity where participants defined the relationship between academic work and the nation in different ways. Interest in this complex intertwining of nationalism and reconstructions of the past has been a major theme in studies of the history of archaeology since the 1980s (e.g. Trigger 1984; Kohl and Fawcett 1995; Díaz-Andreu and Champion 1996). In the context of Finnish archaeology, Derek Fewster (1999, 2002) has applied the concept of 'nationalist paradigm' in describing the history of Finnish archaeology and its conception of the past. The concept has been widely used in studying the relationship between archaeology and the nation or nationalism. The nationalist paradigm could be defined as the frame of both popular and disciplinary discourses which enables them to ask and answer questions on the past.

Although the concept of paradigm has relevance here as the nationalist project was the background to the whole confrontation and a shared source of justification, it is problematic in analysing the small-scale debate over the professorship. It brings the risk of muting negotiations and resistances and hinders seeing the active manipulation and forging of the nationalist paradigm. This has led us to approach our subject microhistorically, tracing major trajectories of nationalism, disciplinary history and ethno-linguistic identity intersecting at a micro level (Ginzburg 1989; Peltonen 2001). Instead of paradigm, we would be more inclined to apply the concept of 'implicit contract' to analyse the interplay between various agents of the event and its historical context and the way the devices of the paradigm are exploited in producing meaning. The concept of implicit contract describes the relationship of the state or nation and academia, and it somewhat overlaps with the concept of paradigm as it is something shared by the scholarly community and remains more or less unarticulated but is still a fundamental basis for academic work. In contrast to paradigm, the concept of implicit contract reveals the benefits given to the parties involved: on the one hand, the contract guaranteed an appropriate past for the nation, and on the other hand, it gave both economic and paradigmatic prerequisites to archaeology. The idea of a contract also emphasises the shared assumptions that the parties for and against the appointment of Rinne had despite their disagreements over the interpretation of the contract. Where there were cracks in the conception of the national contract, the parties involved worked to explicate their differing interpretations on the conditions of the contract.

Archaeology was one of the national disciplines (*kansalliset tieteet*), and it had a duty to give Finns reasons to be proud of their past and find the ancient roots of independent Finland. Already in 1919, when Rinne and Grotenfelt made the initiative for creating a new chair in archaeology, they justified the cause by referring to the importance of archaeology for the study of the nation's past. Even in the frenzy of the debate in 1924 and 1925, no-one denied the importance of the chair for the nationalist project, and in all letters and editorials, the nationalist purpose of the new chair was repeated time after time almost in the same words. The radicals claimed that the contract between the people and the Finnish University would be violated if a person with a doubtful nationalist mind was elected. On the other hand, even the most radical views did not intervene in the way archaeological research was carried out as long as it was derived from the national paradigm since outright interference would have undermined the credibility of academic work.

In the debate, the insoluble differences lay in the ways in which the relationship between academic research and the nation or, rather, between scholarly work and its funding was defined. The battle was fought over appointment policy rather than the content produced by the discipline. In fact, it was very seldom explicitly stated that the possible appointment of Rinne might affect the results produced by the discipline. Only the magazine *Suomen Heimo* (1925/3: 41) and the newspaper *Ilkka* (13.3.1925) published two articles where some traces of content analysis can be detected. In both articles, the author wonders how a deficiently nationalist person could teach historical archaeology at the Finnish University since the discipline has created studies which in many respects follow the lines of the Swedish nationalist policy. However, the claim does not refer exclusively to historical archaeology but to archaeology in general and appears repeatedly in the texts of the Finnish nationalistic movement (e.g. *Aitosuomalainen* 7/1925: 141–43).

The Justifications of Historical Archaeology

After the efforts to establish historical archaeology as an academic discipline failed, it was not until the late 1980s (Taavitsainen 2003: 13) that a renewed but again unsuccessful attempt was made to create a professorship in historical archaeology, this time at the Åbo Akademi. Is the attempt of the 1920s sufficient to explain the situation for the rest of the century? What other factors may also have contributed to the situation where historical archaeology remained non professional outside academia? It would be tempting to associate the marginality of historical archaeology in the academia with the Finnish nationalist conception of the past, where the Middle Ages are the first period of dependency under Swedish domination. However, this interpretation seems inadequate from a Scandinavian perspective as the development of historical archaeology was similar in Sweden and Denmark, where the Middle Ages were fundamental in the creation of national identity (Andrén 1997: 35–38).

Between the First and the Second World Wars, the attitudes towards the Middle Ages and their use in the national project rested on a conception of uniform and teleological history destined to lead to independent Finland, as for instance Fewster (2002) has stated. In nationalist historiography, the Late Iron Age and Early Middle Ages were considered as the last period of an independent, militaristic Finland organised in tribes. The time of the tribes came to an end when

the long subjection under the Swedish rule began, and with the Swedes came Catholic
Christianity. Notwithstanding the possible stamp of Swedish domination and Catholicism,
medieval castles and churches were part of national romanticism and objects of extensive
restoration and renovation work in nineteenth and early twentieth centuries (Gardberg 1984: 65).
Moreover, there was a complementary view of the Middle Ages which emphasised Finland as a
fairly autonomous part of Sweden and its local leaders as imbued with the Finnish spirit. Especially
in the monumental works of the historian Jalmari Jaakkola, the medieval remains were seen as
manifestations of Western culture and Finland as the last citadel of western civilisation against the
eastern threat. The idea that the Middle Ages were a period of European culture or subjugation to
Swedish rule did not automatically exclude attaching national sentiments to medieval monuments
(cf. Fowler 1987: 237–41). The ambivalence the medieval period and its monuments had in
Finnish history made them suitable for the nationalist project.

When the Rettig company's donation set in motion the process to create a chair in historical
archaeology in 1924, archaeological research had been carried out on historical sites in Finland for
nearly sixty years (Sarvas 1977; Taavitsainen 1999: 6). The first excavation at a Finnish historical
site was undertaken in 1867, and before the turn of the century, a few other excavations had taken
place. Furthermore, when the Finnish Antiquarian Society launched its series of nationwide parish
surveys in 1876, historical monuments constituted an organic part of their programme. These
early parish surveys, like the few excavations at historical sites, focused specifically on such
monumental and distinctive remains as churches, monasteries and castles. Also research in the
urban area of Turku fundamentally concentrated on monuments. Remains of buildings or artefacts
found accidentally in the urban area during construction or other development work were
documented or recorded only randomly (Appelgren 1901; Drake 1984: 93–98).

The historical archaeology carried out in the latter part of the nineteenth century did not
differ significantly from contemporary prehistoric archaeology, but the contrast between the two
disciplines increased at the turn of the century. Prehistoric archaeology began to take a more
academic form and become a profession, and the term archaeology became defined primarily as
the study of the prehistoric past (Andersson 1993: 11–15). Anders Andrén (1997: 39–41) has
traced this development to the nineteenth-century notions of the past and how to study it
appropriately. The most important traces of prehistory lay hidden under the ground whereas the
most important expressions of the Middle Ages remained above the ground in the form of
churches, castles or objets d'art deposited in museums. Approaching these traces of the medieval
spirit did not require the efforts of a professional archaeologist but rather the gaze of an art
historian or the sentiment of a historian.

Institutionally historical archaeology was established neither as an academic discipline nor as
a specialized branch of heritage management (Andersson 1993: 13–15). Whereas archaeology
conceived as prehistory was taken into the state organisation of the cultural heritage as a separate
department, archaeological research on historical sites was driven to the departments of cultural
history and historical monuments. Although there were attempts to establish historical
archaeology within academia in the Nordic countries in the 1920s, they never succeeded
(Andersson 1993). In Lund, Otto Rydbeck was appointed as the professor of both prehistoric and
medieval archaeology, but his efforts to develop historical archaeology remained sparse. In
1920–1926, Bengt Thordeman was lecturer of art history and medieval archaeology in Uppsala.
Although documentation of historical remains and excavations at historical sites were carried out
in the early twentieth century, it was not until the latter part of the century that historical
archaeology started gaining institutional currency.

At the Intersection of Individual Identity, Disciplinary Identity and Nationalism

Historical archaeology has needed to justify its existence as a distinctive discipline since its beginnings (Sarvas 1977; Andrén 1997). In Finland, the justification has been a sought from the small amount and fragmentary nature of medieval and even younger written sources. Already in the late nineteenth century, the lacunae of the written sources were compensated for by 'reading' the surviving medieval monuments (Drake 1999: 19–23; Taavitsainen 1999: 9–10). Also Appelgren (1901) and Rinne (1922) in their early twentieth-century manifestos point out the importance of historical archaeology for the nation lacking written sources. Thus the need for historical archaeology was clearly defined in relationship to historiography, which was also a drawback. Historical archaeology could be considered as a complementary discipline in service of the synthetic work done by historians (Andrén 1997: 112–14, 126–28, 150–82; Taavitsainen 1999: 8). This is explicit in the title intended for the new professorship, 'Historical archaeology and cultural history'. Also the assumptions present in the plans and manifestos on creating the chair imply that historical archaeology was not considered to have a sufficiently clearly defined identity and the prerequisites to operate on its own. Creating a chair in historical archaeology independent of cultural history was apparently considered problematic, which made its usefulness for the nationalist project uncertain. Its benefits and necessity for building the nation were not as apparent as with disciplines like historiography or ethnography.

The process of creating the chair in historical archaeology at the Finnish University of Turku was motivated by the need of the newborn state to create national sciences and an appropriate past, which contrasted with the desperate need of the new university for resources. The chair was justified with the same nationalistic arguments as all the other national sciences, but its disciplinary identity was not as established as the others. The sensitive situation became untenable when the identity and suitability of Rinne came under scrutiny, which coincided with wider accusations questioning the national spirit of the university. The accusations exploded into an open battle, where the different lobbies all operated and justified their position in the confines of the nationalist paradigm. Indeed, no-one inside or outside the university denied the suspicious identity of Rinne, and the debate was fought more over the effect the appointment would have on the university in general. The main issue was the interpretation and extent of the contract between people and academia. Initially the situation might have had a different outcome, but after Kaila's article, the university had to secure its ideological and economic basis by a series of drastic defensive actions. It became apparent that appointing Rinne to the professorship was impossible, and the administration had no other alternative than to dissolve plans for the chair in historical archaeology.

Notes

1. In 1985, another philosopher, Ilkka Niiniluoto (1994), began his meditation on the autonomy or freedom of academia by paraphrasing the events surrounding Rinne's pending appointment.
2. Originally, Harva's last name was Holmberg, but in 1927 he changed it to the more Finnish form Harva to conform to the university's language policy (Anttonen 1987: 173).

References

Primary sources

Aitosuomalainen 1924–1926.
Ilkka 1924–1926.
Suomen Heimo 1924–1926.
Turun Sanomat 1924–1926.
Turun Suomalaisen Yliopistoseuran vuosikirja 1924–1926.
Turunmaa 1924–1926.
Uusi Aura 1924–1926.
Valvoja-Aika 1925.
Åbo Underrättelser 1924–1926.

Publications

Alanen, A.J. 1976. *Santeri Alkio.* Helsinki and Porvoo: WSOY.

Andersson, H. 1993. 'Medieval archaeology in Scandinavia', in H. Andersson and J. Wienberg (eds), *The Study of Medieval Archaeology: European Symposium for Teachers of Medieval Archaeology, Lund 11–15 June 1990.* Stockholm: Almqvist and Wiksell International, pp. 7–21.

Andrén, A. 1997. *Mellan ting och text: En introduktion till de historiska arkeologierna.* Stockholm/Stehag: Symposion.

Anttonen, V. 1987. *Uno Harva ja suomalainen uskontotiede.* Helsinki: Suomalaisen Kirjallisuuden Seura.

Appelgren, H. 1901. 'Det underjordiska Åbo', *Finskt Museum* 1901/VIII: 49–65.

Bahne, E. 1950. *P.C. Rettig ja kumpp. 1845–1945: Suomen tupakkateollisuuden vaiheita.* Turku: Rettig.

Cleve, N. 1950. 'Juhani Rinne', *Finskt Museum* 1950/LVII: 5–8.

Díaz-Andreu, M. and T. Champion. 1996. 'Nationalism and Archaeology in Europe: An Introduction', in M. Díaz-Andreu and T. Champion (eds), *Nationalism and Archaeology in Europe.* London: UCL Press, pp. 1–23.

Drake, K. 1984. 'Stadsarkeologisk forskning i Åbo', *Åbo landskapsmuseum: Rapport* 6: 92–101.

———. 1992. 'Medeltidsarkeologi i Finland', *Finsk Tidskrift* 10/1992: 577–80.

———. 1995. *Forntid, nutid, framtid: Åbo stads historiska museum – Åbo landskapsmuseum 1881–1981.* Åbo: Åbo landskapsmuseum.

———. 1999. 'Finlands nya medeltid', *META* 1/1999: 18–23.

Fewster, D. 1999. 'The Invention of the Finnish Stone Age: Politics, Ethnicity and Archaeology', in M. Huurre (ed.), *Dig it All: Papers Dedicated to Ari Siiriäinen.* Helsinki: Finnish Antiquarian Society and Archaeological Society of Finland, pp. 13–20.

———. 2000. 'Fornfolket i nutiden: Arkeologins politiska budskap', in D. Fewster (ed.), *Folket: Studier i olika vetenskapers syn på begreppet folk.* Helsingfors: Svenska litteratursällskapet i Finland, pp. 106–24.

———. 2002. 'Visions of National Greatness: Medieval Images, Ethnicity, and Nationalism in Finland, 1905–1945', in A. Gillett (ed.), *On Barbarian Identity: Critical Approaches to Ethnicity in the Early Middle Ages.* Turnhout: Brepols, pp. 123–46.

Fowler, D.D. 1987. 'Uses of Past: Archaeology in the Service of the State', *American Antiquity* 52(2): 229–48.

Gardberg, C.J. 1984. 'Medeltidsarkeologi i Finland', *Åbo landskapsmuseum: Rapport* 6: 64–70.

Ginzburg, C. 1989. *Clues, Myths, and the Historical Method,* trans. J. Tedeschi & A.C. Tedeschi. Baltimore, Md.: Johns Hopkins University Press.

Huttunen, V. 1968. *Täysivaltainen kansakunta 1917–1939.* Porvoo and Helsinki: WSOY.

Hämäläinen, P.K. 1969. *Nationalitetskampen och språkstriden i Finland 1917–1939,* trans. T. Warburton. Helsingfors: Schildt.

Jäntere, K. 1942. *Turun yliopiston perustaminen.* Helsinki: Suomen kirja.

Klinge, M. 1964. 'Ruotsalaisten eristäytymisliike ja aitosuomalaisuus 1920–luvulla', *Historian Aitta* XVI: 121–44.

Kohl, P.L. and C. Fawcett 1995. 'Archaeology in the Service of the State: Theoretical Considerations', in P.L. Kohl and C. Fawcett (eds), *Nationalism, Politics, and the Practice of Archaeology.* Cambridge: Cambridge University Press, pp. 3–18.

Ligi, P. 1993. 'National Romanticism in Archaeology: The Paradigm of Slavic Colonization in North-West Russia', *Fennoscandia archaeologica* X: 31–39.

Meinander, C.F. 1991. *Carl Axel Nordman*. Helsingfors: Svenska litteratursällskapet i Finland.

Niiniluoto, I. 1994. *Järki, arvot ja välineet: Kulttuurifilosofisia esseitä*. Helsinki: Otava.

Peltonen, M. 2001. 'Clues, Margins, and Monads: the Micro–Macro Link in Historical Research', *History and Theory* 40: 347–59.

Perälä, T. 1970. *Turun Yliopisto 1920–1939*. Turku: Turun yliopisto.

Perälä, T. 1977. *Turun Yliopisto 1939–1974*. Turku: Turun Yliopistosäätiö.

Pihlman, S. 1994. *A Short History of Archaeology at the University of Turku*. Turku: University of Turku.

Rinne, J. 1922. 'Muinaistieteellisiä tutkimustehtäviä Turussa ja sen ympäristössä', *Historiallinen Aikakauskirja* 2/1922: 65–74.

Salminen, T. 1993. 'Suomalaisuuden asialla: Muinaistieteen yliopisto-opetuksen syntyvaiheet n. 1877–1923', *Helsinki Papers in Archaeology* 6.

Sarvas, P. 1977. 'Om historisk arkeologi', *Historisk Tidskrift för Finland* 4/1977: 353–76.

Taavitsainen, J.-P. 1996. 'Onko menneisyydellä tulevaisuutta?', *Kanava* 3/1996: 167–69.

Taavitsainen, J.-P. 1999. 'Historiallisen ajan arkeologia tieteenalana ja antikvaarisena toimintana', *Museoviraston rakennushistorian julkaisuja* 20: 6–14.

Taavitsainen, J.-P. 2003. 'Piirteitä Turun arkeologian historiasta', in L. Seppänen (ed.), *Kaupunkia pintaa syvemmältä: Arkeologisia näkökulmia Turun historiaan*, Turku: TS-Yhtymä and SKAS, pp. 9–22.

Trigger, B. 1984. 'Alternative Archaeologies: Nationalist, Colonialist, Imperialist', *Man* 19: 355–70.

Valkama, L. 1977. 'Alkion ja Koskenniemen kirjeenvaihtoa', *Sananjalka* 19: 128–43.

Vilkuna, J. 2001. 'Time-bound theories about the origin of the Finns', *Acta Borealia* 18(1): 69–80.

Voionmaa, J. 1950. 'Juhani Rinne', *Suomen Museo* 1950/LVII: 69–72.

Chapter 22

Protohistory at the Portuguese Association of Archaeologists

A Question of National Identity?

Ana Cristina Martins

'As in large parts of Europe, archaeology in Lusitania stands before the abstruse issue of "celticism". But here the issue is simplified and emphasized in a particular way'.
F. M. Sarmento (1880: 1)

Abstract

The pioneers of Portuguese archaeology focused on the study of Iron Age hill forts, traditionally known as 'castros' or 'citânias'. Those studies aimed above all at understanding the rise and development of the so-called 'complex societies' in Portuguese territory, thought to result from a long process of mostly internal order, and not from a succession of waves of migration of peoples from abroad. We will, therefore, explore one of the more symbolic examples of this reality, which involved leading members of the Association of Portuguese Archaeologists, principally Francisco Martins Sarmento (1833–1899), an outstanding intellectual from the north-west of Portugal and the central character in this chapter.

Introduction

It is by now well established that the birth of nationalism and the affirmation of liberal ideas have motivated the establishment of archaeology as a scientific discipline, while also dictating and conditioning its internal organisation. Indeed, this close relationship was embodied in the nineteenth-century concept of 'nation', as the basis for a population unity with a right (and duty) to become a (sometimes) powerful political entity, apparently justified by a (desirable and necessary) certain past. And there was an urgent need to know (to recognise), divulge and to praise, and ensure the survival of the ideological programme that had been imposed. This process reached its peak during the nineteenth century, while it was being theorised by all intellectuals searching for a platform stand in a society, which until then had been almost totally dominated by the sword, aristocratic interests and ecclesiastical wishes.

Within this general framework, Portugal was no exception, even if some authors seem to hang on to the idea that the theoretical and practical evolution of archaeology never featured distinctive examples of any nationalistic appropriation of its object of study, and consequently of its multiple interpretations. Nor were there examples of the use of archaeological artefacts as national symbols, nor even a more specific intention of adapting research to certain political concepts of national(istic) background. For those intellectuals, Portugal never witnessed a close connection (woven abroad) between politics and science. This was superfluous, given the long existence of its geographical borders since the thirteenth century AD. But was it really so, or does this assumption result from the fact that Portuguese archaeologists never (excepting some isolated cases) gave this issue the thought it deserves? In fact, the History of Science, in general terms, is a comparatively recent area of study in our country, probably due to almost half a century of institutional repression, during the military dictatorship (1926–1933) and the authoritarian regime of the 'Estado Novo' (1933–1974), that quite intransigently managed and controlled cultural practices, leaving precious little room for any kind of epistemological analysis of scientific enterprises, while the latter were far too attached to the regime, the only entity that seemed able to ensure their development.

It is undeniable that Portugal already held considerable experience in the field of research and preservation of its ancient heritage, including some prehistoric monuments, even if, as in most European countries, until the early nineteenth century attention was primarily focused on the Roman heritage. Still, and certainly inspired by the main Western absolutist models of his day and age, in 1721 King João V (1689–1750) granted the recently formed 'Real Academia de História' (Royal Academy of History) the task of making an inventory of and conserving a vast series of heritage typologies, among which some were clearly archaeological, even if not so reported. But despite this remarkable first attempt at the institutionalisation of recording and preserving the historical and cultural heritage, a long series of events would subsequently sentence its development to a secondary role, in quite an indefinite future. The earthquake of 1755, the successive Napoleonic invasions, the departure of the Court to Rio de Janeiro (Brazil), the simultaneous occupation of Portuguese territory by French and British forces, endless internal wars, exile of members of the most prominent aristocratic houses, widespread anticlerical feelings among the people, and the independence of Brazil (and consequently the loss of its much needed gold) kept the young liberal regime from fully governing the territory according to powerful positivist principles.

Nevertheless, there is little doubt that with the liberal victory of 1833 the first step was taken towards the economic development of the country, and also towards the widening of its spiritual, mental and cultural horizons as one of the few (if not the only) ways of reaching the European intelligentsia, and its devotion to improving the young sciences of the nineteenth century. Still, one of the main reasons for the impasse met by heritage practice in Portugal was the almost complete absence of a consistent cultural policy, perhaps because there seemed to be no real or urgent need to emphasise the importance of preserving the vast and diversified heritage legacy, both from an economical and a cultural point of view. But, as in countries more involved in the Romantic Movement, Portugal also showed a tendency towards historical studies and the stimulation of the achievements of the young archaeological and anthropological sciences, perhaps as a way of establishing a certain (and politically necessary) image of homogeneity in a continental territory revealed by some specific features, like language, behaviour and religion, the only ones that seemed to hold the capacity to justify its cultural and geographical borders, supposedly formed already in medieval times.

After the Paris Exposition Universelle of 1867, the core members of the 'Associação dos Arqueólogos Portugueses' (Association of Portuguese Archaeologists) began to dedicate special attention to prehistoric studies. It is likely that they were influenced and inspired by research being carried out abroad. Their activities stimulated the study of megalithic structures as old Spanish integrationist ambitions were awakening, now reinforced by the unexpected support shown by some of the brighter Portuguese minds. Against this minority tendency, most of the intellectuals educated in enlightened cities like Paris or London, during the so-called 'liberal exile', who had grasped the main lines of aesthetic and philosophical thought, were trying to apply them to different areas of Portuguese daily life, and also to the preservation of the medieval and modern monuments. They also showed great sympathy for the development of archaeological studies, even in a context of apparent governmental indifference towards such specific issues. And this was perhaps the reason why the aim of some academies and associations was to study, publicise and preserve the Portuguese historical and cultural heritage. Still, they did not always show the right attitude towards the recording and conservation of the prehistoric and protohistoric heritage. This was only really affirmed after the IX 'Congresso Internacional de Antropologia e Arqueologia Pré-histórica' (9th International Congress on Prehistoric Anthropology and Archaeology, IX CIAAP), held in Lisbon in 1880.

Facing such a particular context, it is only natural that the pioneers of Portuguese archaeology focused on the study of Iron Age hill forts, traditionally known as 'castros' or 'citânias'. Those studies aimed above all at understanding the rise and development of the so-called 'complex societies' in Portuguese territory, thought to result from a long process of mostly internal order, and not from a succession of waves of migration of peoples from abroad. It was, without doubt, a remarkable example of how archaeological research was widely stimulated as it favoured an ideological programme, at a time when the European voices in favour of a peninsular integrationist policy were multiplying. In this context, the megalithic monuments have played a central role, as they represented the antiquity of the Portuguese nation, while the hill forts of its protohistory were able to reveal the fact that the territory was already united at the dawn of late prehistory. Thus the archaeological study of regions relevant to the designs of the national memory was promoted. The aim was to establish these regions as the ancient 'Lusitania', and attempt to establish a link between their inhabitants, led by one of the most valiant fighters of the Roman Empire, 'Viriatus', and the contemporary Portuguese, their putative heirs. It was important to consolidate the idea that long before the creation of the medieval state, the territory already featured a reality of old, like an ethnic homogeneity linked to the same territorial strip, the sole elements that could legitimate the intimate relationship between nationality and nation.

It is not my intention to fill the pages of this chapter with considerations on some of the most interesting examples of pre- and protohistoric research promoted within the 'Associação dos Arqueólogos Portugueses' during the nineteenth century. Indeed, other papers have already focused on the subject (Martins 2003). I only wish to explore one of the more symbolic examples of this reality, which involved leading members of the Associação dos Arqueólogos Portugueses, principally Francisco Martins Sarmento (1833–1899), an outstanding intellectual from the north-west of Portugal and the central character in this chapter.

'Celticism' in the Imagination of the Nineteenth Century

One striking issue attracts the attention of all those who address the epistemology of nineteenth-century studies of northern hill forts – the different views regarding the ethnic origin of their builders and main users. Considering how little was then known on the matter, the reasons for that controversy must lie in issues other than the strictly scientific. Indeed, we believe that the authors trying to shed some light on this issue were following some of the main European lines of thought, which mostly depended upon political ideologies that featured a strong national tendency. To be sure, Portugal did not need so urgently an ideological platform for its national survival, nor did it need to put an end to some expansionist pretensions that were to be found scattered across Europe, though the old ghost of Iberian incorporation still haunted its borders, deeply desired by some members of the Portuguese intelligentsia. And perhaps this was the reason for the different views on the subject we are discussing. However, this was not the only raison, as other issues equally influenced this divergence, among which the strong feelings of regionalism and localism, thriving of old in some parts of the country. All we are left with, it seems, is a speculative exercise on how

Fig. 22.1 J. Possidónio N.
da Silva (ca. 1857).

such internal tendencies have come to terms with the main lines of the archaeological, anthropological, and ethnological studies of that time, in a context of deep political instability, economical and financial weakness, and consolidation of local authoritarian practices, aimed at aborting any attempt to asphyxiate the strong sense of independence shared by the main rulers of the northern regions.

From an historical point of view, Portugal has always been more in favour of the policies of the United Kingdom, thus spurning France and Germany. Spain, on the other hand, was much closer to those two countries, and all for the revolutionary spirit of Paris, which the Portuguese authorities tried so hard to keep away from their borders, so as to perpetuate their more conservative attitude. Yet, the ideals of 1789 were quickly overthrown by Napoleon's ambitions, which searched in the study of the ancient past for the necessary grounds for its imperialistic practice. Germany was also committed to a geographical 'widening', namely from 1871 onwards, empowered by the 'German idealism' brought forward by a national(istic), moralist and moralising model of 'State', of Hegelian and Fichtenian roots. Clearly these positions had to have an influence on the emerging archaeological studies, particularly concerning the 'Celtic issue', which was then to know two quite different approaches.

Following a certain humanistic tradition, the Germans (with the French and the Scandinavians) seemed to prefer (for a while) the philological studies of the Indo-European world, screening along with the numismatics and epigraphy the more enlightening classical sources, on the subject of reference sites like 'Hallstatt' (1846) and 'La Tène' (1856). Beyond this research line, a second and essentially archaeological approach emerged, to be followed by Possidónio da Silva (1806–1896) (Fig. 22.1), under the influence of the Swedish historian and archaeologist Hans Hildebrand (1842–1913). These scholars met during the Bologna Congress (1871), where Hildebrand, along with the Swedish prehistorian Oscar Montelius (1843–1921) and certainly inspired by the Evolutionist approach of Ch.J. Thomsen (1788–1865) and J.J.A. Worsaae (1821–1885), had established the so-called 'crossed chronology' as an archaeological typology. The sketching of the identifying elements of the recently established understanding of 'culture', or rather, 'Archaeological culture', was now possible, as all the essential conditions seemed to have been brought together. The process was quickly applied to the Celts, which Gabriel de Mortillet (1821–1898), one of Possidónio's great mentors, would (by the end of the century) turn into the protagonists of one of the major invasive movements of European protohistory, almost as if they had established a real Empire, and being integrated in the diffusionist model defended by Possidónio on different occasions (Martins 2003). Nevertheless, it is likely that his contemporaries did not immediately understand the true reach of this position: that the apparent (and desired) distance between the nationalities would in this way be embodied by the presence of a hypothetical internal coherence, revealed by its ethnic, cultural, historical and even biological expressions. And, in this sense, scepticism seemed to grow against the legitimacy of the old concept of 'independent development'. As Possidónio da Silva would stress,

> In the absence of more positive archaeological data, good sense itself would advise us that in matters of imitation the peoples cannot escape the influence of other neighbouring peoples, to which they were linked by trade, common interests and racial kinship, which would have preceded them in the history of the World, even if only from a chronological point of view (da Silva 1890: 131).

In the meantime, this position would be crowned by the works of O. Montelius who, taking advantage of the wide network of railways in Europe travelled to Lisbon in 1879. Showing great enthusiasm for the results on dolmenic structures and materials found in southern Portugal presented by Possidónio during one of the annual sessions of the 'Société Française d'Archéologie', he considered Portuguese archaeological studies '[...] beaucoup plus avancés qu'en Espagne [qui] peut nous donner la solution de bien des questions importantes relatives aux peuples des dolmens.'[1] These 'peoples of the dolmens' would have moved through the European continent from the northern regions, from whence Montelius himself came, though he did not counter the evidence of branching and convergence recognisable in some artefactual types, as Possidónio da Silva suggested regarding the case of the so-called 'caches' of bronze axes found at some places in Portugal:

> Judging not only by the large amount of bronze axes that have been found in our country, but also by their particular shape, considering those that have been found in other nations, I am convinced that this is due to some industry that existed in this part of the peninsula.[2]

The issue was a somewhat delicate one though, even if F. Martins Sarmento stressed that 'the notion that this industry existed in ancient times in our country has a value that nobody can deny'[3] as standing for a specific bronze metallurgy in this peninsular region meant countering the theory that viewed the presence of bronze production in the Iberian Peninsula as a direct and exclusive consequence of some diffusionist process. This situation showed, after all, the dawn of the political use of the data gathered by this new archaeological science, and the emphasis given by some European circles to the concept of a (desired) Semitic cohesion and to the idea that the Aryan race had conceived and materialised the more outstanding cultural innovations of humankind (Duchêne 1996). This was, though, a very delicate issue, one that did not bring the consensus certainly desired by its most enthusiastic supporters. In Portugal, several of Possidónio da Silva's peers have repudiated him, ironically referring that,

> It is politics' turn to take advantage of the archaeological studies, as the emancipation claims of the Schleswig duchy are supported by the notion that archaeology and linguistics prove beyond doubt that the people's origin is purely Scandinavian, and not a single bit German (Ribeiro 1876: 7).

But these apparently discordant voices were the same ones that seemed to validate the 'ex oriente lux' theory, as they claimed, 'Asia is the primeval birth place of the Human species' (da Silva 1876: 83), while stating that,

> Among these superior races, the Caucasus race is no doubt the most superior, the one that developed to the highest degree the philosophy, the sciences and above all the fine arts, being their keeper for over fifty centuries [affirming that the Aryan race would be the] civilizing race by excellence, the only that has left a legacy of architectural monuments in all the countries that it could reach (da Silva 1876: 83).

And so the Western expansionist policy and the differentiation between 'Kulturvolker' and 'Naturvolker' were legitimised within the Associação dos Arqueológos Portugueses, as 'The observation of the facts has been proving everywhere that the uncultured and savage peoples, with few exceptions, are not the result of the degeneration of others higher in civilisation, of others intellectually, morally and industrially more developed' (de Corvo 1883–1884: 63), there being 'this or that tendency to progress: surely, though, some show an obvious incapacity for civilisation, even in its most simple and rudimentary conditions, and therefore there is an incompatibility between their existence and the inevitable expansion of the perfectible Human races' (de Corvo 1883–1884: 63).

Deep down, these views expressed one of the main particularities of the Portuguese intellectual movement in the nineteenth century, notoriously influenced by operating schemes dictated by the French and German academic circles, which replaced the former British ascendancy, as the organisation of the IX CIAAP, and the works of Émile Cartailhac (1845–1921) and Emile Hübner (1834–1901) proved. And from France came one of the central issues of archaeological activity: the Celtic issue, arising out of an internal need for a national(istic) identity that coincided with Gaulish ethnicity and (almost by inference) with the Aryan antecedent of Indo-European background. Gone were the years of overvaluing its association with the mythical Hellenic civilisation, which the German researchers saw as the result of an Aryan invasion proceeding from Germanic lands, and not from eastern locations, as F. Martins Sarmento so strongly defended, perhaps under the influence of the eighteenth-century theories regarding its racial superiority, which generated the so-called 'Aryan myth'.

Fig. 22.2 The Carmo
Archaeological Museum at the
end of the nineteenth century.
AH/AAP.

Fig. 22.3 F. Martins Sarmento
(ca. 1876). (From *Dispersos*,
Coimbra, Impresa da
Universidade, 1933).

Searching for the Pre-Roman Roots of the Portuguese Population:
Francisco G.M. Martins Sarmento

Born to a wealthy family with a long local tradition in the city of Guimarães, in the northwest of Portugal, F. Martins Sarmento was only 20 when he graduated in Law at the University of Coimbra and returned to his home region (Fig. 22.3). Just like his parents, from whom he would inherit a considerable fortune, he favoured the village of Briteiros, facing mount São Romão, where the famous ruins of the Citânia de Briteiros stood (the Briteiros hill fort; see above). Strongly supporting the Romantic Movement and enlightened liberalism, F. Martins Sarmento soon left the family-imposed study of law to become a man of letters, revealing a poetic sensibility that was rare among country gentlemen. His earliest works were published in 1855, one of them under the significant title 'Pátria' (motherland). Also significant were the newspapers where he chose to publish some of his other works: *Renascença* (Renaissance) and *Portugália*, which published works by some of the stronger supporters of the Portuguese cultural revival. It is likely that daily contact with local and regional traditions, which he personally promoted, led him towards a study of their deepest roots. In fact, this seems quite understandable in a context that was still dominated by the Romantic spirit, which generated a true Europe-wide 'Celtmania'. The Romantics cherished the popular, bucolic, religious and mystic values (which were also conservative and paternalistic), resisting the young, industrial, urban and bourgeois society, and constantly praising the relevance of subjectivity in each culture's future, as if there was a common mythology and an intellectual cosmopolitanism that embodied patriotic feelings. In this new Europe, nationalism and archaeological research were promoted in an almost perfect symbiosis, in order to 'create' a past set upon the national unity.

So, after a period of poetic and Romantic literary writing and sociological studies, F. Martins Sarmento began to focus his activities on archaeological research, trying to find the origin of the 'Lusitanos' (the inhabitants of 'Lusitania' and putative ancestors of the Portuguese). The very same purpose led him to the study of popular traditions, as links in a chain that had been broken by time, and which he now tried to re-establish. His aim was to reveal in the present the faded remains of a (more or less) distant past; he was one of the first (perhaps even the pioneer) researchers to apply photography to archaeology, from the late 1860s onwards. Still, what made him notorious in the eyes of the main research centres of that time was his denial of the tradition followed by the humanists, which regarded all material that did not indicate any Roman influence as being Celtic. This awarded him access to some of the major European institutions, such as the German Archaeological Institute, the Belgian Archaeological Academy, and the Madrid Academy of History. Furthermore, the French government granted him the degree of 'Chevalier de la Légion d'Honneur', and he was also a member of the most outstanding Portuguese scholarly societies, such as the 'Real Associação dos Architectos Civis e Archeologos Portugueses', the 'Academia Real das Ciências' and the 'Sociedade de Geografia de Lisboa'.

Apparently supporting the regeneration movement of progressive features then promoted by the country's ruling political class, F. Martins Sarmento showed a very special interest in national and above all regional characteristics. Reason enough, perhaps, for involving himself in the study of the social and economic systems of the first inhabitants of the material reality he considered so unique in the Portuguese archaeological landscape: the protohistoric hill forts. And the long research carried out in the field seemed to confirm his set of ideals, strictly related to the need to recover the collective spirit as an essential element of the Portuguese nationality, affirmed by communities that held a complex social structure, based upon collectivist economic systems. This would, in fact, have been one of the main causes of the differences arising between F. Martins Sarmento and the well-known Portuguese philologist and ethnographer Francisco Adolfo Coelho (1847–1919), deeply influenced by German science Indo-European philological studies, for which he was acknowledged by some internationally renowned theorists.

But, it seems the differences between the two of them were not limited to this theoretical ascendancy. In fact, their divergence may have been of a different kind, an essentially political and social one. Because of his ideological affinities and pedagogical commitment, F. Adolfo Coelho was invited in the early 1870s to give one of the famous 'Conferências do Casino' (the Casino Lectures), at a time when Europe was recovering from the defeat of the second French Empire, the Commune de Paris, the widespread of the International, the rising crisis of the Spanish Crown, while learning new ideals, based upon Herderian and Hegelian historical philosophies, Renanian biblical criticism and the Proudhonian utopic socialist federalism. At the same time, Portugal was facing the labour movement and the discreditation of the constitutional monarchy. And the political sympathies of F. Adolfo Coelho seemingly severely countered the social interests of F. Martins Sarmento, in the setting up of the fundamental conditions for an urgent political, economic and religious renewal of Portuguese society. These could (and/or should) feature a degree of progress, socialism and Peninsular republican federalism. As a matter of fact, we think that one of the primary reasons for the literary and scientific disagreement between F. Martins Sarmento and F. Adolfo Coelho is precisely that latter condition, which can be partly explained by their respective social backgrounds and political sympathies. Though refusing the old Castilian centralism, socialist and republican thinkers like F. Adolfo Coelho seemed committed to attaining the peninsular unity as the only way to ensure the country's internal development and its international standing. And 1868 might have been critical for the most secret wishes of an Iberian union, cherished by the representatives of this 'Geração de Setenta' (the Generation of Seventy).

With the fall of Queen Isabel, the Spanish throne was offered to the Portuguese sovereigns who, with deep patriotic feelings, declined the offer. History pushed back the viability of a political fusion in the Iberian Peninsula, now only attainable through the arts and sciences, which did not know any physical borders imposed from outside their privileged (and truly unique) cosmopolitan and ecumenical position. Indeed, it was probably not just by chance that the 'Conferências Democráticas' were started, two years later, possibly as a way of keeping alive the flame of the Iberian ideal, which would have to face opposition from political interests then thriving within Portugal, and strongly opposing its practice.

What seems to be of utmost interest and relevance here is to understand how ideological beliefs and the likely political affiliations possibly influence (or not) the choice of research subjects and their interpretation by these two intellectual adversaries. And in fact, we begin to get a glimpse of scenery deeply filled with ideological intentions, more or less consciously recognised. Two very distinct stands thus appear before us, both closely related to specific political programme. On one side we see a set of principles valued of old by the main aristocratic stratum of the country, namely in the north and north-west Portugal, in the case of F. Martins Sarmento, which always showed a strong will for freedom of action and thought, whatever the desires of the centralising capital might be. Thus, the vast history of resistance against the permanent winds of Iberian integration blowing from Castilla, as well as the frequent opposition to the absolutist power of some national monarchs and struggles for the implementation of liberalism. For the most outstanding personalities of this region, the reasons for this craving for freedom could take root only in historical foundations of their very own, the features of which would certainly distinguish them from other population groups, not so much within Portugal, but above all from the remainder of the peninsula. And the nineteenth century seemed quite providential for their firm beliefs, as it brought the scientific bases for archaeological practice in the West, allowing for a search of the fields for evidence confirming a long accepted fact: their particular regional character.

It was therefore hardly surprising that the almost unique purpose of F. Martins Sarmento's linguistic, archaeological and ethnological research was the demonstration of views that saw the Lusitanians as not belonging to the so-called 'Celtic family', or the Celtiberians, in whom Madrid's political programme seemed to want to take root. In fact, and seemingly countering the apparent European scientific unanimity on the subject, this son of the north-west designed a research project dedicated exclusively to confirming his theory/belief that the peninsular peoples derived from an Aryan migration – the one that saw the Bronze civilisation emerge centuries before the Celts were to appear on the historical scene: 'To fight the generally admitted 'celticism' of the Lusitanians is my delenda est Carthago' (Sarmento, 1890: 75), focusing on the interpretation of the archaeological remains and on the detailed analysis of Avieno's 'Ora Maritima'. He based his work on some of the major reference works of his time, the contents of which would be partially criticised by F. Adolfo Coelho, due to their apparently being out of date. Most of these references stood for the 'ligurian' thesis (see below). But F. Martins Sarmento was seriously committed to demonstrating that, unlike the Celtiberians, the Lusitanians incinerated their dead, worshipped a wide pantheon, glorified the druids and augurs and built 'oppida'. His methods were the careful scrutiny of the classical sources and of the artefacts found during the many surveys he undertook in the north of the country. Besides, it was in those hill forts that he felt the presence of a strong 'national(istic)' interest, that the contemporary Portuguese seemed to have inherited and which they ought to honour in the present, in the face of the integrationist ambitions, in his view dangerously embedded in some of the country's intellectual circles. But even though he stood for the pre-Celtic nature of the Lusitanians, F. Martins Sarmento was unable to sever himself completely from the generalist tendency of the European scientific community, strongly dictated by the diffusionist conception anchored in the 'ex oriente lux' theory, as his views on the pre-Celtic ethnogenic panorama seem to reveal. From his point of view, the West would have been colonised (long before the arrival of the Phoenicians) by the Ligures, quite likely of Aryan origin, who developed a remarkable civilisation.

The approach to this theory seemed to be the laborious study of one of the main material elements in which he saw the results of the activities of the Ligures: the northern hill forts. Not just these, though, for he saw the Ligures as directly responsible for the expansion of megalithic monument construction, that he thought were erected in Portugal by the same people who built the hill forts, such as the one at Sabroso. This was the only one that did not seem to show any Roman influence (Sarmento 1883–1884: 9, 17). He thus linked those people to the reality of the Bronze Age, establishing a very deep existential continuity, in a completely innovative way in the Portuguese scientific landscape. In his view, those were quite plainly two sides of the same civilisation: the pre-Celtic Aryans, whom he called Ligures (the first representatives of the Aryan civilisation in the West), and the people of the dolmens, the same who, still in his view, had introduced bronze metallurgy into the Iberian Peninsula. Yet, more relevant than these conclusions, would be the fact that these archaeological specimens seemed to denounce the presence of an autonomic feeling, demonstrated by what he thought was a clearly communal organisation, that would have induced its inhabitants to stamp the surfaces of their buildings with a very characteristic (and characterising) decorative grammar, which included circles and spirals (along with swastikas). Contrary to the views of the majority of the members of the XI CIAAP who visited the Citânia de Briteiros in 1880, he was deeply convinced of their antiquity, based upon the revealed surface of the famous 'Pedra Formosa' (the Handsome Stone), a fundamental part of the hill fort's baths (Fig. 22.4). From the round houses, the metallic artefacts and the pottery, F. Martins Sarmento tried once more (and even unconsciously) to adjust material realities to the theory he was trying to validate, establishing parallels between the most frequent ornaments found in the 'castros' and those identified at Mycenae, so as to (re)affirm their Indo-European antecedence, via Greece. Truly, he was the first author to claim the cultural unity of the central regions of Portuguese territory in the pre-Roman era, particularly after his journey to the region where the Lusitanian warrior 'Viriatus' was born, and where he found hill forts he believed similar to those he studied in Minho and Trás-

Fig. 22.4 The 'Handsome' Stone (From *Dispersos*, Coimbra, Impresa da Universidade, 1933, p. 477).

os-Montes (the northernmost regions of Portugal). But the most important seemed to be the fact that, long before the arrival of Celts in the West, all the dolmens region had been rapidly dominated by a chain of Aryan peoples, which integrated it in their own civilisation processes, filling it with monuments and traditions, and consequently with ethnic names:

> The investigation we undertook in some dolmens of the Ancora valley, where, apart from a perfect dolmen, there are also vestiges of four other more, demonstrate that these monuments were utilised even after the Roman conquest. However, the fortified settlements, used as shelter by valley people, have a pre-Roman origin, corroborated by the similarity of its structures with the ones found in Sabroso. Here, in Sabroso, we find the same engravings we detected in the dolmens from North Europe, and, in view of the character observed in the ruins examined by us in Minho (in a relevant number of them) its population must have had the same traditions as those registered in the valley of Ave and Ancora (Sarmento 1883–1884).

In this respect, F. Martins Sarmento seemed to agree with some of his main French mentors, and not just because he had a well-known respect for classical sources, thus approaching the so-called 'historical-archaeologists' rather than the 'geologist-prehistorians'. Besides, the actions undertaken by Alexandre Bertrand (1820–1902) and Salomon Reinach (1858–1932) at the referential 'Musée des Antiquités Nationales', at Saint-Germain-en-Laye, seem to have inspired him in some of his most remarkable enterprises. For instance, the foundation of a museum in the city of Guimarães (northern Portugal), totally dedicated to national, or rather regional and local archaeology, where along with remains from the unavoidable Roman period, emphasis was placed upon some of the more representative artefacts of north-western Portugal's protohistoric past. This was one of the few ways then known to (more or less officially) acknowledge this branch of archaeological studies in Portugal, while functioning too as political propaganda. (Fig. 22.2)

The Lusitanians as the Root of the Nation

It thus seemed as if F. Martins Sarmento was committed to the reconstruction of the putative (and desirable) 'national' origins, raising the role played by the Lusitanians (or pre-Celtic ethnic basis) in the foundation of the Portuguese 'nation': 'If between the Mycenaean and the Roman civilisations there are no traces of a third one, one is forced to admit that the Celts did not bring with them any institutions that deserved to be named civilisation' (Sarmento 1890). As a matter of fact, it is possible that his aims went further than the barriers of 'nationality', but in an opposed sense, for the sites he highlighted in his theory (Briteiros, and above all Sabroso) were located precisely around the town where, according to popular mythology, Portugal had been born. The Minho, and in particular Guimarães, possessed the qualities of those ancient Lusitanian warriors who, like 'Viriatus', fought bravely for the independence of their daily life, under their very own set of values and beliefs. His theory, as much as its materialisation, seemed to stress in a (still) silent way how much the country owed that background, which had built, strengthened and ensured national and international respect for the Portuguese geographical borders. His beliefs drove him further still, to seek the grounds of Galicia and Beira Alta, searching for the final evidence of the great territorial extension he believed to have been occupied by the Lusitanians (and thus countering the most radical anti-Iberists, who opposed the integration of Galicia in the Portuguese administration), roughly extending between these two peninsular regions, one long since independent, the other one in a permanent search for the emancipation lost under Madrid's rule. Galicia's condition of 'finis terrae' did not help the region to maintain its autonomy, but during the nineteenth century Galicia exploited the ideological load of the 'Celticismo galego' (Galician Celticism) as a national founding myth, countering, in this sense, the purpose of F. Martins Sarmento. As a matter of fact, this could be one of the main reasons for his commitment in demonstrating that the so-called 'Estátuas Galaicas' (Galaic Statues/Warriors) possessed an obvious Lusitanian character. That character would explain the differences between Northern and Southern Portugal, as two other major Portuguese intellectuals affirmed, the historians J. P. de Oliveira Martins (1845–1894) and Alberto Sampaio (1841–1908), both close friends of his. For F. Adolfo Coelho, on the other hand, the Portuguese territory was a distinct linguistic unit within the Iberian Peninsula due to a set of shared traditions and customs determined solely by specific geographical features, and not by any political purpose. Besides, he also seemed to subordinate regional studies, to a more general picture of the 'nation'.

Protohistoric archaeology could reinforce the Portuguese regime's mythology, by passing on an image of the Lusitanian ancestors as strong defenders of territorial independence. An example of national dignity, so much needed by the country, particularly when facing issues that had shaken it so much, like the revival of Iberian unity, the 'Mapa-côr-de-Rosa' (the Pink Map) episode and the subsequent and humiliating (1890) 'Ultimatum Inglês' (the British Ultimatum). The latter would dictate the fortune of the decaying monarchy, opening a way for the ambitions of some outstanding personalities of the turn of the century, like F. Adolfo Coelho, even if it was somewhat too late for those (already) 'Vencidos da Vida' (Life's Losers), despite the celebrations of Luíz Vaz de Camões' centennial (c. 1517–1579), the first poet to relate the origins of the Portuguese with the Lusitanians (Guerra, 1993: 90). In fact, it would not be totally wrong to establish a parallel between the efforts of F. Martins Sarmento and the funding of the excavations at the Celtic 'oppida' and hill forts of Mont Auxois and Mont Réa by the French Emperor Napoleon III (1808–1873), keen to strengthen his rule by exploiting national(istic) feelings. Thanks to their privileged geographical position, it was believed that the Lusitanians had one of the purest genealogies among ancient peoples, as they were able to preserve their language, traditions and civilisation until the Roman conquest:

The comparison between Citânia (Briteiros) and Sabroso brings hope of the partial reconstruction of the old pre-Roman civilisation, as soon as we proceed to serious archaeological research. Everything seems to point to the end of Sabroso before the arrival of Roman influence on its site. The Citânia suffered this same control, at least until Constantine, as we can infer from a coin recently found there. And, yet, apart from some Roman objects and inscriptions, we could affirm that the two sites are contemporaneous: the same architecture, the same ornamental style, the same engravings and symbols, etc. It is almost certain that the exploration of all other ruins would reaffirm these same results. Subsequently, we can conclude that Roman civilisation, did not want, or was not able to end with the characteristic routine of previous civilisation, and that, if Lusitânia is ethnologically a privileged land, it is no less from an archaeological point of view, especially in the northern part (Sarmento 1883–1884).

In this sense, it seemed as if F. Adolfo Coelho had sufficient material to disagree with F. Martins Sarmento, at least in what concerned the so-called 'people of the dolmens'. Holding new elements, mostly gathered from the studies promoted by British researchers, so full of confidence in their national potential, F. Adolfo Coelho considered those monuments as Neolithic, while understanding that the production of bronze had been introduced into the Iberian peninsula by non-Aryan peoples. Indeed, for him the ethnographical and ethnological information to be found in the classical texts would be absolutely secondary in the frame of nineteenth-century studies, which gave greater privilege to other sources, more in line with the neo-positivist spirit of that time. In his view, and quite unlike his intellectual rival, research in the field seemed to confirm the absence of the Ligures in the western strip of the Iberian Peninsula, corresponding to Roman Lusitania and to 'Gallaecia'. There also seemed to be a confirmation of Celtic elements in the religious and funerary rituals, agreeing with the views of some German archaeologists who saw the Mycenaean civilisation as the product of an Aryan invasion coming from the north of Europe. We feel, though, that in this context F. Adolfo Coelho would be more interested in finding the substance he needed for sustaining his political and social plan, which he shared widely with his more direct supporters, and which, in his personal case, seemed to make more sense, considering his social background, quite distant from the country's aristocracy. For these firm federalists, the Celtic background could be the archaeological evidence missing in the logic of an ultimate Iberian union, which would so be pushed far beyond any post-Roman congregation, and linked to a hypothetical western empire, fragmented only by reasons external to the will of its main and first creators.

Conclusions

We could be tempted to conclude that one of F. Martins Sarmento's primary intentions when he chose the northern hill forts as one of the preferred subjects of his studies was the integration of Portugal, as a whole, but especially the region where he was born and had grown up, in the wide cultural and psychological context of a world directly and/or indirectly related to the Greek and Roman reality. As the main matrix of western living since classical times, the Greek/Roman civilisations had always symbolised the 'other(s)' through an image of barbarism, opposed to the principles it stood for. And this seemed to be the sense of F. Martins Sarmento's commitment in demonstrating the connection between the inhabitants of hill forts and the Indo-European background, precisely through the Mycenaean civilisation. But the kind of approach he chose could also be interpreted in a rather different way, or, rather, in a much more complementary, and thus richer, way. As he underlined the specific features of a pre-Celtic background, quite close to other European protohistoric realities characterised by the (almost) endless power of the mystic forces represented by the druids, it was as if F. Martins Sarmento wanted to praise a 'modus vivendi' which was closer to ancestral rural Portuguese way of life. On the other side stood a contemporary Europe that was dangerously parting from its primeval and authentic spirit, holding on to things he would consider as anti-natural and ephemeral, regarding the interests of the human innermost life, such as the excessive (?) rationality, artificiality, pragmatism and daily monotony so dear to the Germans, or even to the Industrial Age British. It was as if he aimed to raise the peripheral against the centralism of the country's main cities, under the leadership of Lisbon. And this was perhaps the reason why F. Martins Sarmento, who kept a deep, constant and productive relationship with the European culture of his time, never showed any particular interest in travelling through other landscapes besides the Portuguese ones. Indeed, he travelled little outside the regions of Minho and Trás-os-Montes – his only known journey abroad was a short visit to Galicia, certainly searching for remains that would prove his Lusitanian theory. It thus seemed as if F. Martins Sarmento was truly committed to dressing the culture of the Portuguese north-west in an antiquity filled with the values traditionally recognised in the Hellenic and Atlantic civilisations, even if he thought higher of the former than the latter. In so doing, he brought together such apparently opposed concepts as intellectualism and spiritualism, materialism and religiousness, rationalism and creativity, in an inner struggle against the atheism proclaimed by the fiercest republican and socialist spirits. Perhaps he aimed at some daring (but nonetheless silent) ambition of northern self-rule, possibly in close connection with the political entities of Galicia, with whom he might have (unofficially and secretly) shared some of these wishes.

Notes

1. Instituto dos Arquivos Nacionais da Torre do Tombo (I.A.N./T.T.), *Correspondência scientifica e litteraria mantida com J. Possidónio N. da Silva*, t. XI, em 8.ª, doc. 1767, 1879.
2. Arquivo Histórico da Associação dos Arqueólogos Portugueses (A.H./A.A.P.), *Actas da Assembleia Geral*, n.º 102, 5/7/1881.
3. I.A.N./T.T., Idem, t. XIII, em 8.ª, doc. 2278, 1881.

Archival and bibliographic references

Archives

Historic Archive of the Portuguese Association of Archaeologists (AH/AAP).
Historic Archive of the National Academy of Arts (AH/ANBAL).
General Directory of Historic Buildings and Monuments (DGEMN).

References

Almagro, M. and A. Lorrio. 1992. 'Representaciones humanas en el arte céltico de la Peninsula Ibérica', *II Symposium de Arqueología Soriana* I. Soria, se.
Arnold, B. 1996. 'The Past as Propaganda: Totalitarian Archaeology in Nazi Germany', in R.W. Preucel and I. Hodder (eds.), *Contemporary Archaeology in Theory. A Reader*. London: Blackwell.
Coelho, F.A. 1889. 'Questões ethnogenicas. Lusitanos, ligures e celtas', *Revista Archeologica* 3, sl, se.
Correspondência Epistolar entre Emílio Hübner e Martins Sarmento (Arqueologia e Epigrafia) 1879–1899) 1947. Guimarães: S.M.S..
Corvo, de A. 1883–1884. 'A propósito de Castros', *O Panorama Contemporâneo*. Porto: se.
De Ulisses a Viriato. O primeiro milénio a. C. 1996. ed. J. de Alarcão e A. Isabel Palma Santos. Lisboa: MNA.
Duchêne, H.D. 1996. *The Golden Treasures of Troy. The Dream of Heinrich Schliemann*. London: Thames & Hudson.

Fabião, C. 1989. 'Para a História da Arqueologia em Portugal', *Penélope – Fazer e Desfazer a História* (2). Lisboa: Cosmos.

———. 1993. 'A Idade do Ferro no Norte de Portugal', in J. Medina (ed.), *História de Portugal*, II. Lisboa: EdiClube.

———. 1993. 'Alcácer do Sal', in J. Medina (ed.), *História de Portugal*, II. Lisboa: EdiClube.

———. 1993. 'As Migrações Célticas', in J. Medina (ed.), *História de Portugal*, II. Lisboa: EdiClube.

———. 1993. 'O Passado Proto-Histórico e Romano', in J. Mattoso (ed.), *História de Portugal*, V. Lisboa: EdiClube.

———. 1994. 'Viriato: genealogia de um mito', *Penélope – Fazer e Desfazer a História* (8). Lisbo: Cosmos.

———. 1996. 'Archaeology and Nationalism: The Portuguese Case', *Nationalism and Archaeology in Europe*. London: University College of London.

Gran-Aymerich, E. 2001. *Dictionnaire Biographique d'Archéologie. 1789–1945*. Paris: CNRS.

———. 1998. *Naissance de l'Archéologie Moderne. 1798–1945*. Paris: CNRS.

Guerra, A. 1993. 'As fontes e as Entidades Étnicas', in J. Medina (ed.), *História de Portugal*, II. Lisboa: EdiClube.

———. 1993. 'José Leite de Vasconcelos', in J. Medina (ed.), *História de Portugal*. II, Lisboa: EdiClube.

———. 1993. 'Os Lusitanos', in J. Medina (ed.), *História de Portugal*, II. Lisboa: EdiClube.

———. 1993. 'Viriato', in J. Medina (ed.), *História de Portugal*, II. Lisboa: EdiClube.

Hayden, B. 1993. *Archaeology, the Science of One and Future Things*. New York: W.H. Freeman and Comp.

James, S. 1999. *The Atlantic Celts. Ancient People or Modern Invention?* London: British Museum Press.

Leal, J. 2000. *Etnografias Portuguesas (1870–1970). Cultura Popular e Identidade Nacional*. Lisboa: Pub. D. Quixote.

Lemos, F. de Sande 1999. 'Francisco Martins Sarmento na Arqueologia Portuguesa e Europeia do século XIX', *Actas do Congresso de Proto-história Peninsular*, I. Guimarães: SMS.

López Jiménez, O. 2003. *El Pensamiento Europeo y el Concepto de Celtíbero: 1821–1939*. Oxford: BAR International Series.

Martins, A.C. 1999. 'Francisco Martins Sarmento e Possidónio da Silva. Uma Breve Olhar sobre a Troca Epistolar', *Actas do Congresso de Proto-história Peninsular*, I. Guimarães: SMS.

———. 2001. 'O Associativismo Erudito e o Elogio da Memória Histórica. O Contributo da Associação dos Arqueólogos Portugueses para a Salvaguarda do Património Historico-cultural (sécs. XIX–XX)', *Actas del I Congreso IberoAmericano del Patrimonio Cultural*. Madrid: Asociación Española de Gestores de Patrimonio Cultural.

———. 2002. 'Uma Breve Incursão pelos Primórdios da Inventariação do Património Histórico-cultural Português (1859–1861)', *Arqueologia*, (26). Porto: CEAP.

———. 2003. *Possidónio da Silva (1806–1896) e o Elogio da Memória. Um Percurso Arqueológico no Portugal de Oitocentos*. Lisboa: AAP.

———. 2004. 'O Associativismo Erudito e a Inventariação do Património Artístico e Arqueológico no Portugal Oitocentista. A Real Associação dos Architectos Civis e Archeologos Portuguezes', *Actas do II Congresso Internacional de História da Art*. Porto: APHA.

Matos, Sérgio C. 1998. *Historiografia e Memória Nacional no Portugal do Século XIX (1846–1898)*. Lisboa: Ed. Colibri.

Millán González-Pardo, I. 1983. 'El anticelticismo de Francisco Martins Sarmento', *I Colóquio Galaico-Minhoto*. Ponte de Lima: CMPL.

Pereira González, F. 1999. 'O «Mito Celta» na História', *Actas do Congresso de Proto-história Peninsular*, I. Guimarães: SMS.

Ribeiro, C. 1876. 'A Archeologia', *Boletim de Architectura e Archeologia*, I. Lisboa: Typ. Lallemant-Frères.

Richard, N. 2002. 'Archaeological Arguments in National Debates in Late Nineteenth-Century France: Gabriel de Mortillet's La Formation de la nation française (1897)', *Antiquity*, 76 (291). York: York University Press.

Ruiz Zapatero, G. 1993. 'El concepto de celtas en la prehistoria europea y española', *Los celtas: Hispania y Europa*. Madrid: se.

Sarmento, F.M. 1876. 'Os Gregos no Noroeste da Ibéria', *O Instituto*. Coimbra: se.

———. 1878. 'O Deus Bormânico', *Museu Illustrado*. Porto: se.

———. 1879. 'Acêrca das Escavações de Sabroso (Estudo)', *A Renascença*. Porto: se.

———. 1879. 'Arte Pré-Romana', *O Occidente*. Lisboa: se.

———. 1880. 'No Tempo de Viriato', *A Vida Moderna*. Porto: se.

———. 1880. 'Observações Acêrca do Vale do Âncora', *O Pantheon*. Porto: se.

———. 1880. *Os Lusitanos. Questões de Etnologia*. Porto: Ed. de Autor.

———. 1881. 'A Estátua do Pátio da Morte', *O Pantheon*. Porto: se.

———. 1881. 'A Igreja de Rio Mau', *A Vida Moderna*. Porto: se.

———. 1881. 'O que podem ser os Mouros da Tradição Popular', *O Pantheon*. Porto: se.

———. 1882. 'Os Celtas na Lusitânia', *Revista Scientífica*. Porto: se.

———. 1882. 'Os Marcos Miliários de S. Bartolomeu de Antas', *A Vida Moderna*. Porto: se.

———. 1882. 'Se Antes da Invasão Romana Havia uma Arte entre Nós', *A Arte Portugueza*. Porto: se.

———. 1882. 'Sepultura Pré-histórica em Soalhães', *A Vida Moderna*. Porto: se.

———. 1882. 'Sinais Gravados em Rochas', *A Renascença*. Porto: se.

———. 1883. *Expedição Scientífica à Serra da Estrela em 1881*. Lisboa: Imprensa Nacional.

———. 1883–1884. 'A Propósito de Castros', *O Panorama Contemporâneo*. Coimbra: se.

———. 1884. 'O Deus Bormânico. Subsídio para o Estudo da Mitologia dos Lusitanos', *Revista de Guimarães*. Guimarães: Sociedade Martins Sarmento.

———. 1884. 'O Soldado que Venceu Viriato', *A Vida Moderna*. Porto: se.

———. 1884–1899. 'Materiais para a Arqueologia do Concelho de Guimarães', *Revista de Guimarães*. Guimarães: Sociedade Martins Sarmento.

———. 1885. 'A Argola encontrada em Penela', *Novidades*. Lisboa: se.

———. 1885. 'A Civilização da Pedra Polida no Minho', *Revista Scientífica*. Porto: Sociedade Ateneu do Porto.

———. 1885. 'A Inscrição de Burgãis', *A Vida Moderna*. Porto.

———. 1887. 'Para o panteão Lusitano', *Revista Lusitana*. Porto: se.

———. 1887. 'Deus Tameóbrio', *A Vida Moderna*. Porto: se.

———. 1888. 'A Propósito dos «Roteiros de Tesouros»', *Revista de Guimarães*. Guimarães: Sociedade Martins Sarmento.

———. 1888. 'Antigualhas', *Revista de Guimarães*. Guimarães: Sociedade Martins Sarmento.

———. 1888. 'Os Milários da Trofa', *A Vida Moderna*. Porto: se.

———. 1888. 'Os Milésios da Tradição Irlandesa', *O Reporter*. Lisboa: se.

———. 1888. 'Sôbre as Antigas Cidades da Ibéria', *Museu Illustrado*. Porto, se, 1879.

———. 1889. 'Os Atlantes de Diodoro Sículo', *Revista de Sciencias Naturaes e Sociaes*. Porto: se.

———. 1890. 'Lusitanos, Ligures e Celtas', *Revista Guimarães*. Guimarães: Sociedade Martins Sarmento.

———. 1894. 'O Deus Brigo', *Nova Alvorada*. Famalicão: se.

———. 1894–1895. 'Materiais para a Arqueologia da Comarca de Barcelos. Antas e Antelas', *Revista de Sciencas Naturaes e Sociaes*. Porto: se.

———. 1895. '«Cidade Velha» de Monte-Córdova', *O Archeologo Português*. Lisboa: Museu Nacional de Etnografia.

———. 1895–1896. 'Materiais para a Arqueologia do Distrito de Viana', *Revista de Sciencias Naturaes e Sociaes*, Porto: se.

———. 1896. 'A Propósito das Estátuas Galaicas', *Revista de Sciencias Naturaes e Sociaes*. Porto: se.

———. 1896. 'A Propósito de Valábriga', *Nova Alvorada*. Famalicão: se.

———. 1896. *Antiqua. Apontamentos de Arqueologia*. Guimarães: Sociedade Martins Sarmento.

———. 1899. 'A Arte Micénica no Noroeste de Espanha', *Portugália*. Porto: se.

Silva, A.C.F. da S. 1886. *A Cultura Castreja no Norte de Portugal*. Paços de Ferreira: MACS/CMPF.

———. 1999. 'A Cultura Castreja no Norte de Portugal', *Actas do Congresso de Proto-história Peninsular*, I. Guimarães: Sociedade Martins Sarmento.

Silva, J.P.N. da 1877. 'Monte de Santa Luzia (Vianna do Castello)', *Boletim da Real Associação dos Architectos Civis e Archeologos Portuguezes* 2(4). Lisboa: RAACAP.

———. 1880. 'Machados de Bronze descobertos em Portugal', *Boletim da Real Associação dos Architectos Civis e Archeologos Portuguezes* 3(3). Lisboa: RAACAP.

———. 1887. 'Descobertas recentes de monumentos megalíthicos na Rússia Meridional', *Boletim da Real Associação dos Architectos Civis e Archeologos Portuguezes* 5(6). Lisboa: RAACAP.

———. 1887. 'Monumentos célticos', *Boletim da Real Associação dos Architectos Civis e Archeologos Portuguezes* 6(1). Lisboa: RAACAP.

———. 1877. 'Relatorio acerca das novas investigações archeológicas. Praticadas na província do Minho no mez de Junho do corrente anno nos montes de Afife e S. Roque', *Boletim da Real Associação dos Architectos Civis e Archeologos Portuguezes* 2(4). Lisboa: RAACAP.

———. 1877. 'Relatorio, apresentado na sessão de 14 de Maio da assembleia geral da Real Associação dos Architectos Civis e Archeologos Portuguezes, acerca do descobrimento feito no monte de Santa Luzia em Vianna do Castello, no mez de Abril de 1877', *Boletim da Real Associação dos Architectos Civis e Archeologos Portuguezes* 2(2). Lisboa: RAACAP.

———. 1884. 'Sur les haches en bronze trouvées au Portugal', *Congrès International D'Anthropologie et D'Archéologie Préhistorique*. Lisboa: s/e.

———. 1889. 'Explicação da estampa n.º 85 [placas de xisto da Serra de Ossa]', *Boletim da Real Associação dos Architectos Civis e Archeologos Portuguezes* 6(3). Lisboa: RAACAP.

Skeates, R. 2000. *The Collecting of Origins. Collectors and Collections of Italian Prehistory and the Cultural Transformation of Value (1550–1999)*. Oxford: BAR International Series.

Trigger, B. 1992. *Historia del Pensamiento Arqueológico*. Barcelona: Editorial Crítica.

Chapter 23
Making Spain Hispanic

Gómez-Moreno and Iberian Archaeology

Juan P. Bellón, Arturo Ruiz and Alberto Sánchez

Abstract

The piece of historiographical research presented in this chapter concern one of the most prestigious Spanish historians, archaeologists and art historians of the tweentieth century: Manuel Gómez-Moreno Martínez. The methodological approach taken is based on the analysis of his scientific publications and of the documents kept in his private archive. This chapter is intended primarily to deconstruct this scholar's theories on Spanish prehistory and protohistory, as well as his analysis of the notion of Hispanic culture and its influence on the Spanish academic world of the twentieth century.

A Biography of a Late Follower of The Institución Libre de Enseñanza[1]

Manuel Gómez-Moreno Martínez was born in 1870 in Granada to a rich family of artists who were also in the business of printing. His father, Manuel Gómez-Moreno González, was an educated painter who was in the esteem of the cultural elite of Granada and was also a member of the *Real Academia de Bellas Artes*.

He was a not a brilliant student of Arts. However, a stay in Rome with his father funded by the *Diputación de Granada* between 1878 and 1880, as well as his instruction while on fieldwork at various sites for the *Centro Artístico y Literario* and the *Comisión Provincial de Monumentos* of Granada laid the foundations for a sound practical knowledge of drawing, epigraphy and documentation. These enriched him with an outstanding observation capacity. In 1886 he worked with Hübner on his *Corpus Inscriptionum Latinarum*, and was taught Arab by Simonet. His early publications are about local issues in Granada, and Roman and Visigothic archaeology. He helped his father with the *Guía de Granada*, published in 1892. He taught Sacred History and Archaeology (*Historia y Arqueología Sagrada*) at *Colegio-Seminario de Sacro-Monte* until 1905.

This early stage of his education, undertaken by his father in the context of Granada, was set in a late-nineteenth century background in which the first changes are taking place in respect of the view of science, culture and teaching, following the scheme of the *Institución Libre de Enseñanza*. Some of the most relevant theoreticians, like Giner de los Ríos and Riaño, were close to Gómez-Moreno's family.

Encouraged by Giner de los Ríos, he started his Ph.D. studies at the Central University of Madrid in 1898, but he was not awarded the degree until 1911, for a dissertation on Mozarabic archaeology. The delay was caused by a landmark in Gómez-Moreno's life: the Spanish *Catálogo Monumental y Artístico* entrusted to him by Riaño in 1900. He was appointed for the job without having to sit any exams and against the will of the Royal Academy of Fine Arts, led in this issue by Amador de los Ríos and Rada y Delgado.

The *Catálogos Monumentales* were an old state project whose origins date back to the very creation of the *Comisiones Provinciales de Monumentos* in the mid-XIXth century. They became a reality as late as the early twentieth century thanks to the initiative of reformist politicians like Riaño and Alejandro Pidal, Minister of Major Works (*Fomento*). The Catalogues were intended as a unitary project aimed at a deeper knowledge of the state's heritage, a necessary census for the preservation of the items that could embody the cultural identity of the country (Rodríguez 2002: 75). In 1901, Gómez-Moreno undertook alone the Catalogue of Ávila, and then the ones of Salamanca (1903), Zamora (1904) and León (between 1906 and 1908). After that, the Catalogues were entrusted to several authors, which meant remarkable progress in respect of the final number, if not in respect of the quality or the consistency of the contents.

His withdrawal from the Catalogues did not exclude him from the reforming project started by the politicians supporting the *Institución Libre de Enseñanza* in the first decade of the twentieth century. A far-reaching policy of foundation of institutions for scientific, cultural and teaching research was implemented at that time. An example of these is the *Junta para la Ampliación de Estudios*, which hosted the *Centro de Estudios Históricos*, at which Gómez-Moreno was head of the Section of Archaeology from 1912 to 1936.

He did his teaching at the *Centro*. The Section of Archaeology provided the then few students with a direct teaching method based on supporting lectures with practical sessions using photographs, slides and artifacts and also included outings to the sites under study. It was at the *Centro de Estudios Históricos* where he taught his 'school of archaeology', with followers like Cabré, Carriazo, Camps, Mergelina, Navascués, Mateu, Beltrán and Camón, among others.

In 1913 he became professor of Arabian Archaeology at the Central University in Madrid. He also took part in the process of institutionalisation of archaeology in Spain through the 1911 Act of Excavations and as a member of the *Junta Superior de Excavaciones y Antigüedades*.

From the 1920s onwards, Gómez-Moreno defined his view of Spanish Prehistory based on a privileged institutional and academic position and a detailed ideological programme. His first papers on the subject are 'Ensayo de prehistoria española' (1922) and 'Síntesis de prehistoria española' (1925), both of which remained unpublished until they came out in the *Misceláneas* in 1949. It was also in the 1920s that his research on epigraphy became known. It meant a turning point in the knowledge of Iberian writing, and was studied in further detail in his speech 'Las lenguas hispánicas' given in 1942 on the occasion of becoming a member of the Real Academia Española.

Besides the research done in this period, he was actively involved in institutional, political and teaching projects. In 1929 he became *Comisario de la Exposición Internacional de Barcelona*, in 1930 was appointed *Director General de Bellas Artes* by Minister Elías Tormo, and in 1933 he accomplished one of the major cultural feats of the Second Republic: the Mediterranean cruise aboard the *Bahía de Cádiz* (Gómez-Moreno 1995), a school-ship that put into practice the educational and pedagogical beliefs of the *Institución Libre de Enseñanza*.

In 1934, at the age of 64, he gave up his professorship although he remained as head of the *Instituto Valencia de Don Juan* (1925–1949), and a member of the *Patronato de la Alhambra* and of the Academies (*Historia and Bellas Artes*). He was also a member of the *Junta de Incautación del Tesoro Artístico* during the Spanish Civil War (1936–1939) and, the war over, when he was nearly 70, still carried out some impressive research with such relevant papers as the above mentioned *Las lenguas hispánicas* (1942), *Misceláneas* (1949), and others on epigraphy like *El plomo de Líria* (1953) or *La escritura bástulo-turdetana* (1961).

His professional and political activity under the Second Republic was not an obstacle for the acknowledgement of his research when the Nationalist army won the war in 1939. He was thus awarded the *Gran Cruz de Alfonso X* in 1942 and became Honorary Head of Instituto '*Diego Velázquez*' of the then new *CSIC* (heirs to the *Centro de Estudios Históricos* and the *Junta para la*

Fig. 23.1 M. Gómez-Moreno and M. Almagro-Basch at the Shelter of Cogull (Leida, Spain) (Archive Gómez-Moreno, IGM5378).

Ampliación de Estudios, respectively) from 1944 to 1950. For his research, he was also awarded such important distinctions as the History Award of *Fundación Juan March* in 1956. In general, it is worth mentioning that many of his followers from this time, some of whom had joined the new regime's academic system, like Tovar, Mergelina, Nieto and Gallego Burín, supported him (Fig. 23.1).

The Concept 'Hispanic'

Manuel Gómez-Moreno is a late follower of the *Institución Libre de Enseñanza*. As noted above, he had close ties with Giner de los Ríos, who, with the foundation of the *Institución Libre de Enseñanza* in 1876, had opened the so-called era of *positivist* or *open Krausism*. This era replaced the initial period started by Sanz del Río. With this new period, Giner made it easier to integrate other theoretical trends in the *Institución* in order to lay emphasis on what was defined as an essential objective of the new period: a national pedagogical mission capable of instructing leaders who would carry out, from the political point of view, a National Reform, as Giner wrote in 1880, 'to redeem the Country and bring it back to its destiny' (quotation taken from Tuñón de Lara 1984: 46). This is how *Institucionismo*, truly a life style and a credo, was born (Tuñón de Lara 1984: 45).

From 1907 the *Institución* was strong enough to develop its reform programme from inside the structure of the State. The foundation of the *Junta para Ampliación de Estudios* by Castillejo was the starting point. This was supported by the strong scientific personality of Nobel Prize winner Ramón y Cajal. Shortly afterwards, in 1910, the *Residencia de Estudiantes* and the *Centro de Estudios Históricos* were founded too. After these early decades of the XXth century, the historical and ethical view of history as a whole that had defined old Krausism gave way to a more specialised and limited thematic directory. In this new scheme, the issue of Spain, its crisis awareness, the quest for practical measures to guarantee resolution and an ethical principle for science as a religion, very much like in the early

Krausist period, were the major subjects. The new followers of the *Institución Libre de Enseñanza* that held power were no longer just krausists: positivism and social Darwinism joined the prevailing theoretical schools. Their hallmark was their professional profile as scientists: they became a lay and liberal bourgeoisie highly aware of being an elite as a result of viewing themselves as a learned and educated minority. This elite held radical but non-revolutionary beliefs that supported reform in a monarchic state or, at any rate, a reformist republicanism. They were also aware of the need to go deeper into the traditional values and, as pointed out by Jiménez Frau, the founder of *Residencia de Estudiantes*, to defend them against an invasion of technologisms (Tuñón de Lara 1984: 56).

Gómez-Moreno proposed his synthesis of prehistory in the political and ideological framework built around the *Centro de Estudios Históricos*. The notion of *'Periodo Hispánico'* appears in his discourse for the first time ever (Ruiz *et al.* 2002). According to him, it is a *national reaction* arising between the sixth century BC and the period of Roman domination, geographically located between the basins of the rivers Genil and Júcar (Fig. 23.2), the territory of Mastians and Oretanians:

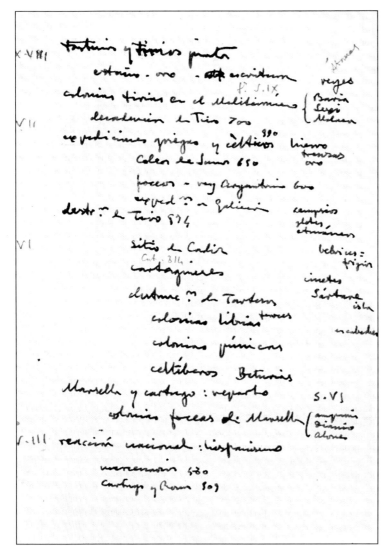

Fig. 23.2 An outline of Spanish protohistory and final 'national reaction' (V–III BC) (Archive Gómez-Moreno).

A highly beneficial consequence of these contacts with the indigenous population was the influence of Eastern art as in the style of Cyprus and Ionia, […] thus giving rise to a new cycle of Spanish culture, strong of character, free to new initiatives that would single them out among other similar schools. This started about the sixth century BC and lasted until the Roman domination […] It is, as a result, unfair to label as Iberian the genuinely pre-Roman Spanish art. This should be termed, more appropriately, *Hispanic* (Gómez-Moreno 1949: 40).

Cabré supported his theory as early as 1925:

There exists an archaeological Spanish period that is characterised by the occurrence of imported Punic, Greek and Italic items, among many others of a local origin retrieved in sanctuaries and, above all, in Andalusian cremation burial sites. This culture has been called Iberian up to now, but this is a deceptive term, since it concerns the southernmost regions, precisely where Iberianism was remote as a result of the interposition of the great Tartessian civilisation; furthermore, that name is necessary for other purposes, namely for designation of our primitive Neolithic art, which for many years remained strong in the region of the river Ebro, that is, Iberia proper, where no other culture above mentioned is present. Consequently, it will be preferred, in accordance with Mr Siret's initiative supported by Mr Gómez-Moreno, to call 'Hispanic' this period with which historical Spanish archaeology starts (Cabré 1925: 73).

The term 'Hispanic' soon became widespread among the students and followers of the 'master', and the proposal appeared again in Mergelina, Fernández de Avilés, Carriazo and, especially, Cabré's work between the 1902s and 1930s. The progression stopped in the late 1940s, when only Nieto remained in support of the proposal. Gómez-Moreno still used the concept in 1949 in his *Misceláneas*, and argued in favour of it as late as 1958 in *Adam y la Prehistoria* (Fig. 23.3):

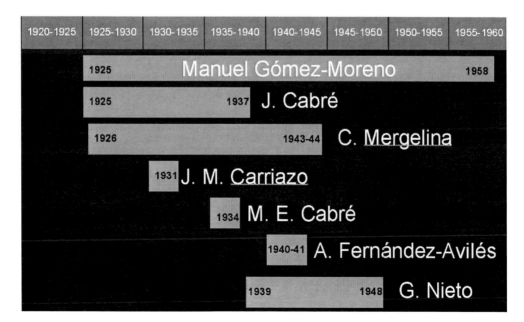

Fig. 23.3 Temporal framework of the Hispanic concept in the Gómez-Moreno school.

[…] This is the reality that hangs in the air over our prehistory, focused on the Tartessian society, the earliest recognisable civilising centre in the European West. Following infiltrations opened the gates to Eastern culture, and melted in a melting pot of unique activities, something like nationalism. But the world became smaller and smaller for men; then came the cycle of conquests, first by peaceful colonies, they determined our *Hispanic* culture, the last independent period, then with the Punics and Romans ruling at will'(Gómez-Moreno 1958: 174).

The proposal of a 'Hispanic Culture' was not welcome in the sphere of the Catalonian school of prehistorians. Bosch Gimpera severely questioned the proposal because it broke with the consensus agreed by the old scholars on the role of the Iberians, and because it did not separate the various ethnic groups in the peninsula while at the same time the term 'Hispanic' referred to a geographical fact. In all, it was not welcome, because it merged together cultures that were totally foreign to the Iberian (Bosch 1932: 558). Gómez-Moreno must have been extremely annoyed, because he replied in a letter:

My dear friend, I have just browsed with attention your last and excellent book on the Etnología de la Península Ibérica. My congratulations! Please forgive my acknowledging receipt of the general contempt towards all my modest archaeological work which you so openly make explicit (Gracia *et al.* 2002).

Gómez-Moreno's dream that his notion of Hispanic culture would reach beyond his school vanished when, in the late 1940s, the Iberists of Bosch Gimpera's school (Pericot, Maluquer, etc.)

Fig. 23.4 Hispanic culture according to Gómez-Moreno.

and the archaeologists of the CSIC, led by García y Bellido, reached an agreement to put an end to the theory of the Celtic origin of the Iberians defended by the Falangist archaeology of Martínez Santa-Olalla and which had been supported also by researchers of Gómez-Moreno's school, like Cabré. The consolidation of the paradigm of the term 'Iberian', as preferred by Bosch, also did away with the proposal of a Hispanic period (Ruiz *et al.* 2003). Gómez-Moreno himself admits so in a note to his synthesis of prehistory in the 1949 edition. This was marked by a widespread criticism of the prevailing positivism in the field, which was not completely unknown to himself as a methodological proposal: 'Instead, they do not lighten the expositive and critical method outlined by my humble essay, just as they do not make me change course, thus staying away of all prehistoric contacts and string-pulling' (Gómez-Moreno 1949).

But back to the conceptual foundations of the proposal, because, as will be shown, the 'master's' intentions were not just to replace one geographical term with another. Under the term 'Hispanic Culture' lie the theoretical foundations of the nationalism of the 1907 generation that supported the *Institución Libre de Enseñanza* (Fig. 23.4).

Beleisa of Beleturgi. The Opposition between the Original Nucleus and the Active Area

Gómez-Moreno set the area where the Hispanic culture developed in the Mastian/Oretanian region. In doing so, as remarked by Cabré, he separated and detached the Hispanic from the Iberian world. In terms of time, it was in fact a process; as noted in his work, in the Neolithic the Iberians held all the geographical area of the Iberian Peninsula. With the term 'Hispanic', Gómez-Moreno created a spatial duality just as Bosch Gimpera did with Catalonia and the native Capsian population with respect to the Iberians: there was an original or passive centre that, by remaining unchanged, kept the essentials of the national spirit (the Iberian area) and there was also a developing or active area which had contacts with outer communities and developed outwards. The Hispanic southeast was the open centre of the most ancient history of Spain. According to Gómez-Moreno, that was the entrance route for Tartessians, Mastians, and that is where the Greeks and the Phoenicians later based their fronts when the Hispanic period was in progress, and where the Carthaginians built their military stations.

On the other hand, the Iberians lost ground until all they retained was the area of the Basque region, Aragón, Valencia and the south of Catalonia. This could be attested by the linguistic evidence that Basque represented as the remains of the original language. The rest was invaded by European barbarian tribes, first the Ligurs, then the Celts. This 1925 view was changed in 1942 to extend the original nucleus to the whole Celt-Ligur-Iberian territory for his speech addressed to the Royal Academy on the occasion of becoming a member:

> Are they [the Iberians of the original nucleus] the Spanish natives? Thus was it said and thus is it confirmed by their primitivism. But I now doubt it: travelling the world I have met the pure Basque in Navarra, maybe in Maestrazgo and in High Aragón, but I also met the 'everyman' in Castilla, the farmer of Gothic fields [...] it all hints that he was also our native, without a history, without a name [...] These peoples, of course, even if always detached from the Iberians, probably were our passive national background, insensitive to invasions (Gómez-Moreno 1942: 20).

In 1928 Gómez-Moreno published *Novela de España*, a work model that pleased the followers of *Institución Libre de Enseñanza*. Reproducing Collingwood's idealism, they tried to recreate the past in their minds, breaking through the limits between the individual and the object whose history is told (Valera 1999: 255). This is how Beleisa, an Iberian female, was born. She embodies in that work the original Spanish woman who discovers agriculture, animal domestication and even founds towns like Beleturgi. The Iberian woman was the symbol of the original Iberian nucleus and of a still barbarian and primitive matriarchal society.

Dorifón the Ionian. The Opposition Between the Civilised Settler and the Spanish Genius

Dorifón is another character in *Novela de España* who appears in the chapter entitled *'Hispánica'*. An Ionian sculptor who travelled across the peninsula long after Beleisa's death and the colonisation of Tartessos, Dorifón concludes that only in Contestia (that is, in Contestania), where he sculpted the *Dama de Elche*, and in Orson, where he sculpted the Osuna reliefs, did he find a civilised society capable of understanding him.

Gómez-Moreno thus submits himself to the diffusionist theories of the time, contradictorily to a concept that must explain the uniqueness of the Spanish spirit. However, he did so based on a dichotomy that confronted whatever Eastern (Egypt, Crete, Cyprus, Phoenicia, Ionia, etc.) with the European spreading element (Ligurs and Celts). Unlike the former, the latter were negative. Gómez-Moreno had publicly argued in the *Residencia de Estudiantes* (Valera 1999: 106) for the importance of the Eastern and Arabian element for the definition of the Spanish element. These were thus not like other catchy elements that had disguised Hispanic art, like the Celtic, Gothic or Renaissance elements, all of them periods when *'the European element enters Spain and tries to seize its spirit'* (Valera 1999: 251).

The contradiction contained in this view of the Hispanic element can be resolved thanks to the concept of Hispanic art. In the foreword to his renowned 1899 manual, Rafael Altamira wrote that his work contained not only external political history, but also internal history. This is why, he argued, he wrote not just a history of Spain but a history of Spanish civilisation, an essential issue for the knowledge of the personality of a people (Altamira 1928). Based on this, Altamira explained the essentials of the role of Dorifón the Ionian, in his case still without distinguishing Iberian from Hispanic art: 'The Iberian plastic arts were the result of the genius of the peninsula fertilised by all the foreign influences mentioned above and, especially, by the Phoenician and the Greek ones. This is why they appear loaded with Greek-Orientalism. The main production centre seems to lie in the SE' (Altamira 1928: 71).

What Altamira explained was the need to study the unvarying, the essence of the Spanish people in its changing looks, that is, the essence of time. This, after all, was total History, as another krausist, Azcárate, had written before (Valera 1999: 102). In that setting, the foreigner's action, the colonising action, consisted in waking up the sleeping genius of the Spanish people. However, in Gómez-Moreno's words, as an artist, the foreigner *'creates emotions and lives off them'* (Gómez-Moreno 1949: 19), which is why Dorifón also partakes of the essence of the Spanish element. Cossio, upon publishing his 1908 book on El Greco, appointed another foreigner the prototype of the Spanish painter (Valera 1999: 93). In any case, a nationalist's acceptance of the foreign factor, however Eastern, as in the case of Gómez-Moreno, bears witness to the followers of the *Institución Libre de Enseñanza*'s sharing the regenerationist concept of fostering of the peoples (Costa 1895). This could be expressed sometimes as the need for a firm hand, a 'tyrant', and sometimes as an educated people that contributed to civilisation. Dorifón embodied the educated elite which the followers of the *Institución Libre de Enseñanza* were so fond of.

Córdoba-born Velaunis. The Opposition between Lost Paradise and the Desired Empire

'Velaunis is the arrogant, indolent Hispanic soul who leaves the field clear and is content with a childishness instead of mastering the situation putting his talent to the service of a productive economy' (Gómez-Moreno 1928: 152). A woman rises as the symbol of pragmatism again in *Novela de España*. Like Beleisa, Attita assumes the reality of her time and rejects quixotic Velaunis to marry a less handsome man. This gender dichotomy, a true separation of work in the

Cervantine style such that male holds political representation and female economic infrastructure, often appears in Gómez-Moreno's work. Yet, it is the male that eventually leads the process, and his quixotic attitude is the cause of his disgrace.

> Hispania, most prosperous, happy and serene, abandoned itself to the enjoyment of all the seductions that trade and its very genius provided it with, and refused to learn the difficult lesson of taking precautions. It did not study, it did not study itself, it was lacking in science and therefore also in awareness of reality. Hispania ignored its geography, the unitary concept imposed upon it by Nature [...]. it was certainly comfortable to live carelessly. Carthago knew well how to take preventive measures destroying Tartesis [sic] and keeping Gadir. Had Hispania succeeded, the horizon would have become its own and neither Rome nor Carthago could have ruled at will in the Mediterranean [...] But for that, a solid, learned and ambitious leading class would have been necessary, and it was totally absent (Gómez-Moreno 1928: 151).

Based on the positivist side of the followers of the *Institución Libre de Enseñanza*, Sales y Ferré proposed that a nation is a living organism defined in four stages: first unity of kin and ethnicity, then unity of territory and government, then unity of language, tradition and clothes, and finally awareness of being a nation (Sales y Ferré 1889–1897). According to Gómez-Moreno, the first stage of the Iberian nation was first formed by the Iberians, and then, as revised in 1942, by the association of Iberians-Celts-Ligurs. This was the Spanish race: unity in diversity 'as regards complexities of noble ancestry, the Spanish population reaches extraordinary limits and, thanks to it, it keeps a powerful vital force to avoid the degenerative stigmata that keeps it fit for the fight against new peoples. A temperate Spaniard is a first quality factor' (Gómez-Moreno 1949: 28).

The second stage is analysed by Gómez-Moreno based on the peculiar geography of the peninsula and on the Tartessian paradigm. The former is, for the author, an unquestionable physical unit detached by the Pyrennees, a unique case in Europe (Portugal is, for Gómez-Moreno, a part of the Spanish nation geographically speaking). The view of the unity of government is a different matter, that is the match between the territory of the peninsula and the government. In his *Novela de España*, the quixotic element so proper to the ethnic group, a paradise that does not long for other territories, and the aversion to military expansionism (according to Gómez-Moreno, the Ligurs would have been easy to integrate as a fighting class) all lead the Tartessian leaders towards an predictable death. This is a missed opportunity to become the first power in the western Mediterranean, the accomplishment of the nation by becoming an empire, as Prat de la Riba (1998) wrote. Tartessos should have worked historically towards the strengthening of the nation: 'Hispania has always been too big for its leaders; it lost its head with Tartessis [sic] and has not recovered it yet; it never looked outwards, while it is always watched from outside for its worse' (Gómez-Moreno 1928: 153).

The 1898 crisis, the end of the overseas Spanish empire, is not far from this view. Gómez-Moreno gives this view in response to the question that the followers of the *Institución Libre de Enseñanza* and regenerationists emphasised as the source of the national ailments: the lack of a leading elite capable of attaining the historical process that Providence had reserved for Spain: 'Providence gave the world to the fights of men, it put war in their hands; but it also gave them a light that eventually leads towards life, a light that from the heights of genius enlightens mankind and shows the way. History, sitting at a side of this way, takes notes and teaches' (Gómez-Moreno 1949: 28).

Interestingly, both of Gómez-Moreno's proposals in archaeology, the Iberian languages and the Hispanic period, are the major features of the third stage of the birth of a nation in the scheme by Sales y Ferré. The researcher aimed his work at the history written by Altamira, the history of civilisation, where genius and the national spirit appear and become a nation. The Hispanic period developed after the Tartessian crisis, at a time when it could hardly be the political expression of an empire, but it still remained as the proof that the Hispanic genius would revive after its own crisis: 'Perhaps, it is only the peoples that went through this salutary experience that are up for the fight and are effective promoters of genius' (Gómez-Moreno 1928: 102).

A Note on the Archives under Study

The Instituto Gómez-Moreno at Fundación Rodríguez-Acosta (Granada)

The archive of *Instituto Gómez-Moreno*, kept by the *Fundación Rodríguez-Acosta*, Granada, result from Gómez-Moreno's prolific professional activity and research. This archive contains his private library, his collections of works of art and archaeological items, and his private documents. The project *'Los archivos de la arqueología ibérica: una arqueología para dos Españas'*, set in the framework of the European projects AREA I (Programme Rafael) and AREA II and III (Culture 2000) has since 2000 worked on the catalogue, description and research on this crucial archive for the history of archaeology in Spain. This was made possible by an agreement between the *Centro Andaluz de Arqueología Ibérica and Fundación Rodríguez-Acosta*.

Based on a preliminary study of the contents, these documents have been separated into various subsets, such as 'Numismatics', 'Epigraphy', 'Catalogues of Monuments', and, most important, 'Iberian Archaeology' and 'Correspondence'. With its 7000 documentary units, now digitised into 12000 computer files, the 'Iberian Archaeology' subsets contains documents resulting from Gómez-Moreno's routine research work. The most common types of documents are photographs and handwritten notes and sketches. These documents, whose description is still in progress, relate to several themes: photographs of Iberian bronze votive offerings, documents on Iberian epigraphy, preparation of various publications, correspondence on his research, field photographs of excavation campaigns, handwritten records or essays on the prehistory of the peninsula, Finally, there is a rather mixed documentary body consisting of press articles on archaeological findings, notes on certain sites, drawings of materials, photographs, carbon copies of engravings, imprints of coins, etc. Altogether, these documents constitute a rich and indeed unique archival source for investigating the history of archaeology in Spain.

Acknowledgements

We wish to thank *Archivo Instituto Gómez Moreno of Fundación Rodríguez Acosta* (Granada) for its cooperation, and Dr Salvador Valera for translating the Spanish manuscript into English.

Notes

1. Many summarising documents on Manuel Gómez-Moreno's life have been published over the years. The most relevant are the one by his daughter Mª Elena in 1995 (Gómez-Moreno 1995), and the *Homenaje a Gómez-Moreno, 1870–1970* by various authors published by the University of Granada in 1972. The latter contains a wealth of research papers as well as autobiographic papers by Gómez-Moreno himself, like his *Autorretrato a los noventa años*, or his *Notas para un curriculum vitae*. Two interesting research papers have also been published recently: one is on his work at the 'Centro de Estudios Históricos' (López-Ocón 1999), the other, by F. Rodríguez, is a wide-ranging review of his various interests and activities (Rodríguez 2002). The *Diccionario Akal de historiadores españoles contemporáneos* also contains a summary of his education, professional and academic activity, major works, and prizes and awards (Peiró and Pasamar 2002).

References

Altamira, R. 1928. *Historia de España y de la Civilización Española*. T. I, 4ª ed. Madrid.

Bosch, P. 1932. *Etnología de la Península Ibérica*. Barcelona: Editorial Alpha.

Cabré, J. 1925. 'Arquitectura Hispánica. El sepulcro de Toya', *Archivo Español de Arte y Arqueología* 1: 73–101.

Costa, J. 1895. *Tutela de los Pueblos de España*. Madrid: Biblioteca Costa vol. 11.

Gómez-Moreno, M. 1928. *La Novela de España*. Madrid: Real Academia de la Historia.

———. 1942. *Las lenguas hispánicas. Discurso de recepción en la Real Academia Española*. Madrid.

———. 1949. *Misceláneas*. Madrid: Instituto Diego de Velázquez, C.S.I.C.

———. 1958. *Adam y la Prehistoria*. Madrid: Tecnos.

Gómez-Moreno, Mª E. 1995. *Manuel Gómez-Moreno Martínez*. Madrid: Fundación Ramón Areces.

Gracia, F., J.Mª Fullola and F. Vilanova. 2002. 58 anys i 7 dies. *Correspondencia de Pere Bosch Gimpera a Lluis Pericot 1919–1974*. Barcelona: Universitat de Barcelona.

López-Ocón, L. 1999. 'El Centro de Estudio Históricos: un lugar de la memoria', *Boletín de la Institución Libre de Enseñanza* 34–35: 27–48.

Peiró, I. and G. Pasamar. 2002. *Diccionario Akal de historiadores españoles contemporáneos: (1840–1980)*. Madrid: Akal.

Prat de la Riba, E. 1998. *La Nacionalitat catalana*. Barcelona: Edicions 62.

Rodríguez, F. 2002. *Humanismo y progreso*. Madrid: Novatores 12. Nivola.

Ruiz, A., A. Sánchez and J.P. Bellón. 2002. 'The History of Iberian Archaeology: One Archaeology for Two Spains', *Antiquity* 76: 184–90.

———. 2003. 'Aventuras y desventuras de los iberos durante el franquismo'. In F. Wulff and M. Álvarez (eds), *Antigüedad y Franquismo (1936–1975)*. Málaga: Diputación de Málaga, pp. 161–88.

Sales y Ferré, M. 1889–1897. *Tratado de Sociología. Evolución social y política*. Vols I and IV. Madrid: Victoriano Suárez.

Tuñon de Lara, M. 1984. *Medio siglo de Cultura Española*. Madrid: Tecnos.

Valera. J. 1999. *La Novela de España*. Madrid: Taurus.

Chapter 24
Virchow and Kossinna

From the Science-Based Anthropology of Humankind to the Culture-Historical Archaeology of Peoples

Sebastian Brather

Abstract

Virchow and Kossinna were prominent figures in German prehistoric research. The year of Virchow's death saw the appointment of Kossinna as associate professor at Berlin university, confirming a shift from an international, anthropologically oriented approach, through 'national archaeology', to a very 'German prehistory'. In this respect, Virchow and Kossinna can be seen as scientific, political and moral contrasts, representing different aims, traditions and times. Otherwise both 'giants' had much in common – in the courses of their life, in their approach to politics, in their militancy for culture history (against political historiography), and in their German nationalist attitude. As this paper will show, Virchow's broad perspective and his methodological caution led to a lasting underestimation of his importance for prehistoric research, while on the contrary Kossinna's influence, negative as well as positive, has long been overestimated.

Introduction

Rudolf Virchow (1821–1902) and Gustaf Kossinna (1858–1931) were two prominent figures in German prehistoric research. Both dealt with prehistory only in the second part of their lives – for approximately thirty years. Although they both worked in Berlin, they probably never met.[1] The year Virchow died (after jumping off a tram at the age of 81 and subsequent pneumonia), Kossinna was appointed as associate professor at Berlin university. This year, 1902, can be viewed as a turning point – from an international and anthropologically oriented field of research through 'national archaeology' to a very 'German prehistory'. In this respect, Virchow and Kossinna may be seen as scientific, political and moral contrasts, representing these different aims, traditions and times. Otherwise both our 'heroes' had much in common – in the course of their lives and in their attitudes. Both were appreciated at home and throughout Europe, and both were very influential in programmatic and methodological terms.

Kossinna is still present in the thoughts of European archaeologists today. He is well known for the invention of the concept of 'archaeological culture' in the early twentieth century, and for his political engagement at the extreme right. Since becoming professor, Kossinna tried to dominate German archaeology, really 'fighting' against all his colleagues. Prominent archaeologists like the Berlin museum director and member of the academy of sciences Carl Schuchhardt (1859–1943), the Silesian Hans Seger (1864–1943), or the Austrian Moritz Hoernes (1852–1911) became 'enemies' of the Berlin professor, due to the unfriendly personal character of

Kossinna who understood their success as his own unfair failure. Scientific networks were contaminated by personal rivalry for decades, and scientific discussion was partly blocked. Nevertheless Kossinna is remembered as an outstanding scholar of the early twentieth century – who had given archaeology a simple, but powerful paradigm often carelessly used even today (if understood not as a modern artificial classification but as a historic reality). This ethnic or national paradigm argued that every geographical difference in archaeology is in every case due to different ethnic groups. Of course everybody argued that this is too simple, but often his concept was followed uncritically.

Virchow played a major role thirty to forty years earlier. In the twentieth century he is appreciated mostly as a famous physician and politician. In archaeology his fame is much smaller, and he is seen as an expert in the whole field of anthropology who failed in some important respects. Chief among these was his refusing to accept the Neanderthal find as the 'missing link' in the line to the origin of man. Virchow was indeed totally wrong, but it was mainly his scientific carefulness that led him to see the Neanderthal man as a pathological anomaly. In many analyses Virchow insisted on careful and systematic observations to reach correct results, resisting all scientific and political pressure. But it was probably not this point, i.e. the absence of simplistic models, which led to a lasting underestimation of Virchow's importance for nineteenth- and twentieth-century archaeology. In Virchow's time archaeology (prehistory), (physical) anthropology and ethnology were bound together, and none of them had yet developed into separate disciplines. Therefore no paradigm could be created and could dominate the field of research. The late nineteenth century was the age of the systematic collecting of material, developing methodological standards, and organising the disciplines – and in so doing Virchow and others erected the basis for all future research.

From this perspective Virchow was at least as important as Kossinna, if not more. Virchow followed a European-wide perspective; he took into consideration every available source material, and therefore invested much energy and time in organising the anthropological science. Kossinna was focused on archaeological finds, especially those he could connect to the ancient Germans. He asked everybody for information on finds, but he only established a vast private collection of published artefacts or those which came to his knowledge, and he created his own society and its journal. Virchow and Kossinna shared many fundamental assumptions, but only Virchow looked for strong scientific arguments and published them. This main difference is only very partly due to the personal characters of both men and rests more in their different scientific approaches. Both researchers represented mainly the international development in science at that time. After the establishment of separate disciplines – archaeology, anthropology, ethnology – at the turn of the century their foundations were of importance. In this process the conditions which were laid out in the later nineteenth century – when an integrated perspective on the *Altertumskunde* dominated – were more and more overlooked during the twentieth century.

A balanced view on Virchow and Kossinna has to take into consideration the scientific circumstances as well as the individual attitude of both men. Seen against the historic and scientific background of that time the two archaeologists could be compared with John Lubbock (1834–1913) and Edward Byrnett Tylor (1832–1917) at the time of Virchow, and with Oscar Montelius (1843–1921) and Vere Gordon Childe (1892–1957) in Kossinna's period (Trigger 1989: 114–95). Nevertheless, they both had a strong influence on the scientific standards which changed from science-based anthropology of mankind to culture-historical archaeology of peoples in the decades around 1900. This development was due to the logic of scientific differentiation and separation, but it also blocked some approaches which were to be rediscovered later. A detailed look at Virchow and Kossinna shows that this dichotomy overlooks important similarities which make more plausible the transition in perspective and method between them.

The Two Protagonists

Rudolf Virchow (Goschler 2002; Andree 2002a) (Fig. 24.1), born in Schivelbein in Pomerania, was a physician. Trained as a medical army officer, he started a meteoric career at the university. In the 1840s he claimed medicine as an applied science, and was promoted by a social network of military personnel and physicians. After an engagement as a liberal politician in the 1848 revolution Virchow became professor in Würzburg in 1849 (Andree 2002b). Ten years later he returned to the Berlin *Charité* where he developed a focus of scientific and political networks. His reputation was grounded on the famous 'Cellular pathology' (Virchow 1858). By institutionalising pathological anatomy Virchow's concept followed a new main trend in medicine in the mid-nineteenth century. For the rest of his life he was engaged in politics, known for his engagement in the *Kulturkampf* against Catholicism and for his opposition to Bismarck. His political horizon remained restricted to the times of the *Vormärz* 1848 (Goschler 2002: 375).

After 1867 Virchow withdrew himself more and more from medicine as a science. His main interest shifted to politics – and physical anthropology, ethnology and prehistory (lake dwellings, Lusatian culture, Slavic material culture and hillforts; Andree 1976a: 57–80). His main interest came from the idea of progress in the history of mankind. It is true that Virchow remained an influential physician and professor of pathology but the kind of medicine he represented became increasingly old-fashioned and conservative. New directions like Robert Koch's (1843–1910) bacteriology outstripped pathology as the leading sub-discipline from the 1880s,[2] while Virchow did not change his views since about 1850. As an authority Virchow became increasingly involved in popularising his scientific approach. Since its founding in 1869/70 Virchow was the *spiritus rector* of the German Society for Anthropology, Ethnology and Prehistory (soon to become the German Anthropological Society [Deutsche Anthropologische Gesellschaff]; Andree 1969). He was active at organising conferences (annual Allgemeine Versammlungen der DAG[3]) and

Fig. 24.1 The second Hissarlık conference, 1890. Standing from left: Virchow, Wilhelm Grempler (1826–1907), Effendi Munif Galib, Heinrich Schliemann (1822–1890), Miss E. Calvert, Wilhelm Dörpfeld (1853–1940), Mad. Babin, Charles Louis Henry Babin (1860–1932), Friedrich Carl Humann (1839–1869); sitting from left: Frank Calvert (1828–1908), Osman Hamdi Bey (1842–1910), Charles Waldstein (then Walston; 1856–1927). (DAI Athen, Neg.-Nr. 1990/94).

exhibitions (*Ausstellung prähistorischer und anthropologischer Funde*, Berlin 1880; *Berliner Museum für Völkerkunde*), establishing journals (*Zeitschrift für Ethnologie; Correspondeznt-Blatt der deutschen Gesellschaft für Anthropologie, Ethnologie und Urgeschichte; Archiv für Anthropologie*), developing research programs (*Prähistorische Typenkarten*, skull form statistics, school statistics) and networks (DAG). Coupled with his control over publications in several journals, all this gave to Virchow considerable influence in, and over, this new field of science.

Gustaf Kossinna (Fig. 24. 2) was born in Tilsit in East Prussia(Schwerin v. Krosigk 1982; Grünert 2002). He studied German philology and obtained his Ph.D. at Strasbourg university, but he claimed as his teacher Karl Müllenhoff (1818–1884) in Berlin. Realising that philology had come to an end in searching for the 'early Germans', Kossinna, driven by Germanomania, shifted to prehistory. The inspiration may have come from Müllenhoff and from his Strasbourg teacher Rudolf Henning (1852–1930), the later son-in-law of Rudolf Virchow. His main interest was therefore one-sided and led to unbalanced interpretations (Brather 2001; Grünert 2002: 71–75; Veit 2000). It took some ten years from his initial interest in 'German archaeology' to his appointment as professor to the first chair of this new discipline in Germany. During this time Kossinna was employed as a librarian at the Berlin Royal library, after having held similar positions in Halle/Saale and Bonn. He gave extensive attention and time to his hobby which led to serious problems with colleagues and bosses. Nevertheless Kossinna had many opportunities for long study trips, although he protested incessantly about alleged 'discrimination' over his activities (Grünert 2002: 58–66).

Fig. 24.2 Gustaf Kossinna at the 11th Congress for prehistory in Königsberg 1930, together with the managing committee of his Society for German Prehistory. From left: Franz Langer (1866–1938), Wolfgang Schultz (1881–1936), Wilhem Gaerte (1890–1958), Hans Heß v. Wichdorf (1877–1932), Kossinna, Ernst Snethlage (1860–1934), Alfred Götze (1865–1948), (from Stampfuß 1935: table 4).

Kossinna's reputation rested on two points: first on his enormous typological knowledge of different artefacts throughout Europe, and second on his methodology, called 'settlement archaeology' (*Siedlungsarchäologie*) – in fact a prehistoric *Stammeskunde*, looking for the earliest origins and settlement areas of peoples (Kossinna 1911). Kossinna based all his interpretations on his huge archive of find spots (Grünert 2002: 75–90) but he never published a sound list of artefacts; therefore while optimists believed in his arguments, pessimists called for proofs. In reality his interpretations remained hypotheses. Like Virchow, Kossinna was engaged in organising the discipline; he founded the German Society for Prehistory (*Deutsche Gesellschaft für Vorgeschichte*), later renamed the Society for German Prehistory, and its journal *Mannus*, both in 1909; the majority of members and subscribers were amateur archaeologists. Kossinna's prehistoric professorship stood at the beginning of the disciplinary institutionalisation at universities in Germany.[4]

Similar Aims and Different Perspectives

Virchow and Kossinna themselves tried to establish a specific picture of their scientific and public life (and later on both became 'giants' through their successors and admirers). These self-images produced some fog which is not easy to see through. Virchow styled himself as a 'natural scientist' whose knowledge gave him authority on political matters – because politics should be nothing else than medicine within a wider framework (a 'social science').[5] He demanded 'scientific politics', and therefore he engaged in politics from 1848 (with an interruption in the 1850s). He wanted political decisions to be seen as matters of 'expert analysis' based on hard facts, not on opinions and alternatives (Goschler 2002: 77–78, 239). Kossinna saw himself as the 'fighter' for German prehistory and the best qualified expert in this field (Kossinna 1919/20). To propagate this emphasis on the alleged high cultural level of the ancient Germans (*altgermanische Kulturhöhe*) became Kossinna's 'mission'.

Nevertheless both were interested mostly in the Bronze Age and the Iron Age – Kossinna in artefacts only, Virchow often in physical remains and ethnological observations, but this difference rested more in the international development towards independent disciplines of archaeology, anthropology and ethnology. Looking for *the* origins and analysing the *early* remains of the indigenous peoples they believed to see much clearer for antiquity and the Middle Ages – in terms of culture and race. On the basis of pottery decorations, Virchow distinguished between 'Germanic' cremations of the Iron Age and early medieval 'Slavic' hillforts and graveyards. From this perspective, Virchow's resistance to research on the Roman past in Western Germany was primarily for 'chronological' reasons, rather than of 'regionalism' as with Kossinna. Nevertheless, the dichotomy of civilisation and barbarism was overlooked – while at the same time different levels of cultural development were stated. Both aired their views with arrogance and with great self-confidence, though both were really poor speakers; soft-voiced, inarticulate and yet verbose – a fact which (surprisingly?) did not seem to affect their popularity. Both connected science and politics, and they were anxious to receive public attention and esteem, from both fellow professionals and amateurs.

'Truth' and 'objectivity' were the main aims of Virchow's scientific worldview, based on 'facts' and 'rules' as universal principles. Therefore the model of modern natural science became the standard (Goschler 2002: 209–210, 242), and Virchow looked for analytical explanations in anthropology (Fig. 24.3). 'Learning by observing' was his motto – in medicine as in prehistory. Just as he had established pathology as a new medical discipline, so did Virchow aim to make of prehistory a new discipline by erecting and guarding disciplinary frontiers (Goschler 2002: 185). Nevertheless Virchow thought that prehistory would never become a separate discipline (Virchow 1874: vii); instead this field should be the object of interdisciplinary research in anthropology, ethnology and archaeology.

I. Absolute Messzahlen.

Aisheim.		Länge.	Breite.	Höhe.	Ohrhöhe.	Horizontale Hinter-hauptslänge.	Gesichtshöhe.	Ober-gesichtshöhe.	Gesichts-breite.	Orbita. Breite.	Orbita. Höhe.	Nase. Höhe.	Nase. Breite.
I.	♀	182·3	146·5 p	127	108	68	115	67·5	90	38	35	50	24·5
II.	♂♀	189	142 t	—	117	64	114	69·5	95	40·5	33	53	26
III.	♀	185	133 p	120	105	60·5	99·5	62·5	87	38	33	48	25
IV.	? ♂	187·5	131 p	128	107·5	71·5	121	70	87	39	31·5	52·5	22
V.	♂	195·5	140 p i	132·5	114	65	112	69	94	40	36	53·5	28
VI.	♀	182	131 p	120·5	105	66	108	63	88	35	31	48	23
VII.	♀	174	130 t	129	106	57	105	68	93	38	36·5	52·5	22
VIII.	♂	190	133 p	129	111	67	—	68	89	38	33	47·5	23
IX.	♀	183	129 t	128	105	62	102	61	92	36	34	45	23
X.	♂	184	138 p	—	106	—	—	70	86	40	37	58	25
XI.	♀	189	142 ? p	—	106	—	110	70	—	40	37	50	—
XII.	♀	186	138 p	—	109	—	—	68	94	39	32	49	23·5
XIII.	♀	183	138 ? p	—	—	—	—	—	—	—	—	—	—
XIV.	? ♀	—	138 p	—	106·5	—	115	67	98	38	31	53	26
XV.	♂	195	146 pt	133	108	65	—	70	101·5	38	31·5	52·5?	28
Monsheim	♀	—	132 p i	—	109	—	—	68	93·5	39	35·5	50	25

II. Berechnete Indices und Capacität.

Alsheim	Längen-breiten-	Längen-höhen-	Breiten-höhen-	Ohr-höhen-	Occipital-Längen-	Gesicht-	Ober-gesicht-	Orbital-	Nasen-	Capacität
I.	80·3	69·6	86·7	59·2	37·3	127·7	75·0	92·0	49·0	1500
II.	75·1	—	—	61·9	33·8	120·0	73·1	81·4	49·2	—
III.	71·8	64·7	90 2	56·7	32·7	114·3	71·7	86·8	52·0	1210
IV.	69 8	68·2	97·7	57·2	38·1	139·0	80·4	80·7	41·9	1200
V.	71·6	67·7	94·6	58·3	33 2	119·1	73·4	90·0	52·3	1610
VI.	71·9	66·2	91·9	57·6	36·2	122·7	71·5	88·5	47·9	1280
VII.	74·7	74·1	99·2	60·9	32·7	112·9	73·1	96·0	41·9	1170
VIII.	70 0	67·8	96·9	58·4	35·2	—	76·4	86·8	48·4	1340
IX.	70·4	69·9	99·2	57·3	33·8	110·8	66·3	94·4	51·1	1140
X.	75·0	—	—	57·6	—	—	81·3	92·5	43·1	—
XI.	75·1?	—	—	56·0	—	—	—	92·5	—	—
XII.	74·1	—	—	58·6	—	—	72·3	82·0	47·9	—
XIII.	75·4	—	—	—	—	—	—	—	—	—
XIV.	—	—	—	—	—	117·3	68·3	81·5	49·0	—
XV.	74·8	68·2	91·0	55·3	33·3	—	68·9	82·8	53·3	—
Mittel . . .	73·5	68·5	94·0	58·0	34·6	120·4	73·2	86·7	48·2	1306
Männer . .	72·7	67·9	95·0	58·1	34·7	126·0	75·5	85·7	48·0	1383
Frauen . .	74·2	68·9	93·4	58·0	34·5	117·6	71·1	89·2	48·4	1260
Maximum. .	80·3	74·1	99 2	61·9	38·1	139·0	80·4	96·0	53·3	1610
Minimum . .	69·8	64·7	86·7	55·3	32·7	110·8	66·3	80·7	41·9	1140
Differenz . .	10·5	9·4	12·5	6·6	5·4	28·2	14·1	15·3	11·4	470
Monsheim- .	—	—	—	—	—	—	72·7	91·0	50·0	—

Fig. 24.3 Anthropometric measurements of skulls from an early medieval row grave cemetery near Worms, carried out by Virchow (from Virchow 1877: 503).

From the standpoint of a scientist Virchow looked for 'hard facts' to address answered questions of research or publicly asked questions. Like many other prehistorians, including Kossinna, he was very interested in the prehistoric origins of modern nations and the racial composition of today's populations; this seemed to be a publicly very important object of research (Virchow 1884). Virchow argued that 'certain physical differences did affect the capacities of various races to adapt to particular environments – and therefore affected the cultures that arose from environmental adaptation' (Smith 1991: 106). Unlike others, Virchow insisted on proofs instead of hypotheses; the 'better argument' should decide between alternative possibilities and opinions, not 'pure patriotism' or 'flying enthusiasm'.[6] Even in the case of assertions he believed to be totally wrong, Virchow called for a scientific analysis. When the French anthropologist Jean Louis Armand de Quatrefages de Bréau (1810–1892) claimed that the attitude of Prussian soldiers during the war of 1870/71 had not been that of noble Aryan Germans, and that this might have been due to the Finnish origin of the Prussians (in terms of race; de Quatrefages 1871), Virchow reacted by organising the famous school statistics (*Schulkinderuntersuchung*). 'In the 1870s, the German Anthropological Society persuaded the German states to record the hair, eye, and skin color of over 6 million German schoolchildren to determine the fate of the fair-skinned, blond, blue-eyed 'classic Teutons' (*classische Erscheinungen des Germanen*) described by Tacitus and the origins of the brown-skinned, brown-haired, brown-eyed individuals who had become so preponderant in Germany' (Zimmerman 2001: 135; 1999). But de Quatrefages' challenge was only a new stimulus, not the main reason for this scientific enterprise.

At the beginning a 'statistical study of skull form in all of Germany' was intended, differentiating between brachycephaly and dolichocephaly, and the origins of races (Zimmerman 2001: 86–107). Because Virchow and the *enquête* commission[7] wanted a survey on a very large scale, it had to be carried out by untrained observers. Teachers recorded the colour of skin, hair and eyes by using tables (*Formulare*).[8] Finally it became clear that Quatrefages was wrong: the blond type was common in northern Germany and should therefore be of Germanic origin (Virchow 1886). The wider effects of these statistics were probably not intended, but they had a profound influence on the public; the racial categories became common as a kind of widespread 'tacit knowledge'. For example, Jewish pupils were omitted from the study to get an 'unadulterated' picture (not to discriminate the Jewish population); interestingly it was not the Jews but parts of the Catholic population in Prussia who became irritated and frightened (Goschler 2002: 341). But how could one argue against racist theories other than by proving them analytically? Virchow himself and his leading colleagues stood firmly against Anti-Semitism (Massin 1996: 88–92).

Towards the end of his life, during the 1890s, Virchow realised that some age-old questions could not be answered by anthropological or prehistoric research. Principally the desire to determine racial differences and to identify ancient peoples seemed to be an insoluble problem. His concepts and ideas did not change, but his clear analytical understanding led Virchow to identify fundamental methodological problems: 'In the case of nationality, all proper questioning comes to an end, as we do not have the language, linguistics as the basis [...] This was our greatest and most important task, and all the time of the century was not enough to destroy what was gradually established by foolish understanding of opinions'.[9] He refused all attempts to ground racial differences on skull measurements and to differentiate between 'German(ic)' and 'Jewish' skulls (Virchow 1896: 24, 26). In some cases Virchow was too cautious (because of methodological reasons and political implications; Smith 1991: 92), for example with respect to the Neanderthal skull and skeleton, which he declared a pathological anomaly (Virchow 1872, 1892; Andree 1976a, 151–64),[10] or in the case of Darwin's theory of descent, which he considered as unproven (Virchow 1863; 1882b). He continued to stand by his opinion with all his authority, however ultimately incorrect. The scepticism led Virchow to focus on cultural traits, a direction that Kossinna took some years later. This perspective made it possible to maintain the concept of human progress as cultural assimilation (and not as biological development), thus separating physical and cultural developments.

The Kossinna 'method' was centred on the prehistory of peoples, especially of the Germanic peoples or tribes. It had a simple axiom, which Hans Jürgen Eggers (1906–1975) later called a 'dogma' (*Glaubenssatz*): 'Distinct archaeological cultures are always congruent with certain peoples or tribes'.[11] Influences from north to south were interpreted as the reflection of Germanic expansion (Fig. 24.4), while in the opposite direction similarities were seen as only superficial imitations. Founded on this 'successful' and 'victorious' paradigm, Kossinna publicly fought for an 'appropriate' appreciation of the 'East German' or 'own' prehistory. His declared 'enemies' were the so-called Romance archaeologists (*Römlinge*) in West and South Germany who dealt with the Roman past along the *limes* (Veit 2000; Wiwjorra 1996).[12] Everything beyond the 'ancient Germans' and their Indo-European 'forefathers' (since the Neolithic) was irrelevant in Kossinna's eyes; even the Slavs as the 'primitive' counterpart are mentioned very rarely in his articles. This concept of a 'pre-eminently national archaeology' – not new, but simple and therefore 'convincing' – was Germanocentric, and it divided prehistoric research in Germany into two parties for a long period of time (Wiwjorra 2002; Grünert 2002: 164–73).

   It is remarkable that Kossinna never worked in the field. His museum approach was similar to that of contemporaneous cultural anthropologists like Leo Frobenius (1873–1938), Fritz Graebner (1877–1934) and Bernhard Ankermann (1859–1943) and their *Kulturkreise* (Zimmerman 2001: 201–216). The enormous museum collections needed categorisation and interpretation. Not surprisingly, Kossinna developed an atomistic view on culture(s), adding some traits of material culture to reconstruct cultural provinces; in some cases only a single characteristic was sufficient to identify a people (Kossinna 1905). This was influenced by anthropology too, but mainly by a nationalist view of history orientated towards culturally homogeneous modern states

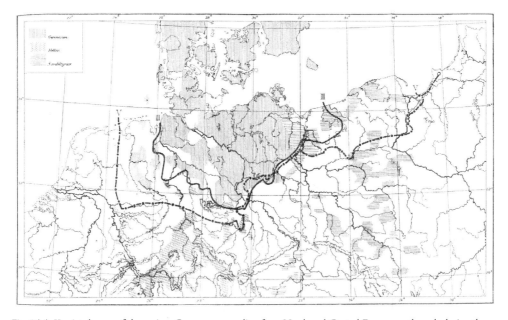

Fig. 24.4 Kossinna's map of the ancient Germans, expanding from North and Central Europe southwards during the Bronze and Iron Ages. Hatching indicates settlements in Bronze Age period II, while different lines mark the 'expension' during periods III to V (from Kossinna 1926–1927: fig. 52).

and their territories with sharp boundaries. Every regional 'culture' was understood as the material reflection of a specific people or tribe, leaving no room for other explanations. Kossinna used the term 'culture group' when he wanted to underline his ethnic approach.

Following the establishment of chronological schemes in the late nineteenth century Kossinna focused on the geographical dimension of prehistory. Knowing the age of artefacts, their connections between different regions were to be analysed. Even today the fixing of objects and structures in time and space are fundamental operations in archaeological research – to find out similarities and differences, continuities and discontinuities, influences and exchange. Kossinna's concept was therefore a necessary one; nevertheless his questioning produced the problem. He looked for nothing other than the settlement areas of different peoples. Despite the fact that there were no particularly homogeneous and distinct cultural groups Kossinna reconstructed such regions, arranging the material according to his strong opinion, sometimes quite arbitrarily (at least in the selection of the material described). The main mistake lay not in the antiquarian categorisation of pottery, jewelry and weapons (the positivist approach in space), but the one-sided questioning (Eggers 1986: 274) which came and comes from a national(ist) view of present and past times.

The 'Kossinna method' should have been 'thoroughly reasoned' and 'frequently tested' which therefore demanded unrestricted validity, as its author constantly claimed. In fact, Kossinna's arguments were risky and unproven – as most experts in archaeology, anthropology and linguistics noticed. But nearly all of them were prepared to believe that Kossinna must be right in the other field; everyone thought the errors would occur only in their own discipline and accepted the fundamental 'ethnic' interpretations. After 1918 his books contained ever increasing passages on the origin of the 'Nordic race' based on prehistoric skulls and actual race typologies by Hans F.K. Günther (1891–1968);[13] no new idea or further explication of published hypotheses could be seen.

Virchow as well as Kossinna argued for studies in culture history – as opposed to the political historiography of Leopold von Ranke (1795–1886) and Heinrich von Treitschke (1834–1896). They both shared a national German attitude (although both were aware of the suggested Slavonic origin of their last names; Goschler 2002: 27; Andree 1976a: 51; Grünert 2002: 18). Although Virchow tried to achieve intensive international cooperation he saw anthropology as a very German field of research. A major reason for the founding of the German Anthropological Society was the Copenhagen Anthropological congress of 1869 because the absence of a national association had prevented the 'appropriate perception' of German anthropologists abroad (Virchow 1871). Virchow was afraid that the main rival, France, could get a dominant role in anthropology. In general, Virchow believed in (natural) science as a 'German science' which could help to unify the split nation, and which was therefore – as a kind of education – important with respect to a national identity (as did 'German gymnastics'; Goschler 2002: 368). It is well-known that Kossinna declared the 'German prehistory a pre-eminently national discipline' (*hervorragend nationale Wissenschaft*; Kossinna 1914) again looking to the west (against France) and to the east (against Poland). But Kossinna used archaeological 'arguments' to strengthen actual political goals, i.e. entering territorial claims against Poland (Kossinna 1919). Even before the First World War Kossinna became a racist chauvinist (*völkischer Nationalist*), and he had many contacts with the extreme right.

Both men were restless positivist collectors. Virchow actively looked for new material to answer specific questions.[14] He occasionally excavated some archaeological sites, but in most cases he initiated anthropological research programmes – measuring skulls and skeletons, discovering physical characteristics of individuals and populations, collecting material for scientific analysis. Kossinna for his part only dealt with collected material in museums, or already published somewhere, and he also drew on information given to him by colleagues, students and amateurs. Kossinna was not in any case very much interested in the contexts of the finds, and his aim

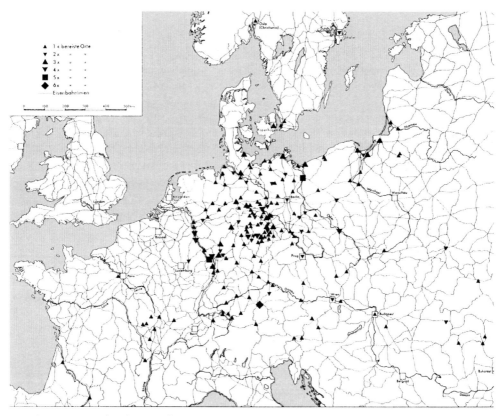

Fig. 24.5 Museums with prehistoric collections visited by Kossinna, who was travelling by railway. (from Schwerin v. Krosigk 1982: 25, map 1).

remained to produce a vast private archive with which to prove and underline his views on Germanic prehistory: and although he was very often asked to published these material arguments, he never did.

Besides collecting, other activities required much travelling. Both Virchow and Kossinna[15] visited many congresses, excavations and museums (see Andree 1976a: 17–48, 57–80; Grünert 2002: 75–90; and here Fig. 24.5 and Table 24.1). Both kept an ongoing correspondence with many people,[16] in line with their intensive efforts at organising the discipline and in popularising its results; Virchow wrote mainly to colleagues and other scientists such as physicians, geologists, palaeontologists, botanists and zoologists – and only to a few well known archaeologists such as Hans Hildebrand (1842–1913), Ingvald Undset (1853–1893), Jens Jakob Asmussen Worsaae (1821–1885), but interestingly not to Oscar Montelius. Kossinna for his part corresponded mainly with numerous prehistorians. In any case, both clearly stood at the crossroads of scientific and political networks which made them well informed and influential.

Impacts and Effects

The historiography of archaeology often sees Kossinna as a 'classic' together with the Australian British archaeologist Vere Gordon Childe. These two prehistorians established the concept of 'archaeological cultures' as a fundamental paradigm which became widespread during the 1920s (Veit 1984); later on Childe tried to eliminate Kossinna's racist connotations. This primarily geographic perspective, with its assumption of homogeneous and distinct cultural areas, led to specific expectations. For those who shared the fundamental assumptions of late nineteenth- and early twentieth-century historiography, it was by searching for ancient people that archaeology could provide historical interpretations, and at the same time demonstrate its public and scientific relevance. Kossinna gave this new discipline of prehistory a rather simple but impressive paradigm at a time when it started its own institutionalisation at the universities. Often – and even today – it is overlooked that 'archaeological cultures' are actually scientific categories which depend on the characteristics considered (Wotzka 1993; 2000).

Because Kossinna posthumously developed into a 'hero' of Nazi archaeology,[17] a so-called 'Kossinna syndrome' arose in German archaeology (Smolla 1979/80; Klejn 1974). Nevertheless 'culture' in a similar sense remained a basic concept neglecting the fundamental methodological problems. A major reason lay in the cautious critique it received during the first decades of the twentieth century. Only some people questioned Kossinna's methodology publicly and plainly as did Karl Hermann Jacob-Friesen (1886–1960) (Jacob-Friesen 1928). The Austrian Moritz Hoernes, for example, viewed a 'Germanic prehistory' with concern, 'soon tracing back the German phylogenetic tree into the palaeozooic formation' (Hoernes 1905: 238 fn. 1). Criticism of Kossinna's opinions remained marginal for two reasons: first, after 1918 his work was increasingly regarded as part of political propaganda (Kossinna 1921; 1926–1927; 1927); secondly, he became embittered and begun to offend personally his scientific opponents (Grünert 2002: 191–94). For this reason his opponents such as Carl Schuchhardt, tended to ignore his theories rather than arguing in detail against them (Grünert 2002: 174–84); this prevented the discipline from holding an intensive debate on the issue – a lacuna that can sometimes still be felt today. Yet Kossinna's statements drew attention and became widespread from the 1920s, as can be seen, for example, in the case of the journal 'People and Race' (*Volk und Rasse. Illustrierte Vierteljahresschrift für deutsches Volkstum*), established in 1926 and edited by well-known scholars of different disciplines.[18]

In personal and scientific terms, Virchow dominated prehistoric research much more than did Kossinna, who remained at least in some respects a social outsider (compared for example with his Berlin opponent Schuchhardt, museum director, member of the Berlin Royal Academy, and personally known to the *Kaiser*). As Virchow became active in anthropology and prehistory in the late 1860s, prehistoric archaeology had grown from a diffuse subject of research into a coherent research field with its own methods and principles (Kaeser 2002). In the evolutionist view of the 1870s and 1880s anthropology, ethnology and prehistory were considered together centred around one subject – the progress of humankind with respect to culture and race (cf. Massin 1996: 97).

Virchow's main methodological contribution lay in his unbiased approach to open and ongoing questions, and in the consideration of all available sources of evidence including different scientific analysis bearing on artefacts, physical remains, material for zoological, botanical, chemical and environmental analysis[19] (which were all matters of no interest to Kossinna). Even the national impetus shared by these anthropologists was no obstacle, encouraged by their interest in the origins of man and the early history of races. Virchow was aware – as was Kossinna – of the impact of anthropological theories and results on the public. But unlike Kossinna, he did not venture into political propaganda but rather tried to argue cautiously on the basis of analytical investigations. Virchow saw the recurrent but fruitless attempts to find national 'types' as the result of political considerations 'foreign to science'; in his eyes actual 'national unity had nothing to do with the results of anthropology' (Massin 1996: 100–101). These two points – Virchow's multiple perspectives and his methodological caution – led in the twentieth century to a lasting underestimation of his importance for prehistoric research.[20] This is especially the case when contrasting his broad perspectives with Kossinna's far simpler paradigm,[21] which has for long led to overemphasise his importance, negatively as well as positively.

By about 1900 anthropology, ethnology and prehistory became separate independent disciplines. The previous organisational cooperation was replaced by separate developments (with respect to university departments, organisations, journals, congresses). In 1899 Virchow sadly wrote about this change: 'when speaking of anthropology, many people do not think any longer of bones and human beings, but of tools, pots, swords, daggers and such-like grave-goods'.[22] Prehistoric archaeology benefited much from the disciplinary separation, but unfortunately thereafter the popular race 'theories' were perceived only from the outside (Weingart et al. 1992) and were no longer a theme of scientific debate within prehistoric research. Another main reason was the then fundamental crisis of classical physical anthropology and its excessive use of skull measurements which came to nothing (Massin 1996: 106–143; Gould 1988: 73–117).

More than his caution in the cases of the Neanderthal man and Darwin's thesis, these structural developments make it clear that Virchow had been a representative of the past, whose arguments now belonged to a discipline that was effectively subdivided. In medicine as well as in anthropology and politics, he was outstripped for at least the last ten years of his life. Kossinna was the one who articulated a spatial concept for the former sub-discipline of prehistory, once its fundamental chronological schemes had been established in the late nineteenth century (notably by Virchow himself) (Gräslund 1987). Unfortunately this specialisation took place in a very simplistic manner, after the defeat of liberalism in Wilhelmine Germany; Virchow, moreover, had been an important and long-standing liberal member of parliament (in the *Preußisches Abgeordnetenhaus* [1862–1902] as well as in the *Reichstag* [1880–1893]).[23]

When critique on the modern age arose, Virchow insisted on the simultaneity of material and moral progress which made him a transitional figure – with no sense for social tensions and ambivalences (Goschler 2002: 373); from his liberal perspective he could trust neither conservatives nor social democrats. Social instabilities and anxieties became widespread within modern German society at the dawn of the twentieth century, and Kossinna's questioning reflected the yearning for a stronghold in the *early* past, at least for a conservative part of society. The main problem remains not the approach itself, but its nationalist or 'ethnic' implications. Virchow's idea of continuous progress was increasingly replaced by the obsessive search for early origins of cultures and races. Regardless of their different characters and personalities, Virchow and Kossinna were exponents of their respective time and of the changing developments in science – from anthropology as a natural science within an imperial synthesis to culture-historical archaeology with its unmistakable national implications.

Notes

1   Grünert (1998) states that Kossinna became active within in the Berlin Anthropological Society only after Virchow's death.

2   As early as in the 1860s laboratories were founded which were bigger and better equipped than Virchow's (Goschler 2002: 382). These new institutions were established to serve the needs of a modern industrial nation – during an 'institutional revolution' in the 1860s (Cahan 1989).

3   These general meetings had him as chairman (as the chairman of the society) in 1871, 1874, 1877, 1880, 1883, 1884, 1886, 1887, 1891, 1893, 1894, 1896, 1897, 1898, 1900. Despite this Virchow was vice-president of the *Congrès International d'Anthropologie et d'Archéologie Préhistorique* in 1872 (Bruxelles), 1874 (Stockholm), 1876 (Budapest), 1880 (Lisbon), 1892 (Moscow).

4   The first full professorship was awarded to Gero von Merhart (1886–1959) at Marburg University in 1928; in general, see Pape 2002.

5   Therefore the metaphors became interchangeable: organism and state, cells and individuals (Weindling 1989; Mazzolini 1988).

6   'Ich bitte darum, dass wir nicht in blossem Patriotismus arbeiten und unsere Aufgabe nicht bloss in schwungvoller Begeisterung zu lösen suchen, sondern dass wir uns die Mühe nehmen, den Thatsachen nachzugehen, und uns die ganze Schwierigkeit des Problems vergegenwärtigen' (Virchow 1885: 125).

7   Members were Virchow, Alexander Ecker (1816–1887), Wilhelm His (1831–1904), Rudolf Albert Kölliker (1817–1905), Wilhelm Krause (1833–1910), Johann Christian Gustav Lucae (1814–1885), Hermann Schaaffhausen (1816–1893), and Hermann Welcker (1822–1897) (Zimmerman 2001: 290 fn. 3).

8   Originally a survey of young recruits was intended but the Prussian military rejected this plan.

9   'Bei der Frage der Nationalität hört eigentlich alles regelrechte Fragen auf, sobald wir nicht mehr die Sprache, die Linguistik als Grundlage haben [...] Das war unsere grösste und wichtigste Aufgabe, und es hat die ganze Zeit des Jahrhunderts nicht ausgereicht, um Alles das zu zerstören, was aus thörichter Auffassung der Meinungen allmählich aufgebaut war' (Virchow 1899, 82–83).

10 Symptomatically, 'monsters' were seen as pathological deviations from the ideal typus (not from the average) (Goschler 2002: 296; Zimmerman 2001: 62–85).

11 Kossinna (1914: 3): 'Scharf umgrenzte archäologische Kulturprovinzen decken sich zu allen Zeiten mit ganz bestimmten Völkern oder Völkerstämmen'.

12 But even Virchow prevented the *Römisch-Germanische Kommission* from expanding its area of research beyond the Rhineland, into 'Germanic' regions (Kossack 1999: 36).

13 Cf. Kossinna (1926–1927: 79–128) with the 'Entstehung der nordischen Rasse'.

14 Cf. the schoolchildren statistics, the lake dwellings, the differentiation between Iron Age (Lusatian culture) and early medieval Slavic remains, and the early medieval hillforts. For Virchow's collections, see Matyssek (2002).

15 Kossinna visited more than 300 sites (Grünert 2002: 90–95). Fieldworkers like Schuchhardt described Kossinna's little interest in archaeological structures (Schuchhardt 1944: 289): 'die Beobachtung im Gelände war nicht Kossinnas Sache'.

16 Within Virchow's estate about 20,000 letters from 2,200 correspondents are preserved (Andree 1976a: 15); letters concerning anthropology, ethnology and prehistory are already published in the following editions Andree (1976b: 9–541) (410 letters); Andree (1991) (ca. 120 letters); Herrmann/Maaß/Andree/Hallof (1990) (622 letters); Wenig (1995) (69 letters). All letters will be published in: Christian Andree (ed.), Rudolf Virchow, Sämtliche Werke. Abteilung 4: Briefe (Berlin et al.). – Kossinna's correspondence is less well preserved (Grünert 2002: 350–62).

17 In his last years Kossinna sympathised with the Nazi party (Grünert 2002: 306–12).

18 By the prehistorians Gero v. Merhart (1886–1959), Ernst Wahle (1889–1981) and Gustav Schwantes (1881–1960), the ethnologist Richard Thurnwald (1869–1954), the race anthropologists Karl Walter Scheidt (1895–1976) ('Schriftleiter' or chief editor) and Eugen Fischer (1874–1967), the geographers Rudolf Gradmann (1888–1962) and Robert Mielke (1863–1935), the philologist Rudolf Much (1862–1936) and others.

19 Schliemann's excavations at Hissarlık gave Virchow the opportunity to use scientific analysis in archaeology, a main reason for Virchow's interest (Virchow 1879; 1882a).

20 Cf. the influence on Franz Boas; see several articles in Stocking (1988; 1996); cf. Geulen (2000).

21 Already Kossinna sharply criticized Virchow (Grünert 2002: 202).

22 Virchow (1899: 83), stated, that: 'wenn man heutzutage von Anthropologie spricht, Viele nicht mehr an Knochen und Menschen denken, sondern an Geräthe, Töpfe, Schwerter, Dolche und was sonst noch in Gräbern getroffen wird'; translation following Fetten (2000: 168).

23 Together with Theodor Mommsen (1817–1903) and others he founded the German Progress Party (*Deutsche Fortschrittspartei*) in 1861.

References

Andree, C. 1969. 'Geschichte der Berliner Gesellschaft für Anthropologie, Ethnologie und Urgeschichte 1869–1969'. In: *Hundert Jahre Berliner Gesellschaft für Anthropologie, Ethnologie und Urgeschichte 1869–1969*. Berlin, 9–142.

———. 1976a. *Rudolf Virchow als Prähistoriker 1*. Köln, Wien.

———. 1976b. *Rudolf Virchow als Prähistoriker 2.* Köln, Wien.

———. (ed.) 1991. *Über Griechenland und Troja, alte und junge Gelehrte, Ehefrauen und Kinder. Briefe von Rudolf Virchow und Heinrich Schliemann aus den Jahren 1877–1885.* Köln.

———. 2002a. *Rudolf Virchow. Leben und Ethos eines großen Arztes.* München.

———. 2002b. *Virchows Weg von Berlin nach Würzburg. Eine heuristische Studie zu den Archivalien der Jahre 1848 bis 1856.* Würzburg.

Brather, S. 2001. s. v. Kossinna, Gustaf. In: *Reallexikon der Germanischen Altertumskunde*[2] 17. Berlin, New York, 263–67.

Cahan, D. 1989. *An Institute for an Empire. The Physikalisch-technische Reichsanstalt 1871–1918.* Cambridge.

Eggers, H.J. 1986. *Einführung in die Vorgeschichte.* München.

Fetten, F. 2000. 'Archaeology and Anthropology in Germany before 1945'. In: Heinrich Härke (ed.), *Archaeology, Ideology and Society. The German Experience. Gesellschaften und Staaten im Epochenwandel* 7. Frankfurt/M., 140–79.

Geulen, C. 2000. 'Blonde bevorzugt. Virchow und Boas – eine Fallstudie zur Verschränkung von "Rasse" und "Kultur" im ideologischen Feld der Ethnizität um 1900'. *Archiv für Sozialgeschichte* 40, 147–70.

Goschler, C. 2002. *Rudolf Virchow. Mediziner, Anthropologe, Politiker.* Köln, Weimar.

Gould, S.J. 1988. *Der falsch vermessene Mensch.* Frankfurt/M.

Gräslund, B. 1987. *The Birth of Prehistoric Chronology.* Cambridge.

Grünert, H. 1988. Gustaf Kossinna und die Berliner Gesellschaft für Anthropologie, Ethnologie und Urgeschichte. *Mitteilungen der Berliner Gesellschaft für Anthropologie, Ethnologie und Urgeschichte* 19, 31–38.

———. 2002. 'Gustaf Kossinna (1858–1931). Vom Germanisten zum Prähistoriker. Ein Wissenschaftler im Kaiserreich und in der Weimarer Republik'. *Vorgeschichtliche Forschungen* 22.

Herrmann, J., E. Maaß, C. Andree and L. Hallof (eds.), 1990, *Die Korrespondenz zwischen Heinrich Schliemann und Rudolf Virchow 1876–1890.* Berlin.

Hoernes, M. 1905. Die Hallstattperiode. *Archiv für Anthropologie N. F.* 3, 233–81.

Jacob-Friesen, K.H. 1928. *Grundfragen der Urgeschichtsforschung. Stand und Kritik der Forschung über Rassen, Völker und Kulturen in urgeschichtlicher Zeit.* Veröffentlichungen der Urgeschichtlichen Abteilung des Provinzial-Museums Hannover 1, Hannover.

Kaeser, M.-A. 2002. 'On the International Roots of Prehistory'. *Antiquity* 76, 170–77.

Klejn, L.S. 1974. Kossinna im Abstand von vierzig Jahren. *Jahresschrift für mitteldeutsche Vorgeschichte* 58, 7–55.

Kossack, G. 1999. *Prähistorische Archäologie in Deutschland im Wandel der geistigen und politischen Situation.* Bayerische Akademie der Wissenschaften, philosophiosch-historische Klasse, Sitzungsberichte 1999/4. München.

Kossinna, G. 1905. 'Über verzierte Eisenlanzenspitzen als Kennzeichen der Ostgermanen'. *Zeitschrift für Ethnologie* 37, 369–407.

———. 1911. *Die Herkunft der Germanen. Zur Methode der Siedlungsarchäologie.* Mannus-Bibliothek 6. Würzburg.

———. 1914. *Die deutsche Vorgeschichte, eine hervorragend nationale Wissenschaft.* Mannus-Bibliothek 9. Würzburg.

———. 1919. *Das Weichselland, ein uralter Heimatboden der Germanen.* Danzig.

———. 1919/20. 'Das siegreiche Vordringen meiner wissenschaftlichen Anschauungen als Ergebnis meiner wissenschaftlichen Methode'. *Mannus* 11/12, 394–404.

———. 1921. *Die Indogermanen I. Das indogermanische Urvolk.* Leipzig.

———. 1926–1927. *Ursprung und Verbreitung der Germanen in vor- und frühgeschichtlicher Zeit.* Irminsul 1. Berlin-Lichterfelde.

———. 1927. *Altgermanische Kulturhöhe. Eine Einführung in die deutsche Vor- und Frühgeschichte.* München.

Massin, B. 1996. 'From Virchow to Fischer. Physical Anthropology and 'modern race theory' in Wilhelmine Germany'. In: G.W. Stocking (ed.), *Volksgeist as Method and Ethic. Essays on Boasian Ethnography and the German Anthropological Tradition.* History of Anthropology 8. Madison, Wisconsin, 79–154.

Matyssek, A. 2002. *Rudolf Virchow. Das Pathologische Museum. Geschichte einer wissenschaftlichen Sammlung um 1900.* Schriften aus dem Berliner Medizinhistorischen Museum 1. Darmstadt.

Mazzolini, R.G. 1988. *Politisch-biologische Analogien im Frühwerk Rudolf Virchows.* Marburg.

Pape, W. 2002. Zur Entwicklung des Faches Ur- und Frühgeschichte in Deutschland bis 1945. In: A. Leube and M. Hegewisch (eds), *Prähistorie und Nationalsozialismus. Die mittel- und osteuropäische Ur- und Frühgeschichtsforschung in den Jahren 1933–1945*. Heidelberg, 163–226.

de Quatrefages, A. 1871. *La Race prussienne*. Paris.

Schuchhardt, C. 1944. *Aus Leben und Arbeit*. Berlin.

Schwerin v. Krosigk, H. 1982. *Gustaf Kossinna. Der Nachlaß. Versuch einer Analyse*. Offa-Ergänzungsreihe 6, Neumünster.

Smith, W.D. 1991. *Politics and the Sciences of Culture in Germany, 1840–1920*. New York.

Smolla, G. 1980. 'Das Kossinna-Syndrom'. *Fundberichte aus Hessen* 19/20, 1979/80 (Festschrift Ulrich Fischer), 1–9.

Stampfuß, R. 1935. *Gustaf Kossinna, ein Leben für die deutsche Vorgeschichte*. Leipzig.

Stocking, G.W. (ed.), 1988. *Bones, Bodies, Behaviour. Essays on Biological Anthropology*. History of anthropology 5. Madison, Wisconsin.

——— . 1996. *Volksgeist as Method and Ethic. Essays on Boasian Ethnography and the German Anthropological Tradition*. History of Anthropology 8. Madison, Wisconsin.

Trigger, B.G. 1989. *A History of Archaeological Thought*. Cambridge.

Veit, U. 1984. Gustaf Kossinna und V. Gordon Childe. 'Ansätze zu einer theoretischen Grundlegung der Vorgeschichte'. *Saeculum* 35, 326–64.

——— . 2000. 'Gustaf Kossinna and His Concept of a National Archaeology'. In: H. Härke (ed.), *Archaeology, Ideology and Society. The German Experience*. Gesellschaften und Staaten im Epochenwandel 7. Frankfurt/M., 40–64.

Virchow, R. *Die Cellularpathologie in ihrer Begründung auf physiologische und pathologische Gewebelehre* (Berlin 1858) = *Cellular pathology* (London 1860) = *Pathologie cellulaire* (Paris 1861) = *La patologia cellulare* (Roma 1863).

——— . 1863. 'Über die Erblichkeit I. Die Theorie Darwins'. *Deutsche Jahrbücher für Politik und Literatur* 6, 339–58.

——— . 1871. 'Rede auf der 2. allgemeinen Versammlung der deutschen Gesellschaft für Anthropologie, Ethnologie und Urgeschichte am 22. September 1871 in Schwerin'. *Correspondenz-Blatt der deutschen Gesellschaft für Anthropologie, Ethnologie und Urgeschichte* 2, 43–47.

——— . 1872. 'Untersuchung des Neanderthal-Schädels'. *Verhandlungen der Berliner Gesellschaft für Anthropologie, Ethnologie und Urgeschichte* 4, 157–65.

——— . 1874. Einleitendes Vorwort. In: J. Lubbock, *Die vorgeschichtliche Zeit, erläutert durch die Ueberreste des Alterthums und die Sitten und Gebräuche der jetzigen Wilden*. Jena, V–VIII.

——— . 1877. 'Reihengräberfeld bei Alsheim (Rheinhessen)'. *Verhandlungen der Berliner Gesellschaft für Anthropologie, Ethnologie und Urgeschichte*, (495)–(504).

——— . 1879. 'Ueber Troja'. *Verhandlungen der Berliner Gesellschaft für Anthropologie, Ethnologie und Urgeschichte. Beilage zur Zeitschrift für Ethnologie* 11, (254)–(281).

——— . 1882a. *Ueber alttrojanische Gräber und Schädel*. Berlin.

——— . 1882b. Über Darwin und die Anthropologie. *Correspondenz-Blatt der deutschen Gesellschaft für Anthropologie, Ethnologie und Urgeschichte* 13, 208–11.

——— . 1884. 'Eröffnungsrede. Ueber ostdeutsche prähistorische Alterthümer'. *Correspondenz-Blatt der deutschen Gesellschaft für Anthropologie, Ethnologie und Urgeschichte* 15, 65–76.

——— . 1885. Ergänzeude Bemerleuugen tu einen Vartrag über die Herkuuft der Germanen. *Correspondenz-Blatt der deutschen Gesellschaft für Anthropologie, Ethnologie und Urgeschichte* 16, 124–25.

——— . 1886. 'Gesammtbericht über die von der deutschen anthropologischen Gesellschaft veranlassten Erhebungen über die Farbe der Haut, der Haare und der Augen der Schulkinder in Deutschland'. *Archiv für Anthropologie* 16, 275–446.

——— . 1892. 'Ergänzungen zu einem Vortrag über die Schädel von Cannstatt und Neanderthal'. *Correspondenz-Blatt der deutschen Gesellschaft für Anthropologie, Ethnologie und Urgeschichte* 23, 90–92, 93–94.

——— . 1896. 'Rassenbildung und Erblichkeit'. In: *Festschrift für Adolf Bastian zu seinem 70. Geburtstage*. Berlin, 3–43.

——— . 1899. Meinungen und Thatsachen in der Anthropologie. *Correspondenz-Blatt der deutschen Gesellschaft für Anthropologie, Ethnologie und Urgeschichte* 30, 80–83.

Weindling, P. 1989. *Health, Race and German Politics Between National Unification and Nazism 1870–1945*. Cambridge.

Weingart, P., J. Kroll and K. Bayertz. 1992. *Rasse, Blut und Gene. Geschichte der Eugenik und Rassenhygiene in Deutschland*. Frankfurt/M.

Wenig, K. (ed.) 1995. *Rudolf Virchow und Emil du Bois-Reymond. Briefe 1864–1894*. Marburg.

Wiwjorra, I. 1996. 'German Archaeology and its Relation to Nationalism and Racism'. In: M. Díaz-Andreu and T. Champion (eds.), *Nationalism and Archaeology in Europe*. London, 164–88.

———. 2002. '"Ex oriente lux" – "Ex septentrione lux". Über den Widerstreit zweier Identitätsmythen'. In: A. Leube and M. Hegewisch (eds.), *Prähistorie und Nationalsozialismus. Die mittel- und osteuropäische Ur- und Frühgeschichtsforschung in den Jahren 1933–1945*. Heidelberg, 73–106.

Wotzka, H.-P. 1993. 'Zum traditionellen Kulturbegriff in der Archäologie'. *Paideuma* 39, 25–44.

———. 2000. '"Kultur" in der deutschsprachigen Urgeschichtsforschung'. In: S. Fröhlich (ed.), *Kultur. Ein interdisziplinäres Kolloquium zur Begrifflichkeit*. Halle/S., 55–80.

Zimmerman, A. 1999. 'Anti-Semitism as Skill. Rudolf Virchow's Schulstatistik and the Racial Composition of Germany'. *Central European History* 32, 409–29.

———. 2001. *Anthropology and Antihumanism in Imperial Germany*. Chicago, London.

Table 24. 1

Virchow's travels concerning prehistoric research (incomplete list). Own excavations in italics; modern place-names as far as possible (arranged after Andree 1976a: 17–48; 1969; 2002: 76–91)

Year	'Solving prehistoric questions' and in the field	Museums and collections
1865	*Lübtow* (Lubiatowo)	
1866	*Daber* (Dobra Nowogardzkie)	
1869	*Lübtow* (Lubiatowo), *Daber* (Dobra Nowogardzkie)	
1871	*Wollin* (Wolin)	
1873	Sprottau, Klein Obisch, *Zaborowo* (Unterwalden), Glogau, Kiel, Hamburg	London
1874	Halle/S., *Zaborowo*	Jena
1875	Regensburg, Muggendorf, Soldin, *Zahsow, Ragow*	Munich, Nuremberg, Bamberg, Schwerin, Prague
1876	Taubach near Weimar, Erd, Toseg/Abony, *Klein Rössen, Falkenberg, Schlieben*	Budapest, Brussels, Leiden, Amsterdam, Utrecht
1877	*Zaborowo*	
1878	Vetschau, Burg near Magdeburg	
1879	Troy, Dümrek, Hanai Tepe, Upik Tepe, İntepe (Erenköy), Istanbul, Bayramiç, Efyilar, Eriulu, Kutlobası, Pınarbası, Ayvacık, Assos, Karanlık, Ucek Tepe, Ilyek Tepe, Besik Tepe, Athens, Santorin, Eleusis, Corinth, Corfu, Bologna, Assignario, Certosa; *Krien-See* near Neubrandenburg	Kensington
1880	*Lübben, Ragow*	Vienna
1881	Breslau (Wrocaw), Lemberg (Lviv), Ostrov, Olviopol', Vandarka, Elisabetgrad, Kharkov, Taganrog, Rostov, Koban, Nolla Koban, Tiflis, Mleti, Mzkhet, Kazanka, Mikhailovo, Kutais, Abastuman	Kharkov, Vladikavkas
1882	Dürkheim, Bodenheim, Saalburg, Frankfurt/M., Heddernheim, Groß Gerau, Suggenthal, Freiburg i. Br., Straßburg, Milano, Kerenzen (Chireze), Obstalden	Hanover, Dornach, Colmar, Stettin (Szczecin), Darmstadt, Karlsruhe, Basel, Konstanz, Hottingen

1883	Otzenhausen, Luxemburg, Worms, Dürkheim, Konstanz, Groß Kühnau near Dessau, Aschersleben, Wilsleben, Ketzin, Basel, Zürich, Neapel, Rome	Treves, Bregenz, Dessau, Bernburg, Halberstadt, Berlin
1884	Gnischwitz, Edinburgh, Hamilton, Glasgow, Prague, Dresden, Heidenau near Pirna, Dux (Ducové), Feldberg, Bernburg, Hagenau	Breslau (Wrocaw), Budapest, Vienna, York, London, Copenhagen, Kiel, Hamburg
1885	Munich, Triest, Bozen, Neuchâtel, Chur, Weisdin near Neustrelitz, Neustrelitz	Innsbruck, St. Gallen, Berne, Biel, Konstanz
1886	Strega, Niemitzsch near Guben, Vettersfelde (Vitaszkowo)	Cottbus, Stettin (Szczecin), Lenzen/Elbe
1887	Friedberg, Werben, Seehausen/Altmark, Oldenburg, Rastede, Zwischenahn, Bremerhaven, Ansbach, Nuremberg, Bamberg, Rothenburg, Schleswig, Heimenschwand, Swizzerland	Mainz, Kassel, Eschwege, Wiesbaden
1888	Athens, Olympia, Pyrgos, Patras, Aegion, Korinth, Nauplia, Mithana, Epidauros, Cleve	Tirgnes
1889	Schönkirchen, Beringstedt, Wendek, Seefeld, Hademarsch, Albersdorf	Görlitz, Kiel
1890	Vienna, Budapest, Belgrade, Istanbul, Troy/ Hissarlık, Pınarbası, Dümrek, Neostori, Karadağ, Ezine (Ine), Krugarer, Zeytinli, Kemer, Sastir, Nuromilou, Sofia, Emsbühren, Rastede, Vechta, Cloppenburg, Oberweiler, Marzell, Heilbronn, Leysin near Aigle, Waadt, Zermatt, St. Nicolas, Lintfluh, Berne	Münster, Osnabrück, Neuchâtel
1891	Danzig (Gdańsk), Tolkemit (Tolkmicko), Hirschfeld (Jelonki) near Elbing (Elblåg), Dörschek, Lenzen (Lecze), Kamp near Krauts-Kuren, Wargen, Wiskiauten (Mokhovoe), Runtau, Kewitten near Tapiau (Gvardeysk), Nidden (Nida), Russ, Werder near Elbing, Löbarken, Ilgengun, Schwarzort (Juodkrante), Ermland, Thorn (Toruń)	Königsberg, Halle/S.
1892	Moscow	
1894	*Groß Wachlin*, Dessau, Visby, Stockholm	
1895	Glückstadt, Wyk/Föhr, Romania, Ivan, Buna, Moitav, Jegerov (Yugoslavia)	Vienna, Prague, Sarajevo
1896	Riga	
1898	Kronstadt (Braov), Hermannstadt (Sibiu), Bologna	Hermannstadt (Sibiu)

Zusammenfassung

Virchow und Kossinna waren prominente deutsche Archäologen. Beide beschäftigten sich erst in ihrer zweiten Lebenshälfte mit der Vorgeschichtsforschung. In Virchows Todesjahr wurde Kossinna a. o. Prof. in Berlin; dies war ein Wendepunkt auf dem Weg von international und anthropologisch ausgerichteten Forschungen über eine „nationale Archäologie' zur „deutschen Vorgeschichte'. Daher können Virchow und Kossinna wissenschaftlich, politisch und moralisch kontrastiert werden, die unterschiedliche Ziele, Traditionen und Zeiten repräsentierten. Doch hatten beide auch viel gemeinsam – in ihrem Leben und in ihren Vorstellungen.

Beide suchten ihr eigenes Bild von ihrem wissenschaftlichen und öffentlichen Leben zu verbreiten. Virchow sah sich als Naturwissenschaftler, dessen Kenntnisse ihm die „große Politik' ermöglichten – weil, Politik nichts weiter als Medizin in einem größeren Rahmen sei. Kossinna betrachtete sich als „Kämpfer' für eine deutsche Vorgeschichtete und den besten Experten auf diesem Gebiet. Die emphatische Haltung hinsichtlich der vorgeblichen „altgermanischen Kulturhöhe' zu propagieren, wurde zu seiner Mission.

Beide setzten sich für kulturgeschichtliche Arbeiten ein – im Gegensatz zur politischen Historiographie von Ranke und Treitschke. Beide teilten ein starkes Nationalbewußtsein (und waren sich ihres mutmaßlich slawischsprachigen Namens bewußt). Obgleich Virchow sich um intensive internationale Zusammenarbeit bemühte, betrachtete die Anthropologie als „deutsche Wissenschaft'. Bekanntermaßen erklärte Kossinna die „deutsche Vorgeschichte' zu einer „hervorragend nationalen Wissenschaft'. Aber Kossinna benutzte archäologische „Argumente' zur Erreichung aktueller politischer Ziele.

Beide Männer waren rastlose Sammler, und sie besuchten zahlreiche Kongresse, Ausgrabungen und Museen. Beide unterhielten eine umfassende Korrespondenz mit vielen Partnern – wegen ihrer intensiven Arbeit bei der Wissenschaftsorganisation und bei der Popularisierung wissenschaftlicher Erkenntnisse. Im 20. Jahrhundert führten Virchows differenzierte Ansichten und methodische Vorsicht zu einer anhaltenden Unterschätzung seiner Bedeutung für die prähistorische Forschung, besonders im Vergleich seiner breiten Perspektiven mit Kossinnas simplem Paradigma. Kossinna dagegen wurde lange Zeit im positiven wie im negativen Sinne überschätzt.

Chapter 25
Dutch Archaeology and National Socialism

Martijn Eickhoff

Abstract

Dutch pre-and protohistory triggered a lot of interest during the 1930s and 1940s among national socialists. In their opinion, this ancient history reflected essential German characteristics in cultural and ethnic-racial senses. For this reason, archaeologic research would provide not only knowledge about the beginnings of history, but also contribute to the regeneration of the 'German character' in the present. This chapter explores the impact of this particular interest from the national socialist side for Dutch pre- and protohistorical archaeology. First, an analysis will be made of the Dutch national identity, with particular attention to the regional, national (Dutch) and supranational (pan-German) levels. Secondly, it will be shown that only against this background, can the response of Dutch archaeologists toward national socialists be fully understood. The idea that the Dutch people had their origins in Germanic people was a common idea in the Netherlands. German officials responsible for cultural affairs merely tried to increase this particular awareness. For archaeologists, it thus became increasingly difficult to ignore the social and political implications of their work. In this chapter this phenomenon is illustrated by four examples. While A.W. Byvanck, F.C. Bursch and P. Felix for various reasons left the ivory tower of academe by stressing nationalistic or national socialistic implications of their archaeological research, A.E. van Giffen tried to hold on to his scientific ideal of objectivity. On the one hand, his positivistic background made him unassailable in his own eyes, while at the same time his insights were most vulnerable for political appropriation by national socialist propagandists.

Introduction

It is well known that during times of social crisis and political revolutions people tend to turn to the past looking for their roots. In Dutch history, several such moments of heightened historical interest can be found, for example during the French invasion of 1795 (Romein 1946: 180–81). Also during the German occupation of 1940–1945, the historical consciousness of the Dutch received a sudden and strong impulse. Especially during the first years of occupation many books and pamphlets appeared in which, speaking of the Dutch national 'character', national identity was analysed and described. With reference to these historical publications, some post-war studies spoke of 'historical resistance' (for some examples see Beyen 2000: 113). This is, however, a rather simplified view of the situation. From the side of the German authorities, these historical activities were not curbed, but outright stimulated.

At first sight this seems a paradoxical situation. Why would German officials responsible for cultural affairs encourage the study of the Dutch past? Was is not, after all, their goal to embed the Dutch people in a Greater Germanic Empire? In order to answer this question, a closer look at the Dutch national identity, its historical dimension and its multiple layers is necessary. Only against this background can it be shown that German officials had a hidden agenda: they strove to make the Dutch people more aware of the ethnic-racial level of their identity. This was expected to set a Germanic regeneration in motion: the embracing by the Dutch people of their Germanic roots.[1] Then, the German officials reasoned, a consciousness would automatically arise that jewish citizens were a threat to Germanic-Dutch society. They also hoped that the Dutch would realise that the national borders were artificial constructions, and not in line with 'natural' ethnic-racial boundaries. Moreover, they expected the Dutch to become national socialists, as this political ideology was deemed an expression of the natural world-view of Germanic people. (Plate 16)

In order to prove the Germanic dimension in Dutch national identity many branches of research – germanistics, folkore studies, physical anthropology, eugenics, archaeology and history – were stimulated or even funded by the national socialists. For Dutch prehistorians, who traditionally approached the early past in a very positivistic way, this had far-reaching consequenses. They were encouraged to continue with their work; there were, for example, important new opportunities for excavations due to the bombing of city centres. And in doing so, archaeologists provided the material that would make the Germanic essence both visible and tangible for contemporary beholders. As a result, archaeoloy was used by the German government to undermine Dutch national unity, to promote the Greater Germanic unity, and to justify their racist population policy in the Netherlands. In retrospect one would therefore expect that, during the occupation years, it was not easy for Dutch prehistorians to remain in the ivory tower of academe. In reality their position was, as will be shown in this paper, much more complex.

National Identity in the Netherlands

Nowadays it is often recognised that identities are mainly constructions; describing or analysing an identity leads – unintentionally but inevitably – into creating, or even inventing one. This is a consciousness that did not exist in the first half of the twentieth century. The historians, linguists, archaeologists and anthropologists then doing research on the Dutch national 'character' were of the opinion, in line with the positivistic philosophy of their time, that this character was a tangible reality. In other words, they thought they were discovering 'essential' information on the cultural and ethnic-racial roots of the Dutch people.

A closer look at the publications on the Dutch national 'character'of the first half of the twentieth century reveals that there were three main levels on which Dutch identity was centered. First, there was the national level, which was directly related to national history, especially from the later Middle Ages onwards. This was the period during which the present national boundaries were defined, including the division into provinces. Second, there was the level of language, which, in cartographic terms, extended beyond the national borders. This unity of language had been the issue of the Greater Dutch Ideal. Adherents of this ideal considered the Franconians as the first speakers of modern Dutch, and they argued for more cooperation, in the political as well as the cultural sense, between the Netherlands and Flanders, the Dutch-speaking part of Belgium (Von der Dunk 1984). The third level of identity was constructed on the basis of ethnic-racial terms, which also transgressed national boundaries. This primarily concerned the Frisian, Franconian and Saxon areas. These Germanic tribes were supposed to have settled in the Netherlands and in parts of Belgium and Germany during the early medieval period of migrations, which would have left ethnic as well as cultural traces in the present inhabitants of these regions. From the second half of the nineteenth century onwards, regional movements aiming to protect and conserve Frisian,

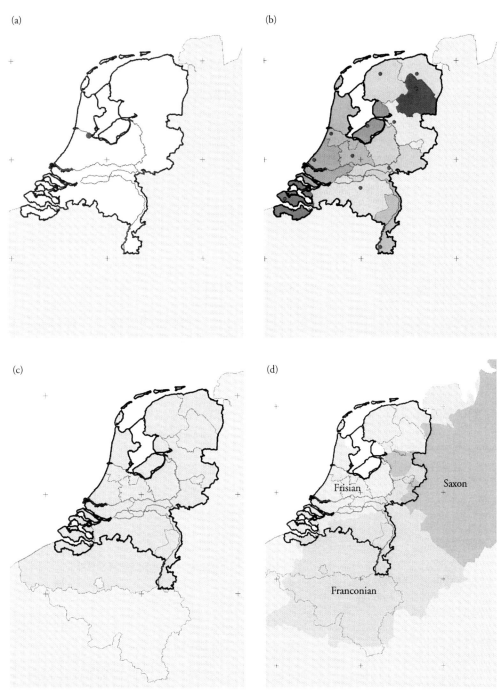

Fig. 25.1 The main levels of Dutch identity. (a) The Netherlands, (b) The Dutch provinces, (c) The Dutch-speaking area, (d) The Frisian, Saxon and Franconian regions.

Franconian and Saxon culture against the growing influence of the national state had sprung up within the Netherlands (Eickhoff 2003a: 158–60). (Fig. 25.1 a–d)

The multiple character of Dutch identity could have resulted in irredentism, being a potentially destructive force working within the nation. When the levels of language and ethnicity are projected a geographical map of the Netherlands, the national boundaries would appear to be unnatural or incorrect. This is not only a modern hypothetical consideration: the American anthropologist Benedict Anderson has pointed out in his study *Imagined Communities – Reflections on the Origin and Spread of Nationalism* that maps contain the power to construct identities (Anderson 2003: 163–85). Still, within Dutch nationalist movements, geographic expanse or national deconstruction were never serious topics of debate. In patriotic historiography, the three aforementioned levels of identity were usually integrated, with the emphasis on the national history of early modern and modern periods, the time during which the national borders had emerged. Often, these historical books referred to the cultural flourishing during the 'Golden Age', the seventeenth century. For these reasons, modern studies mentioned this as a form of 'cultural nationalism' (Bank 1990). Apart from this, the Dutch royal family was another important symbol that stressed the national identity. Schoolchildren were taught that William of Orange was the 'Father of the Fatherland' (Haitsma Mulier and Janssen 1984). Historians were much less interested in folkloristic culture in the Netherlands. At the beginning of the twentieth century, some folklorists complained that it was easier to find out something about the folkore from the Dutch East Indies (Gallée 1903, 1904). In 1918, this changed, when the Dutch Open-Air Museum was founded near Arnhem; a museum dedicated entirely to Dutch folklore. It is important to note, however, that its collection was displayed and ordered according to provincial boundaries, without completely ignoring the existence of Frisian, Saxon and Franconian regions. The national structure of the Netherlands was thus explicitly reconfirmed (Heslinga 1996). The museum also contained one prehistoric object: a stone-coffin grave from the Bronze Age, which had been excavated in the province of Drenthe (Van Erven Dorens 1937). This exhibit pointed out to the visitors, that the origin of folklore was to be found in prehistory. In other words, the Netherlands had witnessed a cultural and ethnic continuity since prehistoric times.

Dutch Archaeologists and National Socialism

Dutch national socialists started to pay attention to the Germanic past during the 1930s. This was especially the case with the foundation *Der Vaderen Erfdeel* (ancestral heritage), a religious-sectarian group of the NSB (*Nationaal-Socialistische Beweging*/National Socialist Movement), the largest national-socialist party in the Netherlands. The members of this foundation, labelling themselves as converted or new pagans, reconstructed and practised ancient Germanic religion through ethnography and folklore. So-called 'zinnebeelden' played an important role in this context; these were folkloristic ornaments that were considered to contain and express pristine religious meaning. A well-known example of such an ornament was the called Irmin-column: a Saxon shrine which was supposed to have been demolished at the order of Charlemagne. For example, a boundary marker from the province of Gelderland dating from the tenth century kept in the Dutch Open Air Museum at Arnhem was considered to contain a depiction of such a column (Fig. 25.2).[2] All this was deemed to be a sign of the continuity of Germanic religion, despite Christian conversion during the Early Middle Ages. The *Der Vaderen Erfdeel* group condemned Christianity openly as a non-Germanic and therefore un-Dutch mentality (Eickhoff 2003a: 240–43). This happened for example in 1939 when the Dutch commemorated that Willibrord – the first evangelist in the Netherlands – had died 1200 years before. After some Catholic priests had coined him as the 'true father of the Fatherland', the *Der Vaderen Erfdeel* group reacted furiously, and not because they considered William of Orange the only one worthy of this

Een merkwaardige grenssteen

In het Openluchtmuseum te Arnhem bevindt zich een grenssteen die vroeger gestaan heeft tusschen de oude hertogdommen Gulik en Gelder. Hij stond op een weiland op de grens van de gemeenten Roosteren en Susteren (Limb.) De steen is uit de 10e eeuw en de namen aan weerszijden zijn in Gotische letters ingebeiteld, met één uitzondering en wel van de l, die vrijwel in het midden van beide woorden voorkomt. Deze vertoont

Links: de grenssteen, zooals hij thans in het Openluchtmuseum te Arnhem staat. Boven en onder: de beide opschriften, met de merkwaardige letter „l".

Fig. 25.2 A boundary marker from the province of Gelderland, considered to contain a depiction of an Irmin column.

title. They stressed that Franconians, Frisians and Saxons had known, long before the arrival of Willibrord, one civilisation and one religion, in the form of the Germanic culture.[3]

In the 1930s the leading Dutch archaeologists had only incidentally contact with the members of *Der Vaderen Erfdeel*. The possible consequences of the national-socialist interest in their field were known to them only indirectly, through the reports on the situation in Germany from their colleagues there, with whom they had been in regular contact from the start of the twentieth century. The prehistorian Albert Egges van Giffen (1884–1973), who had been employed at the State University of Groningen since 1922, knew virtually everyone in German archaeology. He corresponded with his German colleagues, exchanged publications, and was regularly invited for lectures.[4] Some contacts had been established at the beginning of his career. One of these early acquaintances was K.H. Jacob-Friesen, director of the prehistoric department in the Niedersächsisches Landesmuseum of Hanover (Van Giffen 1927: 329). The exchange with the Römisch-Germanische Kommission in Frankfurt am Main began later on, from 1931 onwards.[5] In the second half of the 1930s, Van Giffen also came in contact with Westforschung: the interdisciplinary research conducted in Germany on the concepts of 'Raum' (area), 'Kultur' (culture) and 'Volk' (people) in Germany and its north-western neighbouring countries (Eickhoff 2003b: 178–79). Good relations were also maintained with prehistorians who belonged to the SS-Ahnenerbe, the research department of the SS. For example, in 1937 Van Giffen visited H. Jankuhn's excavations of the Viking city of Haithabu in Schleswig-Holstein. Jankuhn

(1905–1990), an archaeologist focusing on the protohistory, was working in Kiel as a private lecturer and had worked his way up to the position of a respected SS-Ahnenerbe scholar (Kater 1974: 80–81; Steuer 2001). From 1935 Van Giffen corresponded with Hans Reinerth, leader of the Reichsbund für deutsche Vorgeschichte.[6]

As a result of his empirical and scientific methods of research, Van Giffen was known among his German colleagues as the 'best excavator in Europe.'[7] He received much esteem in Germany for his research on terps, especially since he was supposed to have discovered the primitive form of the Germanic (Saxon and Frisian) farmhouse in the terp of Ezinge. In 1938 he was decorated at the University of Cologne with an honorary doctorate for this conclusion. Critics in the Netherlands, however, were of the opinion that he had been compromised by this sign of approval from German academics (Zwarts 1938). Was Van Giffen blind to the political implication that his work was given in the German context? Most probably he was of the opinion that, notwithstanding the evident political use that was made of his results, he could mantain the distinction between science and politics by incidentally pointing out the boundaries. For example, he categorically refused to support the use of archaeological propaganda for national socialism. Even after the German invasion of the Netherlands, his relations with German colleagues remained good. In December 1940, Reinerth was officially received at the Biologisch-Archaeologisch Instituut in Groningen.[8] During the occupation Van Giffen continued working and did not hesitate to take up opportunities offered by the German authorities. He did, however, silent on political matters. The fact that others with whom he worked, did not do so, was no problem in his eyes. This attitude made him invulnerable as well as defenseless. After all, for the national socialist propagandists, the images of Germanicness collected by archaeologists were of primary importance. Scientific research results, and in the case of Van Giffen even the mere mention of his name, lent archaeological propaganda an additional power of persuasion. Van Giffen, however, did not account for this himself and continued making a clear distinction between science and politics.

During the 1930s and the occupation years the archeaologist A.W. Byvanck (1884–1970), working as a professor at the University of Leiden, had no contact at all with members of the foundation *Der Vaderen Erfdeel* and met with less approval in Germany. Byvanck, who was not an active excavator, and who primarily wrote surveys on classical archaeology, had written only one book on Dutch prehistory (see Eickhoff 2003a: 107–120). It was the nationalistically biased *De Voorgeschiedenis van Nederland* (The prehistory of the Netherlands), which was published in 1941 (Byvanck 1941). In this book, he described how the Netherlands had become ethnically unified as long ago as the Neolithic period. The implication of this

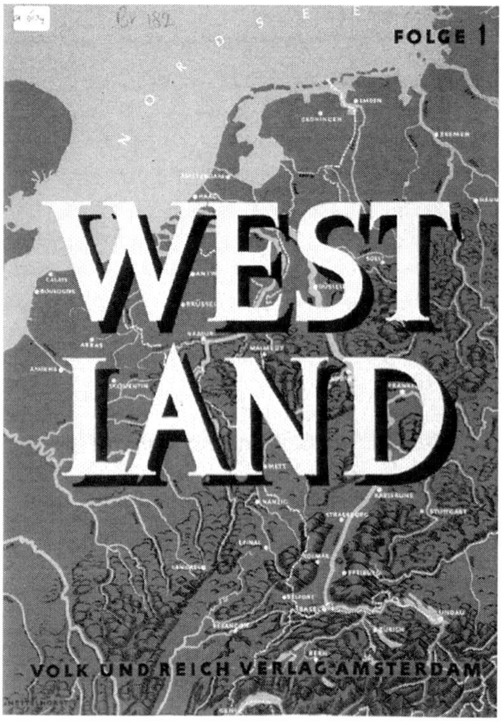

Fig. 25.3 Cover of the *Westland* magazine. The Netherlands are depicted as part of a Greater-Germanic unity.

theory was that the early-medieval Frisians, Franconians and Saxons were political and cultural, but not ethnical entities. Against this background Byvanck was able to develop a nationalistic theory on the Neolithic bell-beakers. He observed in them a certain 'individual' artistic sense, which lent, in his eyes, every such beaker its own character. In line with the idealistic philosophy, he pointed out that this was an expression of the artistic sense which would reach its culmination during the Dutch 'Golden Age'. During the German occupation, Byvancks study was reprinted twice, despite its Dutch nationalistic bias, and despite the photograph of the bell-beaker on its cover (Byvanck 1944). This goes to show that the German authorities welcomed any kind of attention to Dutch prehistory, even if it did not completely match their concept of the Germanic level of Dutch identity. However, the Dutch national-socialistic archaeologist F. C. Bursch (1903–1981) wrote a critical review of the book. He was of the opinion that Byvanck should have used the theories of the German prehistorian G. Kossinna on the genesis of the Germanic people to explain the ethnic (Germanic) unification of the Dutch in prehistoric times (Bursch 1941; on Kossina, see Grünert 2002, Brather this volume).

It was Bursch – from 1929 curator at the Leiden Rijksmuseum van Oudheden (Museum of Antiquities) – who turned out to be one of the few outspoken allies of the German archaeological cultural politics (see Eickhoff 2003a: 60–67, 234–40 and 257–72). The German cultural officials preferred to work with Van Giffen, who enjoyed a higher esteem, and whose work, due to his natural scientific methods, carried more weight in propaganda. But Van Giffen had kept the German cultural officials at a distance. On the other hand, Bursch was more than happy to cooperate with German national socialists. As a result of his good experiences during his studies in Germany in 1931 and 1932, he had started to sympathise with the doctrines of national socialism. Moreover, as a prehistorian he had begun to idealise the Germanic past, and related this to a utopian ideal in which tradition and modernity were harmoniously combined within the context of a Greater Germanic Empire. Bursch even made archaeological propaganda for national socialism, often in collaboration with the SS-Ahnenerbe. This did not only concern publications, but also propagandistic exhibitions and films. Bursch himself held the opinion, that his archaeological propaganda was identical to popularisation, especially since he refrained from the new paganism of the *Der Vaderen Erfdeel* group. According to his Dutch colleagues, however, he made unwarranted concessions to the historical and archaeological truths. For example, Bursch appeared in a scene of a propagandistic film on an excavation, picking up a fragment of earthenware on which a carved swastika could be seen. This fragment was, however, an evident case of forgery. During the occupation Bursch became increasingly isolated due to his political activities. As a consequence he jumped at the offer from the SS-Ahnenerbe to carry out an excavation in the village of Solenoje in Ukraine in the summer of 1943. The aim of this excavation, at which forced labour was used, was to prove that German tribes had settled in the Ukraine as long ago as in prehistoric times (Eickhoff 2006).

During the German occupation of the Netherlands German prehistorians were involved in the production of propaganda as well. The identity-creating power of maps played a central role in this propaganda: the Netherlands were often represented as an integral part of the Greater Germanic unity. An important example of this phenomenon was the magazine *Westland*, which often contained archaeological articles, for example, 'Die Wurzeln des Niederländischen Volkstums' (The Roots of Dutch Ethnicity) by W. von Stokar, an archaeologist from Cologne (Von Stokar 1943, Zondergeld 2003) (Fig. 25.3). Apart from making propaganda, German prehistorians incidentally also undertook excavations in the Netherlands. Von Stokar and his assistant C. Redlich were involved in a number of excavations connected with constructions for the Wehrmacht. One of those was the project on the isle of Walcheren, where in 1943 a bunker was built in a 'vliedberg' (the terp-like remain of a fortress from the tenth or eleventh century). Like the propaganda material, such scientific excavations eventually served the Greater Germanic ideal: Redlich worked on her dissertation on the West Germanic tribes, which was never concluded.[9]

P. Felix: The Prehistorian of the Netherlands of the New Order

One of the great disappointments for the German officials responsible for cultural affairs in the Netherlands was that Dutch academics who worked on topics and ideas which had a central place in the national-socialist world-view, soon appeared not to be the presumed 'natural' allies. This was the main reason why they had started to make archaeological propaganda themselves. But as a result, it was soon decided to raise a new generation of academics. The officials started to look for suitable youngsters who had passed their final exams. They could obtain a grant which enabled them to study in Germany.[10] In the summer of 1940 Von Stokar met a 22–year-old young man called P. Felix during an excursion organised by the Rijksmuseum van Oudheden (on Felix, see Eickhoff 2000). This meeting would have far-reaching consequences. The archaeologist from Cologne realised that Felix was the man they were looking for: a prehistorian of the Netherlands of the New Order. Felix seemed to be predestined and not only because of his intelligence, enthusiasm and looks (blond forelock), but also because he had already attended the Agricultural University of Wageningen from 1936 to 1938. In that period his interest in prehistory and folklore had been aroused and his sympathy for national socialism had developed. Therefore, it did not come as a surprise that Felix accepted the grant from Germany.[11]

Felix's academic programme started in Cologne in 1941 at the institute under Von Stokar. During two semesters he studied prehistory, in which he concentrated on the research of prehistoric clothing and food. Thereafter he got to know the circuit of renowned Ahnenerbe prehistorians of Germany and Austria. In the autumn of 1941 he worked in Wilhelmshaven at the Institut für Wurten- und Marschenforschung under W. Haarnagel. During the winter semester of 1942–43 he attended the lectures of O. Menghin in Vienna. In January 1943 he went to Rostock, where he started to write a thesis on the Dutch Bronze Age. He was supervised by Jankuhn. In this period Felix also worked at the laboratory for palynology under R. Schütrumpf in Berlin-Dahlem, and he made some study tours. He visited the Siebengebirge near Bonn, Burgenland in Austria, Ditmarschen in Schleswig-Holstein, the cities Danzig and Neumünster and the islands Rügen and Usedom. Finally, on 30 April 1945, Felix, who was now 27, obtained his doctorate from the university of Rostock with the classification Magna Cum Laude (Felix 1945: title page). For his thesis Felix had made an inventory of all the bronze objects found in the Netherlands. He drew conclusions that could not be misunderstood. During the Neolithic the builders of the megalithic tombs 'marched' out of North Germany into the Netherlands, later followed by 'die Streitaxtleute' (the people with battle-axes). In the Northern parts of the Netherlands during the Bronze Age the Germanic people developed out of these two tribes, as had happened in North Germany and Scandinavia. Considering the West European influences in the Northern parts of the Netherlands, Felix called the area 'Provinzial-Germanisch' (a Germanic province) (Felix 1945: 153–55, 164 and 171). Felix had obtained his doctorate just in time: one day later the Red Army would take the city of Rostock during the afternoon and seven days later the Third Reich would capitulate unconditionally. By that time Felix had already left Germany by boat.

In september 1945 Felix arrived in the Netherlands and after he was arrested in the city of Enschede he stayed in internment camps until September 1946. A few months later he visited Van Giffen who was excavating at Valkenburg. The meeting was an important moment for Felix: his archaeological future depended on it. Van Giffen was the most powerful archaeologist in the Netherlands. And during the occupation their political opinions might have been directly opposed, but at the same time their ideas on the earliest history of the Netherlands had been very similar. During their meeting, they talked about the publication of his dissertation and the possibility of working again as a prehistorian in the Netherlands. As a result of their conversation Van Giffen received a copy of Felix's dissertation, which he studied intensely. He also got an elaborate Curriculum Vitae in which Felix was remarkably outspoken about his 'scientific and political antecedents'. He said he now recognised the 'manifestations of degeneracy of the Nazi system'. Referring to the Holocaust he spoke of a 'too extreme racial policy', which implied that he did not condemn the racial policy itself. He also kept to the political intentions that guided him when he studied prehistory:

> I am still holding on to my conviction that prehistory is not only valuable as a scholary discipline – but as all history has a meaning for the present and the future. It may be that the knowledge of the culture and history of our earliest ancestors (more than historical accounts with many details) can give to the hurried people at present a feeling of the eternal, of the main lines of development and the ancient ethnical, cultural and economical ties with the areas surrounding us.[12]

Felix showed his cautiousness in speaking of a 'feeling of the eternal', which could be evoked with knowledge of 'our' earliest ancestors. During the occupation years he had written many propaganda articles in which he described how the culture of these earliest ancestors evoked a feeling of respect: respect for 'our own character' which was not contaminated with 'strange influences' and that was bound to 'our blood'.[13] It was clear that Felix's belief in the nature and mission of the Germanic people had not disappeared after 1945: when he could work again as a prehistorian this belief would still be his underlying motive (Eickhoff 2000). After a while Van Giffen made it clear to Felix that he saw no place for him in Dutch archaeology. Van Giffen's motives are not known, although he did take a lot of effort to find work for his own pupils (Bazelmans et al. 1997: 74). As a result, the man who should have been the prehistorian of the Netherlands of the New Order, remained – in spite of his Magna Cum Laude – excluded from the study of Dutch pre- and protohistory for the rest of his life.

Conclusion

The four examples given in this paper of the positions chosen by Dutch archaeologists during the German occupation of the Netherlands at first sight might have been selected rather at random: Van Giffen's attitude towards the German or national-socialist reception of his work, Byvanck's nationalistic interpretation of bell-beakers, Bursch's activities in archaeological propaganda and Felix's prematurely aborted archaeological career. However, these cases share the characteristic that archaeological research was explicitly linked to ethnic entities. It appears that national socialists were not the only ones to do so: in line with positivistic philosophy these ethnic entities were generally seen as tangible realities. But the four examples cannot be thrown together. It had been usual for Dutch prehistorians – in accordance with the ideal of objectivity – not to pronounce upon the immanent political and social dimension of their archaeological research. In that respect, the position taken by Byvanck deviated from the tradition: he left the ivory tower of academe by stressing the national dimension of his work. The same can be said of Bursch and Felix: they emphasized the Greater-Germanic implication of their archaeological research. Van Giffen, however, tried to hold on to the scientific ideal of objectivity. On the one hand, his positivistic background made him unassailable in his own eyes, while at the same time his insights turned out to be most vulnerable for political appropriation by national socialist propagandists.

In the period after 1945 the positivistic approach in Dutch archaeology did not become a topic of debate. However, there were some changes. Prehistoric cultures – without mentioning ethnicity – became the main object of archaeological research, while political engagement was kept at an even greater distance than before. It is hard to point out precisely how these changes were related to the prior experiences of prehistorians under national socialist rule; in the 1950s there was no open reflection on this topic. In the late 1960s this situation of silence ended. Under the influence of Marxism and the students' revolt, knowledge and its political and social implications were increasingly seen as an inseparable unity (Van der Waals 1969). For archaeologists like Van Giffen who, more than twenty years earlier, during the German occupation of the Netherlands, had tried to safeguard the integrity of their profession by staying in the ivory tower of academe – by holding on to the distinction between science and politics – this development mustr have been an alarming reverse of perspective.

Notes

1. For the difference between 'Germanic' and 'German', see Mees (2004: 257).
2. 'Een merkwaardige grenssteen', *Der Vaderen Erfdeel* 3–12 (1939) 191–92.
3. 'Rond de Willibrodus-herdenking', *Der Vaderen Erfdeel* 3–12 (1939) 188–90.
4. See Correspondence archive of the Biologisch-Archaeologisch Instituut (hereafter cited as BAI), GIA, Rijksuniversiteit Groningen; Archive Van Giffen, Lectures, University Library Groningen. For Van Giffen, see Lanting (1973).
5. For the correspondence between Van Giffen and the Römisch-Germanische Kommission, see Archive RGK 19: 578 Frankfurt am Main. For the RGK, see Krämer (1977).
6. See Archive BAI 1935 M-R. For Reinerth and the Reichsbund, see Bollmus (1970: 153–235).
7. Archive Van Giffen, Lectures, University Library Groningen; 'Nederlandsche terpen. Voordracht van Dr Van Giffen in de Universiteit te Berlijn', *Volk en Vaderland* 25/1/1936.
8. Letter dated 13/12/1940, H. Reinerth to A.E. van Giffen, Archive BAI 1941 R-Sto.
9. For Von Stokar, see Hirschfeld (1997: 560–91). For Redlich and her dissertation, see Archive Römisch-Germanische Kommission 19:I.035 Frankfurt a. M. For the *Wehrmacht* excavations, see Eickhoff (2003a: 172).
10. H.E. Scheider, Aktenvermerk-Heranbildung wissenschaftlichen Nachwuchses in Holland, Den Haag 15/10/1940. Schneider B291 – BDC Ahnenerbe, Bundesarchiv Berlin.
11. Proces Verbaal P. Felix 31/7/1946, File P. Felix, Centraal Archief Bijzondere Rechtspleging (hereafter cited as CABR), Nationaal Archief Den Haag. Letter dated 24/11/1946, P. Felix to A.E. van Giffen, Archive BAI, 1947 E-G.
12. Letter of 24/11/1946, P. Felix to A.E. van Giffen, Archive BAI: 1947 E-G; Letter of 7/2/1947, P. Felix to A.E. van Giffen, Archive Instituut voor Pre- en Protohistorie, Universiteit van Amsterdam.
13. 'Wat hunebedden ons te zeggen hebben. Spreker: P. Felix', File P. Felix, CABR, Nationaal Archief Den Haag.

References

Anderson, B. 2003. *Imagined Communities-Reflections on the Origin and Spread of Nationalism.* London: Verso Books

Bank, J.Th.M. 1990. *Het Roemrijk Vaderland; Cultureel Nationalisme in Nederland in de 19e Eeuw,* 's-Gravenhage: Sdu Uitgevers.

Bazelmans, J., J. Kolen and H.T. Waterbolk. 1997. 'On the Natural History of the Peasant Landscape. An Archaeological Dialogue with Tjalling Waterbolk', *Archaeological Dialogues* (4)1: 71–101.

Beyen, M. 2000. 'Natuurlijke Naties? Nationale Historiografie in België en Nederland tussen een "Tribaal" en Sociaal-cultureel Paradigma', in M. Eickhoff, B. Henkes and F. van Vree (eds), *Volkseigen. Ras, Cultuur en Wetenschap in Nederland 1900–1950. Jaarboek van het Nederlands Instituut voor Oorlogsdocumentatie* 11. Zutphen: Walburg Pers, pp. 95–128.

Bollmus, R. 1970. *Das Amt Rosenberg und seine Gegner. Studien zum Machtkampf im Nationalsozialistischen Herrschaftssystem.* Stuttgart: Deutsche Verlags-Anstalt.

Bursch, F.C. 1941. 'Boekbespreking. Prof. Dr A.W. Byvanck, De Voorgeschiedenis van Nederland', *Volksche Wacht* (5)8: 9.

Byvanck, A.W. 1941. *De Voorgeschiedenis van Nederland*, 1st edn. Leiden: Brill.

———. 1944. *De Voorgeschiedenis van Nederland*, 3rd edn. Leiden: Brill.

Dunk, H.W. von der. 1984. 'De Grootnederlandse Gedachte Geen Tic van Excentrieke Heren', *Tijdschrift voor Geschiedenis* (97) 4: 207–213.

Eickhoff, M. 2000. 'De Geest van de Hunebedbouwers. De Nederlandse Pre- en Protohistorie in Wetenschap en Propaganda', in M. Eickhoff, B. Henkes and F. van Vree (eds), *Volkseigen. Ras, Cultuur en Wetenschap in Nederland 1900–1950. Jaarboek Nederlands Instituut voor Oorlogsdocumentatie* 11. Zutphen: Walburg Pers, pp. 32–61.

———. 2003a. *De Oorsprong van het 'Eigene'. Nederlands Vroegste Verleden, Archeologie en Nationaal-Socialisme*. Amsterdam: Boom Publishers.

———. 2003b. '"Zusammenarbeit Dies- und Jenerseits der Deutsch-Holländischen Grenze". A.E. van Giffens Archeologisch Onderzoek in Noord-Nederland (1920–1940), Wetenschappelijke Uitwisseling met Duitsland en de *Westforschung*', in F. Boterman and M. Vogel (eds), *Nederland en Duitsland in het Interbellum. Wisselwerking en Contacten van politiek tot Literatuur*. Hilversum: Uitgeverij Verloren, pp. 175–88.

———. 2006. 'De Nederlandse Prehistoricus F.C. Bursch en zijn SS-Expeditie naar de Oekraïne, Grafheuvelonderzoek achter het Oostfront', in O. Brinkkemper a.o. (eds) *Vakken in Vakken: Achaeologische kennis in lagen. Nederlandse Archeologische Rapporten* 32. pp. 73–84.

Erven Dorens, A.A.G. van. 1937. *Nederlandsch Openluchtmuseum te Arnhem. Geïllustreerde Gids*. Nijmegen: Vereeniging voor Volkskunde.

Felix, P. 1945. *Das Zweite Jahrtausend vor der Zeitrechnung in den Niederlanden*, Ph.D. Dissertation, Universität Rostock.

Gallée, J.H. 1903. 'Wenschvervullend?', *De Nederlandsche Spectator* 52: 415–16.

———. 1904. 'Wenschvervullend?', *De Nederlandsche Spectator* 1: 4–6.

Giffen, A.E. van. 1927. *De hunebedden in Nederland (met Atlas)*. II, Utrecht: Uitgeverij Oosthoek.

Grünert, H. 2002. *Gustav Kossinna (1858–1931) Vom Germanisten zum Prähistoriker. Ein Wissenschaftler in Kaiserreich und in der Weimarer Republik*. Rahden/Wesfalen: Leidorf Verlag.

Haitsma Mulier, E.O.G. and A.E.M. Janssen (eds). 1984. *Willem van Oranje in de Historie, 1584–1984. Vier Eeuwen Beeldvorming en Geschiedschrijving*. Utrecht: HES.

Heslinga, M. 1996. 'Tussen "Stammen" en "Streken". Uit de Voor- en Vroege Geschiedenis van het Openluchtmuseum', *Jaarboek Nederlands Openluchtmuseum*, 97–169.

Hirschfeld, G. 1997. 'Die Universität Leiden unter dem Nationalsozialismus', *Geschichte und Gesellschaft. Zeitschrift für Historische Sozialwissenschaft*, 23: 560–91.

Kater, M.H. 1974. *Das 'Ahnenerbe' der SS 1935–1945. Ein Beitrag zur Kulturpolitik des Dritten Reiches*. Stuttgart: Deutsche Verlags-Anstalt.

Krämer, W. 1977. 'Fünfundsiebzig Jahre Römisch-Germanische Kommission', *Beiheft zum Bericht der RGK* 58: 5–23.

Lanting, J.N. 1973. 'A.E. van Giffen. Education and Official Career', *Palaeohistoria* XV: 13–14.

Mees, G. 2004. 'Hitler and Germanentum', *Journal of Contemporary History* (39)2: 255–70.

Romein, J. 1946. 'Beschouwingen over het Nederlandse Volkskarakter' (1941), *In Opdracht van de Tijd. Tien Voordrachten over Historische Thema's*. Amsterdam: Querido, pp. 172–200.

Steuer, H. 2001. 'Herbert Jankuhn und seine Darstellungen zur Germanen- und Wikingerzeit', in *Eine Hervorragend Nationale Wissenschaft. Deutsche Prähistoriker zwischen 1900 und 1995 RGA-E Band 29*. Berlin New York: Walter de Gruyter, pp. 417–73.

Stokar, W. von. 1943. 'Die Wurzeln des Niederländischen Volkstums', *Westland* I: 18–20.

Waals, J.D. van der. 1969. *Praehistorie en Mythevorming*. Groningen: Wolters-Noordhoff.

Zondergeld, G.R. 2003. '"Nach Westen Wollen Wir Fahren!" Die Zeitschrift "Westland" als Trefpunkt der "Westraumforscher"', in B. Dietz, H. Gabel and U. Tiedau (eds), *Griff nach dem Westen. Die 'Westforschung' der Völkisch-Nationalen Wissenschaften zum Nordwesteuropäischen Raum (1919–1960)*. Münster: Waxmann Verlag. pp. 655–71.

Zwarts, J. 1938. '"Politieke" Opgravingen? Tweeërlei Geschied-Opvatting in het Geding', *Utrechtsche Courant* 7 July.

Index